COLLINS COBUILD

COLLINS Birmingham University International Language Database

English Course

Jane & Dave Willis

with
Debra Powell

Teacher's Book

2

Collins ELT
8 Grafton Street
London W1X 3LA

COBUILD is a trademark of William Collins Sons & Co. Ltd

© William Collins Sons & Co. Ltd 1989

10 9 8 7 6 5 4 3 2 1

First published 1989

Printed in Hong Kong by
Wing King Tong Company Ltd

ISBN 0 00 370035 6

Design: Terry Smith (Student's Book), Gina Smart (Teacher's Book)
Cover design: Richard Morris
Photography: Chris Ridgers
Artwork: Jonathan Allen, Sarah Allison, Laura Boyd, Terry Burton, David English, Mike Mosedale, Kieren Phelps, Paul Shorrock, Clive Spong

This Teacher's Book is accompanied by a Student's Book ISBN 0 00 370033 X, a set of cassettes ISBN 0 00 370036 4, and a Practice Book ISBN 0 00 370034 8. A booklet containing transcripts of the unscripted recordings is included inside the back cover of the Student's Book.

COBUILD is the Collins Birmingham University International Language Database

Acknowledgements *(Figures in brackets refer to sections.)*

The syllabus of the Collins COBUILD English Course is based on the research findings of the COBUILD project at Birmingham University. Editor-in-Chief: Professor John Sinclair.

Liaison between COBUILD and Collins was co-ordinated by Antoinette Renouf. Computer support was provided by Tim Lane.

The authors would especially like to thank the COBUILD team for their detailed research and Michael Halliday and John Sinclair for guidance on the Grammar material. They are also grateful to students at the Cicero Language School, Tunbridge Wells for their advice in 209, and to teachers at the School for their co-operation. Finally, the authors would like to thank family and friends, especially their daughters, Jenny and Becky, for all their help and patience throughout the writing of this book.

Many people read and commented on the manuscript and it is impossible to list them all here. The publishers and authors are especially grateful to the following: Alastair Banton, Martin Mulloy, Georgina Pearce, Debra Powell, Hilary Rees-Parnall and Paula Walker.

The following participated in the unscripted recordings, and provided supporting texts and information to ensure the contextualisation of the recordings was accurate: Stephen Bowden, Jeremy Clear, David Foll, Caroline Frost, Bridget Green, Monica Janowski, Philip King, Danny Lim, Catherine McKinna, Jenny Maxwell, John Mannion, Ken O'Connell, Myf Sinclair and Jenny Vaughan.

Most of those in the published recordings also gave time to be photographed, as did the following: Brendan Barnes, Jane Burnell, Theresa Clementson, Claire Edwards, Marcia Jackson, Sian Mills, Paul Stokes and Maya Wilkie (all 128); Alan Dury (15); Deborah Blackburn and Dave Swabrick (182) and Jane Marr (14, 17).

The following allowed us to take photographs at their homes or premises: Argos Distributors Ltd (117); Stephen Bowden (14); The Trustees of the British Museum (157); Forfars Bakers Ltd, Brighton (42, 47); Caroline Frost (14); General Trading Company (1); John Mannion (1, 14); Playtime Playgroup in St Paul's C.E. School, Brighton (11, 42); St Martins Reference Library (14); The Window Box, Brighton (42); Y.M.C.A., London (2); Varndean School, Brighton (42); Selfridges (126).

The publishers are grateful to the following for permission to use original material in the Student's Book: Automobile Association for extracts from the A.A. Members' Handbook, 1986/87 (Great Britain) edition (7, 134, 198); Sunday Times for permission to redraw their original (18); and Reader's Digest (21, 45, 55, 73, 93, 164, 171, 188); Reader's Digest and T. McGuire (75); Spike Milligan for poems 'The Dog Lovers' and 'Holes in the Sky' (15); Dateline for part of application form (20); Northumberland County Council for extract from Northumberland Gazetteer (35); Country Farm holidays, Worcester for newspaper quotes (35); Just Seventeen, EMAP Metro Publications for extracts (47, 78, 158, 162); A. D. Peters & Co Ltd for poem 'Teachers' by Michael Rosen (58); André Deutsch Ltd for poem 'Juster and Waiter', from 'You Can't Catch Me' by Michael Rosen (64); Guinness Publishing Ltd for three extracts from 1988 Guinness Book of Records (copyright 1987) (63); West Midlands Passenger Transport Executive (now obsolete) for Travelcard text (82); Reader's Digest and Alan Woodward (93); Carcanet Press Ltd for extract from William Carlos Williams, 'The Collected Poems 1909–1939', ed A. Walton Litz and Christopher MacGowan (1987) (95); Roald Dahl for 'The Hitch-hiker' from 'The wonderful world of Henry Sugar', Jonathan Cape 1977 and Penguin 1982 (97, 114, 121, 136, 147, 152, 161, 167, 174, 179, 189, 193); Reader's Digest and A. H. Andrews (103); Guardian Royal Exchange for part of a claims form (108); British Rail for timetable (110); Time Out London Student Guide for extract (110); B.M.W. (121); Reader's Digest and H. Morris (144); Thomson Local Directories, Farnborough GU14 7NU for extract (176); Milk Marketing Board 'Dairy Diary' for extract (178).

The publishers are grateful to the following for the use of photographs: Irish Tourist Board (1, 38); Cheshire County Council (1); Gazette series, Middlesex County Press (7); Catherine McKinna (9, 64); Dateline (20); Britain on View (BTA/ETB) (28, 35, 114, 116, 139, 144, 186, 198); English Life Publications Ltd (28); Sunday Times (39); Bahamas Tourist Board (38); Lyons Maid (42); All-Sport Photographic Ltd (42); Ford Motor Company Ltd (42); Spectrum (49, 51, 62, 69); British Heart Foundation (63); DHSS (63); John Mannion (64); Hoverspeed Ltd (68); Air France (68); Hot-Air Balloon Company Ltd, London SW6 2AG (68); Sealink Ferries (68); Kobal Collection (75); Birmingham Post and Mail Ltd (80); Toshiba (U.K.) Ltd (91); Topham Picture Library (97); Guinness Publishing Ltd (101); Knutz (116); Collins Road Atlas Great Britain (based on Ordnance Survey maps with the permission of the Controller of Her Majesty's Stationery Office, Crown copyright reserved) (134, 198); Ian Brown (134); Police Review (143); Museum of London (191); Mary Evans Picture Library (198); Glasgow University Library (201).

Every effort has been made to contact the owners of copyright material. In some cases this has not been possible. The publishers apologise for any omissions, and will be glad to rectify these when the title is reprinted if details are sent.

Contents

Foreword

The *Collins COBUILD English Course* is a new departure in English language teaching materials. It is a lively and varied Course, using plenty of natural English examples. And it is founded on the very latest evidence of English structure from the COBUILD files.

The authors set themselves a very demanding task. Course materials today attain very high standards of presentation, variety of activity and stimulation to learning. The Course had to meet or beat all these existing criteria, but at the same time it was to be designed around our growing knowledge of the role of the common words in the language.

COBUILD has built up a mass of information from the careful examination of many millions of words, and it offers a new style and balance to a syllabus. Until now it has not been possible to tell which are the most central and typical patterns of the language. Teachers and materials writers have simply not had sufficient evidence, important usages have been missed and some quite trivial material has been prominently taught. Sequencing has been fairly arbitrary, and there is not much agreement between one course and another on what constitutes the first stages of English.

Worst of all there has been for many years in English teaching a loss of respect for the natural patterns of a language. Because of the difficulty of collecting and analysing language that occurs in everyday contexts, teachers have had to accept all sorts of invented or adapted texts. These are grimly defended by some, but there is no virtue in them; they were only made up because it was not practicable to harness real language.

Now it is possible, with a little trouble, to offer the learner plenty of texts in quite natural English, and this Course opens up new experiences in that area.

In particular, the COBUILD Course boldly features spontaneous conversation, language at its most natural. This is the most elusive form of English, and very difficult to get under control for classroom use.

A good course is a remarkable balancing act, and also a miracle of compression. Each activity has to take up only a small amount of space, the vocabulary, grammar, phonology and everything else has to be kept under control, and the whole thing has to vary constantly to keep up the level of interest and excitement. In a series of designing, drafting, piloting and revising stages, the Course has taken shape as a viable classroom instrument.

The ordering of the Course follows a new and carefully designed methodology which has been developed by the authors. In the variation of activities the learner follows a series of steps which give a great deal of learning reinforcement and practice in language skills.

The most precious resource in language teaching is classroom time. Hence it is very important that the choice of what is taught is made very carefully. Using the evidence available from COBUILD, this Course is able to identify the most useful words and patterns, and give the learner an excellent start.

Professor John Sinclair

Introduction

Who is this Course for?

Level Two of the *Collins COBUILD English Course* is the second part of a three-part general English course for adult students. It is designed for early intermediate students, particularly those who have successfully completed Level One of this Course. Level Two takes learners beyond the level of the *Cambridge Preliminary English Test*.

Students who have a good grounding in the basic words and patterns of English will progress rapidly, building up their knowledge and confidence until they can use English to meet a wide range of real needs.

The Course is Complete

Like Level One, Level Two offers a complete package comprising a Student's Book in full colour, with a separate transcript booklet inserted in its back cover, a Practice Book for use in or out of class, a set of cassettes and an interleaved Teacher's Book. The Teacher's Book is designed for easy access by busy teachers, and contains clear and detailed guidance on how the course can be taught, offering a flexible approach to the materials and methodology.

Basic Principles

In devising the methodology for the Course, the authors have adhered to a number of basic principles, which have been at the heart of good language teaching practice for some years. These are:
1 People learn a language most effectively by using the language to do things – to find out information, to solve problems, to talk about personal experiences, and so on.
2 A focus on accuracy is vital. Learners need time to think about the language they are using.
3 As far as possible learners should be exposed to real language.
4 Grammar is learned rather than taught. Coursebooks and teachers provide useful guidelines on the language, but learners should additionally be encouraged to think and deduce for themselves.
5 Learners need strategies for organising what they have learned – they need rules, patterns, and categories.

The *Collins COBUILD English Course* realises these well-established principles through a new language syllabus – a lexical syllabus – that has been drawn from the COBUILD language research project.

The COBUILD Project

COBUILD is the Collins-Birmingham University International Language Database. Using large-scale computer facilities, an editorial team at Birmingham University has worked for seven years, analysing and recording the patterns of use in millions of words of current English text. The Database holds extensive information about how English is really used, and is an authoritative resource that has proved invaluable in the development of this Course.

The Lexical Syllabus

Level One takes 700 of the commonest words in today's English, covering their most important meanings and uses as identified by the COBUILD Project. Level Two reviews these words and goes on to cover 850 new words.

Unlike traditional syllabuses, the lexical syllabus starts from a description of real language. In taking words and their meanings as the core items, the syllabus offers genuine coverage of the most central and typical patterns of English. It also provides a focus for language analysis, which allows students to develop and refine their awareness of the actual grammar of the language.

In the teacher's notes which follow, the lexical aims for each unit are clearly listed, with examples. This overall guidance appears opposite the final page of each unit, which is always called 'Review Page'. Additionally, each section of teacher's notes includes a 'Lexis box', which gives the words to focus on during the activity concerned.

There is a Full Index of the words covered in Level Two on pages 126T–128T of this Teacher's Book.

The Methodology of the Course

The methodology in Level Two follows closely the cycle that was successfully piloted for Level One. It is a task-based approach to learning which takes full account of the need for accuracy. It contains the following components:

1 Input
The Course provides a rich input of *real* language, both written and spoken, which is extensively recycled throughout the Course. This language is carefully selected both to provide a contextualised presentation of the target words for Level Two and to confront learners with the kind of communication problems they are likely to meet when they use the language outside the classroom.

2 Task
Each unit contains several tasks involving both spoken and written language, usually done in pairs or groups. In doing a task learners are primarily concerned with fluency – using whatever language they have to solve a problem, exchange relevant information and so on. The teacher's role is to help them complete the task in English, rather than to make corrections at this stage.

3 Planning and Report
After performing the task each group is asked to present its findings to the class in a spoken or written report. In preparing this report with the help of the teacher, and in presenting it to the class there is a clear focus on accuracy.

4 Focused Listening
Students are also given the opportunity to listen to recordings of native speakers performing the same tasks. This provides important language input and also gives useful hints as to how to go about the task.

5 Language Analysis
Students are engaged in a detailed analysis of aspects of the written and spoken texts to which they have been exposed. This enables them to gain valuable insights into the grammatical and lexical system of English and its basic discourse patterns.

6 Controlled Practice
Controlled repetition of various kinds involves students in practising useful and very frequent combinations of words in English in order to build up their confidence and their ability to produce groups of sounds and intonation patterns accurately and spontaneously.

This methodology ensures that a good deal of responsibility lies with the learners. The teacher's role is to encourage them and offer precise guidance as their students' knowledge of the language develops. It also ensures constant recycling of language material within and across units. The use of real written texts and real recordings means that the common colloquial forms of English, which have a high communicative value, occur again and again. This tendency is reinforced by a careful selection of material based on the COBUILD Database findings.

The net result of this methodology, as demonstrated in the pilot stage of this Course, is that learners become competent in English both quickly and efficiently. Because they learn the English that is really important to their needs they are able to use natural language from an earlier stage.

Unit Organisation

Level Two contains fifteen units, organised in three blocks of five units each. Every fifth unit is a revision unit. Each unit will take between four and six hours to complete.

As with most other courses, there is a gradual shift in emphasis from the spoken to the written form of the language. There is a wide selection of reading material in Level Two, all taken from authentic sources and produced here unchanged. The passages have been carefully selected to provide good coverage of the target language, the 1550 commonest words in English. They are taken from a range of sources to give students experience of the kinds of reading task they are likely to meet outside the classroom. For this reason students are not expected to understand every single word they read. A variety of tasks and exercises accompany the texts and students are encouraged to complete these as efficiently as possible, ignoring any irrelevant difficulties which they may meet.

From Unit 7, the Student's Book features 'The Hitch-hiker' a short story by the well known author, Roald Dahl. The story is broken down into short instalments, each of which is read first for the suspense and enjoyment before being studied more intensively. Students derive considerable motivation from their ability to read and enjoy a short story as written for native speakers of English.

There is a similarly wide variety of written tasks in both the Student's Book and the Practice Book, ranging from single sentence responses to much longer texts. Writing tasks involve the production of stories, instructions, descriptions, summaries, written reports and other forms of writing.

All units follow the methodological cycle outlined above. A detailed description of how to handle this sequence is given in the teacher's notes for Unit 1 (see pages 1T to 3T which follow).

Level Two continues from Level One in encouraging students to think about language for themselves. Again there is a variety of language-focused exercises, to help students to discover the words and patterns of English for themselves:

- Grammar
The first five units review the important grammatical features which were covered in Level One. From Unit 6 onwards the grammar work is organised functionally, under headings like *Cause and Result, Purpose, Time* and *Descriptions.* With few exceptions, the examples illustrating these functional areas are examples which students have seen in context in the Course.

- Language Study
These sections focus on other important aspects of the language and examine examples that have occurred in the recordings and written texts.

- Wordpower
These sections cover particularly common target words which have a number of important meanings or uses, for example the word **way**.

- Preposition Spot
This is a new feature. All teachers know that prepositions are of central importance in English. Level Two treats them systematically, looking at their 'literal' meanings to do with space and time and also at their more 'idiomatic' uses in phrasal verbs, with reference to the particularly important collocations that have been identified in the COBUILD research.

- Phrase-building
This section is also new, and draws students' attention to some of the very common patterns in English. These have been identified by the COBUILD Project as being

vitally important in English, but many of them are omitted in coursebooks. 'Phrase-building' allows students to practise the uses of words such as **fact**, **point**, **problem**, **thing**, and so on, in patterns like *The point is . . .*, *The main thing is . . .*, and so on.

- Lexicon

In Level One, a Grammar Book was included in the back of the Student's Book to provide students with a record of coverage and to initiate important reference skills. In Level Two, there is a Lexicon at the back of the Student's Book, which contains 165 of the target words for Level Two. The main purpose here is to give students a thorough training in dictionary reference skills and the entries in the Lexicon have been chosen with this in mind. In every unit there are exercises which utilise the Lexicon entries.

- Word Study Boxes

These coloured boxes – pink for 'Words to look up' and blue for 'Words to guess' – draw attention to other target words and at the same time train students in inference skills, encouraging them to be more independent.

There is lead-in and summary material for each unit, as in Level One:

- Lead-in Page

The lead-in page at the beginning of each unit normally uses photographs and other pictorial stimuli to promote informal discussion, focusing on the unit topics. This is an opportunity to assess students' knowledge of relevant vocabulary, and to introduce some of the new words that will be used in the coming unit.

- Review Page

Level One had a 'Useful Words and Phrases' section at the end of each unit to provide a summary of some of the important language covered in that unit. Level Two has a review page at the end of each unit, which summarises not only the language of that unit but some of the useful language which has been covered up to that point in the Course.

The Cassettes

The three cassettes at Level Two contain all the recorded material, in the order in which it occurs during the Course. Full tapescripts are given at the back of this book.

The unscripted recordings are an integral part of the Course, and give a very rich input of natural language. Students will rapidly become accustomed to working with them and can also refer to the Transcript booklet as necessary.

Students with time for home study may like to have their own set of cassettes so that they can listen again to the native speaker recordings.

The Practice Book

This book can be used in or out of class and consolidates and extends the Student's Book material. A range of exercises includes items for completion in the book itself. Space has deliberately not been given for longer written exercises, which should be prepared in a separate notebook if possible. There is an answer key at the back of the Practice Book.

Map of Level 2

	TASKS AND TOPICS	TEXTS AND FEATURES	WRITING	SOCIAL LANGUAGE	VERBS/TENSES CLAUSE PATTERNS	NOUN PHRASES PRONOUNS ADJECTIVES PREPOSITIONS ADVERBIAL PHRASES	SPOKEN AND WRITTEN DISCOURSE
Unit 1 So I'm going to move on	Family/work situations: finding things in common. Game: guess where something's hidden. Childhood. Survey: languages you've learnt. Learning a language.	Descriptions of people. Facts about a town. Gazetteer entry for a town. Four people's language learning experiences.	About a person. Explaining the precise position of an item. Descriptions of towns from notes and interview. Personal experiences of learning English.	Introductions. Talking about your background/present situation. Useful classroom phrases.	Questions about past/present/future. Verbs with prepositions: **about, round** etc. Uses of **be**. **Wh-** words: relative clauses and after **say, ask,** etc.	Prepositional phrases; positions of places and objects. Uses of **about.** Time phrases. Expressing degrees of competence.	Spontaneous spoken discourse: starting to speak – phrases referring back; unfinished sentences. Questions and types of answers. Short answers with **not.**
Unit 2 Have you any idea what they're like?	Interests and habits. Describing and identifying people. Sports and injuries. Personalities and compatibilities. Ways of winning money. Animals.	An autobiography. Personal accounts giving overall impression of home life, interests, personality, career, etc. Two poems by Spike Milligan.	A description of someone. A brief autobiography. About yourself: personality and interests.	Talking about where you have lived, studied, worked. Anecdotes about injuries. Anecdotes about good luck and winning things.	Present simple to describe interests/pastimes. Simple past used in biography and anecdotes. Past/present simple forms of **have**. Verbs with **back.**	Adjectival phrases with modifiers: eg *with fairly long straight hair and brownish eyes.* Uses of **bit.** Measurements and distances. Phrases meaning 'whole' or 'part'.	**And, but, so** to link narrative. Intonation and stress to add meaning to qualifiers **quite, a bit, rather,** etc. Responses showing complete or partial agreement.
Unit 3 A good place for a holiday	Describing countryside and scenery. Things to do on holiday. Holiday activities – likes and dislikes. Holiday accommodation. Future holidays.	Two holiday postcards with different purposes. 'Discover the North Pennines' – tourist information leaflet. Opinions on farmhouse holidays. 'B & B. A home away from home'.	Notes about a holiday. Postcard, with indirect request for help. Persuasive description of tourist resort. Future holiday plans. Questions as headings. Describing holiday accommodation. Punctuation.	Discussing past and future holidays and preferences. Ways to avoid answering questions; ways of asking indirectly. 'Hedging'/expressing uncertainty.	'Delexical' uses of **Do, did** eg *We did a lot of walking…..* Speculative phrases with **suppose,** etc. Verbs with time and money, eg **spend.** Referring to the future. Uses of **been.**	Adjectival phrases describing landscapes. Phrases with time/times. Phrases specifying areas, eg *Western Europe.* Phrases with **for.**	Questions to elicit specific narrative information. *That was why/how…* for clarification. A persuasive text. Degrees of certainty: **likely/unlikely?**
Unit 4 They're probably worth the money	Rates of pay for jobs and professions. Jobs done by schoolchildren. Fair pay for women. Speculating about a picture. Discussing endings of stories.	Two jokes: 'At the dentist's'; 'If you call the plumber'. Letter to the Editor: 'Equal Opportunities'. Stephen's summer work. John's future work. Three funny stories: successful or doubtful employees.	Responding to the Letter to Editor about fair pay. Account of someone's work, and jobs past and future. Summarising personal views. Retelling a story from another point of view.	Comparing/evaluating rates of pay. Reacting to and giving opinions, with reasons. Sharing memories.	Phrases with **say, think, know.** Verbs and patterns followed by **to.** Verb forms and other phrases that express 'often', eg **tends to, in general.**	Phrases expressing amounts and comparison in connection with pay. Meanings and uses of any and its compounds. Phrases with **in.** Time phrases, eg *Some days, in between times.* Qualified noun phrases with **to,** eg *nowhere very exciting to go.*	Past narrative with dialogue. Speculation and co-operative discourse. Using specific questions in an interview.
Unit 5 Revision Unit	Schooldays. Favourite subjects. Talk about teachers. Other meanings for parts of the human body, eg *second hand.* Dreams and ambitions – past and present. What you were like as a child.	Poem by Michael Rosen: 'Teachers'. Comment on poem. 'Believe it or not': amazing facts about the human body. Riddles. Poem: 'Juster and Waiter'.	Report on findings of group survey. Notes/report on people's childhood ambitions. Description of yourself as a child.	Sharing past likes and dislikes with reasons. Asking indirectly and dropping hints. Useful classroom phrases. Checking people have understood. Comparing ambitions. Reacting to poems.	More past forms of common verbs. Verbs referring to future plans: **intend, expect,** etc. **Would, 'd,** and other ways to express repeated past actions. Verbs in passive after **was/will be,** etc.	Uses of **that** and **or.** Prepositional and adverbial phrases with **behind, along, away,** to express distance/time/space/discourse. Adjectives with **un-.** Noun phrases describing a picture.	The use of words like **so, well, then,** to link parts of a conversation. Exclamations as responses. Words used in dictionary definitions.

Unit	TASKS AND TOPICS	TEXTS AND FEATURES	WRITING	SOCIAL LANGUAGE	VERBS/TENSES CLAUSE PATTERNS	NOUN PHRASES PRONOUNS ADJECTIVES PREPOSITIONS ADVERBIAL PHRASES	SPOKEN AND WRITTEN DISCOURSE
Unit 6 What do you think's the best way of travelling?	Advantages/disadvantages of forms of transport. Most popular forms of transport. Giving lifts and hitch-hiking. Transport survey: who spends what on travel? Cut-price travel.	Public announcements. Two funny stories about travel. How a hovercraft works. A true story about Michael Caine. Modern legends. Travelcard leaflet.	Transport from your country to another. Advice to foreign visitor about a journey from your capital city. Continuation and summary of a story. Questions enquiring about a travelcard. Report on transport survey.	Anecdotes about difficult journeys. Recommendations about travel. Spoken and written advice. Making suggestions.	Verbs phrases with on. Past tense anecdotes used to give advice. Verb phrases with -ing to express interrupted action, past, habitual and future: eg *I'll be watching TV when you get back.* Present simple for colloquial narrative.	Phrases with on. Uses of way. 'Cause and result', eg use of as, led, to, etc. Neither, nor, so, to express similarity. Nouns from 'talk' verbs, eg explanation (from explain) Use/intonation of really in speech.	Colloquial style in popular writing, compared to formal past narrative. Use of No to express agreement; ways to begin disagreeing.
Unit 7 I'd probably cook an omelette	Talking about food. Describing and identifying food. Cooking for an unexpected guest. Favourite cheap meals. Predicting a story's development. Puzzle: how to cut the cake.	Recipe: scrambled eggs. 'Microwave' leaflet. Stories on eating out. Poem and comments. Serial story by Roald Dahl 'The Hitch-hiker': Part 1. 'Great eaters of the world'.	Simple recipe from your country. Advantages and disadvantages of microwave ovens. Rewriting a story from another point of view. Brief reply to the poem.	Explaining about food in your country. Asking for things in a restaurant. Anecdotes about restaurant experiences. Sharing reactions to poem.	Imperative forms in instructions. Would and past forms expressing hypothesis. By + -ing for manner. More uses of -ing. Verbs to express probability. Who, which, what introducing clauses.	Prefix: **micro**. Uses of by. Noun phrases with give: eg *an impression of, some good advice.* Descriptive phrases: eg *...the woman at the bus-stop with the large umbrella.*	Expressing purposes with to and for, etc. More ways of signalling cause, eg **through**, and unsignalled examples. Understanding/discussing longer literary texts.
Unit 8 I wish I were going with you	Journeys that went wrong. Major causes of motor accidents. Frightening flights. Identifying who was to blame for an accident. Advice in the event of an accident. Working out journey times from a timetable.	Stories: Petrol Tanker; Auto-Pilot; Jumbo Jet Pilot; No claim. Guardian Royal Exchange claim form: – semi-official source. British Rail timetable. Tourist information on London buses. 'The Hitch-hiker': Part 2.	An account of a frightening flight/accident. Comparison of two stories. Enquiries about bus services. A paragraph about 'The Hitch-hiker'.	Anecdotes about journeys that went wrong. Advising a course of action. Speculating on possible outcomes. Comparing personal reactions to a problem. Discussing a story.	Present perfect to ask about experiences. Verbs with off, eg **put off**. Phrases with **lead**. **Should, ought to,** etc for advice/obligation. Time clauses with **while, as soon as, until,** etc, and -ing forms. Meanings of get/got.	Adjectives for describing events and feelings. Meanings/uses of off. Comparative phrases with as...as. Time words and phrases eg **once, some time ago**. Expressions of size.	Language of a semi-official document. Asking/answering enquiries.
Unit 9 Everything you could imagine	Unusual speciality shops; street markets. Bargaining. Comparing systems for transacting/exchanging foreign money. Favourite adverts. Tax-free shopping for tourists. Speculating about a mystery.	'Speciality shops' – magazine feature. Instructions from Argos store catalogue. Advertising jingles. 'The Hitch-hiker': Part 3. Song: 'I discovered a pom pom pom ...'. Instructions for reclaiming VAT – from tourist newspaper.	Two systems of making payment in shops. List of products advertised. Beginning and continuation of story in traditional style. Favourite colours and associations.	Comparing shops/ markets in different countries. Recollections about advertisements and jingles. Stating preferences. Favourite colours.	Imperative informal instructions. Up verb phrases. Hypothesizing in conditional sentences. Past simple for future, hypothetical reference. Causative uses of get and have. Continuous tenses in narrative eg **As I was**.	Quantifying phrases: eg *all you want, just about anyone.* Impersonal use of you and they. Phrases with case eg *in any case.* Other words meaning if, eg *provided.* More phrases with **any**: eg *any longer.*	Colloquial expressions in written narrative dialogue. Educated/uneducated speech. Understanding how character is revealed in dialogue. Narrative structure: starting a story.
Unit 10 Revision Unit	Map reading, route planning/directions. Speculating about a place on a map. Comparing amenities. Summarising/ predicting a narrative. A sense of direction.	Teesdale road map. Gazetteer entries for two towns. 'The Hitch-hiker': Part 4. Useful notices for travellers, tourists, etc. A cockney song.	Notes detailing a route. Describing situation and scenery of small country town. Factual information about a town. Listing suggestions.	Comparing and evaluating routes. Conversation about notices. Feelings about the place you come from. Anecdotes about being lost.	Imperatives, and *I want you to ...* Clauses and phrases expressing cause, purpose, time, etc. Common adverbs ending in -ly. Uses of **come**.	Phrases expressing cause, purpose, time and condition. Phrases/compounds with **ever, whenever**. Prepositions used in abstract sense: eg *it's beyond me.*	Ways of checking you've understood. Starting/ending a discussion or report.

Unit	TASKS AND TOPICS	TEXTS AND FEATURES	WRITING	SOCIAL LANGUAGE	VERBS/TENSES CLAUSE PATTERNS	NOUN PHRASES / PRONOUNS / ADJECTIVES / PREPOSITIONS / ADVERBIAL PHRASES	SPOKEN AND WRITTEN DISCOURSE
Unit 11 I would have let his tyres down	How police are seen. Slang words for police. Traffic regulations. Hypothesising about the past. Excuses for speeding. Identifying people from a description. Handling situations. Parking problems.	Road signs/pedestrian notices. Funny: 'Humour in uniform'. 'The Hitch-hiker': Parts 5 and 6. Stories about parking problems. More signs and notices.	Short summary of a narrative. Parking – problems in a specific area, and possible solutions.	Informal anecdotes about traffic incidents/offences. Appropriate excuses in varying circumstances. Hypothesizing on why something is missing. Comparing reactions to a voice; discussing character.	Verbs followed by over and into. Uses of go/going. Uses of modals: might/could have. Ways of saying but (expressing contrast): eg whereas, though, yet, still, etc. Uses of let.	Prepositional phrases with over and into. Word forms: eg employ, employer, employment, etc.	Narrative sentences that set scene and further the story: eg As a police officer... I come across... Fronting patterns to start explanations eg What I did was... False starts in conversation.
Unit 12 Things for free or almost free	Leisure activities; inexpensive things to do in cities. Comparing amenities in various cities. Types of town accommodation. Funny/embarrassing experiences with children. Summarising/speculating on action in a story.	Tourist information on London amenities from a magazine. 'The Hitch-hiker': Parts 7 and 8. Advice on places to stay in London. Story: 'Babies can be useful'.	Descriptions of tourist attractions. Brochure on leisure activities. Descriptions of pictures required for the brochure. Short report for two different audiences giving advice on accommodation. Critical report on a particular hotel/hostel.	Recommendations to do with leisure activities. Advice on accommodation in towns. Speculating on reasons for people's behaviour.	Can and could for available activities. -ing forms in descriptions. Do for emphasis. Superlatives with the present perfect/past. Uses of break, give. Relative clauses in descriptions. Down verb phrases. Other verbs meaning said/asked eg make.	Pronoun reference and impersonal use of you. Phrases of location. Meanings/uses and phrases with of. Phrases with for. Superlatives in noun phrases: eg One of the most interesting books. Descriptive phrases in complex sentences. Nouns that go with give: eg a speech.	Design of brochure page: relationship between pictures and text. Writing for different types of audience. Using the context of text to infer meanings of words. Features of/attitudes to local dialects.
Unit 13 How did you do that? I never saw you	Practical, 'April Fool' jokes/conjuring tricks. Speculating about the past. Security and crime prevention. Talking about stolen objects. Describing people in a street from memory.	Stories about Hodja. 'The Hitch-hiker': Parts 9 and 10. 'Fight crime and protect your home' – advice/questionnaire from local directory. Crime Prevention article, with list of points.	Sequence of instructions for a trick. Completing questions/filling out a questionnaire. Report on a crime. Description of what was happening at a particular time – street scene.	Anecdotes about practical jokes, tricks. Discussion about crime prevention. Evaluating a questionnaire. Discussion of home security – what could be/should have been done.	Had in past perfect. Verbs of perception. Use of -ing in narrative. Modals, questions, imperative for recommendations. Passive with be/got. Reporting speech; use of that. Uses of whether/take.	Phrases with all/whole. Uses and meanings of from. Phrases building up descriptions of personal belongings. Common colloquial phrases.	Using clues from context to infer meanings. Different registers in public information leaflets on similar subject. Colloquial dialogue in a narrative text.
Unit 14 And he told me I was going to win	Traditional beliefs/superstitions. Customs associated with New Year. New Year resolutions. Fortune-telling. Origins of traditional children's songs. Possible endings for a story.	People's New Year resolutions. Stories about fortune-telling. 'The Hitch-hiker': final two parts. Historical basis of children's songs.	Paragraph about a person's character. Story about a fortune-telling experience. What adults told you as a child about your future.	Discussing things you think lucky/unlucky. Inferring a person's character/attitudes from their behaviour. Personal anecdotes comparing experiences of fortune-telling. Discussing someone's feelings.	The future in the past: eg He said I would... Modals expressing probability, certainty, etc. Clause patterns following ask, tell, etc., eg ask if. Verb phrases: out/after.	Words and phrases expressing certainty/probability/possibility eg Certainly not me. Meaning and uses of thing. Phrases with out and after.	Explanatory texts – origins of songs and folklore. Use of clauses with thing/point/trouble, etc, to introduce an idea to be developed: eg The thing is...
Unit 15 Revision Unit	Descriptions of people and places. Summarising stories. Preparing and performing 'magic'. Stating your case. Warnings and security. How to learn English. Evaluation of Course.	Gazetteer entry for a small town. Song: 'Keep right on'. Instructions for tricks. Warnings/advice to prevent loss or theft. Informational advice about learning English. Security adverts.	Brief biographies. Dramatisation of part of 'The Hitch-hiker'. Written instructions. How a trick works. Notes/summaries of spoken anecdotes. Advice for students. Questionnaire.	Social situations with requests/warnings. Agreeing/disagreeing with reasons. Ways to avoid loss. Sympathising. Finding out other people's opinions.	Verbs of motion to denote passage of time. Uses of verb mind. Modals/other ways of expressing certainty/uncertainty, etc. Expressing hypotheses, with if and would.	Relative pronouns and prepositional phrases to describe people/places. Phrases with mind: eg It's gone right out of my mind.	Turning story into a dramatisation. Summarising a spoken account in writing. Sequence of instructions backed by an explanation. Producing a questionnaire.

So I'm going to move on

This unit serves as a gentle introduction to the methodology and the way a lexical syllabus works. It recycles much of the work done in CCEC 1, and only introduces half as many 'new' words as later units will do.

It aims to build up students' confidence in using English as the medium of communication. Students are given a chance to introduce themselves and find out some things about their classmates if they don't already know them. Even if the class has been together for some time, and already covered CCEC 1, it is still useful to cover this unit, but perhaps more quickly, as it introduces some of the native English speakers you will be hearing on tape and revises a lot of useful language but in different contexts. In this unit students are introduced to words about people and words that help explain the place you come from.

Words marked [L] in the lexical aims boxes for each section in Units 1–15 appear in the Lexicon, and students should be encouraged to look these up. Words marked [T] do not actually appear in the texts, rubric or transcripts for that section, but can easily be introduced by the teacher.

OBJECTIVES

Lexical objectives are in TB10

Grammar and discourse

a Questions referring to past, present and future time. (3)
b Possible ways of introducing answers: **Well**, **So**, **Yes, But** etc. (3,10)
c Prepositions showing spatial relations revised: practising longer sentences made up of 2 or 3 prepositional phrases. (5)
d Verbs plus prepositions in which the preposition that follows changes the meaning of the verb. (6)
e Verb **to be** revised – basic meanings and patterns: **am**, **is**, **are**, **was**, **were**. (8)
f Revision of use of relative pronouns: **who**, **which**, **where**, **when**. (13)
g Use of hesitation markers: **er**, **erm**, **well** etc. (3,10)
h Discourse markers for providing positive feedback: **Mm**, **Aha**, **Oh**. (3,10)

Tasks

a Introducing a friend, giving various degrees of information about their background: work or study, family, where they live. (1)
b Introducing oneself fairly fully. (1)
c Exchanging information about one's background. (2)
d Describing the place you come from or a town you know well (spoken and written). (7)
e Talking about one's childhood, and the way people feel about going back to childhood places. (9,10,11)
f Reading and discussing different British people's experiences of learning foreign languages. (12)
g Classroom language: organising things, giving one's own opinion, asking for clarification etc. (13)

As in CCEC 1, the title of each unit is always a quotation from either the authentic recordings or written texts within the unit. Train your students to look for the title as they work through the unit. This can be done in the form of a competition. Who can spot the title first? This may be difficult for the students to understand in Unit 1, so just wait until the title occurs in Recording 1 and draw students' attention to it.

Course lead-in (books closed)

> **Aims:** 1 To put the students at their ease and to build up their confidence about using English as the main medium of instruction and communication in the classroom.
> 2 To introduce the teacher to the class, as appropriate.

In a monolingual class, the teacher should use English as much as possible to establish it as a viable means of communication.

1 On entering the class, use a suitable greeting. Tell students your name and write it on the board. Tell students what to call you and ask them to repeat the name you want them to use until they feel comfortable with it. Then tell students where you are from – either what country, or what town or village if you are all from the same area.

Notes for SB1 are on 2T overleaf.

1 Who's who?

Aims: 1 To revise introductions.
2 To give initial practice at using linguistic clues like distinguishing between **he/she** and past/present tenses.
3 To give students practice in applying their own knowledge of the world to decipher meanings and do the task.
4 Structure revision (as needed): passive recognition of past and present reference: **is, was, have, used to have, had, work, worked, used to work.**
5 To practise saying where places are in relation to others using phrases with the points of the compass and expressions of relative distance.

Lexis: capital, county, deal, industrial, insurance, introduce, Ireland, job, task (T)
Revision: **a long way from, born, business, called/you can call on me, comes from, country, deal (with)** [L], **in/to the north/south/east/west of ..., map, move/ moving, near, needs** (noun), **not far from, work out**

The purpose of the first page of each unit is to give a general introduction to the theme and some of the vocabulary from the unit. The people the students will be reading about or listening to in the unit are also introduced on this page. The material on these pages is not meant to be dealt with in detail as it will be recycled later in the unit.

SB1a

1 In groups of 3 or 4, students tell each other their names and where they're from – what town, village or country, depending on the circumstances. (Accuracy is not important at this stage – aim to build up students' confidence.)

SB1b

1 Emphasise that Catherine and John are real people, not actors, talking about themselves during their first meeting.

2 Students will probably need you to give them clues for this activity. For example, the statement, 'Before I had the children I was an insurance broker' probably applies to Catherine, because in most cultures, it is the woman whose career is affected when children are born. The plural form, children, means that she has more than one, so the comment beginning 'I've got two...' would probably also apply to Catherine. If students need further help, the tape for 1e could also be played at this point.

3 Students work in pairs, matching each quote to the person they think it is about. Encourage them to help each other and, if they begin to speak in their mother tongue, to use English as much as they can.

4 Pairs report back to the class. Also make sure target lexis has been understood.

Key: John: He comes from Warrington.
How old are your children?
My son's called Joe.
He's about 15 months – just about learning to walk ...
At the moment I'm looking for jobs, maybe moving out of London.
I work in Hillingdon, which is in West London.

Catherine: She was born in Dublin.
How old is she?
Before I had the children I was an insurance broker.
I used to work at a desk and have files of clients ... businesses in front of me and I would deal with their insurance needs.
I've got two ... I've got a three year old, a girl, called Lucy Claire and a nearly one and a half year old, who's called Neil.

SB1c PB1a

Culture note: The Irish Republic is independent of Britain (as opposed to Northern Ireland which is part of the British Isles). England, Scotland and Wales are separate countries within Great Britain. (British, therefore, does not equal English.)

5 You can tell students that all the British places mentioned in this unit are on this page somewhere. Britain is divided into counties: Cheshire is one. Do the students know any others?

6 Give students practice in saying these phrases if they need it. In pairs, students read the rubric and work out what to do themselves. Check the answers with the whole class to see if they found the places and can understand you when you say where they are.

Key: in the north of England: Warrington; in West London: Hillingdon; in central England: Birmingham; in Ireland: Dublin; not far from Scotland: Warrington; quite near Wales: Birmingham, Warrington; in Cheshire: Warrington; near Manchester: Warrington.

Planning   SB1d PB1b

The purpose of this activity is to increase students' confidence and to give them a chance to walk around and talk in English informally and purposefully to more than one person. Communication is more important than accuracy at this stage so don't correct.

7 Students choose a partner to introduce to other students. Give them a chance to ask each other about their work, study and family before they begin the task, using language similar to that in 1b. If all members of the class already know each other, get them to find out about the other person's best friend, wife, sister, brother etc.

8 Copy the survey form below on the board and tell students to complete one of their own after the introductions. The purpose of the form is to motivate students into communicating well enough to remember enough details to write down after talking to people.

NAME	WHERE FROM	WHERE STUDY/ WORK	FAMILY
Student 1			
Student 2			
Student 3			

9 Students walk around in twos and introduce each other to different people, talking about family and where they come from. Encourage students to continue their conversation if they find each other interesting. (The theme 'Jobs and Work' is the topic of Unit 4, so don't let students go into detail about their jobs here. Phrases like: 'I work for Sony' or 'I'm in business' are enough.)

10 Individually, students complete their survey forms. Encourage them to work from memory.

Written report

11 The survey form can be used as the basis for a homework assignment, e.g. 'Write three short sentences about one other person.' Give some help in class to start students off. Tell them to ask you if they want to check that something is right. Two or three sentences is enough at this stage. (This task should be done very simply as a lead-up to the task in 2d.)

SB1e 1e *

12 These are excerpts from the full recording in Section 2. Students listen to the tape to check their responses to 1b, if they have not already done so.

13 Students look up the word **deal** in the Lexicon at the back of their books. Ask them which meaning Catherine is using (in her last statement in recording 1e).

Unit 1
So I'm going to move on

1 Who's who?

a Introduce yourself to the people near you.
Find out their names and where they come from.

b Read the quotations. Say which person you think they are about.

Speech bubbles and captions in the images:

How old are your children?

I've got two . . . I've got a three year old, a girl, called Lucy Claire and a nearly one and a half year old, who's called Neil.

I work in Hillingdon, which is in West London.

She was born in Dublin . . .

He comes from Warrington . . .

At the moment I'm looking for jobs, maybe moving out of London.

John Mannion

Dublin, the capital of the Republic of Ireland.

Catherine McKinna

Warrington, an industrial town in the north of England.

My son's called Joe.

How old is he?

He's about 15 months – just about learning to walk . . .

Before I had the children I was an insurance broker.

I used to work at a desk and have files of clients . . . businesses in front of me and I would deal with their insurance needs.

c Work out where these places are.

Warrington   Dublin   Hillingdon   Birmingham

in the north of England
in West London
in central England
in Ireland

not far from Scotland
quite near Wales
in Cheshire
near Manchester

d Introduce the person next to you to one or two other people in the class. Say where they come from, where they work or study and a little about their family.

1e **e** Listen to the quotations. Find out who says what.

5

2 Background

2a a Listen to Catherine asking John about himself.

What kind of work does he do?
Why does he want to move on?
How far will John's family have to travel if he gets the job he is now applying for?

b Later, we asked John to write about Catherine.

CATHERINE by John

Catherine describes herself as a wife and mother. She has two children, one, Lucy Claire who is three and Neil who is eighteen months. Before having children she worked in insurance. She was born and lived for the first seven years of her life in Dublin. She still has an Irish accent, in reaction to the 'very English' community in which she lived. Her parents moved back to Ireland and so she returns there often.

How much did you know already?
Where do you think she lives now? How do you know?

c Now read what Catherine wrote about John. What additional information does she give us?

JOHN by Catherine

He is a teacher of English at a Catholic school in Hillingdon, London. He comes from Warrington which used to be in the county of Lancashire but is now in Cheshire. He is married with a 15 month old son called Joe who, he says, is just starting to get interesting and mischievous. John is trying to get a new job and is busy sending application forms and CVs all over the country.

d Find out things like this about one or two other people in your class. See if you or they have anything in common with each other.

▸ Write a paragraph about one person, but do not write their name.

Give your paragraph to your teacher to read out loud. Who is each paragraph about?

▸ How many people in your class have things in common with you? Tell each other.

3 Language study

a Questions

2a Write down the questions that Catherine asks John. Do they refer to past, present or future time?

Write down questions that you used when talking to people in section 2d above. What words do your questions begin with?

b so, well, . . .

2a Why does Catherine use the word **so**?
What words does John use to begin his answers? Why?

4 Wordpower

about

How many meanings does **about** have? Look at the cartoons. Who is saying what? Then look up **about** in the Lexicon. What other meanings are there?

Help us to bring about political change.

What I like about him is his sense of humour.

Can you ring back later? We're about to have dinner! Oh, about 9, 9-30 O.K?

A letter from school? Oh, what's it about?

2 Background

Aims: 1 To get students to listen for relevant information and not worry about understanding every word.
2 To get students to infer information which is not explicitly stated and to read for specific (new) information.
3 To give students practice in inferring from context the meanings of unfamiliar lexical items.
4 To give students practice in exchanging more detailed personal information.
5 Structure revision: Reflexive pronouns – herself/ himself, myself, yourself etc., as in 'I bought myself a drink'.

Lexis: community [L], **county, insurance, Ireland, job, leave, live, pleasant, reaction, return, sorry, tape** [T], **text** [T]
Revision: **accent, all over, busy, called, describe, find out, going to** (planning to), **interesting, life, married, moved back to, move on, no chance of (promotion), often, sending, still, trying, with, used to be/is now.**

Listening   SB2a [2a] *

*The purpose of 2a is to introduce students to a **listening** phase and to prepare them for the parallel task in 2d. See the Introduction to the Teacher's Book for information on the general aims and handling of the **input** and **listening** components, especially if you have students who are new to the methodology.*
The course includes both scripted and unscripted recordings. Recording 2a is the first of the unscripted recordings in which native speakers are set a task to carry out, without following a script, in natural language. The people in the unscripted recordings are being themselves – there is no acting or role-playing involved.

1 Students read the questions about John and listen for the answers to them. Play the tape as many times as they need, but bear in mind they will be hearing it again twice for the Language Study. They will need to look at a map of Britain with a scale for the last question. Between playings, allow the students to discuss the answers to the questions in pairs. ILEA refers to the Inner London Education Authority.

Culture Note: Catherine has a very light Irish accent. John has a light North country accent. Both are equally acceptable internationally, and quite clear.

Discussion points: Ask whether people in the north/west of their countries speak the same way as those in the south/east. Do the students themselves have regional accents, or did they when they were younger? Do they change their accents according to the person they are speaking to? (Most people speak differently when back in their own villages for example). Does their accent get stronger or milder when they are with people from a part of the country that they don't like? (Catherine's family reacted against the very English community they lived in by keeping their accents.)

Key: John's a teacher.
He wants to change jobs because there's no chance of promotion where he works now.
If he gets the job in Telford he will have to travel about 150 miles north-west of London.

Reading   SB2b

2 Students read the text about Catherine and discuss the questions.

Key: We knew about Catherine's family situation and her former job as an insurance broker from 1e.
We know she lives in England now because she returns to Ireland often to see her parents.

3 Write the new words from the lexis box on the board and check that the students have understood them. Students work in pairs to guess the meanings of the words from context. Encourage them to ask you if they are really stuck and cannot guess the meaning of a word or phrase.
OR
Find the phrase in which the word occurred in the Lexical Objectives List on page 10T, and give this to the students.

4 Students should keep vocabulary books for new words.

As a general point, the tasks have been designed in such a way as to provide students with an opportunity to process the lexis in the natural course of the activity, or in a subsequent Language Study. A few words may occasionally need pre-teaching; all new words can usefully be revised at the end of each activity.

Reading   SB2c

5 Students read to find the new information about John.

Key: John teaches at a Catholic school.
Warrington used to be in the county of Lancashire.
His son is starting to get interesting etc.

Task   SB2d PB2

*This section is intended to get students used to the **task-planning–report** cycle which is vital to the methodology of this course.*
*The first part of the cycle is the **task** in which students work (in pairs or groups) to find out specific information about each other or to solve a puzzle or problem. Students will inevitably use inaccurate language here, but the aim is to encourage communication rather than accuracy. Correction of mistakes is not advised at this stage.*

*In the second part of the cycle, students **plan** and practise what they are going to say to the rest of the class about their findings. Help and correction are important at this stage to encourage accurate use of language.*

*The third part of the cycle is the **report** itself, when students tell the rest of the class what they have found out. The purpose behind the report phase is to encourage students to want to use accurate language in a formal public situation. Report phases are marked with yellow triangles in the Student's Book.*

6 Students now do the same as they heard Catherine and John doing on the tape. Tell them it is like a short interview. Make sure they choose different people to talk to this time.

7 Students should take brief notes to help them with their writing later on – this interview should enable students to write a paragraph describing the person's background in more detail than they did in 1d.

Planning and report

8 Students study John and Catherine's paragraphs and try to write something similar. Students should not use a name in their paragraph (see below). Help students with their writing at this stage and collect the reports when students have finished.

9 Mix up and read out the descriptions. Ask students to write down who they think it is, not shout out the name.
or
Ask students to read out their descriptions, but give them time to read them through and practise reading out loud first. Students find other people with the same interests, or with something in common, as they listen.

Discussion points: What points do most of the backgrounds have in common? Whose background did the class think was the most interesting or different? Why?

3T

2 Background

2a **a** Listen to Catherine asking John about himself.

What kind of work does he do?
Why does he want to move on?
How far will John's family have to travel if he gets the job he is now applying for?

b Later, we asked John to write about Catherine.

> CATHERINE by John
>
> Catherine describes herself as a wife and mother. She has two children, one, Lucy Claire who is three and Neil who is eighteen months. Before having children she worked in insurance. She was born and lived for the first seven years of her life in Dublin. She still has an Irish accent, in reaction to the 'very English' community in which she lived. Her parents moved back to Ireland and so she returns there often.

How much did you know already?
Where do you think she lives now? How do you know?

c Now read what Catherine wrote about John. What additional information does she give us?

> JOHN by Catherine
>
> He is a teacher of English at a Catholic school in Hillingdon, London. He comes from Warrington which used to be in the county of Lancashire but is now in Cheshire. He is married with a 15 month old son called Joe who, he says, is just starting to get interesting and mischievous. John is trying to get a new job and is busy sending application forms and CVs all over the country.

d Find out things like this about one or two other people in your class. See if you or they have anything in common with each other.

▶ Write a paragraph about one person, but do not write their name. ◀

Give your paragraph to your teacher to read out loud. Who is each paragraph about?

▶ How many people in your class have things in common with you? Tell each other. ◀

3 Language study

a Questions

2a Write down the questions that Catherine asks John. Do they refer to past, present or future time?

Write down questions that you used when talking to people in section 2d above. What words do your questions begin with?

b so, well, …

2a Why does Catherine use the word **so**?
What words does John use to begin his answers? Why?

4 Wordpower

about

How many meanings does **about** have? Look at the cartoons. Who is saying what? Then look up **about** in the Lexicon. What other meanings are there?

Help us to bring about political change.

What I like about him is his sense of humour.

Can you ring back later? We're about to have dinner! Oh, about 9, 9-30 O.K?

A letter from school? Oh, what's it about?

3 Language study

Aims: 1 To revise question forms.
2 To practise recognising questions referring to past, present and future time.
3 Recognition of discourse hesitation markers e.g. **er**, **erm**.
4 Recognition and understanding of markers for providing positive feedback e.g. **Mm**, **Aha**.

Listening   SB3a 2a * PB3

1 Students listen to Recording 2a again. Instruct them to ask you to stop the tape when they hear a question so they can write it down.

2 Students tell you whether the question refers to past, present (usually meaning 'generally true' or 'normally does') or future times.

3 Encourage students to think of other question forms or parallel structures to those Catherine has used.

4 Section 13a on questions could be done at this point.

   Key: Present:
   What do you teach?
   So you teach (or you're teaching) in London?
   Do you work for the ILEA?
   Where's that? Near Birmingham, is it?

   Future: So where will you look, do you think?

   Past: none

SB3b 2a *

5 Students listen for and note down the words that often begin questions and answers. Ask students for other examples like the ones they have heard.

   Key: So seems to have a reviewing effect here: 'having talked about that, let's go on'.
   Well is very often used to gain a bit of time; if you're not sure what to say, or how to say it, especially if there's an explanation to come, not just a short answer.
   John also began answers with: I teach . . .; Mm; No, I work . . . (No = for the ILEA); It is, yes, but we . . . (in response to 'is it?' and introducing a negative).

4 Wordpower

Aims: 1 To introduce students to the idea that some words in English are very useful because they have so many meanings.
2 To extend students' knowledge of the word **about**. Categories 2 and 4–7 in the Lexicon may be new to them. (The Lexicon appears on Student's Book pages 111–125.)

Lexis: about

SB4 PB4

1 In pairs, students try to decide who is saying what. Encourage speculation – there are no 'right' answers.

2 Encourage students to work in their pairs, but independently of the teacher as far as possible.

3 Refer students to the Lexicon. Be prepared to give additional examples for Categories 2 and 4–7.

4 Ask students if they have the same word for all of these uses for **about** in their own language.

Further examples:
2 The thing about X is that he/she always wears smart/ bright etc. clothes.
   What I like about English is that it is understood in many different countries.

5 Can I do it/finish this tomorrow? I'm about to go home/go out/do my homework/start cooking.

6 **go about** = start: What's the best way to go about learning a language? He went about the problem of X as best he could.
   The power cut was brought about by a huge storm.

7 Who is the person in your family who often sits about doing nothing? Who walks about all day? Who leaves books and clothes lying about the room?

   Key: Help us to . . . 6; Can you ring back . . . 5; What I like about . . . 2; A letter . . . 1

5 Where would you hide it?

Aims: 1 Revision of prepositions showing spatial relations.
2 Practising longer sentences made up of 2 or 3 prepositional phrases.
Lexis: repeating [T], **words**

Guessing game lead-in   SB5   PB5

1 Check that students know most of the names of the common furniture in the room. Don't give the words for less common things; students can use a phrase with a word like 'thing', e.g. 'next to the thing in the corner of the shelf on the right.'

2 See if students can read the instructions and play the game. Tell them you will help out if necessary. Students decide on a place in pairs – without pointing to it!

3 Pairs ask each other: 'Would you put it . . . under a book? If the answer is yes, then 'Which book?', 'The book on the left under the cat' and so on.

4 In pairs, students write sentences about where they would hide their objects. Then students exchange sentences to see if they can find each other's objects.

Listening

5 Students listen to the tape and find out where John and Catherine hid their object. Students could practise repeating sentences after the tape, but try to make the activity enjoyable.

6 Game: this activity could be extended to the classroom. For example, ask 2 people to wait outside for a minute. Hide a small coin somewhere. If the 2 people can guess in 3 (or 4) guesses, they can have the money.

Discussion points: Ask students where they/their parents/ grandparents keep/used to keep their keys/English books/valuables/photos.
Do they ever lose things and find them in silly places? Where?

Before going on to section 6 you could do either section 13b or section 8.

6 Language study

Aims: 1 To give students practice in recognising and understanding verbs with prepositions that function as a single lexical item.
2 To introduce students to the idea that the preposition that follows the verb can change the meaning of the verb, e.g. to give up smoking.

SB6

1 In pairs, students work out the meanings of the verbs with prepositions.

Key: 1 omitted   2 think   3 discover   4 give to each person in turn   5 refer to   6 remaining

7 A town you know

The source material for this section is from the Automobile Association Handbook for drivers in the UK. Before starting this section invent AA style entries for nearby towns, including the town you are in. Omit place names and see if students can recognise which towns they are.

Aims: 1 To stimulate discussion.
2 To practise interpreting symbols and abbreviations and in expanding a text which contains them.
3 To practise exchanging information about a place students know well.
4 To practise writing a short description of a place.
Lexis: hotel, partner, population [T]
Revision: abbreviations for days of the week, expressions of distance/position, **main** (biggest), **market, mile** (1 mile = about 1.7 km), prepositions: **with, from, in, on, for.** Other high frequency words, like **roofs**, as needed.

Writing task   SB7a

1 Students should read the description of Hillingdon and study the picture, and then discuss the questions in 7a in pairs, making notes if they like.

2 After discussing the apparent differences with the class, ask students what other differences there might be, e.g. colour of letter boxes, phone boxes, policemen's hats/ helmets, types of buses etc.

Culture note: Early closing (Ec) is on one day a week, usually Wednesday or Thursday; most shops close at 1 p.m. instead of staying open until 5.30 or 6.00 p.m. Some big supermarkets, however, stay open from 8 a.m. to 8 p.m., six days a week. All shops are supposed to close on Sunday. Market days (Md) are usually once a week.

3 Description of Warrington: In pairs, ask students to make a list of the symbols and to guess their meanings. Then give them the Key to symbols from the AA Guide to check their guesses and help them finish their descriptions.

Key: Ec – early closing; Md – market day; *** – hotel classification; rm – number of bedrooms; P – parking on hotel premises (number of cars in brackets); B&B – bed and breakfast; (e) and (f) refer to hotel charges – on the AA scale, (a) is the cheapest, (k) the most expensive.

Planning   SB7b

4 In pairs, students exchange information about a town each knows well. Students use the descriptions of Warrington and Hillingdon as guides to help them decide what information to ask for.

5 Individually, students write their descriptions. Help them write about their partner's town and tell them to follow the text about Hillingdon if they want to. Stress that, because this is writing, you want their descriptions to be as accurate as they can make them.

Report

6 Partners exchange descriptions and check for both grammatical and content accuracy.

7 Optional preposition review: students read about Hillingdon and find all the phrases with prepositions in. Students list them and say what they mean in each case.

Key: of London	on Wednesdays
with a population	in Hillingdon on
of about 230,000	Western Avenue
from Uxbridge	with 64 rooms
from the centre	with bathroom
of London	for about 200 cars

8 The descriptions of a town students know well could be done for homework. Tell them to model their descriptions on what they have done in class.

Where would you hide it?

Discuss with your neighbour the best place in the room on the right to hide something small (like money or keys) if you were playing a game. Decide exactly where you would put it. For example:

In the vase on the bottom shelf of the bookcase on the left of the fire.

Here are some words to help you.

on	between	at the bottom/top
behind	by	next to
below	in	over
beside	in front of	under

See how quickly you can guess which places other people have decided on. Ask them questions. They can only answer 'yes' or 'no'.

▶ Can you write any sentences of twelve words or more to describe where to hide the object? ◀

5 We asked two people where they would choose. Listen and find out if they decided on the same places as you.

Language study ....

Verbs with prepositions

Can you explain what these examples mean?

1 *a b c d f g h – which letter has been left out?*
2 *Work out where these places are.*

3 *Find out their names and where they come from.*
4 *Could you pass the books round please?*
5 *Look up the word about in the Lexicon.*
6 *There are twelve books and ten students. How many books are left over?*

A town you know

Hillingdon is a suburb of London with a population of about 230,000. It is two miles from Uxbridge and fourteen miles from the centre of London. Early closing is on Wednesdays. There is no market Day. The main hotel in Hillingdon is the Master Brewer on Western Avenue, (A40) telephone Uxbridge (0895) 61199. It is a large hotel with 64 rooms, each with bathroom. It has parking for about 200 cars. J.W.
(from facts taken from the AA members' Handbook. 1986/87)

a Hillingdon, where John works, is a typical West London suburb. Could this be a picture of a town in your country? Why not? What things in this photo strike you as being typically English?

What can you find out about the town of Warrington (which is where John originally comes from) from this *AA Members' Handbook* entry? Read the description of Hillingdon above, then see if you can guess what the signs and symbols for Warrington mean.

WARRINGTON 135,568 Cheshire (STD 0925) Map33sj68 EcThu MdWed/Fri/Sat Bolton 21, Chester 21, Liverpool 18, London 190, Manchester 20.
***Fir Grove Knutsford Old Rd Tel 67471 rm38 (18 bath 20 shower)
100P B&B (e) (f)[price range from £35–45]
**Patten Arms Parker St (GW) Tel 36602 rm43 (29 bath 14 shower) 25P B&B (e)

▶ Write a full description for Warrington using the handbook entry. ◀

b Find out about a town your partner knows well. Ask questions and then write a short description. Give it to your partner to check.

Write a description of a town you know well. Make one factual mistake. See if your partner can guess what the mistake is.

7

8 Grammar revision

am, is, are, was, were

Look at these uses of the verb **to be**.

1 Who or what
It's a very pleasant school.
I was an insurance broker.

2 Describing
He's about fifteen months.
She's quite small.

3 Where
It's near Birmingham, isn't it?
That was in Warrington.

4 With -**ing**
He's getting to the more interesting stage isn't he?
At the moment I'm looking for jobs.

5 With -**ed, -en**
He's married.
Where were you born and brought up?

Which category do these examples belong to?

a *John is trying to get a new job.*
b *It's a new town I think.*
c *Now it's in Cheshire.*
d *Hillingdon is a suburb of London.*
e *It's two miles from Uxbridge.*
f *His son is called Joe.*
g *Joe is just starting to get mischievous.*
h *Catherine left Dublin when she was seven.*

9 Childhood

Catherine's family

| guess |
| hated |
| worse |
| long |
| **?** |
| Words to guess |

9a **a** John and Catherine talked to each other about where they were born and brought up, and where they lived as children.

Before you listen, say whether you think these sentences are true or false.

a *John's parents have lived in the same house for more than twenty years.*
b *John enjoyed going to school.*
c *There were no girls at John's secondary school.*
d *John likes going back to Warrington.*
e *Catherine started school in Ireland.*
f *Although she is Irish she has an English accent.*
g *They had a lot of Irish friends as children in England.*
h *Catherine still lives near her mother and father.*
i *She used to live in a small Irish community in London.*

After listening, correct the sentences which are false.

community	over	**L** Words
left/leave	remain	to look up
brought up/		

b How does each of them feel about the community in which they lived as children?
Being away and going back – what does each of them say about this?
8 Where do their parents live now?

10 Language study

a Which phrases don't always refer to past time?

in those days	some time ago
then	at that time
every year	

b Study the transcript of **9a**.

1 Can you find five phrases which show how John felt about his schools and Warrington itself? e.g. *I didn't like it.* Did he give any reasons?

2 When each person starts speaking, what are the first two or three words that they say? e.g. *I was born . . . What was . . . Erm sometimes, . . . Ah! I beg your pardon.*
How do they relate to what has gone before?

3 What do you think they were going to say? Can you finish their unfinished sentences?

What was . . . ? Did you like where you lived?
Was it . . . ?
But living there was . . .
I haven't been back since, really. (since when?)

4 Which one of these words/phrases did Catherine say? Which two others would also be possible here?

Actually   In fact   But   Funnily enough

CM: Oh, I go back there every year . . . _____ I'm going on my holidays there tomorrow!

11 Your partner's childhood

Find out as much as you can about your partner's childhood. Write notes so that you can tell the class about the most important things.

▷ Tell the class about your partner. ◁

Grammar Revision

Aim: To revise the basic meanings and patterns of the verb **to be**.

*Don't try to contrast or explain the traditional differences between the present simple and the present continuous in this section; for example, the verb **to be** plus '-ing' in 'He's getting to the more interesting stage, isn't he?' is also describing.*

SB8 PB8

1 Do a couple of examples with the class to make sure they understand how to approach the exercise. In pairs, students match the examples to the appropriate categories.

2 Additional examples which you can use at any point in the activity (all of which occur later in the book):

1 Who or what?
This is a friend of Becky's.
He was a small, ratty-faced man.

2 Describing
I'm not very tall.
My little sisters were even smaller than me.
The seats inside were darker blue and they were made of leather.

3 Where?
It was in Africa.
I've never been to South America. Have you been there?

4 With -ing
I'm taking my two children with me.
My husband is joining us in a week's time.
I was still living with my family.

5 With -ed, -en
I'm not surprised.
A nuclear scientist is paid reasonably well.
One of the postcards was written in London.

Key: a 4   b 1   c 3   d 1   e 3   f 5   g 4   h 2

Childhood

Aims: 1 To prepare students for the parallel task in section 11.
2 To give students practice in anticipating what they are going to hear.
3 To give students practice in listening for specific information and not worrying about understanding every word.

Lexis: bring/brought [L], **community** [L], **guess, hate, house, Ireland, leave/left, live, long, reaction, remain** [L], **tape** [T], **worse**

Listening   SB9a   9a *   PB9

*Culture note: In Britain now, most schools are comprehensive schools, that is, they take children of all abilities. When John was a child, though, there were commonly two types of schools – grammar schools for the brighter children and secondary modern schools for less academic children. John lived in an area where most children probably went to a secondary modern school. He says that it was bad enough going to an all boys' school, but being a grammar school made it even worse.
Most children, including those in Ireland, start primary school at the age of 5.*

1 Students discuss the true/false questions first and write down T or F (in pencil) for each one before they listen. Then play the tape for them, taking the questions one at a time.

Key: a T   b F   c T   d T   e T   f F   g F   h F   i F

2 Words to guess: These words are less frequent, therefore less important, than the 'Words to look up' (see note 3). Students should use the transcript to guess their meanings from context.

3 Words to look up: Refer students to the Lexicon in the back of the Student's Book. Students select the appropriate meaning for the context of the transcript from the list of meanings given in the Lexicon. The teacher can use this time as an opportunity to help students with the other meanings for the words given in the Lexicon.

4 See if students can give you other words with similar meanings to the 'Words to guess' and 'Words to look up'.

Examples
hated – really didn't like
worse – 'more bad' (which people never say)
long – for very long = for a long time
community – group of people (see Lexicon)
brought – brought over to England = her parents took her away from Ireland; 'brought up' is different: you could say she 'grew up' in Ireland with her parents.
remain – stay, i.e. not lose their Irish identity (retain = keep, not lose)
left = past of verb 'leave'

SB9b

5 Students should try to answer these questions from memory before you replay the tape. Students discuss the answers to the questions in pairs, then use the transcript to check their answers.

Key: John's was a close community; it still feels like home to him.
Catherine was part of a small Irish family in the middle of a very English community, which she implies was not very easy – her parents obviously felt they were in danger of losing their Irish identity.

John left when he was 18, and doesn't often go back, but when he does he still feels at home there.
Catherine goes back to Ireland every year.

John's parents are in Warrington.
Catherine's parents are living in Ireland.

Language study

Aims: 1 To draw students' attention to some of the words and phrases used to refer to past, present and future time, e.g. **then, at that time**.
2 To focus attention on ways of expressing dislike.
3 To show how native speakers use hesitation markers and discourse markers which provide feedback.
4 Understanding the meaning and use of discourse markers: **actually, in fact, but, funnily enough**.

Lexis: ready

SB10a

1 In pairs, students decide on their answers. Ask them to write examples of sentences in which these words or phrases refer to past time and, where possible, present and future time as well.

Key: Examples:
A: I'll leave at 11.00.
B: You can't leave then.
I go/will go there every year.
I graduate in one year and then/at that time I'll think about getting married.

Grammar revision

am, is, are, was, were

Look at these uses of the verb **to be**.

1 Who or what
It's a very pleasant school.
I was an insurance broker.

2 Describing
He's about fifteen months.
She's quite small.

3 Where
It's near Birmingham, isn't it?
That was in Warrington.

4 With **-ing**
He's getting to the more interesting stage isn't he?
At the moment I'm looking for jobs.

5 With **-ed, -en**
He's married.
Where were you born and brought up?

Which category do these examples belong to?

a *John is trying to get a new job.*
b *It's a new town I think.*
c *Now it's in Cheshire.*
d *Hillingdon is a suburb of London.*

e *It's two miles from Uxbridge.*
f *His son is called Joe.*
g *Joe is just starting to get mischievous.*
h *Catherine left Dublin when she was seven.*

---

9 # Childhood

guess
hated
worse
long

?
Words
to guess

Catherine's family

9a **a** John and Cathcrine talked to each other about where they were born and brought up, and where they lived as children.

Before you listen, say whether you think these sentences are true or false.

a *John's parents have lived in the same house for more than twenty years.*
b *John enjoyed going to school.*
c *There were no girls at John's secondary school.*
d *John likes going back to Warrington.*
e *Catherine started school in Ireland.*
f *Although she is Irish she has an English accent.*
g *They had a lot of Irish friends as children in England.*
h *Catherine still lives near her mother and father.*
i *She used to live in a small Irish community in London.*

After listening, correct the sentences which are false.

community	over	**L** Words
left/leave	remain	to look up
brought up/		

b How does each of them feel about the community in which they lived as children?
Being away and going back – what does each of them say about this?
8 Where do their parents live now?

---

10 # *Language study*

a Which phrases don't always refer to past time?

in those days   some time ago
then   at that time
every year

b Study the transcript of **9a**.

1 Can you find five phrases which show how John felt about his schools and Warrington itself? e.g. *I didn't like it.* Did he give any reasons?

2 When each person starts speaking, what are the first two or three words that they say? e.g. *I was born ... What was ... Erm sometimes, ... Ah! I beg your pardon.*
How do they relate to what has gone before?

3 What do you think they were going to say? Can you finish their unfinished sentences?

What was ...? Did you like where you lived? Was it ...?
But living there was ...
I haven't been back since, really. (since when?)

4 Which one of these words/phrases did Catherine say? Which two others would also be possible here?

Actually   In fact   But   Funnily enough

CM: Oh, I go back there every year ... ____ I'm going on my holidays there tomorrow!

---

11 # Your partner's childhood

Find out as much as you can about your partner's childhood. Write notes so that you can tell the class about the most important things.

▷ Tell the class about your partner. ◁

Listening SB10b 9a

2 Students study the transcript individually for the 5 phrases and the reasons John gives for his feelings, and then compare their answers. Ask them if they found the same 5 phrases.

Key: Phrases:
I hated being at school there.
I didn't like it.
It was a boys' grammar school, which was even worse.
... my secondary school I didn't enjoy.
Warrington itself, it's quite a close community ... so you did feel at home.
Reasons he didn't like it:
It was an all boys' grammar school.

SB10b2

This exercise focuses students' attention on: hesitation markers, like 'erm', 'er'; and on words that introduce some kind of feedback to the question or information given, e.g. 'Oh' (as in 'Oh great'), 'Ah!' = 'I see', and 'aha' meaning 'Yes, go on'. It also focuses their attention on 'Well', 'So', question words and frequent collocations like, 'And then I...' and 'But if...'.

3 Students find the words beginning the sentences. Ask students what they say in their own language for words like 'Aha,' 'Oh' and 'Mm'. Point out that these words are used differently in English.

SB10b3

This exercise develops students' predictive abilities and helps them develop better syntax.

4 Students finish the sentences.
Possible answers:
What was it like where you lived?
Was it nice?
But living there was alright/fine/very nice/okay.
... since I left there at the age of 18. At least, I haven't been back for a long visit. Just for a day maybe.

SB10b4

5 Students decide on their answers. Check and discuss.

Key: in fact (said), actually, funnily enough

Discussion points: (see section 11 – don't ask too many personal questions about childhood yet.) What kind of community do most of the students come from? A close community where everyone knows everyone? Or the kind of place where you know a few neighbours, but that's all? Or a scattered farming community? Do students often go back to their childhood home? Do any of them still live in the village or town they were born in?

11 Your partner's childhood

Aims: 1 To encourage discussion about the past.
2 To give students practice in making notes.
3 To give students practice in making a (formal) report to the class on their findings.

*See the aims for section 2, or the general description of **task** aims in the Introduction, for detailed aims and procedures for the **task – report** cycle.*

Task SB11

1 In pairs students do the same as John and Catherine did on tape. Try to arrange it so that they don't talk to the same students as they did for previous tasks.

Planning

2 Help students work in pairs to complete their notes so they can use them to refer to when telling the class about their partner's childhood. You could also hear them saying out loud some of the things they have written down.

Report

3 Students take turns telling the class about their partner: when most pairs are ready, bring the class together. Ask a good pair to start. Before they begin, ask the others to listen to find out which person's childhood had the most in common with their own (this provides a purpose for listening).
Rephrase their report if necessary. If you cannot understand what they are saying, say 'Sorry' as you would in normal conversation.
Be encouraging. Although accuracy is important during the report phase, don't be too insistent on correcting every mistake in these early units. Students' confidence also needs building.

12 Languages you've learnt

Aims: 1 To encourage students to read for interest and relevant details only.
2 To give students an opportunity to react personally to other people's ideas and to relate them to their own feelings and experiences.

Lexis: apart from [L], **(any) degree, foreign** [L], **learning, literature, not, particular, particularly, Russian, Spanish, struggle** [L], **study, tiny (bit)**
Revision: **any more** (any longer), **get by in** (just manage), **(fairly) similar, that's about it**

SB12a PB12a

1 Don't go into these questions in detail (omit them altogether if you want to do 12g below). Instead tell students about your own language learning experiences. Say what languages you can speak, read and write now.

Listening SB12b 12b * PB12

2 Students listen to the tape and take notes about Catherine and Stephen. Suggest they make a table to fill in and give them a framework like the following.

Key:

	CATH.	STEPH.
FRENCH	learnt at school	can get by
GERMAN	learnt at school	no
SPANISH	no	no
ITALIAN	tiny bit	reads a little
RUSSIAN	no	no
LATIN	no	no
OTHER:	a tiny bit of Greek	American
MALAY,		
THAI,		
JAPANESE		

When students have done 12c they can extend this table to include M. West, R. Turner, C. Egerton and E. Turner.

Listening SB12c 12c

3 Students read the introduction to 12c. Ask them if they feel that English people are lazy about learning other foreign languages. How many British people do they know who can speak their language really well/quite well/just a bit? Encourage them to comment if they wish.

4 Students read and then listen to reports 1–4, which are written by British people. Ask students for their reactions to these before they work in pairs to complete the table from 12b.

5 Pairs compare answers. An overhead transparency would provide a good focus for a further class discussion of answers.

Key: M. West: speaks some French and a bit of Russian.
R. Turner: learnt French at school, was taught Latin and German but didn't learn either.
C. Egerton: learnt French and Spanish at school, learnt German at school and university, and speaks Malay and Thai.
E. Turner: studied French, and Latin at school.
All are native speakers of English.

SB12d

6 Students will have already discussed 12b and c in some detail, so go over these questions to summarise.
Class vote: does the class agree that the British are really lazy about learning other people's languages? Let them vote: yes/no/just a bit.

SB12e

7 Students choose the 3 best ways of learning a language individually. Then put the class responses on the board and discuss. Ask students why they have selected their responses and what other ideas they have.

8 Tell students to find some statements in the text that apply to them personally. (Give students a minute to prepare their answers to this.) Then ask them: What are some of the most useful English phrases you know already? When might you/do you have to use English in your own country? Why are you learning English now?

Writing homework SB12f

9 If you have a lower ability class, students might find this framework useful as preparation for the paragraph. See also review page 13c.

Many/most/some people say that . . .	the British never speak . . .
	the British are quite willing to learn . . .
	is fairly easy to learn.
	is quite difficult to learn.

We were taught . . . at school, but . . .

I took a . . . course some/many/two years ago, and/but . . .

I tried to learn . . . but I didn't get very far/do very well/ remember very much.

When I try to speak . . ., it's always/often a . . . word that comes into my head instead.

My . . . has been particularly/quite/very useful.

Planning SB12g

10 Students' survey questions could be based on the conversation between Catherine and John. Students need to find out how many languages the others know and which they are the most fluent in. Encourage them to ask specific questions about skills: listening, speaking, reading, writing; often language learners will be very fluent in some skills and not in others.

11 Students write down some of the questions they will need to ask. Teacher provides input and assistance as needed. If students need more help, refer them to 13a on the review page, but warn them that they must choose questions that make sense, e.g. 'Where did you do?' does not make sense.

12 Students take turns to interview the other members of their groups. Ask them to appoint a group secretary to record results for the group. Help students collate their results simply, e.g. 'Everybody in this group spoke at least two languages, . . . and . . . . One person also speaks . . . . We can all read and write . . . , and two of us can . . . .' and so on.

Report

13 Students either read the results of their surveys to the class or pass around a written report. Written reports could be collected later and put on the wall. The other students read or listen to find out who in the class speaks/has learnt the most languages.

Languages you've learnt

a What languages can you speak? How many foreign languages have you learnt, or tried to learn?

12b **b** Catherine talked to someone called Stephen about the languages they knew. Listen and make a list of the languages they knew, and say how good they were at each.

12c **c** Many people say that the British are very lazy about learning foreign languages, because they think that when they go abroad they will usually be able to find someone who speaks English.
To find out if this was true, we asked a variety of British people from different walks of life about their language learning experiences.
Some of their comments and stories are written here. Read them. Do you think the British *are* lazy about learning languages?

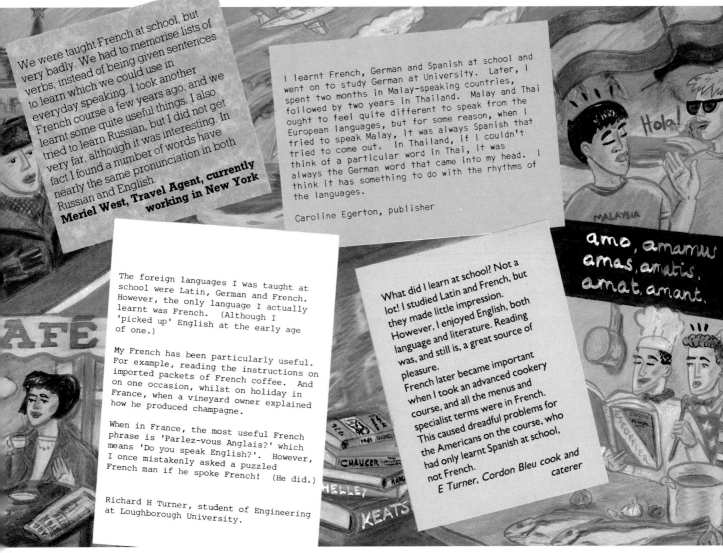

We were taught French at school, but very badly. We had to memorise lists of verbs, instead of being given sentences to learn which we could use in everyday speaking. I took another French course a few years ago, and we learnt some quite useful things. I also tried to learn Russian, but I did not get very far, although it was interesting. In fact I found a number of words have nearly the same pronunciation in both Russian and English.
Meriel West, Travel Agent, currently working in New York

I learnt French, German and Spanish at school and went on to study German at University. Later, I spent two months in Malay-speaking countries, followed by two years in Thailand. Malay and Thai ought to feel quite different to speak from the European languages, but for some reason, when I tried to speak Malay, it was always Spanish that tried to come out. In Thailand, if I couldn't think of a particular word in Thai, it was always the German word that came into my head. I think it has something to do with the rhythms of the languages.

Caroline Egerton, publisher

The foreign languages I was taught at school were Latin, German and French. However, the only language I actually learnt was French. (Although I 'picked up' English at the early age of one.)

My French has been particularly useful. For example, reading the instructions on imported packets of French coffee. And on one occasion, whilst on holiday in France, when a vineyard owner explained how he produced champagne.

When in France, the most useful French phrase is 'Parlez-vous Anglais?' which means 'Do you speak English?'. However, I once mistakenly asked a puzzled French man if he spoke French! (He did.)

Richard H Turner, student of Engineering at Loughborough University.

What did I learn at school? Not a lot! I studied Latin and French, but they made little impression. However, I enjoyed English, both language and literature. Reading was, and still is, a great source of pleasure.
French later became important when I took an advanced cookery course, and all the menus and specialist terms were in French. This caused dreadful problems for the Americans on the course, who had only learnt Spanish at school, not French.
E Turner, Cordon Bleu cook and caterer

d Which of these people do you think is most serious about learning languages?
Which of them do you think has the best sense of humour?

e What do you think is the best way of learning a foreign language?

By reading a lot	Reading a dictionary
Doing grammar exercises	Translating
Trying to speak it, even though you make mistakes	Watching English or American films on TV

f What experience do you have of learning English? Write a short paragraph.

g **Language survey**

Design a survey form. Practise the questions you might ask. Ask other people in your class.

Tell each other which person you think speaks the most languages.
Who has learnt the most languages in the class as a whole?

a Questions and answers

Make questions that you can match with some of the answers below.

Do		What …	do	
Did	you …?	Where …	did	you …?
		How many …		

English, French and some Japanese.
Quite near, yes.
I live about three miles from here.
Not much, just a few words.
Well. I did, yes, but …
Oh, er, about four.
No, outside London.
Well, I used to speak five ..
I work for GEC.
Not really, no.
No, I don't …
No, I didn't, really …

Do you speak English?

b Classroom phrases

Who might say each of these – teacher, student, or either?

Sorry, I didn't understand.
Sorry? Can you say that again?
What's the meaning of …?
Can you guess what it means?
Try and work out what it means.
Excuse me. What does 'community' mean?
I don't know the word for xxxx.
Okay. Your next task is to find …
Shall we start?
We've finished.
Well, that's about it.
I don't know what to say next.
Tell them about …
Ask them about …
On your own …
Help each other.
Excuse me. Can you help me?
Get into groups, and …

c How good are you at languages?

I know a tiny bit of Italian.
I can speak a little Spanish, but not much.
I can get by in French.
I picked up some Greek from travels.
I was taught Latin, French and German at school.
I've forgotten my German.
I can read English all right, but I can't speak much.
I'm quite good at …
I can understand quite a lot of …
But I find it difficult to say what I want to say.
Catherine has a slight Irish accent.

d ????

What's the missing word?

He is married _____ a 15 month old son called Joe.
What words do your questions begin _____ ?
… is a suburb of London _____ a population of …
It is a large hotel _____ 64 rooms, each _____ bathroom and shower.
It has something to do _____ the rhythms of the language.
Do you have anything in common _____ any other students?
… wait a moment and I'll be _____ you.

In which sentences does the missing word mean 'and has'?

e Not

Not much, just a few words.
Not a lot!
Spanish, not French.
Not really, no.
Not many.
Not bad.

I'm not very good at languages.
Finished? Not yet!
It's not time yet.
Not me!
Why not?
Of course not.

f Common uses of wh- words

1 To describe
I work in Hillingdon, which is in West London.
… Americans, who had only learnt Spanish.

2 After words like say, find out, ask
Say where they come from.
We asked John to write what he could remember.

Find 3 sentences like those in 1, and 3 like those in 2.

a Find out their names and where they come from.
b Now read what Catherine wrote about John.
c He comes from Warrington, which used to be in Lancashire but is now in Cheshire.
d He has a son called Joe who, he says, is just starting to get interesting.
e You are often asked to send a curriculum vitae when you are applying for a job.
f Write down questions that you used when talking to people in section 2d above.
g And what about these?
h Decide exactly where you would put it.
i Hillingdon, where John works, is a typical West London suburb.

How many sentences are left over? What are the **wh-** words in them and how are they used?

Important words to remember (34 so far)					
alright	deal L	introduce	particularly	remain L	task
apart L	foreign L	Ireland	partner	Russian	text
bring L	guess	Japanese	pleasant	Spanish	tiny
capital	hate	learning	population	struggle L	worse
community L	hotel	literature	reaction	study	
county	industrial	particular	ready	tape	

13 Review page

Aims: 1 To revise question forms.
2 To make students aware of the importance of using English in their lessons.
3 To revise some of the meanings and uses of **with**.
4 To revise some of the uses of **not**
5 To revise some uses of relative pronouns.

Lexis: alright, **community** [L], **Japanese**, **Spanish**

SB13a PB13a,b

1 If students need more help, you could complete the substitution tables for them and ask them to select the appropriate answers.

SB13c

2 Ask students to learn only the phrases that apply to them or to someone they know well that they might talk about.

SB13d

Key: with

*Students could also look for the verbs that often go with **with**: deal, play, begin, **do** in the phrase 'something to do with . . .' etc. Adjectives like: pleased with, angry/annoyed with, mad with.*

SB13f

1 c, d, i

2 a, b, f, h

e 'when' introduces a time at which something happens.
g 'what' functions in this sentence as a question word.

PB13c is an additional Lexicon exercise.

a Questions and answers

Make questions that you can match with some of the answers below.

| Do
Did | you ...? | What ...
Where ...
How many ... | do
did | you ...? |

*English, French and some
Japanese.
Quite near, yes.
I live about three miles from here.
Not much, just a few words.
Well. I did, yes, but ...
Oh, er, about four.
No, outside London.
Well, I used to speak five ..
I work for GEC.
Not really, no.
No, I don't ...
No, I didn't, really ...*

Do you speak English?

b Classroom phrases

Who might say each of these – teacher, student, or either?

*Sorry, I didn't understand.
Sorry? Can you say that again?
What's the meaning of ...?
Can you guess what it means?
Try and work out what it means.
Excuse me. What does 'community' mean?
I don't know the word for xxxx.
Okay. Your next task is to find ...
Shall we start?
We've finished.
Well, that's about it.
I don't know what to say next.
Tell them about ...
Ask them about ...
On your own ...
Help each other.
Excuse me. Can you help me?
Get into groups, and ...*

c How good are you at languages?

*I know a tiny bit of Italian.
I can speak a little Spanish, but not much.
I can get by in French.
I picked up some Greek from travels.
I was taught Latin, French and German at school.
I've forgotten my German.
I can read English all right, but I can't speak much.
I'm quite good at ...
I can understand quite a lot of ...
But I find it difficult to say what I want to say.
Catherine has a slight Irish accent.*

d ????

What's the missing word?

*He is married ____ a 15 month old son called Joe.
What words do your questions begin ____ ?
... is a suburb of London ____ a population of ...
It is a large hotel ____ 64 rooms, each ____
bathroom and shower.
It has something to do ____ the rhythms of the
language.
Do you have anything in common ____ any other
students?
... wait a moment and I'll be ____ you.*

In which sentences does the missing word mean 'and has'?

e Not

*Not much, just a few
words.
Not a lot!
Spanish, not French.
Not really, no.
Not many.
Not bad.*

*I'm not very good
at languages.
Finished? Not yet!
It's not time yet.
Not me!
Why not?
Of course not.*

f Common uses of wh- words

1 To describe
*I work in Hillingdon, which is in West London.
... Americans, who had only learnt Spanish.*

2 After words like **say, find out, ask**
*Say where they come from.
We asked John to write what he could remember.*

Find 3 sentences like those in 1, and 3 like those in 2.

a *Find out their names and where they come from.*
b *Now read what Catherine wrote about John.*
c *He comes from Warrington, which used to be in
   Lancashire but is now in Cheshire.*
d *He has a son called Joe who, he says, is just
   starting to get interesting.*
e *You are often asked to send a curriculum vitae
   when you are applying for a job.*
f *Write down questions that you used when talking
   to people in section 2d above.*
g *And what about these?*
h *Decide exactly where you would put it.*
i *Hillingdon, where John works, is a typical West
   London suburb.*

How many sentences are left over? What are the **wh-**words in them and how are they used?

Important words to remember (34 so far)					
alright	deal L	introduce	particularly	remain L	task
apart L	foreign L	Ireland	partner	Russian	text
bring L	guess	Japanese	pleasant	Spanish	tiny
capital	hate	learning	population	struggle L	worse
community L	hotel	literature	reaction	study	
county	industrial	particular	ready	tape	

LEXICAL OBJECTIVES

about [see 4], **degree** L, **job**, **leave** L, **little** L, **live** L, **long**, **repeat** L, **sorry** L, **try**, **with** [see 13], **words**.

alright 1 as a signalling word. *Alright, shall we start?*
2 Alright? = Is that all right?
apart L
bring L
capital 1 of a country. *Dublin, capital of Ireland.*
2 sum of money to start a business. T
3 capital letter. *capital A, small b.* T
community L
county 1 small region of Britain and Ireland that has its own local Government (called the County Council, e.g. East Sussex C.C.)
deal L
foreign L
guess 1 to give an answer when you don't really know if it is correct. *It's not easy to guess his age. At a guess, I'd say 45. See if you can guess which person they are about.*
2 to guess correctly. *45! How did you guess?* T
3 **I guess** = I suppose (often American). *I guess I'd better be going.* T
hate 1 to have the strongest possible feeling of dislike. *I used to hate going to lectures. I hate football.*
Also: *I hate to say it . . .*
hotel a building where people stay, usually for a few nights, paying for their rooms and meals. *I was sleeping in a different hotel room every night.*
industrial 1 *an industrial town* (a town with a lot of heavy industry, factories etc. like Warrington).
introduce 1 to formally tell someone the name of another person, when the two people meet for the first time.
2 to tell a group of people the name, the background and other details of someone who is about to speak to them. *Quiet please. May I introduce the speaker tonight.* T
Ireland 1 Name of country. *The North of Ireland and the Republic of Ireland are two separate countries.* Adj: **Irish**.
Japanese 1 language
2 the people of Japan
learning *He found learning languages very difficult.*
literature 1 short stories, plays, novels, poetry etc. that are written down in a language and read for enjoyment. *If you think of English literature, you think of Shakespeare.*
particular 1 one out of many. *If I couldn't think of a particular word in Thai . . .*
particularly 1 *My French has been particularly useful . . .*
partner 1 someone you are doing something with. *Talk to your partner . . .*
Also: *partner in a dance, a marriage partner.*
2 partners in a company share the ownership of it. T

pleasant 1 rather nice and enjoyable in a quiet, gentle way; used of appearance, smell or taste or of an experience. *It's a very pleasant school. A pleasant chat. Pleasant memories.*
2 friendly and likeable character or nature. *. . . said in a pleasant voice, 'Can I help you?'* T
population 1 the people who live in a country. *13% of the population.* T
2 the number of people living in an area. *Pop. 12,000.* T
reaction 1 something that you feel or do because of something that has happened or because you are in a particular place. *. . . still has an Irish accent in reaction to the very 'English' community.*
ready 1 properly prepared to do something. *Are you ready to start?*
Ready when you are! = Let's start!
2 *Lunch is ready.* T
remain L
Russian 1 person or thing belonging to the Soviet Union
2 the language
Spanish 1 person or thing belonging to Spain
2 the language
struggle L
study 1 *He'd once studied chemistry at university.*
2 the activity of studying a subject. *Linguistics is the study of the structure of languages.* T
3 a room in someone's house which is used for reading and studying. *She was downstairs in the study.* T
4 to look at someone or something very carefully and slowly, so that you see every part of it. *I studied a map.* T
tape 1 as in tape-recorder. *Listen to the conversation on tape.*
2 to record speech, music or images. *What's wrong with this machine? It won't tape properly.* T
3 a narrow strip of cloth which is used in sewing, for tying things together etc. *You have to sew name tapes into everything when your child first goes to school.* T
4 a strip of plastic. *Attached by sticky tape.* T
task 1 a piece of work which has to be done and which may be difficult or unpleasant. *The task he thought would take him half-an-hour a day.* T
2 an important and sometimes difficult piece of work which is undertaken for a special reason and is often part of a larger project. *Our first task is to set up a committee.* T
3 in a language classroom, a task is a purposeful activity, like solving a problem or doing a survey. T
text 1 any written material: the main part of a book, the written version of a speech. Also: a listening text. T
2 *textbooks contain facts about particular things (maths).* T
tiny extremely small . . . *a tiny bit of Spanish. . . . a tiny baby.*
worse 1 comparative of bad. *Her marks are getting worse and worse. A boys' school, a boys' grammar school, which was even worse.*
2 more ill than before. *You'll get worse instead of better unless you get back into bed.* T

Have you any idea what they're like?

This unit progresses from description of physical characteristics, and giving an account of past experience in the form of a biographical summary, to exploring character traits and looking at ways that different types of people react to various things, from sports, to injuries, to animals. There are plenty of opportunities here for students to express personal feelings and reactions to situations, as well as to give and understand straight objective accounts and narrative.

OBJECTIVES

Lexical objectives are in TB27

Grammar and discourse

a Recognising different reactions, e.g. exclamations: **Oh dear**; and agreement: **Same here**. (18)
b Phrase-building with adverbs, adjectives and nouns, e.g. '.. not very tall, with fairly long dark hair'. (16)
c Verb phrases with the word **back**. (27)
d Use of simple past tense for past anecdote. Revision of simple past tense questions. (17, 18)
e Revision of the past simple forms and pronunciation of the 30 most common verbs (excluding modals). (19)
f Meanings and uses of **have**, including **have got**. (22)
g Words and phrases that modify adjectives and verbs, to keep something neutral or make it 'stronger'. Words that can do both, depending on pronunciation, e.g. **quite**, **a bit**, **not very**. (16,24,27)
h Revision of measuring expressions: height, length, width, distance, heat, e.g. 'I'm 5 foot 2 inches tall. (20,27)
i Exclamations with **How ...!** and **Oh dear!** (18)

Tasks

a Describing just enough of the physical appearance of someone (including their clothes) so that a stranger would recognise them in a crowd (spoken and written). Students describe themselves in the same way in written form. (15)
b Writing a short biography of oneself after talking it through with a partner. Finding someone else with something similar in their past. (17)
c Past narrative – telling anecdotes about injuries and how they happened. Writing a summary of a spoken anecdote. (18)
d Discussing briefly personal likes, dislikes (including sports and other pastimes) and personality, and describing the type of people or person one gets on with. Writing about oneself. (20)
e Talking and reading about animals, and about people as animal-lovers; describing reactions to different kinds of creatures. (25)(26)
f Finding ways to categorise various creatures. (25)

14 What can you tell from a photo?

Aims: 1 To introduce the general theme of the unit, which is finding out what people are like, what they like doing and how they react to things.
2 To introduce some of the new lexis from the unit.

Lexis: (initial exposure only at this point) **absolutely, academic, bored, boring, character** [T], **consider** [L], **easily** [L], **fairly, fit, hates, health** [T], **healthy, hope, involve, love, mainly, medical, meeting, mostly, nature** [T], **smoke, sport, still**
Revision: **hole, mouse/mice, personality**

Throughout this unit, encourage students to read the rubrics and follow the instructions as far as possible on their own. After they have read them for themselves, but before they actually start a task, you could ask them what they are going to do and how, to check they have understood sufficiently well.

SB14a PB14a

1 Encourage students to ask you for words they don't know as they look at this page to do the task. Explain that there are no right answers. At this stage students can only speculate about these people, but their characters will be revealed gradually through the texts and tasks in the unit.

Listening SB14b 14b *

2 Play the tape so that students can get used to their voices and help to learn their names. Exploit 'I'm so sorry, I've forgotten your name' as a useful phrase.

Key: Monica is the only one not on the tape.
Caroline Frost works for a publishers.
Stephen Bowden is a graduate student in anthropology.

SB14c

3 Let students discuss which 2 sentences apply best to themselves and their partners. Get a few students to read out their choices and comment informally.

Have you any idea what they're like?

John

14 What can you tell from a photo?

a How much can you tell about a person from their looks? Look very carefully at the photos.

Stephen

Caroline

Try to guess which of these people:
- definitely has a sense of humour
- has had to get remarkably fit and healthy since having children
- absolutely hates sport
- is fairly interested in sport but hates football
- enjoys some sports (mostly squash, tennis and swimming) but is not terribly good at them
- makes friends fairly easily
- likes most sociable activities which involve meeting and talking with people
- smokes a lot, and so feels they cannot be considered terribly healthy
- likes food and cooking but mainly eating
- is still at university, after studying one academic subject after another
- is interested in the Arts, especially cinema, and reads a lot
- used to be a medical student but got bored and took up anthropology
- leads a hectic social life and smokes
- seems to like animals
- has been to America and likes football
- loves to travel and hopes to go abroad again soon

Catherine

Monica

14b b You will hear four of these people introducing themselves. Which people? What kind of work do they all do?

c Which two of the descriptions on the left apply best to you? Which two would you guess best applied to your teacher? And your partner?

15 Describe a person

John   Alan   Catherine   Caroline   Monica   Stephen   Jane

> Take turns at describing one of the people
> here today. You must not say their name.
> Can your partner guess who it is?

15a a We asked Monica and Caroline to play this game. Listen and work out which of these people Monica is describing. Does Caroline guess correctly? Then listen to Caroline describing one of these people for Monica to guess.

b Now can you play the same game with a partner? First describe one of the people in the photograph above.
Then look around the class and describe one of your classmates to your partner. Be careful not to look at the person and give the game away!
Finally, play the game again, without mentioning any colours.

c If you had to describe yourself to a stranger so that they would recognise you easily in a crowded place like a hotel, station or airport, what would you write?

> 21 Park Road
> Harefield HW3 4IL
> 12 December '87
>
> Dear Mr Shaw,
> Thank you for offering to come and pick me up on the 22nd. I hope we won't miss each other.
> I'm fairly tall, and not exactly thin. I have long fair hair, and will probably be wearing a dark red jacket.
> I should be at the meeting point by 6.30 p.m. but I may be slightly later.
> Looking forward to meeting you all,
>
> Marie-France

Write the same kind of thing about another person in the class, so that someone else would recognise them easily. Do not write their name.

16 *Phrase-building* ....

Make some phrases and say them quickly.

quite
fairly | tall / short / slim / well-built / plump
rather

reasonably | thin / slim
slightly

medium height
not what you would call thin
not exactly thin

with long hair
with longish hair
with long dark hair
with long dark straight hair
with fairly long straight hair and brownish eyes
with long hair, darkish and straight, and brown eyes
she has longish hair, dark and straight, brown eyes and glasses

I'll be wearing a suit / dress
I'll be wearing a light suit / dress
I'll be wearing a light blue suit / dress
I'll be wearing a light blue suit/ /dress with a flower in my buttonhole

17 Biography

We asked Monica to write a brief biography of herself. She was, in fact, about to set off on a trip to South East Asia, to do some research in Sarawak. Find out how many countries she has lived in.

> I was born in the United States and lived in the Mid West of America until 1962 and I have only been back once since then, when I was fourteen. I've mostly lived in England since leaving America, although I spent two years in Rome while I was still living with my family. I studied History at Sussex University and since then I have been teaching English in Poland and in Malaysia. In 1983 I started postgraduate work in Social Anthropology and I am now doing a PhD at LSE.

Tell your partner the same kinds of things about yourself. Try to find out if you have anything in common.

Now write a short biography for yourself. Don't put your name.

Read other people's biographies. Which person's experience is the most similar to yours?

15 Describe a person

Aim: To describe a person's physical appearance as economically as possible, so that they could be recognised by a stranger in a crowded meeting place.

Lexis: strange, sweet, thin
Modifiers: e.g. **quite, rather, really, very**
Colours: Words ending in **-ish** meaning quite/a bit.
Revision: **accent, fairly, small, stranger, tall**

Listening   SB15a   📷 15a *

1 Give an example by describing one of the people in the picture yourself. (Don't pick Alan or Monica.) Ask the class to guess who it was. Students listen to the tape.

SB15b

2 Start students off by describing someone in the class without looking at the person concerned. You could turn your back on the class to make it more fun. Ask 1 or 2 more confident students to do the same. Replay this game without mentioning colour (to force the students to use more language to do the task).

3 In pairs students take turns describing and guessing. Monitor their work, noting common errors, but no need to correct at this point.

Writing   SB15c

4 Students may use the letter as a model for their descriptions of themselves. Remind them not to write a name on it. As students are writing, provide help and correction as needed, but be encouraging.

5 When students have finished the writing tasks, they write a number on their work (they could choose any 3-figure number – this gives useful practice with numbers and they are unlikely to choose the same as anyone else).

6 Display students' writing on the wall. *or*
Students pass round what they have written. Students read the descriptions and in their notebooks they write down both the number of the description and the names of the people students think are being described. Finally, ask students to give a name to their descriptions so the others can confirm their guesses.

Written homework: Students could describe another student in the class for the benefit of someone who has never seen the student before.

16 Phrasebuilding

Aims: 1 To give students practice in building phrases with adverbs, adjectives and nouns, e.g. . . . not very tall.
2 To give students practice in ordering adjectives.

Lexis: fairly

SB16 PB16

1 Get students to say the phrases in the order that they appear in the book. Make the activity fun by encouraging students to say the phrases as quickly as possible.

2 Check students' pronunciation, paying particular attention to stress, e.g. with LONGish hair, with LONG, DARK HAIR. (The following words could be substituted: short, fair, very, rather etc. was/is wearing a . . . will be in a . . . Introduce the word **extremely** if you need a stronger word.)

3 After doing the practice phrases, students adapt them and apply them to other people in the class or to famous people they all know, like pop stars. One student could give a phrase and the others say if they agree or disagree.

17 Biography

Aims: 1 To introduce students to writing briefly and chronologically about their past lives.
2 To give students practice in reading for relevant information.

Lexis: background [T] [L], **mostly** (mainly), **still, United (States)**
Revision: **academic, research** (studying), **although, been back, since leaving, since then, social** (about society), **until, work**

This section picks up from Unit 1 where students spoke about their childhood, where they used to live and where they went to school. But then, they were also expressing how they felt about them. Here, what is required is an objective summary, of the type that they may need to write for a CV.

1 Students read Monica's biography and tell you what countries she has lived in.

   Key: She has lived in 5 countries altogether. Sussex is in the UK.

For a less able class, it might be useful to ask them to tell you about Monica. Each student could tell you one (different) thing. They will have to reread the text, and change the 'I' to 'She', 'have' to 'has' etc.

2 Encourage students to ask you about yourself. Give them a short biography of yourself. (You don't have to tell them the whole truth!) Or you could talk about someone in your family or a friend you know well. Give only the answers to the questions they ask – don't continue until they ask you something else. Students will probably produce questions like:
Did you . . ./she/he . . .?
When did you . . .?
How long were you there?
After that what did you do?
If students' questions are grammatically inaccurate, rephrase them as you would in normal conversation, but no need to correct overtly at this point.

3 Students could write notes on the facts about you and then arrange them in the order they happened. Test their memories by getting them to read them back to you.

4 Individually, students write a brief (4–5 sentences) biography about themselves. Show them how to use Monica's text to help them by writing on the board key words that will help them see what information to include. e.g.:
Where born?
When?
Where lived most/all of life?
Where/what studied?
Work?

5 Suggest they help each other if they need help, as well as asking you. Go round and be ready to help out both with content and with their use of past and perfect tenses for their biographies. (Students who finish quickly can write a biography for one of the partners they have talked to in class, or for a family member.)

6 Suggest students write out a neat version at home with their names on the back of the paper. Whenever possible, encourage students to produce a final corrected version of their written work (a neat, reasonably accurate final product is much more motivating to students than an untidy 'first draft').

7 Next lesson put the finished biographies up on display and number them. Ask students to identify as many biographies as they can and to find the person who has the most in common with themselves. At this point, you could also ask them to look for a photo of themselves as a child to bring to class ready for Unit 5, section 64.

Sports and injuries

Aims: 1 To stimulate discussion and the exchange of anecdotes.
2 To give students practice in listening for relevant information and ignoring what is not relevant.
3 To provide students with an opportunity to compare their performances with native speakers performing the same task.

Lexis: afterwards, apparent, fall/fell (off) [L], **immediately, into, hurt, knee, metal, nasty, nose, off, pain, painful, whole**
How + exclamations: **How awful/difficult/painful/ terrible!**
Initial exposure to: **break/broke(n), cut/got cut by, immediately, unwell, whole**
Revision: **got hit by, hit, just, My goodness!, nearly, Oh dear!, split, worst**

SB18

The first two activities here lead up to an anecdote-telling session, which is followed by a tape-recording of the group of native speakers doing the same thing.
Most people delight in telling others about how they got their scars, their sports injuries etc, but just be aware that there may be someone in your class who would prefer just to listen.
Don't let the conversations dwell on the morbid side of accidents (note that road accidents are a theme of Unit 8); try to keep the discussion light-hearted as they see whether they can, as a class, outdo this professional footballer. Encourage talk about how they felt at the time, their reactions.

SB18a

1 Groups do this task briefly as an introduction to the cycle of activities in this section. Students will have more chance to develop the theme of sport, if it interests them, later in the section.

SB18b

2 In groups, students decide how many injuries the footballer had. (Make sure students realise he did not get all his injuries at once.) Ask how many injuries each group thought he had had. (Encourage students to ask you for relevant lexis, as they will need to use many of the same words themselves in the next stage of this section.)

Listening [18b]*

3 Play the tape. Students need only listen for the types of injuries and the total number.

Key: The actual number of injuries doesn't really matter – most people seem to think at least 7.
(In fact, the footballer had had several different types of leg injuries. The two round things on his upper arms are joined across his back, to prevent him from raising his arms too high and further damaging his shoulder.)

Task SB18c

*For other words for parts of the body, introduce only the lexis that students ask for (e.g. **shoulder, nose, leg**); there is no need for a complete list here. Also see Unit 5, section 63, where all names for parts of the body are exploited together with their other meanings.*

4 Give students time to think of their anecdotes before they tell them informally in groups. Appoint one student to take notes for the group.

Planning

5 Help students to summarise their anecdotes in groups: e.g. Sarah once sprained her ankle (when she was) walking over some very rough ground in xxx. Pierre is lucky – he's never had any serious injuries. Neither has/ Nor has Y.

Report

6 As groups report to the class, count up the fairly serious injuries on the board. Do the class have more than 8? Do they beat the footballer?

Listening SB18d [18d]* PB18

7 Give students time to match the pictures to the sentences. Students listen to the tape.

8 Allow the class time to compare their own experiences with this group's before going on to do the Language Study in section 19 which is based on the same recording.

Key: 1 Catherine broke her collar bone as a child. Caroline split her chin and had to have stitches in it. Stephen broke a bone in his hand, and tore ligaments in his knee, skiing.
John got some bad cuts.
2 laughed at Caroline's chin – still has the scar!
'Oh dear!' at Stephen having to write his exam with a broken hand.
'Goodness me' at John nearly losing a finger.
3 The picture of the hammer hitting someone's finger.

Language study

Aims: 1 To revise past simple forms and pronunciation of the 30 most common verbs. (The modal verbs are not in this list. They will come later. Also not in this list are **suppose, believe, understand** which, though common in this form are not so commonly used in past form.)
2 To revise the connectors **and, but** and **so**.

Lexis: but, fall/fell [L], **painful**

SB19

*Tell students that in many cases the past tense form of the verb is more common than the present form (esp. **said, called, asked, told** and **fell**).*

1 In pairs, students write the present forms of the verbs. Refer students to the Word List at the back of their books if they really need help. **Break/broke, hit/hit, tear/tore** and **fall/fell** are new.
19a and 19c could be made more interesting if students thought of or found phrases they could say with some of the verbs.

SB19b PB19

2 Individually students fill in the blanks, then compare their answers with those of the person beside them when they have finished. Explain 'supposedly asleep', meaning her family supposed/thought she was asleep, but actually she was awake and in great pain. Also explain **whole**.

Key: and, but, but, and/so, and, and/so

SB19c

3 As in 19a, allow students to use their word lists if they have trouble with this activity.

Key: /ɛ/ said meant left felt helped (add fell)
/ɔː/ thought saw called brought (add tore).
/uː/ knew used
/ei/ came made gave became
/ʊ/ took put looked
/iː/ needed seemed
/ɒ/ was got lost (wanted)
Left over: 7 had, did, worked, found, told, loved, liked

18 Sports and injuries

a Find out what kind of sports the people in your group and their families take part in. How many are (or could be) dangerous sports? Prepare to tell the class.

▶ *Sports Survey* Tell the class. Listen and work out which seem to be the two most popular sports among you all. ◀

b Look at the picture opposite of a professional footballer. It shows all the injuries he has had in his ten-year career. What injuries has he had, and how many?

18b Listen to the group counting up his injuries. Did they get the same ones as you did? Did they get the same number?

c Can you beat the footballer? Get into groups. What injuries have you had between you? (They need not only be sports injuries. Any injuries at all.) Find out what happened in each case.

Have you as a group had more injuries than this footballer?

▶ Plan a summary of your group's injuries to tell the class. ◀

Find out which is the most common injury that people in your class have had.
Can your class beat the footballer?

What do you say in your language if something hurts you? In English we say **Ow!** or **Ouch!**

I nearly chopped my hand off ... my finger off ...

I've never broken anything, but I've had lots of stitches.

I went and split my chin on the metal handle ...

I also tore all the ligaments in one knee.

I've broken one bone in one hand.

I broke my collarbone when I was quite small.

... so far ... just some very nasty cuts.

18d **d** Find out:
1 Which person did which of these things, and how they did it.
2 What were the reactions of the others? What did they say or do?
3 Which drawing is not mentioned at all?

19 *Language study*

a **Verbs in past tense form**
Check that you know the present forms of these verbs.

> lived spent studied started broke
> fell had to spend gave went split
> had to sit and write tore got had

b **and, but, so**
Read the summary of what happened to Catherine, and say where **and, but, so** could fit.

When she was quite small, Catherine fell off her bike _____ hurt herself badly _____ nobody realised how serious it was. She went to bed _____ it was very painful _____ she didn't sleep the whole night. The next morning, they took her to the doctor's _____ he said she had broken her collarbone _____ she had to have it bandaged up.

c Below are 30 common verbs, starting with the most common. What are their past tense forms?

be	say	take	use	like
have	mean	want	give	feel
think	see	put	call	become
do	go	look	tell	help
know	make	find	need	bring
get	come	leave	seem	lose

Put the past tense forms in categories according to their pronunciation. e.g. **gave** and **made** have the same sound.
How many do you have left over?

13

20 Who would you get on with?

> Imagine that you were applying to a
> Computer Dating Agency. Write a short
> piece about yourself to enclose with
> your letter to the Agency.

We asked everyone in the group to
do this task. Read what two of them
wrote about themselves.

*I am 29 years old and work for a publishing
company. I enjoy travel and lived for five
years in Papua New Guinea, where I was a
teacher. Although I intend to stay in Britain
for a few years, I hope to see more of the
world in the next ten – definitely South
America and Africa.*

*I enjoy living on my own although I
love to be with friends and lead a hectic social
life. My main preoccupations are reading,
music, travel and friends. I like food and
cooking – but mainly eating.*

J.

3. Your Interests

Indicate the interests and activities you enjoy by placing a tick ✔ beside
please indicate with a cross ✚. Otherwise leave the box blank ☐

THE MUSIC YOU ENJOY		
Classical		
Opera		
Pop		
Jazz		98.
Folk		99.
		100.
		101.
		102.
		103.

AN EVENING OUT
Theatre
Concerts
Opera/Ballet
Cinema
Dancing
Parties

*My name is Catherine McKenna and I am
32 years old. I was born in December 1953
in Dublin, Republic of Ireland.
I am one of five children and am an identical
twin. I am 5ft 2½ ins tall and have red
hair, blue eyes, fair skin and freckles
and am reasonably slim.
My hobbies include reading, sewing, cinema,
theatre going and most sociable activities
which involve meeting and talking with people.
I also enjoy some sports (eg, squash and
tennis although I am not very good at them)
and swimming and other pastimes like playing
boules or croquet and sitting in the shade on
a sunny day.
I have had a varied career but lastly I
was an insurance broker working for an
International Insurance Broking House
based in Hampton Wick and, of course, the City.
C.M.*

a Think of a friend of yours who
would get on well with one of these
people. Explain to your partner why
you think so.

20b **b** Listen to John and Catherine talking about
what they would write.
What did Catherine say? Did she actually write what
she said she would?

Make a list of what they have in common.

▷ Tell the class. Do you all agree? ◁

c Write about yourself. Start by talking through
with your partner what you want to write.

▷ Write in a similar style to the texts above.
Read each other's and comment. ◁

21 Funny Story

21 San Francisco disc jockey Don Sherwood
tells of an argument in a friend's house after a
weekend of sports television. The wife
complained, 'You love football more than you
love me.'

The husband replied, 'Yeah, but I still love
you more than basketball.'

22 *Grammar revision* ....

have, has, having, had

Look at the sentences 1–10. Find:

a at least two sentences where **have** goes with **to**.
  What do they mean?
b two where someone **has** something in their character.
c two sentences describing someone.
d two where **have** goes with part of the verb like this:
  *I have lived in London for almost as long as I can
  remember.*
e two sentences where **have** means 'own' or
  'possess'.

1 *We had to look in the atlas to find out where it
  was.* (2)
2 *I would need to meet someone who also had a
  sense of humour.* (20)

3 *Do you have any pets?*
4 *Do you have a favourite colour?* (128)
5 *I've never broken anything but I've had lots of
  stitches.* (18)
6 *I do pride myself on having a good sense of
  direction.* (140)
7 *She has dark hair.* (15)
8 *I have a travelcard, so I don't have to pay.* (80)
9 *I have eaten the plums that were in the icebox.*
  (95)
10 *Have you finished?*

In which five sentences could you use **got** after **have**?

20 Who would you get on with?

> **Aims:** 1 To section students practice in expressing likes, dislikes and the type of people they get on with.
> 2 To practise writing descriptions of students' own physical appearance and personalities.
>
> **Lexis: agency, argument, character** [T], **characteristics, computer, funny, international, involve** [L], **love, mainly, meet/met, meeting** [L], **reasonably, shade, skin, tall**
> Revision: **academic, also, cope (with), easily, intellectual, medical, precise, settle**

This section links more directly back to the first page of this unit. It begins to pull together some of the separate smaller tasks that students have done, and build on them, leading up to a full-scale writing task of the same type as Catherine and the others have done.

Reading SB20a

1 The funny story in section 21 could help you set the scene, e.g. Is this a couple who have the same interests, and get on well together in all ways?

2 Help students to understand what the context of the task was – it will be more fun if they understand what a Computer Dating Agency is. Bring in an advertisement from a magazine if you can find one. Do they have them in students' countries? Remind them that they are sometimes just for friendship, not just marriage. Make it clear that the situation is a hypothetical one. Both Catherine and John (who appears later in the tape) are happily married, and are writing and discussing what they would say about themselves if they did apply to such an agency!

3 Students read Caroline's and Catherine's descriptions of themselves. Help students to ignore unimportant words and to guess meanings of words they don't know. Don't 'teach' any that are not on the list unless your students really need them.

4 Students talk informally in pairs or groups about friends of theirs who might get on with one of these people, and give their reasons. Get 1 or 2 students to tell the rest of the class what they think if they are keen to talk.
Students may produce sentences like: 'I've got a friend called . . . who smokes a lot, so he/she might get along with . . .'

Listening SB20b *

5 Students listen to Catherine and John deciding what they would say about themselves if they were genuinely writing such a letter. If it is culturally acceptable, tell them they will be doing the same task and they will probably listen more attentively.

   Key: Catherine actually wrote more than she said she would. But she missed out one thing: the fact that she hates football.

   In common – from what they say on the tape:
   both like talking (John says 'same here' when Catherine mentions talking to people).
   Both like reading – John reads a lot.
   Both hate football – John hates all sport, in fact.

6 Students look back at SB14 and see whether they guessed right about the people from the photos of them.

   Key: definitely has a sense of humour JM
   absolutely hates sport JM
   is fairly interested in sport but hates football CM
   enjoys some sports (mostly squash, tennis and swimming) CM
   likes most sociable activities which involve meeting and talking with people CM
   is interested in the Arts, especially cinema, and reads a lot JM

Planning SB20c PB20

7 To help students with their descriptions, ask them to include some/all of the following:
   a Name, age, where born, where from
   b Physical description
   c Interests, hobbies
   d Education, work experience
   e Hopes/plans for the future

8 If students need more help, put some useful phrases like these on the board:
   My name is . . . and I am . . . old. I was born in . . . in . . .
   Also:
   I am blonde/I have long, blonde hair.
   My hobbies include . . .
   I also enjoy . . .
   I work for/study at . . .
   I hope/plan to . . .

   See also section 27a for some useful phrases.

Report

9 Students could write about themselves at home, then bring their reports in the following day for the others to read. Alternatively, the teacher could read a few reports to the class, and ask them to guess who the report is about.

21 Funny story

> **Lexis: argument, funny**

SB21
See note 1 for TB20a for suggested procedure. The story should be read quickly and for fun.

22 Grammar revision

> **Aim:** To give practice in the meanings and uses of **have**.

SB23 PB22

1 Students read the rubric themselves. Make sure they know what is expected of them. Explain the meaning of **have** = possess. Explain 'have something in the mind' by giving an example like 'I have a good idea!' or 'He had a bad temper'.

2 Students do the activity individually or in pairs.

   Key: a 1,8 (have to = must)
   b 2, 4, 6
   c 2, 6, 7
   d 5, 9, 10
   e 3, 8
   Have = Have got: 2, 7, 8. 3 and 4 could be rephrased 'Have you got . . .?'

23 | Are you a lucky person?

> **Aims:** 1 To foreshadow some themes: going to the horseraces and winning things, that will be occurring in the first episode of The Hitch-hiker in Unit 7.
> 2 To practise exchanging anecdotal narratives.
> 3 To let students express their feelings and reactions.
>
> **Lexis: luck/y, races, win, winning, won**
> Revision: **some** (indefinite, with singular noun = not sure which one)

Listening   SB23 * PB23

1 Students discuss the pictures to set the theme. Ask students if betting on horses is legal in their countries. Do many people watch and bet on horseracing?

Culture note: Advertisers often have competitions to make people buy their products. Community centres and shops often have lucky draws at Christmas. Horse-racing is very popular, and there are betting shops in towns where you can bet even if you can't go to the races.

2 Students find the answers to the first two questions in pairs, then ask other pairs before reporting back. Make a list on the board of ways of winning money. Then find out who the luckiest person in the class is.

Key: Catherine won some money on a big race (a couple of years ago). She felt excited and really really pleased. She was so proud that she jumped up and down.

24 | Wordpower

> **Aims:** To illustrate some meanings and uses of **bit** [L]

SB24 PB24

1 From the drawings, students think of phrases about the people and situation, which contain the word **bit**. If students cannot think of many, they should look at the categories for the word in the Lexicon first. Then students see how many situations they can make up.

*See also section 27f for the word **whole** which is in contrast to **bit** and **part** (except for **bit** category 4).*

Key: suggestions: Bus-stop queue: Two people are chatting a bit, 'The bus is a bit late isn't it?' (they have had to wait a bit for their buses.)
the buses are probably a bit late.
there's one person with a bit of shopping;
it's probably getting a bit late.
the lady with the hat looks a bit angry.
she could be saying 'It's a bit much – 25 minutes late!'
the dog has just bitten the man in the bus queue. He looks a bit scared. The dog's owner doesn't look a bit sorry.

Social scene: she's passing round a cake cut into bits.
she's a bit worried because of the baby under the table.
he speaks a little bit of Chinese.
The Chinese man is looking a bit puzzled.
The baby is playing with bits of Lego, altogether being a bit of a nuisance and making a bit of a mess . . .

25 | Animals

> **Aims:** 1 To let students express their feelings about creatures, and their reactions to what other people think in preparation for later sections.
> 2 To practise identifying and describing animals.
>
> **Lexis: animals, birds, category, condition** [L],
> **creatures, deal, diseases, dog, noise, quite, respond
> (to), response** [T], **spread** [L]

SB25

1 Discussion: How many students are animal lovers? How many hate creatures like mice? What can this tell us about their character? etc.

SB25a

1 In pairs, students identify the animals in the pictures. They do not need to learn *all* these names. Useful names they will need for this unit are: cat, chicken, dog, fish, mouse (hole), rat. Give students a chance to express their reactions to some of these animals.

2 Give examples to introduce some of the language from the tape: Rats tend to live in dirty places, in bad conditions. They are bigger than mice and have very pointed noses/faces. They can spread disease.

3 In groups, students find different ways to categorise them. Give students an example if necessary.

Key: those with 4 legs, those with 2 legs, those with none.
big or small   by what they eat – meat or no meat (grass, seeds etc.)   whether they make nice pets or not   whether you find them only in zoos in this country   whether you can eat them or not   birds and others   birds, mammals, fish and reptiles   mammals (warm-blooded creatures) and others   whether you like them or don't like them.

Listening   25a

4 Play the tape. It is not intended for intensive study.

Key: Caroline and Stephen don't do this task very well. They get sidetracked, and start describing people's reactions to mice and rats. They only get 3 ways: size, type, those that most people like/dislike.

5 Discussion: What pets do the students' families have? Are dogs easy to look after? What creatures do they enjoy seeing in zoos or on TV? What conditions do animals in the nearest zoo live in? Are the zoo animals themselves in good condition? What animals are native to their own countries? Are they considered to be good/bad/useful?

Key: Cats purr. Dogs and big cats (eg lions) growl. Dogs bark. Mice squeak.

26 | Poems by Spike Milligan

> **Aim:** Reading and expressing personal reactions to a poem by a British comic/writer.
>
> **Lexis: animal, cry, energy** [L], **escaped, hole, mad
> (wild), otherwise, writer** [T]
> Revision: **deep/deep freeze/freezer, kept**
> Phrase: **mad with** (because of) **energy**

SB26a 26a PB26

1 Discuss the topic first to give them a mental set for understanding the poem. e.g. What do you need to do for a dog? What happens if a dog doesn't get enough exercise?

2 Students read the poem. Discuss their reactions to it before they answer questions.

Key: 1 F   2 T   3 T   4 T

SB26b 26b

3 Before the second poem, introduce the words **thick** and **thin** by drawing lines on the board.

4 Students listen to the poem until they can recite it from memory. Ask for their reactions to the poem.

Tapescript   There are holes in the sky
               Where the rain comes in
               But they're ever so small
               That's why rain is thin.

23 Are you a lucky person?

How many ways are there of winning money in your country?

Find out if other people in your class have ever won any money, and how. Who is the luckiest person in your class?

23 Catherine won some money two years running. How? How did she feel? What did she do when she heard she had won?

24 *Wordpower*

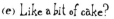

bit

Find someone in the pictures who might be saying or thinking the following:

(a) It's a bit much, 25 minutes late again!

(b) Ow, hey! Your dog bit me!

(c) Have you had to wait a bit?

(d) I got a bit of shopping done.

(e) Like a bit of cake?

(f) Just a small bit, thanks.

(g) Sorry he's making a bit of a mess.

(h) Ah, he knows a bit of Chinese.

(i) Your son is a bit smaller than my son.

Now look up **bit** in the Lexicon.
What other **bits** can you see in the pictures?
What other phrases with **bit** could you make up?

25 Animals

a   Animal categories

How many different ways can you think of to categorise these creatures?

25a Which categories did Caroline and Stephen think of? Who do you think is an animal lover?
Stephen says 'Rats get a really bad deal.' Why?

What animals do these things in English?
purr   growl   bark   squeak

What noises do animals make in your language?

What kind of noises are these?
'The car engine purred quietly . . .'
'What's your name?' the policeman barked loudly.

26 Poems by Spike Milligan

26a   **a   THE DOG LOVERS**

So they bought you
And kept you in a
Very good home
Central heating
TV
A deep freeze
A very good home
No one to take you
For that lovely long run –
But otherwise
'A very good home'
They fed you Pal and Chum
But not that lovely long run,
Until, mad with energy and boredom
You escaped – and ran and ran and ran
Under a car.
Today they will cry for you –
Tomorrow they will buy another dog.

Do you agree or disagree with these statements?

1   This is a poem about people who are nice to animals and who gave a dog a very good home.
2   The poet says that dogs need more than just food.
3   The dog's owners just never took him out for a good long walk.
4   The people in the poem didn't realise what they were doing was wrong.

26b   **b   Holes in the sky**
Now listen to another poem. Learn it.

a fairly, very, quite, a bit etc.

Find the words like **fairly, very, quite, a bit** etc. that go with the adjectives in the phrases.

27a Listen to how they are said. Which words are stressed? There are some phrases where they make the adjective stronger in meaning, and others where the adjective remains fairly neutral. Can you hear the difference? The sentences marked (x2) you will hear twice. How is the meaning different each time?

e.g. *I'm fairly interested in sport.* neutral
Not very tall. neutral
They're ever so small. strong
It's a very pleasant school. strong

She's got a very strange accent.
...squash and tennis, though I'm not very good at them.
English and American, which are fairly similar.
I make friends fairly easily.
It's quite a close community. (x2)
She's quite small. (x2)
They are ever so small.
It was so painful.
It's extremely cold outside.
It can be terribly cold in winter.
...who was not terribly interested in sport.
I absolutely hate sport!
I was really very very unwell.
She looks a bit tired.
You're a bit late!
A bit shorter than you.
A lot shorter, in fact.
Much shorter.
Generally quite healthy. (x2)
It's rather expensive. (x2)
Extremely expensive!
That's quite enough!

b Using measurements

I'm 5 foot 2½ inches tall.
That's about 1 metre 58.
How tall are you? What height are you?
It's 50 metres long and 25 metres wide.
How long is the swimming pool near you?
How wide is it?
It's about 5 miles (8 kilometres) away.
Around 20 minutes away, by car.
How far is your house from here?
It's over 30 degrees Centigrade.
How hot is it where you live now?
How cold is it in winter?

c back

Use the Lexicon to find out what these uses of **back** mean.

a *I've only been back to America once.*
b *...way back when I was a paperboy...*
c *...he was in the back of the police car.*
d *My back garden...*
e *...I backed the car out of the garage.*

Now think of situations when you might hear or say these.

f *Can I have my book back please?*
g *Oh, that music brings back memories!*
h *Can you ring me back later? We're in the middle of dinner.*
i *To come back to what we were saying before, ...*
j *All right then. Go out now, but be back by 11. Okay?*
k *Let's go back to your first point ... the first thing you said.*
l *Never look back!*
m *Stand back.*

d Odd word out?

There is one word/phrase that is the odd one out in each set. Which is it?

a medical, fit, well, unwell, healthy, ill, sick, energy, pain, intelligent, hurt
b university, degree, academic, intelligent, subject, argument
c How awful! Dear me! Oh dear! What a dreadful thing! Great! How terrible! How sad!
d very very, fairly, really, extremely, terribly, absolutely, ever so, dreadfully, awfully

e Absolutely okay or generally all right?

Match these questions with the answers below. They all have at least, two possible answers.

1 *What do you think, then?*
2 *What's he like as a teacher?*
3 *Do you agree?*

a *Yes, on the whole. There are just one or two things...*
b *Really very good. First class.*
c *On the whole, it should work well. But perhaps...*
d *Very pleasant, on the whole.*
e *I think you're absolutely right.*

f Whole or part?

Match 1–7 with the phrases below.
1 *Which piece would you like?*
2 *Will you be at home in the morning?*
3 *There are five more bits to fit in.*
4 *When will you be away?*
5 *Did her father know?*
6 *Which bit of the town is nicest?*
7 *Just in India?*

a *I'll be in the whole day.*
b *Then you've done the whole lot.*
c *The whole family had heard about it.*
d *The whole place is lovely.*
e *Can't I have the whole thing?*
f *The whole of July.*
g *No, in the world as a whole.*

Important words to remember (98 so far)

absolutely	bored	dog	health	metal	sad	United States
academic	boring	easily L	healthy	mostly	shade	whole
afterwards	category	energy L	hole	nasty	sick	win
agency	character	escape	hurt	noise	skin	writer
animal	characteristic	extremely	ill	otherwise	smoke	
apparent	computer	fairly	international	pain	spread L	
argument	condition L	fall L	knee	painful	sweet	
background L	consider L	fell	mad	reasonably	tall	
bird	creature	fit	mainly	respond	terribly	
bit L	disease	funny	medical	response	thin	

Aims: 1 The uses of modifiers like **fairly**, **very**, **quite**, **a bit**.
2 To revise phrases for describing measurement.
3 To revise some of the meanings and uses of **back**.
4 To revise expressions of agreement and approval.
5 To revise the meanings and uses of **whole**.

Lexis: extremely, **ill**, **sad**, **sick**, **terribly**, **whole**

SB27a 27a

The sentences that can have both meanings are recorded twice: the neutral one first, the strong one second.

Key: All are strong except the following which are neutral: *... though I'm not very good at them. ... which are fairly similar. I make friends easily. ... who was not terribly interested in sport. She looks a bit tired. A bit shorter than you.*

SB27b PB27a

1 Students repeat these for pattern practice work, then make up true sentences to describe themselves or the environment.

SB27c PB27b

*This exercise extends students' experience of **back** to verbs which combine with **back**, e.g. **have back**, **bring back**, **go back**.*

Key: a return; b a long time ago – (e.g. back in the 70s ...); c not the front seats of; d not front; e backed out = to come out backwards not forwards

2 Students think of situations where they might hear these phrases, and report back.

SB27d

Key: a intelligent – (others to do with sickness/health).
b argument (the rest are to do with studying).
c Great! (the rest are exclamations used if it is *not* nice).
d fairly (the others are extreme, or strong in meaning).

3 Students could practise saying 'I'm _____ sorry!' (not **absolutely** or **fairly**) and 'It was _____ funny/late.' (not **absolutely**) and 'I'm fairly/absolutely certain that ...'

SB27e

Key: 1 a, b, c, d, e   2 b, d   3 a, c, e

SB27f

Key: 1 e 2 a 3 b 4 f 5 c 6 d

PB27c is an additional Lexicon exercise.

LEXICAL OBJECTIVES

Level 1 words (see page 129T):
how, **love**, **meeting**, **still**.

absolutely 1 totally. ... *You're absolutely right.* (14)
2 certainly. *'You mean prison?' I asked, 'Absolutely,' he said.* (12)
academic 1 the type of work done in school/university. *academic subject*
afterwards 1 after an event, day, time etc. *for a long time afterwards.*
agency 1 *Imagine that you were applying to a Computer Dating Agency.*
animal 1 *No birds or animals came near.*
apparent 1 seeming: ... *the apparent success of arranged marriages* T
2 obvious. *It wasn't something that was apparent.*
argument 1 support for an opinion. *Do you accept this argument?* T
2 a disagreement. *I said no and we got into a big argument over it.*
back L (See SB27c.)
background L
bird 1 ... *birds singing in the trees.*
bit L (See SB24.)
bored *I used to be a medical student but got bored and took up anthropology.*
boring dull, uninteresting. *Are all your meetings this boring?* T
category a set of objects, people etc. with one characteristic in common
character 1 personality or nature. *He has a pleasant character.* T
2 the people in a film, book or play. T
characteristic 1 a typical quality that makes someone easy to recognise. *My physical characteristics*
computer a *Computer Dating Agency* = a dating agency that uses computers
condition L
consider L
creature any living thing that can move
disease illness
dog the animal
easily L
energy L
escape 1 avoid something ... *to escape responsibility* T
2 to get away from a place you don't like. *The dog escaped.*
3 survive something dangerous. *Fortunately we all escaped unharmed* T
extremely very ... *extremely tired*
fairly (See SB27).
fall/fell L
fit 1 right size and shape. *It fits nicely.* T
2 *The clothes fit into one small case.* T
3 healthy ... *fit and well*
funny 1 amusing. *How funny!*
2 odd, strange. *Funny, I didn't know ...*
health 1 how well or ill someone is. *Smoking is dangerous to your health.* T
healthy 1 well, not suffering from illness. ... *a healthy baby.*
hole 1 opening. *Many animals live in holes in the ground.*
hope L
hurt 1 to cause physical pain. *What do you say in your language when someone hurts you?*
2 to make a person feel unhappy. *He didn't want to hurt her feelings.* T
ill unwell, sick. *He's been ill for 2 weeks.*
international 1 involving more than one country. *I was working for an International Insurance Banking House.*

knee *I tore all the ligaments in one knee.*
mad 1 unable to control yourself; *He looked at me as if I were mad.* Also: **madness**.
2 very angry. *Don't be mad at me.* T
mainly 1 used to say that a statement is true to a large extent. *A queue of people, mainly children and old men.*
medical concerned with medicine. *I started off as a medical student.*
meet/met L
metal iron, steel, gold, silver etc. are metals. *Cars are made mainly of metal.*
mostly 1 *The men at the party were mostly fairly young.* (See **mainly**)
nasty not nice. *How nasty!*
noise 1 a sound. *What's that noise?*
2 a loud or unpleasant sound. *Try not to make so much noise. Noisy children.* T
otherwise 1 if you don't/if it isn't. *You should wash five times a day. You're not properly clean otherwise.*
3 in other way(s). *But otherwise 'a very good home'*
pain 1 an unpleasant feeling in a part of your body. *I'm getting a pain in my side.*
2 feeling of deep unhappiness. *I remember, with pain, his tears.* T
painful causing pain. *That was painful.*
race 1 *horse races, motor-racing.*
2 the arms race, the race for power
3 to go very fast. *We raced across London ...* T
4 group of people with the same culture. *The Italians, as a race, love Opera ...*
reasonably to an acceptable degree. *I'm reasonably slim.*
respond 1 to answer. *'May I come in?' 'Of course', she responded.* T
2 to react. *I've never really seen a spider respond to attention.*
response 1 a spoken or written answer. *Please write your responses in the appropriate place.* T
2 a reaction to something. *Hate is an automatic response to fear.* T
sad 1 unhappy or upset. *I enjoyed the film even though it made me feel sad.*
shade 1 out of the sun. *Sit in the shade.*
sick 1 ill. *look after me when I'm sick.*
2 people who are ill. *The care of the sick and the aged.* T
3 very angry. *It makes me sick to see the way they waste our money.*
skin 1 *I have red hair, blue eyes, fair skin and freckles. fairly dark-skinned*
2 *Cook the potatoes quickly with their skin on.* T
smoke 1 use cigarettes. *I smoke, so I'm storing up ill-health.*
2 *The room was full of cigarette smoke.*
spread L
sweet 1 i.e. like sugar. *sweet biscuits*
2 *What kind of sweets do you like?* T
3 The final course of a meal, dessert.
4 nice, pretty. *What a sweet baby!*
tall *I'm not very tall.*
terribly 1 very. *It's terribly cold.*
thin 1 narrow in comparison to the length. *His nose was long and thin.*
2 ... *thin slices of bread* T
United States a country ... *the United States of America*
whole See SB27f.
win 1 *Who's winning the war?* T
2 *Catherine won some money at the races.*
writer a person who writes as a job. ... *the writer and comic Spike Milligan.* T   16T

A good place for a holiday

This unit begins by focusing on holiday places and pastimes. The emphasis here is on holidays in the country. (Unit 12 recycles some of the themes of this unit, but with an urban background and setting.) It involves questions and narratives focusing on holidays and then goes on to look at samples of holiday correspondence. It then looks at holiday areas from a descriptive rather than a narrative point of view. The next stage is planning for a holiday and finally there is a discussion of holiday accommodation. Thus, within the context of holidays, students are given exposure to and practice in narrative, description, correspondence, evaluation and planning.

OBJECTIVES

Lexical objectives are in TB41.

Grammar and discourse

a Producing and responding to past tense questions to elicit a narrative. (29)
b Summarising a narrative. (29)
c **Do** as a delexical verb, especially as used with a quantifier – **do** a lot of/a bit of etc. (32,36)

*A delexical verb is one which must be followed by a word or phrase in order for it to carry meaning, e.g. I'm going to **do** the cooking. (**Make** is also a delexical verb: **make** a decision/journey.)*

d 'That is/was + **wh-** clause' to provide supplementary information or clarification. E.g. that was why we wanted to go. (32,36)
e 'Hedging' phrases and words, e.g. perhaps, I suppose. (33)
f Ways of referring to future time. (38,40,41)
g **Have/had/had been** with present perfect continuous; with the passive; with the meaning **gone to** or **visited**. (37)
h Lexical set: words used to persuade, e.g. ideal, superb, marvellous. (35,39)
i Words that go with both expressions concerning time and expressions concerning money, e.g. spend, afford.

Tasks

a Speculating on and evaluating possible activities. (28)
b Expressing likes and dislikes. (28)
c Asking questions to elicit specific information of a narrative kind. (29)
d Producing a narrative. (29)
e Summarising a narrative. (29,38)
f The tactics of asking questions to elicit information without giving away one's intentions. (30,31)
g The tactics of pre-empting or avoiding questions. (30,31)
h Correspondence involving the achievement of a hidden agenda – getting someone to do something without actually asking them. (33)
i Understanding a persuasive text and recognising words and phrases which have a persuasive intent. (35,39)
j Talking about future plans. (38,40)

28 A nice active week's holiday

Aims: 1 To introduce the general theme of the unit and some of the new lexis.
2 To practise speculating on and evaluating possible activities.
3 To give students practice in expressing likes and dislikes.

Lexis: active, activity [T], **ancient, beach, beautiful, Christian(ity)** [T], **crowded, noisy, north, peaceful, quiet, quietly, swimming, wild**
Revision: **busy, castle, hills, historical, Roman(s), scenery, north-east, walking**

Ask students to bring in pictures of their own country for this section.

Task SB28a

1 In groups students find the appropriate words to describe Northumberland National Park and answer the questions about what tourists might do there.

2 Teacher monitors briskly. Encourage students to ask you for the meanings of words they don't know. As one group identifies the need for a particular word, put it up on the board for other groups to refer to if they wish.

3 Ask groups informally what they each thought. (Rephrase if necessary but it is too early to expect accuracy with new words and phrases. It will all be focused on later.) Practise pronunciation of the lexis (in suitable phrases) as necessary.

4 In pairs students find out what sort of holiday their partner likes and whether he/she would enjoy a holiday in Northumberland. You could give students headings to help them to organise their questions and subsequent informal reports on their own countries (see note 7 below):
Scenery: wild, beautiful . . .
Activities: go walking/climbing . . .
Sights: castles, churches/temples/mosques . . .

5 Ask 3 or 4 students to say what kind of holidays they and their partners like.
How many students think they would in fact enjoy a holiday here? If not, why not?

Background information Holy Island (bottom, left, inset) gets its name from the fact that St Aidan established a monastery there in the 7th century, from which he came to the mainland to convert the inhabitants, the Saxons, to Christianity. The top right hand picture shows Lindisfarne Priory, Holy Island.
The Cheviot is the highest hill in Northumberland (centre top and right – in the background).
Hadrian's Wall (bottom, centre) was built by the Romans during the reign of the Emperor Hadrian in AD 122 to protect England from raids from Scotland.
The two castles are Alnwick (left) and Lindisfarne (centre). The Farne Islands (bottom, left, background) are part of a bird sanctuary where a great variety of seabirds live.

Task SB28b PB28

6 In groups, students decide which features they can see in the pictures and map of Northumberland.
It shouldn't be necessary to pre-teach this lexis – allow students to pool their knowledge and encourage them to ask you as you come around to monitor their groups.

7 Students say briefly how they would describe their own countries and compare them with the picture of Northumberland. They should use pictures of their own country at this point if they have them. See note 4 above for a possible plan.

8 Help students to prepare their reports comparing their country to Northumberland. Encourage them to use language like: X says that in Spain they have ancient buildings and sandy beaches but they don't have hills like these . . ., or: Y says . . . .

9 Groups report back to the class. Encourage them to use whatever pictures have been brought in.

SB28c

Predicting what Jenny did on holiday here will help students to understand the recording about Jenny's holiday in section 29. (Jenny and Jeremy are new characters who appear only in this unit.)

10 Ask students to make their lists of 6 things Jenny and her family might have done on holiday, e.g. swimming . . . .
No need for full sentences at this stage (this will come later in sections 32 and 36).

11 Elicit ideas and make a consolidated list on the board. Students will need to refer to this list in the next section.

Unit 3
A good place for a holiday

Northumberland

28 A nice active week's holiday

a   Whereabouts in England is Northumberland?

Which of these words might be used to describe the Northumberland National Park?

beautiful	noisy	historical
crowded	quiet	ancient
peaceful	busy	wild

How do you think tourists spend their time in this area?
What do you think they go to see?
What sort of holiday do you like?
Do you think you would enjoy a holiday in Northumberland?

b   Which of the following can you see on this page?

mountainous regions	seaside/lakes
areas of forest or woodland	rocky coastline
grassy hills	sandy beaches
desert	small harbours
farmland	large ports
green valleys	ancient buildings

Could any of these pictures be somewhere in your country? Which ones? What kind of scenery is typical of your country? How does it compare with Northumberland?

c   Jenny Maxwell spent a week in Northumberland on holiday with her two children.
Make a list of six things you think they did.

17

29 Jenny's holiday

a   Jenny talked to a friend, Jeremy, about her holiday.

Before they began their conversation they had the instructions opposite. (They did not see each other's cards.)

29a Listen to the tape, and then read the transcript and say how many of the questions you think Jeremy was able to answer.

Listen and read again and count how many questions Jeremy asked. Did he ask four, or more than four?

29b b   Now listen to Jeremy's answers and see if you were right.
How many questions did he answer correctly?

c   Look at the six things you guessed in section 28c. Were you right?

> **Jenny**
>
> Talk to Jeremy about your last holiday. When you think you have told him all the important things, say "And that was how we spent our holiday."

> **Jeremy**
>
> Jenny is going to talk to you about her last holiday. You may ask her a maximum of four questions. At the end of the conversation you must answer as many of the following questions as you can.
>
> a How many people did she go on holiday with?
> b How did they travel?
> c How long was the holiday?
> d Where did they stay?
> e What was the weather like?
> f How did they spend the time?
> g Have they ever been on a similar holiday before?
> h Will they go back to the same place again?
>
> When Jenny says, "And that was how we spent our holiday." that is the end of the conversation.

---

30 Being indirect

a   Avoiding the question

In Britain, people don't like being asked how much money they earn, or how old they are. So if you are asked directly, you try to say something else, or give an answer that is vague, or a joke.

| *Well, how much do you get a month?* | *Not enough!*
Less than you, I expect.
Oh, about what a school teacher normally gets.
Well, it depends . . . |

Think of things you could say if for some reason you didn't want to answer these questions.

1 *How old are you?*
2 *What time did you get home last night?*
3 *Who were you with last night?*
4 *How much money did you actually spend?*
5 *Why didn't you come to the party?*

31 A holiday you've had

Working on your own, make a few notes about a holiday or day out you had recently. Your teacher will divide you into A and B groups and give you further instructions.

b   Asking indirectly

Now think of the different ways of finding something out without asking directly.

Instead of asking: *How old are you?* you could:

1 indirectly find out what year the other person left school etc. and work it out from that.
2 ask questions like *Do you remember when the Beatles first became popular?*
3 give the same information about yourself, e.g. *Well, I'm 43 and . . .*

Think of what might you say in order to find out:

1 how much rent someone pays
2 if they have had a nasty argument lately
3 how much they spent on their last holiday

32 *Language study*

a   do, did

Jenny says: *We did a lot of walking along the coast.*

What did you do on your last holiday?

a bit of climbing   some swimming
a lot of boating   a lot of sightseeing

What do the phrases with **do** mean here?

a *Who does most of the meals in your house?*
b *I'll do the list.*
c *Who does most of the talking in your home?*

b   That was why/how etc.

Jenny and her children had never been to Northumberland. Jenny says:
>   *That was why we wanted to go.*
They did a lot of different things.
>   *That was how we spent our holiday.*

Now look at these.

I liked science subjects but I think that was because the teachers were very much better. (58)
You have to get on a train and come all the way back again. That's why it's always better to catch a taxi.

29 Jenny's holiday

Aims: 1 Questions to elicit specific information.
2 To practise producing and summarising a narrative.

Lexis: active, boat, coast, dry, idea, island, last, lucky, managed, maximum, met, reach [L], **spend, time, top**
Revision: **farmhouse, highest, like, north**

Listening   SB29a   *   PB29

1 Students read Jenny and Jeremy's cards. Before playing the tape get students to speculate on possible answers Jenny might give. (Some of this stage overlaps with 29c.)

2 Students listen to the tape and read the transcript to find which questions they are sure he will be able to answer and which ones they are not so sure about.

3 In their groups students count Jeremy's questions, then check the transcript to find out if Jenny actually gave the answer or if the answer is implied.

Listening   SB29b   [29b] *

4 Students listen to Jeremy's answers. Which ones was he able to answer with confidence? Which ones did he guess or infer?

Key: Jeremy answers a, b, c, f, g with confidence. He infers the answer to e from the word 'dry' and to h from the fact that they enjoyed their holiday. He gets d wrong, though Jenny says 'We stayed in a farmhouse for a week.'

5 Optional: students write brief summary of Jenny's holiday.

SB29c

6 Refer students to their consolidated list on the board and compare their guesses with what they heard on the tape.

When you do the lexis review for this section get students to look up **top** *in the Lexicon. Ask what meaning it has when Jenny uses it (1).*

7 Optional survey: Students find out if anyone in the class as a whole or in their group has ever been: climbing
fishing   to the north of England   swimming in really cold water   etc.
Encourage students to ask for details when the response is 'yes', e.g. Where? Did they enjoy it? etc.

8 Students prepare reports. Teacher monitors. Help them to produce language like:
X has been to the north of England. He/she didn't enjoy it. Nobody has ever been swimming in cold water, etc.

9 Students read reports to the class. The others listen to find how many people have done the same as they have.

30 Being indirect

Aims: 1 To practise tactics for asking questions to elicit information without giving away one's intentions.
2 To practise pre-empting and avoiding questions.

SB30a

1 In pairs students prepare possible answers.

2 Students change partners and take turns asking and giving the answers they prepared with their first partner. Then elicit suggested answers and write them on the board as a basis for further discussion.

SB30b

3 In groups students think of indirect ways of asking questions 1–3. Students will probably need help with this activity.

4 Consolidate students' suggestions on the board.   *or* students prepare and present roleplays to the class.

SB30a   Possible answers

1 Not as old as you think.   2 Not that late.   3 An old friend of mine.   4 Less than I expected.   5 By the time I finished work/dinner it was too late.

Your aim here is not to encourage students to tell direct lies, but to avoid telling the truth in a way which may offend the listener.

SB30b   Possible questions

1 My rent seems to be going up all the time. Does yours?   2 You seem a little tired/upset. Is everything alright?   3 We spent a fortune on our last holiday . . .

31 A holiday you've had

Aims: 1 To give further practice in eliciting information without revealing your intention.
2 Practice in pre-empting and avoiding questions.

SB31   PB31

Instructions for B: Find out as much as you can about what the weather was like. Do this without asking any questions *directly* about the weather. e.g. *not* 'Was the weather cold?' *but* 'Did you need lots of warm clothes?'

Instructions for A: You don't want B to ask many questions. Keep talking so he/she doesn't have time for questions. Pretend to misunderstand. Give misleading answers.

1 Get all the As on one side and all the Bs on another and give them their instructions. If possible let them plan their strategies in separate rooms. The As have fewer strategies to prepare. Ask them to spend their time anticipating questions and planning evasive answers.

2 As students are working take note of what strategies they use. After the task help them to list their strategies. Then round off the exercise by making a list on the board of: questions used by the As.   tactics adopted by the Bs.

32 Language study

Aims: 1 To practise **do** as a delexical verb, especially as used with a quantifier, e.g. **do** a lot of/a bit of.
2 The use of **that is/was + wh-clause** to provide supplementary information.

Lexis: swimming

SB32a   PB32a

1 Elicit and write on the board what students did on their last holiday. Use substitution to focus attention on **do** e.g. We did a bit of sightseeing/some shopping.

2 In pairs students discuss what **do** means in a–c. What words could replace **do**?
Key: a cooks   b write   c carries out/conducts/talks.

SB32b   PB32b

3 Students read and try to produce more examples. e.g. I need English to/for . . . That was why I decided to take a course here.

5 Write up the following and ask students to match them.
Column 1: 1 I liked science subjects but I think
2 But they're ever so small
3 A: It's summer. B: Why? C: Because
4 . . . get on a train and come all the way back again.
Column 2: a that's why rain is thin.
b that's why it's always better to catch a taxi.
c that was because the teachers were very much better.
d that's when it is.
Key: 1 c   2 a   3 d   4 b

Aims: 1 To practise making and understanding an implied request.
2 To practise reading and writing holiday correspondence.
3 To focus on the meaning and use of 'hedging' words and phrases, e.g. **perhaps**, **I suppose**.

Lexis: **country** [T], **miss (you lots)**, **purpose**, **reason**
Revision: **basically**

SB33a PB33

1 After students have read the postcards and speculated on their meanings in pairs, put some of their suggestions on the board. Don't confirm or give away any answers at this stage – this will be the point of further activities. It may help the students to speculate if you put a framework on the board:

Place:
Relationship Munling – Willises/Amanda – Becky:
Holiday?:
Result:

SB33b 33b *

2 Students listen to John and Monica to compare and/or confirm their answers.

Key: Postcard 1
John and Monica guessed correctly that Munling is a friend of the Willises on holiday in Australia, and that she sent the postcard in the hope that they would meet her and her family at the airport.
There is an additional fact that John and Monica did not know. Munling had left her car with the Willises while on holiday and they had offered to meet the family at the airport. The postcard is, therefore, by way of a reminder.

Postcard 2
They were correct in that Amanda was a friend of Becky's; that Becky wanted but was unable to see her off at the airport; that Amanda had gone back to live in Ireland. They did not know that Amanda had spent her final weekend in Singapore with Becky's family.

Listening SB33c 33c *

3 In pairs students speculate about why John and Monica have used the words and phrases in the box.

Key: John and Monica say 'perhaps', 'it sounds as though' etc. because they are not sure; that is, they are speculating or guessing.

Planning SB33d

4 Elicit a few ideas about how to drop hints, e.g.
We don't get back till 10.30 at night. I'm afraid the children will be very tired.
I hope we don't have to wait too long for a taxi/bus at the airport.
It will be nice to get home but I always hate the long busride from the airport.
I wish we'd left our car in the airport carpark, but it's so expensive we couldn't afford to.

It is probably better not to put these on the board in full, otherwise all you have left is a mechanical copying exercise. In groups students write their postcards. Go round and help as necessary.

Report

5 Take finished postcards in and read them out to the class. Ask students to decide how persuasive and subtle they are – a scale of 1 to 5 might be fun here.

Aim: To practise recognising words which can be used both with expressions concerning money and expressions concerning time.

Lexis: **afford**, **lose**, **loss** [T], **spend**, **time**, **waste**

SB34 PB34

1 In pairs students match sentences a–f to the correct lexical categories. Refer them to the Lexicon for further explanation of the categories.

2 Students find the words in sentences g–l which can be used with both time and money.

Key: a 1　b 3　c 4　d 3　e 2　f 5
g afford
h waste
i lose
j spend
k save
l save

3 Ask students if there are words in their own language which can be used with both time and money. In English there is a saying, 'Time is money.' Do they have a similar expression?

a Read the two postcards. Speculate about who the senders are and their reasons for sending the postcards. What do you think will happen as a result of these postcards?

Dear Dave, Jane, Jerry + Becky 3/5
My sister lives very close to this picture. The Blue Mountains are spectacular. We're having a family time here till we leave on Friday 11/5. This is to inform you that we've changed our flight. We're flying direct from Sydney on QF1 e.t.a. 21.10, just in case you're thinking of coming to the airport.
See you soon
Munling

AIR MAIL

DAVE + JANE WILLIS
c/o The British Council
Rubber House
Collyer Quay
Singapore 1
SINGAPORE

Dear Becky,
Sorry you couldn't come to the airport. Miss you lots. Say hi to your parents from me. Thanks for the weekend. Please write. Anne-Clare has my address.
Amanda

BECKY WILLIS
21 FOLLESTONE RD.
MEDWAY PARK.
S'PORE 0513
SINGAPORE

PAR AVION
AEROPHOST
O.E. 78.

O'Connell Bridge, Dublin, Ireland.   Photo: P. O'Toole, John Hinde Studios.

b What do you think about the first postcard?

33b Listen to John and Monica. Did they say the same as you?

c What about the second postcard?

33c Listen to John and Monica again.

Why do they use these words and phrases?

Perhaps	Do you suppose
It sounds as though	I don't know
Maybe	Probably
I suppose so	

d Imagine you are on holiday abroad. You write a postcard to a friend. Your real purpose is to persuade them to meet you at the airport or station. But of course you want to do this without actually asking them directly.
Write the postcard.

time and money

1 **time** = minutes, hours, days, week, months etc.
Mummy and Daddy went back to Ireland some time ago. (4)
It'll rain all the time. (38)
How did they spend the time? (21)

2 to have a ___ time.
It sounds like you had a good time. (29)
We had a dreadful time.

3 **time** = an occasion when something happens

The second time was when we went to eat at a hamburger restaurant.
I've already boarded this flight five times and every time I ended up in Cuba.
This time our friend left a warning note. (150)

4 **time** = two o'clock, 8.30, 17.20 hours etc.
What time is it?   Do you have the time?

5 **times**
The taxi cost five times as much as the bus.

Which category do these examples belong to?

(a) Took a very long time getting there. (21)
(b) People we met on it said they'd been many times before. (29)
(c) Look at the time. We're going to be late.
(d) But next time I knew I could do it. (58)
(e) We had a very busy time at work last week.
(f) My job is a hundred times more difficult than playing the piano. (174)

Spend goes with money as well as time. What other words are like **spend**?

(g) That's very expensive. We can't afford it.
(h) You'd waste a lot of time and you'd feel exhausted when you got there. (69)
(i) Business is bad. We're losing quite a bit.
(j) How much did you actually spend?
(k) If you go by taxi you'll save ten minutes or so.
(l) We are saving for our holidays.

35 Discover the North Pennines

a The North Pennines, as the name suggests, are at the Northern tip of the Pennine Hills, the backbone of England. A spectacularly beautiful and undiscovered area, some of the wildest open landscape left in England.

Read through the passage below and find phrases that could act as captions for the pictures.

Northumberland is a paradise for everyone who enjoys the open air. There are magnificent walks over hills, moors and dales, including a rugged stretch of the Pennine Way, and in summer you can bathe from miles of smooth sandy beaches. The streams and rivers of Northumberland provide some of the finest trout and salmon fishing in Britain, and there is excellent sport along the coast for sea anglers. With the sea or the moors for a background, you can play golf on superb courses, and there are good facilities for other sports and pastimes, including pony-trekking, sailing, gliding, tennis and bowls. Horse-racing, Association and Rugby football can be enjoyed in nearby Newcastle.

If you are thinking of a motoring holiday, there's no better place than Northumberland, where parking problems are few, and you can drive for miles without seeing another car. In fact there are several roads where you are more likely to surprise a pheasant or a hare than to pass another vehicle. Wherever you decide to stop you can always be sure of finding comfortable accommodation, a good meal, and a real warm-hearted Northumbrian welcome – Northumbrians have a reputation for being the most hospitable folk in Britain. There's plenty of entertainment too, especially in the larger towns. National ballet and opera companies visit the region regularly, and there are first-class theatres in Newcastle …

provide
guesthouses
farmhouses
ideal
atmosphere
excellent value

?
Words to guess

WHERE TO STAY

Hotels, inns, guesthouses and farmhouses provide a wide choice of accommodation.

What the critics say …

A farmhouse holiday is ideal for a family – good food, a friendly atmosphere and a lovely setting.
– Carol Chester, Daily Express

Excellent value for good food, peace and quiet and beautiful scenery.
– Paul Hughes, Daily Mirror

discover
choice
finding

L
Words to look up

open air
streams
region
pastimes
fishing
comfortable
accommodation
plenty
regularly

?
Words to guess

b Think of a tourist place that you know very well. How many of these phrases might be used to describe it? Choose any five phrases and complete them.

There's no better place than … excellent sport/ shopping/entertainment … magnificent … superb … can be enjoyed … You can always be sure of finding … There's plenty of … There are good facilities for … There is/are first-class … The people have a reputation for … Ideal for … a wide choice of … excellent value for …

36 *Phrase-building* ·

Make some sentences from the first table and after each one add a suitable comment from the second.

We did	some a fair bit of quite a lot of a lot of plenty of too much far too much	sunbathing. fishing. shopping. walking. climbing. sightseeing. driving.		That's	how why	you	got so tired. have no money left. saw so much. enjoyed yourselves. got so many things. spent the time.

35 | Discover the North Pennines

Aim: To practise understanding a persuasive text and recognising words and phrases that have a persuasive intent.

Lexis: accommodation, atmosphere, beach, beautiful, beauty [T], **choice** [L], **choose** [L], **comfort** [T], **comfortable, discover** [L], **find, fish, fishing, friendly, guest(house), ideal, likely (to), lovely, north, pass, plenty (of), provide** [L], **quiet, quietly, region, regular(ly), sand, streams, value, wide**
Revision: **excellent, pastimes**

Lexicon: **discover**: List 3 different things you can 'discover'.

SB35a

1 Students find the phrases to match the captions individually and compare their answers in pairs. Monitor the students, helping out with words where necessary.

2 Students report their answers to the class. Check that students have understood the important lexis during the feedback session.

Key: Magnificent walks over hills, moors and dales. In summer you can bathe from miles of smooth sandy beaches. Some of the finest trout and salmon fishing in Britain. Good facilities for . . . sports. There are several roads where you are more likely to surprise a pheasant or a hare than to pass another vehicle. You can always be sure of finding comfortable accommodation, a good meal, and a real warm-hearted Northumbrian welcome.

3 Words to guess: In pairs students work out the meanings from the way they are used in the text.
Words to look up: in pairs students find the appropriate categories for these words in their Lexicons.

4 Monitor the class carefully while they are doing these activities and be prepared to explain the meanings of any words, particularly those that they cannot guess from context.

5 Tell students to go through the critics' comments and list or underline the words which tell you that something is very good.

Key: ideal, good, friendly, lovely, excellent, beautiful

Task   SB35b   PB35

6 Students work individually to think of a place and complete 5 phrases to describe it accurately.

7 Students describe the place they have chosen to their partner. Monitor the pairs, while they are giving their descriptions, helping out where needed.

8 Students read their descriptions out to the class.

9 Students could write a tourist brochure entry for homework.

36 | Phrase-building

Aims: 1 To give students practice in the use of **do** as a delexical verb.
2 Further practice in 'That is/was + **wh**-clause' structures.

Lexis: do/did

This is not an entirely mechanical drill. Students should not produce for example:
We did a bit of swimming. That's why we have no money left.
. . . That's why we spent the time.

SB36

1 Begin with listen and repeat practice, then let students read sentences for themselves.

2 Ask students to close their books and see how many sentences they can remember. If you like you can ask them to write 3 sentences down and see how many different ones they have got, or if any students have got the same one.

3 Optional: Go on to vary the tense of the verb:
We're going to do a lot of shopping.
We usually do a bit of swimming.
etc.

37 Grammar revision

> **Aim:** To practise **have/has/had been** with present perfect continuous; with the passive; with the meaning **gone to** or **visited**.

SB37 PB37a,b,c

1 Students read the rubric and try to understand for themselves how to do the exercise in pairs. Monitor their progress and help out where necessary.

2 Students report back. List their findings on the board.

   Key: been to = gone/visited in b, c, f, i,

3 Ask students to look at the sentences and to tell you which verb always precedes **been**.

   Key: been is always preceded by **have/has/had**.

4 Ask students to find sentences in which **been** is used with **since, ever** and **never** and to infer or guess, if they don't already know, what these words mean in the sentences.

   Key: since (b, c, d)   ever (f, g)   never (i)
   since – refers to a period of time from a fixed point of time, either stated explicitly or inferred from context, in the past, to the present; **ever** – at any point in your life; **never** – not at any time

5 Point out the other 2 uses of **been** in these examples. (There is no need to go into the meaning of these forms in detail; it's sufficient for students to realise that 'visited' or 'gone to' is not the only meaning for **been**.)

   Key: Other forms with **been**: verb in **-ing** (d); verb in **-ed** (j): **been** = past participle of **be** (a, h)

38 Future holidays

> **Aims:** 1 To practise talking about future plans and to introduce students to ways of referring to future time.
> 2 To practise listening for gist and ignoring details.
>
> **Lexis: Christmas, expect, (looking) forward, join/joining, lucky, provide** [L], **relaxed/relaxing, wet** [T]

Listening   SB38a *

1 In pairs students speculate about whether Catherine or Stephen said a–d. Students give their reasons. Ask them what other comments could take the place of 'How lovely!' Emphasise that it is Stephen who is talking about his holiday.

2 Students listen to the tape to check their answers. Ask students what they remember about Stephen's holiday.

   Key: Catherine says a, b and c. Sentences a and c are identifiable as comments on what Stephen tells her. Sentence b is a question about travel arrangements and therefore likely to be Catherine. Sentence d expresses what Stephen will do on his holiday.

Listening   SB38b *

3 Tell students you are going to play the recording about Catherine's holiday. Ask them to take brief notes of her plans. Play the tape. What notes were they able to take? Aim to get the gist, not detailed information, from them.

4 Individually students find phrases in the transcript. Put these phrases on the board. What do the phrases all have in common? (They all refer to future time). Don't go into a detailed explanation as this will be the point of section 40. Note **mainly** occurs twice.

Key: my next holiday is tomorrow   I'm taking my two children with me   My husband is joining us in a week's time   I'm going to be driving most of the time   we're going to stay with my parents   it's mainly going to be a very relaxing bucket-and-spade holiday for the children   mainly I think it's just going to be a very relaxing time   I'm looking forward to it.

Planning   SB38c   PB38a,b

6 Discuss possible questions as a class before students prepare them individually. With a slower class, do section 40 first. In pairs, students ask one another their questions and take notes.

Report

7 Students write their reports individually. Monitor their work. Collect their work. Read out a few scripts. Can the class guess whose work it is? Ask them to listen for the holiday they would most like to take themselves (apart from the one they have described for their partner).

39 Board and lodgings

> **Aims:** 1 Further practice in using language of persuasion.
> 2 To practise reading for the gist of a paragraph.
>
> **Lexis: accommodation, bed, board** [L], **guest, king, opportunity, queen** [T], **range, royal, separate**

Lexicon: Students look up the word **board**. What meaning does it have here? How many other meanings can they recall?

SB39

1 Ask students to pick out the 'persuasive' words in the text. Make a consolidated list of their suggestions on the board.

2 In pairs, students write the question headings. Monitor pairwork, encouraging them to write accurate question forms. When pairs have finished, have them read a few of their questions aloud to the class. The others should listen to find out if their questions were roughly the same as the ones read out, or very different.

3 Lead a class discussion of the questions that follow to prepare students for the writing task. You might talk about your experiences in foreign countries to start them off.

Planning and report

4 Help students as they work in groups, preparing plans for the writing task, but let them finish for homework.

40 Language study

> **Aim:** More intensive practice in recognising and understanding ways of referring to future time.

SB40

1 Students refer to the transcripts and the text in section 39 to find the ways of referring to future time. Put their findings on the board. Focus students' attention on the ways of referring to future time by grouping them under the following headings:

   Simple present tense: e.g. is tomorrow ... (Focus attention on the use of words **next** and **tomorrow** to signal reference to future time.)

   Going to: e.g. I'm going to the West Coast of Ireland ...

   Present continuous tense: e.g. I'm taking my two children ...

   Modal will: e.g. It'll rain all the time ...

been

Sometimes **been** means 'gone to' or 'visited'. How many sentences are there here where **been** means 'gone to' or 'visited'?

Have you been there before?
I don't know London. I've never been.

a *How long have you been away from there?* (9)
b *I haven't been back since.* (10)
c *I've only been back once since.* (17)
d *Since then I have been teaching English.* (17)
e *We'd been collecting firewood for a bonfire.* (18)
f *Have you ever been to a zoo?*
g *Have you ever been bitten by a dog or a snake?*
h *So the weather must have been sunny and nice.* (29)
i *I've never been to Charles de Gaulle airport.* (69)
j *His stories have been translated into many languages.* (97)

38 Future holidays

38a **a** Stephen is telling Catherine about his next holiday. Who do you think says these things?

a *That sounds really lovely.*
b *Why can he get you tickets?*
c *How lovely!*
d *I'll just laze in the sun.*

Listen and see if you were right.

38b **b** What are Catherine's plans? Find the phrases with these words in the transcript.

next holiday	with my parents
with me	for the children
in a week's time	mainly
most of the time	looking forward

c Work with a partner. Ask five questions to find out what your partner will do for their next holiday. Take notes and then write a short piece about your partner's holiday.

39 Board and lodgings

Write a question to act as a heading for five of these paragraphs, e.g. What is B&B? Is breakfast included?

BED BREAKFAST & EVENING MEAL

Can tourists find anything like B & B in your country?
How much does it cost for a comfortable bed for the night?
Is that more or less than B & B in Britain?
What food is there that is typical of your country and that tourists like?

> Write something similar about holiday accommodation in a country that you know well.

'B & B'. A HOME AWAY FROM HOME
Bed and Breakfast, or B & B as it is often known, is a form of holiday accommodation for which Britain is world-famous.

It gives you the opportunity to stay in a private house that has one or two spare bedrooms, or a small guest house.

And it also gives you the chance to make friends and see some of the most attractive and less well-known parts of the country ranging from John O'Groats to Land's End.

In most cases it will be run by the owner who lives on the premises and you will be treated as a royal guest.

The welcome will be warm and friendly but your privacy will be respected and you can have all your meals in a separate dining room.

In addition to a comfortable bed, your host will prepare you an English breakfast fit for a King.

Prices range from £7 to £16 per night.

Contact your local BTA for information on budget accommodation.

40 *Language study*

Look at the transcripts for sections 38a and 38b. How many ways of referring to the future can you find? e.g. *I'm going to have a holiday.*

a   What do these sentences have in common?

1 *You will be reading about two people.*
2 *What do you think they are going to say?*
3 *I intend to stay in Britain for a few years.*
4 *Tomorrow they will buy another dog.*
5 *My next holiday is tomorrow hopefully.*
6 *If I'm lucky my roommate will be able to get us tickets.*
7 *My husband is joining us in a week's time.*
8 *We're flying direct from Sydney on QF1.*
9 *I'll go home when I've finished this.*
10 *We'll come round and say 'Goodbye' before we leave.*

b   Punctuation

Match these, then see if you can find one example of each of these punctuation marks on this page.

a comma	' '
a full stop	;
an apostrophe s	.
a question mark	( )
an exclamation mark	–
quotation marks/inverted commas	,
a semi-colon	:
a colon	/
a hyphen	?
a dash	's
brackets	!
dot dot dot	-
a stroke/slash	...

c   Which meanings of these words are used here? Check in the Lexicon.

1 *I found Chinese very difficult to learn. I expect you will, too.*
2 *I've got no idea which person on the board of directors to ask.*
3 *There's such a wide choice of banks – go to the one which will give you the top rates of interest if you want to save money.*
4 *I was working in the garden when I discovered this funny black object.*
5 *It was hidden in a small space right under a tree root, and was very difficult to reach.*
6 *The person next door said it would be a good idea to contact the museum who might be interested in the strange object.*
7 *Although I tried several times to phone them, I couldn't reach the man I needed to speak to.*

d   northern, southern, eastern, western, European

What words commonly follow these?

Western Europe will be cold with snow in some northern parts. Southern areas of Eastern Europe will be warmer but heavy falls of snow may effect European airports.

e   likely, unlikely

Say whether you think these things are:

(almost/practically) definite/certain
likely/probable   possible
(almost/practically) impossible   unlikely

1 *Catherine enjoyed her holiday in Ireland.*
2 *Jenny and her family will be going back to Northumberland.*
3 *Stephen had a good holiday in Bermuda.*
4 *If you go to Ireland you will be able to do a lot of sunbathing.*
5 *If you go to Bermuda it will rain all the time.*
6 *If you stay in a B & B you will be well looked after.*
7 *The Willises went to meet Munling and her family.*
8 *You will be going on holiday sometime in the next year.*
9 *You will be going abroad.*
10 *You will enjoy your holiday.*

f   What's the missing word?

1 *I've lived in London _____ years.*
2 *Where are you going _____ your next holiday?*
3 *You can drive _____ miles without seeing ...*
4 *... breakfast, fit _____ a king.*
5 *It's ideal _____ a family.*
6 *... a good place _____ walking.*
7 *B & B accommodation _____ which Britain is world-famous.*
8 *What does it cost _____ a bed?*
9 *What's _____ homework?*

Which examples answer the question WHY, which HOW LONG and which WHAT/WHO FOR?

Important words to remember (164 so far)

accommodation	central	dry	king	queen	southern
active	choice L	eastern	likely	quiet	spend
activity	choose L	European	lovely	quietly	stream
afford	Christian	expect L	lucky	range	swimming
ancient	Christmas	fish	managed	reach L	unlikely
atmosphere	coast	fishing	maximum	region	value
beautiful	comfort	friendly	northern	regular	waste
beauty	comfortable	guest	opportunity	relaxed	western
beach	crowd	ideal	peace	royal	wet
board L	dangerous	island	plenty	sand	wide
boat	discover L	join	provide L	separate	wild

Aims: 1 To revise ways of referring to the future.
2 To revise punctuation marks in English.
3 To revise useful lexis.
4 To revise some ways of expressing certainty/uncertainty.

Lexis: central [T], **eastern, European, southern, western, wet** [T]

SB41a

Key: All the sentences refer to the future.

SB41b

Aim: To recognise English punctuation marks.

SB41c PB41b

Key: **1** find 3, expect 1 **2** idea 4, board 2 **3** choice 2, top 2, interest 2 **4** discover 2, **5** reach 3 **6** idea 2, interest 4 **7** reach 2

SB41d

Key: areas, parts (of a continent or country).

SB41e

The purpose of this activity is primarily to promote discussion.

Note alternative forms: certainly/definitely; probably; possibly (but *not* 'impossibly')

SB41f PB41a

Key: for

LEXICAL OBJECTIVES

Level 1 words (see page 129T):
bed, country, find, L, **for** (see SB41), **forward, idea** L, **interest** L, **last, miss, pass, time** (see SB34), **top.**

accommodation 1 . . . *a form of holiday accommodation.*
active 1 *an active member of a club*
2 in operation . . . *an active volcano*
3 energetic . . . *active week's holiday.*
activity 1 . . . *high economic activity.* T
2 things you spend time doing . . . *cultural/leisure activities.* T
3 . . . *the activities of a group.* T
afford See SB34.
ancient 1 *Ancient Greece*
2 very old. . . . *an ancient building.*
atmosphere 1 feeling a place has . . . *a friendly atmosphere.*
2 air around the earth. T
beach *miles of smooth, sandy beaches.*
beautiful 1 . . . *beautiful scenery.*
2 skilful; well done. *'Lovely!' he cried. 'Beautiful! Keep going!'* [10]
beauty 1 *a beauty spot* = a beautiful place T
2 a person: *a beauty queen.* T

board L
boat a vessel for travelling on water. *We went out in a boat one day . . .*
central 1 most important part . . . *the central character in the film.*
2 controlling headquarters of an organisation. *Central Government.* T
3 geographical. *Central London.* T
choice L
choose L
Christian 1 person who believes in Jesus Christ. T
Christmas Christian festival when the birth of Jesus is celebrated.
coast where the sea meets the land. . . . *on the east coast.*
comfort 1 . . . *hotels chosen for their comfort.* T
2 *the comforts of home.* T
3 something that makes someone feel less unhappy. . . . *comforting thought.* T
comfortable *The hotel was large and comfortable . . .*
crowd 1 a large group of people. *A big crowd gathered.*
Also **crowded**
2 *a whole crowd of* = a large amount; informal. *A whole crowd of people . . .* T
3 gather closely together. *The boys crowded round him . . .* T
discover L
dry 1 *Is the paint dry yet?*
1.1 *He dried his feet with the towel . . .*
1.2 dry the dishes. *I'll wash up and you can dry . . .* T
2 . . . *a dry summer*
3 dull and uninteresting . . . *a dry book.* T
eastern 1 *Eastern Europe*
2 from the Far East. *Eastern culture.*
european The European Economic Community (EEC).
expect L
fish 1 a creature that lives in water
2 to pull something out of somewhere else *I fished out my passport from the bottom of the bag.*
fishing the sport or business of catching fish. *The fishing industry*
friendly welcoming. . . . *warm and friendly*
guest 1 someone invited to someone else's home. *We had a couple of guests staying overnight.*
2 *Be my guest* = I'll pay for this. T
ideal perfect. *A farmhouse holiday is ideal for a family.*
island 1 piece of land surrounded by water. *Holy Island: a tiny island cut off from the mainland.*
join 1 *My husband is joining us in a week's time.*
king 1 *King George 6th.*
2 *Elvis is the king of Rock and Roll.* T
likely probable. . . . *roads where you are more likely to surprise a pheasant or a hare than to pass another car.*
lovely wonderful; beautiful. *a friendly atmosphere and a lovely setting*
lucky fortunate. *If I'm lucky, my room-mate next year will be able to get us tickets.*
managed 1 succeeded, . . . *never managed to get to the top.*
Can you manage = Do you need help?

maximum 1 the most or highest number. *a maximum of 4 questions* [12]
northern . . . the Northern Hemisphere.
opportunity 1 chance. *It gives you the opportunity to stay in a private house.*
2 *trying to increase employment opportunities for school-leavers.* T
peace 1 without worry. . . . *peace and quiet and beautiful scenery.*
2 period of time in which there is no war. . . . *when the world is at peace.* T
plenty 1 a large amount; enough. *There's plenty of entertainment.*
2 *We are using new technology to help us along the road to peace and plenty.* T
provide L
purpose reason for doing something. *Your real purpose is to persuade them to meet you . . .*
queen *Queen Victoria*
quiet 1 *Peace and quiet*
2 saying nothing. *There was nothing to say to this so she kept quiet.*
3 secret. *And you keep quiet about what you saw tonight.*
quietly *'I'm going to do it,' I said quietly.*
range 1 *Prices range from £7–£16 per night.*
2 . . . *cover a wide range of subjects.* T
reach L
region 1 an area. *Ballet and opera companies visit the region regularly.*
regular/ly *regular visits.* T
relax 1 without tension. *It's going to be a very relaxing time.*
2 to loosen. *He relaxed his grip.* T
royal connected with a king or queen. . . . *the royal palace.* . . . *treated as a royal guest.*
sand *In summer you can bathe from miles of smooth sandy beaches.*
separate 1 apart from other things or people. *You can have all your meals in a separate dining room.*
2 distinct from, not the same as *Ireland is a separate country from Britain.*
southern see Eastern, Northern
spend spend time and money
stone a stone. *I picked up a stone.*
stream 1 a small river. *The streams and rivers of Northumberland.*
2 *She stood in the doorway, tears streaming down her face.* T
3 *A steady stream of questions.*
swimming *swimming in the cold sea*
unlikely See SB41e.
value 1 *The value of money.* T
2 importance. *I don't think it would be of much value.*
3 worth buying. *Excellent value for good food, peace and quiet . . .*
waste See SB34.
western See eastern
wet 1 weather: rainy. *A wet night.* T
2 *I don't want to get my feet wet.* T
wide 1 . . . *wide open spaces.*
2 . . . *about seven inches long and about four inches wide . . .* [13]
3 *a wide range . . .* [15] T
wild 1 *wild horses.*
2 far from towns. *The wilder parts of Scotland.*
3 very stormy weather. T
4 excited. *Now the crowd was wild.* T

They're probably worth the money

The themes of this unit cover issues such as rates of pay for different types of jobs and professions, fair pay, and equal pay for women and men. Students are asked about the lowest paid jobs in their countries, and about the kind of work involved in their present job (or past or possible future job). For light relief there are some funny stories and there's a 'keyhole picture' game, which appears at 3 different places in the unit, the 'keyhole' revealing more each time, as students guess who this man might be. Within the context of jobs, conditions and pay students are asked to describe, evaluate and compare. The picture game involves speculation and cooperative discourse, and the stories recycle anecdotal narrative.

OBJECTIVES

Lexical objectives are in TB57.

Grammar and discourse

a Meaning and use of **any** and compounds (**anybody, anyone, anywhere** etc); also compounds with **-body: anybody** etc. (56,57)
b Phrases expressing amounts and comparison in connection with money and pay. (44)
c Common uses in discourse of phrases with verbs: say, think, know. (44)
d Meaning of time phrases, e.g. some days, in between times, once. (52,53)
e Understanding past narrative with dialogue. (45,55)
f Ways of expressing reasons why particular jobs should be better paid than others. (43)
g Use of question forms (to gain specific information about someone's work). (52)
h Phrases with adjectives and verbs which take **to**: tend/appears/able; happy/hard to etc. (54)
i Words and phrases which express the notion of 'often'/'usually' using 'tend to', 'in general' etc. (57)
j Meaning of **in** in phrases which refer to time and place, e.g. in ten years, in the sky. (50)

Tasks

a Discussion, comparison, and evaluation in the context of job conditions and pay. (42,43,46)
b Understanding and telling anecdotes and exchanging experiences. (55)
c Evaluating and responding to magazine correspondence; making recommendations for action. (47)
d Cooperative problem solving; converging on a solution as more information is supplied. (49,51)
e Describing the type of work you do/did/would like to do and how you feel about it. (52)
f Drafting a written summary from information obtained through a spoken interview. Summarising personal views. (52)

42 Well paid or badly paid?

Aim: To introduce the themes and some of the lexis which will be dealt with in this unit.

Lexis: **anybody** (it doesn't matter who you are), **dentist, earns, engineer** [T], **generally** (in general), **handles, (at) least** [L], **minister** [T], **profession, scientist, tend to, union** [L], **wage, worth**
Revision: **best, expected, pay** (earnings), **receive, should, worst**

SB42

1 Introduce a few further examples, e.g. the Prime Minister, an engineer. Students discuss in groups what jobs these people are doing and decide which statements they agree with.

2 Write target lexis, revision words or generally useful words on the board as students ask about them.

   Key: Jobs and professions: nurse, young girl baby sitter/child minder, teacher, baker's assistant, waitress, ice-cream seller, professional footballer, car assembly worker (factory worker), plumber, dentist, shop assistant (florist).

3 Discuss questions about best and worst paid professions briefly – they are discussed in more detail in section 43.

4 Students work out what £1.20 an hour is in their currency. Add a proportion to allow for inflation, e.g. 5% per year.
   1986 1.20
   1987 1.25
   1988 1.30 etc.

5 Encourage cross-class comparison of rates of pay for the various professions. Also encourage discussion about rates of pay for difficult, dangerous jobs like coalmining. Do students think they should be higher/lower?

   Explain what a workers' union is. For example, the National Union of Teachers in Britain. Unions like these help workers to get better pay and conditions.

6 Students look in the Lexicon for the other uses of **professional, worth** and **least**.

Background: The word 'salary' comes from 'salt' because in the very early days, especially in the mines, workers were not paid in money, but were given salt, which was absolutely necessary for their well-being.

They're probably worth the money

42 Well paid or badly paid?

How many different jobs and professions can you
find on this page? Which would be the best paid in
your country? Which would be the worst paid?
Which *should* be the best paid, do you think?

```
Mr. Matthew Stewart,
The Manager,
National United Bank,
57 High Street,
Risborough,
RB1 5AP.
```

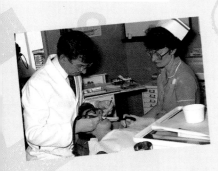

Which of these statements do you agree with, if any?

a *'Anybody who handles money tends to get paid a
lot.'*
b *'Dentists are well paid; they're probably worth the
money though.'*
c *'Teachers are definitely underpaid.'*
d *'Anybody who's paid more than me is probably
overpaid.'*
e *'In general, women receive the same pay for the
same work as men.'*

f *'... women have a slight advantage; they tend to
get tipped more generously than men.'*
g *'Anybody who is expected to work eight and a half
hours a day should be receiving more than just
£1.20 an hour.'*
h *'The Union would probably insist on a wage of at
least £108 per week.'*

L profession/al
   worth
   least

23

43 Best paid and worst paid

a   Look at the list of jobs below.
In groups, discuss which are the three best paid jobs and the two worst paid in your country. Write a list.
Do you think that any of the jobs on the list are overpaid or underpaid in your country?
Have you any idea which are the best and worst paid in Britain?

> a nurse in a hospital
> a miner at the coalface
> a shop assistant
> a car assembly worker in a factory
> a bank manager
> a dentist
> a schoolteacher
> a plumber
> a top professional footballer
> a nuclear scientist

▷   Tell the class what you have decided.   ◁

Listen to the other groups and see if they think the same as you.
How many groups had the same person at the top of their lists?

43b   **b**   What did Caroline and Stephen think? Draw a table like this one, and fill it in after you have listened.

Best paid	....
Worst paid	....
Overpaid	....
Underpaid	....

Compare their opinions with:

what you think about your country.
what you decided about Britain.

44 *Language study* ············

44a   **a**   Listen to Caroline and Stephen talking about the schoolteacher and the nurse. How many times do they use the words **say, think** and **know**? What phrases do they use with them?

b   How many ways could you categorise these phrases?

> *paid reasonably well*
> *get a lot of money*
> *Too much!*
> *paid a lot*
> *the lowest*
> *are underpaid*
> *were the worst paid*
> *gets even less*
> *get well paid*
> *the same pay*
> *get less pay*
> *earn more than just £1.20 an hour*
> *at least £108 a week in wages*
> *the salary is just not enough*
> *can earn as much as $200 a day*
> *a low income*
> *a highly paid job*
> *gets a good salary*

45 Two jokes

a   **At the dentist's**

Do you like going to the dentist? Why not? How much does it cost (roughly) to have a tooth out in your country?

Compare prices with other students.

What could be the last four words of this joke? Decide what you think they are then tell the class.

> A woman went to a dentist in Baghdad to have a tooth out and was told it would cost the equivalent of £30.
> 'But that's ridiculous! she said. 'My husband has to work two hours for that.'
> 'Madam,' the dentist replied, 'If you like, I _____ _____ _____ _____.'

b   **If you call the plumber . . .**

The five parts of this joke have been mixed up. Can you work out the joke?

45c   **c**   Listen to the jokes.

46 When I was a paperboy

What kind of work can schoolchildren or young students do in your country to make some money? Tell each other.

Caroline and Stephen talk about their jobs as baby-sitter, paperboy and factory-worker. Stephen also mentions a friend who's a waitress.

Put their jobs in order from worst paid to best paid.

46   Listen and see if you were right.

Aims: 1 To provide practice in the skills of discussion, comparison and evaluation.
2 To provide practice in the skills involved in reaching a cooperative decision.
Lexis: anybody, handle, low(est), nuclear, nurse, professional [L], **science** [T], **worst**
Revision: **definitely, high, less, less than, money, more than, must be/must get, no idea, over/underpaid, probably, top, worth**

Task SB43a

1 In groups students discuss the questions and note their answers. Encourage them to use a similar table to 43b.

2 Check that students understand the difference between best paid and overpaid (paid too much for what they do).

If the class is mixed nationality, you could put them in groups according to where they come from. Also, if some jobs don't exist in some students' countries, get them to substitute similar ones, e.g. quarry worker for coal miner.

3 Students report back briefly. Encourage them to give reasons for their opinions, e.g. Coal miners should be better paid because it is dangerous and unpleasant work.

Listening SB43b 43b *

4 Students listen to the tape of Stephen and Caroline and complete the table in groups.

Key: Best paid: footballer, bank manager, nuclear scientist, (possibly dentist)
Worst paid: shop assistant, car assembly worker
Overpaid: footballer, bank manager
Underpaid: teachers, nurses
Stephen and Caroline are more or less right, apart from the footballer; they are like actors – the best of them are very well paid, the worst very badly.

5 Get groups to tell you informally how their opinions compare with what they heard on the tape.

SB44 PB43

Aims: 1 To study the common uses in discourse of phrases with the verbs **say, think** and **know.**
2 Understanding phrases expressing amount or comparison in connection with money or pay.

Lexis: high(ly), income, low, nurse, partner, wages, worst

SB44a 44a * PB43

1 Students refer to their transcripts to find the words and phrases **say, think** and **know** occur in.

Key: Caroline uses **think**: Dentists are well paid, I **think**.
Caroline uses **know**: It's hard to **know**, isn't it?
Stephen uses **say**: Who are both I would **say** underpaid.   I'd **say** the shop assistant and the car-assembly worker were probably the two worst paid.
Stephen uses **think**: But I **think** a shop assistant probably gets even less.   I **think** the footballers are probably overpaid   I **think** bank managers are overpaid . . .
Stephen uses 'know' in: I don't **know** whether it's . . .

SB44b

2 In pairs students find as many ways of categorising the phrases as possible. (They all express a degree of quantity or amount of money or pay.)
Possible ways: **a** paid a lot   not paid much   reasonable   other (e.g. the same) **b** paid too much   not paid enough   reasonable/neutral
Students could add to this list and make pairs of phrases with opposite meanings: e.g. too much, not enough   at least, at the most etc.

Aims: 1 To give practice in understanding narrative.
2 To give students practice in listening for the order of events in a narrative and for specific information within the narrative.

Lexis: dentist, equivalent (of), fixed, joke, neither (did I), surprised, system, trouble [L]
Revision: **ridiculous**

SB45a 45a

1 Set the scene: lead the discussion about going to the dentist's.
Discussion points: ask students if they have much trouble with their teeth. How often do they go to the dentist? How much does it cost? Does the Government help pay for treatment? (In Britain, children under 16 or in full-time education get free treatment.) Do they enjoy going to the dentist? If not why not?

2 Students read the story and try to work out the last 4 words for themselves, then tell each other their answers.

3 Play the tape which has the whole story with the original ending.

SB45b 45b

4 Make sure students know what a plumber does. Ask if it is highly skilled work; do you need to be highly educated to be a plumber? How much do plumbers charge in the students' countries for a house call?

5 Students do the puzzle in pairs.

6 Students listen to the tape to see if they have the same order.
Discussion point: you could ask the students for stories about plumbers or any similar experiences they have had when they think they have been overcharged. Have they ever had trouble with any water systems where they live?

SB46 PB46

Aims: 1 To practise the skills of discussion, comparison and evaluation (of children's and younger students' jobs).
2 Structure: if it wasn't for the tips, she wouldn't be getting much at all. If it wasn't for the . . . = Without the . . . If she didn't get the . . .

Lexis: dollars, factory, low, tend, waiter, waitress
Revision: **mainly, pretty awful**

Task SB46

1 In groups students tell one another about their experiences and list the types of work younger people can do to make money.

2 Students speculate about how to order the 4 jobs in terms of pay. (It's a cake factory, if they want to know.)

Listening SB46 46 *

3 Before they listen to the tape, warn students it won't be absolutely clear from what Stephen and Caroline say exactly which order the jobs come in.

4 Suggest students make a note of how they get paid for each of the 4 jobs. Also ask them which person they think did which job.

Key: Stephen was a paperboy; he didn't say how much he was paid, but he said it was the lowest paid work he did. Stephen also did babysitting for 6 pence an hour when he was eight! This was paid even less.
Caroline worked in a cake factory for not much more than 'a pound an hour'.
Stephen's friend works as a waitress and claims she can sometimes get as much as $200 in a day (including tips – i.e. her basic pay is probably very little).

24T

47 Equal opportunities

Aims: 1 To practise evaluating and responding to correspondence of the type one would find in a magazine.
2 To practise making recommendations for action.

Lexis: amount, basic, earn, equivalent, especially, fair, generally, hear, heavy [L], **(at) least** [L], **often, opinions, union** [L], **wages**
Revision: **even if they are ... , in general, not always possible to ... , on the other hand**

Reading SB47a PB47

1 Ask the students if any of them have ever written a letter to a magazine or newspaper, and if so, what about.

2 Tell students that in this particular magazine recently, there had been a lot of correspondence about unemployment, and poorly paid work and bad conditions. The editor asked other readers to write in with their experiences. This school leaver did just that. Don't give the game away by mentioning he/she as you tell them about the person who wrote the letter.

3 Students read on their own first, then in pairs, to work out the answers to the first two questions.

4 Ask the class whether they think the writer is a woman or a man. If they don't agree, tell them to read the last paragraph very carefully: 'I'm one of them' One of whom? (5 million working women who earn less than £108 a week). 'Decency threshold' means the minimum amount which you need in order to live and eat.

   Key: a a young woman (working women – I'm one of them)
   b There will have been deductions for tax, and National Insurance, otherwise she would be getting £48 per week, times 4, = £192 per month.

5 Words to look up: Students find the correct categories for these in their Lexicon. Also exploit any new lexis or useful phrases that have not come up in the activities.

6 In groups students discuss what kinds of things they could write. Be prepared to offer suggestions: remind them about unions – the writer could perhaps ask her union for advice. If the writer's not a member of her union, they should join and become a member. They should insist on somewhere to sit. A half-hour break is not long enough. Assist the groups with their writing, correcting as necessary. (If the class is a good one, ask them to write the whole letter. Otherwise some sentences giving the group's opinions and advice is enough.)

7 Collect the students' advice/letters. Read them out to the class if you have not had time to correct all their work, correct as you read.

Listening SB47b 47b *

1 Students listen to Caroline and Stephen doing a similar task. Tell students that they knew the writer was a woman.

   Key: Stephen agreed that women in general don't get the same pay for equivalent work as men. They both agreed it wasn't fair. And that this job at the bakery was also underpaid.
   On the other hand – Stephen
   I don't think that should make that much difference. – Stephen

48 Wordpower

Aim: To focus on the meanings of the world **clear**.
Lexis: clear/clearly [L]

SB48

1 Students look at the pictures and say which things are **clear** or not very **clear**, and which things have been done **clearly**. (You have probably been using the word **clear** in everyday classroom interaction, e.g. 'That's nice and clear, good.' (when evaluating written or spoken reporting work) or 'Is that clear?' If so, point this out.)

2 In pairs students match the phrases with the pictures.

3 Students look up the word **clear** in the Lexicon and match the phrases with the categories. Ask them which examples might be the most useful for them in class (cat. 1), and in business (cats. 1,2).

   Key: 1 b,g   2 f   3 e,d   4 h,i   5 a   6 c

49 Keyhole picture

Aim: To give practice in the skills involved in cooperative problem solving; and converging on a solution as more information is supplied.

Lexis: anywhere, chin, completely [L], **hang** [L], **or, pair, piece, plastic, scene** [L], **scientific, string, surprise** [L], **wrong**

Students may have looked ahead and seen the whole picture in Unit 5 already. So it is important to set this task in such a way that:
a) those who know already do not tell the others yet.
b) it is made more of a challenge. We do not simply ask students what they think; we ask them to predict what John and Catherine will say about each picture. (They see them in strict order, smallest first, and don't see the complete picture till the very end.)

Listening SB49a 49a *

1 Students look at the small keyhole picture and say what they think John and Catherine thought and said about him at that stage.

2 Students to listen to the tape and make a list of the things John and Catherine think they can see and in pairs compare their lists.

   Key: business person, someone scientific.
   They see his glasses, a piece of rope or a tie (hanging down from his chin), people behind – a pair of jeans?, a window. NB they don't actually see a microscope.

Listening SB49b 49b * PB49

3 Students look at the keyhole picture in 49b and predict what John and Catherine will say about what he could be doing, then share their predictions with the rest of the class before they listen to the tape.

4 Students listen to the tape and note the things they think the man could be doing.

   Key: Five different things:
   1 looking into ...
   2 talking to somebody who's getting in or out of a car
   3 taking something out of a car
   4 putting something into a car
   5 loading the boot of a car

John now thinks the man is in a boat, and that he's a fisherman. Maybe he thinks the pieces of rope are fishing equipment.

Task

5 In pairs students discuss their ideas about what the man could be doing, and whether they agree with John. They write down their ideas and report back to the class.

47 Equal opportunities

a Letter to the Editor

Read this letter which was written by a teenager who had just left school and started work. Was it a young woman or a young man who wrote it?

I thought you might like to hear about my job in a bakery. I start work at 6 am, at the latest, and often work past 3 pm. That's at least 8½ hours work each day (I'm allowed a half hour break). Often the work is unpleasant – standing up all day, working near hot ovens (especially in summer), carrying heavy weights about – flour, baking trays, etc.
From my basic 40 hour week I get £1.20 an hour, which I think is awful. OK, so this is my first job, straight from school, but I do think my wages are bad. In an average four-week month I get to take home only about £160.
I saw in *Just Seventeen* that 5½ million working women earn less than the 'decency threshold' wage of £108 a week. Well, I'm one of them and would like to hear other readers' opinions.

HB, Worcester

> **L** heavy
> least
> union

If this person gets £1.20 an hour, and works an eight and a half hour day, how does that work out at £160 a month?

What are your opinions? What do you think this person should do?

> Together plan what you would put in a letter to send to the Editor responding to HB's letter. Write about three sentences, giving your opinions, and one or two pieces of advice, but don't write the whole letter.

Read your opinions and advice out to the class. Did you all suggest the same kind of things?

b Fair pay?

> Read the letter about the job in the bakery. In general, do you think women receive the same pay for the same work as men? What do you think about this particular job in this letter?

47b Listen to what Caroline and Stephen thought. Would you agree with them?
Who said these phrases?

On the other hand.
I don't think that should make that much difference.

48 *Wordpower*

clear, clearly

Which phrases could go with which person or which picture?

(a) The line of its footprints was clear.
(b) I hope that's clear.....
(c) The sea was so clear you could see everything on the bottom.
(d) Large areas of forest were being cleared.
(e) It was not clear whether the meeting had begun or not.
(f) Women are clearly underpaid in some jobs they do.
(g) Sorry but I'm not clear about what we have to do....
(h) Could you possibly write more clearly?
(i) The table needs clearing.

Look up the word **clear** in the Lexicon.

49 Keyhole picture

a Discuss what kind of job this person might do.

49a What jobs do John and Catherine think he might do?
Make a list of the things they think they can see.

e.g. *something hanging down from his chin*

b Looking at the picture above, what might the man be doing at this moment? What do you think John and Catherine will say? They mention five things he could be doing.

49b What five things do they think he could be doing?
Do you think John is 'completely wrong'?
Tell the class what you think now.

> **L** completely   piece
> hanging   scene

25

50 *Preposition spot* ··········

in

In can refer to *time* and *place*. Find the phrases with **in**, and say which they refer to. When they refer to time, what do they mean?

a ... *less injuries than he had in about ten years* (18)
b *There are holes in the sky where the rain comes in.*
c *My husband is joining us in a week's time.* (38)
d ... *the highest hill in Northumberland* ... (29)
e ... *and we went out in a boat one day* ... (29)
f ... *especially in summer* ... (47)
g ... *a plumber who fixed everything in about half an hour* ... (45)
h *I was born in 1956 in Warrington* ... (9)
i ... *a competition in which the first prize was one week* ...
j ... *if someone dropped in unexpectedly and stayed for a meal* ... (86)

What about these phrases? What word does the **in** go with?

k ... *who wasn't terribly interested in sport* ... (20)
l *Even taking part in sport?* (20)
m ... *what do they have in common?* (20)
n *In fact there are several roads where* ... (35)
o *In addition to a comfortable bed* ... (39)
p *I think in general they don't (get equal pay).* (47)
q ... *some difficulty in finding a successful position.* (52)
r ... *just in case you're thinking of coming to the airport.* (33)
s *He was in such a hurry that* ... (136)

51 Now what?

Discuss in groups what you now think the man does and where you think he is. What are all the things that he has with him? Tell the class.

51 John and Catherine discuss this picture, then finally they look at the whole photograph. What else can they see? What particular things complete the picture?

52 About your work

a We asked Stephen and Catherine to do this task.

> If you have a job, write a short account of the work you do. Are you happy with this job/type of work? Or you could write about someone else.
>
> If you do not have a job, write about what you would like to do, or have done in the past, and say very briefly what it involves. (max. 10 lines).

Read what Stephen wrote and find out how many different types of work his present job involves.

> Really I am a student, but during the summer I work to make some money. This summer I am working for my father's publishing company, doing odd jobs. Some days I am the receptionist, on other days I make the tea. In between times I use the word-processor to send letters to authors and other publishers. Once I had to show a visitor from Korea around the office, another time I was commissioned to draw maps and illustrations for a new book. But most of the time I am filing invoices and stuffing envelopes. It's OK for the summer, but I wouldn't want to do it every day of my life.

L odd
draw

my father's publishing company

Aims: 1 To focus students' attention on prepositional phrases with **in** referring to time and space.
2 To focus students' attention on some of the words which are commonly used with **in**.

Lexis: **less**

SB50 PB50

1 Students read the rubric and work in pairs. If necessary do an example with them: students find one phrase where **in** refers to time and one where it refers to space.

2 Go over students' answers, putting them on the board. Ask students to provide an alternative word or phrase for **in** when it refers to time.

Key: a time – a ten-year period   b place   c time – a week from now   d place   e place   f time – during   g time – a half-hour period   h time – during place i time – during the competition   j place   k **interested in** sport/animals/travelling   l **taking part in** sport   m have **in common**   n **in fact**   o **in addition to**   p **in general**   q **difficulty in** finding/paying/seeing/ remembering names   r just **in case** you're thinking/the building catches fire   s **in such a hurry** that . . ./to cross the road

51 **Now What?**

Aim: Further practice in cooperative problem solving and converging on a solution as information is supplied.

Lexis: **(a) fair**, **or**, **somewhere**, **surprise** [T]

This section continues the **keyhole puzzle** *from section 49. In this section we have a larger picture, and a tape of John and Catherine looking at this picture and at the final one (in Unit 5 on page 31).*

SB51 *

1 Students speculate about the man from what they can now see in the Keyhole picture. Encourage discussion by asking the students: What could the scene behind him be? Can they now see what the things round his neck are used for? (Tying the balloons.) Students should report back to the class informally before they listen to the tape.

2 Before they listen to the tape, ask students to listen for what John and Catherine say about the complete picture.

3 When students have heard the tape, they should try to describe the whole picture (which they have not seen yet) from John and Catherine's descriptions.

If students don't know 'balloons', get other students to explain.

4 Students look at the complete picture in Unit 5 on page 31. Encourage discussion about the picture, e.g. how much were they able to guess about the picture? Do students agree that he's at the back of a fairground? Maybe he's preparing his balloons before the start of a day walking round the streets selling them.

5 Some students close their books and try to describe the complete picture from memory, while others are allowed to see the picture in Unit 5, and evaluate their performance.

6 Discussion: Ask students about when they have balloons in their own countries. Have they any stories about balloons? Were they ever frightened of them when small? (In case they burst and made a loud bang!)

7 Possible writing task: Students report on their guesses (or John's predictions) about the keyhole picture.
e.g. First we thought it was . . . Then we thought . . . Then we noticed . . .
If you assign the task for homework, give students class time to begin the task in groups.

52 **About your work**

Aim: To give students practice in describing the type of work they do/did/would like to do, and how they feel about it.

Lexis: **apply(ing)**, **brief(ly)**, **company(ies)**, **department**, **difficulty**, **draw** [L], **during**, **experienced**, **joy**, **lack(s)**, **once**, **process**, **senior(ity)**, **successful**
Time phrases: **another time**, **between times**, **during the summer**, **every day**, **for the summer**, **in between times**, **most of the time**, **on other days**, **once**, **this summer**

Reading   SB52a PB52a

Students could describe someone else's work if they have never had a job or don't know what they want to do, as Catherine did here. Students read and analyse what Stephen and Catherine wrote before they write their own descriptions.

1 Students read about Stephen's work and count up how many different odd jobs he does/has done at the company. Encourage them to guess the words they don't know, as far as possible.

Key: works as a receptionist, makes tea, uses the word-processor, sends letters to authors and other publishers, shows visitors around the office, draws maps and illustrations, filing invoices, stuffing envelopes.

'stuffing envelopes' is very colloquial; it means putting letters in envelopes ready to be sent off.

2 Language study: check students understand the meanings of the 10 time phrases here, so that they could use them in their own writing if they wish to.

3 Words to look up: students look up in their Lexicons the appropriate categories for the words as they are used in Stephen's description. Be prepared to explain other categories to the students if they ask you.

The verb **draw** *has many other uses. Ask students to look it up. Where would they be if they were about to* **draw** *some money? How would they be feeling if the exams were* **drawing** *near? How can buses* **draw**? *What other things can* **draw**?

4 Students listen to the tape and write brief notes of the main points about John's situation afterwards.

5 Students read Catherine's summary to see whether she has included all the points they made a note of.

6 Ask students if any of them have experience of using a word-processor. If so, can they explain the difference between a word processor and a typewriter? Let students listen for the explanation John gives after the words: It's just a queston of ...'

Key: A word-processor will store on disc what is typed into it so when you want a copy, it can be printed directly off the disc. It is also possible to make corrections without retyping the entire document. John uses a word-processor to type his job applications. This means he can apply for lots of jobs even though he only has to type his application papers once.

Writing task   SB52c

Students should do the interview in pairs, so that they can help each other with the questions and with the writing up afterwards.

9 In pairs, students prepare questions. Give help when necessary but allow students to prepare the questions mainly on their own. (Students have already prepared interview questions for other tasks so should be getting to the stage where they can work more independently.)

10 Students move around the class finding other students to interview. Provide help as necessary when they prepare their reports, particularly with time phrases, as these are one of the Lexical aims for this section. Students read and check one another's finished reports.

Written report

11 Students' written reports about themselves or a friend could be done for homework.

SB52d

Key: trying to
application **forms**
successful position
difficulty in
relatively **young**/Other examples: new/cheap/well paid

---

53 Language study

> **Aim:** To give students further intensive study of time phrases, e.g. during the summer, once.

SB53a

1 Students find the time phrases in the transcript. For further practice students could write true sentences of their own using some of these phrases.

Key: during the summer, this summer, some days, on other days, in between times, once, another time, most of the time, for the summer, every day of my life

SB53b

Key: on one occasion

---

54 Grammar revision

> **Aims:** 1 To practise discriminating between phrases in which **to** is preceded by verbs, and phrases in which **to** is preceded by adjectives, e.g. go back to; happy/hard to.
> 2 To focus attention on the use of **to** for describing purpose.
>
> **Lexis: dentist, manage(d), to**

SB54 PB54

1 Point out to students that the exercise includes **to** for motion, as in the example, 'go back to Ireland'; and **to** as part of the infinitive as in 'want to'. They are grammatically different but similar in meaning because both show a goal or target of some kind.

2 Divide the class into two groups – those that look at Set A, and those that look at Set B on Page 29. Go round groups, helping out as necessary.

3 When the two groups have finished, put students in pairs, with one from the Set A group and one from the Set B group, so that they can compare their answers.

Key to set A:
a
3 used to   4 intend to   5 hope to   6 wanted to
7 going to   8 decide to   11 had to   12 trying to
14 went to   15 has to

b
1 sorry to   2 difficult to   9 possible to

c
10, 14

13 and 16 are left out.

Key to set B:
a
2 go down to   3 have to   5, 6 get to   6 managed to
9 tends to   11 expected to   12 seems to
14 appear to   15 belong to

b
1 important to   2 able to   5 lucky to   8 happy to
10 hard to

c
2, 16

7 and 13 are left out.

52b b Catherine talked to John about the whole process of applying for jobs and about the job he had applied for in a school in Telford.

1 Find out exactly what post he wants in Telford, and if he thinks he'll be successful in getting it. Make brief notes.
2 What can a word-processor do that a typewriter cannot? How does this help John?

After their conversation, Catherine wrote about John.

John is trying to get a new job – and is busy sending application forms and CVs all over the country. He wants a promotion to Head of Department, but as he is still relatively young and lacks seniority, he anticipates some difficulty in finding a successful position.

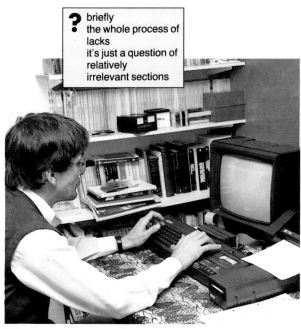

? briefly
the whole process of
lacks
it's just a question of
relatively
irrelevant sections

I discovered the joys of word-processing the other day.

c In pairs, interview two other people in your class. Find out something about the work they do, or a job they have done or may do.

▷ Together, write a few lines about one of them. Then give it to them to read and check.

▷ Write a few lines on the same subject about yourself or a friend.

d Read Catherine's text on John again to find the phrases that go with the words in the box.

| trying | successful | relatively |
| application | difficulty | |

a Can you find nine or ten phrases that refer to time in Stephen's piece on page 26? Write them down.
e.g. *during the summer*

b What's another way of saying **once**?

Verbs and adjectives with 'to'

The class should be in two groups – one group of A students, and one group of B students.
Look carefully at these phrases with **to** in them.
A students look at set *A* below, while B students look at set *B* on page 29.

a How many *verbs* can you find that are often followed by **to**? Write a list of them.

b How many *adjectives* are there (e.g. *happy to*)? Write them down too.

c In which examples does **to** mean 'in order to', ('for the purpose of')?

Compare lists. Do you have any similar examples?

Which **to**'s are left over? What do these phrases mean?

Set A. Examples with 'to'

1 *... a very pleasant school and I'd be sorry to leave it ... (2)*
2 *... very difficult to tell anybody anything about me. (20)*
3 *She used to work at a desk. (1)*
4 *Although I intend to stay in Britain for a few years ... (20)*
5 *I hope to see more of the world ... (20)*
6 *That was why we wanted to go. (29)*
7 *You weren't going to tell me that ... (29)*
8 *Wherever you decide to stop you can ... (35)*
9 *... it is possible to visit the ...*
10 *I use the word-processor to send letters ... (51)*
11 *Once I had to show a visitor round ... (52)*
12 *John is trying to get a new job ... (52)*
13 *He wants a promotion to Head of Department ... (52)*

14 *A woman went to a dentist in Baghdad to have a tooth out ... (45)*
15 *My husband has to work two hours for that. (45)*
16 *... stood around with nothing to do. (55)*

27

55 Success or failure??

Read these stories, and try to work out how best to complete them. Write your ideas down.
Read them out to each other.

A On his first day selling ice-cream in the cinema, an assistant sold more during the interval than anyone had ever done before. When this success was repeated day after day, the manager decided to keep an eye on him. He found that ten minutes before the interval the enterprising assistant _____.

C Upon returning to his office, my husband stopped at his secretary's desk to see if there were any messages for him. There were none but he couldn't help noticing a note to his secretary from a recently hired young clerk-typist. It read: 'Dear Ida, I'm in the lounge. _____ coffee break. Sally.'

B In the sweet shop, one sales assistant always had customers lined up waiting while other assistants stood around with nothing to do. The owner of the shop asked the popular one for her secret. 'It's easy,' she said. 'The other assistants scoop up _____ of sweets and then _____. I always scoop up _____ and then _____.'

55 Listen to the complete stories and see what the missing words actually were.

Discuss in groups.

1 Does anyone in your family eat a lot of sweets? Are they good or bad for you? Why?
2 What does ice-cream make you think of? Has it any associations or memories for you? Has ice-cream ever melted and made a mess over your clothes?
3 Do you know anyone who tends to be rather lazy, like Sally in the story here? In what ways are they lazy?

▷ Write a brief account of what your group thought about one of these topics. ◁

Write it clearly, then pass it round for other groups to read. Then tell each other briefly about any other interesting ideas you had.

▷ Tell one of the stories again, but from the point of view of one of the other characters in it. ◁

e.g. *I'm the manager of the local cinema here. Last winter, we employed a new assistant. Part of his job was to sell ice-cream during the interval. This young man sold so much more ice-cream than ...*

56 *Phrase-building*

... stood around with nothing to do.

Think of some places you have been to recently. Make some sentences about them using these ideas.

e.g. I sat in the dentist's waiting room with nothing to read.
I went to my friend's house and we had so much to talk about.

Where could you add words like **interesting, exciting, special, cheap, really nice** etc?

There was / We had / ... with	nothing / something / a lot / lots / quite a lot / quite a few / lots of things / so much	to	eat/drink/read/look at/do.

There wasn't / ... without / We didn't get/find	much / anything / anywhere / anything	to	see/buy/eat/visit/go.

Success or failure??

> **Aims:** 1 To practise understanding narrative.
> 2 To practise informal discussion and narrative.
>
> Lexis: **assistant, decided, during, easy, failure, message, nothing (to do), secret** [L]**, secretary, sell, success(ful), wake**

SB55 ⬜ 55 PB55

1 Students read the stories and work out what the endings could be. Supply them with any words they need.

2 In groups, students read their endings out to one another. Students could be asked to vote on the best ending for each of the stories.

Listening 55

3 Students listen to the tape. For Stories A and C, ask them to write the ending they hear. For Story B, ask them to summarise what they hear.

   Key:
   Last lines:
   . . . the enterprising assistant turned the heating up.
   The other assistants scoop up more than a pound of sweets and then start taking away. I always scoop up less than a pound and then add to it (ie – this has the psychological effect of making customers think they are getting extra . . .)
   Wake me up for coffee break. Sally.

4 Students discuss one or two of these topics in groups, and write about one of them as a brief report.

5 Written task: telling one of the stories from a different point of view. This could be done for homework, but give students time in class to start the task.

---

56 **Phrase building**

Phrases like these can be very useful, particularly because you can also put a qualifying word (adverb or adjective) in, e.g. with nothing much to do/nothing of interest/interesting to do, nothing beautiful to see, a lot of good things to see/buy etc.

Students practise phrases from the table and make up true sentences about places they have visited.

Review page

> **Aims:** 1 To revise some uses of **any** and **anybody**.
> 2 To revise some of the meanings of **often** and **tends to**.
> 3 To revise some useful lexis.
>
> Lexis: **awful, decision, earnings, management, nobody, somebody**

SB57

1 Point out that the '-body' ending means the same as '-one' as in 'anyone', though it's less common. The main meaning of 'any' is 'it doesn't matter which/who etc as in 'anybody who . . .' or 'any time'.

   Key: doesn't appear to go anywhere, does it? – negative and interrogative
   Anything you need – interrogative
   Anything that's not clear? – negative and interrogative

SB57b

   Key:
1 Profession, decision – the others are people

2 Equivalent, unions – the others are to do with money

3 In my opinion, On the other hand – are not necessarily introducing points expressing *general* truths

4 Failure, awful – the others are positive, successful aspects.

5 Headquarters, at least – all the others are about bad conditions. 'At least' is neutral and its meaning depends on what words are used with it.

SB57c

This may need some teacher guidance. The aim is purely to give a little more exposure to other uses of these common words.

1 When students have finished the activity, ask them to look up the meanings of 4 words in the Lexicon.

   Key: wrong wrong   secret secret   [L]
   decision decision   success successful
   take take   application applying
   easy easy   trouble trouble   [L]
   draw drew   [L]   process process
   away away   complete completely [L]
   especially especially

   PB57 is an additional Lexicon exercise.

   SB57e Set B Examples with **to** see section 54.

LEXICAL OBJECTIVES

Level 1 words (see page 129T):
anyway, **during**, **especially**,
everybody, **in** (see SB50), **less**, **neither**,
nothing, **nuclear**, **often**, **once**, **or**,
process, **system**, **to** (see SB54), **wrong**.

amount 1 *same amount of work*
2 *the fees amounted to £2,000*
anybody See SB57.
anywhere See SB57.
apply 1 *applying for a job in Telford.... application forms.*
2 **apply to**: concern. *This scheme does not apply to visitors leaving by air.* [9]
3 to use.... *apply the death penalty.* T
assistant 1 one who is second in authority.... *baker's assistant*
2 shop assistant
awful 1 bad... *the job was pretty awful*
2 ill: *I feel awful.* T
3 used for emphasis. *Awfully hot*
basic L
brief/ly 1 lasting a short time.... *a brief look at the paper. I saw him briefly.* T
2 in a few words.... *say very briefly.*
chin ... *something hanging down from his chin*
clear L and SB
clearly L (See SB48)
company 1 *my father's publishing company*
2 *I enjoy the company of animals* ...
completely L
Customer ... *customers lined up waiting*
decide/d to choose to do something. *The manager decided to keep an eye on him.*
decision *The Government announced their decision on the future of railways.* T
dentist person who treats people's teeth
department a section in an organisation. *Head of Department*
difficulty problem(s).... *some difficulty in finding a successful position.*
dollar ... *twenty dollars an hour*
draw(ing) L
earn *5½ million working women earn less than* ...
earnings pay received from a job
easy 1 not difficult. *It's easy*
2 relaxed.... *an easy manner.* T
engineer a person who designs and constructs machinery, roads etc. T
equivalent having the same use, size etc.... *the same amount of work or equivalent work* ...

experienced one who has worked at a job for a long time... *an experienced mechanic*
factory place where things are produced with machines. *My worst pay was in a cake factory* ...
failure 1 lack of success. *She was a bit of a failure at her job.*
2 ... *the government's failure to insist on fair pay for women.*
3 *a power failure/engine failure.* T
fair reasonable. *Do you think that's fair? fair wages*
fixed 1 repaired.... *called a plumber who fixed everything.*
2 arranged, ... *fixed a meeting*
general L
generally usually, in general
handles deals with. *Anybody who handles money tends to get paid a lot.*
hang/hanging L
heavy L
highly to a great extent. *Highly paid*
income money earned or brought in from other sources.... *an income of £200 a week*
joke a funny story
joy 1 pleasure. *The joys of parenthood*
2 luck. *Any joy at the Job Centre?*
lack 1 doesn't have any. *He's still young and lacks seniority.*
least L
low 1 not high from bottom to top. *A low wall.* T
2 close to the ground/sea. *Fly low over the beach.* T
3 small in number or amount. *Low pay*
manage 1 to succeed (See Unit 3)
2 to control an organisation or business. *Bank manager*
management 1 the management: those who control an organisation or business
2 ... *the management of money.* T
message 1 a piece of information. *Any messages for him?*
2 the main idea. *It's important that everybody should get the message.* T
minister a person in charge of a particular government department. *The Minister of Health and Social Security.* T
nobody 1 not a single person ... *nobody to look after me when I'm sick.* [02]
2 *Nobody wears mini skirts nowadays.*
opinion what you believe about something. *I ... would like to hear other reader's opinions.*
pair 1 two things that are intended to be used together.... *a pair of shoes*
2 two people who are together. *They*

would be seen walking in pairs.
2 business partners
piece 1 a bit or part. *He tore both letters into small pieces. ... a piece of string.*
2 **in one piece**: not harmed. *'How is he?' He's in one piece. Don't worry.'* T
plastic chemical material: light in weight and does not break easily. *Plastic bags*
profession career. *How many different jobs and professions can you find* ...?
professional L
scene
science 1 Physics, chemistry, biology etc. *I liked science subjects* [05]
scientific 1 *scientific studies.* T
2 careful and systematic. T
scientist *a nuclear scientist*
secret L
secretary *My husband stopped at his secretary's desk to see if there were any messages.*
sell *On his first day selling ice cream in the cinema, an assistant sold more* ...
senior 1 holding an important position. Also **seniority**: *He is still relatively young and lacks seniority.*
2 older. *She was at least fifteen years his senior.*
somebody = someone. *There's a seat for somebody to sit down.*
somewhere used to refer to a place. *Is he in a carpark somewhere?*
2 approximately. *Somewhere between 55,000 and 60,000 men.* T
string 1 thin cord. *That piece of string*
2 row.... *a string of beads*
success 1 doing well. *When this success was repeated day after day the manager decided to keep an eye on him.*
2 becoming rich, famous, powerful. *His next film 'Jaws' was a tremendous success.* T
successful ... *a successful attempt to land on the Moon. ... a successful writer*
surprise/surprised L
trouble L
union L
wage ... *a wage of £108 a week*
waiter a man who serves people in a restaurant
waitress a woman who serves people in a restaurant
wake *Wake me up for coffee break.*
worst superlative of bad. *Which two are the worst paid?*
worth *They're probably worth the money though.*

a   any, anybody, anyway, etc

Look at these sentences with **any**. How many of them are negative or interrogative sentences?

He stopped at his secretary's desk to see if there were any messages for him. There were none.
Anybody who handles money gets paid a lot.
Anybody who's paid more than me is overpaid!
An assistant sold more ice-cream during the interval than anyone had ever done before.
That piece of string doesn't appear to go anywhere, does it? It's just hanging ...
That's what I would say, anyway.
A: When shall we come? B: Any time you like.
A: Where shall we sit? B: Anywhere. It doesn't matter where.
Is there anything you need to ask? Anything that's not clear?

anybody, everybody, somebody, nobody

b   Odd ones out

Find two odd ones out in each group.

1 businessman, General Manager, profession, secretary, Head of Department, the Management, scientist, decision
2 rates of pay, fair pay, equivalent, earnings, Unions, wages
3 In general, On the whole, In my opinion, Usually, On the other hand, Normally, Generally, It tends to be ...
4 failure, highly paid, professional, successful, business-like, awful, worth the money
5 low paid, unsuccessful, bad working conditions, trouble with, Headquarters, at least, the worst, badly paid, pretty awful

c   Game: Spot the pairs!

Can you find twelve pairs of similar words? Is each word in the pair used with the same meaning?

We've got it completely wrong.
We've made the wrong decision.
A difficult decision to take.
Hey, wait a minute! Take it easy!
Is it easy to draw maps?
The bus drew away before I could get on.
It's nice to go away, especially in summer.
Can you keep it secret? Especially the bit about me.
What was the secret of her success?
I hope your application is successful.
John has gone to a lot of trouble applying for jobs.
The trouble is, the whole process is a long one.
It takes time to complete such a process.

d   often, tends to

Which of these sentences are true as far as you are concerned?

Often my work is unpleasant.
I often work past 6 p.m.
Anyone who handles money tends to get paid a lot.
Rats tend to live in unattractive conditions.
I think women tend to get better tips than men.
Do you know anyone who tends to be lazy?
I tend to worry about ... I lie awake at night thinking.
I tend to wake up early in the morning. Do you?
I often wake up late.

e   Set B. Examples with 'to' (see page 27)

1 *... that half an inch is very important to me. (20)*
2 *... will be able to get us tickets to go down to Jamaica ... (38)*
3 *... you have to expect rain ... (38)*
4 *I'm looking forward to it. (38)*
5 *Very lucky to get to the top of it ... (29)*
6 *... had never managed to get to the top ... (29)*
7 *In addition to a comfortable bed ... (39)*
8 *... we will be happy to help select the holiday.*
9 *Anybody who handles money tends to get paid a lot ... (42)*
10 *... it's hard to know isn't it? (43)*
11 *I think anybody who is expected to work eight and a half hours a day ... (47)*
12 *Seems to be a street scene (49)*
13 *... it looks like a window behind him to me. (49)*
14 *... that piece of string doesn't appear to go anywhere ... (49)*
15 *... could it belong to the door of the car? (49)*
16 *... during the summer I work to make some money. (52)*

Important words to remember (238 so far)

amount	completely L	equivalent	joy	partner	senior	worst
anybody	decided	experienced	lack	piece	somebody	worth
anywhere	decision	factory	least L	plastic	somewhere	
apply	dentist	fair	low	profession	string	
assistant	department	failure	manage	professional L	success	
awful	difficulty	fixed	management	scene L	successful	
basic L	dollar	generally	message	science	surprise L	
brief	draw L	handles	minister	scientific	surprised L	
chin	earn	hang L	nobody	scientist	trouble L	
clear L	earnings	heavy L	nurse	secret L	union L	
clearly L	easy	income	opinion	secretary	wage	
company	engineer	joke	pair	sell	wake	

technology   economics

home economics

music

business studies

Unit 5
Revision Unit

languages

sport/PE (physical education)

[58] ## Schooldays

maths

art

history

biology

science

geography   chemistry   physics

a Favourite subjects

In groups, tell each other a little bit about your
favourite subject at school. Also which subjects you
like or liked the least and why.

▶ Summarise the findings of your group survey
so that you can report to the class. ◀

Find out:

1 the most popular subjects
2 the least popular
3 the most common reasons why people dislike
   certain subjects
4 whether the men and women in the class like the
   same subjects

[58a] Compare your findings with Catherine's group.
Write notes about Caroline, Stephen and John.

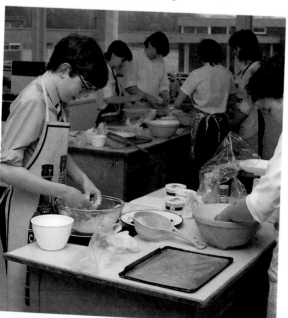

b Talk about teachers

What kind of things do schoolteachers complain
about in your experience? Are they always right?

[58b] Do you agree with what Rodge (Roger) says in
this poem? He is talking about what it's like being a
pupil at Primary School.

TEACHERS

Rodge said,

'Teachers – they want it all ways –
You're jumping up and down on a chair
or something
and they grab hold of you and say,
"Would you do that sort of thing in your own home?"

'So you say, "No"
And they say,
"Well, don't do it here then."

'But if you say, "Yes, I do it at home."
They say,
"Well, we don't want that sort of thing
going on here
thank you very much."

'Teachers – they get you all ways,'
Rodge said.

Michael Rosen

We asked Stephen to write what he thought about
this poem.

I remember thinking that way about
teachers. After class, or on the way home, I
would work out what I should have said to
the teacher, to shut him up completely. But
when it happened, I never had any reply at
all. I had to just sit back and take it.
But next time, I knew I could do it!

This is a consolidation unit, which aims to recycle the most useful lexis and language areas from Units 1–4 in wider contexts. The aim of all consolidation units (5, 10 and 15) is also to build up students' confidence. Each consolidation unit is followed by a test. The unit begins by focusing on subjects studied at school. Within this context students practise expressing preferences and giving reasons for those preferences. They go on to discuss attitudes towards others – in this case their teachers at school. The next stage illustrates how a lexical set, parts of the human body, may have a range of extended meanings. These meanings are discussed and the range of the lexical field is compared with the same field in the native language. There is focus on the past, the students' childhood, both from an anecdodal narrative point of view and in the expression of ambitions and wishes. Next there is a test of memory which involves students in working cooperatively to elaborate on one another's ideas to reconstruct the picture of the balloon man from Unit 4. This is followed by speculation on the character in the picture, his personality and way of life. There are two short poems about childhood to read and react to at different points in the unit, and an optional task where students compare physical appearances – in this case describing themselves as they looked when small children.

Some students need to bring photos of themselves as small children, or family photos without themselves in, for a description and recognition game in section 64.

OBJECTIVES

Lexical objectives are in TB67

Grammar and discourse

a Past narrative (more common verb forms revised) and description of habitual action in the past, with **used to** and **would/'d**. (65)

b Expressions of like and dislike (with past reference), giving reasons. (58,59)

c A study of how the words for various parts of the body are used with other meanings. (63)

d Nominal groups with adjectives, qualifiers, words like part/bit/piece of; and relative clauses, to describe objects, buildings, past looks/appearances. (62)

e Expressions of existence and location with 'There is/are/was/were.' (62)

f Revision of phrases describing personal appearance (past reference). (64)

g Ways of expressing reactions, e.g. Great! My goodness! (59)

h Revision of the passive. (66)

i Meaning and use of the prefix **un-**. (67)

j Common words and phrases used in dictionary definitions. (67)

k Classroom language: how to start and end a task in English, seeking the cooperation of others; also ways of querying understanding. (67)

Tasks

a Expressing preferences and giving reasons for those preferences. (58)

b Expressing and justifying attitudes. (58)

c Discussing and comparing the meanings of words. (63)

d Further practice in exchanging anecdotal narratives. (58)

e Describing past and present wishes and ambitions. (64)

f Working cooperatively to define and reconstruct a scene. (62)

g Speculating on someone's character and way of life. (62)

h Describing feelings about and attitudes towards a past event. (64)

i Describing the way someone appeared in the past. (64)

j Making and refusing requests indirectly. (60)

58 Schooldays

Aims: 1 To give students practice in using past narrative in the form of anecdotes and describing past habitual actions and attitudes.
2 To practise reading to understand attitudes.
3 To practise using expressions of like/dislike (with past reference), justifying attitudes and giving reasons.

Lexis: danger, dangerous [T], **favourite, mathematics, movements, physical, thank**
Revision: **at the back, a bit/bits, favourite, got, pretty** (modifier), **reasons, that, used to**

Task/report SB58a 58a* PB58a

1 Ask one person in each group (preferably the most talkative person) to be the group leader. The leader's role is to encourage the others to talk and to share in the planning of the summary prior to the report phase. The leader's main role is to share out the talking and planning between the others. This is to ensure that students who, up to now, have been shy of talking get a chance to perform well in this unit and gain confidence.

2 After each report, the findings for the whole class could be written up under the four headings for the survey.

Listening SB58a 58a

3 Play the tape. Students compare their findings and make notes about Caroline, Stephen and John.

Key: Caroline: liked English because she liked writing stories; disliked maths because she was bad at it and tended to get behind, and probably PE (physical education) because she had a sadistic teacher.
Stephen: liked science subjects because the teachers were good, maths and English because he could do them; disliked languages (French, Latin, Greek) because the teachers were poor and he used to get behind.
John: disliked sport because he had a sadistic teacher.
Both Caroline and Stephen liked English.

SB58b 58b PB58b,c

4 Give one or two ideas to start students off: getting to school/lessons late, running in the school corridors, hair too long/short, not wearing correct uniform.

5 As the groups report informally, make a list of things on the board that teachers seemed to complain about.

6 Discuss whether it seemed that teachers at primary school and secondary school were always right, whatever you said. (This is to prepare the ground for understanding the expression: 'Teachers – they want it all ways'.)

7 Possible extension: Find out what excuses students used to give if they were caught breaking rules.

8 Students listen to and read the poem at the same time. In groups, students write a few sentences in reaction to this poem, then read what Stephen thought. Ask them if they ever felt and did the same; do they think that Stephen really did answer back next time?

'shut him up' (Shut up!) is very colloquial English and is usually a rather rude way of saying 'Stop talking/making so much noise'

Language revision

should have said (didn't say but wanted to)
the three uses of **to**: after **said**; **in order to**/shut him up); after **had** (to show obligation)
time phrases: **after class, on the way home, when it happened, next time**.
reply as noun. cf **No reply** when trying to telephone someone who is not in.
would meaning past habit (**used to/always**)

59 | Language study

Aims: 1 Revision of expressions for like and dislike, and for surprise.
2 To revise the meanings of some linking words as they are used in context.
3 To analyse how to keep a conversation going with response like: **Oh really? Did you?**

Lexis:
Revision: **got**, **like**, **that**, **those**

SB59a [58a]* PB59a

1 As this section is mainly revision, focus only on points which prove problematical for students.

2 When students have finished the activities in this section, ask them what kinds of things Catherine said in her role as leader of the group: Why don't you start? Why was that? Oh really? Did you? (to keep the conversation going).

Key: 1 subjects like French, things like maths and English
2 got to say = obligation, must   have to say it got worse and worse = became/grew
Greek got a bit, you know = became/grew
I got a bit behind = fell behind
3 the ones that we liked – relative clause = which
but I think that – referring back to the whole situation, liking science subjects   'better in that' – refers just to science subjects   weren't that helpful – colloquial = so helpful   But why was that? – refers to situation 'I hated it'   so uncontrolled that – result   they do that even now – refers to action – 'write dreadful reports'
4 like: I liked writing stories/science subjects. I liked science subjects
quite like: I didn't mind things like maths …   I didn't like those as much.
not liking at all: the least favourite was always maths.
… it was pretty disastrous, really.   … which I really didn't like at all.   What did you dislike? Well, French …   My least favourite subject was sport. I hated it.
Surprise: 'Oh really?' and 'Did you?' show the preceding information surprised them.
Also expressing surprise: Oh, my goodness!   Did you really?   My God!

Ask what expressions students use in their own language.

SB59b PB59b,c

1 Students underline the phrases in their books. Encourage them to ask you if they don't understand how or why any of the linking words are used. (The final 'then' meaning 'in that case' may be new.)

2 See section 67d.
Other revision points from this recording:
amounts: a little bit, quite a lot, a bit
modifiers: pretty disastrous, really didn't like, the most dreadful, not that helpful, much better, a bit behind.

60 | Asking indirectly and dropping hints

Aims: 1 To practise the tactics of asking someone to do something indirectly.
2 To practise the tactics of indirectly refusing a request.

Lexis: for good (for ever)
Understanding only: **dropping hints**, **indirectly**, **repaired**

Task SB60

1 Divide the class into groups A and B. In groups, students prepare their requests and responses. Monitor groups' work assisting where necessary. If students are finding this task difficult, refer them to Unit 3 section 31, where they practised a similar strategy.

Report SB60

2 Students could take turns role-playing some of the situations in front of the class for the report phase of the activity.

Possible answers

a I'm a bit low on funds/money until I get paid next week.
b I give up. I just can't understand how to do this homework.
c I've had this car serviced X times and they still haven't found what's wrong with it.
d Do you know that the smoke in a room is as dangerous for non-smokers as it is for smokers? I've just been reading about it in the newspaper.
e Oh dear – the smoke is making my eyes run.
f There's a great film on at the cinema tonight.
g Same as a.
h I have to get to the bank but I don't have any transport.

61 | Language study

Aim: To highlight common phrases and verbs by focusing on the word **or**.

Lexis: follow [L]

SB61 *

1 Play recording 61 and ask students to stop you when they hear the word **or**.

2 Students practise the phrases, repeating after the tape. Point out that the phrases 'or somebody', 'or something', 'or somewhere' are used when we don't need to be very precise.

Key: Five examples: in **or** out of a car; **or** he's taking something; the Queen **or** somebody; **or** maybe he's putting something; a bag **or** something.
It comes at the beginning or middle of a sentence (or at the end of an unfinished sentence).

62 | Balloon man

Aims: 1 To practise working cooperatively to define and reconstruct a scene.
2 To practise speculating on someone's character and way of life.
3 To practise the meaning and use of nominal groups with adjectives, qualifiers, words like **part/bit/piece of**; and relative clauses, to describe objects, buildings, past looks/appearances.
4 Meaning and use of expressions of existence and location with **There is/are/was/were**.

SB62 PB62

1 Give them one minute to look at the picture. With books shut do the examples with them so they get the idea. Further examples: there was part of an air cylinder in the car boot, made of metal.

2 Write each phrase up on the board as they give you an item from their list. Count up the number of items the class remembered.

Language study

58a **a** Find the transcript for 58a.

1 Look at the sentences in the transcript with **like**. Which two '**like**'s have a different meaning from the others?

2 Find four examples of the word **got**. Does it have the same meaning in each case?

3 Find seven examples of **that**. How many different meanings does it have here? What about the word **those**?

4 Find about six more phrases that tell us how much or little they liked their subjects. Write two more in each column of a table like this.

like	quite like	not liking it at all
my favourite was English		*the least favourite was Maths*

Then add any other phrases you know expressing 'like' or 'dislike' in the suitable columns.

What information surprised Catherine? How do you know?
Which of these expressions also express surprise?

Oh, my goodness!   Did you really?
Ouch!   My God!
How sad!

b   Find phrases with these words in the poem in section 58b.

or   so   and   well   but   of   ... then

60 # Asking indirectly and dropping hints

Oh dear! The smoke is making my eyes run!

Very sorry. I've nearly finished it.

Group A students together think of ways you could ask people indirectly to do the following things to help you.

Group B students together think of ways to answer A, politely, avoiding the issue, and not doing what the other person will be asking.

a A wants to borrow some money from B.
b A wants someone to help them do some homework.
c A's car has gone wrong – it needs to be repaired.
d A wants B to stop smoking in the office for good.

A and B students in pairs practise some of the situations above.

Then change over, and do the ones below.

e A wants B to put his/her cigarette out now.
f A has no-one to go to the cinema with.
g A lent B some money and now wants it back.
h A wants to borrow B's bike/car.

Language study

or

Look at this example:

JM: . . . Is it a tie? Or, is it a piece of rope or something?

61   Listen again up to the phrase 'a plastic bag'. How many examples of **or** can you hear? Where does it come in the sentence? What words follow it?

62 # Balloon man

Memory challenge

Look at the picture for one minute. Close your books. How many things can you remember? Make a list. Say where they were and what colour.

e.g. *a piece of grey string, round the man's neck*

63 The human body

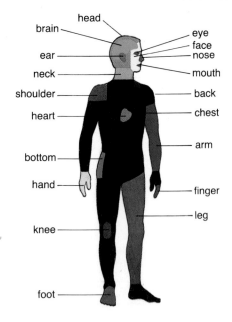

Parts of the human body

a Other meanings

Find three meanings for the word **head** and two for the word **foot**. If you are talking about the human body in your own language how do you say **head, hand, heart, foot, leg, arm**?
What other meanings do these words have in your language?

63a Look at the pictures and then listen to John and Monica talking about them. How many of the uses of these words do they find? Which ones do they miss?

b Useful phrases

When do you think you might use the phrases below? For all except one, there is a possible situation given on the right but they are mixed up. Which one is missing?

1 *Could you hand me that one please?*
2 *Oh dear, I can't face it!*
3 *Keep an eye on this for me please.*
4 *The body was pale blue.*
5 *Where are you heading for?*
6 *Could you give me a hand?*
7 *Right in the heart of Africa.*
8 *On the other hand, …*
9 *In my heart I knew she was wrong.*
10 *It's two feet wide and roughly six feet long.*
11 *I got it second hand.*
12 *You must ask headquarters.*

a When you want someone to look after something.
b When you want someone to help you.
c When saying how big something is.
d When you really don't want to do something.
e When you want someone to pass something.
f When you want to know where somebody is going.
g Saying where a place is.
h When you want to give the opposite point of view.
i When talking about a car.
j If you need the permission of head office.
k When you buy something which isn't new.

c Believe it or not!

Allen Doster, from New York, self-employed, donated 1,840 pints of blood between 1966 and 1986.

Brain of Britain Quiz
The youngest person to become 'Brain of Britain' on BBC radio was Anthony Carr, aged 16 …

Give blood – save a life!
The National Blood Donors' Association

Heart stoppage
The longest recorded heart stoppage is a minimum of 3 hr 40 min in the case of Miss Jean Jawbone, 20, who was revived by a team of 26 in the Health Sciences Centre, Winnipeg, Canada on 8 Jan 1977.

The British Heart Foundation

Look after your heart!

YOU CAN SUBSTITUTE HEART VALVES WITH PLASTIC ONES AND HIP JOINTS WITH METAL ONES.

THE OPERATIONS, HOWEVER, REQUIRE ONE THING FOR WHICH THERE IS NO SUBSTITUTE
BLOOD
AND THERE'S ONLY ONE PLACE WE CAN GET IT FROM
THE NATIONAL BLOOD TRANSFUSION SERVICE
"We're asking you to help us"

d Riddles

Do these riddles first, then write some more for your friends to answer. (The pictures above may help you.)

What has a face but no eyes?
What has feet, a back, sides and arms but no hands?
What has a mouth and runs, but can't eat, speak or walk?

The human brain as compared to a sheep's brain.

63 The human body

Aims: 1 To show how the words for various parts of the body can be used with other meanings.
2 To compare these uses across other languages (to give students practice in talking about language).

Lexis: arm, blood, body, brain, chest, ear, face, finger, heart, human, knee, leg, neck, nose, part, shoulder, teeth [T]
Revision: **feet, hand, head, leg**

Listening SB63a [63a]* PB63a

1 Check that students know the basic meanings of the words for parts of the body that are new to them.

2 Give students plenty of time to study this page and draw their own conclusions, before you play the recording.

   Key: Parts of the body that John and Monica found: head of a pin; eye of a needle; mouth of a tunnel; seat of a chair; face of a clock; foot of a mountain; headmaster's door; legs of a table/chair; finger on that sign; arms of a chair; back entrance sign.

   Additional expressions shown in pictures:
   back seat of car
   neck of a bottle
   mouth of a river and a neck of land,
   shoulder of a mountain
   cliff face
   armchair with back, arms and feet,
   watch/clock with hands, face and second hand
   Valentine card has heart
   two long guns (arms) that could be shouldered

   We also say the leg of a race or a journey, but this is quite rare (e.g. How long will the first leg take?).
   'Door handle' and 'handling money' come from the word 'hand'.

SB63b

3 Students do the exercise and practise saying the phrases. Get students to tell you which 3 phrases they think they will find the most useful and why.

   Key: 1 e 2 d 3 a 4 i 5 f 6 b 7 g 8 h
   9 missing   10 c   11 k   12 j

SB63c

4 Ask students how many parts of the body they can find in the texts. (This activity is mainly for interest and fun.)

   Key: blood; heart; jawbone; brain

SB63d PB63b

5 Students could write some more riddles to ask each other.

   Key: a mountain or clock; an armchair; a river

64 Childhood

Aims: 1 To practise expressing past and present wishes and ambitions.
2 To revise phrases used to describe physical appearances (see Unit 2).
3 To practise exchanging past anecdotes, talking about character and personal experiences.
4 Reading and understanding a poem.

Lexis: attention [L], **career, childhood, consequences, dream, grow** [L], **happy** [T], **odd** [L], **partly** [L], **push** [L], **relationship** [L], **unfortunately, wait.**
Revision: **come true, didn't really have, direction, ever, expect us to have, just, member of family, taken** (exams, subjects), **university.**
Phrases: **a bit childish; a couple of; do you ever say …?; don't really like; lend me a hand, will you?; pretty handy** (fairly useful); **years ago**

Listening SB64a [64a]* PB64

There will be no intensive study of this transcript, but discussion about why Catherine could not become a doctor will help to highlight the target lexis. You may also like to highlight the revision phrases above, and use the Lexicon for the words marked [L].

1 Students make their own personal list of dreams and ambitions. This is to set them thinking, and give them time to remember. While listening to the tape, they will probably remember other things that they can then add to their own lists. So there is no need to get students to report their lists at this stage.

2 Before playing the tape ask students which person they think wanted to be a doctor. Stop at John saying 'My parents didn't expect us to have career ambitions' and check that students have understood.

   Key: Catherine wanted to be a lady-doctor, and John just wanted to be taller, sane and healthy.

3 Introduce the idea of parents who are 'pushy', i.e. over-ambitious, for their children. Ask students if they thought John's parents were the 'pushy' type or not.

4 In groups students ask one another about childhood dreams and ambitions. (Before they start, you could give them a little more time to complete the lists they began before listening.)

5 Groups prepare their reports. Provide help with lexis as needed – there is likely to be much variation between the groups' topics.

6 Each group reads their report to the class. Other groups jot down people's ambitions, to see if any one profession came out as most popular.
   (This activity revises the lexis from Unit 4 concerning jobs, professions, training etc.)

SB64b

7 In pairs, students tell one another about their ambitions. The reporting back on this should be brief and informal.

SB64c

Students who have brought in photographs of themselves or families should hand them in before this task starts. Mix them up and display them, but with no names showing. Put a letter by each one, a – z.

8 Students write a short description of themselves as small children, e.g. I used to have short black hair. I used to be rather fat/fatter than I am now. I was tall for my age etc. Help students as necessary.

9 Number the finished descriptions and display them on the wall. Ask students to wander round, read the descriptions, and match them to a person in the class and, if possible, to a picture. Expressions like **My goodness, How funny!, You looked so different!** etc may be useful.

SB64d [64d]

10 Ask about students' childhood nicknames – what their family used to call them, and friends (or enemies!) at school. Why were they called that?

11 Tell students they won't understand the title of the poem until they have actually read it, but ask what they think it means – tell them that 'Juster' is a made-up word. Do they know what **just** and **wait** mean normally?

12 Students listen to and read the poem at the same time, then comment in groups. Ask if the same happened to them as children. Does it happen now? Did they like helping their parents in the house? What jobs did they do? Groups report back about their comments.

Listening SB64e [64e]*

13 Optional listening: Catherine and Stephen comment on the same poem.

   Key: Neither Catherine nor Stephen like the poem much. Stephen thinks that as a child he would do as he was told. Catherine thinks she was helpful.

In the Practice Book there's a poem by the same author about a child who is always asking questions, which could be read to the students.

65 Language study

Aim: To make students aware of the various ways of expressing something that happened repeatedly/ habitually or always in the past.

Lexis: used to, would

SB65 PB65

1 Use as a further example: 'I used to work at a desk and have files of clients' businesses in front of me and I would deal with their insurance needs.' (From page 1.)

2 Students do the activity in pairs.

   Key: would means **used to.**
   Ways of expressing habitual past action:
   use of **would** or **'d** (new to students), **used to** (revision), simple past tense.

There are two examples from Monica's recording in the test.

66 Grammar

Aim: To focus on meanings and forms of the passive with various time references.

SB66 PB66

1 Ask students what a–j have in common. (A form of the verb **to be** followed by another verb.)

2 Also ask them in how many of the sentences they could answer the question **by whom?** or **by what?** Point out that in a. we know who wrote the postcard (Becky's friend). Ask if we know who does/did all the other things from what is in the sentence. (only in h.). Therefore, we use the passive when it is not important who has done or performed the action.

3 Students should do the activity individually, then check their answers with a partner.

   Key: 1 d 2 c 3 b 4 f 5 a 6 h
   7 i 8 e 9 g 10 j

4 Optional: All the contexts have occurred in Units 1–5. You could ask students to choose 1 or 2 and explain where they come from and what they refer to.

Childhood

John   Catherine

a   Dreams and ambitions

> What were your childhood dreams and
> ambitions? What did you want to be when
> you grew up? What were your parents'
> attitudes? Write down one or two things
> that you can remember.

Read the card. Write notes about yourself.

64a Listen to John and Catherine. Take notes.

Tell one another about your childhood
dreams and ambitions.

How many people in your class actually carried out
what they wanted to do as a child? Who had the most
ambitious parents?

Choose two different people in your class
and write a short report about their
ambitions and whether or not they have been
fulfilled.

b   Present dreams and ambitions

Tell your partner what your present dreams and
ambitions are.

*I hope to ... I intend to ... I'd like to ... I'm ...
I may ... I think I'll ... I'm definitely going to ...
I hope I'll be able to ... I expect I'll ...
I won't ... I hope I won't be ... I'm not going to ...*

c   What were you like as a child?

Write a few lines describing what you looked
like when you were a small child. Don't put
your name. Give it to your teacher.

64d   d   Juster and Waiter

My mum had nicknames for me and my brother.
One of us she called Waiter
and the other she called Juster.
It started like this:
she'd say, 'Lend me a hand with the washing up
will you, you two?'
and I'd say, 'Just a minute, Mum.'
and my brother'd say
'Wait a minute, Mum.'
'There you go again' – she'd say,
'Juster and Waiter'.

Michael Rosen

64e   e   What did Catherine and Stephen think of this
poem? What were they like as children?

---

65   *Language study* ····················

What does **would** (or **'d**) mean in these sentences?

She'd say, 'Lend me a hand with the washing up ...' (64)
And I'd say, 'Just a minute Mum.' (64)
And my brother'd say 'Wait a minute, Mum.' (64)
*On the way home, I would work out what I should
have said to the teacher.* (58)

Look at these sentences and see what other ways you
can find of expressing the same meanings.

a JM: *I hated being at school there. It was an all
boys school and I didn't like it.*
b *When we lived in Rome, we used to go out to
the Auburn Hills.*
c CF: *... I used to sit at the back ...* (58)
d SB: *I didn't mind things like maths and English
because I could do them ...* (58)
e JM: *Sport ... I hated it!* (58)
f CM: *If anybody ever asked me what I wanted to
be, career-wise, I always said I wanted to be a lady
doctor.* (64)
g CM: *I don't think I used to say 'Just a minute.'*

---

66   *Grammar* ····················

Verbs in the passive: what or who was/will be/has been ..?

Match the phrases below with those on the right to make complete sentences.

1 In Britain, people don't like
2 Catherine
3 Hadrian's Wall
4 Have your childhood dreams ever
5 One of the postcards
6 In most cases, the B & B
7 Fill in the blanks and then see which words
8 When talking to Jenny about holidays, Jeremy
9 A woman who went to a dentist in Baghdad
10 Which of these words

a was written in Ireland, by Becky's friend.
b was built in northern Britain in AD 123.
c was born in Ireland.
d being asked how old they are.
e was only allowed to ask three questions.
f been fulfilled?
g was told it would cost £30 to have a tooth out.
h will be run by the owner.
i are left over?
j can be used to describe Northumberland National
Park?

a Words in definitions

... is an object used for ...
a living creature found in ...
having the quality of ...
a large quantity/amount of ...
a natural material used for ...
an action which involves ...
to a large degree or extent
a part of ...

Which defining words (**object,
living creature, quality, quantity/
amount, material, action, degree**)
would you use in defining the
following?

very	lucky
book	plenty
pen	healthy
metal	wet
quite a lot	plastic
horse	a great deal
sense of	successful
humour	highly educated
beautiful	paper
escape	foot
rat	extremely
fishing	wall

Which words have you defined
as objects? What are they usually
made of?

b Words with un-

If you put **un-** on the front of these
words, what will they mean?

e.g. **unhappy** = not happy, sad

happy	pleasant	fit
well	lucky	able
attractive	healthy	

Find pairs of words that are
opposite in meaning.

e.g. The opposite of **unhealthy** is **fit**.

unhealthy	lucky
unusual	lovely
unattractive	fit
unpleasant	famous
unlucky	common
unable	nice
unknown	able
	well known

c Prepositions

behind

1 *There are people behind him.*
2 *The reasons behind his action
were clear.*
3 **to get behind** = to be late doing
something
*Oh dear – we're a bit behind –
look at the time!*

Where could the word **behind** fit in
these sentences?

a *When driving a car you should
always know what is you.*
b *I don't know what is the
suggestions in his letter.*
c *I got in some subjects.*

along

Do you have the same word in
your language for **along** in all these
sentences?

1 *... did a lot of walking along the
coast ...*
2 *... some way along there, not
far.*
3 *The police came along ...*
4 *Come along, hurry up!*
5 *Bring your friends along!*
6 *We went along with his
arguments.*
7 *I knew all along they had been
wrong.*

away

Find which examples:
1 mean at a distance from
someone or somewhere.
2 give a distance in space or time

a *He was away for quite a bit and
rarely saw his family.*
b *It's about five miles away.*
c *Around twenty minutes away,
by car.*
d A: *When will you be away?*
B: *The whole of July.*
e *Can you put your books away
now?*
f *She looked away as he spoke.*
g *They turned away and walked
off.*
h *The end of term is two weeks
away.*
i *He gave all his money away.*

d Classroom language

What have the phrases in each set
got in common?
When might you say them?
Read the sentences stressing one
word in each. See if your partner
can hear the stressed word.

1
Why don't you start?
Do you want to start or shall we?
Well, you start ...
Shall I start?
Shall we begin?
All right, I'll start, then.
Could you begin?
Let's start now.
Okay, you start off ...
It's time we started to write ...

2
Right, that's it then.
We've done ours.
Ours is done.
Have you finished?
We've done half.
I've nearly finished.
We need another two minutes.
Could we finish it later?
We've finished ours.
I've done mine, and checked it.
It's time you stopped!

3 (Guess the last word!)
Was that clear?
Did you follow his argument?
*Were you able to follow what they
said?*
Did you get it?
Did you __d__s__n_?

e Verb forms (past and after 'to')

Past Which verbs have the same
vowel sound in them? Divide them
into four groups. Which word is
left over?

After **to** What form of each verb
would be used after **to**?
e.g. *I want to grow.*

grew	said	shone
forgot	drove	dreamt
read	knew	met
wrote	woke	lost
spoke	won	spread

Important words to remember (281 so far)

attention L	definition	heart	neck	quantity	unpleasant
blood	dream	human	nose	relationship L	unusual
brain	ear	humour	object	sense L	usual
career	favourite	knee	odd L	shoulder	
chest	finger	leg	partly L	teeth	
childhood	follow L	material	physical	unable	
consequence	grow L	mathematics	push L	unhappy	
danger	happy	movement	quality	unknown	

Aims: 1 To revise common defining words.
2 The prefix **un-** to create opposites.
3 To revise **behind, along, away**.
4 Revision of useful classroom language.

Lexis: **definition, humour, material, object, quality, quantity, sense** [L], **unable, undo, unhappy, unknown, unpleasant, unusual, usual**

SB67a PB67a

Key: Objects: book, pen, paper (newspaper) foot, wall
Living creatures: horse, rat **Quality:** sense of humour, beautiful, lucky, healthy, wet, successful, highly educated (See Lexicon). **Quantity/amount:** very, quite a lot, plenty, a great deal, highly, extremely, educated, a foot (measurement) **Material:** metal, plastic, paper **Action:** escape, fishing **Degree:** very, quite a lot, a great deal, extremely

SB67b PB67b Key: unusual – common, unattractive – lovely, unpleasant – nice, unlucky – lucky, unable – able, unknown – well known/famous

SB67c PB67c Key: Behind: a what is behind you. b what is behind the suggestions... c got behind in some subjects.
1 and 2 give direction. **Along:** In 3 and 5 **along** can be left out without changing the meaning. In 4 **come along** means **hurry**. In 6 **to go along with** means **to agree with** or **to pretend to agree with**. In 7 **all along** means **all the time**.

Key: a 1 b 2 c 2 d 1 e 1 f 1 g 1 h 2 i 1

SB67d PB67d Key: SET 1: all deciding who will begin a task, .
SET 2: all to do with finishing a task.
SET 3: all ways of asking if someone has understood.
Missing word: **understand**.
Show students that almost any word can be stressed – it all depends on the meaning and on what has gone before.

SB67e PB67e Key: /uː/ grew, knew, /ɒ/ forgot, shone, lost, /ɛ/ read, dreamt, met, spread, said /əʊ/ wrote, spoke, drove, woke, odd one out – won /ʌ/
After **to:** The infinitive: grow, forget, read, write, speak, say, drive, know, wake, win, shine, dream, meet, lose, spread.

LEXICAL OBJECTIVES

Level 1 words (see page 129T):
along (see SB67), **arms, away** (see SB67), **body, face, feet/foot, hand, head, part** L, **thank, wait, would**.

attention L
blood 1 *What blood group are you?*
brain 1 *We don't know how the brain works.*
2 intelligence. *He's got his mother's brains. ... brainy*
career 1 job. *Careerwise, I always said I wanted to be a lady doctor.* [05]
2 all the jobs in your working life
chest 1 top, front of your body, between your neck and waist. ... *a chest X-ray*
2 a large, heavy box ... *an oak chest.* T
3 **get something off your chest** = tell people what you are worrying about. T
childhood time of your life in which you are a child. ... *childhood dreams*
consequences results. ... *I'd do what I was told or suffer the consequences.*
danger 1 possibility that someone may be harmed. *Danger! Keep away!* T
2 something that can hurt you. *Cigarette smoking is a danger to your health.* T
dangerous likely to hurt or harm you. ... *the most dangerous time when you're on a plane is take off and landing.* [08]
definition 1 statement explaining the meaning of a word
dream 1. *I dreamt you were ill. In his dream he was sitting in a theatre watching a play.*
2. an imaginary situation which you would very much like to become real. *... childhood dreams ...*
ear 1 *He whispered in Philip's ear.*
2 **ear for music or language** = able to hear, interpret and reproduce its sounds accurately. T
3 willingness to listen to what someone is saying. ... *a sympathetic ear ...* T
favourite the one you like the best
finger *He held the handkerchief between his finger and thumb.*
follow L
grow/grew L
happy contented, pleased. ... *I was happy just to get out of the house ...*
heart part of the body
human 1 noun/adj: *the human body, human life/being/condition/nature*
2 adj: *it's only human to make mistakes.*
humour 1.1 **sense of humour** = ability to see that things are funny. *She had no (sense of) humour at all.*
1.2 *the English sense of humour*
2 temper. *I'm in a bad humour.* T
knee the place where your leg bends.
leg 1 Part of the body.
Also: *trouser legs; legs of a chair etc.*
material 1 a solid substance, e.g. stone, iron, metal, plastic

2 cloth, e.g. for making clothes etc.
3 material possessions of this world, rather than emotions etc. *The material comforts of life.*
4 equipment. *... cleaning materials.* T
mathematics arithmetic, algebra, geometry etc. *I didn't mind things like maths and English ...* [05]
movement 1 a group or organisation. *The trade union movement.* T
2 moving something. *Caroline's movements are so uncontrolled ...*
neck 1 part of the body
2 part of a dress, sweater etc. *a round neck, a V neck*
Something that goes narrow at one point. ... *a neck of land*
nose part of the face ... *a broken nose*
object 1 something that has a fixed shape or form, but that has no life of its own; a thing. *A board is a flat object.*
2 aim; purpose. *The object of their visit.*
3 the thing or person that a particular action or activity affects ... *concerned with the object of his love.*
4 grammatical term; *'him' is the object of the verb 'I saw him'.* T
5 to oppose. *Some people object to all boys' schools.*
odd L
partly L
physical connected with a person's body. ... *physical strength*
2 physical characteristics or surroundings = the objects etc. around one. ... *appalling physical conditions in prisons ...*
push L
quality 1 used to refer to how good or bad something is. *The quality of the photograph was poor.*
2 of a high standard. *Choose them for their quality, ... and hospitality.* [03]
3 something abstract like kindness. ... *the qualities they look for in a teacher.*
quantity amount, number of something. *any quantity, a large quantity of ...*
relationship L
sense L
shining *Because the sun's shining.*
shoulder 1 part of the body. *He looked over his shoulder.*
2 to accept responsibility for a problem. *Many of us would rather that someone else shouldered the responsibility.*
tooth/teeth *Sweets are bad for your teeth.*
2 the teeth of a comb, saw, zip etc.
unable not able to
unfortunately *Unfortunately, I must have forgotten it somehow.*
unhappy not happy
unknown not famous
unpleasant not pleasant
unusual fairly rare **usual** opp. unusual

What do you think's the best way of travelling?

The unit is based on transport and travel. Students begin by talking about difficult journeys in an anecdotal narrative vein. They go on to identify and discuss forms of transport and to speculate on the characteristics of these different forms, listing recommendations and giving detailed advice for a particular journey familiar to them.

There are stories and puzzles incorporating a variety of types of texts including a semi-technical description of a hovercraft. Students read and listen to a couple of 'modern legends'. This is the kind of story, existing in all cultures, about something, usually horrific, that happened to 'a friend of my boyfriend's mother' – always convincing but rarely true. The theme of this particular 'modern legend' is 'The Vanishing Hitch-hiker'. In addition to giving practice in understanding and producing narrative this section helps to prime students for the serialised story which begins in Unit 7, which also concerns an element of mystery. After this there is a class survey which involves students in the costing of their own transport, initiated by a parallel survey on tape, followed by a formal presentation of results. Finally there is a study of an information leaflet about a travel card which offers savings over buying a ticket in the usual way. Students read this critically and evaluate the offer, and then describe similar facilities for cheap travel in their own countries.

OBJECTIVES

Lexical objectives are in TB84

Grammar and discourse

a Ways of giving advice – direct and indirect. (69,70,84)
b Meanings of **really**: as an intensifier,
  to mark a contrast with some supposed state of affairs,
  to give assurance of the truth of a statement. (70)
c The use of **on**: referring to place, referring to a means of transport, referring to time, with the meaning 'about' (a book **on** transport), used to reinforce the idea of a continuing action (to **go on** doing something), and common phrases with **on**. (72)
d Revision of ways of making suggestions. (83)
e The use of **way**: referring to manner, means and method, meaning direction, distance or route. (74)
f Expressions of cause and result. (76)
g The use of continuous tenses for an action or state that is interrupted in some way. (77)
h Features of style in colloquial written narrative. (78,79)
i Meaning and use of verbs used for travelling. (81)
j The use of **no** and other devices for expressing agreement. (84)
k A study of a set of verbs and related nouns used to express different kinds of **talk**: e.g. explain/give a clear explanation, enquire, make an enquiry. (84)
l Use of **neither**, **nor**, **so** to mark similarity in responding phrases. (84)

Tasks

a Producing a narrative involving a series of difficulties and the final outcome. (68)
b Identification and discussion of the characteristics of different forms of transport. (68,69)
c Understanding and making recommendations for a particular journey. (69)
d Giving advice in writing (71)
e Understanding short humorous narratives and predicting the outcome of an incomplete narrative. (73)
f Recognising essential information in a semi-technical description. (73)
g Understanding and producing anecdotal narrative. (75)
h Discussion of folklore and legend. (78)
i Predicting the ending of a narrative. (78)
j Identification and comparison of costs. (80)
k Evaluation of an information leaflet and production of statement containing information on a parallel topic. (82)

35T

68 Forms of transport

> **Aims:** 1 To stimulate anecdote telling about journeys.
> 2 To introduce the theme of travel.
> 3 To give students exposure to travel announcements made in English at ports, stations, airports.
>
> **Lexis:** (preliminary introduction only) **air, aircraft/ aeroplane, although,** (no) **charge,** (first) **class, each, executive, exhausted, form** (of), **fuel, gas, horrible, include, including** [T], **major, oil, rate** [L], **reduced, service(s)** [L], **ship, transport, way** (method, means)
> Revision: **boat** (boat-train), **by air/car/plane** etc, **cycling, driving, fairly, ferry, hitch-hiking, hovercraft, pretty, sea** (on a ship), **spend, train, flying, waste**

The distance record in 1987 for hot air balloons was over 700 miles.

SB68a,b PB68a,b

1 Promote as much discussion as possible. Allow time for anecdotes, especially if any students have experience of the more way-out forms of transport. In groups students list advantages/disadvantages of forms of transport.

SB68c

2 In groups students discuss the signs in red. Put new lexis on the board as it comes up in the class discussion.

Key: The red signs advertise package holidays (where a travel company books travel and accommodation for you), except for KLM EXECUTIVE CLASS and FIRST CLASS SERVICE, which refer to flights only.

Listening SB68d 68d

3 Play the tape and pause where students want to discuss a noise or announcement. Do not tell them if they are right until they have all written their list. Most native speakers discussing this tend to use a lot of modals (it must be, it could be, it might be) to express degrees of certainty. Encourage this.

Key: 1 Air France announce the departure of flight AF807 to Paris ... (airport).
2 Bicycle passing, ringing its bell.
3 Man telling car driver which row to park in on a ferry.
4 Victoria Coach Station, announcing the 121 coach to Paris at 2100 hours: 'Please check in at the continental lounge.'
5 Train leaving – doors slamming.
6 Car stopping and driver asking hitchhiker where he wants to go (to Dover).
7 Plane announcement: 'Passengers' attention is directed to the safety instructions for this aircraft ...'
8 Motorbike going from tarmac up a ramp.
9 'The last call for the 12.30 sailing to Calais. Foot passengers are requested to go through immigration to the departure lounge.'
10 Woman checking in for hovercraft 519 leaving at 11.00 hours for Calais.
11 Ship's siren making departure signal.

SB68e

4 Refer students to a map if they have no ideas on how to get from London to Paris. This is a similar task to recording 69, so they should attempt it seriously. The quotations are from the transcript for section 69. The ???? stand for words denoting forms of travel. When students have discussed the quotes in groups, make a list of different methods of transport on the board.

Key: All quotations could be advantages except for **very tiring, waste a lot of time, exhausted**.

SB68f **Key:** Types of fuel/power. Missing word: petrol.

Unit 6
What do you think's the best way of travelling?

> Or boat, I suppose, but that ** doesn't take y long, does it?

> I believe that's quite quick.

68 Forms of transport

a What is the longest or most complicated journey you have ever been on? Tell the class about it.

KLM EXECUTIVE CLASS

b What are the advantages and disadvantages of each of these forms of transport in the pictures?

c What could the signs be advertising?

NO CHARGE FOR CHILDREN UNDER 5

68d **d** On the tape you will hear different sounds and announcements associated with the forms of transport on this page. Write down what places and sounds you think you hear.

SUNSHINE HOLIDAYS
BOOKING FORM
Name ....
Address ....
....

> I always prefer ???? 'cause I don't like having to sort of walk too much.

> You have more time to spend in Paris.

> Although it was more expensive, it meant we had more time there.

HOVER*SPEED*
The Motorway to Europe

Car and Passenger Services
Dover to Calais & Boulogne

> It's nice and quick.

> I haven't got a ????
> Nor have I.

DOVER

> I think that would be very tiring. Horrible.

> I suppose the cheapest way would be go to by ????

> You feel exhausted when you got there.

> Would you take your ????

> If I had a lot of time, yes …

1st Class tickets →
Excess fares, Seasons →
⇄ Travel Centre →
Buses & Taxis →
← Platforms 9 to 19
← Victoria Place-shopping
← Victoria Place-eating
Tickets →
← Gatwick tickets
← Gatwick Express

NO FUEL SURCHARGE

e How many ways can you think of of travelling between London and Paris? Write them down.

Read the quotations and try to guess what means of transport are being talked about. (You will find out later whether you are right.)
Find three quotations that mention an advantage, and two that mention a disadvantage.

> Although, early July, … it might be fairly pretty going by ????

> You waste a lot of time.

f Types of fuel/power

What's missing?

oil   gas   air   steam   electricity   wind

L rate class form

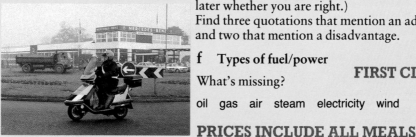

FIRST CLASS SERVICE

PRICES INCLUDE ALL MEALS

69 London to Paris in early July

Bridget, Jenny and Danny all live and work in London. We asked them to discuss the best way of travelling to Paris.

69a **a** First Bridget asked Jenny. How many forms of transport did they mention? Did they recommend one particular way?

69b **b** Listen to their summary. Did they mention the same forms of transport as they had in their discussion?

69c **c** Next Bridget asked Danny. What advice did Danny give? How many reasons did he give?

d Now go back to section 68, and read the quotations again. Can you now say which form of transport they were about? How many did you guess right?

70 *Language study*

a **Giving advice**

Read the transcripts for section 69 carefully. Pick out seven useful phrases you might use if you were starting to give advice to someone.
e.g. *Well, I actually did that last year. We . . .*

b **really**

Put the word **really** into these sentences. (There is more than one possible place in each sentence.)

It depends on the time you've got.
That would mean having a car.
It depends on how long you've got, though, doesn't it?
Well, I don't know.

70b How is the word **really** said in these sentences? What does it mean in each case?

Erm, God, this is really difficult.
I really like that one.

And how is **really** used here?

I quite like the red one but I really wanted blue.
Hi, Mike. I was really looking for Roger, but you'll do.
It's quite warm. Do you really think it'll rain?

71 From your country to ___

Decide on a country near your own that people sometimes travel to. How many ways are there of getting from your own country to the capital city of the nearby country? Write down two or three different ways of travelling there, making notes of the advantages and disadvantages of each way.

Tell people in your group what you have written. Explain the advantages and disadvantages clearly. Let them decide which way they would choose.

Tell the class about your decision.
What were the most popular forms of transport among students in other groups?

Write a short paragraph giving advice to a foreigner new to your country on how to get to another capital city from yours.

69 London to Paris in early July

Aims: 1 To practise understanding recommendations and the reasons given for making them.
2 Understanding language used when taking differing circumstances into account, e.g. depends . . .

Lexis: although, because, believe, depend [L], **discuss, discussion** [T], **exactly** (I agree), **exhausted, form, horrible, mention, no** (I agree), **nor** [L], **one/someone** (impersonal 'you'), **plane, previous** [T], **suggest, suggestion** [T], **though, travel, way**
Revision: **anyway, does it? have you?, in fact, I've done it**

Bridget, Danny and Jenny appeared in Book 1 but are new to Book 2.
Bridget lives and works in London as a personal assistant in a London company. She shares a flat with a friend.
Jenny is a freelance writer and editor and works for large publishing companies. She has an office at home in her flat. Danny lives in South London and has a small design business, with his brother. They work from a studio in Central London, designing leaflets, brochures etc for shops and other companies.

Listening   SB69a [69a]* PB69

It may be necessary to explain **compromise** *(she means the train is comfortable and not too expensive) and* **confined to** *(you have to take the ferry if you go by train).*

Key: They mentioned:
plane, bus, train, boat, hovercraft, ferry, car.
They seemed to feel that the train would be the best compromise.

Listening   SB69b [69b]*

Key: In their summary they did not mention the bus (they felt they couldn't recommend the bus anyway) or boat (understood – going by car one has to take the boat/ferry). They added 'cycle'.

Listening   SB69c [69c]*

Key: Danny gave 3 reasons for preferring flying: two personal ones – doesn't like walking, hasn't been to Charles De Gaulle airport in Paris. One general one – nice and quick, so more time to spend in Paris itself.

SB69d

1 Ask students to refer to the quotations on the previous page. They should be able to do this on their own – it will be good consolidation. Students can check by reading the transcript.

70 Language study

Aims: 1 To show that giving advice is often done by telling the other person about one's own personal experience of having done something similar and, depending on whether it was successful or not, recommending a similar or different procedure.
2 To revise the uses of **really**. (Its very common pragmatic use (to delay, show hesitancy or to make things less dogmatic) is very difficult to explain. The best way to demonstrate this is through intonation and gesture.)

SB70a PB70

1 Discuss the example. Here, Jenny is saying that what they did last year (go by plane) is good general advice for anyone who wants to save time.

2 Point out that: 'Well I actually did that . . . last year/month' etc is a good general 'opener'. Demonstrate how you can change 'did that' to 'bought one' – ask them what they could say if they wanted to recommend a car that they/a friend had already bought: 'Well, I/a friend of mine actually bought one of those last year.'

Key: Other useful phrases (with suggested alternative contexts in brackets) might be:
1 It really depends on the time you've got available (money)
2 although it was more expensive . . . (bigger/better quality etc.)
3 I suppose the cheapest way would be to . . . (easiest, safest etc.)
4 I believe the train (the book by x) is quite quick (good).
5 In fact I know it is, I've done it (read it, seen it on TV).
6 Or boat, (other object, e.g. book) I suppose . . .
7 I suppose one could . . ./I suppose you could . . .
8 . . . it doesn't take very long, does it? (cost very much, does it?) (It's not too far, is it?)

Research suggests 'traditionally taught' patterns (e.g. 'Why don't you', 'If I were you') form only one part of a much more complex interaction.

SB70b [70b]

3 Students do this exercise in pairs.

Key: (Only one position at a time!) It **really** depends on the time you've got **really**. That would **really** mean having a car **really**. It **really** depends **really** on how long you've got, **really** though **really**, doesn't it **really**? Well, I **really** don't **really** know **really**.

4 Students listen to the tape.

Key: The word **really** is usually stressed when it means 'very' or 'in actual fact'. In its pragmatic use, it sometimes makes up a single tone unit on its own, especially where it is at the end of an utterance. In these examples **really** means 'very, very', or something even stronger, e.g. 'Erm, God, this is really difficult'.
In the last examples, it means 'in actual fact', 'actually'.

71 From your country to____

Aims: 1 Describing advantages and disadvantages.
2 To practise giving advice in writing.

Lexis: explain

Task   SB71 PB71

1 Students make notes on their own, then discuss in groups. (Quieter students are more likely to put forward their views if they have time to prepare them.) If students come from the same country, get some groups to choose different nearby countries, for variety.
If there are some countries represented by only one student each; put those students together. They can each prepare their own report by explaining what they want to say to each other first. Then they can help each other plan a short report about each country.
Remind students to take into account different types of travellers – the well-off businessman who is short of time and the penniless student are two extremes.

2 Groups report to the class. Remind students to keep a tally of the types of transport recommended as they listen to the reports.

3 Students write their reports in groups. Provide assistance and correction as necessary at the group writing stage. After completing the reports, students could read each other's and compare recommendations. Collect written reports for further correction.

72 Preposition spot

> **Aims:** 1 To focus on the meanings and uses of **on**.
> 2 Understanding common phrases containing **on**.

*When used in phrasal verbs, **on** often has the meaning of 'continuing further, progressing'. However there are many other uses that simply defy generalisation. These will need to be pointed out as they occur in later units.*

SB72a

1 Students do the activity individually then discuss and compare answers in pairs.

> **Key:** form of transport: g
> place: b
> time: d
> topic: c
> continuing: a, l, m
> with verb: i, j, k
> e and so on = etc.
> f to keep an eye on = to watch
> h base on = to take as starting point

SB72b PB72

2 To extend the activity, focus attention on the common verbs that precede **on**: get, depends, based, spend.
> **get on** = succeed, perform well
> **get on with** = be good friends with
> How are you getting on? = How much success are you having in what you are trying to do?
> **on my/your/his own** = by myself/yourself etc. (i.e. without help/company)
> Write the phrases on the board and ask students to explain or paraphrase their meanings. Also elicit further examples from students.
>
> **Key:** 1 b 2 c 3 a 4 e 5 d 6 g 7 f

---

73 Stories and a picture

> **Aims:** 1 To help students understand short humorous narrative and predict the outcome of an incomplete narrative.
> 2 To practise recognising the essential information in a semi-technical description.
>
> Lexis: **base, deep, pause, thought, vehicle**
> Revision: **able/unable to, across, agency, keeps ... in place, return/single ticket, ring** (circle of), **run on** (a fuel), **skirt, travel**

Reading SB73a PB73

1 Students read the stories on their own and discuss the last lines in groups. Get them to read out their best last lines before giving them the answer. The key is given on page 42, but the lines are not matched with the correct stories.

> **Key:** A return ticket please: 'To here, to here'.
> A quick trip: 'I see, thank you,' ... hung up, satisfied.

SB73b

2 See if anyone in the class can explain how a hovercraft works. Then let the students do the labelling exercise and discuss. You will probably have to give a quick demonstration of 'cushion' of air, 'fans' and 'jets'. (They are not target words!)

3 Further practice: Try this guessing game. Students work in pairs. One student thinks of a form of transport; their partner must try to guess what it is in 3 questions with Yes/No answers.
   e.g. (Hot air balloon)
   1 Does it run on petrol? (No.)
   2 Does it travel on roads? (No.)
   3 Does it fly? (Yes. So it must be a ...)

---

74 Wordpower

> **Aim:** To look in detail at the word **way**.
>
> Lexis: **manner, way**

*The word **way** ranks as the third most frequent noun in English (after **time** and **people**). The largest category of the word **way** is the word used as a 'sub-technical' noun; it is a 'dummy' word, empty of meaning on its own. Compare 'He walked purposefully towards us' and 'He walked towards us in a purposeful way'. The word 'way' doesn't really add any meaning; it allows a change of emphasis within the sentence. It often occurs in phrases like 'The way we think', 'Their way of life'.*

SB74 PB74

1 Help students with the meanings of the definitions here, then ask them to assign the examples to each category.

> **Key:** The numbers refer to the category numbers.
> a 1 b 1 c 3 d 2 e 3 f 2 g 1 h 1 i 3

2 Further practice: Ask students if they know any other expressions with **way**, e.g. **way out** (exit), 'Is this the right **way** to do this exercise?' 'Is there another **way** to say this?' etc. Use the phrase 'By the way' at times during the lesson yourself, changing the topic on purpose, and see if students notice.

3 Optional: Do a practice drill based on 'I like the way X smiles/walks/writes/sings/dresses/eats/talks ... etc, using students' names or names of singers, pop groups, other teachers etc.

4 Ask students to look up in the Lexicon other largely sub-technical nouns like **form** which is a target word for this unit.

37T

Preposition spot

a on

On can refer to:
a form of travel/transport (e.g. *on a bus/plane*)
a place where something is (e.g. *on the table*)
time (e.g. *on Sunday*)
subject or topic (e.g. *books on travel*)
On can mean continuing or going further (e.g. *go on, carry on*)
On is used with some verbs (e.g. *depend on*)
Find at least one example of each in the examples below.

a *... no chance of promotion there, so I'm going to move on.* (2)
b *... and we had to look on the map ...* (2)
c *We did a survey on languages we had learned.*
d *On one occasion, while on holiday in France ...*
e *... interested in the cinema, and the theatre and so on.* (20)
f *The manager decided to keep an eye on him.* (55)
g *We're flying direct from Sydney on QF1.* (33)
h *... if you base it on the cost of petrol and parking ...* (82)
i *Who spends the most/least money on travel?*
j *It depends on the time you've got available.*
k *I switched on the car radio.* (97)
l *He got in and I drove on.* (97)
m *'Go on then.'*

b Match phrases with similar meanings.

1 *Hold on! Hang on a minute!*	a very busy
2 *There was a policeman on duty.*	b wait a second
	c working there
3 *I can't come, I've got so much on.*	d after some time
	e please – hurry
4 *Come on!*	f most of the time
5 *Later on.*	g in the future
6 *From now on.*	
7 *It's been raining on and off all day.*	

Stories and a picture

a Can you guess the missing endings?

> **A return ticket, please**
> I work in a railway ticket office. One day, a man came up to my window and asked for a return ticket. After a long pause I finally said, with mounting impatience, 'To where? To where?' There was another long pause. Then, after some obvious deep thought, he replied, _____, _____.

> **A quick trip**
> One woman telephoned a travel agency and asked, 'Can you tell me how long it takes to go by plane from Paris to London?'
> 'Just a minute, Madam' said the employee.
> _____, she replied, and _____, _____.

b How does a hovercraft stay up in the air? Label the parts in both figures using words from the definition.

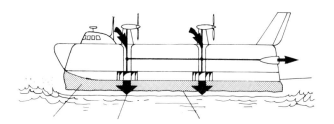

Figure 1   Hovercraft

> **Hovercraft**   a vehicle that is able to travel across both land and water on a cushion of air. The cushion is produced by fans or a ring of air jets. A skirt around the base of the vehicle keeps the cushion of air in place.

Figure 2   Airjets

Wordpower

way

Look up **way** in the Lexicon. Which meanings does **way** have in these examples?

(a) This word can be used in many different ways.

(b) I like the way he sings that song. It's really good.

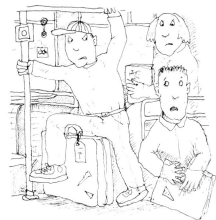

(c) After class, or on the way home...

(d) The cheapest way would be to go by bus. (68)

(e) Sorry, is that in the way?

(f) It's interesting the way computers have changed our lives.

(g) I can remember thinking that way about teachers. (58)

(h) The American way of life is very different.

(i) I can go back the way I came.

75 **Like a lift?**

Do you ever give lifts to people, or get lifts from people?
Have you ever hitch-hiked? Tell each other.

Exhausted at the end of two days filming in a
small part at Pinewood Studios, I found that
no transport back to London was available
and began the four mile walk to Uxbridge
station in the rain. Then a limousine stopped
beside me.

'Like a lift into London, lady?' enquired the
smiling chauffeur.
'You're very kind,' I said. 'Are you sure?'
'Just carrying out the boss's orders,' he
replied. 'Every day he says to me when I've
dropped him: "Don't know when I'll finish –
I'll get back on my own. You just take the
car and drive home anyone who's walking."'
'What's your boss's name?' I asked
thankfully as the car purred softly on.
'Eh? It's Michael – Michael Caine.'

L part
life
drop

? enquired
carry out
filming boss
beside orders
softly

76 *Grammar* ....

Cause and result

In the first examples, the part expressing *cause* is
coloured. The other part expresses the *result*.

1 a sentence
consequently *He was very tired.* **Consequently he
fell asleep.**
as a result *Britain is quite a small country.* **As a
result travel is quick and easy.**
that's why ... *but they're ever so small.* **That's why
rain is thin.**

2 a clause
because **I don't have a journey to work** *because I
work at home.* (80)
and *John is trying to get a new job* **and is busy
sending application forms all over the place.** (2)
as **We chose to go by plane** *as it meant we had more
time in Paris.* (69)
so *There's no chance of a promotion there,* **so I'm
going to move on.** (2)
so ... that *I was so proud (that)* **I jumped up and
down.** (23)
since **I suppose that would come out the same way**
*since people seem to prefer cats and dogs to snakes
and spiders.* (25)

3 a phrase
as a result of *As a result of this postcard* **I think
Becky will write back.** (33)
because of A: *Why can't you starve in the desert?*
B: **You can't starve in the desert** *because of the sand
which is there.* (Can you explain this joke?)

as *As a visitor* **you can take tax-free goods home.**
with *Until, mad* **with energy and boredom,** *you
escaped.* (26)

4 words meaning 'cause' or 'result'
make *His pointed ears* **made him look like a rat.**
result *Shorter periods of use* **can result in fuel bill
savings.** (91)
cause *What* **was the cause of the accident?**
lead to *A serious illness* **led to his losing his job.**

5 no marker
I don't want that one. *It's too expensive.*
Until, mad with energy and boredom, **you escaped.** (26)

Look at the sentences below. Say which part expresses
cause and which *result*.

a We had never been to Northumberland before.
   That's why we wanted to go. (29)
b We went by plane. As a result we had more time in
   Paris.
c My favourite was always English because I liked
   writing stories. (58)
d It's a very pleasant school, and I'd be sorry to leave
   it. (2)
e ... a woman ... looking a bit angry as it's one in
   the morning by then. (78)
f I can't see the TV with you standing in front of it!
g He worked hard and did very well as a result.
h Finally, tired out, they fell asleep.

77 *Phrase-building* ....

77

Think of times when you are
interrupted, or when things happen
while you are busy doing other
things. Make up some true
sentences.

I He	was	in the middle of busy	cooking dinner doing my homework watching TV having a meeting	when ...
I'll be I'm usually				

75 Like a lift?

Aims: 1 To practise understanding and telling anecdotes.
2 Reading and inferring word meanings from context; dictionary reference practice.

Lexis: boss, drop [L], **enquire/enquiry** [T], **exhausted, lift, soft, softly**
Revision: **available, carrying out, film star, get back** (home), **kind, part** (role in a film), **rain, sure**

SB75

1 Students read the anecdote on their own. Refer them to the picture of Michael Caine and ask if they have ever met anyone famous like a film star. Ask some general questions to see if they have understood:
What's the writer's job? (actress – but not famous!)
Do you think she is well off? No. Why? No car. Doesn't phone for a taxi. Sets out to walk 4 miles to the station. Who offered her a lift?

2 Ask students to guess the meaning of 'limousine', 'chauffeur', 'purred softly on'.

3 Words to look up: Students look the words up in their Lexicon and find the appropriate categories (all minor meanings). Help students to understand when to use the major meanings of **lift** and **drop** which are new words and don't occur later in the book.

4 Words to guess: Students guess their meaning from context.

76 Grammar

Aims: 1 To show that notions of cause and result can be expressed at different levels:
1 by two separate adjacent sentences
(. . . Consequently . . .),
2 by two clauses within one single sentence
(. . ., because, . . .),
3 by a phrase (e.g. as a result of . . .),
4 by one word (e.g. make, cause).

Lexis: cause, result

SB76 PB75, 76

1 To help students to understand the relationship, get them to ask questions beginning with **why** that can be answered by the coloured part of the examples, e.g Why did he fall asleep?
This technique will help them do the other examples.
Ask students to provide their own sentences like the ones in the examples.

2 Show students other ways of expressing cause and result. For example: 'And' (e.g. He was tired and fell asleep while studying.)
and 'with' (e.g. mad with energy).
Sometimes, there is no word or phrase marking or expressing this notion, as in: 'Finally, tired out, they fell asleep.' (Note the use of commas, which can help signal an unmarked relationship.)

3 Optional: Exploit the joke: Why can't you starve in the desert?
Because of the **sand which is** there.
(Say it out loud – and it sounds like **sandwiches** . . .)

Key: a C R
b C R
c R C
d C R
e R C
f R C
g C R (*Note that 'as a result' could be omitted and cause/ effect relationship would not be affected.*)
h C R

4 Optional: The song 'She'll be Coming Round the Mountain' could be sung at this point. This is a song often sung on journeys. Ask students to make up more verses with the pattern:
She'll be wearing . . .
She'll be singing . . . when she comes.

The pattern illustrates the form of the verb in section 77, but is a different use of that form.

77 Phrase-building

Aim: To practise using the continuous tense to describe an action or state that has been interrupted in some way.

*The continuous tenses (past, present and future) highlight the continuity of a state or action which is then 'interrupted' by something or someone else. **Busy** and **in the middle** of emphasise the continuity and necessity of the action, and seem to be used only when an interruption is unwelcome. (You are unlikely to say: I was busy watching TV when he rang.)*

SB77 77 PB77

1 Students listen to and repeat recorded examples. Focus on obtaining accurate pronunciation.

2 Encourage students to think of times when they were/are often/may be interrupted while doing other things, so they can make up some true sentences about themselves.

It's true! It happened to a friend of mine ...!

Aims: 1 To prepare students for reading and enjoying longer passages of narrative – the serialised story begins in the next unit.
2 To stimulate story-telling.
3 To highlight stylistic differences between: a 'chatty' colloquial written narrative (typical of spoken story-telling) and a more formal account of the same story taken from a more serious book.

Lexis: angry, associated, cousin, dead angry (colloquial), **dying to go** (colloquial), **explanation, modern (legend** = well-known story), (read the) **rest, role, throughout**
Revision: **disappear, ghost, vanish**

Reading and listening   SB78a 78a   PB78

The main aim of this section is to help students enjoy reading the story for themselves, so the lexis study and any formal language work should be left for later. Encourage students to accept general comprehension rather than detailed study of the text.

1 After initial discussion, students read or read and listen to the first part of the story. Ask students to close their books and discuss what has happened, and what they think will happen next. (Duran Duran was a famous pop group.)

2 In groups students discuss how the story could end, choose the best ending and write a continuation of the story. Monitor and provide assistance where necessary. Encourage students to write their continuations in the same informal spoken narrative style as the first half of the story; they should use the present tense which is typical of this style.

3 Groups read their endings to the rest of the class. A vote could be held on the best ending.

Listening   SB78b   78b *

4 With their books still closed students listen to the recording of John and Caroline for the differences in John's story.

5 Students read the last section which is lower down the page. Discuss their reaction to the ending – did they enjoy it?

6 Optional further practice: To encourage a more detailed understanding of the text, and to provide and feed in target lexis, ask students to look at the first paragraph of the story and write 5 Wh- questions. Students write the answers to their questions in full and keep them as a key. In groups students write down the answers to one another's questions from memory, then compare the two sets of answers. You could suggest a scoring system: 2 marks for each fair question (1 for content, 1 for accuracy); and 2 for each correct answer.

Language study

Aims: 1 To highlight the difference between colloquial style and more formal written style.
2 To give practice writing summaries in a different style from the original (in this case a more formal style).

Students should realize that the story in section 78 is written in a very colloquial style, whereas the version in 79a is much more formal. They should write their summaries of section 78 in the more formal style.

Key: Main differences:
use of present simple tense/past simple tense
sentence length: longer in the colloquial version
colloquial words and phrases:

COLLOQUIAL	FORMAL/USUAL WAY
swear blind	say they definitely happened
So how come ...?	So how is it that ...?
really weird	very strange
the other week	a few weeks ago
this girl	a girl
or something	or something similar
off they go	they set off
have a nice chat	have a conversation
feeling daft – it sounds so ...	feeling silly, because it sounds
softens up*	stops being angry
the bloke	the man
My bet is ...	I'm absolutely sure
but, own up*,	if you told us the truth
mate's	close friend's
complete codswallop*!	completely untrue.

* very colloquial expressions.

The story in Practice Book 78 is a possible, more formal, version of a similar story.

It's true! It happened to a friend of mine ...!

a Do you ever hear stories beginning 'A funny thing happened to my ... sister's boyfriend's cousin. Or somebody ...'? Do you believe in ghosts? Can people or things really vanish?
Read the first part of the story.

Dogs in the microwave, rats in the curry, murderers on car roofs and disappearing hitch-hikers all play starring roles in modern legends. They're those 'true stories' we tell each other and swear blind they happened to our best friend's sister. So how come exactly the same tales have travelled half way around the Western World? Phil Sutcliffe tells the stories – and tells us why we tell them too.

78a George: 'Something really weird happened to this friend of my sister's the other week. He lives down in Southampton and he's driving back from a Duran Duran concert when he sees this girl standing by the roadside hitching. He stops and it turns out he's going right past her door – she tells him the address, 110 Acacia Gardens or something, and off they go. She sits in the back as if she's a bit cautious maybe, but they have a nice chat. Then, when they're getting close, he can't quite remember the quickest way. He pulls up at a traffic light and turns round to ask the girl – but she's vanished.

What do you think has happened to the girl? And what does George's sister's friend do next?

▶ Plan a continuation of the story, explaining what happens to the girl. Read it to the class.

78b **b** Listen to what Caroline and John think might have happened. John tells a slightly different story. How different?

78c **c** Read on.

'Of course, he's amazed, he can't think how she got out without him noticing. Anyway, he goes round to the address she's given him and a middle-aged woman in her dressing-gown answers the door, looking a bit angry as it's one in the morning by then. He stammers out what happened – feeling daft, it sounds so stupid – but the woman softens up and tells him he's the sixth person who's come along with the same story. The girl answers the description of her daughter who disappeared two years ago after telling her friends at a party that she was going to hitch-hike home!'
Tracey: 'No! I don't believe it.'
George: 'No, honestly, it's really true. The bloke told my sister ...'
Well, maybe, George. My bet is it didn't happen to your sister's friend though. I know you have to keep it simple to let a story flow along but, own up, wasn't it your sister's friend's mate's cousin ... who heard it from someone, forget who exactly, who read it in a newspaper, so it must be true?
In other words 'The Vanishing Hitch-hiker' is a modern legend. It has been told, and believed, a million times throughout Britain, America and Europe with only the place names changing. And it's complete codswallop.

---

79 ## *Language study*

Colloquial style

a Look at this version of the same story.

This happened to one of my girlfriend's best friends and her father.
They were driving along a country road on their way home from the cottage when they saw a young girl hitch-hiking. They stopped and picked her up and she got in the back seat. She told the girl and her father that ...

In what ways is the language different?

▶ Write a summary of the whole story in section 78 in the same style. ◀

b Find the colloquial words and expressions below in the text and guess what they mean. Can you find four more?

So how come ...?   Anyway,
really weird   friend's mate's cousin
this girl   complete codswallop

80 Transport survey

a We asked a small group of people who live in Birmingham to do a group survey on how much they spent on travelling to work, on average, per week, and how much time each person spent travelling.

Myf was the chairman. She had to fill in the form below, and check her figures afterwards.

Travel to work or place of study			
Name	Jane	Philip	Ken
Job or study area	writer	research Student	lecturer
Place of work/study	home	Birmingham University	College of Further Ed
Means of transport			
Distance/time taken			
Cost per day			
Cost per week			

80a Listen to Myf doing her survey and find out which person spends the most money and takes the most time.

80b **b** Listen to Myf checking her figures. Is she right?

c How accurate do you think Philip's figures are for running a car? Has he included everything? Find the information given by the AA (Automobile Association) in section 82.

Ken says, 'I have a Travelcard so I don't have to pay.' What do you think he really means?

d Now do the same kind of survey in groups.

> Prepare a report. Tell the class which person in your group spends the most and the least money, and who takes the most and the least time on their regular journeys. Which people in the whole class spend most/least?

81 Language study

a Verbs meaning travel of some kind

Look at the transcript from section 80a. Find thirteen or fourteen phrases with a verb, which show some kind of coming or going. What other words are there with the verb? Why?

I leave at (**at** – because it is followed by a time – 8 a.m.)
to come in (**in** = into work)

b Why does Myf change to the past tense when she does her checking through in section 80b?

c Does the word **come** always mean move or travel?

82 Travelcard

a Read these questions about the Travelcard and write four more.

1 Can you use it on trains as well as buses at no extra cost?
2 Will it still make travel cheaper, even if you own a car?
3 What if you're a student in full-time education? Can you get a cheaper rate?

> Tell each other what your extra questions are. Then write three more.

b Read the brochure on page 41 and try to find the answers to all ten questions.

How many questions out of the ten can you now answer?
Write the answers down and compare them with other people's.

c Travel in your country

Do you have any cut-price tickets? How do the different forms of transport compare in cost and comfort? What might foreign visitors need to know about ways of travelling around your country? Discuss with your group.

> Write notes for a short report or talk, then tell the class. Find which country offers the cheapest/most comfortable travel.

d Put the words in the column on the left in the correct phrases. Check them against the brochure itself and make sure you know what they mean.

base	*at no _____ cost*
endless	*a _____ ticket*
extra	*bus _____*
major	*For _____ if you travel . . .*
charges	*if you _____ it on petrol alone*
rush	*_____ hour jams*
valid	*parking _____*
instance	*complete the _____ form*
special	*Travel _____*
Centres	*the opportunities are nearly _____*
land	*watch the planes _____ and take off*
services	*theatres and _____ sports events*
attached	*_____ all day until 11.29 pm*

Aims: 1 To practise identifying and comparing costs.
2 To practise listening for relevant information only.
3 To practise scanning for specific information.

Lexis: (Automobile) **Association, because, figure** [L], **listen, properly, taxi** [T], **total** [T]
Revision: **a bit ahead of, come/get in,** (the answer) **comes to . . ., get here/home, go out, in the rush hour, out and back, per/a day.** Expressions of length of time and distance.
Phrase: **what I do is, . . .**

SB80 PB80

In Practice Book 80 there are some quick arithmetical problems to get students into the right mind for this exercise.

Listening SB80a

1 Tell students that Myf and Ken and Philip live in Birmingham in the West Midlands. Ask what they can find out from the form that Myf has started filling in.

2 Students fill the form as they listen. Let students compare figures then listen again. Don't tell them any right answers yet – they can listen to Myf checking, and compare totals.

Key: refer to table in section 80:
Means of transport – car, bus
Distance/time taken – 3 miles/20 min 5 miles/45 min
Cost per day – 40p 74p   Cost per week – £2.80 £4

Listening SB80b

Key: She is right.

Reading SB80c

4 Point out that it seems odd that the Travelcard comes to more than the costs of running a car (considered to be far more expensive than a bus). Ask students to skim read the leaflet on the opposite page headed **I drive a car** to find out if Philip's figures are accurate: ask students to work out how much Philip's car journeys were actually costing him. They should base their calculations on the AA's lower figure, for petrol and parking, at 10p a mile. Estimate that he does 4 miles on his 'roundabout' route.

Key: Philip says he lives 3 miles away but he does a bit extra ('a roundabout route') in the mornings because he takes the children to school. So say he does one 4-mile trip and one 3-mile trip per day, that comes to 7 miles at 10p a mile = 70p a day = £3.50 per week. Still slightly less than Ken's busfares, but more than he thought.
Ken means that he pays for his Travelcard monthly in advance. (With a more able class you could also get them to work it out at the higher £8.75 rate)

Task SB80d

5 Make sure students are not working with people they normally travel with. There is a form in the Practice Book for students to use. If there are students who stay at home and rarely travel, they can take the role of interviewers.

6 In groups students work out the cost of travelling, per week, either to work or to English lessons, and the average time spent on travel. Students can do their calculations with reference to their present situation, or (if they are away from home) they can work out how much time and money they would normally spend at home on such journeys.   *or (more difficult):*
Students work out the cost of all the journeys they make in an average month, and divide it out to get the average cost and time spent on travel per week, for each person.

7 Groups read their reports to the class, while the other groups take notes of the largest and smallest amounts of time and money spent. Finally, which students spend the most and the least time/money travelling?

Aims: 1 To examine different ways of expressing travel and movements to and from a place in a general sense.
2 To focus on the meanings of the prepositions that are commonly associated with each verb.

Key:
a Verbs meaning travel of some kind:
have a long way to go   don't have a journey   I take the children to school (to = because the phrase is about location)   about 20 minutes . . . to come in (in = to work)   I come by bus (by = showing method of transport)   I leave at about 8 o'clock (at = because phrase is followed by time)   I arrive at . . . (at = because phrase is followed by time)   coming by car (by = showing how or method of transport)   for getting here (here = to work)   to come in (in = into work)   to go out (out = home)   for coming to work   to get here (here = to work)   to get back (back = home)

b Myf changes to past tense because she is speaking of the survey details which are already written down.

c 'That comes to four pounds a week' is about mathematical calculations, not about travel.

---

 82 **Travelcard**

Aim: To train students to read actively, with particular questions in mind.

Lexis: adult, airport, attach, base (it on), (Travel) **Centres, charges, endless, explain, extra,** (for) **instance, land, major, publish, services, special** [L], **Transport** (Executive), **valid, watch, with**
Revision: **be sure and bring, even if . . . still,** (nature) **centres, historic, once** (you have), **opportunities, own a car, take in** (include), **take off, Why not watch . . .**

SB82a PB82a

1 Students write their questions. Check these are accurate, and encourage them to check one another's.

Reading SB82b PB82b

2 Students read the brochure and find answers to their 10 questions. They should write the answers down and pass them round to see if other pairs think they are correct. Encourage pairs to examine each other's answers to see if they are the same in meaning, even if not in form.

3 Words to look up: Students find the appropriate categories in their Lexicon.

*hop on/off = get on or off easily and quickly; colloquial. Similar in register to **pop** in 'I'll pop over and visit you tomorrow', meaning come over, for a short visit. (See cartoon in section 84c).*

Task SB82c
This differs from the earlier task in that this is travel within the student's own country.

4 In groups students prepare reports. Monitor groups, providing assistance where needed. When groups present their reports, others listen for the country which offers the cheapest/most comfortable travel.

SB82d
This activity highlights most of the target words for this section.

Key: extra, special, services, instance, base, rush, charges, attached, Centres, endless, land, major, valid
Bottom of SB41: The Travelcard itself doesn't become cheaper, but each journey taken costs less, if you average out the cost.

83 Language study

Aims: 1 To revise ways of making suggestions.

SB83

1 Refer students to **What places can I visit?** in the Travelcard leaflet. Elicit both the places mentioned and the language of suggestion from them and put the latter on the board.

2 Get students to suggest places of interest, restaurants etc. in the area, or in their own country, to other members of the class.

3 See section 84d for further practice.

TRAVELCARD

Travelcard is a special ticket – your ticket to ride cheaply on buses and trains in West Midlands county.
It can be used on all West Midlands passenger transport and most Midland Red bus services within the county. It is also valid on local and Inter-City train services within the county at no extra cost. You can hop on and off a bus and train as many times as you like with Travelcard.
And, of course, with a Travelcard you don't need to worry about having the right change. The more you use it, the cheaper it becomes.

Adult county wide travelcard

1 week	£5.00
4 weeks	£16.00
13 weeks	£46.50

...lcards valid ALL DAY until 11.29pm

I DRIVE A CAR. HOW CAN A TRAVELCARD HELP ME?

Even if you own a car, a Travelcard can still save you time and money. For instance, if you travel 10 miles to work each day, commuting with a Travelcard could cost you as little as 4p a mile. Compare that with AA motoring mileage costs of 25p, or, if you base it on petrol and parking alone, 10p a mile.
And think of the rush hour jams, the frustration and the parking charges you'll avoid. Don't forget that many of our local rail stations have free 'park-and-ride' car parks. Just sit on a train or bus, read your paper and arrive relaxed.

How do I get a travel card?

Just complete the attached form and take it to any of the places listed here. (For 16-18 year olds in full-time education – ask at Travel Centres for a separate form.)
You will be issued with a Photocard which costs you 35p.
Be sure and bring a passport size colour photograph of yourself (photographs may be obtained at all our Travel Centres see below). Once you have a Photocard, your Travelcard can be renewed at any of these outlets.

WHAT PLACES CAN I VISIT?

The opportunities for getting about with your Travelcard are nearly endless.
You can visit stately homes, museums and art galleries, historic buildings and cathedrals. There are leisure parks, zoos, gardens, nature centres etc.
Why not watch the planes land and take off at Birmingham's new International Airport?
You can go to theatres and major sports events, exhibition centres and on shopping trips too.
Plan an excursion to take in a country walk or picnic.
Or use it to visit friends and relations.

(leaflet published by West Midland Passenger Transport Executive)

Can you explain:
The more you use it, the cheaper it becomes.
Is it really true?

---

83 | *Language study*

Suggestions

How many suggestions does the leaflet make about places to visit, using a Travelcard? What exactly does it say about each of them?

a although

JV: *We chose to go by plane – although it was more expensive, it meant we had more time there.*
DL: *Paris? ... I'd suggest flying. Although in early July, it might be fairly pretty going by train.*
RHT: *The only language I actually learnt was French, although I picked up English at the early age of one.*

b Agreeing or disagreeing?

A: *Very tiring ... Horrible!* B: *Exactly!*
A: *I haven't got a car.* B: *No, no, nor have I.*
A: *It doesn't take long, does it?* B: *No, ...*
Well, I'm not too sure.
Yes, that's true.
Yes, but ...
What a good idea!

c neither, nor, so (to mark similarity)

A: *I don't like it!* B: *Neither do I.* C: *Nor do I.*
A: *I like that one!* B: *So do I.*
A: *I wanted that one.* B: *So did I.*

Now suggest answers for these sentences, expressing similarity/agreement.

I came early.
I wasn't late.
He never arrives on time.
She's always late.
I wouldn't buy that one.
She hasn't brought her money.

I'd pop over and see you more often, Laura, if it wasn't for the journey.

d Advising, suggesting or instructing

Talk about problems you sometimes have. Offer each other advice.

Why not / You can / Why don't you	go ...(?) / ask ...(?) / talk to ...(?)

What about / How about / Have you thought of / Have you tried	going ...? / asking ...? / talking to ...?

e Verbs and nouns involving talk

Most of these words involve telling someone something, or talking about something together. Which one involves asking for information? Which one means to say something briefly or shortly?

Verbs
discuss suggest enquire
explain advise describe
mention decide
inform agree

Do you know the nouns associated with these verbs? Notice how they are used. Can you suggest a way to complete some of the sentences?

They	gave / offered	a good description of ... / a quick explanation as to why ... / some good advice on ... / some clear information about ...

They made		a good suggestion about ... / the right decision about ... / an agreement on the rates ... / no mention of his name at all. / an enquiry about the train times.

We had a		good discussion on ... / nice chat about ... / long conversation about ... / horrible argument over ...

A decision/agreement was finally reached.
The girl answered the description of her daughter.

Which last line goes with which story?
'I see, thank you,' and hung up, satisfied.
'To here, to here!'

Key (73a)

Important words to remember (349 so far)

adult	cause	exhausted	lift	reduce	thought
agreement	charge	explain	major	result	throughout
aircraft	cousin	explanation	manner	role	total
airport	deep	extra	mention	services L	train
although	depend L	figure L	nor L	ship	transport
angry	discuss	gas	oil	soft	valid
associated	discussion	horrible	pause	softly	vehicle
association	drop L	include	plane	special L	watch
attach	endless	including	previous	suggest	
base	enquire	instance	properly	suggestion	
based	enquiry	journey	publish	taxi	
boss	executive	land	rate L	though	

Aims: 1 To revise the uses of **although**.
2 To revise the use of **no** to agree and **yes** to disagree.
3 To revise ways of advising, suggesting and instructing.
4 To revise nouns and verbs which describe functions of speech.

Lexis: **agreement, although**

SB84a

Although is also treated in section 155.

SB84b

It is important that students realise that in English one can agree by saying **no***, and disagree by saying* **yes, but . . .**

SB84c

1 Mention to students that the second woman could be saying 'So would I.' 'I don't like it **either**' could also be given as input.

SB84d

2 After pattern practice using the substitution tables, students could be asked to prepare their own short dialogues.

SB84e

3 Ask students if they can think of any other nouns that could be used with the verbs in the table.
E.g. gave/offered (clear) instructions had a (long) talk/(big) disagreement

Point out that when one uses **give some advice** *instead of the verb* **advise***, one can easily add an adjective to describe the kind of advice, e.g. useful, good, terrible. The same goes for all these phrases with verb* **give/make/have** *etc. plus noun – they are more flexible in use, which is probably why they occur more frequently than the simple verb.*

Key: enquire, mention
PB84 is an additional Lexicon exercise.

LEXICAL OBJECTIVES

Level 1 words (see page 129T):
air, because of, centre, each, form L, **listen, modern, on** (see SB72), **one, rest** L, **travel, way** L (see SB74), **with**.

adult 1 *Adults only – no children.*
2 Suitable for adults not children. *A sort of adult joke shop . . .* [9]
agreement 1 a formal document. *Agreements on nuclear weapons . . .* T
2 *There was no general agreement on the timing . . .* T
aircraft 1 aeroplane. *a light aircraft*
airport a place where aircraft land and take off.
although basic meaning: introduces a fact or comment that makes another part of the sentence rather surprising.

We went by plane, although/though it was more expensive.
angry annoyed. *A middle-aged woman . . . answers the door, looking a bit angry as it's one in the morning.*
associated 1 *There are a lot of ghost stories associated with hitch-hikers.*
2 *I always associate windmills with Holland.* T
association group with a common aim or interest. *British Medical Association*
attach 1 join. *Complete the attached form.*
base/based 1 bottom or underneath part. *. . . the base of the vehicle . . .*
2 *. . . mileage costs of 25p, or, if you base it on the cost of petrol and parking . . .*
3 a military base T
boss person in charge
cause 1 *. . . cause and effect.*
2 aim. *. . . the cause of world peace . . .* T
charge 1 (verb) *Tax is charged on most goods at the rate of 15%* [9]
2 (noun) *No extra charge for . . .*
3 **in charge** = in control. *I'm in charge of the office when the boss is away* T
class L
cousin the son or daughter of your aunt/uncle
deep 1 *. . . deep water; deep in the forest* T
2 serious. *. . . after some obvious deep thought . . .*
depend L
discuss to talk or write about something in detail
discussion *. . . the subject under discussion . . .* T
drop/dropped L
endless seemingly without an end. *The opportunities . . . are endless.*
enquire 1 to ask (formal). *'Like a lift into London?' he enquired.* [6]
2 *I want to enquire about train times.* T
enquiry noun: *What number is Directory Enquiries?* T
executive 1 a person (or committee) employed by a business at a senior level. *West Midland Transport Executive*
2 adj: *an executive chair*
exhausted very tired
explain *Can you explain the situation?*
explanation *the most logical explanation would be . . .*
extra additional. *No extra charge for . . .*
figure L
gas 1 substance like air; can be a fuel. *gas cooker*
2 (American) petrol
horrible 1 very unpleasant, awful. *That would be very tiring, horrible!* [6]
2 extremely. *. . . horribly expensive* T
include/ing *The AA gave figures that included costs of insurance, petrol . . .*
instance 1 for example: *For instance, if you travel . . .*
2 case. *. . . numerous instances of family arguments . . .* T
journey travel. *. . . journey to work*
land verb: *watch the aeroplanes land and take off* [6]
lift 1 to raise. *He lifted the baby out with both hands.* T
2 *We took the lift up to the fourth floor. Ski lift* T
3 give someone a lift in a car. *Like a lift into London?*

major 1 most important. *. . . major sports events.*
2 a rank in the army, above captain. *He was a major by the age of 34.* T
manner 1 the way you behave. *Her voice and manner changed . . .* T
2 social behaviour: *children should be taught good manners* T
3 type: *all manner of things* T
mention 1 to talk about very briefly. *What types of transport did they mention?*
2 *'Thanks for your help!' 'That's okay. Don't mention it!'* T
3 when adding extra information: *'I'd like eggs or cheese and wine, not to mention bread and fruit . . .'* T
nor L
oil 1 *. . . the cost of petrol and oil.*
2 verb. *He oiled the clock.* T
pause 1 to stop speaking. *He paused for a moment, then went on . . .* T
2 a moment of silence. *A long pause*
3 a rest. *He worked without a pause.* T
plane see **aircraft**.
previous the one before. *Go back to the previous page and read . . .* T
properly correctly and satisfactorily: *I can now write these properly*
publish *. . . published by West Midlands Transport . . .*
rate L
reduce make smaller. *. . . reduced rates*
result 1 *As a result of this postcard . . .* [3] *Cause and result*
2 shorter periods of use can result in fuel bill savings . . . [7]
role 1 position one plays in society. *In her role as mother, she . . .* T
2 part in a film or play *. . . starring roles in modern legends.* [6]
services L
ship 1 *. . . go by ship or plane?* [6]
2 *We want to ship this back to our country . . .* T
soft/ly 1 something that changes shape or bends when touched: *a soft bed* T
2 gentle, quiet. *She spoke softly.*
3 kind. *She's got a soft heart.* T
special L
suggest 1 *I'd suggest flying* [6]
2 *The North Pennines, as the name suggests, are at the northern tip of the Pennine hills.* [3]
suggestion *That's an interesting suggestion.* T
taxi *Let's take a taxi!* T
though 1 see **although**
2 however. *It really depends how long you've got, though, doesn't it?* [6]
thought 1 idea. *. . . a tempting thought.* T
2 *after some obvious deep thought . . .*
throughout through the whole of. *. . . throughout Britain, America and Europe . . .* [6]
total *What are the total costs?* T
train 1 form of transport *. . . by train* [6]
2 *. . . a highly trained doctor . . .* T
transport vehicle or system (bus etc.) used for travelling from one place to another [6]
valid *Travelcards valid all day up to 11.29 p.m.* [6]
vehicle such as a car, bus, bike. [6]
watch 1 *Why not watch the planes . . . at Birmingham's new airport?* [6]
2 time piece. *He placed the watch carefully on the leather tray . . .* [13]

I'd probably cook an omelette

This unit is based on the topic of food – choosing, cooking, buying, stating preferences, eating out, anecdotes about food and eating and so on. A major new component in this unit is the first instalment of a short story, 'The Hitch-hiker, by Roald Dahl. This story, which is given in the original version, without simplification or editing, is serialised over the remaining nine units. It exposes students to a longish narrative and gives them an opportunity to develop the skills of prediction and to handle meanings within an extended context.

OBJECTIVES

Lexical objectives are in TB102

Grammar and discourse

a Use of **would** in hypothesising. (86,90)
b Use of the imperative in written instructions. (87,88)
c The word **give** in its literal, extended and delexical uses. (92)
d Expressions of purpose. (87,94)
e The uses of **by** with an agent after the passive, with verbs in **-ing**, and stating time and place. (96)
f Common phrases with **by**. (96)
g The meaning of **-ing**. (98)
h **-ing** in descriptive phrases. (98,99)
i **wh-** words in relative clauses and in indirect questions. (102)
j Review of expressions of cause and result. (102)
k Expressions of probability. (102)

Tasks

a Identification, speculation and comparison. (85)
b Hypothesising about courses of action in given circumstances. (86)
c Understanding and giving written instructions (for a recipe). (87)
d Stating preferences. (89)
e Itemising and comparing costs. (89)
f Understanding a semi-technical description and statement of advantages and disadvantages. (91)
g Discussing and expressing advantages and disadvantages. (91)
h Understanding and producing anecdotes. (93)
i Reading a poem and expressing reactions to it. (95)
j Understanding an extended narrative. (97)
k Producing a brief description from memory of a written text. (97)
l Predicting the development of a narrative. (97)
m Discussion and speculation within the context of problem solving. (100)

85 Talking about food

> **Aims:** 1 To promote discussion on the subject of food, students' preferences, their beliefs about food and their attitudes towards it.
> 2 To introduce the lexis appearing later in the unit.
>
> **Lexis: cup, fork, fruit, knife, milk, plate, restaurant, salt, spoon, sugar**
> Revision: **café, dish, menu**

It is difficult to predict the lexis that will be needed here since the aim is to encourage students to talk about food that is typical of their own country. Thus the word 'kebab' is likely to figure in Turkey and the Middle East, 'pasta' will be necessary in Italy and so on.

Discussion   SB85a–d PB85a,b

1 Discuss the illustrations. These focus on the fact that many different national cuisines are available in Britain and can be used to lead into a discussion of what is available in the students' own country. This may involve a good deal of introductory teacher talk. Remember that teacher talk provides students with valuable exposure provided students are interested and are making a serious effort to understand what is said.

2 Students discuss some of the subjects in groups or pairs and report their findings. Monitor the discussions, helping with lexis and other problems.

As the discussion develops you may want to pursue other aspects of the topic. Here are a few suggestions:
Are there any vegetarians in the class? What do they eat?
What does a strict vegetarian eat?
Some religions and races do not eat pork. Others (the Chinese for example) eat a lot of pork. Do students know of any other taboos in the way of food and drink?
How many ways do the students have of cooking eggs?
Have any of them have ever eaten anything strange or unusual?
What do they eat on festive occasions?

SB85e

3 To introduce the guessing game on meat, fruit and vegetables it may need be necessary to list possible questions on the board and for the teacher to think of the first item of food. In a multi-cultural class ask students to think of an item commonly eaten in Britain.
Students can only ask questions which have Yes/No answers, e.g. Is it a fruit of some kind? It is a local fruit?

SB85f PB85c

4 The missing item is the salt. Elicit from students and write on the board ways of asking a waiter for an item they need: e.g. Is there any/Could we possibly have some ... please, do you have any/a ... etc. Also ask students how they could mime something, or explain it somehow, if they didn't know the name for it. This can be fun.

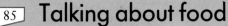

I'd probably cook an omelette

85 Talking about food

a What sort of food would you get in each of these restaurants?

b What are the most typical dishes in your country?

What do you normally have for breakfast?

If you met a foreigner who was coming to your country for the first time, what local dishes would you recommend?

c How much do you know about food in Britain? What do you think it is like? Do you know any dishes that are typically British?

d What food and drink is good for you? What things are bad for you? What foods have most Vitamin C in them?

e Think of a kind of meat, fruit or vegetable. See if your partner can guess what it is. See how many questions it takes.

f Imagine you are about to have a meal in a restaurant. What very basic thing is missing? How would you ask for it?

43

86 Cooking for an unexpected guest

a We asked Jenny, Bridget, David and Danny what they would cook from the fridge or store cupboard for an unexpected guest. This is what they said.

Sausages and baked beans.
A cheese flan and baked potatoes.
An omelette.
Rice and vegetables.

Which dishes do you think the men chose and which do you think the women chose?

86a See if you were right.

Can you summarise what they said?

b Find out which of these meals people in your group would like best. Take a vote to see which was the most/least popular.

c What would the people in your group cook for an unexpected guest? Explain to the class. Listen and decide whose meal you would like best. Take a vote.

87 A recipe

a Here is a recipe for scrambled eggs which appeared in the teenage section of a Sunday newspaper. Read the first part and work out how much you would need for three people.

Scrambled eggs for breakfast

The trick to getting nice soft scrambled eggs is to cook the eggs over a very low heat and to turn off the heat about two minutes before you think the eggs are ready. Scrambled eggs should be soft and creamy not hard and lumpy.

The seasoning given here is for one egg. To cook for more than one person, just multiply the ingredients.

You will need:

One egg per person
2 tablespoons milk
A knob of butter
¼ teaspoon salt
Shake of pepper
Saucepan
Small bowl
Fork
Large spoon

Look at the four stages for the recipe. Can you number them in the correct order?

a To get creamy scrambled eggs, be careful at this stage. As soon as the egg in the pan is thick and there is almost no liquid egg left, turn off the stove. Keep stirring to continue the cooking. The heat in the pan will cook the egg to the right consistency.

b Place the pan over the lowest heat possible and put the knob of butter in. Stir the butter around the pan.

c As soon as the butter starts to melt, pour in the egg. Keep stirring the egg in the pan with a spoon to mix the cooked egg with the uncooked part.

d Break the egg into the bowl and add the milk, salt and pepper. Beat the egg gently just to mix in the ingredients.

87a Listen and see if you got the stages in the right order.

L appeared stage thick

b Write a recipe for a simple dish that is popular in your country.

Tell each other about it.

88 *Language study*

Instructions

A recipe is a set of instructions. When giving instructions we often use these verb forms. There are ten forms like the examples on the right in the scrambled eggs recipe. Can you find them all?

Think of a kind of fruit or vegetable.
See if your partner can guess what it is.
Listen to Jenny's summary.
Work in groups.

Aims: 1 To illustrate the use of **would** for a hypothetical situation.
2 To practise hypothesising about a course of action in given circumstances.

Lexis: cook, imagine [L], **imaginative, now** (used to claim the listeners' attention), **rice, shut, supposing, vegetable**
Revision: **because, especially, I'd prefer, I'd rather, probably, someone; something, what if?**

Listening   SB86a [86a]* PB86a, b

1 In groups students look at the pictures, identify the items of food and speculate about who prepared them. To help them, ask questions like 'The cheese flan would probably be quite difficult to cook. Who do you think could have cooked that – one of the men or one of the women?' 'One of them would cook a vegetarian meal. Who do you think that is?' and so on.

2 Give students time to reach a group decision about the men and the women. Go round and check with them. Summarise the groups' guesses on the board. This will give you a chance to use **would** – 'Okay, you think the men would cook the . . .'

3 Students listen to the recording and check their answers.

Bridget – sausages and baked beans
David – rice and vegetables
Danny – omelette
Jenny – cheese flan and baked potatoes

4 Students summarise in their own words what the people on the recording said, e.g. Danny said he'd probably cook an omelette. Put students' responses on the board and focus on the use of **would**. (Explain that the speakers are using **would** because they are talking about a hypothetical situation, something which has not yet happened, but might.)

5 Use the tape and/or the transcripts to do some pattern practice on **would**. Practise forms like:
What would you do?
Would I have to cook them something?
I'd probably cook an omelette.
I'd prefer to take them out.

SB86b

6 In groups students vote on the most popular meal.

Task   SB86c

7 Give students time to think about what they would cook before they go into groups. Students should explain briefly what they would prepare. (Note that writing recipes comes up in section 87.) Encourage them to give reasons for their choice, e.g. because the meal is quick or inexpensive to prepare/is a traditional dish etc.

8 Encourage them to use **would** correctly when they are preparing their reports, and when they read them to the class, e.g. X says he/she **would** cook . . .

Aims: 1 To give exposure to the vocabulary of a number of basic food items.
2 To practise understanding and producing the format of a set of instructions, in this case a recipe.
3 To illustrate the use of the imperative in instructions.
4 To illustrate the use of **to** to show reason or purpose.

Lexis: appear[L], **appearance** [T] [L], **cream, egg, fork, heat, large, mix, mixture** [T], **salt, section, simple, soft, spoon, stage** [L] (at this stage, the first stage, the next stage etc), **thick** [L]
Revision: **just** (multiply), **keep stirring, should be**

Reading and listening   SB87a [87a] PB87

1 Explain the word 'recipe' and phrase 'shake of pepper'. Students read through the recipe and ask for words that they need. Realia to illustrate some of the lexis would be helpful.

2 In pairs students rearrange the jumbled stages. If they are having any difficulty refer them to the accompanying pictures.

3 Students listen to the tape of someone reading the recipe to check their answers.

Key: b d c a

4 Ask them to read the whole recipe and underline instances where **to** is used to show reason or purpose.

Key: To cook for more . . .
To get creamy scrambled . . .
Keep stirring to continue . . .
a spoon to mix . . .
just to mix . . .

5 Words to look up: Students look up the words in their Lexicon and find the appropriate categories for the meanings the words have in the recipe.

Writing   SB87b

6 Review the use of the imperative when giving instructions. It may be worth pointing out that it does not necessarily come first in the sentence or clause, e.g.: If you want a good breakfast, cook up some scrambled eggs.

7 Students could make notes about their recipes individually, then explain them to a partner. The partner must write down the recipe from the other person's oral instructions, not from their written notes. Remind students that the written recipes should be accurate.

*Although this exercise seems to focus on the imperative this is actually a secondary aim. It is primarily a way to get students to focus once again on a number of very common words and forms such as: **be careful; keep stirring; place; just**.*

SB88

Key: The eleven imperatives are:
be careful at this stage
turn off the stove
Keep stirring
Place the pan over the lowest heat possible
put the knob of butter in
Stir the butter around the pan
pour in the egg
Keep stirring the egg
Break the egg into the bowl
add the milk, salt and pepper
Beat the egg gently

89 | Your favourite cheap meal

Aims: 1 To practise stating preferences.
2 To practise itemising and comparing costs.

Lexis: compare, favourite, meat, pound, whereas.
Revision: **about ... or so, actually, asked them how much, asked what ..., I should think, in fact, it depends, more than ..., probably, you could always ...**

SB89a 89a * PB89

1 Students read the introductory paragraph and prepare their answers in pairs. If you want to give students a bit of help you could tell them that the cost of the dishes at home would be about £1.50 and £1 (we do not hear the cost of Danny's pie and mash). The cost of the dishes at a restaurant would be £3.04, £4 and £4. This makes the task much easier since they now simply have to decide which price goes with which dish.

SB89b 89b *

2 Students present their answers, but you should not confirm them. Let them first listen to Jenny's summary and compare their answers. (They will not be able to do this in every case since Jenny does not give the cost of Danny's dish.)

Key:
David – £1 at home, £4 out
Bridget – £1.50 at home, £4 out
Danny – £3.04 (Presumably when he says 'My pie and mash would cost me 76p' he means 76p each, so that times four would be £3.04.)

Task SB89c

This exercise differs from 86c in that, in the former, students were asked to plan for an unexpected guest. In this exercise they are being asked to describe their favourite cheap meal.

3 Individually students work out what meal they would prepare cheaply for 4 and itemise the cost.

4 In groups, students tell others about their meals, and decide which meal would be the best value. Groups report back on the meal they chose, and the whole class votes on the best cheap meal to serve for 4 people.

90 | Language study

Aims: 1 To study intensively **would** used for making a hypothesis.
2 To show that the past tense is used for hypotheses.

PB90a PB90

*Make it clear to the students that the participants are not going to cook these things. The first set of examples exemplifies **would** and also the past tense.*
Supposing they arrived after the restaurants had shut.

SB90

Key: The verbs are in the past tense, but they do not refer to past time. They are in the past tense, because they are part of a hypothetical or conditional statement about the future. Further example: If it rained (tomorrow), I'd be astounded. It's been dry for weeks now.

SB90b

Key: Would is the 'past' form of **will** and is therefore used for hypothesis. (c.f. 90a.)

91 | Microwave ovens

Aims: 1 To practise understanding a semi-technical description and statement of advantages and disadvantages.
2 To practise discussing and expressing advantages and disadvantages.

Lexis: absorb, advantage, by, contact [L], device, fear, heat, issue, largely, mains, model, shut, test [L], wave
Revision: **ideal, include, problem, produce, rather, safety, several**

SB91 PB91

This is a very condensed text which will be difficult in places for the students to understand. Emphasise to students that it is an unsimplified text. Be prepared to give them lots of help and encouragement.

1 Draw students' attention to the picture. Elicit from them as much as possible about microwave ovens (possibly by referring back to 'dogs in the microwave' in Unit 6, section 78).

2 Work intensively through the first paragraph giving students a lot of help. Students will probably bring their own knowledge to bear. One way to handle this would be to build up a labelled diagram on the board as you go through the text.

3 The second paragraph is easier. Help students by asking them to identify 3 advantages. There are 4 identifiable advantages altogether:
ideal for defrosting and reheating,
reduces cooking time,
saves on fuel bills,
keeps vitamins and minerals.
Students work in pairs. Then bring the class together to make a consolidated list.

4 Before reading the third paragraph ask students about the dangers of microwave ovens. (The main danger is of waves escaping and 'cooking' something outside the oven. In the early days of microwave ovens there were stories of people having their kidneys cooked – although these were almost certainly 'vanishing hitch-hiker' stories.) Ask students what could be done to counter this possible danger. Ask them about official organisations which check these things and certify safety standards. They can then check their ideas against the text.

5 Word study

Key: a convert   b vibrate   c penetrate
'Micro' means very small.
A microcomputer is a computer which, by comparison with earlier models, is very small in size.

6 Words to look up: Students find the appropriate categories in their Lexicon.

7 Students in groups list the advantages and disadvantages of microwave ovens. Monitor briskly. Students should be able to express the advantages easily enough, but they might need help with the disadvantages: microwaves can be dangerous, but they are safe enough if you buy an approved model and have it serviced regularly.

8 Students report their lists of advantages and disadvantages, and say whether they think a microwave would be useful for them or not.

9 Students in groups prepare an explanation of the workings of a microwave and present it to the class. Remind them that it might be useful to provide a diagram in support of their explanation.

Your favourite cheap meal

a   Jenny asked the others what they would cook for their favourite cheap meal for four people.
David chose baked potatoes with a filling of cheese and Jenny said she would do scrambled eggs on toast. Danny said he wouldn't cook anything himself. He would go out for some pie and mashed potatoes.
Jenny then asked them how much it would cost to cook these things at home and how much it would cost if they went out to a café or restaurant.

89a   Make notes about how much each meal would cost. Compare your notes with a friend.

▷   Tell the class.   ◁

89b **b**   Listen and see if you were right.

c   What would members of your group cook and how much would their meals cost?

▷   Tell the class. Whose dish would be the best value for money? Take a vote.   ◁

90

Microwave ovens

st Midlands County Council
sumer Services Department
/our Service
mer 1985   Issue 8

ow do they work?

icrowaves work by using a device called a magnetron to convert mains ectricity into microwaves. These are short waves, rather like radio waves. ney bounce off the metal sides of the oven and are absorbed by the food. he microwaves then produce heat by friction and this is caused by the ater molecules in the food vibrating against each other very quickly. everal million microwaves will penetrate the food every second.

What are the advantages?

They are ideal for defrosting and reheating foods quickly. Microwaves can also reduce cooking times for certain foods quite drastically, and the shorter periods of use can result in fuel bill savings. Food cooked in a microwave oven retains more vitamins and minerals which are often lost through cooking in water or destroyed through prolonged cooking.

The safety factor

Early fears about safety have now been largely dispelled. On most modern models, the door has to be firmly shut before the oven will operate, and similarly, once the door is opened the microwaves stop being produced. Any microwave for sale in the UK must comply with Safety Regulations which include stringent tests for electrical safety and microwave leakage.* Ensure your safety by getting microwave ovens serviced regularly, and if you have any problems contact us and we'll try to help.

*Look for the BEAB label and BS 3456 approval.

90

Language study ···········

Would

a   Look at the verbs in colour. What tense are they in? Do they refer to past time?

JV: Are we ready? Yes. Erm, now what would each of you cook if someone dropped in unexpectedly and stayed for a meal in the evening?

JV: What would you cook, David?
DF: Whatever vegetables happened to be there.
JV: Supposing they arrived after the restaurants had shut.
JV: But, er, and if you'd made it at home . . .

Why are they in the past tense?

b   Look at these sentences. What does **would** mean? Why is it **would** not **will**?

We asked Jenny, Bridget, David and Danny what they would cook for an unexpected guest.

JV: What would you do Danny?
DL: Would I have to **cook them something**, because I'd prefer to take them out for a meal.
JV: It says here 'What would each of you cook
DL: Erm . . .
JV: So, to summarise, Bridget would cook **sausage and beans**, Danny would cook **an omelette**, David would cook **something exotic that he'd rustled up from bits in the fridge**, and I would cook **a cheese flan**.

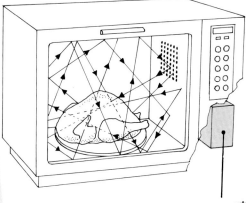

In here is a magnetron: a device which converts or changes mains electricity into microwaves.

> **Word study**
>
> Which of the three words below means:
> a) change into   b) shake very fast
> c) get right inside
>
> penetrate
> vibrate
> convert
>
> Which part of the word **microwave** means 'very small'?
> What is a microcomputer? (It is often simply called a 'micro'.)

contact
fears
largely
test

List the advantages and disadvantages of microwave ovens. How many in your group think that a microwave would be useful for them? If a microwave oven costs about £250, how many of you think it would be worthwhile for you to have one?

92 Wordpower

give   an impression of being angry   good advice on....   something out   directions to someone

Find a person here who could be giving (or be about to give):

a speech
a party
a funny look
a nice smile
a wave
a kiss
a push
a present
something up

93 Eating out

Which story goes with this picture?

93a a Losing weight?

Lunching at a restaurant, I ordered the special low-calorie dish. Then I ordered apple pie. The waitress told me there was none left.
As I got up to go, I saw the same waitress serving apple pie to another table. Seeing my expression, she came over and explained, 'I just couldn't let you eat that pie after you had ordered the slimmer's lunch.'

93b b Pub food

One evening we decided to go out to eat at a small pub, which turned out to be very busy. Noticing a woman reading the menu, I kept an eye on her until she put it down. Rushing over, I muttered, 'May I?' and brought it back to my friends. Triumphantly, I opened the menu to reveal – a photograph album!

> Plan how you would tell this story from the point of view of the woman with the photograph album. In groups, write her story. Read it to the other groups.

> Now write the first story from the waitress's point of view.

93c c Was the fast food fast?
Catherine reads a story.

93d d What was Catherine given for free?

> e Has anything funny ever happened to you in a restaurant, or have you ever got something for nothing? Discuss in groups, then choose the best story to tell the class.

94 Grammar

Purpose

We often use **to** and **for** to express purpose.
*Keep stirring the egg in the pan ... Why? What for?
...to mix the cooked egg with the uncooked part.*

I have eaten the plums which you were probably saving ... Why? What for? ... for breakfast.

Look at these sentences. Which phrases answer the question 'Why?' or 'What for?' Which of these phrases do not have **to** or **for**?

a *We gave Jeremy a set of eight questions to look at.* (29)
b *There are good facilities for other sports and pastimes.* (35)
c *But during the summer I work to make some money.* (52)
d *A woman went to a dentist in Baghdad to have a tooth out.* (45)
e *My husband stopped at his secretary's desk to see if there were any messages for him.* (55)
f *Wake me up for coffee break.* (55)
g *This is just to say I have eaten the plums.* (95)
h *They are ideal for defrosting and reheating foods quickly.* (91)
i *To cook for more than one person just multiply the ingredients.* (87)
j *The door has to be firmly shut before the oven will operate.* (91)
k *Ensure your safety by getting microwave ovens serviced regularly.* (91)
l *You'd better go to bed now or you won't wake up in the morning.*

92 Wordpower

Aims: 1 To draw attention to the double object after **give**:
We gave **Jeremy a set of** ...
I gave **him my driving licence**.
Give **me a sheet of paper**.
2 To illustrate the use of **give** with words like **advice**, **information**, **directions**, **push**, **kiss**, **wave** and to highlight other delexical uses: **give** + opportunity; chance; a look; a smile. (See Collins Cobuild English Language Dictionary for explanations.)

Lexis: speech,wave

SB92 PB92

93 Eating out

Aims: 1 To practise understanding and producing anecdotal narrative.

Lexis: advantage, among, beer [T], **bottle, companion, express** [L], **expression** [T], **large, twice, wine**
Revision: **as** (when); **explained, just, kept an eye on**; **let, noticing, ordered, serving, special**

SB93a/b 93a 93b PB93a

1 In groups students look at the picture and say what they think is happening. Ask them to read and decide which story goes with the picture.

2 Monitor and try to find a group or pair who have obviously grasped what is required and ask them to retell the stories to the rest. Optional: Get the students to act out the stories.

3 Retelling story: Encourage students to imagine how the other woman must have felt. Monitor and correct group. Groups pass their stories round to other groups for comparison and peer correction.
Students could do the second writing task for homework.

Listening SB93c 93c * SB93d 93d * PB93b

4 Explain the phrase 'on the house', then ask students to read the instructions for this task. Students tell the class whether they have ever had any experiences like the two they have just read about. (If there are a lot of volunteers take one or two before the listening and one or two after.)

   Key: a free bottle of wine for changing tables; much larger hamburgers then they had ordered free.

Task SB93e

6 Students think of their stories individually, then go into groups and exchange anecdotes. Groups decide on the best story and tell the class. The class then votes on the best anecdote. Optional: A free drink, coffee etc. for the student with the best anecdote!

94 Grammar

Aims: 1 To illustrate the uses of **to** and **for** to express purpose.
2 To illustrate that the expression of purpose can come at the beginning of the sentence: To cook for more than one person ...
3 To draw attention to less common ways of expressing purpose:
The trick to getting ... is to ...
The door has to be firmly shut before the oven will operate. = To operate the oven shut the door.
Ensure your safety by getting ovens serviced. = To ensure your safety get ovens serviced regularly.

SB94 PB94

1 Ask students to underline the expressions of purpose. Focus on the fact that these can come at the beginning or end of a sentence, e.g. We gave Jeremy a set of questions **to look at**.
   To cook for more than one person just multiply the ingredients.

2 Ask students to paraphrase the expressions of purpose in j–l.

   Key:
   j To operate the oven the door has to be ...
   k To ensure your safety get ...
   l To be sure of waking up in the morning ...

46T

95 A poem

Aims: 1 To give students the satisfaction of enjoying a poem which is unsimplified and unedited.
2 To give them an example of language used evocatively rather than pragmatically.
3 To encourage them to express their own feelings.

Lexis: appealing, cold, image, impact, presented, simple
Revision: **delicious, probably, so**

Reading SB95a 95

1 Students read the poem. Check their understanding by asking them to tell you in their own words what happened in the poem.

2 Students read Caroline and Jenny's comments and then say what they think themselves.

3 Ask students if there are any poets in their own language who write with this kind of simplicity.

Task SB95b

4 In pairs students write a reply to the poem. Students read their finished replies to the class.

96 Preposition spot

Aims: 1 To highlight the uses of **by**: with an agent after the passive, with verbs in **-ing**, stating time and place.
2 To draw attention to the other common phrases with **by**:
by ____self; by the way, get by; by no means; to go by.

SB96 PB96

Key:
1 i, j
2 c, f, g
3 d
4 e
a to get by = to manage
b by no means = not at all
h by myself = alone
k by the way (marking a change of topic)

A poem

THIS IS JUST TO SAY...

I have eaten
the plums
that were in
the icebox

and which
you were probably
saving
for breakfast.

Forgive me
they were delicious
so sweet
and so cold.

William Carlos Williams

We asked two people to say what they thought about this poem. This is what they said.

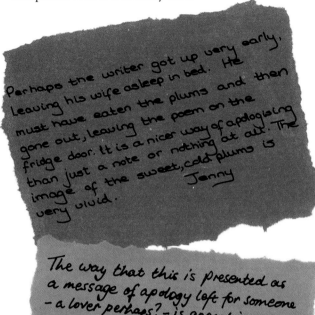

Perhaps the writer got up very early, leaving his wife asleep in bed. He must have eaten the plums and then gone out, leaving the poem on the fridge door. It is a nicer way of apologising than just a note or nothing at all. The image of the sweet, cold plums is very vivid.
Jenny

The way that this is presented as a message of apology left for someone – a lover perhaps? – is appealing. Very simple language, evocative – the plea 'forgive me' has a lot of impact but the excuse doesn't exactly exonerate him!!
Caroline

a What do you think about the writer? Would you forgive him for eating the plums?

b What do you think about the poem itself?

▷ Write a reply to his note. (It does not need to be a poem.) ◁

Preposition spot ....

by

1 showing who or what does something
The microwaves are absorbed by the food. (91)
B & B – in most cases it will be run by the owner. (39)

2 answering the question 'How?'
Microwaves work by using a device called a magnetron... (91)
They only deal with enquiries by letter.

3 answering the question 'When?'

By the time we got downstairs they were already halfway down the street. (178)

4 meaning 'near' or 'next to'
I would probably wait by the car. (150)

Find <u>two</u> examples for category 1, <u>three</u> for category 2 and <u>one</u> example for categories 3 and 4.
Write down the other four phrases with **by**. What do they mean?

a *I can get by in French...* (12)
b *I'm fairly interested in sport, but by no means football.* (20)
c *We went up by car.* (29)
d *She answers the door, looking a bit angry, as it's one in the morning by then.* (78)
e *He sees this girl standing by the roadside hitching.* (78)
f *They produce heat by friction...* (91)
g *Ensure your safety by getting microwave ovens serviced regularly.* (91)
h *I was driving up to London by myself.* (97)
i *There'll be a left turn followed by an immediate right.*
j *I was approached by an American mother...* (144)
k *'By the way,' I said, 'why did you lie to him?'* (161)

The Hitch-hiker

a Roald Dahl is a well known British writer, famous for his short stories, many of which have been dramatised and shown on television. He has written successful children's books as well as two novels.
His books have been translated into many languages and have become best-sellers all over the world.

| 97a |

PART 1

I HAD A NEW CAR

I had a new car. It was an exciting toy, a big B.M.W. 3.3 Li, which means 3.3 litre, long wheelbase, fuel injection. It had a top speed of 129 m.p.h. and terrific acceleration. The body was pale blue. The seats inside were darker blue and they were made of leather, genuine soft leather of the finest quality. The windows were electrically operated and so was the sun-roof. The radio aerial popped up when I switched on the radio, and disappeared when I switched it off. The powerful engine growled and grunted impatiently at slow speeds, but at sixty miles an hour the growling stopped and the motor began to purr with pleasure.

I was driving up to London by myself. It was a lovely June day. They were haymaking in the fields and there were buttercups along both sides of the road. I was whispering along at seventy miles an hour, leaning back comfortably in my seat, with no more than a couple of fingers resting lightly on the wheel to keep her steady.

Ahead of me I saw a man thumbing a lift. I touched the footbrake and brought the car to a stop beside him. I always stopped for hitch-hikers. I knew just how it used to feel to be standing on the side of a country road watching the cars go by. I hated the drivers for pretending they didn't see me, especially the ones in big cars with three empty seats. The large expensive cars seldom stopped. It was always the smaller ones that offered you a lift, or the old rusty ones, or the ones that were already crammed full of children and the driver would say, "I think we can squeeze in one more."

The hitch-hiker poked his head through the open window and said, "Going to London, guv'nor?"

"Yes," I said. "Jump in."

He got in and I drove on.

b Can you remember?

Read the first paragraph of the story very carefully. Try to remember as much as you can about the writer's car. If you want, you can ask your teacher a few questions to help you remember.

Close your books and write down what you can remember.

| 97b | See how much Catherine and Stephen remembered. Did they do as well as you?

c What next?

Have three tries to see if you can guess the next question the driver asked the hitch-hiker.

| 97c | Make a note of the three guesses Catherine and Stephen made.

You will find out in the next Unit who was right.

| 97a | Now listen to the story once more.

Aims: 1 To give students practice in understanding an extended narrative.
2 To give students practice in predicting the development of a narrative.

Lexis: **conversation** [T], **details**, **driver**, **empty**, **engine**, **excited** [T], **exciting**, **field**, **fine**, **fuel**, **genuine**, **genuinely** [T], **imagine** [L], **motor**, **pale**, **pleasure**, **powerful** [L], **terrific**, **touch**, **wheel**
Revision: **back**, **especially**, **inside**, **just**, **offered**, **quality**, **seldom**, **switch**, **top**

This is a new component: from now on there will be instalments of this story in every unit. Explain to students that the story has not been simplified or edited in any way. It is a measure of their progress that they are now able, albeit with difficulty, to read a story written for native speakers of English. Point out that they cannot expect to understand every word of the first reading. The important thing is that they get enough of the gist to enjoy the story.

Reading   SB97a [97a] PB97a,b

1 Students read the introductory paragraph about the author and talk about the title of the story. Ask if they remember the hitch-hiker story in Unit 6, section 78.

2 Students look at Part 1 – I had a new car. How do they think the man will be feeling? Draw students' attention to the top right-hand picture:
What kind of a car is it? Ask them to say as much as they can about the car. Go on to see if anyone understands the abbreviation 3.3 Li.

3 Put the words 'acceleration', 'sun-roof' and 'popped up' on the board and ask students to look out for these when they read. Ask them to see if they can infer the meanings. Demonstrate the words 'growled', 'grunted' and 'purred'.

4 Students read the first paragraph. (Part 1 is split into three smaller sections which should be read one at a time, silently first, then with the tape. Don't let students worry about the new lexis. Get them to guess the meanings if they can. Otherwise explain briefly, and only write the target words up on the board as they crop up.)

5 Draw attention to the middle picture before asking students to read the second paragraph.

6 Students look at the bottom picture. Ask students *before* they read:
Why does the driver stop for the hitch-hiker?
What sort of cars usually stop for hitch-hikers?
What about large expensive cars?
(This gives students a purpose for reading.)

Listening   SB97b [97b]*

7 Students reread the first paragraph. Make a consolidated list of the details they can remember. Leave the list on the board while they listen to Catherine and Stephen.
Students tick off the things that Catherine and Stephen remembered.

SB97c [97c]

8 Students make 3 guesses about the next question the driver asked the hitch-hiker. Ask them to keep these as they will need them in the next unit. Then play the recording of Catherine and Stephen's guesses. Alternatively, play the recording before the students make their guesses and ask them to decide which of Catherine and Stephen's suggestions is the best one.

9 See section 102e for a diagram of a car for students to label.

98 Language study

Aim: To give students practice in identifying the uses of **-ing**.

SB98 PB98

Key: The following **-ing** forms occur in the passage:
an exciting toy – 4
the growling stopped – 6
I was driving – 1
They were haymaking – 1
I was whispering along – 1
leaning back – 5
fingers resting on the wheel – 4
I saw a man thumbing a lift – 2
to be standing – 1
for pretending – 3

99 Phrase-building

Aim: To give students practice in using the verb + **-ing** form to form descriptive phrases.

SB99a

1 To make this more interesting, you might put students into groups and give them a time limit of 3 minutes. At the end of the time limit, find out which group was able to find and write down the most descriptive phrases.

SB99b `99b`

100 Cut the cake

Aims: 1 To give practice with discussion and speculation within the context of problem solving.
2 To give exposure to and practice in discussing alternative courses of action.

Lexis: **across**, **circle**, **cut**, **divide**, **division** [T], **equal**, **knife**, **line** [L], **twice**
Revision: **across**, **I should think**, **right**, **smallest**, **the best way to ...**, **what next?**

SB100a

1 Students discuss the problem in pairs. (They will probably get the answer right away or not at all, so there will probably not be a great deal of discussion.)

Listening SB100b,c   * `100c` *

2 Students listen to Jenny and David's attempt to solve the problem before they give their own answers. (Jenny and David are rather unimaginative. There is no difficulty in completing the task with four cuts.)

3 Ask if any of the students can do better. If so ask them to explain.

Key: There are two ways of making eight equal pieces from three cuts:
1 Make a cut across the middle to divide the cake into two equal pieces.
2 Make a second cut at right-angles to the first so that you have four equal pieces.
3 Place the four equal pieces one on top of the other so that you can divide each one into two separate pieces by cutting downwards through all the four pieces.
or
Danny's solution:
1 and 2 as above.
3 Cut through the cake sideways as if cutting through a bread roll. This will give you eight equal pieces.

Listening SB100d `100d` *

4 Tell students that Danny found a three-cut solution before they listen to the tape. Ask them to listen carefully for the third cut.

5 Word study: Students refer to the Lexicon to confirm their answers. Ask them what other meanings they found for **line** in the Lexicon.

101 Great eaters of the world

Aims: 1 To give students practice in reading for interest.
2 To practise speculation and discussion.

Lexis: **bread, sandwiches**

This section is simply intended to provoke as much talk as possible. You might provoke more discussion by asking students if they know of anyone who has eaten anything very strange – possibly as a child – or of any feats of gluttony.

Key: 14 hard-boiled eggs in 58 sec
38 soft-boiled eggs in 75 sec
13 raw eggs in 1.0 sec

21 hamburgers
22 meat pies
40 jam sandwiches

98 | *Language study* ....

-ing

1 after part of the verb **be**
...which you were probably saving for breakfast. (95)

2 after **see, hear, watch** etc.
I saw the waitress serving apple pie. (93)

3 after **by, of, from** etc.
It is a nicer way of apologising than just a note, or nothing at all. (95)
Microwaves work by using a device called a magnetron. (91)
They are ideal for defrosting and reheating foods quickly. (91)

4 describing someone or something
It must be an interesting job. (189)

5 adding to the main part of the sentence
Perhaps the writer got up very early, leaving his wife asleep in bed. (95)
Noticing a woman reading the menu, I kept an eye on her until she put it down. (93)

6 as a noun
It was a great concert. The singing was very good.

Find words with **-ing** in the story in section 97. Which categories do they belong to?

99 | *Phrase-building* ....

a Look at the picture above. You can see:

a man waiting for a bus/standing in the rain
a woman holding an umbrella

How many phrases like this can you make about the picture?

b Memory game

[99b] Listen to the memory game. Can you remember some of the things they said?

Now you play the game in groups.

100 Cut the cake

a What is the smallest number of straight cuts you have to make with a knife in order to cut this cake into eight equal pieces?

Explain to another pair how you decided to cut the cake. Which pair got the best answer? How did they do it?

[100b] **b** We asked David and Jenny to do this. How many cuts did they make? How do you think they did it?

[100c] **c** Listen and see how they did it.

[100d] **d** Jenny asked Danny to see if he could do any better. How many cuts did he make?

Jenny says 'None of us had that spatial awareness where you thought of cutting it across ways.' How do you think Danny cut it? Can you draw what he drew?

> **Word study**
>
> How many meanings can you think of for the word **line**? Think of three places where you would find lines. Check in the Lexicon.

101 Great eaters of the world

a What do you think Michel Lotito (b.15 June 1950) of Grenoble, France, did with these things?

10 bicycles
a supermarket trolley
7 TV sets
6 chandeliers
a light aircraft

Did he buy them, sell them, cook them, steal them, make them, eat them or break them?

b Another great eater is Peter G. Dowdeswell of Earls Barton, Northamptonshire, who was born in London on 29th July 1940. He doesn't eat TV sets or bicycles but he can eat more food and eat it faster than anyone else in the world.

Which numbers do you think go in the blanks?

Peter Dowdeswell has eaten:

_____ hard-boiled eggs in 58 sec
_____ soft-boiled eggs in 75 sec
_____ raw eggs in 1.0 sec

| 13 | 14 | 38 |

_____ 100g hamburgers in 9 min 42 sec
_____ 156g meat pies in 18 min 13 sec
_____ 15.2 × 9.5 × 1.2cm jam sandwiches in 17 min 53.9 sec

| 40 | 22 | 21 |

49

a who, which, what

1 used to describe something or someone
   ...a foreigner who was coming to your country.
   vitamins which are often lost through cooking...
2 after words like **tell**, **ask** etc.
   See if your partner can guess what it is.
   We asked Jenny, Bridget, David and Danny what they would cook.
3 after **this is, that is**
   This is what they said.

Which category do these belong to?
a *...his short stories, many of which have been dramatised and shown on television.*
b *This is what they said.*
c *We asked Caroline and Jenny to say what they thought about this poem.*
d *Work in groups and find out which of these meals people would like best.*
e *I have eaten the plums which you were probably saving...*
f *Jenny asked the others what they would cook.*
g *...a small pub, which turned out to be very busy.*

b Cause

Heat is caused by the water molecules vibrating against each other.
Shorter periods of cooking can result in fuel bill savings.
Vitamins are often lost through cooking in water.
Once the door is opened the microwaves stop being produced.
Roald Dahl is famous for his short stories.
I always stopped for hitch-hikers. I knew just how it used to feel.
I hated the drivers for pretending they didn't see me.

Find some more expressions of cause.

c probably, perhaps

How do we show we are not quite sure of something?
How many ways can you find?
How much do you think it would cost?
I suppose it's about 50 p.
It would probably cost you four times as much as that.
About 70p I should think.
It seems that for most people their favourite cheap meal is something that is probably going to cost about a pound or so, maybe one pound fifty.
So the driver might ask him where he had come from.
I suppose he could ask him where he was going.
I would imagine that either it will be...

d To do with food

Can you divide these words into four groups?

egg	café	melt	knife	hotel
teaspoon	cook	salt	pie	mix
milk	stove	restaurant	add	pepper
pour	pan	stir	coffee	pub
fork	cheese	potatoes	cream	

e Parts of a car

Which part is which?

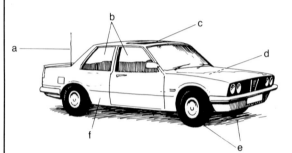

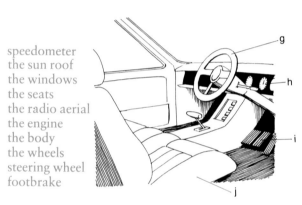

speedometer
the sun roof
the windows
the seats
the radio aerial
the engine
the body
the wheels
steering wheel
footbrake

What were they like? Which of the above can be described by these expressions?

1 *pale blue*
2 *long wheelbase*
3 *powerful*
4 *comfortable*
5 *electrically operated*
6 *top speed of 129 m.p.h.*
7 *made of leather*
8 *darker blue*
9 *of the finest quality*
10 *terrific acceleration*
11 *which popped up...*

Key (101a) He ate them!

Important words to remember (427 so far)

absorb	contact L	equal	heat	pale	stage L
advantage	conversation	excited	image	plate	sugar
among L	cook	exciting	imagine L	pleasure	terrific
appeal	cream	express L	impact	powerful L	test L
appear L	cup	expression	issue	presented	thick L
appearance L	cut	favourite	knife	restaurant	touch
beer	device	fear L	largely	rice	twice
bottle	divide	field	line L	salt	vegetable
bread	division	fork	meat	section	wave
by	driver	fruit	milk	shut	wheel
circle	egg	fuel	mix	simple L	whereas
companion	empty	genuine	mixture	speech	wine
compare	engine	genuinely	model	spoon	

Aims: 1 To review the use of **wh-** words in relative clauses and indirect questions.
2 To review expressions of cause and result.
3 To review expressions of probability.

Lexis: Words associated with food and parts of a car.

SB102a PB102

Key: 1 a, e, g 2 c, d, f 3 b

SB102c

Key: do you think   I suppose ...
about   probably   About ... I
should think   It seems that ...
probably ... about ... maybe might
I suppose X could ...   I would
imagine that ...

SB102d

Key: Group 1: items of food
egg, milk, cheese, salt, potatoes, pie, coffee, cream, pepper
Group 2: utensils, implements for cooking
teaspoon, fork, stove, pan, knife
Group 3: methods of cooking (verbs)
pour, cook, melt, stir, add, mix
Group 4: places to eat
café, restaurant, hotel, pub

SB102e

Key: a – radio aerial 11; b – windows 5; c – sun roof 5; d – engine 3, 6, 10; e – wheels; f – body 1, 2; g – steering wheel; h – speedometer; i – footbrake; j – seats 4, 7, 8, 9.

LEXICAL OBJECTIVES

Level 1 words (see page 129T):
across, cold, details, fine, give (see SB92), **large, mains, now, pound.**

absorb 1 take in. *The microwaves are absorbed by the food.*
2 use up. *Salaries will absorb most of the profits.* T
advantage *It was to the owner's advantage to have us moved from our table.*
advantage *It was to the owner's advantage to have us moved ...*
among L
appeal 1 to ask for. *We appealed for help.* T
2 to attract. *The way this is presented as a message of apology is appealing.*
appear L
appearance L
beer an alcoholic drink T
bottle a container for liquids. ... *a bottle of wine.*
bread ... *a loaf of bread.*
by See SB96.
circle 1 a round shape. *The best way to start would be to draw a circle.*
2 verb: *The Earth circles the sun.* T
companion *My companion and I were having four ounce hamburgers.*
compare *Work out how much it would*

cost to cook that meal ... at home and compare with a restaurant price.
contact L
conversation ... *some conversation between the two of them.* T
cook 1 *I'd probably cook an omelette.* T
2 *Are you a good cook?* T
cream 1 a fatty liquid taken from milk
2 mix together to form a smooth substance. T
Also: **creamy.** ... *eggs should be soft and creamy, not hard and lumpy.*
cup 1 a container for liquids. *John put his cup down on the table.*
2 a prize. *The World Cup* T
cut 1 *You must cut the cake to divide it into eight equal pieces.*
2 to make less. *Our coffee break has been cut to fifteen minutes.* T
device 1 something designed for a particular purpose. *Microwaves work by using a device called a magnetron*
2 *She would use any device ... to make a bit of money.* T
divide 1 *Cut that cake to divide it into eight equal pieces.*
2 *Divide 7 into 35; divide 35 by 7.* T
division 1 *The division of the cake into eight parts ...* T
2 a disagreement. *There is a lot of division among the leaders.* T
driver ... *guess the next question the driver asked the hitch-hiker.*
eggs *scrambled eggs for breakfast*
empty *having nothing in it. ... big cars with three empty seats.*
engine a machine. *The powerful engine growled and grunted impatiently.*
equal 1 the same size or standard. *Cut the cake into eight equal pieces.*
2 have the same rights. *All men are equal.*
3 *Two plus two equals four.*
excited 1 very happy. *I nearly swerved the car into a milk truck I was so excited.* [14]
exciting *I had a new car. It was an exciting toy.*
express L
expression 1 an expression of anger. T
2 *She's always using slang expressions.* T
fear L
field 1 *A field of corn. On the sports field.*
2 ... *an expert in the field of grammar.* T
fork 1 *Small Bowl, Fork, Large Spoon*
2 *When you come to a fork (in the road) turn left.* T
fruit *Think of a fruit, meat or vegetable. ... an apple.*
fuel substance used for heat or power. *Shorter periods of use can result in fuel bill savings.*
genuine real. *They were made of leather, genuine soft leather ...*
genuinely *She was genuinely surprised.* T
heat 1 make hotter. *Heat the eggs ...*
2 *The microwaves then produce heat by friction.*
image 1 something you can see in your mind. *The image of the sweet cold plums is very vivid.*
2 the way one appears to other people. *He gave the image of a true friend.* T
imagine L
impact 1 effect. *The plea 'Forgive me' has a lot of impact.*

2 *His bullet-proof vest absorbed the impact.* T
issue 1 to give. *You will be issued with a photocard which costs 35p.* [6]
2 an edition of a newspaper or magazine. *At Your Service. Summer 1985 Issue 8.*
3 one of the most important issues nowadays is nuclear disarmament. T
knife 1 *What is the smallest number of straight cuts you have to make with a knife? Knife and fork*
largely almost completely. *Early fears about safety have now been largely dispelled.*
line L
meat *fresh meat and vegetables.*
milk 1 ... *a glass of milk.*
2 *I have to milk the cow.* T
mix 1 combine. *Mix the cooked egg with the uncooked part.*
2 ... *mixing business with pleasure.*
mixture 1 a variety. ... *a mixture of languages.* T
2 a combination. ... *a mixture of water and bleach.* T
model 1 a representation. *We always make a model before going on to make the real thing.* T
2 system. *Europe should try to follow the Japanese economic model.* T
3 a particular type. *On most modern models ...*
pale 1 *The body was pale blue.*
2 *You look terribly pale.* T
plate ... *plates of sandwiches.*
pleasure 1 enjoyment. *The motor began to purr with pleasure.* [7]
2 *It's always a pleasure reading his books.* T
powerful L
presented *The way this is presented as a message of apology is appealing ...*
restaurant *What sort of food would you get in each of these restaurants?*
rice a food.
salt ... *salt and pepper*
section part. ... *the teenage section of a newspaper.*
shut 1 *The door has to be shut before the oven will operate.*
2 ... *the restaurants had shut.*
simple L
speech 1 *speech and writing* T
2 a formal talk. ... *give a speech.*
spoon ... *knife, fork and spoon*
stage L
sugar *Have some coffee, and help yourself to sugar.*
terrific 1 wonderful. *Your new house looks terrific.* T
2 great in amount or degree. ... *terrific acceleration.*
test L
thick L
touch *I touched the footbrake and brought the car to a stop.*
twice *I'd go once, twice, three times.*
vegetable *Think of a fruit meat or vegetable. ... a potato*
wave 1 *Peter waved his hand ...*
2 a wave of water, short wave radio, microwave
wheel 1 a circular object, like the steering wheel of a car
2 *He wheeled his bicycle up the hill.* T
whereas while; used to show contrast
wine an alcoholic drink

I wish I were going with you

The unit opens with a general discussion of accidents and mishaps, their causes and consequences, and the procedures associated with them. Next the students read two parallel stories of a fatal mistake during a journey by air. This leads into a discussion of attitudes towards air travel during which students listen to two native speakers before going on to relate incidents which have informed their own attitudes.

They then consider the probable causes of road accidents, discuss the causes of particular accidents and apportion responsibility for them. This is followed by a discussion of preferred courses of action in the event of an accident. Students then piece together the course of an accident from a number of clues. Further work on procedures to be followed after an accident focuses on a semi-official text written by a motor insurance company. This gives students an opportunity to check on the outcome of their earlier discussion.

The focus then shifts to stories of journeys by public transport which went wrong. Here students speculate on what happened and then check their speculation against a recording. They go on to discuss what hypothetical outcomes might have been the result of a different course of action or events. Finally, in this section, they make a comparison of two similar events, identifying similarities and differences. This is followed by an activity in which students talk about how they would react to a given situation before reading about another reaction with a comical twist to it.

OBJECTIVES

Lexical objectives are in TB115

Grammar and discourse

a Present perfect used to talk about previous experience: Have you ever...? (103)
b Adjectives describing attitudes to situations and events (frightened, embarrassed etc). (103)
c Adjectives describing situations and events (frightening, embarrassing etc). (103)
d The meanings and uses of **off**. (105)
e Distinguishing between advisable and mandatory courses of action, e.g. **should** and **must**. (108)
f Offering advice on various possible courses of action, including **should** and **ought**. (109)
g Comparative phrases with **as ... as ...** (111)
h Expressions of time revised and introduced. (113)
i Lexical set: adjectives of size. (115)

Tasks

a Reading an anecdotal narrative. (104)
b Discussing attitudes to an uncomfortable or frightening experience. (104)
c Speculation on a narrative concerning an unpleasant experience. (104)
d Listening to and understanding a story. (104)
e Identifying the cause of accidents and allocating responsibility. (106)
f Identifying and giving advice on the preferred course of action after an accident. (106,108)
g Reading a semi-official document and offering advice on the same topic. (108)
h Comparing the official version of a document with students' own ideas. (106,108)
i Producing and understanding accounts of mishaps involving journeys on public transport. (110)
j Comparing two similar events involving these mishaps and identifying similarities and differences. (110)
k Discussing other possible outcomes of these mishaps. (110)
l Speculating on students' own likely reaction to a given situation. (112)

103 Has it ever happened to you?

Aims: 1 To introduce the themes and lexis for this unit.
2 To practise the present perfect as used to talk about past experiences, as in 'Have you ever ...?'
3 To practise adjectives describing attitudes to situations and events.
4 To practise adjectives describing unfortunate situations and events.

Lexis: accident, annoyed, annoying, frightened, frightening, instead, involved (in) [L], **should**
Revision: **at work, cause, realise**

SB103a PB103a,b

1 Begin by discussing the 6 pictures. The students identify what has happened and, if relevant, what is going to happen.

2 In pairs students talk together about which of these things have happened to them. Monitor closely, helping where necessary, and find students who will have useful contributions to make to the general class discussion.

3 Ask students to talk about their experiences. Be prepared to rephrase and clarify. You may also have a story of your own to contribute.

SB103b

4 Do this briefly, as these questions form the basis of the activities in section 108. Introduce necessary lexis.

SB103c

5 Treat this as a class discussion, using the opportunity to introduce ideas and lexis which will be needed later in the unit.

SB103d

6 In pairs students work on the story. If they are having trouble refer them to the picture of a petrol tanker. Either pairs or the teacher reads out the endings to the stories. Class votes on the best ending.

SB103e,f

7 Encourage students to ask you if they are not sure of the meanings of these words. Write up the words on the board in two groups:
frightened   frightening
embarrassed   embarrassing
etc. to make the point that experiences are described by **-ing** adjectives, and the way we feel by **-ed** adjectives.

I wish I were going with you

Has it ever happened to you?

Has your bus or car ever broken down?

Have you ever missed the last bus home and had to walk instead?

a   Have you ever done any of these things?
Has any of these things ever happened to you?

b   What should you do if you are driving and you have an accident? What information and documents should you exchange with the other driver? Who should you notify?

c   What are the most common causes of accidents in your country?

d   Can you complete this story?

The driver of one of my firm's petrol tankers called in on his two-way radio one day: 'I'm stuck on the bypass.' 'What's the trouble, mate?' enquired the radio operator.

e   What words might you use to describe an accident?

pleasant	lucky
frightening	unpleasant
embarrassing	horrible
exciting	awful
annoying	interesting
terrible	nasty

f   How might you feel when you are involved in an accident?

frightened	sorry
pleased	terrible
embarrassed	unhappy
excited	angry
worried	interested
annoyed	awful

Have you ever gone to sleep on a bus or train and gone beyond your stop or station?

Have you ever got on the wrong bus or train by accident and not realised until it's too late?

Have you ever run out of petrol?

Have you ever been involved in or witnessed an accident?

51

104 A frightening flight

a Which of the following can you find in the picture? the pilot/captain, the crew, the controls, the cabin, the cockpit/flight deck, the passengers, the security door, the aisle.

b Have you ever heard a story like this before?

THE AUTO-PILOT
The flight ran several times a week taking holiday-makers to various resorts in the Mediterranean. On each flight, to reassure the passengers all was well, the captain would put the jet on to auto-pilot and he and all the crew would come aft into the cabin to greet the passengers.

Unfortunately, on this particular flight the security door between the cabin and the flight deck jammed and left the captain and crew stuck in the cabin. From that moment, in spite of the efforts to open the door, the fate of the passengers and crew was sealed.

Here is another story on the same subject. Can you think of words that would fill the gaps?

JUMBO JET PILOT
A show-off Jumbo Jet _____ put the controls on _____ in mid-flight and took his entire _____ for a stroll back down the aisle to meet the _____. He then discovered the cockpit door had _____ itself and he had _____ the key.

104b Listen to the two stories and see if you chose the same words for the second one.

Do you think these stories are true?

Word study
Match the words or phrases on the left with the words/phrases with similar meaning on the right.

their *fate was sealed*	lost
mislaid the keys	jammed shut
then *discovered*	whole
locked itself	nothing could be done
his *entire* crew	attempts, trying
his *efforts* to open	found

▷ **c** Discuss in groups any frightening flight you have had or have heard about or seen on TV. Choose one story to tell the class.

104d **d** How do Stephen and Catherine feel about flying? What does Catherine's husband think are the most dangerous parts of a flight?

e Make a story with these words. Tell each other.

friend	air hostess	missed her connection
bad experience	frightened	back to Heathrow
home to Texas	pilot	engines on fire
noticed	window	pointed this out

104e See if your story is the same as Stephen's. (His girlfriend lives in Texas.)

L controls	experience
various	suddenly
business	noticed

105 *Preposition spot*

off

1 something or someone is removed from somewhere or leaves somewhere
You can hop on and off a bus or train. (82)
Do you want to take your coat off?

2 at a distance from, or quite near to
Her house is just off Western Avenue.

3 not doing a particular activity; a person or machine not working; no longer available etc.
The football match was called off.
...when I switched off the radio...
Tuesday is my day off...

Which categories do these examples belong to?

a *There's this road off to the right.* (131)
b *Turn off the heat.* (87)
c *I'm not afraid of landing and taking off.*
d *I fell off my bicycle.* (18)
e *Off they go.*

Find the sentences which have phrases similar in meaning to the phrases in the box below.

f *I tried to phone again, but we were cut off.*
g *Oh dear – the button's come off.*
h *Sportsday was put off until the following weekend.*
i *The party finally went off very well.*
j *Except that Alice went off with Janet's boyfriend.*
k *I used to like pop music but I've gone off it now.*
l *Phew – I'm afraid this milk has gone off.*
m *He's fairly well off now in his new job.*

fallen off	was successful
not held	gone bad
the line went dead	don't like any more
made friends with	has enough money

A frightening flight

Aims: 1 To discuss attitudes to an uncomfortable or frightening experience.
2 To practise reading with comprehension anecdotal narrative.

Lexis: business, captain, connect [T], **connection, control** [L], **discovered, effort, entire, fate, flight, flying, frightening, notice** [L], **passenger, pointed** (out), **several, stick/stuck, sudden, suddenly, various** [L]
Revision: **a little, a little bit, maybe, mixture, really**

SB104a

1 In pairs students identify the people and parts of the aircraft in the picture. Make sure they understand the lexis before going on to the story.

Reading and listening SB104b 104b PB104a

2 Students read the first story. Check they have understood it by asking them to retell it briefly in their own words. Ask them if they have heard any similar stories. Students complete the second story, then listen to the recording of the stories to compare their suggestions.

Key: pilot, automatic, crew, passengers, locked, forgotten
Other words may be possible.

3 Word study

Key: 1 nothing could be done   2 lost   3 found
4 jammed shut   5 whole   6 attempts, trying

Task SB104c

5 In groups, students find out if anyone has a good, true story to tell. If not, they should tell one from a film or television programme. Help students while they decide on their story.

6 Allow one or two students to tell their stories to the class. Ask the class to decide if they think the stories are true or not.

Listening SB104d 104d * PB104b

7 Students listen to Catherine and Stephen and take brief notes to answer the questions.

Key: Stephen enjoys flying. Catherine finds flying quite boring, apart from taking off and landing, but her husband tells her these are the most dangerous aspects of flying.

Task and listening SB104e 104e *

8 Individually students make up a story with the words, then work in pairs, telling a partner. Have one or two students tell their stories to the class.

9 Students listen to Stephen's story and compare it with their own.

Preposition spot

Aim: To illustrate some of the meanings and uses of **off**.
Lexis: off

SB105 PB105

1 Students do these activities in pairs.

Key: 1 c, d, e   2 a   3 b

f   the line went dead
g   fallen off
h   not held
i   was successful
j   made friends with
k   don't like any more
l   gone bad
m   has enough money

'I simply didn't look'

Aims: 1 To practise speculating on the cause of events and allocating responsibility.
2 To practise identifying and giving advice on a preferred course of action.
3 To revise the meaning and use of the present perfect in 'Have you ever . . .'
4 To practise identifying the cause of accidents and allocating responsibility.
5 To practise distinguishing between advisable and mandatory courses of action, e.g. **should** and **must**.

Lexis: blame, fault, involved, laugh, laughter [T], **simply**
You may also wish to set up a lexical set to do with accidents: **avoid, bump, crash, hit, miss, skid, swerve**
Revision: **around about, completely, imagine, not even, once, take place**

Task   SB106a PB106

1 Students describe what has happened in each of the pictures, and who they think was to blame. (It may be worth allocating pictures to groups before the presentation stage so that they do not have to prepare all three in detail.)

2 If students need help with lexis, interrupt them and bring the class together to help – it is probably better to do this than to try to provide all the lexis at the beginning.

3 Group spokesmen present their findings. Provide linguistic help where necessary. Make a note of the advice they would give in each case so it can be compared with the advice in section 103.

SB106b

4 This is necessary preparation for the reading task in section 108. Explain all the words students need to know. In groups students look at the 10 sentences and say whether they agree or disagree with each one. After students have worked out their answers lead a class discussion in order to get a consensus. Make a note of that consensus so it can be compared with the advice given in section 108. There's no need to give students the answers to these yet, but do focus their attention on the uses of **should** and **must** if it is appropriate to do so during the discussion, e.g. for point 6, it may not be possible to move the car to the side of the road, so **must** should be changed to **should**.

SB106c [106c]

The sound effects are to stimulate students to talk and speculate on what was happening in order to prepare them for hearing Jenny's account.

5 Play the tape straight through and ask for initial impressions.

6 Play the tape again with pauses for students to discuss in pairs and ask for lexis.
The sounds in sequence are:
car door being unlocked, door closing again, engine starting, reverse gear going in, accelerating up drive, then a crunch – two cars hitting – a female voice – saying OH NO! etc. Engine cuts out. Handbrake on, car door opening, closing; pause – as damage is being inspected.

7 In pairs or groups students work out what happened in the sound sequence. Make sure students include details such as: when/where it took place and the cause . . . (if they can get that far) and help with lexis. Students may or may not guess Jenny's story – this is not the main point of the task. *Any* story they make from these sounds is acceptable at this stage, so encourage all versions equally.

8 Students listen to each other and compare stories. Encourage them to look at the pictures and see if they relate to Jenny's story. (The motorbike fairly obviously does not fit. The second picture is a possibility but does not account for the knocking, voices, etc.) Don't be tempted to comment especially on which ones are more like Jenny's. Keep the suspense going.

Listening   SB106d [106d]*

9 Students listen to the recording and compare what actually happened with their own versions. Ask them to look back at pictures earlier in the unit to see if they can find out which shows what happened to Jenny. If necessary refer them back to the yellow picture in the top left hand corner.

Wordpower

Aims: 1 To illustrate the forms and uses of words with **lead**; leader, leading; leadership.
2 To focus on suffixes: **-er**; **-ing**; **-ship**.

Lexis: lead [L], **leaders, leadership, leading**

SB107 PB107

1 See if students can paraphrase or tell you in their own words what **lead** means in the examples before referring them to their Lexicon.

Key: a 10   b 3   c 5   d 7   e 5   f 8   g 9
Manchester's leading . . . 5; . . . your leader 7; . . . the wrong lead . . . 4; . . . a leading insurance company 6; I'll lead the way. 2.

2 Optional: Elicit: other third-person words like **leader**, e.g. driver, manager, reader, runner, teacher, writer.
nouns like **leadership** e.g. friendship, (in cases of) hardship, relationship (avoid less frequent words like 'citizenship').
adjectives like **leading** e.g. boring, exciting.
and nouns, e.g. teaching, writing.

'I simply didn't look'

a Have you ever been involved in an accident like one of these? Who do you think was to blame in each of these?

b Look at these sentences about what you might do in the event of an accident. Say whether you agree or disagree with each one.

You will find out later what advice a leading insurance company gives.

1 You should get the other driver's name and address.
2 You must get the name and address of an independent witness.
3 You should make a note of the make and number of the other vehicle.
4 If you are to blame you should say so.
5 You should not discuss who is to blame.
6 You must move your car to the side of the road so as not to interrupt the traffic.
7 You must report the accident to the police within 24 hours.
8 You do not have to make a report to the police but it is a good idea to do so.

9 You must report the accident to your insurance company as soon as you can.
10 If you are responsible for the accident you must fill in an Accident Report Form.

106c c Jenny once had a really silly accident. Listen. What happened?

106d d Listen to Jenny's account of it. What did Bridget say? Whose fault was it? How did she hit the other car? Which of you guessed what happened to her?

---

107 ## Wordpower

lead

What do the words with **lead** mean in these examples?

(a) What an interesting life you lead!
(b) There's a narrow path leading up the mountains.
(c) We set off with George in the lead.
(d) The country did well under the leadership of the new president.
(e) At the begining of the race he led by over ten metres.
(f) He has played the leading role in many Shakespearean productions.
(g) The incident almost led to war....

Now check in the Lexicon and say which category number goes with each example of **lead/led** etc.

108 After an accident

What should you do in your country after an accident? Must you tell the police? Should you take the other person's insurance certificate? What information should you obtain? Now read what an insurance company advises. Is it the same procedure in your country?

G **R** **E** **Guardian Royal Exchange**

Member of the Insurance Ombudsman Bureau

MOTOR VEHICLE CLAIM FORM

This claim form should be RETURNED DIRECT to your GRE Claims Bureau or Local Office.

Policy (or Certificate) No. ....

G.R.E. Office or Agent to whom you paid your last premium ....

A INSURED

Name.............................

Address (Private).....................

....

Address (Business) ....

Trade or Occupation (if more than

Is the Insured registered (or liabl

B DRIVER

Name...........................

Address ....

ADVICE ON ACTION TO BE TAKEN AFTER A MOTOR ACCIDENT

It is suggested that these notes be kept with your insurance certificate.

AT THE SCENE OF THE ACCIDENT

Keep calm. Do not discuss who was to blame. If there is no injury, move your car to the side of the road so as not to disrupt traffic flow.

A. Obtain the following information:
1. Name and address of the other driver.
2. Name and address of other driver's Insurers.
3. Insurance Certificate Number.
4. Name and address of independent witness.
5. Make, owner and registration number of other vehicle.
6. Sketch a diagram of the accident (including measurements, directions, etc.).
7. Weather and road conditions at the time.

B. Note the date and time of the accident.

C. Provide your own particulars to anyone who has reasonable grounds for wanting them.

AFTER THE ACCIDENT

You should report to:

1. The police as soon as possible but not later than 24 hours after the accident if there is personal injury or damage to government property. If there is no injury a police report is optional by either party, but remember that the party making an official statement is in a better position than one who does not.

2. Your insurers as soon as possible even if you do not intend to make a claim — this is a condition of your policy.

(a) Report any statement made at the scene of the accident by any one of the parties.
(b) You will be required to complete an Accident Report Form, obtainable from your Insurers upon request.

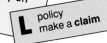

L policy
make a **claim**

Word study

Match the words that are similar in meaning. Which is the odd one out?

action	any reason
be to blame	what to do
disrupt traffic flow	in a better position
obtain	party
grounds	be in the wrong
better off	get hold of
person	must
will be required to	if you ask
upon request	tell the police
make a statement	officially what happened

---

109 *Language study* ....

should

1.1 used to say what it would be right to do or to have done
What should you do after an accident? (108)
Scrambled eggs should be soft and creamy. (87)
If she was working 8½ hours a day they should have paid her more than £1.20 an hour.

1.2 often used in this way to give advice
After an accident you should report to the police.
You should have reported the accident.

2.1 used to show that something is likely to happen
In early July the weather should be fairly nice. (69)

2.2 or something that was expected to happen
Bridget should have arrived at her station at about 19.50. (110)

3 often used with **think**
About 70p, I should think, for four people. (89)

ought

Ought has the same meanings, apart from 3. The difference is that **ought** is followed by **to**.

Which categories do these sentences belong to?

a *Anyone who works 8½ hours a day should receive more than just £1.20 an hour.* (42)
b *I would work out what I should have said to the teacher.* (58)
c *Jenny should have looked where she was going.*
d *We should be there by seven fifteen, I should think.*
e *Are we on the right road? We ought to have another look at the map.*
f *You shouldn't drive so fast! You'll have an accident one day.*
g *You say Jim's only 25? I should have thought he was older than that.*

Aims: 1 To practise reading a semi-official document offering advice on a preferred or necessary course of action.
2 To practise comparing an official version of a document with students' own ideas. (See section 106.)
3 To practise distinguishing between advisable and mandatory courses of action, e.g. **should** and **must**.

Lexis: action, conditions, flow, grounds, independent, insurance, measure(ment), party, policy [L], **required, state** [T], **statement, traffic, witness**
Revision: **directions, injury, intend, owner, particular, personal, reasonable, report, scene**

SB108 PB108

1 Discuss the students' answers to section 106a in the light of the advice given in the document.

The document is difficult and requires a very detailed reading. Be ready to help, either by monitoring quickly or by bringing the class together.

2 Discuss the students' answers to the questions. In the light of the leaflet shown here it is suggested that the answers to section 106a should be as follows:
1 True.
2 This is a good idea, especially if you feel you are in the right, but it cannot be a 'must'. There may not be an independent witness, or they might be unwilling to give their name and address. If you are in the wrong you may not want to involve an independent witness.
3 True.
4 No. The leaflet says 'Do not discuss who was to blame.' If you say anything about this it may be quoted later by someone else and taken as evidence that you were in the wrong. Note that the leaflet here is issued by an insurance company. Obviously the company will want to prevent its clients from doing anything which might lead to a case being found against them.
5 True
6 No. If there has been no injury then you *should* push your car to the side of the road, but you are not obliged to. If there has been some injury to one of the parties you must not move your car:–
If there is no injury move your car to the side of the road. Make it clear to the students that there is a difference between what you *should* or *should not* do and what you *must* and *must not* do.
7 You *should* make a report to the police, but it is not *necessary* unless there has been some personal injury.
8 True.
9 True.
10 True. You can get this form from your insurers on request.

3 In groups students make notes about what they should do in their own country after an accident.

4 Students prepare their reports. Provide assistance as needed. Put the headings **must do** and **should do** on the board and when groups deliver their reports put their advice on the board under the appropriate column.

5 Words to look up: Students look up the appropriate categories for this context in the Lexicon.

6 Word study:

Key: action – what to do
be to blame – be in the wrong
disrupt the traffic flow – *odd one out*
obtain – get hold of
grounds – any reason
better off – in a better position
person – party
will be required to – must
upon request – if you ask
make a statement – tell the police officially what happened

Aim: To illustrate some of the meanings and uses of **should** and **ought**.

Lexis: **ought, should**

SB109 PB109

1 Students do this activity in pairs. Review answers and emphasise to students that **should** is much more common than **ought**. If they ask you which they should use, say 'When in doubt use **should**.'

Key: a 1.1   b 1.1   c 1.2   d 2.1/3   e 1.1   f 1.2   g 3

110 Unfortunate journeys

Aims: 1 To produce and understand accounts of mishaps involving journeys on public transport.
2 To compare two similar events and identify similarities and differences.
3 To discuss alternative outcomes.
4 To practise reading and understanding timetables.

Lexis: **catch**, **caught**, **serve**, **setting**, **similar**, **supposed** [L], **tired**
Revision: **describe**, **fall asleep**, **go wrong**, **set out**

Reading and listening   SB110a [110a]* PB110

1 In groups students look at the timetable and work out how long it should take to get from Charing Cross to Wadhurst and from Wadhurst to Hastings. Tell students who might not know that Charing Cross is a large train station in London.

Key: It depends which train you get. A fast train (e.g. the 17.58 from Charing Cross) takes 56 minutes to get to Wadhurst, and then 30 minutes to get to Hastings. A slower train (e.g. the 18.45) takes 56 minutes to Wadhurst, and then 44 minutes to Hastings.

2 Students listen to the tape to find out what went wrong.

Key: She fell asleep and went all the way to Hastings, then had to come back.

SB110b

3 In groups students use the timetable to answer the questions.

Key: 19.50. Bridget probably got the 20.00. from Hastings and got to Wadhurst at 20.36. This would mean that she was nearly an hour and a half late.
If her train had been ten minutes late, she would probably have missed the 20.00. She would then have caught the 21.02 and got back to Wadhurst at 21.36, nearly two and a half hours late on a one hour journey.

4 One or two students should explain what they have decided.

Listening   SB110c [110c]*

5 Students listen to tape of Bridget and Danny.

Key: Danny advised Bridget '. . . it's always better to catch a taxi, 'cause he'll wake you up when you get home.'

Listening   SB110d [110d]*

6 Students listen to Jenny's story for similarities and three differences. Ask students for their conclusions and make a consolidated list.

Key: Jenny's story is basically very similar in that it involves someone falling asleep and going past their stop. It is different because:
the journey was on a bus.
it was after an office party, and therefore probably later than Bridget's journey after work.
the bus went right to the end of its journey and then right back again before Jenny's friend was woken up.
Bridget woke up herself. Jenny's friend had to be woken up.

7 Words to look up: Students use their Lexicons to look up the appropriate categories for this context.

SB110e

8 When students have asked each other their questions they can then ask you, the teacher, to see how much you can remember.

111 Phrase-building

Aim: To practise comparative phrases with **as . . . as . . .**

SB111 PB111

1 Students should make some sentences from the substitution table. Practise accurate stress of '*nearly* as *hard* as . . .' as necessary. Students should make up similar but true sentences about themselves.

2 Point out that the **as . . . as . . .** expression can be followed by:
1 a name or a noun phrase (*John, your father*)
2 1 + an auxiliary verb (*your father did*)
3 2 + an adverbial (*your father did yesterday/when he was younger*)
4 the word **possible** (very common)
Also the **as . . . as . . .** expression can be preceded by words like **almost**, **nearly**, **twice**, **three times** or by **not**, **not quite**, **not nearly**, e.g. 'Doesn't work nearly as hard as . . .'

3 Students do the exercises in pairs.

Key: a 4   b 5   c 2   d 7   e 1   f 6   g 3

110 Unfortunate journeys

a Bridget's family live in the village of Wadhurst in Sussex. Look at the timetable.
How long does it take by train from Charing Cross to Wadhurst? How long does it take to Hastings?

110a Listen to Bridget's story. What went wrong?

b Bridget got the 18.01 from London, Charing Cross, so she should have arrived at Wadhurst at about 19.15. Work together from the timetable to find out:

what time she got to Hastings
what train she caught back to Wadhurst
what time she got back to Wadhurst
how late she was

CHARING CROSS	dep	**17 58**		18 01h	18 45	19 45	20 45	21 45
Waterloo East	dep	**18 01**		18 04h	18 48	19 48	20 48	21 48
CANNON STREET	dep	**17 44t**		18 20	——	——	——	——
London Bridge	dep	**17 48t**		18 08h	18 28t	19 22t	20 22t	——
Sevenoaks	dep	**18 16t**		18 36h	19 15	20 15	21 15	22 17
Tonbridge	dep	**18 35**		18 46h	19 24	20 24	21 25	22 27
High Brooms	dep	**18 41**		19 00	19 30	20 30	21 31	22 33
TUNBRIDGE WELLS	dep	**18 47**	18 52	19 05	19 35	20 34	21 35	22 37
Frant	dep	——	18 56	19 09	19 39	20 38	21 39	22 41
Wadhurst	dep	**18 54**	19 00	19 13	19 43	20 42	21 43	22 45
Stonegate	dep	——	19 06	19 20	19 49	20 48	21 49	22 51
Etchingham	dep	**19 03**	19 11	19 25	19 54	20 53	21 54	22 56
Robertsbridge	dep	——	19 17	19 28	19 57	20 56	21 57	22 59
Battle	dep	**19 12**	19 25	19 36	20 05	21 04	22 05	23 07
Crowhurst	dep	——	19 28	19 40	20 09	21 08	22 09	23 11
West St.Leonards	dep	——	19 33	19 45	20 17	21 13	22 14	23 16
St.Leonards (W.Sq)	dep	**19 21**	19 36	19 48	20 20	21 16	22 17	23 19
HASTINGS	arr	**19 24**	19 38	19 50	20 22	21 18	22 19	23 21

HASTINGS	dep	**16 36**	16 53	17 49	18 57	20 00	21 02	22 02	
St.Leonards (W.Sq)	dep	**16 38**	16 55	17 51	18 59	20 02	21 04	22 04	
West St.Leonards	dep	——	16 58	17 54	19 02	20 05	21 07	22 07	
Crowhurst	dep	——	17 04	18 00	19 08	20 11	——	22 13	
Battle	dep	**16 48**	17 08	18 04	19 12	20 15	21 15	22 17	
Robertsbridge	dep	——	17 15	18 11	19 19	20 22	21 22	22 24	
Etchingham	dep	——	17 19	18 15	19 23	20 26	21 26	22 28	
Stonegate	dep	——	17 24	18 20	19 28	——	——	22 33	
Wadhurst	dep	**17 05**	17 31	18 29	19 35	20 36	21 36	22 40	
Frant	dep	——	17 35	18 33	19 39	——	——	22 44	
TUNBRIDGE WELLS	arr	**17 12**	17 39	18 37	19 43	20 43	21 43	22 48	
High Brooms	arr	**17 16**	17 43	18 41	19 47	20 47	21 47	22 52	
Tonbridge	arr	**17 21**	17 48	18 46	19 52	20 52	21 52	22 57	
Sevenoaks	arr	**17 31**	18 00	18 59	20 03	21 03	22 03	23 14t	
London Bridge	arr	**18 04s**	18 40t	19 40t	20 43t	21 42t	22 40t	23 43t	
CANNON STREET	arr	**18 09**	——	——	——	——	——	——	
Waterloo East	arr	**18 09s**	18 28	19 29	20 29	21 29	22 29	23 50t	
CHARING CROSS	arr	**18 12s**	18 32	19 32	20 32	21 32	22 32	23 52t	

What if her train had arrived in Hastings ten minutes late? She would have missed the _____.
She would have got the _____ and arrived back at _____.
Then she would have been _____ late.

▷ Tell the class what you have worked out. ◁

c Bridget also told Danny about her journey.

110c What advice did Danny give?

110d **d** Listen to Jenny's story. In what way was it similar to Bridget's story?

▷ Write down three differences between the two stories. ◁

Bridget fell asleep on a train, but Jenny's friend

L experience you can **imagine** Where are you **supposed** to be going?

e Buses

Red Buses serve Central London and are a great way to see the city, you are, however, advised to get a bus map (free from bus and tube stations) before setting out. Fares are similar to tube fares.
Greenline buses run from Central London – usually from Victoria Coach Station or Regent Street – to most towns within 20 miles of London's borders, including Oxford, Cambridge, Windsor and Canterbury. Details on 222 1234.

Write down three questions that people might ask about travelling on these buses. (You should choose questions that can be answered from the information given here.)
Close your books and ask each other questions. How many can you answer?

111 Phrase-building

Look at these phrases with **as ... as ...**

John works	*almost*	*as hard as his father.*
	nearly	*as hard as his father did.*
	almost twice	*as hard as his father did when he was a young man.*

Can you match and complete these sentences?

a *I have lived in London for*
b *We asked him to find out*
c *I won the next year but*
d *Fill in*
e *The taxi costs*
f *You can hop on and off a bus*
g *You should report to the police*

1 *five times as much as the bus.*
2 *not as much as I'd won the first year.*
3 *as soon as possible.*
4 *almost as long as I can remember.*
5 *as much as possible about Jenny's holiday.*
6 *as many times as you like with a Travelcard.*
7 *as many boxes as you can.*

Make up some more examples yourself.

55

112 No claim

a Imagine that you were driving into a car park when you bumped into a parked car and scratched it all down one side. You could not find the driver of the other car to tell him what had happened. What would you do:
if there were no witnesses?
if there were a number of witnesses?

▷ Tell the class. ◁

112b **b** Now read on and find out what one driver did when this actually happened.

> Returning to the car he had left in a nearby car park, a friend of a cousin of mine was rather perturbed to find one side of the vehicle all scratched and dinted. Seeing a note on the windscreen, he breathed a sigh of relief, for he thought that the culprit had left his name and address so, at least, he could make a claim for the damage against the other driver's insurance company. However, on opening the note, his relief turned to dismay when he read:

Dear Driver,

I have just run into your car and made a hell of a mess of it. As a crowd has gathered, I am forced to appear as if writing you this note to apologise and to leave you my name and address. As you can see, however, this I have not done.

A Well Wisher

113 *Grammar*

Time

Expressions of time answer questions like 'When?', 'How long?' or 'How often?' These questions can be answered by:

1.1 a clause
I left when I was eighteen. (2)
I was born and lived until I was seven in Dublin. (2)
I spent two years in Rome while I was still living with my family. (17)
As soon as the butter starts to melt, *pour in the egg.* (87)
I just couldn't let you eat that pie after you had ordered the slimmers' lunch. (93)

1.2 with -ing
Before having the children *she worked in insurance.* (2)
I've lived in England since leaving America. (17)
Lunching at a restaurant *I ordered the special low-calorie dish.* (93)
Seeing my expression *she came over and explained.* (93)

2 a phrase
Mummy and Daddy went back to Ireland some time ago. (2)
She was born and lived for the first seven years of her life in Ireland. (2)
And it wasn't diagnosed until the next day. (18)
I've never broken any bones so far. (18)
I hope to see more of the world in the next ten years. (20)
This summer *I am working for my father's publishing company.* (52)

3 a word
I haven't been back since. (2)
But it's still *home.* (2)
I've never *broken any bones.* (18)
Once *we'd been collecting firewood for a bonfire.* (18)
Have you ever been to Northumberland before? (29)

Look at these sentences. Read out the time expressions. (You should find sixteen.)

a *I was brought over here when I was seven.* (2)
b *She may have sneaked out while he wasn't looking or when his attention was distracted.* (78) (two expressions)
c *Noticing a woman looking at the menu I kept an eye on her until she put it down.* (93) (two expressions)
d *Supposing they arrived after the restaurants had shut?* (86)
e *Before having children I had a varied career.* (20)
f *I have lived in London for almost as long as I can remember.* (20)
g *Seeing a note on the windscreen, he breathed a sigh of relief.* (112)
h *He sold more during the interval than anyone had ever done before.* (55) (two expressions)
i *Upon returning to his office my husband stopped at his secretary's desk.* (55)
j *I actually did that last year.*
k *Report to the police as soon as possible.* (108)
l *On opening the note his relief turned to dismay.* (45)
m *Finally he called a plumber.* (45)

No claim

Grammar

Aim: To speculate on one's likely reaction to a given situation.

Lexis: against, apologise, apology, appear, appearance [T], **claim** [L], **force, gather, hell, mess**

Aim: To illustrate ways of expressing time.

Task SB112a

1 In pairs students speculate on a decision. Give them a few minutes to reach a decision then begin to go round and monitor.

Report

2 Listen to individual students and make a consolidated list. Possible courses of action:
drive off as quickly as you can,
leave a note for the driver with your address and telephone number,
make a report to the local police station including the number of the other car,
leave a message with the carpark attendant.
Make sure that you discuss possibilities both with and without witnesses. Before going on to the reading try to get a class consensus.

Reading SB112b 112b

3 Students give their reactions to the note.

SB113 PB113

1 Ask students to identify words introducing time expressions:
when, while, after, since, before, for, upon, as soon as, on, once, finally.
You may also ask students to identify expressions which do not have an introductory word: Words in **-ing** (noticing, lunching etc.) this summer, one day, twice a week, last year, tomorrow.

Key: a when I was seven
b while . . ., when . . .
c noticing . . ., until . . .
d after . . .
e Before having children
f for almost as long as I can remember
g seeing a note
h during the interval . . . had ever done before
i upon returning
j last year
k as soon as possible
l on opening
m finally

> **Aim:** To give students further practice in understanding an extended narrative.
>
> **Lexis: business, course, enormous, fool, fun, huge, human, machine, pocket, pointed, race, silly, slightly, stare/staring, through, wish** [L]

SB114a [114a] PB114

1 Students look at the pictures in pairs. Encourage them to ask you questions while they are looking at the pictures. Obviously you do not want to give them the answer, but they may have trouble with some lexis such as **hat**, **cap**, **enormous**, and ask for your help with these.

2 Ask students to give their answers with reasons.

   Key: The hitch-hiker is shown in the top left picture. The others are unacceptable because:
   Bottom left has no pockets;
   top right has a brown coat;
   bottom right hasn't got a cloth cap.

3 Students read the extract and then refer to the 3 questions they wrote in the last unit and check if they were right.

SB114b/c [114c]*

4 In groups students write down as much as they can remember about the hitch-hiker. Books closed. Consolidate students' suggestions before playing the tape of Catherine and Stephen.

   Key: Stephen and Catherine remembered: ratty-faced; grey teeth; pointed ears; cap; grey jacket; big pockets. They said he had shifty-looking eyes whereas the writer says he had 'quick eyes'. These expressions are similar in meaning: both imply that he kept looking round him quickly and did not look anyone straight in the eye. They did not miss anything important, but they did not mention that his eyes were dark and clever, and that it was these eyes that made him look like a rat. Also his jacket was greyish rather than grey, and his pockets were more than big, they were enormous. This cap may not have been grey.

SB114d

5 Get students to offer their own suggestions and put these on the board before playing the tape of Stephen and Catherine. Take a class vote on which is/are the most likely possibilities.

   Key: The writer does not reveal why he is going to Epsom. Stephen and Catherine think that he may be a pickpocket or that he may be interested in horses, even though he does not bet on them or even watch them run.

At this stage you do not want the students to focus too clearly on the fact that he might be a pickpocket, so you need to offer a number of alternative possibilities. Perhaps he is a private detective who goes to keep an eye on pickpockets, dishonest bookmakers etc. Possibly he is a blackmailer who goes to find things out about rich people who win a lot of money at the races. He could be a tipster – someone who pretends to know a lot about horses and persuades people to pay him for advice on which horse is likely to win. That might explain why he despises people who bet on horses, because he knows that it is only the bookmakers and tipsters who really make money out of racing. He may be something more ordinary like a carpark attendant or a beggar, or, since there are bars and restaurants at the races, he could be a waiter or a barman. Since he is very small he might even be a jockey. He says that he does not watch the horses run. This does not mean he does not ride them.

114 The Hitch-hiker

a Read the next part of the story and say which of these pictures is the hitch-hiker.

You made three guesses in the last Unit about what questions the driver might ask the hitch-hiker. What are they? Read and see if you were right.

 114a

PART 2

A SMALL RATTY-FACED MAN

He was a small ratty-faced man with grey teeth. His eyes were dark and quick and clever, like a rat's eyes, and his ears were slightly pointed at the top. He had a cloth cap on his head and he was wearing a greyish-coloured jacket with enormous pockets. This grey jacket, together with the quick eyes and the pointed ears, made him look more than anything like some sort of a huge human rat.

"What part of London are you headed for?" I asked him.

"I'm goin' right through London and out the other side," he said. "I'm going to Epsom, for the races. It's Derby Day today."

"So it is," I said. "I wish I were going with you. I love betting on horses."

"I never bet on horses," he said. "I don't even watch 'em run. That's a stupid silly business."

"Then why do you go?" I asked.

He didn't seem to like that question. His little ratty face went absolutely blank and he sat there staring straight ahead at the road, saying nothing.

"I expect you help to work the betting machines or something like that," I said.

"That's even sillier," he answered. "There's no fun working them lousy machines and selling tickets to mugs. Any fool could do that."

b Close your books and write down as much as you can remember about the hitch-hiker.

114c **c** How much did Stephen and Catherine remember? Did they do as well as you?

d Does the hitch-hiker tell the writer why he is going to Epsom?

114d See what Stephen and Catherine think. What do you think?

a size

How many words (or parts of words) to do with size can you find in these sentences?

He was a small ratty-faced man with grey teeth.
He was wearing a greyish-coloured jacket with enormous pockets.
... made him look like some sort of a huge human rat.
The large expensive cars seldom stopped.
A jumbo jet pilot
A microcomputer

b while

While you are in full-time education, you can get a special student travel pass.
I spent two years in Rome while I was still living with my family.

Where does the word **while** fit into these sentences?

1 *the dinner's cooking we could have a drink*
2 *I'd like to do a lot of travelling I have some money*

What other meanings does **while** have? Look in the Lexicon.

c Lexicon words

Look these words up in the Lexicon and say what they mean here.

account   *Listen to Jenny's account of her accident.*
How much is there in your account?

claim   *You should report the accident to your insurers, even if you do not intend to make a claim.*

control   *He gives us a lot of trouble. He has no self-control.*

grounds   *Give your particulars to anyone who has reasonable grounds for asking for them.*

involve   *I enjoy social activities which involve meeting and talking with people.*
Bridget had a similar accident involving a lorry.

machine   *I expect you help to work the betting machines.*
Do you have a washing machine at home?

policy   *This is a condition of your policy.*
Do you support your government's policy?

simply   *I simply didn't look.*
I simply don't believe you!

supposed   *Where are you supposed to be going?*
You are supposed to report the accident to your insurance company.

wish   *I wish I hadn't got caught in the rain.*

d make or let?

1 *A crowd gathered and _____ him write this note to apologise to the car owner.*
2 *Did your parents _____ you stay out until midnight when you were 15?*
3 *My parents always _____ me get home by 10.30. It was awful.*
4 *The doctor's at the door. Could you _____ him in?*

e get and got

Which meanings do **get** and **got** have in these sentences (1–20)?

a have/possess   e reach/arrive at
b must/have to   f receive
c have in mind   g obtain/buy
d grow/become

How many sentences do not have any of these meanings? What do the phrases with **get** and **got** mean in these cases?

1 *She's got a daughter called Lucy Claire.*
2 *I've got absolutely no idea!*
3 *I started off as a medical student but got bored.*
4 *...Joe, who is just starting to get interesting.*
5 *Very lucky to get to the top.*
6 *When we get there, we're going to stay with my parents.*
7 *I still like to travel whenever I get the chance.*
8 *She'll be able to get us tickets to go to Jamaica.*
9 *We've got to look at a picture of a footballer.*
10 *If you get stung by a bee or a wasp ...*
11 *I think women do get less pay.*
12 *Bank manager – he must get well paid!*
13 *Women tend to get tipped more generously than men.*
14 *For a 40 hour week I get £1.20 an hour.*
15 *How do I get a Travelcard?*
16 *Do you think she actually had got out of the car?*
17 *'Jump in!' He got in and I drove on.*
18 *As I got up to go, I saw the same waitress ...*
19 *Supposing she got the 18.45 from Charing Cross, she should arrive ...*
20 *I haven't got a car.*

Important words to remember (489 so far)

accident	connect	frightened	lead L	required	sudden
account L	connection	frightening	leader	serve	suddenly
action	control L	fun	leading	setting	supposed L
annoyed	effort	gather	machine L	several	tired
annoying	enormous	hell	measure	silly	various L
apology	entire	huge	notice L	similar	wish L
blame	fate	independent	ought	simply L	witness
captain	fault	insurance	passenger	slightly	
catch	flow	involved L	pocket	staring	
caught	flight	laugh	pointed	statement	
claim L	flying	laughter	policy L	stick	

Aims: 1 To revise the lexical set for adjectives of size.
2 To revise the meanings of **while**.
3 To revise and contrast the meanings of **make** and **let**.
4 To revise the meanings and uses of **get** and **got**.

Lexis: account [L]

SB115a PB115

Key: small, enormous, huge, large, jumbo, micro

SB115b

Key: While the dinner's cooking . . .
. . . while I have some money.

SB115d

1 made   2 let   3 made   4 let

SB115e

Key: 1 a   2 c   3 d   4 d   5 e   6 e
7 f   8 g   9 b   10 d   11 f   12 d
13 d   14 f   15 g   16 leave
17 enter   18 stand   19 catch   20 a

LEXICAL OBJECTIVES

Level 1 words (see page 129T):
business L, **course, experience** L,
force, ground L, **instead, party, should**
(see SB109), **state, through, while** L,
wish L.

accident 1 a chance event. *It was very lucky. We met quite by accident.*
2 *Jenny once had a really silly accident.*
account L
action 1 something done to achieve something or to deal with something. *He decided on immediate action.*
2 a movement of your body. *I watched his every action very carefully.* T
annoyed fairly angry. *He seemed to be annoyed about being wakened up.*
annoying *It was annoying because it meant I had to wait for another train.*
apology something that you say or write to tell someone that you are sorry. . . . *a message of apology left for someone.* [7]
Also apologise . . . *writing to apologise*
blame 1 to think or say someone is responsible for something or caused it. *Who do you think was to blame . . . ?*
2 *If you are in the wrong you must take the blame.* T
3 *You could hardly blame them.*
captain 1 the person in charge of a ship or aeroplane. . . . *the captain and crew.*
2 a middle ranking officer in the army
3 *Who is the captain of Manchester United?* T
catch/caught 1 *The police never caught them.* [13] *Did you catch any fish?*
2 to catch a bus, train etc. *That's why it's always better to catch a taxi.*

3 *We were caught in the rain.* T
claim L
connect 1 join two things together. *A is connected to B.* T
2 Two planes or trains connect if one arrives in time for you to catch the other. *This connects with the 3.30 to Birmingham.* T
3 Two things are connected if you often think of them together or if they go together. *You will hear 10 different announcements connected with the forms of transport on this page.* [6]
connection As **connect** above 1. *Look, you can see the connection.* T
As 2. *She'd missed her connection in New York to Texas.*
As 3. *There's no connection.* T
control L
effort 1 energy that people put into their work. *They were given a bonus to reward their effort.* T
1.2 *In spite of efforts to open the door, the fate of the passengers and crew was sealed.*
enormous 1 extremely large. . . . *a greyish-coloured jacket with enormous pockets.*
2 . . . *an enormous success.*
entire 1 the whole of. *He took his entire crew for a stroll to meet the passengers.*
fate 1 *I eagerly accepted the job fate offered me.* T
2 . . . *the fate of the passengers and crew was sealed.*
fault 1 to be responsible or to blame for something. *Whose fault was it? What was the cause of the accident?*
2 a mistake. *She was wrong, even though it wasn't her fault.* T
3 **at fault** = to blame. *If you are at fault you must accept the blame.* T
flight 1 *The flight ran several times a week . . . On each flight . . .*
2 the act of running away. . . . *the thieves took flight.* T
flow move smoothly like a liquid. *The traffic usually flows smoothly.* Also: the traffic flow
flying 1 travelling through the air. *The plane was flying through a storm.* T
2 travelling in an aircraft. *My girlfriend is very frightened of flying.*
frightened afraid. *My girlfriend is very frightened of flying.*
frightening *Have you ever had a worrying or frightening flight?*
fun 1 something pleasant and enjoyable. *She got a lot of fun out of hiking.* T
1.1 *There's no fun working those machines.*
gather 1 to bring together. *All right, gather your things together and put them away.* T
2 to come together. *A crowd has gathered.*
3 *I gather you've got a new job.* = someone has told me you've got a new job. T
hell 1 **a hell of a** = very great, considerable. *I've just run into your car and made a hell of a mess.*
2 an angry exclamation. *Oh hell! It's*

broken. [Note: **hell** is mildly rude.] T
huge very large. *He looked like a huge human rat.*
independent 1 separate, not connected. . . . *an independent witness*
insurance an agreement in which you pay money to a company which agrees to pay you in the event of accident, illness etc. *Now read what an insurance company advises.*
involved L
laugh to make a sound which shows you are happy. *I had to join in and laugh as well.*
laughter act or sound of laughing. *There was a lot of loud laughter.*
lead See SB107.
leader See SB107.
leading See SB107.
machine L
measure determine the exact size or extent of something. T
Also **measurement**: the result you obtain by measuring something. *Sketch a diagram of the accident (including measurements . . .)*
notice L
ought See SB109.
passenger . . . *the fate of the passengers and crew was sealed.*
pocket *He was wearing a greyish-coloured jacket with enormous pockets.*
pointed coming to a sharp end. *His ears were pointed*
policy L
required 1 want or need. *Do you require anything else?* T
2 **you are required to** = you must. *You will be required to complete an Accident Report Form.*
serve 1 *Red buses serve Central London.*
2 *Dinner is served.* T
setting out beginning a journey. *Get a bus map before setting out.*
several 1 a few. . . . *several minutes*
silly 1 foolish, not sensible. *Jenny once had a really silly accident.*
similar like something else. *A friend of mine had a similar experience.*
simply L
slightly fairly. *His ears were slightly pointed.*
staring looking. *He sat there staring straight ahead at the road . . .*
state say or write (formal). *State your name and occupation.* T
statement 1 *Report any statement made at the scene of the accident.*
stick Fix something so that it cannot move. . . . *left the captain and crew stuck in the cabin.*
sudden happening unexpectedly. *There was a sudden knock at the door.* T
suddenly unexpectedly. *She suddenly saw that one of the engines was on fire.*
supposed L
tired 1 needing rest. *I was very tired and I fell asleep.*
2 **tired of** = bored with. *I'm tired of watching so much television.*
various L
witness bystander, onlooker. *Name and address of an independent witness.*

Unit 9 Everything you could imagine

The unit opens with a general discussion of shopping based on a number of unusual shops. The discussion covers choosing gifts (especially local specialities), bargaining, markets and shopping procedures that may be specific to a particular country or locality. There is a detailed look at procedures for making payment in two shops in Britain, both of which operate an unusual system. Later there is a discussion of advertising and advertising jingles, focusing on the kind of appeal associated with different products. The Hitch-hiker picks up this theme when the driver is asked to test out the advertisers' claims for his BMW. Shopping as a tourist or by post (mail order from overseas) is the next topic, and in particular how, as a tourist, to take advantage of tax-free offers available in Britain, and possibly in other countries. Finally a discussion of favourite colours involves the kind of language commonly used in a shopping context.

OBJECTIVES

Lexical objectives are in TB130

Grammar and discourse

a Quantifying phrases expressing totality and near totality. (116)
b Understanding the imperative in formal instructions. (117)
c Impersonal 'you' and 'they' in informal instructions. (117,118)
d The uses of **up**, particularly with phrasal verbs. (119)
e The uses of **case** including such phrases as **in case**, **in any case**. (123)
f The use of continuous tenses for interrupted actions. (125)
g Causative **get** and **have**. (127)
h Colloquial phrases: common and unusual. (122)
i Narrative structure: starting a story. (125)
j Conditional sentences focusing particularly on: hypothetical statements, introductory words other than **if** (e.g. **provided**). (129)

Tasks

a Understanding and explaining systems and procedures in speech and writing. (116,117)
b Comparing systems and procedures. (116,117)
c Sharing casual recollections to do with preferences of a trivial nature. ('This reflects a very common casual social situation.) (120)
d Evaluating general claims of the kind found in advertisements. (120)
e Understanding and predicting narrative. (121)
f Understanding how character is revealed in dialogue. (121)
g Further analysis of procedures involving choosing an appropriate course of action in different circumstances. (126)
h Understanding and acting on detailed instructions. (126)
i Stating preferences and speculating on general preferences and the reasons for them. (128)

116 Places to buy things

Aims: 1 To stimulate discussion – comparing types of shops and systems of buying in different countries.
2 To practise scanning for specific information.
3 To focus on quantifying phrases showing totality and near totality, and on phrases denoting the opposite.

Lexis: bargain, design, equipment, fashion, hardly any, intend (to), no matter how/what, presents, store, supply, tradition, traditional, trendy (in fashion), **very few, whatever, whom** [T]
Revision: **a good idea to . . ., anyone, from . . . to . . ., imagine, strange** (bizarre)
Words and phrases meaning all/everything: **all, anything, every, everything, it doesn't matter which/who . . ., whatever . . . you're after**

Knutz The shop name 'Knutz' is pronounced 'nuts', which is slang for someone who is mad or crazy.

SB116a/d PB116

1 Students read the extracts and note down any ideas they have in response to the discussion questions. Then encourage group or class discussion, in preparation for a short oral or written report.

2 After discussing their own country, ask students which London shop they would go to for the items drawn around the page. Deal with lexical problems as they arise.

3 Discussion: Did students notice that the golf clubs and tin opener are left-handed? How many people in the class are left-handed? Do they have difficulty using normal things? (The signs and notices round the page introduce lexis and themes from later in the unit, about tax-free goods etc. They are revised in section 142 as well. Deal with these as students ask about them.)

4 Optional further practice: Students decide what they would buy for their classmates. No need to restrict them to what they can buy from these particular shops. Students react to the presents suggested for them.   *or*
Ask students which family members and friends they would normally buy presents for if they went on holiday or to London. They should make a list. When students report to the class, ask the others to listen for what kinds of things are the most popular as presents.

5 Language study:
1 Give the students the phrases 1–5 from section 116. Ask them to match the phrases 1–5 with the one that is closest in meaning from a–e.
1 just about anyone
2 whatever you're after
3 all your wants, no matter how bizarre
4 everything in this shop
5 everything you could imagine
a all the goods here
b nearly everyone
c absolutely anything you can think of
d no matter what you're looking for
e anything you need, however strange it is

Key: 1 b 2 d 3 e 4 a 5 c

2 Ask students what the following phrases have in common:
very few, hardly, any, not many.

Key: The phrases all refer to a small quantity or number.

3 Ask students the difference between **few people** and **a few people**.

Key: Though both refer to a small number, the former is negative in meaning (i.e. not many), as if the speaker expected or hoped for more, while the latter is more positive (i.e. some).

59T

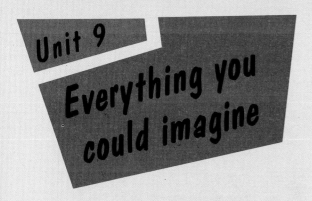

Unit 9
Everything you could imagine

Places to buy things

a Do you have any shops like these in your country? Where would you go to buy such things?

b What other things might the joke shop sell? Has anyone ever bought you something as a joke?

c What kinds of markets do you have in your capital city? And your local town? Do you or your family ever shop in these markets?

d In Britain you can never bargain in shops, and only very occasionally in the markets. The prices are usually fixed. Do you have to bargain in your country? Talk about a bargaining experience.

All prices include VAT

Speciality SHOPS

From buttons to books, from left-handed scissors to clothes for little women, London has shops that cater for the most specialised interests. Here is a selection.

THE LEFT-HANDED SHOP

65 Beak Street, W1 (Oxford Circus tube).
Open: Mon–Fri 10.30–5, Sat 10–2.
When people say London can supply all your wants, no matter how bizarre, they're talking about places like this. Everything in this shop is designed to be used by people who use their left hand. You'll find scissors, tin-openers, pens – everything.
Scissors £2.75; corkscrews £1.85; tin openers from £2.

NO REFUNDS WITHOUT RECEIPTS

kNUTz

1 Russell Street, WC2 (Covent Garden Tube)
Open: Mon–Fri 11–8, Sat 12–8, Sun 12–6.
A sort of adult joke shop where you'll find something to annoy just about anyone you know.
Exploding matches 69p each; self-lighting candles from 35p.

EXPORT DEPARTMENT

Lillywhites

24–36 Regent Street SW1 (Piccadilly Circus tube).
Open: Mon–Sat 9.30–6, Thurs 9.30.–7.
The largest sports store in London, Lillywhites looks more like a department store than a speciality shop. Whatever sports equipment or clothes you're after, they'll have them, or know where you can find them.
Shorts £9.50; running vests £4.50; tracksuits from £24.95.

Street markets are a real tradition in London. They are scattered all over the city and its suburbs . . . Here's one of the best:

Portobello Road (Notting Hill Gate or Ladbroke Grove tube). Open: Fri, Sat 7–5.

Always a good idea to get down the road early if you intend to snap up the bargains. Notting Hill end is antiques, the middle is fruit and veg, under the Westway there are trendy second-hand clothes and the bottom end sports gear – everything you could imagine.

TAX-FREE SHOPPING FOR VISITORS TO BRITAIN!

Unit 9

117 Systems for paying in shops

a   We asked Bridget and David to do this task.

> In a supermarket, you choose what you want, put it all in a trolley or basket, then take it to the cashier by the exit. The cashier rings it up on the till, tells you how much it is, then takes your money. You pack your shopping into a box or bag, and that's it.
>
> In your local shop, you usually ask the shop assistant for what you want. He or she gives you your things in a paper bag, and takes your money.
>
> Do you know any shops with different systems for payment?

▷ What is the procedure for buying things in the shop nearest to your own home? ◁

David and Bridget talked about Foyles, the famous London bookshop. Foyles has an unusual system for payment. Try to put these stages in order to show how it works.

a   Leave the book with the assistant and take the bill to a cashier's desk.
b   Take the book to an assistant who will give you a bill.
c   Take the receipted bill back to the assistant and get the book.
d   Pay for the book and get your bill stamped.
e   Find whatever book it is you want.

117a   Now listen to David and see if you were right.

b   There are also places in Britain where you can shop from a catalogue. One of these is called Argos. Can you put these stages in order?

a   Fill in the selection form, giving the catalogue number and quantity.
b   Take the goods home – it's as easy as that.
c   Check what you want from the master catalogue at the Selection Desk in the Showroom.
d   Your purchases will be sent up from the stockroom while you make payment.
e   Take your completed form to the point marked 'Service'. Our staff will be pleased to help if you need assistance.

 marked post

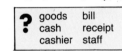 goods   bill
cash   receipt
cashier   staff

117b   Now listen to David talking about Argos and see if you are right.

▷ **c**   Prepare a short summary of both systems. ◁

117c   Listen to David and Bridget summarising the systems used in Foyles and Argos. Bridget makes one mistake. What is it?

d   Have you ever bought anything from a catalogue, either in a shop like Argos or by post?

▷ Do you know of any other shops that have a different system? Can you explain what system they use? ◁

▷ How do you go about exchanging foreign money? ◁

118 *Language study*

Phrases with prepositions

a   Can you put these words in the right order to make the phrases David uses?

1 *from a catalogue you buy*
2 *the front of in the shop*
3 *a form out you fill*
4 *the number down you take*
5 *you go a cash system through*
6 *they do a computer with something*
7 *they enter into a number the computer*

b   Who is David talking about in section 117 when he says 'you' and 'they'?

60

117 Systems for paying in shops

Aims: 1 To give students practice in describing and understanding a procedure: listing the stages in a process and highlighting the relevant relationships between them.
2 To give students practice in understanding the imperative in formal instructions.

Lexis: bill, box, cash, catalogue, enter, exit, fill (out a form), goods, make (payment), [L], mark(ed) [L], master (main), receipt, show (how/that), staff, until, whatever
Revision: **get** (causative): **get it stamped, get** (receive), **send/sent, services** [L], **special, they** (a group of unknown people), **thing, you** (anyone)

Task   SB117a 117a* PB117

1 Students read through the task card with the introductory text about the supermarket and the local shop. They then talk about their local shops in their home town or village, and each group can tell the class briefly about one of them.

2 Foyles: In pairs students work out a possible order. Ask students to read out the sentences to each other in the order they have decided. Don't tell them the correct answers until they have heard the tape and got them for themselves as far as possible.

Key: e, b, a, d, c

Task   SB117b 117b*

3 Use the picture to introduce the idea of mail order shopping, if students are not already familiar with it. Point out to students that the picture in their book shows the first stage in the sequence. Students repeat the procedure for 117a.

Key: c, a, e, d, b

Report   SB117c 117c*

4 In groups students prepare a summary of the procedures. Ask a couple of groups to present their summaries. Then they can listen to Bridget's summary more critically, and compare it with their own.

Key: Bridget's mistake: 'you get a receipt for what you've paid for . . .'. Rather, when you pay, the receipt you have been given by the assistant is stamped.

5 Words to look up/guess. Students find the correct category for the words to look up in the Lexicon and guess the meanings of the words to guess from the context. **Post** is included here because the theme of ordering by post (mail order) from a catalogue, (see also 117d below), may have cropped up.

Task   SB117d

6 Treat this as a class discussion. Encourage students to tell each other if they or anyone in their families has ever bought anything out of a catalogue, by post, without seeing it first. Were the goods thus bought what they really wanted? Were they well enough described in the adverts in the catalogue?

7 In groups students do the same as Bridget and David. If they really don't know about any shops or restaurants with unusual systems, they could describe the procedure for exchanging foreign money in a country they know. Help them prepare a summary for the class. This could be either spoken or written.

118 Language study

Aims: 1 To show that prepositions are sometimes used with a noun e.g. **from a catalogue**, and sometimes used to extend a verb, e.g. **to fill out a form**.
2 To illustrate the use of the impersonal **you** and **they** in informal instructions.

Lexis: fill

SB118a PB118

1 Students complete the exercise in pairs and refer to the transcript to check.

2 Ask students which prepositions could be omitted without drastically changing the meaning of the sentence (though grammatically they must be retained).

Key: 1 you buy from a catalogue
2 in the front of the shop·
3 you fill out a form
4 you take down the number
5 you go through a cash system
6 they do something with a computer
7 they enter a number into a computer

SB118b

Key: The word **they** is used to refer to an unknown group of people of which the speaker and listener are not members.
You is used to mean 'anyone at all'.

119 Preposition spot

Aims: 1 To help students recognise phrasal verbs with **up** where the meaning seems to have no connection with the meaning of the verb on its own.
2 To show how **up** often intensifies the meaning of the verb, e.g. **cut it up** = cut into a lot of pieces, **eat it up** = eat it all.
3 To give students practice in discriminating between the two uses.

Lexis: up

*In the examples where **up** intensifies the verb, it is sometimes, though not always, grammatically possible to omit **up** altogether.*

SB119a PB119

1 Students do the exercise in pairs. Check class answers and elicit that in these examples **up** extends the meaning of the verb but is not responsible for a resulting change in meaning.

Key: standing up, wake me up, driving up to, mixed up

SB119b

2 In pairs students identify those sentences in which **up** could be omitted without a significant change of meaning, and those in which it could not.

3 Students should try to guess the meanings of the phrasal verbs from context. (They should notice that some phrasal verbs have more than one meaning, e.g. **turn up**.)

Key: Examples where **up** merely gives the verb a more specific context without changing its meaning:
2 grow up = to grow from a child into an adult
3 washing up = washing all the dishes from the meal
Examples where **up** changes the meaning of the verb:
1 turned up
4 turn up
5 pulls up
6 picks up
7 did up

SB119c

4 Students match the sentences with the words or phrases in the box individually, then check their answers in pairs.

Key: 1 d 2 f 3 e 4 c 5 b 6 g,k 7 i 8 j
9 a 10 h

120 Advertising

Aims: 1 Sharing of casual recollections to do with preferences of a trivial nature. (This reflects a very common casual social situation.)
2 To practise evaluating general claims of the kind found in advertisements.

Lexis: ability, advertising, analyse, analysis [T], **before, clean, cover** [L], **kids, (it doesn't) matter, product, recognise, taste, treat** [L], **wonderful**
Revision: **absolutely hate it, almost as old as ..., awful, come to mind, enough to, how annoying, recently, still, surprised, that** (all uses, inc. relative)

This theme of evaluating advertising claims also occurs in the episode of the Hitch-hiker in section 121.

SB120a

1 Ask students to identify the products in the pictures. Write the words for these up on the board.

2 In groups students discuss which product goes with which slogan. Don't supply right answers at this stage. Find out which slogans they like best, and whether there are any they find silly or annoying.

Listening   SB120b [120b] *

3 Students listen first simply to identify which are the jingles that Catherine's group talked about. Then they can listen again to see which comments go with which advert.

Key: 8 advertisements:
1 The dirt said hot. The label said not. Ariel gets it clean.
2 A finger of fudge is just enough to give your kids a treat.
3 Only the crumbliest, flakiest chocolate tastes like chocolate never tasted before.
4 A million housewives every day pick up a tin of beans and say, 'Beanz meanz Heinz'.
5 There are two men in my life. To one I am a mother, to the other I'm a wife.
6 Cadbury's take 'em, and they cover them with chocolate.
7 Smartie people are happy people. They smile all the while.
8 Only Smarties have the answer.
Comment 1 – Fudge advert
Comment 2 – Heinz
Comment 3 – Ariel
Comment 4 – chocolate

4 Words to look up and guess: Students find the correct category for the words to look up in the Lexicon and guess the meaning of the words to guess from context.

Report   SB120c

5 Limit students to one favourite advertisement slogan. It can be in their own language or, if they know any, in English.

6 When reporting to the class, students should explain what the advertisements in their own language mean in English so that people who have come from or been to other countries would recognise the same advertisement in another language.

7 As students listen, they should make a list of the products mentioned in the reports. Ask students how far they think the advertisements state the truth.

SB120d

8 Ask students what kinds of things they, or people in general, look for when purchasing a car. Ask them if they can think of any advertising slogans which appeal to any of these wants. List criteria and slogans on the board. Ask students if they think these advertising claims are always truthful. (Do this fairly quickly as a class activity to prepare students for section 121.)

up

a Where could you add the word **up** in the sentences below? What difference does it make? A lot or not much?

Often the work is unpleasant – standing all day. (47)
Wake me for the coffee break. (55)
I was driving to London by myself. (97)
The waitress got the orders mixed. (93)

b What about these examples? How does the word **up** change the meaning of the verb? For instance, in the sentence: *I gave up smoking* **gave** does not mean the same as in: *I gave her a book for her birthday.*

1 *The enterprising assistant turned up the heating.*
2 *It was not a very pleasant place to grow up in ...*
3 *Lend me a hand with the washing up, will you ...* (65)
4 *They probably will turn up.*
5 *He pulls up at a traffic light ...* (78)
6 *... the man who picks up a hitch-hiker ...*
7 *Then he returned the book to its pocket and did up the button.*

c Find a word or phrase below which means something similar to the phrases with **up** in the examples.

a	*decide*	g	*finish*
b	*repairing*	h	*give a bed to*
c	*think of*	i	*doing* (probably
d	*introduced*		something bad!)
e	*fit and strong enough*	j	*getting better*
f	*was faced with*	k	*be quick*

1 *He brought up the subject of equal pay for women.*
2 *He came up against some huge problems.*
3 *Sure you're up to it?*
4 *Can you come up with a plan by tomorrow?*
5 *He was doing his old car up, to sell it.*
6 *Eat it up! Hurry up!*
7 *What were the kids getting up to?*
8 *Things are looking up.*
9 *Make up your mind!*
10 *Can you put me up for a night?*

120 # Advertising

a What kinds of products do you think each of these is advertising?
Can you find the slogans which advertise each item here?

A finger of fudge is just enough to give your kids a treat.

12 Shredded Wheat
THE ORIGINAL BRANFIBRE CEREAL

PERSIL WASHES WHITER

DRINKA **PINTA** MILKA **DAY**

There are two men in my life. To one I am a mother, to the other I'm a wife.

new system
Persil automatic
10p

HEINZ BAKED BEANS

Smartie people are happy people – they smile all the while. Only Smarties have the answer.

GO TO WORK ON AN EGG

WHOLE NUT
Cadbury's FLAKE

The dirt said HOT. The label said NOT. ARIEL gets it clean!

ARIEL
OUTSTANDING CLEANING EVEN AT LOWER TEMPERATURES

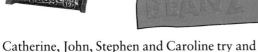
Cadbury's Fudge

BEANZ MEANZ HEINZ

120b **b** Catherine, John, Stephen and Caroline try and remember some advertising jingles and slogans. They write eight on their list. Which ones?
They make these comments about four of them. Which group of comments goes with which advertisement?
What other comments do they make?

Cadbury's take 'em and they cover them with chocolate.

6 EGGS SIZE 1

smarties

? housewife
clean
dirt
label
taste

CM: I think that's quite a nice one.

SB: They don't have that on TV any – still, do they?
CM: No.
CF: Erm, Yes. I saw it recently.
CM: Do they?
CF: Yes. I was very surprised.

JM. The one that I find most irritating is [...]
JM. I absolutely hate it.
CF: Oh, that's awful.
JM. I'd forgotten what it's for but I remember how annoying ...

SB: ... which if you try and analyse it grammatically makes no sense at all.
CM: But it's quite a tongue twister.

Only the crumbliest flakiest chocolate tastes like chocolate never tasted before.

L cover
treat
sense
while

c What is your favourite advert? Tell the class about it. As you listen to the others make a list of the products.

d What about car adverts? What kind of things do they say? Are they always truthful?

121 # The Hitch-hiker

121a

PART 3

THE SECRET OF LIFE...

There was a long silence. I decided not to question him any more. I remembered how irritated I used to get in my hitch-hiking days when drivers kept asking *me* questions. Where are you going? Why are you going there? What's your job? Are you married? Do you have a girl-friend? What's her name? How old are you? And so on and so forth. I used to hate it.

"I'm sorry," I said. "It's none of my business what you do. The trouble is, I'm a writer, and most writers are terribly nosey parkers."

"You write books? he asked.

"Yes."

"Writin' books is okay," he said. "It's what I call a skilled trade. I'm in a skilled trade too. The folks I despise is them that spend all their lives doin' crummy old routine jobs with no skill in 'em at all. You see what I mean?"

"Yes."

"The secret of life," he said, "is to become very very good at somethin' that's very 'ard to do."

"Like you," I said.

"Exactly. You and me both."

"What makes you think that I'm any good at my job?" I asked.

"There's an awful lot of bad writers around."

"You wouldn't be drivin' about in a car like this if you weren't no good at it," he answered. "It must've cost a tidy packet, this little job."

"It wasn't cheap."

"What can she do flat out?" he asked.

"One hundred and twenty-nine miles an hour," I hold him.

"I'll bet she won't do it."

"I'll bet she will."

"All car makers is liars," he said. "You can buy any car you like and it'll never do what the makers say it will in the ads."

"This one will."

a Where is the hitch-hiker going? Do we know why he's going there? Why do you think he answered like he did?

How would you react if you were the driver? Would you keep on talking? Or leave him alone? Read on and find out how the writer reacted and why.

b Do you think the car can really do 129 miles an hour (approx 205 kmh)?

c What do you think will happen next?

121c Do you agree with what Caroline and Stephen think?

---

122 # *Language study*

a Very colloquial expressions

Find phrases in the story that mean:

1 this particular car
2 want to know all about other people in detail
3 at top speed
4 a large amount of money
5 uninteresting work
6 people

b Common phrases

Find these phrases in the text and explain what is meant by them.

And so on and so forth.
The trouble is,
You see what I mean.
None of my business,
It's what I call a ...

c The way he speaks

Look carefully at these short extracts. In what way are these extracts different from the original story?

"Writin' books is okay," he said. "It's what I call a skilled trade. I'm in a skilled trade too. The folks I despise are those who spend all their lives doin' crummy old routine jobs with no skill in 'em at all. You see what I mean?"

"You wouldn't be drivin' about in a car like this if you weren't any good at it," he answered. "It must've cost a tidy packet, this little job."

"All car makers are liars."

121a Listen to the story again, and pay attention to the way the hitch-hiker speaks. What does this tell you about him?

122c What do Caroline and Stephen feel about this?

Aims: 1 To practise summarising past narrative (the story so far).
2 To practise understanding and predicting narrative.
3 To practise understanding how character is revealed in dialogue.

Lexis: able (to), claim, economy, exactly (in agreement), **(so) forth, liar, lying, silence, skill, trade** [L], **wheels, wind**

Ensure students answer a before b after reading.

SB121a 121a PB121

1 In addition to the discussion points here, ask students what they think the hitch-hiker could be thinking; what it is that makes him avoid the driver's questions. The question 'How would you react if you were the driver' is to help students project themselves into that situation before they read on.

2 Let students read on, and then listen if they wish to.

SB121b/c 121c *

3 Students discuss the questions in groups and report back informally before they listen to Catherine and Stephen's views on the same topic.

Key: With reference to fuel economy, a car will do what the manufacturers say it will in perfect conditions, e.g. on flat roads with no wind.

Aim: To help students differentiate between the colloquial phrases that are useful to learn, and those which are slightly too unusual or non-standard for them to use themselves. (They may well need to understand such phrases if they ever travel to Britain.)

Lexis: basically, self-taught, skill, uneducated
Revision: **accent, the way he speaks**

SB122a

1 Students work in pairs underlining the phrases in the transcript. Students report back informally to the class.

Key: 1 this little job
2 are terrible nosey parkers
3 flat out
4 a tidy packet
5 crummy old routine jobs
6 folks

These phrases are probably too colloquial for most situations that students will find themselves in.

SB122b

2 Students work in their pairs. Help students work out what they mean. (All these phrases are useful.)

Listening SB122c 121a 122c *

3 Students compare the extracts with the original. Then ask them to listen to the story again to see what they can tell about the hitch-hiker's background from his pronunciation, i.e. where he comes from and what sort of education he has had.

4 Students listen to Catherine and Stephen. Ask them to listen as well for the features of the hitch-hiker's speech that Catherine and Stephen pick out.

Key: The extracts are here grammatically correct while those in the original text are not. It is interesting to note that Catherine and Stephen did not notice these grammatical slips; it may be because they are fairly common among native speakers!
The hitch-hiker has a London accent (slightly cockney – from the East End of London).
Catherine and Stephen think he is self-taught, i.e. uneducated.
They notice that:
He drops his **h** and **th** sounds at the beginning of words.
He misses out the end of the **-ing** sounds.
He uses the word **very** a lot.

Wordpower

> **Aim:** To illustrate some of the meanings and uses of **case**.
>
> Lexis: **case**

*Students may have met the word before but in its least common meaning – a container of some kind, e.g. **suitcase**, **brief case**, **pencil case**. **Case** is in fact a very common word and is used most often in phrases like: **in this case**, **in that case**, **in which case** ... etc, where, in itself, it is devoid of meaning. It refers to a topic or a set of circumstances which have been or are about to be mentioned. For this reason, it may be a difficult word for students to acquire. This is why so many examples have been included.*

SB123 PB123

1 Ask students to think whether they have one word for all these categories of meaning in their own language.

> **Key:** a 1   b 1   c 2   d 3   e 2   f 1.1
> ... just in case ... 3; The case against ... 4; In case of ... 3.

---

124 **Song**

> **Aim:** To stimulate discussion and student enjoyment.
>
> Lexis: **box**

SB124

1 Read the words aloud. Then ask one or two students to do the same for rhythm and stress practice.

2 Students discuss the questions in groups. Get the best groups to report their ideas.

---

125 **Phrase-building**

> **Aims:** 1 To focus students' attention on a feature of narrative structure: a commonly used way of starting a story.
> 2 To practise the use of continuous tenses for interrupted actions.

SB125

This activity could well be turned into a game of Consequences by following this procedure:

1 One student in a group starts the first paragraph (the one they did for the phrase-building) right at the top of a piece of paper. Then they fold the top part over towards themselves, several times so that it covers all the writing. They then write the word He/She/They (so that it shows), depending on whether the person they've written about is male or female and then pass the paper on to someone else.

2 The next person should write what was said by that person/people – <u>without</u> looking at what has been written already. The student then folds up the paper, covering all the writing, and passes it on.

3 The next person should write a reply then fold it up and pass it on.

4 The next person writes 2 sentences for the end of the story, beginning:
So we ...
So what we did was, ...
The result was, ...
As a result, ...

5 When each person in the group has written something they fold the whole bit of paper up and give it to you.

6 The result should be some entertaining 'nonsense' stories! Mix them up and give one out to each group to open and read.

Wordpower

case

Look up **case** in the Lexicon.

Try to explain exactly what situation the word case refers to in each example.

(a) If you buy from Argos, you can only see things in the catalogue, but this is not the case with Comet; in Comet you can see the goods on the shelves and try them first.

(b) 'My house isn't on fire, officer.' 'In that case,' he said, 'you've got yourself into a nasty mess!' (147)

(c) Daughter: Sorry if I woke you up by ringing so late. Mother: It doesn't matter. In any case, you should always phone if you are going to be back late.

(d) It's not likely to rain. But I suppose I'd better take this just in case it does.

(e) A: Africa? It'll be terribly hot. B: I don't care whether it's hot or cold. I'm going in any case.

(f) We asked a lot of people about cutting a round cake into eight pieces with the smallest number of cuts. In every case except one, they answered four. What about cutting a square cake into eight pieces? Would it be the same answer in this case?

"IN THE CASE OF A POWER CUT DO NOT USE LIFTS."

THE CASE AGAINST

NUCLEAR ARMS
TUESDAY JUNE 23RD.
ALL WELCOME

We're flying direct from Sydney on QF 1 eta 21.10, just in case you're thinking of coming to the airport.

"IN CASE OF EMERGENCY BREAK GLASS"

Song

124

124 Sing the song and then discuss what you think the *pom pom pom* was.

I discovered a pom pom pom...

As I was walking down the beach
One bright and sunny day,
I saw a great big wooden box
Afloating in the bay.
I pulled it in
I opened it up
And much to my surprise
I discovered a pom pom pom
Right before my eyes.

▶ What do you think he did next? Decide, then tell the class. ◀

Phrase-building

125

As I was...

Look at the first two lines of the song. This is a very traditional opening to a song or a story. Can you think of other ways you could start a story, based on the same pattern?

As I was... (action)...(place)...(time)

or

...(time) *as I was...* (action)...(place)

I saw
I heard...,... (name and description of a person)
I met

Write the beginning of the story and then ask someone else in the class to carry on.

126 Tax-free shopping

a Although you can find bargains in London it's not generally a very cheap place to shop. But if you know how to get tax relief you will be able to save some money. Even if you can't actually go to Britain yourself, you can always get things by mail order, by writing direct to the shops concerned.

This extract from a tourist newspaper explains how to buy things tax-free if you are not living in Britain. In what ways could it help you, or someone you know?

In Britain, Value Added Tax (VAT) is charged on most goods at a standard rate of 15%. Some stores offer relief from VAT under the Retail Export Scheme. This means that, provided you export what you have bought, you can have the VAT amount refunded to you.

These are the ways to obtain relief from VAT:

a Many London stores are able to send goods direct to an overseas address, free of VAT.

b Under the Personal Export Scheme, you may, as a visitor, have goods which you have bought in Britain delivered, free of tax, direct to the port by which you are leaving the country, for exportation as baggage. (This scheme does not apply to visitors leaving by air.)

c The Over-the-counter Export Scheme, also known as Retail Export Scheme. There is a form that must be filled in by the shopkeeper and shown, together with the goods, to the Customs Officer at the airport when you leave UK. This scheme is only for things that can be carried on the plane as hand luggage.

It is advisable to tell the shop that you want to claim refund of VAT before making your purchase. You will need to show your passport, so don't forget to take it with you when you go shopping.

A VAT reclaim desk in a London store

b True or false?

1 *You can't buy things free of VAT unless you live outside the UK.*
2 *You are not allowed to use the 'Over-the-counter' Export Scheme unless you can carry the goods on to the plane as hand luggage.*
3 *Many London stores are able to send things direct to your home address overseas, but not unless you have actually been to the store yourself.*
4 *You may not use the 'Over-the-counter' Export Scheme unless you are leaving by sea.*

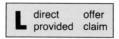
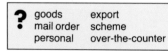

L | direct offer
provided claim

? | goods export
mail order scheme
personal over-the-counter

c Imagine you want to make the following purchases in London. Say whether it would be worth reclaiming VAT and if so under which scheme assuming:

1 that you were leaving Britain by sea
2 that you were leaving by air

Work it out then tell the class what your group thinks.

127 *Language study*

Have things done for you

Have you had your hair done? It looks great. When did you last have your house painted? It looks terrible!

Find phrases with **get** or **have** which mean:

a there is no need to do it yourself,
b you can't/don't do it yourself.

Under the Personal Export Scheme, you may have goods delivered direct to the port by which you are leaving the country.

You take the bill to a special cash desk, pay, and get it stamped.

...under the Retail Export Scheme. This means that, provided you export what you've bought, you can have the VAT refunded.

If you live overseas, you can order things by post and have them sent directly to your home address, free of VAT.

If you ever go to London, you can have a suit made at Moss Bros. You could get your hair cut and styled at Vidal Sassoon. You could even have your fortune told by Madame Sharp in Rupert Street.

Tax-free shopping

Aims: 1 Further analysis of procedures involving choosing an appropriate course of action in different circumstances.
2 To give students practice in understanding and acting on detailed instruments.

Lexis: able to, abroad [T], **bargain, before, direct** [L], **export, goods, if ever, mail (this) means (that), offer** [L], **passport, port, provided (that), relief, save, scheme, shown, store, suit, tax, under, unless**
Revision: **(don't) forget (to), free of (tax), if so . . .,**
known as, most (goods), you may (you are allowed to),
Understanding only: **assuming that** (if)

Reading SB126a

1 Check that students know what **tax** is. Do they have purchase tax on things they buy in their countries? What things in particular? How much or what percent?

2 Ask students what the notices mean. Ask them in which situation they are most likely to be, at some time in the future. (Buying by post? Going to Britain and leaving by sea/plane?)

3 Ask students to read through the text for themselves. Which scheme might be the most useful for them, personally?

SB126b

4 Go through the text with them making sure that they have understood the conditions for each scheme. The 'true or false' exercise is a good way of introducing a discussion which will highlight the different conditions.

Key: True: 1, 2   False: 3, 4

Task SB126c

5 Students should do the task individually, then compare their answers with others.

Key: If you were leaving by sea, you could take all six under scheme b, or have them sent direct to your home under scheme a if they were too big for you to manage on board ship. If leaving by air you could only take the small things under scheme c: the home computer – if it was small enough, the camera, and the suit, the rest would have to come under scheme a.

6 Monitor while students are deciding what they would do. Try to identify one or two areas of disagreement which can be exploited in subsequent discussion.

Language study

Aim: To practise the use of causative **get** and **have**: to have something done, rather than doing it yourself.

Lexis: get, have, post, suit

The examples from the text all refer to the present or indefinite future. Hence the two examples in italics refer to past time.

SB127 PB127

1 Ask students, 'When did you last have your photo taken?' (e.g. for a passport or ID card). Get students to compare any documents they may have on them which have photographs, and ask if they took the photos themselves or if they had them taken.

2 Students read the rubric and find the phrases in the Student's Book in pairs. Put students' examples on the board.

3 Students think of at least 3 other sentences where **get** and **have** are used in the same way, causatively. Ask them if they have a similar structure in their own language. (Don't worry if they don't get the form right at this stage – so long as they understand the difference in meaning it is enough for now.)

4 The Practice Book gives more basic practice and ideas for them to ask each other about. You could turn this into a class survey if you wanted to.

Key: you may have goods delivered,
and get it stamped,
you can have the VAT refunded,
you can . . . have them sent directly to your home,
you can have a suit made; you could get your hair cut and styled; you could even have your fortune told

128 Favourite colours

Task SB128a

1 Students should follow these instructions on their own. The guessing must be done in silence, to make it more fun. There need be no reporting at all until after students have heard the tape.

Listening SB128b 128b*

2 If the picture might give them any clue, students could be referred to an early picture of Catherine and Stephen (page 12) and asked to guess their favourite colours. Students listen and makes notes so they remember Stephen and Catherine's favourites, and what colour they thought was most popular.

Key: Catherine's favourite colour is blue. She thinks it's most people's favourite. Stephen doesn't really have a favourite colour.

Task SB128c

3 Allow students to react to the tape. Then have them walk round the class to ask each other about their favourite colours. Did any people guess any childhood favourites? Ask students if anybody's favourite colour as a child was different from what it is now. Finally, find out which is the most popular colour in the class.

SB128d 128d*

4 Use the exercise to focus on some of the new lexis. Students check the transcript for answers.

Key: blue, popular, majority, say, something, say, against, tend, bright, with, matter

129 Grammar

SB129a PB129

1 Introduce the concept of hypothetical condition. Ask students to answer the first example question. Then ask them a few more hypothetical questions, e.g.: 'If somebody gave you a million pounds (or any other currency), what would you do?', 'Imagine you ran the country. What changes would you make?' Ask students to ask you some similar questions.

2 Students find the other ways of introducing a condition individually, then compare their answers with a partner.

Key: 1 Imagine... 2 Provided... 3 assuming... 4 In the case of... 5 providing... 6 Supposing... 7 unless... 8/9 as long as...

SB129b

3 Students discuss in groups, then report their answers to the class.

Key: Would and the past tense describe things that are not true, but imaginary (hypothetical). If you wish to show clearly that something is hypothetical rather than real you can do so by using **would** and the past tense. The present tense must be used for things that are real, as in 'I have a sense of humour'.

Favourite colours

a Without talking, write down your own favourite colour(s). What used to be your favourite colour as a child? Was there any particular reason? If so, write one sentence saying why.

Look around the class. Without asking anyone, try to guess four or five other people's favourite colours, and write them down.

Then write down what you think is the most popular colour for clothes. (If you saw a large crowd of people together, what colour would the majority be wearing?)

128b **b** Listen and find out what Stephen and Catherine's favourites are.

c Go round and ask the four or five people in your class what their favourite colours are.

128d **d** Listen again carefully to the conversation. What words have been missed out of these extracts?

CM: And I don't know why I like _____, except it's – I think it's probably the most _____ colour for . . . a _____ of the population.
CM: Well, If you look at any group of people together, like _____ in a football stadium or _____ like that . . .
CM: If you go shopping do you not particularly choose _____, a blue shirt _____ a pink shirt?
SB: . . . most clothes I buy _____ to be khaki or olive or grey, and then I have things with _____ colours to go _____ them so – and it's very much a _____ of mood . . .

---

128 ## Grammar

Conditional sentences

a Conditions are often introduced by **if**.

If you met a foreigner who was coming to your country for the first time, what local dishes would you recommend?
If I had a lot of time, yes, that might be quite a good idea. (69)
If we get sunshine that's just a bonus. (38)

But how many other ways of introducing a condition can you find?

1 *Imagine you are going to London. Make a list of the people for whom you would buy presents.*
2 *Provided you export what you have bought, you can have the VAT amount refunded to you.* (127)
3 *Under which system would you claim VAT assuming you were leaving Britain by sea?*
4 *In the case of a power cut do not use the lifts.*
5 *You can see everything from outside providing you are willing to walk.* (157)
6 *Supposing they arrived after the restaurants had shut.* (86)

7 *You can't buy things free of VAT unless you live outside the UK.* (126)
8 *You can get a 'Cheap Day Return' ticket as long as you start your journey after 9.30.*
9 *As long as you are not living in Britain, you can buy things free of tax.*

b How many occurrences of **would** can you find in the passage below? How many past tenses? Why do we have **would** and the past tense here?

Imagine you were applying to a computer dating agency to find a partner. Tell the person with you what you would say about yourself.
JM: *First thing on my list would be that I have a sense of humour. I would need to meet somebody who also had a sense of humour. I'd want to meet somebody who was interested in the cinema, and the theatre and so on. And, somebody who read a lot . . . because I do. And who wasn't terribly interested in sport, because I absolutely hate sport.* (20)

a Lexicon words

Choose the appropriate words to complete the sentences. (Some words are used more than once.) Then look them up in the Lexicon. Say which categories they belong to as they are used here.

cover, direct, marked, matter, show, supply, treat

1 Take your completed form to the point ____ Service.
2 When you ____ that you have paid you can take whatever it is you want to buy and leave with it.
3 Have you got enough money to ____ the hotel bill?
4 People say that London can ____ all your needs, no ____ how bizarre.
5 Cadbury's take them and they ____ them with chocolate.
6 A finger of fudge is just enough to give your kids a ____.
7 ... then I have things with bright colours to go with them, so it's very much a ____ of mood.
8 Some London stores are able to send goods ____ to an overseas address.

offer, post, provided, show, shown, trade

9 Some stores ____ relief from VAT under the Retail Export Scheme.
10 This means ____ you export what you have bought, you can have the VAT amount refunded to you.
11 A form that must be filled in by the shopkeeper and ____ to the Customs Officer at the airport.
12 You will need to ____ your passport.
13 Writing books is what I call a skilled ____. I'm in a very skilled ____ too.
14 Using a mail order catalogue you can buy things through the ____ without even going to the shop.
15 ____ Unions try to improve working conditions for their members.
16 Britain does quite a lot of ____ with Eastern Europe.

b any more/further/longer

Make some sentences.

We decided not to	go on	
We don't intend to	discuss the matter	any more.
I don't think I'll	write	any further
I'd rather not	watch TV	any longer.
Being 65 she's unable to go jogging		

c What are the missing words?

1 What makes you think I'm any ____ at my job?
2 Imagine you want to make the ____ purchases in London.
3 Even ____ you do not intend to make a claim you should notify your insurance company.
4 Make a list of people for ____ you might buy presents.
5 Your purchases will be ____ up from the stockroom while you make payment.
6 The poem makes a good point about people ____ dogs.

7 What make of ____ was the writer of the hitchhiker story driving?

What word appears in all these sentences? What other phrases do you know with this word? Check in the Lexicon.

d Odd word out?

Find the word or phrase whose meaning is quite different from the other words in these sets. Explain.

1 smell, sight, taste, hearing, running, touch
2 gets it clean, that's awful, how annoying it is, most irritating, I absolutely hate it
3 the most popular, very fashionable, liked by the majority, trendy, traditional
4 staff, cashier, shopkeeper, trade union leader, equipment, boss, master
5 abroad, airport, overseas, another country, foreign country
6 bill, cash, change, receipt, goods, payment, postbox
7 very few, hardly any, not many, quite a lot

	Important words to remember (551 so far)				
ability	clean	forth	passport	skill	uneducated
abroad	cover L	goods	popular	staff	unless
advertising	design	intend	port	store	whatever
analysis	direct L	kids	post L	suit	whom
bargain	economy	mail	product	supply	wind
basically L	enter	majority	receipt	taste	wonderful
bill	equipment	make L	recognise	tax	
box	exit	mark L	save	trade L	
case	export	master	scheme	tradition	
cash	fashion	mood	self	traditional	
catalogue	fill	offer L	silence	treat L	

SB130a PB130

1 Point out to students that the exercise is split into two sections: 1–8 and 9–16. Lexicon words to be used are given at the beginning of each section.

Key: 1 marked 5   9 offer 5
2 show   10 provided 2
3 cover 4   11 shown
4 supply, matter 2 12 show
5 cover 1   13 trade, trade 3
6 treat 4   14 post 1
7 matter 1   15 Trade 4
8 direct 1   16 trade 1

SB130b

2 any more, **any further** and **any longer** are not completely interchangeable in these examples. Note that **any further** can have the literal meaning of distance, e.g. 'We decided not to go on (travel) any further', or can mean **any more**, as in 'We don't intend to discuss the matter any further'.

3 Ask students to produce true sentences of their own.

SB130c

Key: 1 good   2 export   3 if   4 whom   5 sent   6 keeping   7 car
The word **make** is the common word.

SB130d

Key: 1 'running' is not one of the five senses
2 'gets it clean' is the only one that does not express dislike
3 'traditional' is the only one that does not express popularity
4 'equipment' is the only one that is not a person
5 'airport' could be in this country – all the rest are abroad
6 'postbox' is the only one not to do with making a purchase
7 'quite a lot' is the only phrase which does not refer to a small amount

LEXICAL OBJECTIVES

Level 1 words (see page 129T):
able, **before**, **ever**, **exactly**, **few**, **fine**, **get**, **have**, **if** (see SB129), **matter** L, **part**, **present**, **provided**, **providing**, **say**, **show**, **under**, **until**, **up** (see SB119).

ability 1 quality or skill. *Do Smarties have the ability to make people happy?*
2 intelligence. *. . . children of all abilities.* T
abroad in/to a foreign country. *Some shops abroad . . .* T *. . . to go abroad* T
advertising *What kinds of products are they advertising?*
analysis the process of considering something in detail. *. . . grammatical analysis.*
Also: **analyse**
bargain 1 Noun: something you can buy cheaply. *It was a bargain at £2.*
2 Verb: to negotiate
basically L
bill 1 *Pay for the book and get your bill stamped.*

2 *The Beatles were top of the bill.* T
box 1 container. *. . . a box of matches*
2 a square shape on a form. *Tick in the box marked X.* T
bright 1 bright in colour. *I like things with bright colours. bright blue eyes*
2 intelligent. *. . . a bright girl* T
case See SB123.
cash 1 Noun: *Are you paying cash?*
2 Verb: *Can I cash this cheque?* T
catalogue a book containing a list of things you can buy. *. . . giving the catalogue number*
clean 1 not dirty. *'Ariel gets it clean.'*
2 *I will try and regularly clean the kitchen.* [14]
cover L
design 1 to plan and make. *Everything in this shop is designed to be used by people who use their left hand.*
2 *. . . the best of British design* [12]
direct L
economy careful spending or use of things to save money. *Cars advertise 'fuel economy' when they don't use much petrol.* [9]
Note: Main two uses of **economy** *'the British economy'* etc. are covered in SB Level 3.
enter 1 to go/come into. *He entered the room/conversation . . .* T
2 to start. *He entered university/politics at the age of 18.* T
3 *They enter the number into the computer . . .*
equipment *sports equipment*
exit way out of a building or place
export to sell something to another country. *Provided you export what you have bought . . .* Opp. of **import**.
fashion 1 manner. *. . . in his usual friendly fashion.* T
2 currently popular style of clothing, make-up etc. *British fashion* T
Also: **fashionable**
fill 1 *to fill a bottle* T
2 *Fill in the selection form.* [9]
forth a rather old-fashioned word common only in a few phrases. **and so forth** = and so on. **back and forth**
goods things that are made to be sold. *deliver the goods direct to . . .*
intend mean, plan. *. . . get down the road early if you intend to snap up the bargains.*
kids children. Informal use. *. . . give your kids a treat.*
mail 1 letters, parcels etc. delivered by the post office
2 **the mail** = system used by the post office for dealing with letters etc.
Also: **mail order** *a mail order firm*
majority 1 the number of people or things that form more than half of a larger group. *. . . for the majority of the population* Opp. of **minority**.
2 the majority in Parliament. *The Labour Party won by a small majority.* T
make/made L
mark L
master 1 the person who has authority/control. *. . . the dog's master.* T
2 a skilled worker. *. . . the master baker* T
3 main/most important. *master catalogue* [9]
mood 1 the way you feel about things *What colours you wear – it's a matter of mood.* [9]

2 *She's in a bad mood today.* T
offer L
passport travel document
popular liked, approved of by a lot of people. *The most popular colours . . .*
port area where ships load and unload. *. . . direct to the port by which you are leaving the country.*
post L
product *What kinds of products are being advertised?*
receipt paper that shows you have paid for something. *Take the receipt to . . .*
recognise 1 *We probably wouldn't recognise them.*
2 = understand *I recognise that you must be very tired.* T
save 1 *If you know how to get tax relief you will save money.*
2 to avoid the need for. *This will save you a lot of trouble in the future.* T
scheme a plan. *Personal Export Schemes*
self combines with adjectives and nouns to refer to:
1 something you do yourself. *self-taught*
2 something that happens automatically. *self-locking doors* T
silence 1 a pause because nobody is speaking. *There was a long silence.*
2 absolutely no noise at all. *The audience was silent.* T
skill 1 knowledge and ability *. . . routine jobs with no skill in them.*
2 a type of work which requires special training. *Learn the skill of painting.* T
staff employees. *Our staff will be pleased to help.*
store 1 a shop. *London Stores*
2 a store cupboard T
3 to put away and keep safe. *Computers can store an awful lot of information.* T
suit 1 an outfit for a man or woman consisting of a matching jacket and trousers/skirt. *. . . a smart grey suit.*
2 *That dress really suits you.* T
supply 1 to provide. *People say that London can supply all your wants . . .*
2 *. . . supplies of food for Africa.* T
taste 1 *It tastes like chocolate never tasted before.*
2 *She has good taste in clothes.* T
tax money you have to pay to the government. *. . . free of tax. He's taxed at the rate of 30%.* T
2 **taxing** = difficult. *We faced new and taxing problems.* T
trade L
tradition a belief or custom. *Street markets are a tradition in London.*
traditional 1 *a traditional song* [6]
2 using old-fashioned methods. *. . . a fairly traditional school* T
treat L
uneducated has not received any education. *He sounds uneducated.*
unless if not; except when. (See SB129.)
whatever 1 *You choose what/whatever you want*
2 *There was no reason whatever for them to behave like that.* (See Unit 10.)
whom used in formal English. *. . . people for whom you may want to buy a present*
wind windy weather. *a straight road with no wind . . .*
wonderful very nice/good. *. . . a wonderful world*

Revision unit

This revision unit has wider range of activities than most units and involves students actively using the language they have learnt. The unit begins with listening to and giving directions from a map. There is an opportunity to describe a place and compare two country towns. The Hitch-hiker is preceded by a summary of the story so far, which includes three factual mistakes for students to spot. A section on useful notices recycles target lexis and gives opportunities for role-play. There is a song about London followed by an informal discussion on tape about sense of direction. Then students discuss the same topic.

OBJECTIVES

Lexical objectives are in TB142

Grammar and discourse

a Instructions; the imperative and 'I want you to . . .'. (132)
b Common adverbs ending in **-ly**: **actually**, **only**, **immediately**, **obviously**, **eventually**, **usually**, **totally**, **utterly**, **probably**, **certainly**, **fairly**, **suddenly**. (132,141)
c Expressions of cause, purpose, time and condition. (135)
d Ways of starting and ending a discussion or report. (137)
e Use of **ever**, **whatever**, **whenever**, etc. (141,142)
f Use of **come**. (142)

Tasks

a Giving directions/instructions. (131)
b Monitoring and checking on information received. (131)
c Describing a place. (133)
d Comparing two places. (134)
e Saying how you feel about where you come from. (139)
f Summarising a narrative. (136)
g Predicting the development of a narrative. (136)
h Recognising useful notices. (138)
i Discussion on personal abilities and attributes. (140)

131 Map reading

Aims: 1 To practise giving directions/instructions.
2 To illustrate monitoring and checking on information received.
3 The use of **could/would have** for unfulfilled possibility.

Lexis: become, **branch**, **castle**, **come across**, **continue**, **cross**, **distance** [T], **eventually** [L], (**so**) **far**, **immediately** [L], **middle**, **onto**, **turn(ing)**

Task and listening   SB131a 131a* PB131

1 Caldwell is on the right-hand edge of the map, north of the A66. Students work in pairs. Point out the task is simply to list roads and villages. (Students will give complete directions for the second part of the journey after they have listened to Catherine's directions for the first part.)

2 Put on the board the routes the students decided on. Expand these in class discussion: 'Okay, along the B6274. That's north along the B6274 as far as Winston' etc. Make it clear there is more than one route. When one or two students have described their routes, lead into a class discussion on the best route. Summarise this route on the board in preparation for the next stage.

3 Students listen and compare their route with Catherine's. (This recording goes only as far as Staindrop. This is so students can speculate again on the second part of the journey, before hearing Catherine's version.)

4 Ask students why Stephen repeats Catherine's words (B6274, across the A67, A688 Staindrop). Repetition is a common way of giving feedback on instructions and showing whether or not we have understood.

Task and listening   SB131b 131b*

5 In pairs students work out a route from Staindrop to Middleton. Again, make a note of the student consensus before listening to Catherine's route.

Key: Catherine chose to go to Middleton via Eggleston.

Listening   SB131c 131c*

7 Students work in pairs. Draw attention to 'We could have taken an A road. That would have taken you into Barnard Castle.' pointing out that the **could/would have** form is used for a possibility which was not fulfilled.

Key: Catherine might have gone by a major road, the A688, but she chose instead to take the 'scenic route'.

Task   SB131d

8 Students could be asked to do this for homework. You may like to do section 132 first, though. Students could also draw a map and refer to it, if they would find it easier.

132 Language study

Aim: 1 To focus attention on adverbs ending in **-ly**.
2 To practise forms used in instructions.

Lexis: actually, **eventually**, **immediately**, **only**

SB132a PB132

1 Students use the transcripts to check.

Key: 1 eventually 2 actually 3 only 4 immediately

SB132b 132b*

2 Students work individually, then compare answers in pairs. Finally students check their answers with the tape.

Key: I want you to head north on the B6274.
You just go straight across there.
I want you to turn left in Eggleston.
You come to a little town.
You should immediately come to a little village.

133 What's it like?

Aim: To practise describing places.

Lexis: behind, **camp(ing)**, **obvious**, **obviously** [T] [L], **rather/than** (for comparisons)
Optional: **common**, **moor**, **scenic**, **valley**, **waterfall**

It should not be difficult even for inexperienced map users to find 5 relevant statements to describe Middleton. Encourage experienced map users to explain how they know that Middleton is in a valley etc.

Task   SB133 PB133

1 Students work in pairs. Monitor very briskly at this stage, to help with both map reading and lexis.

2 Students explain their list to another pair, then report their observations. List the points on the board.

Listening   133*

3 Ask students to tick off the points Stephen makes and also to add any they may have missed.

Key: . . . a fairly small village at the foot of a valley . . . probably very scenic, with Middleton Common behind it . . . on a river . . . on a tributary of the River Tees . . . near waterfalls and camping sites . . . little windy roads . . . quite hilly . . . must be sheep farming country.

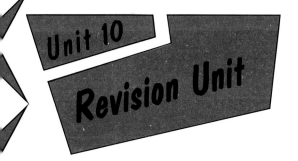

Unit 10
Revision Unit

Map reading

a From Caldwell

Look at this map and work out how to get from Caldwell to Middleton-in-Teesdale. Make a list of the roads you would use and any towns or villages you would go through.

131a Did Catherine give the same route as you?

Listen again and make a note when Stephen repeats Catherine's words.

b ... to Middleton-in-Teesdale

Work out directions for the rest of the journey.

▶ Tell the class and together decide on the best route. ◀

131b Listen and check. Did Catherine choose the same route as you?

c What other route could she have chosen? Why do you think she chose the route she did?

131c Listen and check.

d Plan and give directions for a journey in your own country.

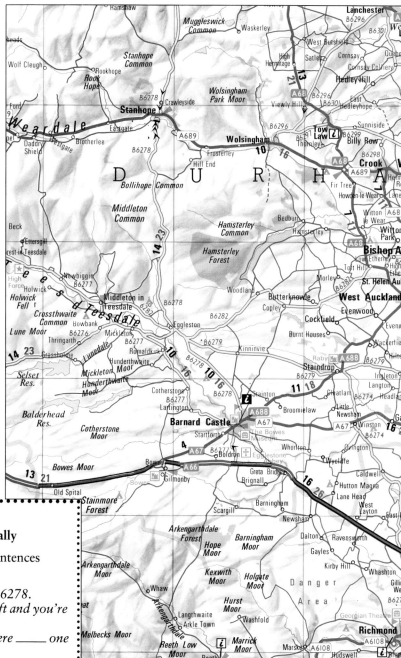

132 *Language study*

a actually, only, immediately, eventually

Use these words to complete the four sentences below.

1 *And the B6279 _____ runs into the B6278.*
2 *The 6278 _____ comes in from the left and you're coming down from the right.*
3 *When you say left in Eggleston, is there _____ one road?*
4 *I want you to turn left and then _____ right onto the B6282.*

b Instructions

132b Match these parts of sentences to give instructions.

I want you to	go straight across there.
You just	come to a little village.
I want you to	a little town.
You come to	head north on the B6274.
You should immediately	turn left in Eggleston.

133 What's it like?

Look at the map of Middleton with your partner. Do you think it's flat or hilly? Nice scenery or industrial? What do you think it looks like? Write down five things about it.

Compare your list with another pair.

▶ Tell the class what you have written. ◀

133 Did you get the same as Stephen?

134 ## How does it compare?

How does Middleton compare with Barnard Castle?

> BARNARD CASTLE 5,016 Co.Durham Map40NZ01 EcThu Md Wed/alt Tue Alston 32 Brough 18 London 244 Middlesbrough 31 Newcastle upon Tyne 45 Scotch Corner 5 **King's Head 12/14 Market Pl Tel Teesdale (0833) 38365 rm20 bath no dogs 25P B&B(c)(d)

Write five sentences, three of which are true, and two of which are false. Read them to your partner.

What can you write about Middleton from this entry in the *AA Member's Handbook*?

> MIDDLETON-IN-TEESDALE 1,200 Co Durham Map 40NY92 EcWed Md cattle alt Tue Alston 22 Barnard Castle 10 Kendal 44 London 254 **Teesdale Market Pl Tel Teesdale (0833) 40264 rm14 (7bath)P B&B(b)

135 ## *Grammar*

Cause, purpose, time, condition

In the last four units we have looked at words, clauses and phrases expressing:

1 cause *There's no chance of a promotion there,* so *I'm going to move on.* (result)
2 purpose *We gave Jeremy a set of eight questions to look at.*
3 time *Before having the children she worked in insurance.*
4 condition *Provided you export what you have bought you can have the VAT amount refunded to you.*

Cause / result because ...	There's no chance of promotion there,
Purpose in order to ...	to look at
Condition if ...	Provided you export what you have bought
Time when / how long etc	Before having the children

Find more examples in the sentences on the right. Which of the coloured expressions belong in which part of the table?

a *The A688 goes through Staindrop and* then *at the end there's this road off to the right.* (133)
b *The 6279 fades out* at this stage *and the 6278 takes over.* (133)
c *As long as you keep to the speed limit* you'll be all right.
d *You can buy things VAT free* since you are not living in Britain.
e *There are lots of camping-sites around,* so it must be quite scenic. (134)
f *In ten seconds* or so *we were doing ninety.* (136)
g *If I look up somewhere on a map to find out where I'm going, I can work out what I'm supposed to be doing and so I don't worry about that. And* when I came here *I looked it up in the A–Z* before leaving home, *and then I checked the map* in the underground station *when I got off, and had no trouble at all.* (140)
h *He saw a man hitching a lift and,* remembering the days when he used to do the same, *he stopped.*
i Finally, *after some time, he told the writer he was in a skilled trade.* (136)
j *I heard a police siren.* It was so loud *it seemed to be right inside the car.*
k *The policeman raised his hand* to order them to stop.
l *The ratty-faced man was going to Epsom* for the races. (136)
m *Catherine couldn't sleep* for the pain in her shoulder.

Aims: 1 To practise comparing two places.
2 To practise writing expressions of comparison.

Lexis: **castle**

Aim: To revise expressions of cause, purpose, time and condition.

Lexis: **since**

Task and writing   SB134 PB134

1 Refer students to the map to find Middleton-in-Teesdale and Barnard Castle. Then tell them to look back at the AA symbols in Unit 1, section 7, and refresh their memories of what the symbols mean. In pairs students work out what the AA descriptions of Middleton-in-Teesdale and Barnard Castle mean.

2 Ask students to make their comparisons orally before writing their sentences down. You could lead students very gently into the exercise by beginning with an oral true/false exercise:
Middleton is much smaller than Barnard Castle.
They are both about 200 miles from London.

Key: Abbreviations used:
EcWed – early closing Wednesdays, Md – Market day,
alt Tue – alternative Tuesdays,
(See Unit 1, TB section 7.)

3 Individually students write the 5 sentences comparing the two places, then exchange them with a partner for true/false check.

4 As a final check, ask each student to read one of their sentences aloud to the class, who will decide if the statement is true or false.

More examples of these expressions can be found in the Grammar sections in the previous four units. To help students recall these, ask them to review the Grammar sections in Units 6–9 for homework <u>before</u> the lesson on which you do this exercise. Make sure students know both uses of **since** *– time and cause.*

SB135 PB135

Key: Cause:
d
e
h   remembering the days . . . = because he remembered the days . . .
j   It was so loud = Because it was so loud . . .
m for = because of
Purpose:
g   to find out
k   to order them to stop
l   for the races
Condition:
c   as long as = if
g   If I look up
Time:
a
b
f
g   when I came here . . .
     before leaving home . . .
     and then . . .
     when I got off
i   Finally, after some time . . .

Aims: 1 To practise summarising a narrative.
2 To practise predicting the development of a narrative.

Lexis: ask, **beside**, **beyond** [L], **challenge**, **far**, **fast**,
flash, **forward**, **guy** (colloquial for 'man'), **immediately**,
law, **motor**(-cycle), **order**, **press**, **prove**, **races**, **shout**,
spot, **within**
Revision: **since**

SB136a PB136

1 Students work in pairs. Make a list on the board of the
mistakes they find.

Key: The three mistakes are:
the car was blue not grey
the passenger was wearing a cap, not a hat
he said that he did not watch the horses run, he was not
even interested in horses

Reading and listening   SB136b/c 136b 136c *

2 Ask students to repeat their predictions from the previous
unit before they read the passage. Ask one or two
students to summarise the story for you orally.

Key: Stephen and Catherine guessed correctly, but they
expected the writer to take up the challenge earlier.

Task and listening   SB136d 136d *

3 Before listening to the tape initiate a discussion about
what kind of man the writer is. Is he law-abiding or is he
likely to take risks? Is he likely to have been in trouble
before? How good a chance would he have of getting
away if he tried to run? Is he likely to run that kind of risk?

4 Ask students if they have ever been caught speeding.
What did they do? Did they consider, if only briefly, not
stopping?

Key: Stephen and Catherine feel that the writer will
probably stop both because he is law-abiding and also
because he would not have much chance of getting away
anyway. They say that they would not have gone at 129
m.p.h. in the first place but that they would certainly pull
over if there was a policeman beside them.

Task and listening   SB136e 136e *

5 Students prepare their questions in pairs. Make a
consolidated list and ask students to pick out the most
likely questions.

Key: Stephen and Catherine suggested that the
policeman will ask the driver:
to show his licence
if he knows what speed he was doing
if the car is his
what the registration number is
where he lives
what his address is
where he is going in such a hurry
where he is coming from
what his business is
to show all his documents

The Hitch-hiker

a   The story so far

Can you spot three mistakes?

The writer had just bought a new car – a smart grey BMW – and he was driving up to London on a nice summer day.

On the way he saw a man hitching a lift, and, remembering the days when he used to do the same, he stopped, asked the man where he was going, and offered him a lift.

The passenger was a 'small ratty-faced man'; he was wearing a greyish jacket and hat. He said he was going right through London to Epsom for the races, since it was Derby Day.

When the writer asked him why he went to the races he said he wasn't going to bet, he just went to watch the horses run. Then he just sat and said nothing until the writer asked him what work he did. Finally, after some time, he told the writer he was in a 'skilled trade' but he still didn't say what work it was.

They started talking about the car, and the passenger asked the writer if it would really go as fast as the manufacturers said it would in the adverts . . .

 b   Now read on . . .

c   Without looking back, summarise what happened. Had you guessed?

 Did Stephen and Catherine guess?

d   What do you think will happen next? Will the driver stop, or will he drive on even faster? What would *you* have done in that situation?

> Tell the class, and make a list of other students' suggestions.

 Did you say the same as Stephen and Catherine?

e   If the policeman orders the driver to stop, what will he say to him?

> Make a list of what he might say and tell the class.

 Compare your ideas with Stephen's and Catherine's.

PART 4

'GO ON! GET 'ER UP TO ONE-TWO-NINE'

"What can she do flat out?"

"One hundred and twenty-nine miles an hour," I told him.

"I'll bet she won't do it."

"I'll bet she will."

"All car makers is liars," he said. "You can buy any car you like and it'll never do what makers say it will in the ads."

"This one will."

"Open 'er up then and prove it," he said. "Go on, guv'nor, open 'er right up and let's see what she'll do."

There is a roundabout at Chalfont St Peter and immediately beyond it there's a long straight section of dual carriage-way. We came out of the roundabout on to the carriage-way and I pressed my foot hard down on the accelerator. The big car leaped forward as though she'd been stung. In ten seconds or so, we were doing ninety.

"Lovely!" he cried. "Beautiful! Keep goin'!"

I had the accelerator jammed right down against the floor and I held it there.

"One hundred!" he shouted . . . "A hundred and five! . . . A hundred and ten! . . . A hundred and fifteen! Go on! Don't slack off!"

I was in the outside lane and we flashed past several cars as though they were standing still – a green Mini, a big cream-coloured Citroën, a white Land-Rover, a huge truck with a container on the back, an orange-coloured Volkswagen Minibus . . .

"A hundred and twenty!" my passenger shouted, jumping up and down. "Go on! Go on! Get 'er up to one-two-nine!"

At that moment, I heard the scream of a police siren. It was so loud it seemed to be right inside the car, and then a policeman on a motor-cycle loomed up alongside us on the inside lane and went past us and raised a hand for us to stop.

"Oh, my sainted aunt!" I said. "That's torn it!"

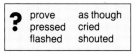

?	prove	as though
	pressed	cried
	flashed	shouted

L beyond

137 *Phrase-building*

Starting and ending a discussion or report

a Find the phrases from the box below which complete what Stephen and Catherine actually said.

> a ... 'Can I see your licence?'
> b ... came into his mind.
> c ... 'Do you know what speed you were doing ...?'
> d ... ask to see the driver's licence.

SB: I think the first thing he will do is ...
CM: Or I think the first thing he might say is ...
CM: And then he might say ...
CM: And anything else that ...

What phrase started their discussion?

b Look at the sets of phrases and sentences in boxes A-D. Which sets do you think would come near the beginning, and which near the end of a discussion or report? Complete four phrases in C.

B

We have	three main points in our report: ...
We've got	two things to say: ...
We thought of	three things: ...

C

	is ...
	was ...
The first thing	*he'll do is ...*
	he did was ...
	we want to say is ...
	to do is ...

A

I don't think	there's anything else.
	there's anything else we wanted to say.
	we've missed anything out.
	there's anything else to add, is there?
I think	that's all. Okay?
	we've covered every point, haven't we?

D

Is		say?	I think that was all.
Was	there anything else to	add?	Oh – the point about the ...
Have we covered	everything?		I think so.
	most things?		I would have thought so.

138 Useful notices

Where might you see these? Make a list. Choose five of these places, and imagine a conversation you might have there.

e.g. Cashier: Do you have any change?
Customer: Hang on ... I might have. Let me see.

SMALL ADS

In case of FIRE

CASHIER

NO REFUNDS WITHOUT RECEIPTS

One piece of hand luggage only

ECONOMY TRAVEL

CUT PRICE OFFERS!

UK Passport Holders Only ➡

Next showing 8.30

VAT REFUNDS

EEC Passports

CUSTOMS OFFICER

TRADITIONAL BRITISH FOOD

PAY HERE

BOX OFFICE

137 Phrase-building

Aims: 1 To practise ways of starting and ending a discussion or report.

Lexis: ask

SB137a

1 Students match the sentence halves. Ask them to guess what phrases they think began the discussion before they check the transcripts to check their answers.

Key: a And then he might say, 'Can I see . . .?'
b And anything else that came into his mind.
c Or I think the first thing he might say is, 'Do you know . . .?'
d I think the first thing he would do is ask to see . . .
Phrase which started their discussion:
I think the first thing he would do is . . .

SB137b

2 In pairs students write sentences containing the four phrases. Monitor their pair work. Have a few students read their sentences aloud to the class.

Key: A near the end   B near the beginning   C near the beginning   D near the end

138 Useful notices

Aims: 1 To revise and extend uses of useful lexis from earlier units.
2 To help students to understand notices and encourage them to try and read notices that may prove of use to them.

Lexis: box, case, cut, economy, officer, passport, receipt, traditional

1 Students should discuss where they might find the notices in pairs. As there are rather a lot of notices, they could be divided up amongst pairs.

2 In pairs students write short conversations of 2–3 lines. Help them to write suitable English. Ask each pair to practise and act out one of their conversations for the class.

Key: Notices could be found in a shop, restaurant, airport/port, theatre/cinema, travel agency, or any public building. (Some of these signs could be found in several types of place.)

139 A Cockney song

Aim: To give intensive listening practice.

Lexis: maybe, sing, wherever

SB139 [139]

1 Ask students to read the rubric and infer what a 'cockney' is: someone who lives in (the East End of) London.

2 Play the song once for the students and ask them to listen for pleasure and general meaning.

3 In pairs students try to fill in the blanks from memory, but tell them you will play the song for them a second time very shortly.

4 Play the song, pausing the tape so students can fill in the blanks.

5 Discuss the picture which shows pearly kings and queens. The Pearly Kings and Queens Association was formed in 1910 to work for charity. Originally pearly kings were elected to protect the interests of street traders. The origin of their pearl buttons has never been fully explained, but is believed to be an imitation of 'toffs' (rich people).

Key: 1 love
2 think of
3 funny
4 because

140 A good sense of direction

Aim: To practise listening to and having an informal discussion focusing on personal abilities and attributes.

Lexis: respect, sense, step [L], totally, turning, wherever

Task SB140

1 Clarify the meaning of 'sense of direction' by talking about your own. Include a story about how you once got lost, or about how you found your way in difficult circumstances.

2 Students discuss the questions in pairs.
It may be necessary to prompt discussion with a few questions:
Do you get lost often/sometimes/occasionally?
When you go to a new place how long is it before you can find your way around?
How often do you need to do a particular journey before you can remember it?
Which member of your family is best at directions?
Can you work out your way on a map and then follow the route from memory?
Can you think of one or two occasions when you got lost or found your way in spite of difficulties?

3 Give individual students a chance to talk. Aim to promote general discussion rather than individual performance, since the topic is more appropriate to informal chat than formal presentation.

Listening SB140 [140]*

4 Students listen to Catherine and Stephen and make brief notes on what they say.

Key: Catherine thinks she has a good sense of direction. She's never been really lost. In the middle of a city she looks for the sun and follows that.
Stephen also thinks he has a good sense of direction, but he relies a lot on maps and landmarks.

141 Language study

Aims: 1 Further practice of common adverbs ending in **-ly**.
2 To illustrate the meaning and use of **ever**.

Lexis: behind, fairly, obviously, suddenly, totally

SB141a

Key: 1 fairly, probably
2 completely, utterly
3 really
4 usually, suddenly
5 obviously, usually
6 probably
7 certainly

SB141b

1 Students read the rubric and decide where **ever** goes without the teacher's help. Students do the exercise in pairs.

Key: 1 Do you **ever** say 'Just a moment?'
2 Have you **ever** been involved in an accident...?
3 if **ever** anybody asked me...
or
if anyone **ever** asked me...
4 if you **ever** go to London./if **ever** you go to London.
5 I don't think we'll **ever** be able to go.
6 did you **ever** stay away from school?
7 I've lived there **ever** since.
8 happily **ever** after.

139 A Cockney song

Which of these words go best in the gaps?

like/love
think of/talk about
a kind of/funny
since/because

Maybe it's because I'm a Londoner

Maybe it's because I'm a Londoner, that I _____ London so.
Maybe it's because I'm a Londoner, that I _____ her wherever I go.
I get a _____ feeling inside me when I'm walking up and down,
That maybe it's _____ I'm a Londoner, that I love London town.

[139] Listen and check.

Do you feel the same way about your town or city?

140 A good sense of direction

Do you have a good sense of direction, or do you get lost? What do you do if you lose your way? Have you ever been totally lost?
Tell each other.

[140] What about Catherine and Stephen?

141 *Language study*

a More words ending in -ly

Put these words in the first three sentences.

fairly totally really probably utterly

1 *Well, it looks like a _____ small village at the foot of a valley. So it's _____ very scenic with Middleton Common behind it.* (133)
2 *Have I ever been lost? Well, not _____ and _____ lost.* (140)
3 *It sounds _____ weird, but in the middle of a city would look for the sun and follow that.* (140)

And these in the last four.

usually (2) certainly suddenly
obviously probably

4 *But _____ there are landmarks and you _____ realise that ... maybe you're heading the wrong way.* (140)
5 *He's _____ ... a man, who is _____ well within the law.* (136)
6 *I _____ wouldn't have gone at 120 miles an hour.* (136)
7 *If there was a policeman beside me, telling me to pull over or flagging me down, I would _____ pull over.* (136)

b ever

ever = at any time (no matter when ...)

If you ever go to London, you could have a suit made at Moss Bros.
Do you ever shop in your local markets in your country?
Have you ever been totally lost?
A: *Have you ever had an accident?*
B: *No, touch wood, never.*

Where could you put the word **ever** in these sentences?

1 *Do you say 'Just a moment?'* (64)
2 *Have you been involved in an accident like one of these?* (106)

3 *When I was very young, if anybody asked me what I wanted to be I always said a doctor.* (64)
4 *You can save a lot of money if you go to London.*
5 *I don't think we'll be able to go.*
6 *When you were a child, did you stay away from school?*

In these two sentences **ever** means 'always'. Where does it go?

7 *My parents came to live in England and I've lived there since.*
8 *Children's stories often end: 'And they lived happily after.'*

71

a whatever, wherever, whenever, however

1 in place of what, where, when or how
You choose what/whatever you want.
You can go where/wherever you like.
We save money how/however we can.
I visit her when/whenever I can.

The **-ever** form is emphatic (it doesn't matter what/where/when/how).

With this meaning **whatever** is often followed by a noun.
A: *What would you cook?*
B: *Whatever vegetables happened to be in the fridge.*

2 introducing a separate clause meaning 'It doesn't matter what/who/when/how/where ...'
She'll never agree, whatever you say.
You'll still be late, however you go.
Wherever they are, we'll never find them.
I think he's a fool, whoever he is.

3 when you are not sure who, where, when
They've just bought a new house or flat or whatever.
If she's still in Singapore ... or wherever ...
I'll be round about seven or whenever ...

4 whatever is often used to emphasise a negative sentence or a sentence with the word **any**
There was no reason whatever for them to behave like that.
There is no time whatever for playing games.
You can ask about any subject whatever.

Which category do these sentences go in?

a *We had no time whatever to enjoy ourselves.*
b *You can, you know, bulk buy or whatever it is.*
c *Whatever you do, don't forget your ticket.*
d *Maybe it's because I'm a Londoner that I think of her wherever I go.*
e *I read whatever books I could find.*
f *You can't get a free ticket, whoever you are.*
g *The hitch-hiker was ready to accept a lift from whoever happened to be passing.*
h *We never managed to do anything, however hard we tried.*

b above, against, behind, below, beneath, beyond

Find five sentences where the words in red refer to place. What do you think the other sentences mean?

1 *Middleton is a few miles beyond Egglestone.*
2 *Just sign your name beneath mine.*
3 *You can't drive a car in Britain below the age of seventeen.*
4 *Is there anybody down below?*
5 *You can see Middleton in the valley, and the hills behind it.*
6 *They are behaving very strangely. I wonder what's behind it.*

c come

Look at these uses of the word **come**. In which sentences does **come** involve moving from one place to another? What does it mean in the other sentences?

He comes from Warrington.   *This came to 25p a mile.*

(not movement = was born/brought up in; his family lived there)   (not movement = works out at, the solution is)

1 *There are holes in the sky where the rain comes in.*
2 *We'll do the word 'mind' when we come to Unit 15.*
3 *Sorry you couldn't come to the airport.*
4 *What ambitions do you have? How far have they come true?*
5 *I try to come in a little bit ahead of most of the traffic.*
6 *We'll deal with that problem when it comes up.*
7 *So how come exactly the same tales have travelled halfway round the Western world?*
8 *The pilot and crew would come into the cabin to greet the passengers.*
9 *I had to wait for another train to come back again.*
10 *But if you know them, why not? If they come to mind.*
11 *The B6278 comes in from the left.*
12 *I don't think anything else came into his mind.*
13 *Can you guess what's going to come next?*

7 *It's on that shelf, above the dictionary.*
8 *I don't understand it – it's totally beyond me.*
9 *He was against the idea of driving through the town centre.*

Important words to remember (589 so far)

against L	camp	fast	onto	step L	whichever
ahead L	castle	flash	press	totally	whoever
below L	challenge	guy	prove	towards L	within
beneath	continue	immediately L	respect	turning	
beside	cross	motor	shout	upon	
beyond L	distance	obvious	sing	whenever	
branch	eventually L	obviously L	spot	wherever	

Aims: 1 To revise the meanings and uses of: **whatever, whenever, wherever, however**.
2 To revise some of the uses and meanings of prepositions commonly associated with place, e.g. **above, behind**.
3 To revise the uses and meanings of **come**.

Lexis: against [L], **ahead** [L], **below, beneath, towards** [L], **upon, whenever, whichever** [T], **whoever**

SB142a

1 Also introduce **whichever** and **whoever**.

Key: a 4 b 3 c 2 d 1 e 1
f 2 g 1 h 2

SB142b PB142

2 Also teach **ahead** as the opposite of **behind** e.g. He's **ahead** of me in English.

Key: Prepositions meaning place:
1, 2, 4, 5, 7
(**below** and, less commonly, **beneath** also have the general meaning of **less than** – **above** can mean **more than**.)
Other meanings:
3 below the age = less/younger than
6 what's behind it = what is causing them to behave that way
8 it's totally beyond me = I don't understand it at all
9 against the idea = opposed to the idea

SB142c

Key: **come** involves movement in sentences:
1, 3, 5, 8, 9
Other meanings:
2 come to = finish the units up to
4 come true = been realised
6 come up = occurs
7 how come = why
10 if they come to mind = if you think of them
11 come in = joins
12 = I don't think he thought of anything else
13 come = happen

LEXICAL OBJECTIVES

Level 1 words (see page 129T):
above L, **actually, ask, behind** L, **come** (see SB142), **far, however** (see SB142), **law, middle, than**.

against L
ahead L
below L
beneath under. *Sign your name beneath mine.*
beside 1 next to. . . . *a policeman zooming up beside him.*
beyond L
branch 1 branch of a tree. T

2 of a company, shop, family. *Some branches of Barclay's bank are open on Saturday mornings.* T
3 take a fork in a road. *I want you to branch off to the right onto a B road again.*
camp also **camping site**: a place where people stay in tents on holiday. . . . *it's near waterfalls and camping sites . . .*
castle a large strong building where you are safe from your enemies; very common in English place names. *Barnard Castle.*
challenge 1 to suggest that someone cannot do something even though they claim they can. *The hitch-hiker challenged the driver to do 129mph.* Also a noun: *The driver might have taken the challenge.*
2 to suggest that something is untrue. *I must challenge your statement.* T
3 to offer to fight or compete with. *He even challenged me to a race.* T
continue 1 if you continue something or if you continue doing/to do something you keep doing it. *Keep stirring to continue the cooking.* [7] *The orchestra continued to play.*
1.1 if something continues, it goes on. *The lesson continued for an hour. The road continued for five miles.* T
2 often used when someone is speaking. *'I'm leaving,' he said. 'And what's more,' he continued, 'I'm not coming back.'* T
cross 1 go from one side to the other. *You cross the A67.*
2 **It crossed my mind.** = I thought of it. T
3 A cross = + T
4 You can cross your fingers, arms etc. T
distance 1 how far it is from one place to another. *I haven't been able to gauge the distance, but it isn't very far.* T
2 in the distance = a long way away T
eventually L
fast 1 quick. . . . *a fast car.*
2 quickly. *The passenger asked if it would really go as fast as the manufacturers said.*
flash 1 a very bright light. . . . *a flash of lightning.* T
2 to turn a light on and off very quickly. *Flash your lights.* T
3 Photographers use a flash. T
4 in a flash/quick as a flash = very quickly T
5 to move very quickly. *We flashed past several cars as though they were standing.*
guy man. *The guy got in and he started boasting about his new car.*
immediately L
motor 1 engine. . . . *motor-bike*
2 a car
3 also **motorist/motorway**
4 to motor = to travel by car T
obvious 1 clear, easily seen. . . . *obvious deep thought . . .* [6]
obviously L
onto 1 *He tossed the book onto the desk.* T
2 to show the place towards which someone moves. *You branch off onto a B road again.*
3 to get onto a bus or train T
4 to go/move onto a new subject T
press 1 to push down. *He pressed the*

doorbell. T *I pressed my foot hard down on the accelerator.*
2 **press for** = argue strongly for. *He continued to press for a peaceful solution.* T
3 **the press** = the newspapers. *The British press.*
prove 1 *I think the only thing he can do is to prove that the car can go to 120 miles an hour.* [9] *Open her up then and prove it.*
2 to turn out. *I'm sure this song will prove very popular.* T
respect 1 to have a good opinion of. *He was respected for his honesty.* Noun: *I have a lot of respect for his honesty.* T
2 to accept or go along with. *I will respect your wishes/traditions.*
3 **in this respect/in one respect/in many respects** are used to refer to a particular aspect or detail. *I think I've got a good sense of direction in that respect.*
shout cry out or speak very loudly. *'A hundred and twenty,' my passenger shouted, jumping up and down.*
sing 1 to sing a song. *There were some children singing in the Smartie advertisement.*
spot 1 a round mark. . . . *a white blouse with red spots. A dirty spot.* T
Also: *spots of rain, spotlight* T
2 a place. *A nice spot for a picnic. A beauty spot.* T
3 a small amount of. *I think I'll do a spot of work.*
4 to find, notice. *Can you spot one mistake?*
step L
totally completely. *Have I ever been lost? Well not utterly and totally lost.*
toward(s) L
turning a road leading away from another road. *I've sometimes taken the wrong turning in Newhaven.*
upon 1 used in phrasal verbs: **come upon, look upon,** etc.
2 in formal English **upon** can replace **on** in some instances. *She was sitting in a chair with a mangy cat upon/on her knee.* T
3 *There were thousands upon thousands of people arriving . . .* T
whenever (See SB142.)
wherever (See SB142.)
whichever 1 used to indicate that it doesn't matter which of the possible alternatives is chosen. *Choose whichever one you prefer.* T
2 used when you specify which of a number of possibilities is the one you mean. *Use whichever of the other three dyes is appropriate.* T
whoever 1 used to refer to someone you are unable to identify precisely. *Come out, whoever you are . . .* T
2 used informally to refer vaguely to someone. *Then I give the report to the director or accounts manager or whoever.* T
within 1 within a time, measurement. *within two hours, a man who remains well within the law.*
3 inside . . . *within the four walls, . . . within city boundaries* T

I would have let his tyres down

This unit covers a variety of angles on the police and ways of handling minor traffic offences.

Most languages have many slang words for police, and television and society hold several different images of the police. These are discussed early on. Students compare basic traffic regulations and exchange anecdotes about any incidents – parking fines, speeding etc. that they or friends have been involved in. There is a simulation game where they take on roles as witnesses, and there are chances to brainstorm about acceptable excuses to suit a range of differing circumstances.

There are two episodes of The Hitch-hiker which, in this unit, assume a fairly central position, so as to advance the story line more quickly. The preceding activities will have helped prepare students for the themes and language they will meet in the story, and the recordings. Students discuss parking and are asked to prepare a short formal report and recommendations for the traffic flow for a place in their own country.

Selections of common notices from public places appear at two points in this unit and help to consolidate common uses of some of the target words.

OBJECTIVES

Lexical aims are in TB156

Grammar and discourse

a Modals **might** and **could** with **have** + **-en/-ed**. (144, 150, 151)

b Sentences in a narrative which both establish the situation and further the narrative. (144)

c The use of commas to separate situations from narrative. (144)

d Meanings and uses of **over** and **into**. (146)

e Meanings and uses of **go** and **going**. (148)

f Fronting patterns such as 'What I did was . . .' (149)

g Ways of expressing contrast, e.g. **but**, **while**, **however**. (155)

h To show how spontaneous conversation still progresses cooperatively even after 'cancellations' have been made by one speaker. (154)

Tasks

a Description and discussion of rules and regulations. (143)

b Producing anecdotes. (143)

c Explaining origins and derivations. (143)

d Speculating on the possible reasons for a given outcome. (144)

e Producing and understanding descriptions of people. (144, 147)

f Giving reasons or excuses. (145, 153)

g Predicting behaviour. (147)

h Speculating on someone's character. (147)

i Proposing and discussing action to be taken in given circumstances. (150)

j Speculating on what course of action would have been taken in imagined circumstances. (150)

k Speculating on people's reactions to particular events. (152)

l Understanding a detailed sequence of events, and being able to identify an unknown item from a specific description. (152)

143 The cops are coming

> **Aims:** 1 To practise describing and discussing rules and regulations.
> 2 To practise telling anecdotes.
> 3 To practise explaining origins and derivations of words.
>
> **Lexis: allowed** [L], **court, duty, fine, level, limit, offence, officer, rule, sharp** [L], **speed** (**limit**), (**parking**) **ticket, warning**
> Revision: **charged with** (formally accused of doing something illegal), **image, in each case, popular**

SB143 143a* **PB143**

1 Ask the students what words they have for the police in their language. Decide whether these are affectionate terms or whether they give a bad image of the police.

2 Play the cassette. Caroline and Monica have been asked to think of slang words in English for the police beginning with the letters B, C, F, L and R. They manage to get four of these: B – **bobby**; C – **cop/copper**; L – **the law**; R – **rozzer**. They do not get F – **fuzz**. The term **bobby** is an affectionate name for the police normally used by people who are well disposed to them. It comes from Sir Robert Peel, who started the British Police Force – Bobby is a short form of the name Robert. **Cop/copper** is a more neutral term but tends to be used by people who don't like the police much. **Fuzz** is definitely used by people who don't like the police. The term **rozzer** is rarely used.

SB143b

3 Students may need help with lexis here although many of the possible words are well know to them: **friendly/ unfriendly**; **honest/dishonest/corrupt**; **strong/weak**; **clever/stupid**; **efficient/inefficient**; **helpful** etc.

SB143c

4 Draw students' attention to the three dictionary definitions on this page. (**fr.** = from, giving the derivation of words. **ca**. 1700 means that the term was first used around the year 1700. Romany is the language spoken by gypsies.)

SB143d

5 Ask students to give reasons for their replies.

SB143e

This exercise introduces target lexis by getting students to look at common notices and giving practice in explaining them. It should stimulate discussion and anecdote telling to introduce themes that will occur in the Hitch-hiker episode and be useful for the subsequent discussion.

6 Students discuss the questions briefly in groups and then report back informally. Students might also be interested in discussing regulations and penalties for driving under the influence of alcohol, both in their own countries and in Britain. (In Britain, there's a 30 m.p.h. speed limit in towns and built-up areas; on wider roads in built-up areas this can be 40 m.p.h. The limit on dual carriageways and motorways is 70 m.p.h.)

SB143f

7 In pairs students discuss the signs and then report back informally. Encourage students to compare these signs with signs in their own country.

SB143g/h

8 Students discuss the questions in groups and then report back informally. Younger students may prefer to talk about their old school rules and what they were allowed and not allowed to do.

I would have let his tyres down

GIVE WAY

NO TROLLEYS Fine up to £200

NO DOGS ALLOWED

The Police Force was founded in Britain by Robert Peel

143 The cops are coming!

Watch out! The cops are coming!

What's up!

The law! Quick! This way!

ROAD CLOSED

LOOK BOTH WAYS

One way

143a a Cop is a slang word for 'police'. How many words do you have meaning 'police' in your language? Do you hear these words a lot on TV? What image do you give of the police in each case? Do they all have exactly the same meaning?

b What image do you get of the police from popular television programmes?

c Look on this page and find three slang words in English, meaning police. Do you know how they originated?

No right turn ahead except buses

P

← Pay at machine Display ticket inside windscreen

Every day 9am - 6pm

Maximum speed 20

REDUCE SPEED NOW

d Would you like to be/have been a police officer?

METROPOLITAN AREA POLICE STATION PLEASE REPORT TO THE OFFICER ON DUTY

WANTED

bobby: a policeman (*fr.* Robert Peel, the founder of the modern police force).

Dual carriageway ahead

DANGER KEEP CLEAR

Waiting limited to 10 minutes on Railway business only

No Parking

Motorists failing to comply with parking restrictions on Railway property are liable to prosecution under Byelaw 25

9.30 BBC
Cagney and Lacey
The two first ladies of the New York Police Department. Starring **Sharon Gless** as Christine Cagney and **Tyne Daly** as Mary Beth Lacey

Traffic rules and regulations

e What are the speed limits in your country? What fines are you likely to get if you go over them and get caught?

f Look at the road signs and notices on this page. Can you explain what they mean?

Look, there's a bobby on the corner. Why don't you ask him?

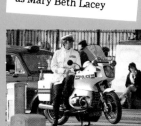

COUNTY COURT

and I look forward to seeing you on the 5th as we discussed on the phone.

Yours sincerely,

Bobby

Robert Green

rozzer: a policeman (possibly *fr.* Romany *roozlo*, strong).

copper (cop): a policeman (*fr.* cop: to catch, arrest *ca.* 1700).

g Have you ever had a parking ticket? Or been in a vehicle that has been stopped for speeding? What happened?

h Do you know anyone who has been charged with a traffic offence and has had to go to court, or been fined, or lost his/her licence?

73

144 Cops or bobbies?

a   Humour in uniform...

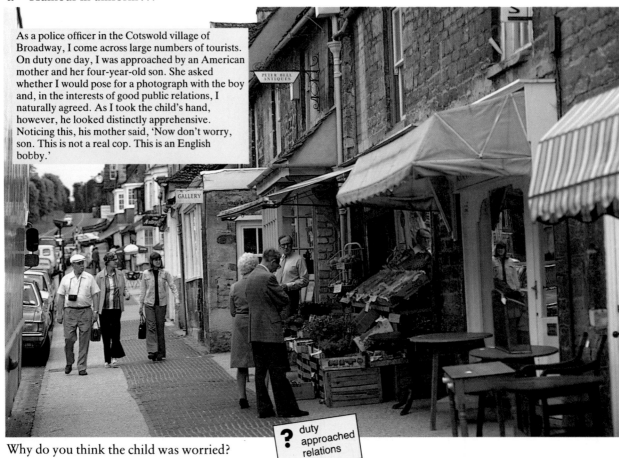

As a police officer in the Cotswold village of
Broadway, I come across large numbers of tourists.
On duty one day, I was approached by an American
mother and her four-year-old son. She asked
whether I would pose for a photograph with the boy
and, in the interests of good public relations, I
naturally agreed. As I took the child's hand,
however, he looked distinctly apprehensive.
Noticing this, his mother said, 'Now don't worry,
son. This is not a real cop. This is an English
bobby.'

Why do you think the child was worried?

? duty
approached
relations

144a Before you listen, guess which words will be
stressed. Then listen and see how it is read.

b   The witness game
Look carefully at the picture above. Imagine that just
after this photo was taken, the man coming out of the
shop discovered that his wallet was missing from his
pocket.

Discuss what might have happened. Write down
three ideas.

e.g. *He might have dropped it while visiting the
village.*

145 What's your excuse?

What excuses might you make if you were stopped
for speeding? Write down two that are not on the list
below.

▶   Tell the class whose are the best.   ◀

*I'm on my way to hospital where my _____ is
seriously ill...
I didn't realise there was a speed limit on this road.
I have to post an urgent letter.
My house is on fire and I've got to get there fast.
My wife/sister/friend is having a baby.
I was just trying out the car to see if it would do
129 miles an hour like the manufacturers said.
I'm not used to this car and I didn't realise it was
going so fast.*

? urgent
not used to
realise

146 *Preposition spot* ··········

over, into

*...there's one over there.
Like a lift into London, lady?* (75)
Place the pan over the lowest heat possible... (87)

Find four sentences that need **over** and four which
need **into**.

a   *...we spent _____ an hour there...*
b   *I don't think anything else came _____ his
    mind.*
c   *...telling me to pull _____.* (136)
d   *That's 50 miles an hour _____ the limit!* (147)
e   *...to convert mains electricity _____
    microwaves.* (91)
f   *Rushing _____, I muttered, 'May I?'* (93)
g   *I once backed _____ my neighbour's car.* (106)
h   *...and the B6279 eventually runs _____ the
    B6278.* (131)

Find phrases below which express a similar idea to
one of the phrases in the box.

1   *It's a good book once you get into it.*
2   *They're both really into Yoga.*
3   *The company's being taken over by...*
4   *Go into the plans very carefully.*
5   *Their age doesn't come into it...*

like a lot / love	examine in detail
have started	has nothing to do with it
change ownership	normal

144 Cops or bobbies?

Aims: 1 To practise speculating on the possible reasons for a given outcome.
2 To practise producing and understanding descriptions of people.
3 To practise the modals **might** and **could** with **have + -en/-ed**.
4 To focus attention on sentences in a narrative which both establish the situation and further the narrative.
5 To illustrate the use of commas to separate situation from narrative.

Lexis: approach, duty, number (amount), **officer, real, relations**
Revision: **come across** (meet), **however, noticing** (realising).

Reading and listening   SB144a [144a] PB144

1 Draw attention to the dictionary definitions in section 143.

Key: The child was worried because he had probably only seen really 'mean' and frightening cops on TV, and didn't realise that policemen can be friendly.

3 Words to guess: Students should be able to guess the meanings of the words.

4 Language study: Drawing attention to the commas highlights both when we use them and when we don't (third sentence – no comma before 'and'). Ask students to circle the commas in the text and to explain their function. Here they separate the first part of the sentence, which gives the situation, from the main point which continues the story.
Point out to students that all sentences in this story (apart from the last 2, which are purposely short to gain effect) are in two parts. Also point out the uses of **as** . . ., and the **-ing** on 'Noticing'.

5 Students should first read the text quietly themselves, limiting the stresses to the key word and one other in each phrase. You could ask them to put / marks between phrases.
e.g.
/ As a polICE OFFicer / in the COTSwold village of BROADway /
or even
/ As a polICE officer in the Cotswold village of BROADway /

6 Play the tape for students to check their predictions about the stressed syllables.

Key: AS a polICE Officer / in the COTswold VILlage of BROADway, / I COME acROSS / LARGE NUMbers of TOURists. On DUTy one DAY, / I was appROAched / by an AMERican MOther / and her FOUR-year-old SON. / She ASked whether I would POSE / for a PHOtograph with the BOY / AND, / in the INterests of GOOD PUBlic relAtions, / I NAturally agrEED. / AS I TOOK the CHILD's HAND, / howEVER, he LOOked disTINCtly APPreHENsive. / NOticing THIS, / his MOther SAID, / 'Now DON'T WORry, / SON. / This is NOT a REAL COP. / THIS is an ENGlish BOBby.'

Task   SB144b

7 In groups students discuss what might have happened to the money and prepare sentences. Students may need words like: could have . . ., as well as, might have . . ., may have . . ., probably, possibly etc.

8 Groups read their sentences to the class. The others decide on the most popular/funniest theory.

9 Further practice: Ask students to assume the money was stolen. Students should look at the places in the picture and use their imagination to think what the people could have been doing in the village when the theft occurred.
either   Ask them to tell each other exactly what they would tell the police officer. Suggest they don't say which person they are and let the others guess their identity. But they must give at least one clue.
or   Give out cards with roles on them – one of which is the thief. Put students in groups with one or two people in the roles of police officers, and let them act it out. Can the police and the others find the thief?
(The second method entails thinking of advice you would give to the person who lost the money, e.g. 'Are you sure you didn't leave it on the bus/in the shop where . . .' etc.)

145 What's your excuse?

Aims: 1 To practise giving reasons or excuses.
2 To prepare for the next part of The Hitch-hiker.

Lexis: excuse, realise, urgent, used to (familiar with)

Task   SB145

1 Check the students understand the excuses in their books. In pairs they should prepare two others.

2 Students could change partners with students from another pair and role-play a situation where one of them has been stopped by a police officer for speeding. Students should use the excuses they have prepared.

Key: Other possible excuses, serious or funny:
I have an urgent meeting/appointment/etc.
I'm a film star and I'm due to appear in the studio at . . .
My speedometer has gone wrong.

3 Bring the class together for an informal report on the excuses. Ask students to vote on the best excuses.

4 Words to guess: Students guess the words in pairs.

146 Preposition spot

Aim: To practise the uses of **over** and **into**.

Lexis: into, over, overseas [T]

SB146 PB146

1 (a–h includes and extends meanings covered in Book 1; 1–5 introduces new phrasal verbs.) Students answer a–h individually and then check their answers in pairs. Give students a few further examples, e.g. **overseas**.

Key: Sentences needing **over**: a, c, d, f
Sentences needing **into**: b, e, g, h

2 In pairs students answer 1–5. (The phrases in the box all contain highly frequent words which should be revised.)
Key:
get into = have started   go into = examine in detail,
. . . 're . . . into = like   doesn't come into it = has
   a lot/love   nothing to do with it
taken over = change
   ownership

3 Point out that 'ownership' is similar in form to 'leadership' (see section 107). Introduce the phrase **pull into** the side of the road (slow down and drive into the side). It occurs in the next Hitch-hiker episode.

Aims: 1 To practise producing and understanding descriptions of people.
2 To practise understanding and predicting the behaviour of a fictional character.
3 To practise speculating on a person's character.

Lexis: approach(ing), careful, careless [T], **finally, guilty, jump, lean(ed), let, meaty** (bulky), **pull (up onto)** [L], **raise** [L], **real, reasonable, seat, slowly, standard** (usual, average), **voice**
Revision: **I can't imagine him being . . ., pretty mean, remarks, So you never know!**

(Point out that trousers is a more usual word than breeches, which are shorter and worn for riding motor bikes.)

Reading SB147a PB147

1 Let the students read silently up to 'sit tight and keep mum' (keep mum = stay silent) and then say in one sentence what the policeman did.

2 Ask students to imagine that they are the policeman and write questions he might ask. Make sure students keep their lists, because most of what they guess will probably not occur until the next episode in this unit. (He is not a very typical policeman, spending so much time asking sarcastic questions.)

3 Students read on up to 'mean as the devil' and discuss which picture of the police officer is the most accurate, and tell one another in pairs. Ask them to give reasons for their choice.

4 Let them read silently to the end. Did the policeman ask the questions they expected? (No, he was listing common excuses for speeding in a sarcastic way.)

Key: Top left picture

Listening SB147b [147b]

5 Students listen to the taped version of the episode for enjoyment. Ask them for their feelings about the police officer, and if the policeman's voice affects their opinion of him at all.

Task

6 Check that the students remember the hitch-hiker's advice. (They can refer back to the text if they need to.) Ask students whether they think the hitch-hiker's advice was good, and why. (There is some psychological evidence to suggest that it is better to get out of the car so you are talking to the policeman on the same level as he is. This gives you more confidence. However it also takes away some of the feeling of superiority and power from the policeman, so it may be better to stay sitting down and say nothing, except perhaps to apologise politely.)

7 In groups students discuss how they would have handled the situation. Help them to prepare their reports. Get the class to vote on the best method when the groups report back.

Listening SB147c [147c]*

8 Students refer to the episode as they listen to the tape of Catherine and Stephen.

Key: They remembered 6 details, and commented 'Sounds like the standard American cop'. The only detail they forgot was 'wide cheeks'.

SB147d/e [147e]*

9 Students discuss the question in pairs and report back informally, giving their reasons. Ask them to compare their speculations with what Stephen and Catherine thought.

Key: They don't think the policeman will be lenient because he has been mean and sarcastic, and it wouldn't be reasonable anyway.

10 The summary could be done for homework.

11 Optional: Let the students act out this episode in groups of 3, each reading one part.

a Which of these pictures of policemen do you think is the most accurate?

PART 5
'THIS IS REAL TROUBLE...'

The policeman must have been doing about a hundred and thirty when he passed us, and he took plenty of time slowing down. Finally, he pulled into the side of the road and I pulled in behind him. "I didn't know police motor-cycles could go as fast as that," I said rather lamely.

"That one can," my passenger said. "It's the same make as yours. It's a B.M.W. R90S. Fastest bike on the road. That's what they're usin' nowadays."

The policeman got off his motor-cycle and leaned the machine sideways on to its prop stand. Then he took off his gloves and placed them carefully on the seat. He was in no hurry now. He had us where he wanted us and he knew it.

"This is real trouble," I said. "I don't like it one bit."

"Don't talk to 'im any more than is necessary, you understand," my companion said. "Just sit tight and keep mum."

Like an executioner approaching his victim, the policeman came strolling slowly towards us. He was a big meaty man with a belly, and his blue breeches were skin-tight around his enormous thighs. His goggles were pulled up on to the helmet, showing a smouldering red face with wide cheeks.

We sat there like guilty schoolboys, waiting for him to arrive.

"Watch out for this man," my passenger whispered. "'Ee looks mean as the devil."

The policeman came round to my open window and placed one meaty hand on the sill. "What's the hurry?" he said.

"No hurry, officer," I answered.

"Perhaps there's a woman in the back having a baby and you're rushing her to hospital? Is that it?"

"No, officer."

"Or perhaps your house is on fire and you're dashing home to rescue the family from upstairs?" His voice was dangerously soft and mocking.

"My house isn't on fire, officer."

"In that case," he said, "you've got yourself into a nasty mess, haven't you? Do you know what the speed limit is in this country?"

"Seventy," I said.

"And do you mind telling me exactly what speed you were doing just now?"

I shrugged and didn't say anything.

When he spoke next, he raised his voice so loud that I jumped. *"One hundred and twenty miles per hour!"* he barked. "That's *fifty* miles an hour over the limit!"

L pull
raise
voice

? stroll
meaty
guilty

147b **b** What sort of person is the policeman? Do you like his voice? Listen for the advice the hitch-hiker gave the driver.

Do you think the hitch-hiker's advice was good?
If you had been the driver, would you have stayed sitting in the car?

> Tell other groups how you would have handled the situation.

147c **c** How many details did Stephen and Caroline remember about how the policeman looked?

d Is he the kind of policeman who might be very reasonable, and say 'Well, never mind' and let the driver off? Or is he likely to take him to court?

147e **e** See what Caroline and Stephen think about his character.

> Summarise this episode in three sentences.

148 Wordpower

go/going

What about these? In your language do you use the word **go** in these situations? When does **go** mean to move from one place to another? When does it not?

I'm going to let his tyres down!

(b) Who's that going by?

(c) Once you've started you must go through with it.

(d) But there are still two years to go!

(e) How are things going? How's it going?

(a) A: Wow! this price has gone up! We should go into this with the agent. B: Well, you don't expect prices to go down, do you?

The television's gone wrong!

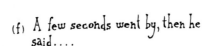

(f) A few seconds went by, then he said....

(g) A: How did that story go? B: Shall I tell you? A: Yes. Go ahead!

(h) They went to sleep.

(i) She went out with her first boyfriend for years.

(j) Oh dear – the milk's gone off! It's so warm.

(k) She's going to University in October.

(l) I've really got to go now. Bye!

(m) A: I've gone off the idea. B: Yeah – I don't like it now, either.

149 Phrase-building

When speaking, we sometimes start explaining something like this:

Well what	I you she	did said thought told X meant to do should have done should have said could have done would have done	was, ...

Well, what I		normally do always say 'm always telling her think	is, ...

Find some ways of introducing these phrases:

a ... *go to work by bus and save the petrol money.*
b ... *'Don't waste money on clothes.'*
c ... *took/take/taken the kids to school first, then ...*
d ... *'Come half an hour earlier.'*
e ... *get/got less money out of the bank.*
f ... *have lunch around 12, then ...*
g ... *you could borrow the car and drive to ...*

Now think of some more examples like these.

Well, what I usually do is, have lunch around 12 ...
Well, what she should have done was, take less money out of the bank.

148 Wordpower

> **Aim:** To practise the meanings and use of **go** and **going**.
>
> Lexis: **go/going**

SB148 PB148

1 Ask students which examples could be captions to the pictures.

2 Students should discuss the questions in groups.

   Key: gone up – get more expensive
   go into – discuss in detail
   go down – get less (cheaper)
   going by – walking past
   go through with – finish
   two years to go – two years before it's finished/the time comes
   things going? – How's life?
   went by – passed
   story go – what was the story
   go ahead – start to tell me now
   went to sleep – fell asleep
   went out with – was friends with
   gone off – gone bad
   going to – attending
   to go – to depart
   gone off – lost enthusiasm for
   going to – that's what I'll do
   gone wrong – stopped working

149 Phrase-building

> **Aim:** To practise fronting patterns such as 'What I did was, . . .'

SB149

1 Refer students to the transcript for section 80, in which Philip says:
   'We live about 3 miles away from the University, and what I do is I take the children to school in the mornings so . . .'

2 Point out that this is a common way of introducing a spoken explanation – especially if there has been some complication – as in the example above.
   Fronting devices can also be used to give more emphasis to a statement, as in: 'What I said was she shouldn't be allowed out so late . . .'
   Other common fronting devices are 'What happened was, . . .', 'What it means is . . .'
   Other fronting devices, 'The point/thing/trouble is . . .' will be covered in Unit 14 (sections 195, 196).

3 Students find ways to complete these openings. Point out that not all endings will fit every opening sequence. 'Well' is not compulsory, but it is quite commonly used to introduce an explanation. The stress falls either on the **I/you** etc. or on the **should/would** etc. depending on meaning.

4 Finally students make up similar sentences that are true for themselves, on similar themes. Possible themes: comparing evening routines, ways of getting to class in different weathers, ways of preparing for a family visit etc.

> **Aims:** 1 To practise speculating on what course of action would have been taken in imagined circumstances.
> 2 To practise the use of modals **might**, **would** and **should** with **have + -en/-ed**.
> 3 To practise proposing and discussing action to be taken in given circumstances.
> 4 To practise cooperative discussion and problem solving.
>
> **Lexis: allowed, block, damage, finally, inside/ (outside), legal(ly), let (down), polite, problem, realised, return, surely, very**
> Revision: **face to face**

Reading   SB150a

1 Use the story for fun and to introduce the problem. Check that students understand that a double yellow line means 'No Parking'. Students tell the class what they think the plumber should have done.

Task   SB150b 150b *

2 Students work in groups to discuss the problem. Students may need you to supply words like: clamp, tow away, give him a ticket, let the air out of the tyres, scratch the paint.

3 As the groups reports to the class, the students should note down each other's best ideas. Then, when they hear the recording, they can tick off those that Stephen and Catherine also mention. (Don't worry if students do not, or cannot, when speaking, produce the form 'I would have ...' there is a Language Study on this point in the next section.)

4 Play the tape in two parts, stopping after 'Oh you're not right' and asking: 'What were they **going** to say?' As students listen, they can tick off any ideas that are the same as they have had, and note down any new ones. (Students may recognise the title of the unit, which appears in this recording.)

   Key: Stephen says he would: 1 Let down the tyres. 2 Inform the police who would fine him or give him a parking ticket. 3 Get the police to tow him away. Catherine would: 1 Inform the police. 2 Get legal advice from a friend. 3 Find a chance to talk to the driver.

Task and report

5 Students tell one another about the parking problems in their own countries, and groups' members suggest possible solutions. Help students in their groups to prepare a brief written report.

6 Groups read their reports to the class. The others should listen to see if any other groups have cited the same parking problems as theirs.

7 Words to guess and look up: Students do these in pairs.

> **Aim:** To provide more intensive practice of modals **might**, **would** and **should** with **have + -en/-ed**.

SB151a PB151

1 Make sure students realise that these actions, e.g. stopped, let tyres down etc., did not actually occur, but could/would have done if the circumstances had been different at that time in the past.

SB151b

Key: The words and phrases in colour all mean 'If ...'

2 Students look at the contexts and rephrase them with an **if** clause to make this clear, e.g. **then** = **if** he **had** let the tyres down (but he didn't).
   Other common phrases meaning **if** to look out for: in those circumstances ... in circumstances such as these ..., in a similar situation ... = if you were/had been in those circumstances ...

Parking problems

a

A plumber who had parked on a double yellow line placed a note reading 'Plumber working inside' under a windscreen wiper of his car. When he returned, he found a parking ticket under the other wiper with a note: 'Traffic Warden working outside.'

What should he have done in the circumstances?

b　Read about this parking problem and discuss what you would have done in the circumstances.

A friend of ours had a garage that opened directly on to a side-street near a main road in the centre of town. One morning he found that someone had parked in front of his garage door so that he couldn't get his car out. He left a polite note explaining the situation, and went to work by bus. Next day the same car was parked in the same place. Our friend left a less polite note. The same thing happened the next day. This time our friend left a warning note. But next day exactly the same thing happened again.

What do you think our friend did?
What would you have done?

> Tell each other:
>
> what the police can do in such circumstances as these?
> what you would have done, if you had been the person blocked in?

150b　Did Stephen and Catherine have similar ideas to yours? What was Catherine going to say after 'Surely, surely not unless...'?
Make notes of the three things they each suggested.

Do you have parking problems anywhere in your country? If so tell each other and try to suggest solutions.

> Write out a statement of the problems, and possible solutions.

Language study ....

would/could have _____

a　Find the verb phrases with **have**. Do they refer to the past, present or future? Do they refer to something that actually happened?

b　The phrases in colour have one meaning in common. What?

1 *What would you have done* in that situation? (136)
2 'I would have stopped.' (147)
3 'If you had been the driver, would you have stayed sitting in the car?' (147)
4 'If it was me, I would have let his tyres down.' (150)
5 'I probably wouldn't have waited for four days.' (150)
6 'I would also have told the local police.' (150)
7 'He could have got the police to tow it away...' (150)
8 'I wouldn't have done any damage like smash the windscreen.' (150)

9 'I would have sought advice from some friend who could have given me the legal bits of it...' (150)
10 'Then I would have let the police know, and then, I think, had they not done anything, I would have...' (150)
11 He was going to let the tyres down, but he realised that then the car couldn't have moved.
12 'I probably wouldn't have gone at 120 miles per hour.' (136)

What about these?

13 The policeman must have been doing about a hundred and thirty. (147)
14 He must have eaten the plums and then gone out. (95)
15 She's late. I suppose she might have missed her train.

a While reading, stop at a few points and discuss how the writer must be feeling.

PART 6

'ME? WHAT'VE I DONE WRONG?'

He turned his head and spat out a big gob of spit. It landed on the wing of my car and started sliding down over my beautiful blue paint. Then he turned back again and stared hard at my passenger. "And who are you?" he asked sharply.

"He's a hitch-hiker," I said. "I'm giving him a lift."

"I didn't ask you," he said. "I asked him."

"'Ave I done somethin' wrong?" my passenger asked. His voice was as soft and oily as haircream.

"That's more than likely," the policeman answered. "Anyway, you're a witness. I'll deal with you in a minute. Driving-licence," he snapped, holding out his hand.

I gave him my driving-licence.

He unbuttoned the left-hand breast-pocket of his tunic and brought out the dreaded book of tickets. Carefully, he copied the name and address from my licence. Then he gave it back to me. He strolled round to the front of the car and read the number from the number-plate and wrote that down as well. He filled in the date, the time and the details of my offence. Then he tore out the top copy of the ticket. But before handing it to me, he checked that all the information had come through clearly on his own carbon copy. Finally, he replaced the book in his tunic pocket and fastened the button.

"Now you," he said to my passenger, and he walked around to the other side of the car. From the other breast-pocket he produced a small black notebook. "Name?" he snapped.

"Michael Fish," my passenger said.

"Address?"

"Fourteen, Windsor Lane, Luton."

"Show me something to prove this is your real name and address," the policeman said.

My passenger fished in his pockets and came out with a driving-licence of his own. The policeman checked the name and address and handed it back to him. "What's your job?" he asked sharply.

"I'm an 'od carrier."

"A *what*?"

"An 'od carrier."

"Spell it."

"H-O-D C-A-. . ."

"That'll do. And what's a hod carrier, may I ask?"

"An 'od carrier, officer, is a person, 'oo carries the cement up the ladder to the bricklayer. And the 'od is what 'ee carries it in. It's got a long 'andle, and on the top you've got two bits of wood set at an angle . . ."

"All right, all right. Who's your employer?"

"Don't 'ave one. I'm unemployed."

The policeman wrote all this down in the black notebook. Then he returned the book to its pocket and did up the button.

"When I get back to the station I'm going to do a little checking up on you," he said to my passenger.

"Me? What've I done wrong?" the rat-faced man asked.

"I don't like your face, that's all," the policeman said. "And we just might have a picture of it somewhere in our files." He strolled round the car and returned to my window.

152b **b** Listen to the story being read. Try to remember everything the policeman did.

c **Memory test!**
What details did the policeman write down, and where did he write them? Then what did he do?

152c Which of the two, Caroline or Stephen, remembered best? Write notes of the details they remembered.

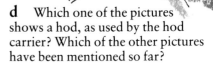

d Which one of the pictures shows a hod, as used by the hod carrier? Which of the other pictures have been mentioned so far?

e Do you think the passenger really is a hod carrier? Would that count as a 'skilled trade'?

152e See what Stephen and Caroline think.

> Summarise how you think the driver and the hitch-hiker are probably feeling.

152f **f** What do Caroline and Stephen say about how the characters feel?

L	sharply	bound up
	produced	feel
	bothered	feeling

?
snapped
unbuttoned
replaced
wonder
strike

Aims: 1 To practise speculating on people's reactions to particular events.
2 To provide practice in understanding a detailed sequence of events, and being able to identify an unknown item from a specific description.

Lexis: bothered, bound (up with), breast (-pocket), brick, building, careful(ly), confidence [T], **confident, cool, copy, count, countless** [T], **employ(er), feeling** [L], **front, licence, official(ly), produce** [L], **replace, return(ed), sharp(ly)** [L], **sink(ing), site, speed(ing), suspicious** (shady), **throw, unemployed, very, voice, wood**
Revision: **anyway, as soft and oily as ..., deal with you, fished in his pockets** (spent some time feeling in them to find something, slightly colloquial), **handed it back, landed, more than likely** (very likely, obviously) **succeed, the best way to get by** (manage to live), **wouldn't go round telling a policeman**

SB152a

1 Check that students still have (or remember) the list of questions that they made in section 147. Discuss the last episode briefly. Did he ask those questions, in fact?

2 Students silently read up to 'I gave him my driving-licence' which is the first point at which students should stop and discuss the driver's feelings. (The first part of recording 152f is of Stephen and Catherine discussing how the driver must be feeling at this point in the story. You could, if you wish, bring this forward and play it now.)

SB152b 152b

3 Let students read along as they listen to the story. Give them time to reread if they wish to – just once – before they do 152c.

SB152c 152c *

The point of the memory test is to make sure students remember these details at the very end of the whole story, when we find out what the hitch-hiker has done. Otherwise the ending may lose some of its impact.

4 Students in groups discuss and note down what they can remember. Play the recording of Catherine and Stephen for students to compare answers with.

Key: Catherine didn't remember the policeman had written some things down on the ticket – she only remembered the notebook. Between them they seemed to remember everything, though.

SB152d

5 The description of the hod could be used, at a later stage, as an example for students to follow in a guessing game, in which students are asked to describe other strange objects for the class to guess or draw.

Key: The second picture.

SB152e 152e *

4 Refer students back to Unit 9, where the hitch-hiker tells the driver he is employed in a 'skilled trade'. Students could vote – how many believe the hitch-hiker is an unemployed hod carrier? (Some students may find it strange that a hitch-hiker/hod carrier actually has his own driving licence.) Students listen to the tape of Stephen and Catherine.

Key: They agree that hod carrying is not a skilled job, but think that he might do a skilled job ('whatever he does that is very hard') in his spare time.

SB152f 152f *

Tell students that at the beginning of recording 152f Catherine and Stephen are looking at the beginning of the episode and talking about the driver, then the 'little man' (i.e. the hitch-hiker), then both.

The best excuse?

> **Aim:** To provide further practice in giving reasons or excuses.
>
> **Lexis: excuse, exercise, invite, personal**
> Revision: **circumstances, turn up** (attend), **accept** (an invitation), **personal, formal/informal**

SB153

1 Treat this activity in a fairly light-hearted way. Give the class an example situation, e.g. A good friend has asked you to go to a fancy dress party, but you don't like the idea of wearing a costume. What would you say? Elicit some suggestions from the class.

2 In groups students choose 5 situations and think of excuses for them. Groups present some of their suggestions informally to the class. Pay particular attention, when assisting students in their groups and when giving feedback, to the register students have used; they should use an acceptable degree of formality for the situation.

3 Further practice: In pairs students prepare short dialogues around one or two of the situations, and act these out for the class.

 Language study

> **Aims:** 1 To show how spontaneous conversation still progresses cooperatively even after 'cancellations' made by one speaker.
> 2 To highlight useful phrases and target words.

SB154

1 Students study the transcript individually, then compare their suggestions with a partner.

   Key: (possible continuations)
   CM had been going to say which details he had written down, but she couldn't remember, so she turned the topic (using a 'fronting device' as in section 149) to where he had written them.
   SB: the fact that he's unemployed.
   CM: check on the files . . . (She couldn't remember the word.)
   CM: Where did he put . . . the notebook. (She changes from a question to a statement.)

Grammar

> **Aim:** To illustrate some ways of expressing contrast, e.g. **but, while, however**.

SB155 PB155

1 Students match the sentences or sentence parts in pairs and then find the word or phrase in each which signals contrast.

2 Optional further practice: When students' answers have been checked and discussed, go over the punctuation for some of the linking words. Students could also be asked to choose 3 of the examples and rewrite them, using a different way of expressing contrast.

Key: a 6 but
b 5 however
c 3 although
d 4 though
e 2 whereas
f 1 Mind you
g 7 Despite, still (Note that 'still' is optional in this sentence.)

a 7 but
b 2 however
c 4 although
d 3 though
e 6 yet
f 5 not
g 1 but
h 8 In spite of

153 The best excuse?

Choose five situations from a-h. What excuses could you use in these circumstances? Think of two or three for each one. Be as polite as is appropriate – you mustn't cause offence!

a *You forget an invitation to a friend's birthday party. They ring you the next day to ask why you didn't turn up.*
b *You arrive twenty minutes late for an important meeting because you got up too late.*
c *You turn up for a meeting on the wrong day.*
d *You do the wrong exercise for homework.*
e *You forget to do your homework.*
f *You don't want to accept an invitation (personal reasons)*
    a: *to a rather formal dinner.*
    b: *to a friendly dinner.*
g *Someone asks you to help them prepare food for a party. You don't really like the person concerned...*
h *You're asked – at the last minute – to attend an urgent meeting but you have something else (personal) planned, although it is in work time...*

In groups, decide on the best excuse for each circumstance.

Language study

Read these extracts from the transcript of 152c and notice where they stop (–), change their minds, and start again. Write down what you think they had been going to say.

SB: What details did the policeman write down, and where did he write them?
CM: He wrote down . . . – well, where he wrote them was in his, his notebook.
SB: But he wrote down . . . the passenger's name, address, occupation, and the fact that he's –
CM: occupation, and the fact that he's unemployed.
SB: in his notebook.
CM: Yes, and he's going to check them on his – when he gets back to the station.
SB: Yeah.
CM: Where did he put it – did – and he returned his notebook to his pocket and he did up the button didn't he?
SB: To his pocket. Yeah.

155 *Grammar*

Ways of saying 'but...'

Can you match these parts?

a *This time our friend left a warning note.*
b *She asked whether I would pose for a photograph with the boy and I naturally agreed.*
c *We chose to go by plane because, although it was more expensive*
d *Coach services are frequent*
e *In a restaurant it would probably cost twice as much,*
f *People usually like mammals better than reptiles or insects.*
g *Despite losing their way there*

1 *Mind you, rats are mammals.*
2 *whereas Danny's meal would probably cost more to make at home. (89)*
3 *it meant we had more time.*
4 *though the travelling time is longer than by train.*
5 *As I took the child's hand, however, he looked distinctly apprehensive. (144)*
6 *But the next day exactly the same thing happened again. (150)*
7 *they still arrived on time.*

What about these?

a *I would have let his tyres down*
b *I am forced to appear as if writing you this note to apologise and to leave you my name and address.*
c *I enjoy living on my own*
d *'It's really true. This bloke told my sister.' Well, maybe, George.*
e *The weather was hot*
f *I have pink and blue shirts*
g *I won the next year*
h *In spite of the efforts to open the door*

1 *but not as much as I'd won the first year. (23)*
2 *As you can see, however, this I have not done.*
3 *My bet is it didn't happen to your sister's friend though. (78)*
4 *although I love to be with friends. (20)*
5 *not green. (128)*
6 *yet rainy and unpleasant.*
7 *but I probably wouldn't have waited four days. (150)*
8 *the fate of the passengers and crew was sealed. (104)*

How many ways are there of saying **but**?

a Odd one out

1 skilled worker, holidaymaker, officer, driver, passenger, builder, building site, employee, policeman

2 sunny, cool, cold, warm, hot, personal

3 enormous, fat, huge, large, big, dangerous

4 at top speed, fast, slowly, in a hurry, rush, quick, urgently

b Match the opposites

Check the words marked (L) in the Lexicon for their other meanings.

sharply (L)	safe
slowly	against the law
urgent	push (L)
pull (L)	tiny
enormous	warm
dangerous	softly, kindly
legal	not important
reasonable	fast/quickly
cool	relaxed
bothered	dropped (L)/lowered
raised (L)	placed carefully
threw carelessly	unreasonable

c Where might you see or hear these notices?

Only five standing passengers allowed.

DANGER

URGENT

PUSH

These seats are meant for elderly and handicapped.

Lifejacket under your seat

PULL

The driver is not allowed to talk to passengers.

Sorry, credit cards not accepted.

. . . found guilty of driving under the influence of alcohol.

£1 coins not accepted.

Smoking is not allowed during take-off or landing.

Speed limit 25 mph

Produced by Waver Products Ltd, G.B.

This machine accepts 5p, 10p, 20p, 50p coins.

Standard size 46p Large size 50p

Please produce passport or means of identification.

L	allowed	pull
	push	produced

d What word can fit all these gaps?

I would have _____ his tyres down.
He was going to _____ all the air out of his tyres.
Then I would have _____ the police know.
Do you think they'll get _____ off?
I just couldn't _____ you eat that pie.
_____'s turn the page.
_____'s find out who it is.
_____ him go .
Please would you _____ me go early today?
Did your parents _____ you stay out after midnight when you were just sixteen?

Saying: _____ bygones be bygones.

In which three sentences could you use the word 'allow to' to give the same meaning? Notice we say 'Allow X to ...'

e Word forms

employ	employment	employee
employer	unemployed	unemployment

Which form fits where?

1 *The company used to provide _____ for over 200 workers.*
2 *They now _____ only 120, of whom 12 are new _____*
3 *So there are now 92 more people in the village _____, and looking for jobs.*
4 *Other local _____ are also cutting back on labour costs.*
5 *The official figures for _____ are rising daily.*

Important words to remember (656 so far)

accept	confident	finally	officer	replace	suspicious
allow L	cool	formal	official	rule	throw
approach	copy	guilty	overseas	return	ticket
block	count	influence	personal	safe	unemployed
bothered	countless	invite	polite	seat	urgent
bound L	damage	jump	produce L	sharp L	voice L
breast (pocket)	duty	lean	pull L	sink	wood
brick	employ	legal	raise L	site	
careful	excuse	licence	real	slowly	
careless	exercise	limit	realise	speed	
circumstances	fat	minor	reasonable	standard	
confidence	feelings L	offence	relations	surely	

SB156a PB156

Key: 1 building site – only one not a person
2 personal – the others are all to do with weather
3 dangerous – the others are all to do with size
4 slowly – the others are all to do with fast speed

SB156b

Key: sharply – softly, kindly
slowly – fast/quickly
urgent – not important
pull – push
enormous – tiny
dangerous – safe
legal – against the law
reasonable – unreasonable
cool – warm
bothered – relaxed
raised – dropped/lowered
threw carelessly – placed carefully

SB156c

1 Give students a further example: 'No alcohol/tobacco sold to **minors**'. (In Britain a minor is anyone under 18 years of age. In many countries the age of majority is 21.)
Suggested answers: doors, buses, airplanes, coin-operated machines (cigarette, laundry etc.), restaurants, shops, on product labels, roads.

SB156d Key: Missing word: let

SB156e

Key: 1 employment   4 employers
2 employ, employees 5 unemployment
3 unemployed

LEXICAL OBJECTIVES

Level 1 words (see page 129T):
building, feel, front, going (see SB148),
inside, into (see SB146), **let, number,
over** (see SB146), **problem, used to,
very**.
accept 1 . . . *accept an invitation*
2 **accept a situation** = face up to it T
3 take. *They don't accept cheques.* [15]
allow L
approach 1 come near. *He opened the car door as she approached.*
2 *I was approached by an American woman and her four-year-old son.*
block 1 a large building. *He owns two square blocks in Minneapolis.*
2 a large solid piece of stone or wood T
3 to prevent something from moving. *It's very difficult to block a bicycle.*
bothered troubled. . . . *the driver is feeling . . . bothered and worried.*
bound L
breast (pocket) = front pocket
brick a rectangular block used for building. . . . *a bricklayer on a building site.* T
2 a brick wall T
careful 1 a warning. *Be careful!*
2 . . . *more careful driving*

careless without paying attention.
circumstances 1 the situation. *What excuses would you give in these circumstances?*
2 the cause. *What were the circumstances of the accident?* T
confidence noun. See **confident**.
confident Adj.: 1 sure, certain. *He was confident that he would succeed . . .* T
1.1 . . . *the type of person that is extremely confident in all he does.*
cool 1 . . . *a long cool drink.* T
2 something that looks or keeps you cool. . . . *a cool material, a cool colour.* T
3 unemotional. *He's probably feeling quite cool and relaxed.*
copy 1 *He tore out the top copy of the ticket.*
1.1 one book, magazine etc. *Just buy a copy of Time Out magazine.* [15]
2 *I copied down his name and address.*
count 1 *He counted up to 3.* T
2 add up. *He counted his money.* T
3 is regarded as. *I wouldn't count a hod carrier as a skilled worker*
countless very many. *He sent countless letters to the newspapers.* T
damage *I wouldn't have done any damage like smash the windscreen . . .*
duty on duty, off duty = working
employ pay someone to work for you. *He was employed as a secretary.*
excuse 1 *What excuses would you give if you were late?*
2 justification for an action. *Jenny said, 'There was no excuse at all.'*
exercise 1 *Dogs need daily exercise.* [2]
2 *Do exercise 1 for homework.*
fat 1 overweight. *The policeman was fat.*
2 cooking substance. *Butter is fat.* T
feelings L
finally 1 eventually. *After a long pause, he finally said . . .* [6]
2 lastly. *Finally he replaced the book in his pocket.*
formal correct and serious . . . *a formal dinner party . . . a formal speech.*
guilty 1 feeling unhappy because you've done something wrong. *We sat there like guilty schoolboys.*
2 *He was found guilty of passing on secret papers to the Soviet Union.* T
influence 1 *What will be the influence of the little ratty man?* [10]
2 **under the influence of** *Driving under the influence of drink/alcohol.*
invite *He had been invited for dinner.*
jump 1 *The horse jumped over a stream.* T
1.1 to move quickly and suddenly. *Out jumped two policemen.* [11]
1.2 to move suddenly because you have been frightened. *He raised his voice so loud that I jumped.* T
lean 1 Verb: *He leaned the machine sideways on its prop stand.*
2 Adj.: not fat. . . . *a very lean man.* T
legal 1 involved with the law. . . . *the British legal system.* T
2 allowed by the law. . . . *not legally allowed to park.*
licence official document which gives you permission to do something. *driving-licence*
limit 1 Noun: the largest or smallest extent/amount allowed. . . . *over the speed limit.*

2 Verb: *We must limit the number of cars in towns.* T
minor not serious. . . . *a minor offence.*
offence a traffic offence.
officer important person within an organisation. . . . *a police officer.*
official . . . *officially a hodcarrier*
overseas abroad. *overseas students =
students from abroad* T
personal 1 The Personal Export Scheme – a scheme for individuals rather than companies. [9]
2 private. . . . *personal reasons*
polite thoughtful, correct. *He left a polite note explaining the situation.*
produce L
pull L
raise L
real genuine. *This is not a real cop.*
realise *I didn't realise there was a speed limit on this road.*
reasonable 1 fair. *I don't think it would be reasonable anyway.*
2 acceptable. *The price was reasonable.* T
relations 1 **in relation to** *Wages are low in relation to the cost of living.* T
2 *In the interests of good public relations . . .*
3 . . . *visit friends and relations.* [6]
replace *Finally, he replaced the book in his tunic pocket . . .*
return 1 *When he returned, he found a parking ticket.*
2 *He returned the book to his pocket.*
rule 1 *Traffic rules and regulations.*
2 a statement describing what usually happens. *The rules of English pronunciation.* T
safe 1 not causing physical harm. *Is it safe to overtake?* T
2 *Keep your passport in a safe place.* T
seat 1 place to sit. . . . *the front seat*
2 a seat in Parliament. *The Labour party had a majority of 10 seats.* T
sharp L
sink 1 to go downwards. *The sun sank below the horizon.* T
2 to become less. *The value of the dollar has sunk.* T
3 *Just a sort of sinking feeling.*
site a piece of ground or place used for something. . . . *a building site* T
slowly 1 not quick/fast. *The policeman came strolling slowly towards us.*
2 *He's a bit slow = He's not intelligent*
speed rate at which something moves. *What speed were you doing?*
standard 1 the level or quality. *Work was of a high standard.* T
2 normal. *Standard size 46p*
surely to express surprise, or to contradict. *They can ticket him! Surely not!*
suspicious not trusting. *He is probably a bit suspicious of him.*
throw 1 *Throw the book in the air. . . . throw a bucket of water over it.*
2 *Hope they won't throw him in prison.* [12]
ticket 1.1 piece of paper that shows that you have paid for something. *Display ticket inside windscreen.*
1.2 a parking ticket
unemployed 1 people who have no jobs. . . . *3 million unemployed*
urgent for immediate attention
voice L
wood . . . *bits of wood. Made of wood.*

Things for free, or almost free

The basic theme of the unit is leisure activities, particularly inexpensive attractions in the city. The unit opens with a discussion of inexpensive pastimes in London – art galleries, sightseeing and so on. Students later extend this to their own countries. To round this off there is an exercise which involves planning a page in a tourist brochure, and later on a day out in a town they know.

The theme extends to include accommodation. Students swap experiences and give advice for visitors to their own capital city. There is more work on discussing the outcome of anecdotes. The first part of The Hitch-hiker story provides a context for speculating on the reasons for people's actions and the consequences of those actions. The second part gives practice in inferring the meaning of words from context. This is reinforced with a recording of native speakers speculating on words and meanings, a valuable exercise for the language learner.

OBJECTIVES

Lexical aims are in TB170

Grammar and discourse

a **Can** and **could** for available activities and amenities. (158)
b Pronoun reference and the impersonal **you**. (158)
c **-ing** forms and prepositional phrases in descriptions. (159)
d **On the left**, **on the right**, **at the top** etc. – phrases of location. (159)
e Meanings and use of **of** (160)
f Meanings and use of **do**, particularly the emphatic use. (163)
g Superlatives with the present perfect. (166)
h Meaning and use of **break**. (168)
i Relative clauses in descriptions. (169)

Tasks

a Discussing and compiling a list of activities. (157)
b Comparing amenities in different cities. (157)
c Understanding tourist information. (157, 162)
d Making suggestions and recommendations to do with leisure activities. (159)
e Describing scenes involving varied activities. (159)
f Discussing design and presentation. (159)
g Suggesting reasons for people's actions. (161)
h Predicting the consequences of those actions. (161)
i Making suggestions and recommendations to do with accommodation. (162)
j Predicting the outcome of an anecdote. (164)
k Discussing and inferring the meanings of words from context. (167)

Tell students in advance that for Section 159 they might like to bring pictures, photos, or drawings of a town they know well to make a page similar to this lead-in page. You will need to supply scissors, paper and glue.

---

157 Free – or almost

> **Aims:** 1 To practise discussing and compiling a list of activities.
> 2 To practise comparing amenities in different cities.
> 3 To practise reading tourist information with understanding.
>
> **Lexis: (in) advance, almost, arts, artist, audience, collection, comedy, design, event, exhibition, feed, frequently, hall, mean, museum, painting, politics, programme, religion, religious** T, **sight (-seeing), theatre, unit, view(s), willing, wonder** [L]
> Revision: **legal**
> Phrases: **take what comes; call in (go to the place itself, not just telephone)**

An s.a.e. *= a stamped addressed envelope (a common abbreviation found in adverts)*

SB157a PB157a

1 Direct students' attention to the pictures. Ask them to work in pairs to identify what is happening and to make their list. Lead from this into a general class discussion possibly leading to a consolidated list.

SB157b

2 Similar to exercise 157a. The aim here is to extend the conversation to a comparison which includes a discussion of the ways in which some cities have a unique character.

SB157c/d PB157b

3 Students could work in pairs to decide on 3 interests that they share and 3 places they would like to go together. Lead into a class discussion in which the whole class decides on one place they would all like to go if they were having a class outing. (This exercise is intended to recycle the words in the list, all of which are very common. Try to cover as many as possible when you move into class discussion.)

Listening SB157e *

4 Before students listen to the tape, focus their attention on the picture of Trafalgar Square. Students listen to Catherine and Stephen discussing things a tourist can do for nothing or next to nothing in London.

Key: The things mentioned:
feed the pigeons in Trafalgar Square
sit on a park bench
go to Covent Garden and listen to the street entertainers
just walk around the markets there
go to museums and art galleries
get a bus pass or underground pass
walk along the Thames.
walk down all the famous streets in London sightseeing

Task SB157f PB157c

5 A further recycling of the words in the list. Students work in pairs to make their lists. Ask them to include any activities <u>not</u> in exercise 157c which might also be free in their own countries.

6 Students report back. Make a consolidated list of students' suggestions on the board.

Unit 12
Things for free, or almost free

157 Free – or almost

a Imagine you are in a big city on holiday. What can you do for free or almost free? Make a list.

b All the pictures here are of people and places in London. Compare your list with what you can do in London.

ENTERTAINMENT

RUPERT STREET THEATRE, Rupert Street, W1 (Oxford Circus tube). Tel 485 6224. A small theatre run by an actor's co-operative who just ask that you pay what you can afford. Comedy, avant-garde, musicals.

BUSKERS. Not strictly legal, but can still be found in many a tube station (Leicester Square, Piccadilly, South Kensington, Green Park and Bond Street) or street corner (Leicester Square, Shaftesbury Avenue). For organised street entertainment, Covent Garden Piazza is a must.

SPEAKER'S CORNER. Hyde Park W1, (Marble Arch tube). Since 1972, people have travelled from far and wide to give vent to their views on politics, the price of butter, religion, anything, and they're still doing it on Saturdays and Sunday afternoons.

GUILDHALL SCHOOL OF MUSIC AND DRAMA. Barbican EC2. Tel 628 2577. Recitals to the public lunchtimes and evenings. Call in at the main entrance in Silk Street for a free programme of events. Open: Mon–Fri 8–9, Sat 8–3.

TV SHOWS. Ever wondered how all that laughter gets in the can?* Yes, it's real live audiences and if you'd like to be part of one apply (well in advance) to the following addresses. Specify your preferred programmes, but you have to take what comes, usually comedy shows, game shows and sitcoms.

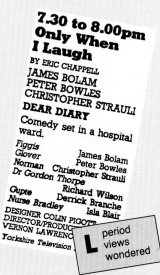

7.30 to 8.00pm
Only When I Laugh
BY ERIC CHAPPELL
JAMES BOLAM
PETER BOWLES
CHRISTOPHER STRAULI
DEAR DIARY
Comedy set in a hospital ward.

Figgis	
Glover	James Bolam
Norman	Peter Bowles
Dr Gordon Thorpe	Christopher Strauli
Gupte	Richard Wilson
Nurse Bradley	Derrick Branche
	Isla Blair

DESIGNER COLIN PIGOTT
DIRECTOR/PRODUCER
VERNON LAWRENCE
Yorkshire Television

L period views wondered

Enclose an sae. Ticket Unit, BBC, Broadcasting House W1; Ticket Unit, Thames Television, 149 Tottenham Court Road W1 . . .

* on to the TV film recording (the film is kept in a 'can')

MUSEUMS AND ART GALLERIES

BRITISH MUSEUM. Great Russell Street WC1 (Russell Square or Tottenham Court Road tube). Tel: 635 1555. Mummies from Egypt and sculptures from Greece are but a few of the millions of treasures housed here. Details on noticeboard inside main door. Open: Mon–Sat 10–5, Sun 2.30–6.

TATE GALLERY. Millbank SW1 (Pimlico tube). Tel: 821 1313. Major collections of British paintings of all periods and an important collection of foreign sculpture, prints and printings. Open: Mon–Sat 10–5.50, Sun 2–5.50.

THE DESIGN CENTRE. 28 Haymarket SW1 (Piccadilly Circus tube). Tel 839 8000. The best of modern British design in fascinating and frequently changed exhibitions. Open: Mon, Tues 10–6, Wed–Sat 10–8, Sun 1–6.

THE TATE GALLERY
MODERN MASTERS
on permanent display

? in advance audience call in

c Which of these things do you like? Where might you choose to go?

theatre	play	paintings
art collections	zoo	concert hall
comedy show	art gallery	exhibition hall
design exhibition	music	fashion show
exhibitions	museum	animals

d Look at the words above. Choose the three things you like best.

157e e Which places and things did Stephen and Catherine suggest? Any of the same things as you thought of? Any of the places on this page? Make a neat list of their suggestions.

f Which of the things listed in section 157c are free or almost free in your country?

81

158 Language study

Feed the pigeons in Trafalgar Square.

Look at the transcript for section 157e.

a In the transcript which words or phrases come before **do it, sit, go to, walk around, see, eat, go to, get a, walk along, walk down, to walk, take a bus** (1–4 words)? How do these words affect the meaning?

b Look at the part of the transcript in square brackets [ ]. Who do the words **they, them** and **you** refer to?

c Which words follow the word **I**?

159 Free in your country?

a Choose a town that you know and think of how you might spend a day there without spending much money.

▶ Tell the class about it. ◀

Listen to the other groups and take notes.

Write about your suggestion. Then choose two things the other groups told you about, and write descriptions of those, too. (Look at the way things are described on the first page of this unit.)

b Describe a picture
From memory, say a sentence describing one of the pictures in 157. Can someone in your class tell which picture it is?

c Plan a page of a brochure intended for one of these two audiences:

either fairly well-off tourists or businesspeople on expenses
or penniless students or hard-up travellers.

In groups produce a page of a colour brochure (similar to the first page of this unit) about a town or city other than London. Suggest three or four places or activities suitable for the audience you have chosen. Plan the page design carefully so that it will look attractive to your readers.

Decide exactly what pictures you would want, then write a description of each one so that an artist could draw it, or so that a picture researcher could find a photograph as close as possible to what you want.

160 Preposition spot

of

1 with quantity (to answer the question 'How many?' or 'How much?')
There's an awful lot of bad writers around. (121)
... a packet of cigarette papers ... (167)
It's none of my business what you do. (121)

Can you think of some other words like **lot, packet** and **none** to complete these phrases?

... a _____ of people ...
... a _____ of water ...
... _____ of the people ...

2 with part of a whole (to answer the question 'What part?')
... along the edge of the paper ... (167)
... watching him out of the corner of one eye. (167)
... a small village at the foot of the valley.

Can you think of other words to complete these phrases?

... _____ of the story
... _____ of the page
... _____ of the day
... _____ of the garden

3 after some adjectives
Is it something you're ashamed of? (167)
I'm about as proud of it as anyone could be. (167)
We're all being very suspicious of him. (167)
You can always be sure of finding comfortable accommodation. (38)

Can you think of anything the driver and the hitch-hiker in *The Hitch-Hiker* might be ashamed / proud / suspicious / afraid / frightened / jealous of?

4 in phrases like these
... a sense of
... a result of
... in spite of
... a means/way of

Can you complete these sentences?

a *Do you _____ direction?* (140)
b *I haven't had to use Joe as _____ jumping queues.* (165)
c *From that moment, _____ the efforts to open the door, the fate of the passengers was sealed.* (104)

Language study

> **Aims:** 1 To practise the use of **can** and **could** to describe available activities and amenities.
> 2 To practise understanding pronoun reference and the impersonal **you**.
>
> **Lexis:** art (**galleries**), **feed**, **museum**, **willing** (**to**)
> Revision: **can**, **could**, **doesn't cost that much** (doesn't cost a lot), **down the streets**, **I mean ...**, **next-to-nothing** (virtually nothing, almost nothing), **providing that**

SB158a PB158

1 Students do the activity individually and then discuss their answers in pairs.

> **Key:** The words are **can** and **could**. They are used here to show what it is possible to do in the sense of what is available.

SB158b

2 Students work in pairs.

> **Key:** First occurrence: Or **they** could go to Covent Garden – **tourists**
> Second occurrence: there's a lot of **them** and **they**'re very good – **buskers**
> Third occurrence: **they** can just walk around the markets – **tourists**

When we identify pronoun references we do not simply look back to see what was the last noun mentioned. We also take account of the sense of the text.
*The word **you** does not refer to Catherine. It means 'anyone at all'.*

SB158c

Key: The words which follow **I** are 'think' and 'mean'. Ask students why they think the speakers used these expressions. 'I think' and 'I mean' are very common in casual speech when people are working out their ideas as they talk.

Free in your country?

> **Aims:** 1 To practise making suggestions and recommendations to do with leisure activities.
> 2 To practise describing scenes involving varied activities.
> 3 To practise discussing design and presentation.
> 4 **-ing** forms and prepositional phrases in descriptions.
> 5 To practise phrases of location. e.g. **on the left**, **on the right**, **at the top** etc.
>
> **Lexis:** artist, design
> Revision: **carefully** (with care), **different walks of life**, **exact**, **gathered around**, **hard-up** (poor), **throwing**, **well-off** (not poor)

Task   SB159a PB159

1 Students work in groups. Give them time to make their decisions before you step in to help them prepare their report.

2 Students present their reports orally to the class. It is important for the others to take notes of the presentations so that they can write a report of what others have decided.

3 Students work in groups to prepare their written reports. Monitor group work, providing assistance where needed. Groups' written reports can be collected for checking later, as students will already have heard the oral reports.

SB159b

4 This should be fun and a challenge. Give students a minute to think about this but, of course, don't let them refer back to the pictures.

SB159c

5 Group project (You might like to group students for this according to where they have come from and what pictures they've brought.): Students choose suitable pictures and write relevant captions and paragraphs. They will need your help. It must be accurate! They can also describe pictures they would like artists to draw for them. Point out that layout, too, is important.

6 Students should work together while planning, but the writing could be done individually.

7 When the projects are finished (students could finish them outside the class) put them up round the wall for others to read.

Preposition spot

> **Aim:** To illustrate and practise the meaning and uses of **of**.
>
> **Lexis:** edge, of
> Phrases: **as a means of**, **as a result of**, **a sense of**

SB160 PB160

1 Students work individually, then compile their answers in groups.

> **Key:** people: lot, crowd, group ...
> water: cup, glass, litre, lot ...
> the people: some, many, a few, a lot ...

2 If you want to make the exercise easier, give students the list of words in the key and simply ask them which goes with which noun: story, page, day, garden. Make it clear that the words you are looking for here are general words and not words which apply specifically to books, like 'chapter' or 'page'.

> **Key:** story: beginning/middle/end
> page: top/bottom/middle/edge/left/right/corner
> day: beginning/middle/end.
> garden: middle/bottom/top/corner/end/edge/side/left/right

3 If the class is talkative, you might get them to talk about things they themselves feel ashamed/proud/suspicious etc. of. You might also ask them about things they were proud (frightened etc.) of as children. This is basically a pattern practice exercise, but that is no reason why it should not be extended to a class discussion.

4 **Key:** a ... have a sense of ...
b ... a means/way of ...
c ... in spite of ...

Aims: 1 To practise suggesting reasons for people's actions.
2 To practise predicting the consequences of those actions.

Lexis: addition, additional [T], **altogether, bar(s), belief** [T], **believe** [L], **break** [L], **care, court, due** (**care and attention**) [L], **encourage, file(s), lie, lip, mean, memory, pleased, (into) position** [L], **positive, prison, serious** [L], **seriously** [T], **signal**
Revision: **along with** (together with), **to appear** (**in court**), **by the way . . ., I/you mean, managed to**

Task   SB161a [161a]* PB161

1 Before they read the story students discuss the questions in pairs and report back. When you are summarising students' reports you can stress ways of expressing possibility and probability:
Good, so you think he'll **probably** have to pay a fine and he **might** lose his licence.
Put students' suggestions on the board so they can be compared with Stephen and Catherine's, and with what is actually in the text.

Key: The policeman took the driver's name and address, the number from the number-plate of the car, wrote down the details of the offence, and then took the hitch-hiker's name, address and occupation.

2 Students listen to the recording of Stephen and Catherine and compare their suggestions.

Key: Stephen and Catherine said:
SB: So he'll probably get a fine, and an endorsement on his licence.
CM: . . . Don't you get fined something like a pound an hour over – not a pound – a pound per mile per hour over the speed limit.
SB: per mile per hour over the speed limit. So it would be about a fifty pound fine. Something like that.
CM: What might the police find out about the passenger from their files?
SB: Well, that he had a previous criminal record.

Reading   SB161b [161b]

3 Let students read and comment on their guesses. Then they could listen and read along. Pause while they look up the words. Ask them for all the ways of referring to prison: lock you up, in the clink, behind bars.

SB161c [161c]*

4 Students work in groups. Put their suggestions about what he will say to his solicitor on the board. Then play the recording of Catherine and Stephen.

Key: They thought the hitch-hiker's lie must be about his being a hod carrier, because that is not a skilled trade. They thought the driver's punishment would be a big fine and an endorsement, but they didn't think he would go to prison.

Points he would make to his solicitor:
what speed he was going
the maximum legal speed
that he pulled over as soon as he was signalled
that he had a witness who was in the car with him
the name and address of the witness
They remembered the hitch-hiker's name but not his address.

5 Word study: Ask students to find three more phrases with **for**, two near the beginning and one near the end.

Key: 1 b 2 c 3 a
Additional phrases with **for**:
for a very long time
for several years
for just speedin' = because of

The Hitch-hiker

a   Do you remember what the policeman did after he had stopped the writer for driving at 120 m.p.h. on the motorway?

What punishment or penalty do you think the driver will get? (Do you think he'll have to pay a fine? If so, how much? Will he lose his driving licence altogether? Or even go to prison?)

What might the police find out about the passenger from their files?

Tell each other what you think.

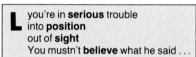 What did Stephen and Catherine think? The same as you?

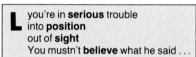**b**   Read on and see how well you guessed.

> L you're in **serious** trouble
> into **position**
> out of **sight**
> You mustn't **believe** what he said . . .

c   What lie was the driver talking about? Why do you think the hitch-hiker lied?

So what punishment do you think he will get?

What do you think he will say to his solicitor? Make a list of points he will probably include.

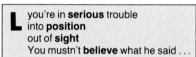 Did Catherine and Stephen think the same as you? Did they remember the hitch-hiker's name and address correctly?

> **?** I'm **positive**
> You **mean** prison?
> his **lips**
> behind the **bars**
> criminals who **break** the law
> **pleased** about that
> see you in **court**

Find the words or phrases from Words to look up and Words to guess which mean:

very sure or absolutely certain
happy
so they could no longer see him
very bad
in prison
it's not true

PART 7

'IN SERIOUS TROUBLE'

"I suppose you know you're in serious trouble," he said to me.
"Yes, officer."
"You won't be driving this fancy car of yours again for a very long time, not after *we've* finished with you. You won't be driving *any* car again come to that for several years. And a good thing, too. I hope they lock you up for a spell into the bargain."
"You mean prison?" I asked, alarmed.
"Absolutely," he said, smacking his lips. "In the clink. Behind the bars. Along with all the other criminals who break the law. *And* a hefty fine into the bargain. Nobody will be more pleased about that than me. I'll see you in court, both of you. You'll be getting a summons to appear."
He turned away and walked over to his motor-cycle. He flipped the prop stand back into position with his foot and swung his leg over the saddle. Then he kicked the starter and roared off up the road out of sight.
"Phew!" I gasped. "That's done it."
"We was caught," my passenger said. "We was caught good and proper."
"I was caught, you mean."
"That's right," he said. "What you goin' to do now, guv'nor?"
"I'm going straight up to London to talk to my solicitor," I said. I started the car and drove on.
"You mustn't believe what 'ee said to about goin' to prison," my passenger said. "They don't put nobody in the clink for just speedin'."
"Are you sure of that?" I asked.
"I'm positive," he answered. "They can take your licence away and they can give you a whoppin' big fine, but that'll be the end of it."
I felt tremendously relieved.
"By the way," I said, "why did you lie to him?"

> **Word study**
>
> Match the phrases in the left-hand column with the one in the right-hand column which has a similar meaning.
>
> 1 *come to that*   a *for a short time*
> 2 *into the bargain*   b *if we are going to talk about that*
> 3 *for a spell*   c *in addition to everything else*
>
> Find three more phrases with 'for'.

Hotels in London are pretty pricey and you get what you pay for. Cheap hotels (£20 and under per night) are all too often not 'nice' places to be in at all. But if you have no choice, or are set on booking in, here are some general guidelines to follow:

* Book in advance.

* Ask the advice and opinions of friends who've stayed or lived in London. [ ]

THE LONDON TOURIST BOARD will provide invaluable information and advice, but only deal with enquiries by letter. Write to them at 26 Grosvenor Gardens SW1. They also give a free advance booking service.

* Be prepared to pay up to £40 a night.

* Remember, sharing a room brings the cost down, so plan your trip with a friend. [ ]

EMERGENCIES If you do find yourself in London with no place to stay, ring one of the following:

THE PICCADILLY ADVICE CENTRE on 930 0066 or the **HOUSING ADVICE SWITCHBOARD** on 434 2522 and they will put you in touch with a night shelter or … [ ]

a What advice would you give to a stranger in your capital city about finding a reasonably priced room for the night?

What range of accommodation is there available in your capital city?

In groups decide which town or city to write about.

▷ Prepare a short report giving suitable advice both for a visiting student and for a reasonably well-off tourist.

Find out from others in your class what advice they have given.

b Compare the advice you gave with the advice given here about London. What kind of person is this advice aimed at?

c Find someone in your class who has stayed (or who knows someone else who has stayed) in one of these types of accommodation.

| a luxury hotel | a guest house |
| a cheap hotel | a hostel |

Find out what it was like.

▷ When you have enough details, write a short critical report of it. Your last paragraph should give would-be travellers advice on whether or not to stay there.

Show your report to the person you interviewed, and ask if it is a fair report.

Finally, read each other's reports. Take a vote on the two best and the two worst places to stay.

163 *Language study* ·······························

: **do, did etc**

: Find all the examples of **do, don't, does, doesn't, did** and **didn't**. All the extracts are from this unit.

: Which ones can you miss out? Which ones can you shorten when you write or speak? Which ones would you need to say in full? Why?

a *If you do find yourself in London with no place to stay …*
b *So, there's really quite a lot to do.*
c *But they can still do it for nothing or next-to-nothing!*

d *It doesn't cost that much to get a bus pass …*
e *Well no … I don't think people get sent to prison.*
f *Don't you get fined something like a pound an hour?*
g *'Phew!' I gasped. 'That's done it.'*
h *'By the way,' I said, 'why did you lie to him?'*
i *What job do you think he does?*
j *'So what do you do?' I asked him.*
k *Doesn't strike me really as a surgeon.*
l *'Do I look like a copper?' 'No,' he said. 'You don't.'*
m *'I don't really care one way or the other.' 'I think you do care,' he said.*
n *I didn't like the way he read my thoughts.*
o *Didn't he say that?*
p *'Well, what do you think?' he asked.*
q *Yes, that was how they did it.*
r *How do you think it ends?*

163 Now listen to a–r.

162 Cheap accommodation in town

> **Aims:** 1 To practise making suggestions and recommendations to do with accommodation.
> 2 To practise understanding tourist information.
>
> **Lexis: advance, advice, prepare(d), set, visitor** T
> Revision: **a fair report, be prepared to . . ., deal with, put you in touch with . . ., pretty** (fairly), **range of, reasonably priced, (advance booking) service**

Task SB162a

1 Ask students to imagine that they are giving advice to a traveller who has arrived at the airport in their capital city and is looking for somewhere to stay. Provide some input by leading a class discussion listing the types of accommodation available with approximate prices. Explain that they should give advice about where to find addresses and where to get advice (possibly from a tourist information board).

2 Students work in groups. Monitor their progress, providing assistance where necessary.

3 Groups could exchange finished reports. Encourage them to ask one another questions.

Reading SB162b

4 This is obviously aimed at someone who has to be a bit careful with money and presumably at someone who does not know London very well. In fact, it is from a European magazine called *Just Seventeen*, which caters for teenagers.

Task SB162c

5 Students should try to find someone who is not in the groups they normally work with.

6 Reporting on the accommodation for 'would-be' travellers is a difficult exercise. Monitor briskly. At the end you can either ask students to read their own paragraphs, or you can pick one or two particularly good ones to read out yourself. If most are good, you could exhibit them on the wall.

163 Language study

> **Aim:** To illustrate the meanings and use of **do**, particularly the emphatic use.

SB163 [163] PB163

Key: The sentences in which **do** can be missed out are:
a 'if you **do** find yourself in London . . .' and
m 'I think you **do** care'
In each of these the word **do** is emphatic. The sentences would still be grammatical if **do** were left out, but it would change the emphasis.

The forms **don't**, **doesn't** and **didn't** are nearly always shortened in speech and very often in informal writing – for example in friendly letters. **Do** (before 'you')/**did** are often reduced in speech to **d**' sounding like a /dʒ/, but not if they are emphatic.

> Further practice: In j and m **do** is emphasised, while in the others it is reduced. In j the sentence would not be grammatical if **do** were left out – the emphasis is only phonetic. When students have finished the exercise ask them to listen to the tape and tell you in which two sentences **do** is pronounced most clearly.
> When students have finished the exercise, ask them to find other sentences where **do** could be stressed phonetically to change the emphasis of the sentence.

Babies can be useful ...

> **Aim:** To give students practice in predicting the outcome of an anecdote.
>
> Lexis: **add(ed)**, **behave**, **enable** [L], **film**, **plain** (clear that) [L], **poor**, **shake**, **source** [L]
> Revision: **causing**, **get boarded** (**onto planes**), **worst thing I've ever seen**
> Phrases: **get/enable ... to ...**; **some relatives of ours/ his/hers**, **come in useful as ...**, **jumping queues** (not waiting in a queue until it is your turn; pushing in, in front of people who were there first.)

Task SB164a

1 Students write their endings in pairs and then show them to another pair.

Listening SB164b 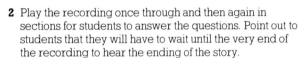*

2 Play the recording once through and then again in sections for students to answer the questions. Point out to students that they will have to wait until the very end of the recording to hear the ending of the story.

> **Key:** John and Monica think the couple got the baby to cry.
> John says about his son: ... I haven't had to use Joe, **as a means of** jumping queues ... if I got Joe to be really ... badly **behaved** ... I could get him to sort of make people leave the room and ... **enable** me to get ... to the front ...
>
> John says about his relatives: ... They used to make them run **around** and they'd get boarded onto planes or onto boats more quickly because they were **causing** so much fuss.
>
> The last line of the story is: **Shake** little Johnny.

Task SB164c

3 Students work in groups, with group members deciding which member in the group has the funniest story to tell. Groups report back and the class votes on the best story. (This exercise may go well or it may be rather slow. To help things along it would be a good idea if you had a story of your own to start things off. If students obviously have little to contribute run it as a class discussion rather than as group work.)

 Language study

> **Aim:** To recycle useful lexis from the transcript.
> Lexis: **around**, **behave**, **poor**, **shake/shook**

SB165a/b [164b]

1 Students should try to fill in the missing words without referring to the transcript. Play this section of the tape a couple of times, for students to check their answers.

> **Key:** as a source of, as a means of, behaved, enable, around, causing, Shake, shook, Poor

---

166 **Phrase-building**

> **Aim:** To practise noun phrases with superlatives used both with the present perfect tense and simple past form (if a definite past time is referred to).

SB166 PB166

1 Encourage students to produce accurate stress and pronunciation as they say the phrases.

2 Get each student to make 5 true sentences from the table. (This is mainly a pattern practice exercise, but you may be able to broaden it out into class discussion.)

Babies can be useful …

a Read this story about the couple and their baby, who was called Johnny. How do you think it ends? Write down two different endings. Show each other.

> A couple took their three-month-old son to the cinema with them. On the way in, the usher said they would have to leave if the baby cried. 'But we'll refund your money,' he added.
>
> After watching the film for half an hour, the husband turned to his wife. 'Well, what do you think?' he asked.
>
> 'It's the worst thing I've ever seen!'
>
> ....
> ....

164b **b** How do John and Monica think the story will end?

What does John say about his son Joe? Is he usually badly behaved?
What does John say about some relatives of his who travelled a lot with their two sons?

Listen carefully as they read the last line of the story. How does it end?

c Have you ever had an embarrassing or funny experience with a small child?

▷ Tell the class about it. Who had the most embarrassing or funniest experience? ◁

Language study ·············

Useful words

a Can you find where the words and phrases below fit in John and Monica's conversation? Look up the words with (L) by them in the Lexicon.

around (L)	as a means (L) of
behaved (L)	poor
causing	shake / shook
enable (L)	as a source (L) of

JM: Er … Yes, they can be useful _____ disruption, I suppose, babies.
MJ: Do you find?
JM: Well, erm, I haven't had to use Joe _____ jumping queues but I'm sure if I got Joe to be really, erm, badly _____ I could get him to sort of make people leave the room and, er, _____ me to get to the front of queues in waiting rooms I suppose. This is apparently what erm, some relatives of ours used to do all the time. They had two sons and they used to make them run _____ and they'd get boarded onto planes or onto boats more quickly because they were _____ so much fuss.
MJ: Gosh, yes. Let's have a look and see. '_____ little Johnny.' Yes. That was how they did it. They _____ him and he cried.
JM: Mhm.
MJ: _____ little Johnny.
JM: Yes. Right.

164b **b** Listen again and check.

Key (164b): 'Me too,' he agreed.
'Shake little Johnny.'

Phrase-building ·····································

Say these phrases quickly.

How many sentences can you make?

The best film	I have ever seen … I have seen this year … I saw last year … I saw as a child …
One of the best / worst	films … books … stories … journeys … things …

The worst	**film**		seen
The best	**meal**		had
The nicest	**book**		heard of
The silliest	**song**		been to
The longest	**food**	I've ever	read
The most interesting	**story**		eaten
The most expensive	**person**		heard
	journey		bought
	day out		met

is …
is called …
is about …
was …

The Hitch-hiker

a Read on. Stop after a few lines (it says *Stop here*) and discuss what trade the hitch-hiker could be in.

c Later, you will find that some words have been blacked out. Can you guess what the words were? Talk together and decide what words they could be, or what they might mean.

167d **d** What words did Stephen and Catherine think went in the blanks?

e Now what job do you think the hitch-hiker does? What jobs need skilled hands? Can you think of four? If you don't know the word, try to describe what the person actually does.

167e Do you agree with Stephen and Catherine? Do you think the hitch-hiker was in a 'crooked' trade too? Or was he simply an unemployed hod-carrier on his way to the races?

167d **167e** **f** Listen carefully for the words from the list that Stephen and Catherine use, and try to catch the word or phrase that goes with them.

kind	disappeared
quite	altogether (L)
plain (L)	strike (L)
edge	not the point (L)
appeared	

Word study

Check all the possible meanings of the words marked (L) in the Lexicon. Which meaning do they have in the transcript?

What do these words and phrases have in common?

went	told him
asked	answered
cried	

---

g Can you say what the hitch-hiker did so that someone else can act while listening to you?

h In groups, rewrite the dialogue between the driver and the hitch-hiker so that both the hitch-hiker and the driver sound very educated.

PART 8
'IT WAS QUITE FANTASTIC'

"Who, me?" he said. "What makes you think I lied?"

"You told him you were an unemployed hod carrier. But you told *me* you were in a highly skilled trade."

"So I am," he said. "But it don't pay to tell everythin' to a copper."

"So what *do* you do?" I asked him.

"Ah," he said slyly. "That'd be tellin', wouldn't it?"

"Is it something you're ashamed of?"

"Ashamed?" he cried. "Me, ashamed of my job? I'm about as proud of it as anybody could be in the entire world!"

"Then why won't you tell me?"

Stop here **167b** **b** Discuss what trade he could be in. Do you agree with what Stephen thinks? Could the hitch-hiker be proud of a job that is illegal? Do you think that's why he wouldn't be willing to tell the police about it?

"You writers really is nosey parkers, aren't you?" he said. "And you ain't goin' to be 'appy, I don't think, until you've found out exactly what the answer is?"

"I don't really care one way or the other," I told him, lying.

He gave me a crafty little ratty look out of the sides of his eyes. "I think you do care," he said. "I can see it on your face that you think I'm in some kind of a very ▆▆▆▆ trade and you're just achin' to know what it is."

I didn't like the way he read my thoughts. I kept quiet and stared at the road ahead.

"You'd be right, too," he went on. "I *am* in a very ▆▆▆▆ trade. I'm in the ▆▆▆▆ ▆▆▆▆ trade of 'em all."

I waited for him to go on.

"That's why I 'as to be extra careful 'oo I'm talkin' to, you see. 'Ow am I to know, for instance, you're not another ▆▆▆▆ in plain clothes?"

"Do I look like a ▆▆▆▆?"

"No," he said. "You don't. And you ain't. Any fool could tell that."

He took from his pocket a tin of tobacco and a packet of cigarette papers and started to ▆▆▆▆ a cigarette. I was watching him out of the corner of one eye, and the speed with which he performed this rather difficult operation was incredible. The cigarette was rolled and ready in about five seconds. He ran his tongue along the edge of the paper, stuck it down and ▆▆▆▆ the cigarette between his lips. Then, as if from nowhere, a lighter appeared in his hand. The lighter flamed. The cigarette was lit. The lighter ▆▆▆▆. It was altogether a ▆▆▆▆ performance.

"I've never seen anyone roll a cigarette as fast as that," I said.

"Ah," he said, taking a deep suck of smoke. "So you noticed."

"Of course I noticed. It was quite fantastic."

He sat back and smiled. It pleased him very much that I had noticed how quickly he could roll a cigarette.

i What kinds of dialects do you have in your country? Try to describe some of the features of one of them to the class.

e.g. *They don't say the -ing on the ends of words properly. They tend to drop their Hs at the beginning of words. Some people from London say a V sound instead of a TH sound.*

167   The Hitch-hiker

> **Aim:** To practise discussing and inferring the meanings of words from context.
>
> **Lexis: altogether, care, disappear(ed), edge, evidence, kind, later, lie(d), operation, performance, plain, pleased, proud, quite, remarkable, smile, strike, willing, wonder**
> Revision: **appeared, not likely to . . .**

Reading   SB167a/b * PB167

1 When the class have stopped reading ask them for their suggestions about what the hitch-hiker does and put these on the board.

2 Students listen for Stephen's suggestions on tape and say whether or not they agree with him.

Key: Stephen thinks he could be a thief. They both agree that he probably makes his living illegally, and that's why he won't speak to the police about it.

SB167c

3 Students read the rest of the text through once for enjoyment. Then, in groups, students try to infer the missing words from the context of the passage. Assist students in their groups, but don't give the answers away as students will be listening for these later. The point is for students to guess the *meanings* of these words by looking at the context and using their own knowledge. They should not be expected to guess the exact words – some are very colloquial, e.g. copper.

SB167d 🔲* 🔲

4 Students listen to Stephen and Catherine's suggestions and compare them with their own. Play the recording of the story. When students have heard the tape, ask them to tell the class how many of their suggestions were the same as the one they heard on tape.

Key: Stephen and Catherine's suggestions: crooked, crooked, most crooked, copper, copper, roll, stuck, flicked/flared, disappeared, magnificent/professional/polished

Text: 'I'm in some kind of a very peculiar trade and you're just achin' to know what it is.'

'I am in a very **peculiar** trade. I'm in the **queerest peculiar** trade of 'em all.'

'Ow am I to know, for instance, you're not another **copper** in plain clothes?'

'Do I look like a **copper**?'

He took from his pocket a tin of tobacco and a packet of cigarette papers and started to **roll** a cigarette.

He ran his tongue along the edge of the paper, stuck it down and **popped** the cigarette between his lips.

The lighter **flamed**.

The lighter **disappeared**. It was altogether a **remarkable** performance.

SB167e 🔲*

5 Students work in groups. Encourage them to try to get their ideas across and to make as long a list of guesses as possible.

Key: This is what Stephen and Catherine said:
CM: . . . I think a safebreaker.

. . .

CM: Or a pickpocket.
SB: . . . conjurer?
CM: . . . surgeons need skilled hands.

SB167f 🔲* 🔲*

6 The aim of this activity is to highlight the common phrases used with these words. Students work in pairs.

Key: SB: . . . I'm in **some kind of** a very blank trade.
SB: 'Cause he's obviously **quite interested** in it. The driver is **quite interested** in what the trade is.
CM: Or a copper.
SB: Yeah.
CM: In **plain clothes**.
CM: . . . he ran his tongue along **the edge of the paper** . . .
CM: I'd say it would be stuck. And as if from nowhere **a lighter appeared in his hand.**
SB: . . . **the lighter disappeared**. It was **altogether a** . . .
CM: **Magnificent** (performance).
SB: **Doesn't strike me** really as a surgeon.
CM: But that's **not the point!** What jobs need skilled hands?
Word Study: They are all words for describing speech/the way something is said or the reason for saying it.

SB167g

7 This refers to the largest paragraph in this episode where he's rolling the cigarette. Try to persuade one of the students to come to the front of the class and mime the hitch-hiker's actions while the class says what he did next, e.g. He got out a tin of tobacco (from his pocket).

SB167h

8 Students work in pairs. The dialogue may be too long for each pair to do all of it. Divide it up and ask each pair of students to do one or two of the hitch-hiker's sentences.

SB167i

9 Discussion: Almost all societies have dialect groups. If you know of such groups in your students' society you can give a bit of help, possibly by going through and analysing one dialect group and then asking the students to do another.

10 Ask students to come out and show on the board the difference between the educated and the dialect form.

168 Wordpower

> **Aim:** To practise the meanings and uses of **break**.

SB168 PB168

1 Discuss the questions at the beginning of the exercise as a class and talk about the pictures. Ask students which pictures have sentences to go with them.

2 Students work in pairs on a–i. The most important thing at this stage is that they produce some sensible guesses; they do not have to be correct. For example a 'broken home' could be a very old and shabby house, or it could be a family which has no money.

   Key: a) a broken home – a family in which the parents are separated or divorced
   b) broken up with – they are no longer friends
   c) broke down – lost control of herself, could not prevent herself crying
   d) break up – finish
   e) broke out – began
   f) broken into – forced open so that thieves could enter
   g) am broke – have no money
   h) An **outbreak** always refers to something bad – an epidemic of illness or crime for example
   i) broke out of – escaped from
   broken marriages – marriages where the couples have divorced
   waves breaking on the shore

3 Encourage students to use the Lexicon entries and ask you questions about them.

169 Grammar

> **Aims:** 1 To practise **-ing** forms and prepositional phrases in descriptions.
> 2 To practise relative clauses in descriptions.

SB169 PB169

1 Point out to students that there is more than one correct way to combine the sentences. Assist them while they work in pairs. When students have finished, put their suggestions on the board. Encourage discussion on the different correct ways of writing the sentences.

   Key: 1 John is a teacher of English at a Catholic school in London.
   2 I was born in Warrington which is a small industrial town in Lancashire in the north of England.
   3 The hovercraft is a vehicle which is able to travel across both land and water on a cushion of air.
   4 Rupert Street Theatre is a small theatre run by an actors' cooperative who just ask that you pay what you can afford.

Wordpower

break

Think of three things that break easily.
Have you broken anything recently?
What time do you normally have a break?

The *Collins COBUILD English Language Dictionary* defines **break**'s first meaning like this.

> break/ / breaks, breaking, broke, broken
> 1 When an object breaks, or when you break it, it splits into pieces as a result of an accident, for example because you have dropped it or hit it too hard. EG *He has broken a window with a ball ... She stepped backwards onto a coffee cup and saucer, which broke into several pieces ...*

What do you think is meant by **break** in these examples?

(a) She comes from a broken home.
(b) He's broken up with his girlfriend.
(c) She broke down and cried.
(d) When does your school break up for the summer?
(e) War broke out in Europe in 1914.
(f) The house next door was broken into and everything of value was taken.
(g) I'm sorry, I can't come out. I'm broke.
(h) An outbreak of ...
   (Is this likely to be good or bad?)
(i) He broke out of prison in broad daylight.

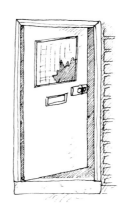

Now look up **break** in the Lexicon and read the examples there. Some come from this book and some from the *Collins COBUILD English Language Dictionary*. Did you guess the meanings?

Grammar

Descriptions

See how these descriptive sentences are made up.

It was a pale blue car with electrically operated windows and dark blue seats made of leather.

The car was pale blue.
It had windows.
The windows were electrically operated.
It had dark blue seats.
The seats were made of leather.

Can you make up one long descriptive sentence from these short sentences?

1 *John is a teacher.*
  He teaches English.
  He teaches at a Catholic school.
  The school is in London.

2 *I was born in Warrington.*
  Warrington is in Lancashire.
  Warrington is a small town.
  It is an industrial town.
  It is in the north of England.

How many ways of describing can you find in your sentences?

Ahead of me I saw a small, ratty-faced man in a greyish jacket, who was thumbing a lift.

Ahead of me I saw a man.
He was small.
He was ratty-faced.
He was wearing a greyish jacket.
He was thumbing a lift.

3 *The Hovercraft is a vehicle.*
  It is able to travel across land.
  It is able to travel across water.
  It travels on a cushion of air.

4 *Rupert Street Theatre is small.*
  It is run by an actors' cooperative.
  They just ask that you pay what you can afford.

a   down (and opposites)

In which sentences can you use one of these phrases, instead of the phrase with **down**, to make it mean the OPPOSITE?

push . . . up	been repaired
pick . . . up	up
speeding up	put some air into . . .
	makes it more expensive

. . . she put the menu down.
Has your bus or car ever broken down on a motorway?
. . . it helps them to keep down crime.
. . . I would have let his tyres down but . . .
He took plenty of time slowing down.
Sharing a room brings the cost down . . .
. . . they were already half way down the street.

b   Ways of saying 'said', 'asked'

Which of these words could you put into each space?

added	wanted to know	asked
agreed	told me	explained
replied	wondered	answered
nodded	smiled	
pointed out	went on	

'Tomorrow's a good day for me. All right, then. I'll do it,' he _____.
'Difficult to tell her age. How old could she be?' he _____.
'Terrific! It must be because of the warm weather,' she _____.

c   Getting/making/enabling people (to) do things

Which of these verbs must be followed by 'to' when it has this meaning?

If I got Joe to be really badly behaved . . .
I could get him to make people leave the room . . .
. . . and to enable me to get to the front of queues . . .
They had two sons and they used to make them run around . . .
Did your parents make you get home by midnight?

d   give

Find phrases with **give** where it means 'say something', 'write', 'hand', 'stop', 'look at'. Which phrases are left over? What do they mean?

1 Staying in a B & B gives you the chance to make friends.
2 What advice did Danny give?
3 How many reasons did he give?
4 If you'll just give me a sheet of paper . . .
5 She should give up smoking.
6 The seasoning given here is for 1 egg.
7 You haven't given me any idea of how long this is.
8 He gave me a crafty little ratty look out of the sides of his eyes.
9 He gave me one of his sly little ratty smiles.
10 Give as many details as you can.
11 He gave the impression he was afraid of us.
12 Give it a kick!

e   Lexicon words

Look up these words in the Lexicon and then find which sentence you could use them in, and what form of the word is appropriate. Use some words twice.

believe	operation	plain	serious	view
due	period	point	sight	

1 Listen, it's not funny – I'm quite _____ about this matter.
2 It's an important _____ and one which must be taken seriously.
3 That motorway accident was _____ to careless driving.
4 All in all he spent a _____ of five weeks in hospital after his _____.
5 If you take a tourist bus, you can see many of the _____ of London for free, and you get a good _____ if you go upstairs.
6 I like the man, – he's got a lot of good _____ , but I shall never agree with his _____ on politics.
7 I like ____ colours for carpets – not flowery designs .
8 She's 87? I don't _____ it! She only looks about 50.
9 Your local travel agent may be a good _____ of information.

Important words to remember (721 so far)					
add	believe L	evidence	performance	religion	unit
addition	break L	exhibition	period L	religious	view
additional	care	feed	plain L	remarkable	visitor
advance	collection	file	pleased	serious L	willing
advice	comedy	film	politics	seriously	wonder L
altogether	court	frequently	poor	shake	
arts	disappear	lie	position L	sight L	
artist	due L	lip	positive	signal	
audience	edge	memory	prepare	smile	
bar	enable L	museum	pride	source L	
behave	encourage	operation L	prison	strike	
belief L	event	painting	programme	theatre	

Aims: 1 To revise important lexical items.
2 To revise lexical opposites.
3 To revise ways of describing speech functions.

Lexis: down, position [L]

SB170a PB170

Key: put down – picked up, broken down – been repaired, keep down – keep up, let down – put some air into, slowing down – speeding up, brings down – makes it more expensive, half way down – half way up

SB170b

Key: agreed, replied, nodded, smiled, went on, answered, wanted to know, wondered, asked
added, replied, pointed out, smiled, went on, explained

SB170c

Key: enable, get/got

SB170d

Key: 2 say something
3 say something
4 hand
5 give up – stop
6 write
7 say something/write
8 look at
9 look at
10 say something/write

Phrases left over:
1 gives you the chance to – enables you to
11 gave the impression – appeared to be
12 give it a kick – kick it (Delexical use as in 'Give him a kiss,' meaning 'Kiss him'.)

SB170e

Key: 1 serious 2 point 3 due
4 period, operation 5 sights, view
6 points, views 7 plain 8 believe
9 source

LEXICAL OBJECTIVES

Level 1 words (see page 129T):
almost, down (see SB168), **hall, kind, later, mean, point** L, **quite, set.**

add 1 *Break the egg into the bowl and add the milk...* [6]
2 *Add up the bill...* T
3 said. *'But we'll refund your money', he added.*
addition *In addition to a comfortable*
bed, your host will prepare... [3]
additional *This is an additional reason for not leaving.* T
advance *Book your room well in advance.*
advice *Ask the advice or opinions of friends...*
altogether 1 all in all. *It was altogether a fantastic performance.*
2 in all. *How many injuries have you had as a group, altogether?* [2]
arts 1 *... museums and art galleries.*
2 *When I was at school, I took only arts subjects.* [5] *Bachelor of Arts* T
artist *a painter, entertainer etc.*
audience *a group of people who attend a performance. ... a live audience*
bar 1 *sandwich/hotel bar*
2 *iron bar.* Also: *prison bars. ... behind bars*
behave/behaviour L
belief L
believe L
break L (See SB168.)
care *to be concerned about. I don't really care one way or the other.*
collection *a huge collection of art*
comedy *a light-hearted play or film. Comedy shows*
court 1 *place where legal matters are decided. I'll see you in court.*
2 *tennis court* T
disappear 1 *The lighter disappeared.*
2 *to stop existing. It was only the dinosaurs that disappeared...* T
due L
edge *the edge of the paper/road etc.*
enable L
encourage *He'll say that the man encouraged him to do it.*
event 1.1 *something that happens. ... the events leading up to the war* T
1.2 *... major sports events* [6]
evidence *anything that causes you to believe that something is true ... with fresh evidence*
exhibition *... frequently changed exhibitions*
feed *to give food to. Feed the pigeons in Trafalgar Square.* [12]
file, it's on file = *we have a record of it. police files*
film *a moving picture. After watching the film for half an hour...*
frequently *often. ... frequently changed exhibitions*
lie/lay 1 *I lie awake at night.* [14]
2 *... several books lying on the table* T
3 **lie/lied** = *not to tell the truth. What makes you think I'm lying?*
lip *He popped the cigarette between his lips.*
memory 1 *I have a bad memory for names. What a memory!*
2 *I quote from memory.* T
3 *a computer memory* T
museum *The British Museum*
operation L
painting *British paintings of all periods*
performance *... a performance of*
Macbeth. *... a remarkable performance* [12]
period L
plain L
pleased 1 *Pleased to meet you.* T
2 *It pleased him very much that I noticed how quickly he could roll a cigarette.*
politics *to do with government. ... give vent to their views on politics.*
poor 1 *without money. Rich or poor?*
2 *Poor little Johnny!*
position L
positive 1 *'Are you sure of that?' I asked. 'I'm positive,' he answered.*
2 *used to add emphasis. I usually find cooking a positive pleasure.* T
prepare 1 *They were expecting me. A room had been prepared.* T
2 *Be prepared to pay up to £40 a night.*
prison *I don't think people get sent to prison these days.*
programme 1.1 *scheme. ... a research and development programme* T
1.2 *a television or radio broadcast. Specify your preferred programmes...*
proud *I'm proud of my job.*
religion *Buddhism, Christianity, Hinduism, Islam etc.*
religious 1 *to do with religion. ... religious instruction* T
2 *The woman was very religious.* T
remarkable *... a remarkable performance.*
serious L
seriously *What I think is important, quite seriously, is that people should know the facts.* T
shake 1 *They shook him and he cried.*
2 *His mother's death had shaken him dreadfully.* T
sight L
signal *He pulled over as soon as he was signalled.*
smile *The man gave another of his sly ratty little smiles.*
source L
strike 1 *Workers went on strike for better pay.* T
2 *The young man struck his father and accidentally killed him.* T
3 *give an impression. Doesn't strike me really as a surgeon.*
theatre *London theatres and cinemas are quite expensive.*
unit 1 *a single, complete thing. ... to treat the world as a unit.* T
2 *a group of people who work together. Ticket Unit, BBC, Broadcasting House.*
view 1 *opinion. To give vent to their views on politics...*
2 *... there is a fine view of the sea.* T
visitor *guest. She was a frequent visitor to our house.* T
willing 1 *You can see everything from the outside for nothing if you're willing to walk.*
2 *... a willing student* T
wonder L

How did you do that? I never saw you

This unit deals with practical jokes and conjuring tricks and goes on to look at security and crime prevention. The lead-in page requires students to explain how things are done (in this case how practical jokes and tricks are carried out) and to complete some short anecdotes. The next section looks at these two aspects of communication – instruction-giving and narrative – in more detail. The first Hitch-hiker episode gives intensive practice in inferring the meanings of words from context as well as the usual prediction exercises. There is an intensive reading passage from a public information leaflet about home security, after which students build up their own questionnaire questions, and use them to carry out a survey. Students are asked to prepare and then evaluate descriptions of personal items so that if they did ever lose something, they would know how to give a relevant description to the police or lost property office. A speed-reading exercise based on advice and instructions regarding personal and home security gives practice in reading for specific items of new information, and comparing its content with that of their own questionnaire. The theme continues with a recorded description of two burglaries and their consequences; the students getting a chance to recount similar experiences. In the tenth episode of The Hitch-hiker, we are given a dramatic demonstration of what the hitch-hiker actually does for a living.

OBJECTIVES

Lexical aims are in TB184

Grammar and discourse

a Use of questions, imperative forms and modals in advice and instructions. (171)
b Use of conditional expressions to contextualise advice and explanations. (171)
c Meanings and use of **had**, particularly in the past perfect tense. (173)
d Inference of meaning from context. (174,179)
e The meanings and use of **from**. (175)
f Weighting of information according to its relevance for a particular purpose. (176,178)
g Patterns following verbs of perception. (181)
h **that** clauses. (183)
i **-ing** forms, particularly their common uses in narrative. (180)
j Passive expressions with **be** and **get**. (184)

Tasks

a Explaining a set of procedures. (171)
b Speculating on and predicting the end of a joke and some stories. (171)
c Giving and understanding advice and instructions in speech and writing. (172,176,178)
d Understanding discussion of the meanings of words and how they are inferred. (174)
e Writing and completing a questionnaire. (176)
f Comparing the results of a questionnaire. (176)
g Producing and understanding descriptions of personal belongings. (177)
h Predicting the content of a public information leaflet and reading it to compare its contents with another, similar text. (176,178)
i Understanding spoken narrative. (172,178)

171 Jokes and tricks

> **Aims:** 1 To practise explaining a set of procedures.
> 2 To practise speculating on and predicting the outcome of jokes and stories.
> 3 To give further practice in anecdote-telling.
>
> **Lexis: belong, burn, contents, lend, mess, moon, pregnant, solve, thus**
> Understanding only: **burgled**

The items on the lead-in page lead up to explanations and other extension work on the next page, so don't encourage students to look ahead. Do sections a–h in any order you like. There is at least one picture for each of a–h. Ask students if they can distinguish them. Just let students speculate for now. The top left-hand picture is explained in 172b. Most of the explanations for the stories and puzzles in this section are given in section 172.

SB171a/b PB171

1 Encourage students to speculate and to share ideas and experiences of conjuring tricks and practical jokes. Allow them to make notes if they wish, so they can remember what they thought. Students should discuss the questions in pairs then report back informally.

SB171c

2 In pairs students speculate on a possible ending for the story. Encourage them to note down their ideas. Pairs report back informally while the others listen for what they think is the best ending to the story. The ending is in section 172d. Tell students they will read it later.

SB171d

3 Some students may need 'April Fool's Day' explained to them (April Fool's Day, April 1st, is a day when people traditionally play tricks on each other). If you have one, give them an example of a joke that you have played on someone, or of one that has been played on you.

SB171e

4 In pairs students speculate on a possible ending for the story, which is: The Hodja replied, 'The moon, because the sun only shines during the day when it's light anyway.' (The Hodja is a famous figure in Middle Eastern folklore, and many stories exist about the man.) Do students know any other famous figures in folklore?

SB171f

5 Direct students to the bottom left-hand picture. Explain to students that the banana is 'magic' because when the magician peeled it it was already in four pieces (one for each of the children in the picture). It's enough at this point to raise the question of how the trick was done. Students will be given more information to work out an explanation for the trick in section 172.

SB171g

6 Point out to students that they will be reading the ending to this story in the next section. (The theme of personal security – burglaries, pickpockets etc. – is fully dealt with later on, so avoid lengthy stories on these themes: the lexis, however, should be introduced if possible.)

SB171h

7 Optional: Encourage students who know how to do a particular trick to perform it in class.

8 Words to guess: Write the following words on the board and ask students to guess the meanings from the context of the stories: **contents, burgled, thus, solved, belong/lent, pregnant, burning** (from the picture).

How did you do that?
I never saw you

Jokes and tricks

In Vienna, we lived next door to a young couple. One evening the wife, white as a sheet, called me over to her flat saying that it had been burgled. All the cupboards and drawers were open, with the contents scattered about the floor. She wanted to call the police, but I advised her first to inform her husband. And thus the case was solved: . . .

a Have you ever watched (or performed) any conjuring tricks? Describe some.

b Find some practical jokes on this page and say what you think is about to happen.

c Read the story about the room that's in a mess. What could have happened? How will the story end?

d Do you have a day like April Fool's Day?

e Do you know the answer to the question the Hodja is asked? What do you think he might say? What reason could he give?

f How could the trick with the banana have been done?

g Why did the Hodja give his friend the small pot?

h Do you know any card tricks? How are they done?

WATCH OUT, THERE'S A SPIDER ON YOUR BACK

EEK!

APRIL FOOL!

The Sun or the Moon

One day someone asked the Hodja which was more useful, the sun or the moon. The Hodja thought for a moment then answered . . .

The Hodja and the Pots

One day the Hodja borrowed a big cooking pot from one of his friends. After a while he took it back to his friend's house and gave it back to his friend together with a small pot. 'Thank you very much,' said his friend. 'But what about this small pot? It doesn't belong to me.'
'Oh, yes,' said the Hodja. 'When you lent me the big pot it was pregnant and the little pot is the baby, so it does belong to you.'
'Well thank you very much,' said his friend and took both pots.

NOW SEE THIS MAGIC BANANA ALREADY IN FOUR PIECES FOR FOUR CHILDREN HERE!

172 What was the trick?

a The Hodja's pots

Summarise what you think the Hodja will do next. Exchange ideas with your friends.

Rearrange these paragraphs to complete the story.

> 1 Excuse me, but could I have my big pot back?' he asked.

> 2 But after three weeks the Hodja had still not returned the big pot, so the friend went round to the Hodja's house.

> 3 Next day the Hodja asked if he could borrow the big pot again. Of course his friend agreed, hoping that he would get another small pot.

> 4 The Hodja shook his head sadly. 'But of course pots die,' he said. 'You believed me when I said your pot was pregnant, and if pots can get pregnant they can certainly die.'

> 5 'What do you mean?' said his friend. 'Pots don't die. I don't believe you. I want my pot back.'

> 6 'Oh dear,' said the Hodja. 'I'm afraid I have some very bad news for you. Your big pot is dead.'

L dead
   die

b April Fool

172b John told Monica about a joke they played once, when he was at university. Which picture in section 171 illustrates this tale?

Can you complete this sentence of John's?

JM: . . . she said 'I didn't know _____ to sort of _____ through it like jumping out of a hoop, you know, _____ a hoop, or, erm, _____ to ignore it and just sort of calmly, erm, tear it _____.'

c The Magic Banana

Did you work out how the banana trick could be done?
If not, here are some clues to help you.

All you need is a needle and some relatively strong thread. Choose a fairly ripe banana. Thread the needle. Carefully push . . .

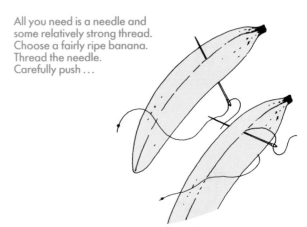

▶ Work out and write the rest of the instructions. Exchange ideas with the rest of the class. ◀

d What had happened in Vienna? What guesses did you make? Were you right?

> . . . her husband had dropped in briefly while she was out, to look for his driving licence.

173 Language study

had

a In each example below there are two or more things that happened. Which thing took place first?

1 *One evening the wife, white as a sheet, called me over to her flat saying that it had been burgled.*
2 *Her husband had dropped in briefly while she was out (before she got back), to look for his driving licence.*

Now what about these sentences from other units?

3 *The assistant sold more ice-cream in the interval than anyone had ever done before. (55)*
4 *And I won the next year but not as much as I'd won the first year.*
5 *. . . they arrived after the restaurants had shut. (86)*
6 *The pilot then discovered the cockpit door had locked itself and he'd mislaid the key. (104)*
7 *One morning he found that someone had parked in front of his garage door. (150)*

b In what ways are **had** or **'d** used in the story below?

173b

SB: Well, my girlfriend's very frightened of flying, and she had a bad experience. [Describes how plane engine caught fire.] And they had to take the plane back to Heathrow.
CM: Does that mean that nobody else had noticed?
SB: I think maybe the pilots had noticed, but certainly nobody else on board had noticed, [ ] so they drugged her up with [ ] valium for the next flight, by when she'd missed her connection in New York to Texas and so she had to go on . . .

172   What was the trick?

Aims: 1 To read a story intensively in order to reassemble it.
2 To practise assembling a set of instructions.

Lexis: corridor, dead, die, ignore, magic, tear(s), whether

The four different activities can be done quite quickly, as a follow-up to and consolidation of the lead-in page.

Reading   SB172a   PB172

1 Students reassemble the story individually, then compare answers in pairs. When discussing students' answers, ask students to justify their ordering by referring either to cohesive devices or to the coherence of the story.

   Key: 3, 2, 1, 6, 5, 4

Listening   SB172b   [172b] *

2 Students listen to the tape and choose the picture which illustrates it. Ask students to complete the sentence, then play the tape again for them to check their answers.

   Key: The top left-hand picture. Words missing: whether, jump, through, whether, down.

Task   SB172c

3 Students work out a solution in groups. Remind students of the picture at the bottom left corner of SB171. You might turn the activity into a competition, offering whatever prize you think suitable to the first group to work out the answer.
Possible instructions:
i) Choose a fairly ripe banana (if possible, one with brown spots on its skin – these will disguise any holes made by the needle).
ii) Thread the needle. (Use the thread double if it's not very strong.)
iii) Decide how many pieces you want the banana to be in, when you later take the peel off.
iv) Notice how most bananas have four 'sides'; insert the needle into the corner of one side, carefully push it along just inside the skin, but not through the actual fruit, and out of the next corner. Pull the needle through but leave a length of thread hanging.
Push the needle back into the same hole, and along the next side of the banana, and out at the next corner. Make sure you leave the end of the thread hanging all the time. Do this twice more. Now you should have the needle and the original end of the thread coming out of the same hole.
v) Take hold of both ends of the thread and pull firmly but gently; the thread should cut through the inside of the banana without leaving a mark, and come out again.
vi) The banana is now in two pieces inside its skin.
Repeat the above procedure in order to cut the banana again, lower down, however many times you wish.

Task   SB172d

4 Most students will think there has been a burglary. Get one or two students to summarise the story briefly and to tell the class again what they think happened before they read the last line.

5 Ask students if anything similar has ever happened to them or to a friend.

173   Language study

Aim: To practise the meanings and uses of **had**, particularly as it is used in the past perfect tense.

SB173a   PB173

1 Students read and discuss the examples, and then report back in the form of a class discussion.

   Key: The action with the **had** or **'d** happened before the other action.

SB173b   [173b] *

2 Remind students of Stephen's story in section 104e. Ask them if they remember what happened to his girlfriend when she was flying.

   Key: Other ways of using **had/'d**:
1 with a noun, e.g. had a bad experience, had a good look, had a long read.
2 must, e.g. they had to take the plane back to Heathrow. And so she had to go on . . .
3 past perfect, as 173a above. E.g. nobody else had noticed.
. . . by when she'd missed her connection . . .

Aims: 1 To give further practice in understanding discussion of the meanings of words and how they are inferred.
2 To give practice in following and discussing a narrative.
3 To show students that they can get the main gist of the story without understanding all the words.

Lexis: elegant, fantastic, fool, marvellous, round [L]
Revision: **give up** (stop trying), **make sure** (that) . . .

Reading   SB174a/b PB174

1 Explain to students that some words (mainly uncommon words) have been blacked out, and that *later* they will have to try to guess what meaning these words might have, by thinking about that part of the story and looking at the words and phrases around it.

2 Students read the extract first and do not listen to the story being read until the end (f). When students have read the extract, get them to summarise the jobs the writer thought of. They can jot down any ideas they have about the missing words but don't need to go into them in depth until later.

   Key: Possible jobs: piano player, brain surgeon, watchmaker, conjurer, card player.

SB174c

3 In groups students try to answer the questions. Get several groups to report what they thought.

Listening   SB174d   174d *

4 Tell students that they are unlikely to get exactly the same words as are used in the story; the important thing is that they get a similar or appropriate meaning. Let students listen to Catherine and Stephen talking about the words they think might fit and compare lists.

   Key: Here we give possible words that could fit, together with the original word used by the writer.
   slim and long and **elegant**, (beautiful, skilful, quick)
   Any **twerp** can learn to do that. (fool, child, simple-minded person)
   There's **titchy** little kids . . . (tiny)
   You do **conjuring tricks**. You're a **conjurer**. (magic tricks, magician)
   A **conjurer**?
   . . . going round **crummy** kids' parties (unpleasant, useless, boring, silly)
   . . . deal yourself **marvellous** hands. (fantastic, really good, cheating, top-class, winning)
   Me! A rotten **card-sharp** (card player, cheat)
   That's a miserable **racket** if ever there was one. (illegal activity)

SB174e   174e *

5 Students listen to Stephen and Catherine reading the key to the missing words.

SB174f   174f

6 Students listen to the dramatised version being read aloud and compare the words they guessed with what is on the tape.

a What kind of work did you think the hitch-hiker might do? Summarise the ideas you had after reading the last episode. See if you thought of any of the jobs the writer guesses at here.

b As you read, you will notice that some of the words in this episode have been blacked out. Discuss what meaning you think they have.

c Where did he get the belt from? What do *you* think? Was it really the driver's belt? Was there a bag or suitcase of clothes in the car that the hitch-hiker had managed to open? Had the driver taken his belt off, before he'd picked up the hitch-hiker, so as to be more comfortable when driving? Or what?

d What did you think the missing words meant? Write down as many ideas for each one as you can. Tell each other.

174d Listen to Stephen and Catherine. Did they mention any of the words you thought of?

174e **e** Listen and see how many words: they managed to guess right you managed to guess

Then compare the meanings. Find out which ones are too colloquial for you to use.

174f **f** Listen to the episode being read.

PART 9
'ANY *** CAN LEARN TO DO THAT!'

"You want to know what makes me able to do it?" he asked.
"Go on then."
"It's because I've got fantastic fingers. These fingers of mine," he said, holding up both hands high in front of him, "are quicker and cleverer than the fingers of the best piano player in the world!"
"Are you a piano player?"
"Don't be daft," he said. "Do I look like a piano player?"
I glanced at his fingers. They were so beautifully shaped, so slim and long and ▇▇▇, they didn't seem to belong to the rest of him at all. They looked more like the fingers of a brain surgeon or a watchmaker.
"My job," he went on, "is a hundred times more difficult than playin' the piano. Any ▇▇▇ can learn to do that. There's ▇▇▇ little kids learnin' to play the piano in almost any 'ouse you go into these days. That's right, ain't it?"
"More or less," I said.
"Of course it's right. But there's not one person in ten million can learn to do what I do. Not one in ten million! 'Ow about that?"
"Amazing," I said.
"You're darn right it's amazin'," he said.
"I think I know what you do," I said. "You do ▇▇▇ ▇▇▇. You're a ▇▇▇."
"Me?" he snorted. "A ▇▇▇? Can you picture me goin' round ▇▇▇ kids' parties makin' rabbits come out of top 'ats?"
"Then you're a card player. You get people into card games and you deal yourself ▇▇▇ hands."
"Me! A rotten ▇▇▇!" he cried. "That's a miserable ▇▇▇ if ever there was one."
"All right. I give up."
I was taking the car along slowly now, at no more than forty miles an hour, to make quite sure I wasn't stopped again. We had come on to the main London–Oxford road and were running down the hill toward Denham.
Suddenly, my passenger was holding up a black leather belt in his hand. "Ever seen this before?" he asked. The belt had a brass buckle of unusual design.
"Hey!" I said. "That's mine, isn't it? It *is* mine! Where did you get it?"

91

175 | Preposition spot

from

1 a starting point in time or space; the place or person where something or someone originates
So you come from Ireland ...
Water from the river.
From 10 to 2p.m.

2 the idea of separation, leaving, being away or apart or removed from (in place or time)
My first job, straight from school.
The money was taken from her bag.
Some stores offer relief from VAT under the ...

Look at these examples. Which phrases with **from** refer to a place? Which to a time? What do the others mean?

a *... fourteen miles from the centre of London.*
b *JM: You're Irish. CM: You've guessed from my accent! (9)*
c *... can't think of anywhere where it's different from here.(117)*
d *Track-suits from £24.99.*
e *I like green, I'm not too keen on yellow, but apart from that, red, blue, ... (128)*
f *He copied the name and address from my licence. (152)*

g *... he was suspicious of him from the very beginning ... (152)*
h *Huge collection of art, dating from 1300 to 1900.*
i *The police try to prevent people from breaking into houses.*
j *It isn't expensive – far from it ...*
k *He caught a cold from walking home in the rain.*

176 | Survey

How safe is your property?

This is taken from the Community Pages of a Local Directory from an area just north of London, where many new roads have been built and where crime is on the increase.

Read the advice, then work in groups to copy and complete the questions on the questionnaire. (Don't write in any answers.)

Then give the questionnaire to another group to fill in.

Finally exchange questionnaires and read each other's. Which group seems to have the safest homes? Which was the best questionnaire?

THOMSON LOCAL DIRECTORY
COMMUNITY PAGES WITH AA, MAPS AND Post Office POSTCODES
THE MAIN DIRECTORY
NAMES & NUMBERS AND INDEX
ISLINGTON-HARINGEY AREA
1987-88

Fight Crime and Protect your Home

Do you support a burglar? Your home could be a criminal's wages for the day. You don't have to be rich or own a lot of possessions to be worth a thief's attention, and we all have things of sentimental value, even if they are worth little or nothing in hard cash.

You should be able to answer "yes" to all the questions listed under General Precautions. If you can't, take immediate steps to put things right. And remember, when in doubt, ask at your police station for your Crime Prevention Officer. His advice is free.

GENERAL PRECAUTIONS

	YES	NO
1 Do you tell your newsagent when you're going to be ....?	☐	☐
2 Do you always lock the garage door when you ....?	☐	☐
3 When you're out for the evening, do you ....?	☐	☐
4 When you go out, ...?	☐	☐
5 If you go on holiday, do you ask ....?	☐	☐
6 Do you tell the police when ......?	☐	☐

YOUR PROPERTY

7 Have you photographed ....?	☐	☐
8 Have you made a note of the serial numbers of ....?	☐	☐
9 ... your bicycle or car when you ....?	☐	☐
10 ....?	☐	☐
...................?	☐	☐

L protect steps support

? crime criminal rich hard cash in doubt crime prevention

Word study

Match words and phrases with similar meanings.

1 precautions	a	if you're not sure
2 don't have to	b	safety measures
3 when in doubt	c	pay for someone's food, drink, clothes ...
4 protect	d	needn't
5 support	e	not valuable
6 worth little	f	make it safe

177 | If you lost your ...

a If you lost your purse or wallet could you describe it?

Think of something that you have with you today. Describe it in great detail to your partner, so that they can write a good description of it.

REWARD
ANSWERS TO NAME PRINCE
POST CARD
LOST
A black leather wallet
High St Area
REWARD OFFERED   TEL 62910
POST CARD
WANTED

b Decide what a good description should generally contain. Add two more things to those below to make a list.

the material it is made of

size or measurements

177c **c** How well does Caroline describe her purse?

What information does she give that is not relevant?

175 Preposition spot

> **Aim:** To introduce more of the common phrases and
> uses of **from**, with their common collocations, e.g. **apart
> from the fact that . . ., far from . . ., from side to side**

SB175 PB175

1 Introduce the activity with some further examples, e.g.:
1 I come from X. Where do you come from?
2 I've lived away from my family for x years now. Have
you ever lived away from your family?
Point out that in 1 you are talking about a starting point and
that in 2 you are referring to a separation.

2 Students read the examples and do the activity
individually or in pairs.

> **Key:** Place: a, f (origin)   e apart from
> Time: g, h,   i prevent from
> Other: b   j far from it
> c different from   k = as a result of
> d = origin/starting point

176 Survey

> **Aim:** To give students practice in writing and
> completing a questionnaire for use in class.
>
> **Lexis: area, community, crime, criminal, doubt,
> doubtful** [T], **fight** [L], **lock, precaution, protect,
> support** [L], **valuable**
> Revision: **attention, little** (a very small amount), **should
> be able to take steps to, worth**

Task SB176 PB176

*Outline procedure: Each group reads the blurb on the
questionnaire then drafts the remaining questions to complete the
questionnaire and passes it on, so that another group can actually fill
in their questionnaire and report their findings to the class. Finally
the questionnaires themselves can be read and commented on – by
other groups – with reference to content and clarity of questions.*

1 The intitial blurb on *Fight Crime and Protect your Home*
contains a large number of target words. Ask students to
read this, and go over any problems they may have.

2 Point out that the questionnaire here is incomplete where
the . . . occur. Ensure that students realise that the answers
to all the questions should be **yes** – that is *if* the people
concerned have made their homes secure enough. Also
point out to students that some of the points on the
questionnaire will need 2 or 3 sentence completions.
(The original questionnaire is at the back of the Practice
Book. However the aim is not to guess what was on the
original; students' own ideas may be far more suitable to
their environment. Section 178 deals with a similar topic.)

3 When students have discussed the task and have begun
to write their questions, go around to check that they are
appropriately correct before students hand them over to
another group to fill in.

4 Groups exchange questionnaires and discuss how to fill
them in truthfully; get students to share the interviewing
round the group and draw one column for each person, or
to put a tick for each person in the correct box, Yes/No.
Each person should answer every question.

5 When they have completed the questionnaire, they can
plan an oral report about their group to give the class.

6 After the report, allow time for a general summing up and
evaluation stage – what should most people's households
do in order to improve the security of their homes?

7 Finally, suggest that all the questionnaires are passed
round or displayed on the walls, so that any differences
can be noted.

8 Word study: **Key:** 1 b   2 d   3 a   4 f   5 c   6 e

177 If you lost your . . .

> **Aims:** 1 To practise producing and understanding
> descriptions of personal belongings.
> 2 To practise assessing what type of information is
> relevant to such a description.
>
> **Lexis: contents, foolishly, possible, possibility** [T],
> **possibly** [T], **relevant**

Ripped off *is an informal slang phrase meaning cheated over the
price, i.e. forced to pay too much for it.* ***You were done*** *means the
same, and is also very informal.
Pierre Cardin is a famous fashion designer and in some countries,
clothes, bags etc. bear the name Pierre Cardin even if they are not
designed by him, just so that they can be sold at a higher price.*

Task SB177a PB177

1 Ask students to imagine they have lost something that
they normally carry round with them (a bag, briefcase,
wallet, purse, diary, notebook, address-book, watch, coat,
jacket, umbrella etc.). (Make sure they don't look at the
object they have chosen – this is partly a memory
challenge; generally, if you lose something, you have to
describe what it looks like from memory.)

2 After students have done the task once, get them to
change partners and describe something different. (If you
wish, students could listen to the tape before they perform
the task.)

Task SB177b

3 Students work in pairs. When they have finished make a
consolidated list of their suggestions on the board.

> **Key:** material it's made of,
> size, or measurements, plus:
> shape
> colour
> condition – old, new-looking etc.
> any distinguishing features – label, writing on it.
> contents – if it is a container of some kind.
> You would also have to say where you thought you had
> lost it.

Listening SB177c 🔊*

4 Students could note down the points Caroline makes
about her purse as they listen.

> **Key:** Irrelevant information – Caroline needn't have
> mentioned how or where she bought it, or the fact that she
> was 'ripped off' . . . However these details do make it more
> interesting for the listener.

5 Optional parallel tasks: *EITHER* choose a small place, a
picture in the building, a person that all students are
familiar with or a classroom item that they can't see. Get
students to write a description of it in as much detail as
possible. They can then read each other's descriptions
and compare the content. Finally, show students the
place, picture, person, object and ask them to decide
which description was the most accurate.
OR – Ask each student to put their purses, wallets or bags
all together in a pile on a table in front of the class. They
should then take turns to describe one of the objects that
are there, so that the owner will recognise it.

Crime prevention and burglaries

Aims: 1 Reading to predict the content of a factual text.
2 To practise speed reading for new items of information.

Lexis: affair, attempt(ed), attitude, authority, certain, crime, doubt, ensure, local, locked, negative, precaution, prevent(ion), proper, questionable, (came) round [L], **security** [L], **shock, stolen, take (place),** other phrases with **take, valuable**

Reading   SB178a PB178

1 Ask students to guess what the text on crime prevention will say by discussing statements 1–6 and writing T or F. Discuss students' ideas before they read, but don't give them the answers. Students read the first part of the text to check their guesses. (The True/False exercise is to prepare students for the first part of main reading task).

Key: 1 T 2 F 3 F 4 T 5 T 6 T
Most people agree that 6 best sums up the general message.

Speed reading   SB178b

2 Students should look back at their questionnaires in section 176 to refresh their memories. Then ask them to read and take quick note of any additional points mentioned here. There is no need for them to worry about any item of information they think they have covered in their own questionnaires. (Since all the questionnaires that students produce will be slightly different, there is no set key for this task; different students will take different times, according to how much information is new.)

Report

3 When students have finished listing the points new to them, they should work in groups to prepare a short spoken report of the new items that they thought most useful. Groups report to the class on the new points.

4 Further discussion:
Where would you hide anything valuable?
Have you ever had anything stolen from a parked car?
How could you improve the security of your own home?
Is there anything you should have done years ago?

Listening   SB178c   [178c] *

Monica tells Caroline about her burglaries. Her account is highly spontaneous and not very organised; students will have to listen more than once to sort out which burglary was which. Warn students there will be empty spaces in the table provided – we get far less information on the first burglary than the others.

5 Make sure students read the questions before they listen to the tape. (This will give them a purpose for reading.)

Task

6 Ask which students in the class know of someone who has been burgled. Arrange students in groups so there is at least one person with a story in each group. Get the group members to find out as much as possible by asking them questions. The informant should then leave the group.

7 The groups then write a report (without talking to the informant any more) to tell the class. Alternatively, allow them to ask the informant one more question.

8 The informants could make a group of their own, exchange stories and choose one to write up.

9 The informants should give their report last so that the other students can identify which story has been reported twice.

a Which are these likely to be – true or false?

1 *The crime rate is generally on the increase.*
2 *It cannot happen to me – my house is secure enough.*
3 *It's up to the police to improve matters; it's not my affair.*
4 *A thief needs only two or three minutes to break in, take what he wants, and leave your house again.*
5 *Most burglaries are carefully planned.*
6 *Crime prevention concerns everyone.*

Now read the text below and discuss which of the above statements are true and which are not.
Which point from above sums up the message of the text best?

> Whether we like it or not, the fact is that the crime rate is going up in almost all areas. The Police are doing their part to keep it down – but there is more that can be done to assist them – BY US ALL.
> It is negative to take the attitude that "It cannot happen to me" or "It is not my affair".
> It is important to realise that most robberies, especially in homes, are opportunist and take place in a few minutes.

which of these do not apply?

b Speed reading

Read the list below through, once, quickly, and try and remember any points which were not covered in your version of the questionnaire in section 176.

Check with your partner.

Read for a second time and take note only of the advice that you hadn't thought of previously.

> *Please take note of these points:*
>
> 1 Make certain that your home is really secure, even when you are only away for a short period. Close and lock ALL windows and doors. Get proper locks. Secure all outbuildings.
>
> 2 Tell the Police, milkman, newsvendor and neighbours when you will be on holiday and cancel milk and newspapers.
>
> 3 Keep your garage door closed and locked and secure any ladders.
>
> 4 Do ALWAYS lock your car, or other vehicle, and hide valuable items or goods in the boot. Ensure that nothing is visible.
>
> 5 Take care with your handbag and luggage.
>
> 6 Take all precautions when answering the door. DO NOT allow strangers into your home without proper authority. If you are in any doubt, inform the Police.
>
> 7 Make certain you do not part with any cash for goods delivered to your house without being absolutely certain you are getting what you pay for.
>
> 8 Report to the Police any questionable telephone calls.
>
> 9 Contact the Police when you see or hear anything suspicious. Dial 999.
>
> 10 Contact the Crime Prevention Officer at your local Police Station for any free Crime Prevention advice you think you might need.
>
> *Written with the assistance of Police Crime Prevention Officers.*

**? ** attitude / make certain / proper locks / proper authority / part with ... / valuable / visible / questionable

Word study
Find five phrases with the word take on this page.

c Monica and her husband Kas had two break-ins, one after another, and also one attempted burglary.

178c Listen and find the answers to the questions.

	1st	2nd	Attempted
What was stolen?			
Were they in the house at the time?			
What time did it happen?			
Who phoned the police?			
What damage was done?			
Did they catch the burglars?			
Did they know who did it?			

Have your family or any friends of yours ever had anything stolen? Find someone in your class who has, and ask them questions about it, so you can write a report about what happened. What should they have done to prevent such a thing happening?

179 The Hitch-hiker

a If the hitch-hiker had got the driver's belt, what other things might he have got, and how? Think of four things.

179a What things do you think Stephen and Catherine will say? Guess, and then listen.

179b **b** Had you guessed correctly? What things had he taken? Does he give a reason for doing this? Now listen to the episode being read.

179c **c** 'The question is, why's he doing this?' Listen and fill in the blanks.

to _____ the other guy.
to _____ him what he can do.
to answer his _____ about what sort of job he does.
Well, he's a _____.

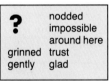

nodded
impossible
around here
grinned   trust
gently   glad

Word study

Match the colloquial words in the column on the left with their meanings in the column on the right.

catch on	good-quality thing
guy	steal
flog	man
nick	friend
pal	sell, give away
nice bit of stuff	realise, understand
get rid of	sell

PART 10

'NICE BIT OF STUFF, THIS'

1 He grinned and waved the belt gently from side to side. "Where d'you think I got it?" he said. "Off the top of your trousers, of course."

2 I reached down and felt for my belt. It was gone.

3 "You mean you took if off me while we've been driving along?" I asked, flabbergasted.

4 He nodded, watching me all the time with those little black ratty eyes.

5 "That's impossible," I said. "You'd have had to undo the buckle and slide the whole thing out through the loops all the way round. I'd have seen you doing it. And even if I hadn't seen you, I'd have felt it."

6 "Ah, but you didn't, did you?" he said, triumphant. He dropped the belt on his lap, and now all at once there was a brown shoelace dangling from his fingers. "And what about this, then?" he exclaimed, waving the shoelace.

7 "What about it?" I said.

8 "Anyone around 'ere missin' a shoelace?" he asked, grinning.

9 I glanced down at my shoes. The lace of one of them was missing. "Good grief!" I said. "How did you do that? I never saw you bending down."

10 "You never saw nothin'," he said proudly. "You never even saw me move an inch. And you know why?"

11 "Yes," I said. "Because you've got fantastic fingers."

12 "Exactly right!" he cried. "You catch on pretty quick, don't you?" He sat back and sucked away at his home-made cigarette, blowing the smoke out in a thin stream against the windshield. He knew he had impressed me greatly with those two tricks, and this made him very happy. "I don't want to be late," he said. "What time is it?"

13 "There's a clock in front of you," I told him.

14 "I don't trust car clocks," he said. "What does your watch say?"

15 I hitched up my sleeve to look at the watch on my wrist. It wasn't there. I looked at the man. He looked back at me, grinning.

16 "You've taken that, too," I said.

17 He held out his hand and there was my watch lying in his palm. "Nice bit of stuff, this," he said. "Superior quality. Eighteen-carat gold. Easy to flog, too. It's never any trouble gettin' rid of quality goods."

18 "I'd like it back, if you don't mind," I said rather huffily.

19 He placed the watch carefully on the leather tray in front of him. "I wouldn't nick anything from you, guv'nor," he said. "You're my pal. You're givin' me a lift."

20 "I'm glad to hear it," I said.

21 "All I'm doin' is answerin' your question," he went on. "You asked me what I did for a livin' and I'm showin' you."

180 *Language study*

a Phrases with 'all/whole'

Which meaning does each have? (Para. = paragraph)

1 *the whole thing* Para.5   a suddenly
2 *all the way round* Para.5   b the belt
3 *now all at once* Para.6   c I'm simply...
4 *All I'm doin' is...* Para.21   d right round

b -ing

There are 17 verbs ending in -**ing** in Part Ten. (But remember the hitch-hiker pronounces most of his **ing**- endings as -**in'**.) Can you find 12 and say exactly who or what they refer to? How many can you find with a comma (,) in front? (e.g. *He nodded, grinning.*)

The Hitch-hiker

Aims: 1 To practise reading for understanding and enjoyment.
2 To practise reading to infer the meaning of lexical items from context.

Lexis: around, bend, fantastic, gentle [T], **gently, glad, gold, impossible, mind, nod(ded), question, stuff, trust, undo**
Phrases: **all at once, do for a living, if you don't mind, it was missing, never any trouble, the whole thing**
Revision: **'d** (would)

SB179a [179a]* PB179

1 Students should discuss what else he could have taken from the driver before they listen to the story. Put students' suggestions on the board so they can compare their ideas with what actually happens in the story. Possible items: driver's wallet, glasses, contents of pockets, ring, jewellery, baggage etc. (If students don't think of it, suggest 'shoelace' as a possibility, as if you were making a joke, so they understand the word when it comes up in the story.)

2 Students listen to the tape and add Stephen and Catherine's suggestions to the ones already on the board.

   Key: Stephen and Catherine suggest: wallet, watch, tie.

SB179b [179b]

3 Students listen to and/or read the story and note the items the hitch-hiker took. When students have said what the hitch-hiker took, ask them why they think he is behaving in this way.

   Key: watch, shoelace

SB179c [179c]*

4 Ask students to read the sentence extracts before they listen to the tape (this gives them a reason for listening) and then to answer the question by filling in the blanks.

   Key: impress, show, question, pickpocket

5 Word study

   Key: catch on – realise, understand
   guy – man
   flog – sell
   nick – steal
   pal – friend
   nice bit of stuff – good-quality thing
   get rid of – sell, give away

Point out to your students that the words in italics are very colloquial, inoffensive (in most situations) slang words.

Language study

Aims: 1 To revise the meanings of phrases with **all** and **whole**.
2 To bring together the many uses of the **-ing** form, as used in narrative, and to draw particular attention to the patterns:
with the comma, e.g. He nodded, watching . . . He asked, grinning.
after see/hear etc. e.g. I'd have seen you doing it. I didn't see you bending down. (There does not always need to be an **-ing** form here. The infinitive is sometimes used if the action happens and is over quickly, or if the speakers wents to give this impression.)
3 To clarify who or what the **-ing** form is referring to.

SB180a

1 Students will need to refer back to the story and see what these phrases refer to in context.

   Key: 1 b 2 d 3 a 4 c

SB180b

Key: 17 verbs with **-ing** endings are:
1 driving – we
2 watching – the hitch-hiker
3 doing – you
4 dangling – shoelace
5 waving – shoelace
6 missing – anything
7 grinning – the hitch-hiker
8 missing – shoelace
9 bending – the hitch-hiker
10 blowing – the hitch-hiker
11 grinning – the hitch-hiker
12 lying – the watch
13 getting rid of – it
14 giving – me a lift
15 doing – see 16
16 answering – 15 and 16 refer to each other
17 showing – what he did for a living
2, 7, 10 and 11 – have commas in front

181 Phrase-building

> **Aim:** To give students practice with phrases and clauses that can follow verbs of perception like **see**, **hear**. (There does not always need to be an **-ing** form here. The infinitive is sometimes used if the action happens and is over quickly, or if the speaker wants to give this impression. See Table 2.)

SB181 PB181

1 After initial practice with these sentences, encourage students to imagine situations where they might need to use them. e.g. Did they notice how the conjurer did the trick? How the pickpocket managed to snatch a wallet? How did the burglars get away? etc.

182 How observant are you?

> **Aim:** To give further practice in describing people and happenings, and justifying a cause.

Task SB182a

1 In pairs students put the pictures in order and then report back informally, giving reasons for their ordering. Ask one or two students to tell you what they remembered about the people in the picture.

> **Key:** Left 1 right 2
> We noticed a girl with dark hair and a blue coat coming out of the Underground. In the second picture she has already bought a newspaper, so she must have come out etc.

Task SB182b

2 Students take a minute to study the pictures and practise saying things about what was happening in them. Then they should close their books and tell their partner what was happening around them. Ask one or two students to report back to the class.

Report SB182c

3 Students' written descriptions could be done for homework.

4 Optional game: Half the students are told to move things around, say things to people, sing a song etc. – all at the same time, but just for one minute or even less. The other half of the class watches and then says what they remember different students doing.

183 Grammar

> **Aims:** 1 To practise **that** clauses introduced by verbs of saying, thinking and similar verbs, e.g. see, understand.
> 2 To show that **that** is usually omitted.

*Clauses introduced by **that** are usually taught under the heading of 'reported speech'. This is an unfortunate misnomer since these clauses are actually much commoner after words like **think**, **see** and **know** than after **say** and **tell**. Another serious mistake, associated with the notion of reported speech, is to encourage students to believe that we try to reproduce as far as possible the wording of the original speech. This is what happens if we work with the traditional exercise which involves changing from direct to reported speech by manipulating personal pronouns, tenses and time and place adverbials. What we actually do is report the content of words or thoughts in a way appropriate to the purpose of the report. In some cases, in a court of law for example, it may be important to attend to actual wordings, but these cases are very rare and exceptional. We normally simply give the gist in whatever amount of detail is necessary.*

*Something else which is often taught is that the tense of the verb in a **that** clause depends on the tense of the verb introducing the clause. This is not, in fact, the case. The statement 'I'm just tidying up in here' could be reported as:*

*'He says he **was** just tidying up, but it looked to me as if he was trying to find something.'*

Likewise there are many instances of a verb in the past tense introducing a clause with the verb in the present tense. Actually there is nothing unusual about tenses in reported speech. They behave in the same way as other tense uses. You can test this quite simply by finding a passage in reported speech and removing the reporting verbs. You will find that it makes no difference at all to the tense patterns. Those verbs introduced by a past tense reporting verb are usually past tense not because they were said in the past, but because they <u>happened</u> in the past.

*Roughly speaking the verbs which are followed by **that** clauses can be classed as verbs of **saying** (**tell**, **promise** etc.) and of **thinking** (**know**, **believe**, **see**, **understand** etc.). There are however many other verbs such as **show**, **mean**, **make certain**, which do not seem to fall neatly into either category.*

This exercise, therefore, aims to illustrate these two points about these clauses:

they can follow a wide range of verbs, relatively few of which have anything to do with speech.

*the word **that** is often, even usually, omitted.*

We have deliberately avoided any exercise which involves manipulating various parts of the language, and in particular we have avoided anything which involves changing tenses. Reported speech is often difficult not because that's the way it is, but because coursebooks and grammar books make it difficult.

SB183 PB183

1 Elicit further examples from the students by asking them questions about things that people or characters have done or said earlier in the book, e.g. What did the policeman ask the hitch-hiker? What did the hitch-hiker say about his profession? How many times did Monica say her house has been broken into?

> **Key:** a discover b expect c tell d see e mean
> f tell g find h mean i imagine j realise k make certain l make sure m know.
> Sentences without **that** to introduce the clause: a, b, f, h, i, l, m.

181 *Phrase-building*

Make up a sentence, then imagine a situation where you might need to say something similar, and think of what might come next.

> 'You never saw anything – you never even saw me move an inch…'

I	didn't see	anything	at all.
We	never saw	anyone	like it/that/him/her.
They	never heard	a thing	, not a single person/thing.

I	never even	saw/see	anyone	walk by/past…
We	didn't even	heard/hear	anybody	come in…
They	certainly didn't	noticed/notice		talking to…

They		realised that		
We		remembered that		
He	suddenly	noticed that	somebody had come/opened/taken…	So…
She		saw that	somebody was/had been waiting/standing…	
You		told me that		

182 How observant are you?

a What order were these photos taken in? Say why you think so. Close your books and see how much your partner noticed about the people in the picture.

b Imagine that you were one of the people in the picture. Close the book and say what you noticed happening around you just as the photo was taken.

c Write a description of what was happening around you just as the photo was taken.

183 *Grammar*

Saying, thinking etc.

After verbs of *saying* and *thinking* we often have a report of what was said or thought. This is sometimes, but not often, introduced by the word **that**.

He'll say that the man encouraged him to do it. (161)
The policeman said (that) he was going to check on him. (152)
I think (that) I know what you do. (174)
I thought that the driver might have taken the challenge. (136)

There are many other verbs that work in the same way as **say** and **think**, e.g. **know, remembered, showed, found, realised, was sure**…

Read these sentences and find other verbs like these. How many sentences do not have **that**?

a *The Jumbo Jet pilot discovered the cockpit door had locked itself.* (104)
b *I expect you help to work the betting machines or something like that.* (114)
c *My husband … tells me that the most dangerous time on a plane is take-off.* (104)
d *She suddenly saw that one of the engines was on fire.* (104)
e *This means … that you can have the VAT amount refunded to you.* (126)
f *He finally told the writer he was in a skilled trade.* (121)
g *One morning he found that someone had parked in front of his garage door.* (150)
h *That doesn't mean he's not a hod carrier.* (152)
i *I would imagine that's one of the more menial jobs on a building site.* (152)
j *It is important to realise that most robberies … take place in a few minutes.* (178)
k *Make certain that your home is really secure.* (178)
l *I was taking the car along slowly … to make sure I wasn't stopped again.* (174)
m *He knew he had impressed me greatly with those two tricks.* (179).

95

a whether

Read on and see whether you guessed right.
He couldn't have known whether or not he was lying.
Whether we like it or not, the fact is that the crime rate is going up.

Put the word **whether** into these sentences:

She asked I would pose for a photograph with the boy.
There's always something going on in London, it's day or night.
I didn't know to sort of jump through it or to ignore it. (twice)
We never did get to find out the car could do 129 m.p.h.
I can't remember his jacket was black or dark blue.

b The passive

Notice the forms in the verb phrases.

. . . saying her flat had been burgled.
She didn't say whether anything of value had been taken.
Both times the video was stolen.
The dogs don't get burnt because they jump through the hoops so fast.
The banana was already cut into four pieces . . .
. . . taking the car along slowly, to make sure I wasn't stopped again.
Caroline didn't get paid for about four months.
Phone numbers of local police stations will be listed in the local press.

Now put these words and phrases into the right order to make sentences.

1 *We twice in the burgled last few months were*
2 *The were videos both rented*
3 *What order taken photographs were in the ?*
4 *got never thieves caught The*
5 *Listen to read the being episode*
6 *Have you burnt ever got cooking while a meal ?*

c Odd words out

1 grinned, nodded, laughed, joked, smiled
2 looked, glanced, stared, caught
3 in doubt, unsure, impossible, uncertain, doubtful, questionable
4 crowded, lonely, alone, on your own
5 burning, on fire, strong, hot
6 prevent, try, attempt
7 things, stuff, security, personal property, contents
8 valuable, gold, leather, plastic
9 fantastic, terrific, marvellous, terrible, great
10 glad, happy, pleased, shocked

d ????

The same word (but different forms of it) is missing from each sentence.

It is negative to _____ the attitude that 'It cannot happen to me.'
Please _____ note of these points.
_____ all precautions when answering the door.
Most burglaries _____ place in a few minutes.
Watching . . . and even _____ part in sport.
You must _____ a decision quickly.
I've sometimes _____ the wrong turning.
They broke the window and they came in and _____ the video.
It _____ me about twenty minutes I suppose to come in.
I was _____ the car along slowly now.

e Lexicon words

Look up the words below, and see which sentences they fit.

around	question	step	stuffed
burning	round	strong	support

1 *The first _____ is to look in the papers for job adverts.*
2 *Then go _____ all the job centres and ask.*
3 *No point in just sitting _____.*
4 *He was out of work, but still had to _____ his daughter.*
5 *She was very tall and easily _____ enough to do the job.*
6 *The _____ was, how did the fire start?*
7 *There was no-one _____ at the time.*
8 *It had been a _____ hot day, though.*
9 *She _____ the things quickly into the bag.*

Important words to remember (779 so far)					
affair	corridor	fool	locked	prevent	strong L
area	crime	gentle	marvellous	proper	stuff
around	criminal	gently	mess	property	support L
attempt	die	glad	moon	protect	tears
attitude	doubt	gold	negative	questionable	thus
authority	doubtful	greatest	nod	relevant	trust
belong	elegant	ignore	possibility	round L	undo
bend	ensure	impossible	possibly	security L	valuable
burn L	fantastic	lend	pregnant	shock	
contents	fight L	local	precaution	solve	

Aims: 1 To revise the uses of **whether**.
2 To revise passive expressions with **be** and **get**.
3 To revise the meanings and uses of **take**.
4 To recycle and revise useful words.

Lexis: **burn** [L], **great**, **greatest** [T], **property**, **strong** [L]

SB184a

Key: She asked **whether** I would pose for a photograph with the boy.
There's always something going on in London, **whether** it's day or night.
I didn't know **whether** to jump through it or **whether** to ignore it.
We never did get to find out **whether** the car could do 129 m.p.h.
I can't remember **whether** his jacket was dark blue or black.

SB184b

Key: 1 We were burgled twice in the last few months.
2 The videos were both rented.
3 What order were the photographs taken in?
4 The thieves never got caught.
5 Listen to the episode being read.
6 Have you ever got burnt while cooking a meal?

SB184c

Key: 1 nodded – the others are all to do with laughter or amusement
2 caught – the others are all to do with looking or watching
3 impossible – the others are all to do with doubt
4 crowded – the others are all to do with being alone
5 strong – the others are to do with heat or burning
6 prevent – the others are to do with making an effort to accomplish something, while prevent means to try to stop someone doing something
7 security – the others are to do with objects or possessions
8 valuable – the others are all types of material
9 terrible – the others are ways of showing extreme approval
10 shocked – the other reactions are all positive

SB184d

Key: take   take the attitude . . .   take note . . .   Take all precautions . . .   take place . . .   taking part . . .   take a decision . . .   taken the wrong . . .   took the video . . .   took me about . . .   taking the car . . .

SB184e

Key: 1 step   2 round   3 around
4 support   5 strong   6 question
7 around   8 burning   9 stuffed

LEXICAL OBJECTIVES

Level 1 words (see page 129T):
certain, **dead** L, **from** (see SB175), **possible**, **question**, **take** L, **whether** (see SB184).

affair 1 an event. *The wedding was a quiet affair.* T
2 *It's not my affair.* = It's nothing to do with me.
area 1 a particular part of a place. . . . *an area just north of London.*
2 size. *What's the area of your piece of land? About 600 square metres.* T
around in the area. See **round**. *Anyone around here missing a shoelace?*
attempt 1 to try. *They attempted to break in by battering the door down.*
2 . . . *an attempted break in.*
attitude the way you think and feel about something. *It is negative to take the attitude that 'It cannot happen to me'.*
authority 1 *The British Tourist Authority*
2 *Do not let someone into your home without proper authority.*
belong *It doesn't belong to me.* = I don't own it.
bend 1 *I never saw you bending down.*
2 *a bend in the road* T
burn L
contents the things inside something/somewhere. . . . *the purse and its contents.*
corridor a long passage. *She opened the door . . . and the corridor wasn't there . . .*
crime an illegal action, e.g. theft. *Fight crime and protect your home.*
criminal 1 person who commits a crime
2 *He had a criminal record.* [12]
die/dying 1 *He knows he's dying.*
2 informal: to really want. *I'm dying for a cup of tea.* T
doubt uncertain. *If you are in any doubt call the police.*
doubtful 1 unlikely, uncertain. . . . *a doubtful future.* T
2 *I was doubtful about accepting.* T
elegant pleasing and graceful in appearance. . . . *elegant fingers.*
ensure make certain that. *Ensure that nothing is visible (when you leave your car).*
fantastic 1 informal: very good, nice, large. *He's got fantastic fingers.*
fight L
fool 1 someone who is silly or stupid. *Any fool could do that.*
2 *to make a fool of someone* = to play a trick or joke to make them seem silly. *April Fool's day.*
gentle/gently 1 *She smiled gently.* T
2 a slow, even movement. *He waved the belt gently from side to side.*
3 a landscape with soft shapes and colours. *A common would be more gentle than a moor.* [10]
glad pleased. *I'm glad to hear it.*
gold a precious metal. . . . *a ring made of gold.*
greatest superlative of **great** T
ignore to take no notice of. *I didn't know whether to ignore it.*

impossible 1 not possible. *That's impossible!*
2 very difficult, hopeless. . . . *an impossible situation* T
lend *The Hodja's friend lent him a big pot.*
local concerned with a small area of the country. . . . *the local police station*
locked 1 to close a door with a key. *Lock your car. Lock all doors and windows.*
marvellous excellent, wonderful. *a marvellous job*
mess *in a mess* = untidy. *Read the story about the room that's in a mess.*
moon *The sun or the moon*
negative 1 giving the answer **no**. *He gave a negative answer.* T
2 *It is negative to take the attitude . . .*
nod to move your head up and down to mean: yes. '. . . *driving alone?' I asked. He nodded, watching me . . .*
possibility *We must accept the possibility that we might be wrong.* T
possibly . . . *to drive as fast as he possibly could.* [15]
2 perhaps. *Could you possibly open a window/lend me £5?* T
precaution safety measure. *Take all precautions when answering the door.*
pregnant expecting a baby
prevent to stop something from happening. *Crime Prevention – to try to stop crime.*
proper 1 real. *Get proper locks.*
2 correct. . . . *proper behaviour* T
property 1 things belonging to a particular person. *Protect your personal property.*
2 piece of land belonging to someone. T
protect keep safe. *Protect your home.*
questionable doubtful. *Report to the police any questionable phonecalls.*
relevant *What information does she give that is not relevant?*
round L
security L
shock 1 *Monica said the burglary was quite a shock.*
2 make you very upset. *Shocked by her husband's death . . .* T
3 an electric shock T
solve to find an answer. *And thus the case was solved . . .*
strong L
stuff 1 material. *Nice bit of stuff this.*
2 to pack something into a small space. *He . . . stuffs it in his pocket.* [14]
support L
tear 1 *She didn't know whether to tear the paper . . . It was torn already.*
2 *She cried for ages, the tears streaming down her face.* T
thus therefore. *And thus the case was solved.*
trust *I don't trust car clocks.*
undo unfasten, open. *You'd have had to undo the buckle . . .*
valuable worth a lot of money, time etc. *Hide valuable items . . .*
whether (see SB184.)

And he told me I was going to win

The theme of this unit is traditional beliefs and superstitions. The first section encourages students to discuss the theme within the context of their own culture and to compare this with attitudes in Britain. They go on to look at customs associated with the New Year, particularly the custom of making New Year's resolutions. Students are given written and spoken input on the basis of which they discuss the resolutions made by others and decide what they might resolve themselves. They go on to look at fortune-telling within the context of a personal anecdote. This is followed by a joke based on fortune-telling. They look at traditional children's songs and see how these have a historical basis which is far from childish. Throughout this treatment of the theme students are encouraged to narrate their own experience and to make speculations and comparisons. The final episode of The Hitch-hiker is treated in two parts in this unit.

OBJECTIVES

Lexical aims are in TB197

Grammar and discourse

a Ways of expressing the future involving prediction. (188)
b The meanings and use of **out**, including some phrasal verbs. (187)
c Pointing to the ending of an anecdote to contradict or reinforce a particular conclusion. (188)
d Expressions of probability and possibility. (192)
e The meanings and uses of **thing**. (195)
f Language patterns with **ask**, **tell**, **know** etc. (194,197)
g The future in the past. (188,197)
h The meanings and use of **after**, including some phrasal verbs. (197)

Tasks

a Anecdotal narrative used in support of an argument or point of view. (185)
b Expression of comparison and contrast between attitudes and cultures. (185)
c Explaining behaviour. (185)
d Advice and promises within the context of New Year's resolutions. (186)
e Inferring people's appearance, attitudes and behaviour. (186,193)
f Comparing experiences and arguing for a particular conclusion on the basis of the comparison. (188)
g Predicting the outcome of an anecdote. (188)
h Predicting the outcome of a narrative. (189)
i Understanding and explaining the origins of folklore. (191)

185 Do you believe it?

Aims: 1 To practise anecdotal narrative used in support of an argument or point of view.
2 To give students practice in explaining behaviour.
3 To practise expressions which compare and contrast attitudes and cultures.

Lexis: belief [T], **believe**, **fortune match**

The object of section 185 is to encourage as much talk as possible. You may need to talk about your own experiences in order to encourage the students to talk.

SB185a PB185

1 Draw attention to the different aspects of the theme – fortune-telling, lucky/unlucky numbers etc. Give the students plenty of chance for discussion in pairs or small groups. Some of the pictures may need explanation:

Many hotels do not have rooms numbered 13 because a lot of people refuse to sleep in a room with an 'unlucky' number.

Similarly people often say 'Touch wood' and touch some wooden object to bring luck. If you ask someone how they have done in an examination, for example, they might say 'Oh, quite well, I think. Touch wood.' The origin of this is not known.

Water diviners claim that they can discover underground sources of water by 'feeling' or divining the water with a branch from the hazel tree. When they come across a source of water the branch begins to twist in the diviner's hand of its own accord. This may seem supernatural, but there is overwhelming evidence that some people do have this power.

This is a very old saying which claims that red sky at night precedes good weather and red sky in the morning very bad weather. The truth of this may depend on where you happen to live. There are many other observations which are supposed to tell us about the weather. Birds flying very low mean rain; seagulls far inland in winter mean a spell of bad weather, and so on. No doubt all cultures have these observations, some of them reliable and some very doubtful.

How many people believe in flying saucers? . . . that there is intelligent life on other planets?

It is a custom in Britain to say 'Bless you' when someone sneezes. It is said that this has its origin in the old belief that when someone sneezed their soul left their body for an instant. If the devil or some evil spirit happened to be about it would snatch the soul and carry it off. For this reason people said 'Bless you' to protect the sneezer against evil. Even though hardly anybody still believes this many people still say 'Bless you'.

SB185b

Suggested answers: Crystal ball, cards, tea-leaves, coffee-grounds, palmistry (lines on hands), astrology (the stars, particularly on your birth date), phrenology (bumps on the head), opening the Bible or some other book and reading the first thing that strikes your eye. These are the commonest in Britain, but no doubt the class as a whole will come up with several others.

SB185c

Within most European cultures the number 13 is considered unlucky and the number 7 is considered lucky. The number 3 is also often considered to be a lucky number. Ask the students if they have a lucky number, colour, day etc. Some people think it is a sign of good luck if a black cat crosses your path. Others claim that it is a sign of very bad luck, because black cats were associated with witchcraft and the devil. It is a matter for discussion what students believe in, but the fact is hardly anyone is totally without superstition.

SB185d

Key: In the 1914–18 war it was very dangerous to light a number of cigarettes from one match. An enemy sharpshooter might catch sight of the match lighting the first cigarette; the second would give him time to take aim and he would fire at the third. Because of this some people still refuse to light three cigarettes from one match.

And he told me I was going to win

185 Do you believe it?

a Find the following things on this page:

some things that are supposed to be lucky
some things that are supposed to be unlucky
some things that you believe in
some things that you don't believe in

b How many ways of telling fortunes can you think of?

c What things are considered lucky or unlucky in your country?

d In Britain some people think it is unlucky to light three cigarettes from one match? Can you think why? Do you know the explanations for any other superstitions?

186 New Year's resolutions

a In most societies there are many traditions, beliefs and superstitions associated with the New Year. Often they are to do with making a new start. In many parts of Britain, for example, we welcome the first visitor of the new year as a bringer of good luck for the whole year. In some countries they clean out the house at the end of the year to sweep out the bad luck and make a fresh start. In many countries people make 'New Year's Resolutions' – they resolve to give up the bad habits of the old year and to do everything better in the future.

Here is a list of possible resolutions. See if you can choose one for yourself, one that would be good for another member of your family and one for a friend.

Give up smoking.	Answer letters promptly.
Go on a diet.	Get up early in the mornings.
Spend less money.	Try not to lose your temper.
Be tidier.	Drive more carefully.
Watch less television.	Try not to worry too much.

b Catherine wrote down three resolutions for herself and three for her husband.

> For Peter (husband)
> 1) Be tidier – hang up clothes.
> 2) Be more assertive with the children.
> 3) Try to be more sociable.
>
> Me
> 1) Be more relaxed.
> 2) Be stricter about keeping up with personal correspondence.
> 3) Find some occupation away from the home.

Stephen wrote down three for his flatmate.

> 1) Give up smoking. After all, it is making me unhealthy too.
> 2) Stop dieting. A 19 inch waist is small enough and malnutrition makes illness even more likely.
> 3) Stop worrying about the rent. We both get a monthly cheque from the university to pay for it.

And Caroline wrote three for a close friend.

> 1) Give up smoking
> 2) Have more self-confidence
> 3) Lose some weight

Look carefully at the resolutions above. Which of the four people:

> is not very friendly?
> needs to lose weight?
> is slim, but wants to lose more weight?
> is bad at answering letters?
> is not strict enough with the children?
> smokes too much?
> worries too much?

The first visitor of the New Year in Scotland

c Monica thought of three resolutions for her husband, Kas. She told Caroline about the first two she made and her reasons for them.

MJ: Mm. Well, for Kas I've got, er, I will try not to –
CF: Who's Kas?
MJ: Kas is my husband.
CF: Right.
MJ: I will try not to finish everything at the eleventh hour. He always finishes everything at the absolute last minute. Like at the moment he's finishing off an MA thesis he's been doing for four years, and we're leaving the country, erm, Friday week, and he's in Cambridge at the moment, erm, reading through the, erm, the computer script for it. He still needs to get it corrected and bound and submitted. Erm, I will always reply to letters within two weeks of receiving them. In fact he never replies to letters at all normally. I have to reply to his letters.

Who is Monica actually talking about each time she says 'I...'? Herself or her husband Kas?

What were the first two resolutions?

186c Now listen to all three resolutions. What was the third one?

186d **d** Monica then gave three resolutions for herself.

> Write down as much as you can about Monica from this recording.

e Close your books and see how much you can remember about the people who have made resolutions, or had resolutions made for them.

186 New Year's resolutions

Aims: 1 To practise giving advice and making promises within the context of New Year's resolutions.
2 To give students practice in inferring people's appearance, attitudes and behaviour from what is said about them.

Lexis: after (all), bad, close, closely [T], **correct, diet, dirty, end(ing), habit, new, normally** (in the normal way), **occupation, rent, resolution, resolve, somehow** [L], **strict, sweep, temper, washing, weight, welcome, worry**

Task SB186a

1 Introduce the topic by asking students how they spend the New Year and what customs they observe.

2 Students read the first paragraph. Check that they have understood the main idea, in particular the idea of New Year's resolutions.

3 Ask students to read through the list of resolutions. Help them with explanations where necessary. Tell them they may add to the list if they wish to, before choosing resolutions for themselves, a relative and a friend.

4 Ask students to report on their decisions and make a consolidated list on the board.

Reading SB186b

5 Students read through what Catherine and Stephen have written and try to answer the questions which follow.

Key: 1 Peter is not very friendly – Catherine wants him to be more sociable.
2 Caroline thinks her friend needs to lose weight.
3 Stephen's flatmate is slim (a 19 inch waist) but is still dieting to lose more weight. Stephen thinks she should stop dieting.
4 Catherine is bad at answering letters. She needs to keep up with personal correspondence.
5 Peter is not very strict. Catherine thinks he needs to be more assertive with the children.
6 Stephen's flatmate smokes too much. Stephen is worried because this is bad for *his* health too. Caroline's friend also smokes too much.
7 Catherine worries too much. She should try to be more relaxed. Stephen's flatmate worries unnecessarily about money. Possibly Caroline's friend worries too. Caroline says she needs more self-confidence.

Reading and listening SB186c *

6 Students read the short excerpt from the transcript to find the first two resolutions. Ask students to tell you who the 'I's' in the transcript refer to. This exercise is made more difficult by the fact that when Monica is making resolutions for Kas she pretends to *be* Kas. When she says:
    I will try not to finish everything at the eleventh hour.
and
    I'll always reply to letters within two weeks of receiving them.
the word 'I' refers to Kas. But when she says:
    I have to reply to his letters.
the word I refers to herself, Monica.

Key: Monica's first two resolutions for Kas are:
Not to leave everything to the last minute.
To reply to letters within two weeks of receiving them.

7 Play the tape and ask students to listen for the third resolution.

Key: The third resolution is:
To leave his dirty clothes tidily and to empty the pockets.

Task SB186d [186d] *

8 Students work in pairs. Make a consolidated list of their suggestions. Some of the things they might write about Monica:
She is very untidy in the kitchen.
She never cleans the kitchen.
She never washes up.
She worries too much.
She is careless with money.

SB186e

9 Ask students in pairs to write down sentences on a piece of paper from memory about the people they have been talking about. Take in the pieces of paper and make questions from them for the class to answer. For example if one pair has written:
Caroline's friend should give up smoking.
Ask the question:
Name one person who should give up smoking.

187 Preposition spot

> **Aim:** To illustrate some of the meanings and uses of **out**.

1 Students read the rubric and work in pairs to do the exercise. When they have finished, ask them if they can think of further examples for any of these uses of **out**.

Key: a 1 b 3 or 4 (calculate) c 4 d 3 e 3 f 3 g 3 h 2

188 Fortune-telling

> **Aims:** 1 Anecdotal narrative used in support of an argument or point of view.
> 2 To practise comparing experiences and arguing for a certain conclusion on the basis of the comparison.
> 3 To practise ways of referring to the future which involve prediction.
> 4 To practise pointing to the ending of an anecdote to contradict or reinforce a particular conclusion.
> 5 To give students practice in predicting the outcome of an anecdote.
> 6 To give students practice in discussing the future in the past.
>
> **Lexis: ball, breath, breathe** [T], **concern(ed)** [L], **dear, early, end, handsome, lot, palm, persuade, remember**

Listening   SB188a 188a * PB188

1 Students work in pairs to find the mistakes.

Key: The three mistakes are:
She thought 200 rupees was 'quite a lot of money', not 'very cheap'.
She met a New Zealander who had been to the same fortune teller, but she met him in Delhi, not in New Zealand.
She was told that she would win £40,000 in a lottery, not £400,000.

Task   SB188b

2 If possible, introduce the topic by telling the class about an occasion on which you had your fortune told, or about when someone you know had theirs told. It might also be fun to bring in a newspaper or magazine which has people's fortunes as told in the stars, and read out what it says for different members of the class. Ask students whether they think the predictions are likely to come true or not. If you do not have an English magazine or newspaper you could use one in the native language as a starting point.

3 Find out from students who has had their fortune told and had it come true, and who has not. If possible, group students so that each group has one of each. Groups write their reports and report back to the class. The class should vote on the best story.

Listening   SB188c 188c *

4 Ask students if they think what happened to Caroline was just coincidence/chance or not. Ask them to give reasons for their opinions. Do they agree with John?

Key: Caroline was told that she would have an accident on a motorbike. This did come true.
John says he doesn't believe in fortune-telling because he believes in free will, so it's not likely that things can be preordained or destined to happen.

Reading   SB188d

Mayor John Lindsay, who was Mayor of New York from 1966 to 1973, was very handsome.

Key: The final line is:
What do I do about my husband and the three kids?

Task   SB188e

5 Students might need a prompt list to help them:
do well at school
go to University
be very tall
be very small
be a teacher/doctor etc.
(The forms **was going to** and **would** are commonly used in talking about how people in the past viewed the future. We can, of course also use modals like **might** and **could**. See section 197b for further practice of these forms.)

6 This could be done as a homework activity, but give students some time in class to start. Monitor students' work, helping out as necessary.

Preposition spot

out

1 away from the inside, or away from home or work
We decided to go out to eat at a small pub. (93)

2 extended away from its usual place
He held out his hand, and there was my watch lying in his palm. (174)

3 used to complete or intensify the meaning of a verb
We never did get to find out whether the car could do 129 miles an hour. (193)

4 together with a verb to produce a new meaning
Have you ever run out of petrol? (103)

What categories do these examples belong to?

a *We went out in a boat one day and saw seals and things.* (29)

b *You can work it out roughly from the information he gives on the tape.*

c *He stops and it turns out he's going right past her door.* (78)

d *She called over an air hostess and pointed this out . . .* (104)

e *The first shop assistant writes out the bill . . .* (117)

f *Fill out a form for it . . .* (117)

g *Watch out for this man.* (147)

h *Out jumped two policemen.*

188 Fortune-telling

a Read this account of Caroline having her fortune told.

Caroline had her fortune told in Delhi, in India. It cost her about 200 rupees, which she thought was very cheap. She was told that she would go back to India and that she would be married soon. She was also told that she would win £400,000 in a lottery. None of this came true, and Caroline realised that the fortune teller was a rogue when she met a friend in New Zealand who had been to Delhi and had been told exactly the same things.

188a Listen to Caroline talking about having her fortune told. This is what she actually said. There are three mistakes in the paragraph above. Can you find them?

JM: Have you ever erm . . . had your fortune told?
CF: Mm. Yes. In India.
JM: Oh yes.
CF: Mm. In Delhi. A very plausible rogue. Accosted me in the street and took me off to this little carpet shop. And he was so charming, as only Indian men can be.
JM: Mm.
CF: Erm. He persuaded me to part with – I can't remember how many rupees now. I think it was about 200, which is quite a lot of money. And then proceeded to tell me all sorts of wonderful things. He told me, by this time next year – this was last year, I think it was in June actually – I would be married.
JM: Are you?
CF: And back in India. No, no, no. And I liked the idea of being back in India very much. And he told me I was going to win forty thousand pounds in a lottery, and various other things.
JM: Did anything come true?
CF: Absolutely nothing. I then went back to the hotel and found a New Zealander who'd had the – exactly the same story.

b Do you know any stories concerned with fortune-telling? Talk in a group and try to find one case where a fortune came true and one where it didn't.

▷ Write down the best story and read it to the class. ◁

188c **c** Caroline also had her fortune read in the tea leaves. What was she told? Did it come true? What did John say about palm reading?

Look at this tea cup. Can you see any significant shapes in it? What do you think they might mean?

188d **d** Madame Wawanda

Mme. Wawanda tapped her crystal ball nervously and began to speak. 'You soon will meet a tall, handsome man who looks something like Mayor John Lindsay,' she told the young woman. 'He owns 94 producing oil wells, two square blocks in downtown Minneapolis, and a yacht with a crew of 34. He will marry you and you'll be happy forever after.'
'Sensational!' breathed her ecstatic customer. 'But tell me just one more thing: . . .'

Can you put these words in order to complete the story?

about and do do husband I kids my the three what ?

e What did different people (e.g. your teachers at school, your parents, your friends) say about your future when you were younger? What did *you* think you would do?

▷ Write some sentences about what people told you about your future. ◁

189 The Hitch-hiker

PART 11

A FINGERSMITH

a Summarise the things the hitch-hiker has taken from the driver. What else might he have got? Now what do you think his trade is?

189a Make a list of the things Stephen and Catherine mention. How many of them are things that the hitch-hiker has already taken?

189b **b** How do you think the driver is feeling now? How would you be feeling in such a situation?

c The next episode is the final episode. How do you think the story will end? Think for a moment then tell each other any ideas you have. Can you think of two possible (alternative) endings?

1 "What else have you got of mine?"
2 He smiled again, and now he started to take from the pocket of his jacket one thing after another that belonged to me – my driving-licence, a key-ring with four keys on it, some pound notes, a few coins, a letter from my publishers, my diary, a stubby old pencil, a cigarette-lighter, and last of all, a beautiful old sapphire ring with pearls around it belonging to my wife. I was taking the ring up to the jeweller in London because one of the pearls was missing.
3 "Now *there's* another lovely piece of goods," he said, turning the ring over in his fingers. "That's eighteenth century, if I'm not mistaken, from the reign of King George the Third."
4 "You're right," I said, impressed. "You're absolutely right."
5 He put the ring on the leather tray with the other items.
6 "So you're a pickpocket," I said.
7 "I don't like that word," he answered. "It's a coarse and vulgar word. Pickpockets is coarse and vulgar people who only do easy little amateur jobs. They lift money from blind old ladies."
8 "What do you call yourself, then?"
9 "Me? I'm a fingersmith. I'm a professional fingersmith." He spoke the words solemnly and proudly, as though he were telling me he was the President of the Royal College of Surgeons or the Archbishop of Canterbury.
10 "I've never heard that word before," I said. "Did you invent it?"
11 "Of course I didn't invent it," he replied. "It's the name given to them who's risen to the very top of the profession. You've 'eard of a goldsmith and a silversmith, for instance. They're experts with gold and silver. I'm an expert with my fingers, so I'm a fingersmith."
12 "It must be an interesting job."
13 "It's a marvellous job," he answered. "It's lovely."
14 "And that's why you go to the races?"
15 "Race meetings is easy meat," he said. "You just stand around after the race, watchin' for the lucky ones to queue up and draw their money. And when you see someone collectin' a big bundle of notes, you simply follows after 'im and 'elps yourself. But don't get me wrong, guv'nor. I never takes nothin' from a loser. Nor from poor people neither. I only go after them as can afford it, the winners and the rich."
16 "That's very thoughtful of you," I said. "How often do you get caught?"
17 "Caught?" he cried, disgusted. "*Me* get caught! It's only pickpockets get caught. Fingersmiths never. Listen, I could take the false teeth out of your mouth if I wanted to and you wouldn't even catch me!"
18 "I don't have false teeth," I said.
19 "I know you don't," he answered. "Otherwise I'd 'ave 'ad 'em out long ago!"
20 I believed him. Those long slim fingers of his seemed able to do anything.
21 We drove on for a while without talking.

190 *Language study* ....

What should the hitch-hiker have said? Correct the coloured words.

e.g: *Pickpockets is coarse and vulgar people.* (are)

1 *It's the name given to them who's risen to the top.*
2 *You simply follows after 'im and 'elps yourself.*
3 *I never takes nothin' from a loser.*
4 *I only go after them as can afford it.*
5 *It's only pickpockets . . . get caught.*

Aim: To give students practice in predicting the outcome of a narrative.

Lexis: after, blind, cry, end, expert, false, final, impress(ed), invent, jacket, leather, president, proud, queue, rich [L], **right, ring, rise, such**

Aim: To focus students' attention on dialectical deviations from standard syntax.

SB190

Key: 1 It's the name given to **those (people)** who **have** risen to the top.
2 You simply **follow** after **him** and **help** yourself.
3 I never **take anything** from a loser.
4 I only go after **those that/people who** can afford it.
5 It's only pickpockets **that/who** get caught.

Reading and listening SB189a *

1 Students work in pairs. Put their suggestions on the board before they read or listen to the tape. Students should make a list of Stephen and Catherine's suggestions as they listen.

Key: The things mentioned by Stephen and Catherine are: shoelace, watch, belt (these are the things we know he has already taken); wallet, tie-pin, tie, vest, driving licence, key ring, the change from his pockets.
The complete list of things the hitch-hiker has taken is: shoelace, watch, belt, driving-licence, key-ring with four keys, some pound notes, coins, letter, diary, pencil, cigarette lighter, ring.

SB189b 189b

2 Students discuss this in pairs. Put their suggestions on the board, encouraging them to give reasons. This activity should produce some useful lexis. (In section 193 students will listen to Stephen and Catherine discussing this question.)
Suggested answers: threatened, worried, amazed, surprised, impressed

Task SB189c

3 Give students a few minutes to think about this before they go into groups. Encourage each group to come up with as many suggestions as possible. Groups report back on their ideas. Ask the class to vote on the most likely suggestion. (Students will be listening to Stephen and Catherine discussing the ending in section 193.)
Possible endings:
The hitch-hiker takes the policeman's notebook etc. (This, of course, is the real ending.)
The hitch-hiker steals something from the driver. (Difficult to think of anything which would provide an appropriately satisfying ending.)
The hitch-hiker, instead of picking the driver's pocket, put something into the driver's pocket, e.g.:
a note apologising for what has happened and some money to pay the fine. He has stolen the money from the policeman.
They drive on a bit further and find that the policeman has crashed.

191 | Two children's songs

Aim: To help students understand and explain the origins of folklore.

Lexis: hold, origin, protect, sail, sink

SB191

This is intended as an exercise in reading for information and interest. It is also intended to generate some discussion.

SB191a

1 Focus students' attention on the drawings. Ask them to tell you what they see. Ask them if they think the picture could be a basis for a cheerful children's song.

SB191b

2 Students listen to the song. Tell them that the big ship which sailed on the Atlantic Ocean was the Titanic.

Many children's songs and rhymes are about unhappy subjects and are sometimes rather cruel–
Three blind mice,
See how they run.
They all ran after the farmer's wife,
She cut off their tails with the carving knife,
Three blind mice.
– even though the tunes are lively and the songs are sung with great enjoyment and laughter.

3 Students work in groups. Ask them to tell each other about songs they sang. Ask them, if possible, to write the background to one of these. Monitor students' group work. Ask the groups to report back when they have finished the task. The others could listen and vote on the saddest or most interesting background.

192 | Grammar

Aim: To focus students' attention on ways of expressing probability and possibility.

SB192   PB192

1 Ask students to find the 6 sentences in which the writer expresses certainty and to tell you which words show the writer is certain. Then ask them to find the expressions of uncertainty. Students could work individually then compare their findings with a partner.

Key: Sentences in which the writer is certain of what he/she is saying:
a   certainly
d   must have
h   certainly
j   certainly
p   must be
t   must have

Ways of expressing uncertainty:
b   I suppose; may
c   Perhaps
e   might
f   Maybe
g   Maybe
i   probably
k   Perhaps
l   Perhaps
m   may have
n   could be
o   probably
q   might
r   probably
s   could have
u   Maybe

The sentences all have in common the use of:
may ⎫
must ⎪
          ⎬ **have**
might ⎪
could ⎭
to refer to past time.

191 Two children's songs

a

Ring, a ring o' roses,
A pocketful o' posies,
Hish-a, hish-a
All fall down.

This is the first song many English children learn. They play a game in which they hold hands in a circle and dance round, until the last line, when they all fall down – usually with lots of shouting and laughter.

Not many children know the origins of this song, and they might not play so happily if they did. It was first sung over three hundred years ago during the Great Plague, an epidemic which swept across Europe, killing millions of people. The first line:

Ring a ring o'roses

refers to the red circles on the skin. These first signs of the disease looked like rings of red roses. The second line:

A pocketful o' posies

refers to the fact that people carried pockets of flowers with them in the belief that these would protect them against the plague. But most people caught the disease and as it took hold they developed a sneezing cough:

Hish-a, hish-a.

And the last line, of course, describes how they all fall down – dead.

b

The big ship sailed on the Ally-Ally-O
The Ally-Ally-O, the Ally-Ally-O.
The big ship sailed on the Ally-Ally-O
On the last day of September.

The big ship sank to the bottom of the sea,
The bottom of the sea, the bottom of the sea.
The big ship sank to the bottom of the sea
On the last day of September.

This is another children's dancing song, and this too has special meaning. The Ally-O is the Atlantic Ocean. This song was first sung over seventy years ago. Can you think of a big ship that sank to the bottom of the Atlantic Ocean?

What songs did you sing as a child? Were there any which had unusual origins like the two above? Although *The Ally-Ally-O* has a cheery tune and is a children's dancing song it is about something quite tragic – a ship being sunk and all the people drowned. Did you have any cheery songs about sad events?

192 *Grammar* ....

Probability and possibility

Look at these 22 sentences. Can you find 6 where the speaker or writer feel sure of what they are saying?

How many ways can you find of expressing uncertainty?

What do sentences b, d, m, q, s and t have in common?

a A: *Who do you think is the healthiest?*
  B: *Certainly not me!*
b *I suppose she may have sneaked out while he wasn't looking.* (78)
c *Perhaps the writer got up early ...* (95)
d *He must have eaten the plums and then gone out, leaving his wife asleep in bed.* (95)
e *Think of three things the driver might ask the hitch-hiker next.* (95)
f *Maybe he is a pickpocket.* (114)
g *Maybe the pilots had noticed, ...*

h *... but certainly nobody else on board had noticed.* (104)
i *It's probably very scenic with Middleton behind it.* (133)
j *I would certainly pull over.* (136)
k *Perhaps there's a woman having a baby.* (147)
l *Perhaps your house is on fire and you're dashing home to rescue the family from upstairs.* (147)
m *He may have had experience as a hod carrier.* (152)
n *He could be a thief that's proud of his trade.* (167)
o *He'll probably get a fine and an endorsement on his licence.* (161)
p *The lie must be about being an 'od-carrier.* (161)
q *What else might he have got?* (189)
r *You're probably quite right.*
s *I wonder what could have happened.*
t *The policeman must have been doing 130.*
u *Maybe it's because I'm a Londoner, that I love London so.* (139)

[193] The Hitch-hiker

a How do you think the driver is feeling now?

[193b] **b** Before you listen, choose three of the words and phrases that you think Stephen and Catherine might use to describe how the driver is feeling:

excited	sort of frightened
nervous	impressed
pleased	very angry
a bit of a fool	

c Compare the endings you thought of in section 189c. Which two do you think are the most likely?

[193c] Did you think of the same as Stephen and Catherine?

[193d] **d** Now listen to the story.

PART 12

'IT'S ALWAYS NICE TO BE APPRECIATED'

"That policeman's going to check up on you pretty thoroughly," I said. "Doesn't that worry you a bit?"

"Nobody's checkin' up on me, he said.

"Of course they are. He's got your name and address written down most carefully in his black book."

The man gave me another of his sly, ratty little smiles. "Ah," he said. "So 'ee 'as. But I'll bet 'ee ain't got it all written down in 'is memory as well. I've never know a copper yet with a decent memory. Some of 'em can't even remember their own names."

"What's memory got to do with it?" I asked. "It's written down in his book, isn't it?"

"Yes, guv'nor, it is. But the trouble is, 'ee's lost the book. 'Ee's lost both books, the one with my name in it *and* the one with yours."

In the long delicate fingers of his right hand, the man was holding up in triumph the two books he had taken from the policeman's pockets. "Easiest job I ever done," he announced proudly.

I nearly swerved the car into a milk-truck, I was so excited.

"That copper's got nothin' on either of us now," he said.

"You're a genius!" I cried.

"'Ee's got no names, no addresses, no car number, no nothin'," he said.

"You're brilliant!"

"I think you'd better pull in off this main road as soon as possible," he said. "Then we'd better build a little bonfire and burn these books."

"You're a fantastic fellow," I exclaimed.

"Thank you, guv'nor," he said. "It's always nice to be appreciated."

193 The Hitch-hiker

> **Aim:** To give students practice in inferring people's attitudes.
>
> **Lexis: announce, brilliant, cry, end, ending, excited, fact, fellow, final, hold, nervous, pick** [L], **relief, remember, worry**
> Revision: **yet**

To keep the suspense going, do a–c before they read the story.

SB193a/b 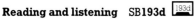 * PB193

1 Remind students of the work they did for section 189b before you let them read the end or play the tape.

   Key: Stephen and Catherine describe the driver as: nervous, a bit of a fool, (very) impressed.

SB193c [193c] *

2 Ask students to remind you of the endings they wrote for section 189, and of the ones they thought were most likely. Play the tape for them before they read the story.

   Key: Stephen and Catherine guessed that the hitch-hiker would pick the policeman's pocket. The only other thing they thought of was that perhaps the driver simply dropped off his passenger and that was the end of it.

Reading and listening   SB193d [193d]

3 When students have read and listened to the final episode ask them for their reactions to the story. Would they like to read more of Roald Dahl's work? If students are enthusiastic, mention that there was a television series of Roald Dahl's stories, called 'Tales of the Unexpected' which students might be able to obtain on video cassette.

Language study

Phrase-building

Aim: To practise language patterns with **ask** and **tell**.

Aim: To practise words in addition to **thing** which highlight the importance or the important aspect of what is being said.

SB194a PB194

1 Students work on these in pairs. Help them to make generalisations from the work by asking them which of these words follow **ask** when we are:
asking a question where the answer is yes or no;
asking a question where the answer is *not* yes or no;
making a request.
Alternatively ask students to group the examples under the headings: *questions* and *requests*.

Key: Words following **ask**: what, where, to, how much, whether.
The basic generalisation is that asking a question involves **if** or **whether** for a yes/no question, otherwise one of the **wh-** words.
Making a request involves **to**.
There are borderline cases such as 'He asked me if I would help him,' which presumably reports a request, but the basic generalisation works well enough.

SB194b

2 Students do the exercise in pairs. Again help students to make generalisations from these examples by asking which of these examples report answers to a question (2,3); which report statements (4,5); and which report an order (1).

Key: Words following **tell**: to, where, why, that, I.
where: why; how much (and other **wh-** words when what is told is an answer to one of these question words).
– that (for other statements. NB **that** can be omitted: See nos. 4 and 5.)
– to (with you, me, etc.) (for an order)
– noun or noun phrase (when describing what is being told i.e. a story, a lie: See no. 3)
Basically, therefore, **to** reports an *action* of some kind; **that** (sometimes omitted) reports a statement; and **wh-** words report questions (after **ask**) or statements (after **tell**).

SB196a

1 Ask students to produce one or two sensible sentences from the table before they go into their pairs. (The practice with **point**, **trouble**, **problem**, **question** is straightforward pattern practice. Students should not, however, produce:
'The **trouble/problem** is you can find whatever you want' since **trouble** and **problem** are only used to introduce things you don't like.) Students practise saying these sentences to their partner for a few minutes. Then ask them to close their books and say them from memory.

SB196b

2 This could be done as individual writing practice.

Wordpower

Aim: To practise some of the meanings and uses of **thing**.

SB195 PB195

1 Students work in pairs, discussing which examples go with the pictures. Ask if they have the same word in their own language for each of the uses.

Key: a 2 b 1 c 1 d 3.2 e first thing (none of these categories) f 3.2 g 2

Language study ∙∙∙

a ask

The writer asked him why he went to the races. (136)
The passenger asked the writer if it would really go as fast as the manufacturers said. (136)
We then asked him to find out as much as possible about Jenny's last holiday. (29)

Look at these sentences. What words like **to, why** and **if** come after **ask**?

1 *I suppose he could ask him what he was doing.* (97)
2 *The driver might ask him where he'd just come from.* (97)
3 *I think the first thing he will do is ask to see the driver's licence.* (136)
4 *Jenny then asked them how much it would cost to cook these things at home.* (89)
5 *She asked whether I would pose for a photograph with the boy.* (144)

b tell

You told me that it was you and the two children who went on holiday. (29)
She rings it up on the till, tells you how much it is, then takes your money. (117)

What words come after **tell**?

1 *If there was a policeman beside me, telling me to pull over, I would certainly pull over.* (136)
2 *I'm sure you told me where you stayed, but I can't for the life of me remember where.* (29)
3 *Phil Sutcliffe tells the stories – and tells us why we tell them too.* (78)
4 *She was told that she would go back to India.* (188)
5 *He told me I was going to win forty thousand pounds.* (188)

Wordpower ∙∙

thing

1 replacing another word or phrase
She likes to eat sweet things.
Think of three things the driver might ask the hitch-hiker next. (97)

2 referring to the situation in general or life in general
Hi! How are things with you?
Business is bad. Things don't look good.

3.1 introducing an idea that you want to develop
But tell me just one more thing: what do I do about my husband and the three kids? (188)
I think the first thing he might say is 'Do you know what speed you were doing?' (136)

3.2 highlighting the importance or the important aspect of what you are saying
The thing is, he has a skilled job.
The silly thing is, the car was parked at the time.

Look at these phrases using the word **thing**. Do they belong to category 1, 2 or 3?

(a) The news is bad today. Things are very worrying.
(b) We went out in a boat one day and saw seals and things. (29)
(c) Has any of these things ever happened to you? (103)
(d) The important thing is you must report the accident.
(e) Could you bring it first thing tomorrow?

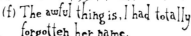

(f) The awful thing is, I had totally forgotten her name.

(g) I'm afraid I've got no time. Things are very busy at present.

Phrase-building ∙∙∙

Here are some other words which are used in the same way as **thing** category 3 (see section 195).

a Make up five sentences and try to remember them.

b Now make up some similar sentences about things in your country.

The	fact point trouble problem	is	living in London is more expensive. transport's easy in Central London. it's difficult to park your car. shopping is such fun, you spend too much. you can find whatever you want.
The	question trouble problem	is	how to get home after 11 o'clock. where to park. what to eat and where.

a   ask, tell, know

Look at these sentences with **ask**, **tell** and **know**.

1 *He told him (that) he was a hod carrier.*
2 *He asked him why he was going to London.*
3 *The policeman told him to move over.*
4 *The driver knew (that) he was speeding.*
5 *He knew where he was going.*

The words below can be used in sentences like those above, as shown in brackets. For example **inform** can be used in sentences 1 and 2, but not 3, 4 or 5, **remember** can be used in 4 and 5, but not 1, 2 or 3.

Read the sentences above once or twice, but instead of the verbs in colour, try out some of the different verbs from below. Think about what your new sentences now mean.

inform (1, 2)	think (4)	know (4)
tell (1, 2, 3)	believe (4)	learn (4, 5)
ask (2, 3, 5)	mean (4)	remember (4, 5)
advise (3)	explain (4, 5)	notice (4, 5)
invite (3)	guess (4, 5)	say (4, 5)
order (3)	find (4, 5)	see (4, 5)
want (3)	hear (4, 5)	understand (4, 5)
agree (4)	imagine (4, 5)	wonder (5)

Complete these sentences. (Try using two different verbs in each.)

a *He stopped the car and _____ the hitch-hiker to get in.*
b *The driver _____ why the hitch-hiker was going to the races.*
c *The driver _____ his passenger that he was a writer.*
d *The driver _____ (that) he was a writer.*
e *The hitch-hiker _____ the writer what job he did.*
f *They _____ that the policeman was a dangerous looking man.*

b   He told me I was going to . . .

Caroline says:

He he told me I was going to win 40,000 pounds.
He told me by this time next year I would be married.

Which of these things did Madame Wawanda *not* tell her customer?

1 *Madame Wawanda told her she was going to meet a tall handsome man.*
2 *He would marry her.*
3 *They were going to have four children.*
4 *They would live happily forever after.*

c   after

1 later, during the period of time following the time or event mentioned
She likes to eat sweet things after lunch.
After my return home I wrote him a short letter every week.
The day after tomorrow.

2 if you are after someone or something you want them or it for some reason
I think the police are after him.

3 if you go after someone you follow them
She ran after him as quickly as she could.

4 with a verb to make a new meaning
Who's looking after the baby?

Which of the following sentences belong to which categories?

a *I only go after those who can afford it.*
b *Supposing they arrived after the restaurants had shut.*
c *He started to take out of his pocket one thing after another.*
d *She's a clever girl. She takes after her mother.*
e *He will marry you and you will be happy forever after.*
f *Give up smoking, after all, it is making me unhealthy too.*

d   Lexicon words

Use your Lexicon to say what the words and phrases in colour mean. In what sense are they used here?

1 *She is a dear friend of mine.*
2 *He has been picked for the Olympic Games.*
3 *That's all right as far as I am concerned.*
4 *I like to eat cakes, but they're very rich.*
5 *This one is cheap. The other is much dearer.*
6 *In fact the song is concerned with the Plague.*
7 *That glass holds just over a litre.*
8 *We are all very concerned about unemployment.*
9 *Newspapers seldom give all the facts.*
10 *Get hold of it!*
11 *The only way to get rich is by working for yourself.*
12 *Somehow he managed to pick the policeman's pocket.*
13 *This is a bargain I picked up in the sale.*
14 *The government ought to tax the rich more heavily.*

	Important words to remember (830 so far)				
announce	cry	fortune	normal	relief	sweep
ball	dear L	habit	occupation	rent	temper
blind	diet	handsome	origin	resolution	washing
brilliant	dirty	impress	palm	resolve	weight
breath	ending	invent	persuade	rich L	welcome
breathe	expert	jacket	pick L	rise	worry
closely	false	leather	president	sail	
concern L	fellow	match	proud	somehow L	
correct	final	nervous	queue	strict	

Aims: 1 To revise the meanings and uses of words like **ask**, **tell** and **know**.
2 To give further practice in understanding expressions used to describe the future in the past.
3 To revise some of the meanings and uses of **after**.
4 To revise useful lexis.

Lexis: **after**, **rich** [L]

SB197b PB197

Key: Madame Wawanda did not tell her they were going to have four children.

SB197c

2 Students work in pairs.

Key: a 2   b 1   c 1   d 4   e 1
f set phrase – after all

SB197d

Key: 1 someone I am very fond of : 4
2 chosen : 1
3 where it affects me : 2
4 containing a lot of fats, eggs, cream etc. : 3.1
5 costing a lot : 5
6 about : 3
7 contains : 2
8 worried : 1
9 things that really happened : 1
   or
   information or knowledge : 2
10 take hold : 4
    or
    take in your hands : 1
11 having a lot of money or possessions : 1
12 I do not know how but . . . : 1
13 found : 2.3
14 people who are rich. : 1.1

LEXICAL OBJECTIVES

Level 1 words (see page 129T):
after, **bad**, **close**, **fact** L, **hold** L, **lot**, **new**, **out** (see SB187), **remember** L, **right**, **ring**, **such**.

announce 1 *It was announced on the radio that the Prime Minister will be making a speech this evening.* T
2 *'Easiest job I've ever done,' he announced proudly.*
ball 1 round object used in games
2 anything round. *Mme Wawanda tapped her crystal ball.*

blind 1 unable to see. *They lift money from blind old ladies.*
2 unable to understand. *He is completely blind when it comes to understanding someone else's point of view.* T
breath Noun: the air you take into your lungs T
breathe Verb: *He drops him off in London and breathes a sigh of relief.*
brilliant 1 an extremely clever person. *'You're brilliant!'*
2 *a brilliant career* = a very successful career
3 bright. *. . . a brilliant colour/light*
closely 1 near, tightly. *The children moved in more closely around him.*
2 strongly. *My family were closely connected with the theatre.* T
concern L
correct 1 right. *The correct answer . . .*
2 to put right. *He still needs to get it corrected and submitted.*
cry 1 to weep. *They said they would have to leave if the baby cried.* [12]
2 to call out loudly. *'Caught!' he cried, disgusted. 'Me get caught!'*
dear L
diet to eat only certain food, usually in order to lose weight. *Go on a diet*
dirty 1 not clean. *. . . the dirty clothes basket*
2 unfair, unkind. *. . . a dirty trick.*
early 1 *very early in the morning.*
2 *The meeting was at seven, but most people . . . arrived early.*
ending the last part of a book, story etc. *Can you think of two possible alternative endings?*
expert someone who is a very good at something. *I'm an expert with my fingers, so I'm a fingersmith.*
false 1 not true. *Do you think her statement is true or false?* T
2 not real. *I could take the false teeth out of your mouth if I wanted to.*
fellow 1 a man, usually used affectionately. *'You're a fantastic fellow,' I exclaimed.*
2 *. . . a fellow student.* T
final last, coming at the end. *The next episode is the final episode.*
fortune a lot of money. *He has made a fortune out of his books.* T
2 luck. *He wished them good fortune.* T
3 someone's future. *How many ways of telling fortunes can you think of?*
habit something you do regularly. *They resolve to give up the bad habits of the old year.*
handsome good looking (used normally of a man). *You soon will meet a tall, handsome man.*
impress surprised and admiring. *'You're right,' I said impressed.*
invent *The telephone was invented by Alexander Graham Bell.*

jacket *He started to take from the pocket of his jacket . . .*
leather made of cured animal skin. *He put the ring on the leather tray . . .*
match 1 *Is it unlucky to light three cigarettes from one match?*
2 a game or contest. *. . . a football match*
3 *The colours don't match very well.*
nervous *I don't think he's feeling nervous*
normal usual. Also 'normally' = usually. *In fact he never replies to letters at all normally.*
occupation a job. *Find some occupation away from the home.*
origin the beginning of something, or the way it began. *Not many children know the origin of this song.*
palm 1 a tree which grows in hot countries. T
2 the inside surface of your hand.
persuade to use argument or authority to get someone to do something. *He persuaded the driver to open the car up.*
pick L
president *President of the Royal College of Surgeons*
proudly pleased with oneself and one's achievements. *He spoke the words solemnly and proudly . . .*
queue to wait in a line for something. *. . . watchin' for the lucky ones to queue up and draw their money.*
relief 1 *He drops him off in London and breathes a sigh of relief.*
2 *Tax Relief* T
rent *stop worrying about the rent.*
resolution Noun: *In many countries people make 'New Year's Resolutions'.*
resolve Verb: to make a decision. *They resolve to give up the bad habits of the old year.*
rich L
rise *It's the name given to someone who's risen to the top of the profession.*
sail *The big ship sailed on the Alley-Alley-O.*
somehow L
strict 1 severe. *Do you know someone who is not strict enough with the children?*
2 a law that must be obeyed. *There ought to be stricter laws on guns.* T
sweep *In some countries they clean out the house at the end of the year to sweep out the bad luck.*
temper angry way of behaving. *She has a very bad temper.*
washing *I have to do all his washing you see.*
weight 1 *It was . . . 30 tons in weight.* T
2 **put on** or **lose weight** = change your body weight
welcome greet. *We welcome the first visitor of the New Year . . .*
worry *Stop worrying about the rent.*

The unit begins with practice in talking and writing about people giving both biographical information and physical description. This is followed by descriptions of places. There is some dramatisation work on The Hitch-hiker story, followed by a song. Summary practice is combined with listening comprehension focusing on personal anecdotes. A final Wordpower exercise on 'mind' gives students a chance for some role-play. There is practice in giving and understanding instructions for tricks. Next comes stating opinions and giving supporting information. A discussion of personal security provides a context for giving and understanding advice. To round up, there is some advice offered by a class of students in a language school in Britain, and students are ask to design a questionnaire to evaluate their course.

OBJECTIVES

Lexical aims are in TB210

Grammar and discourse

a Relative pronouns, prepositional phrases and other devices for producing complex sentences describing people and places. (198,199)
b Verbs of motion used to describe passage of time. (201)
c Imperative with instructions. (204)
d **ask to** and **ask if**. (204)
e Expressions of opinion followed by **that** clause. (205)
f Pointing to a personal anecdote to show its relevance in support of a point of view. (205)
g **If** with **would**. (206)
h Expressions of advice. (206,209)
i Asking for and giving evaluation: **What do you think ...? I think ...** (210)
j Expressions of possibility, probability and certainty. (207)
k Meanings and uses of **mind** as noun and verb. (203)

Tasks

a Giving biographical information. (198)
b Describing people. (198)
c Describing places. (199)
d Producing a dramatised version of a story. (200)
e Summarising a story. (202)
f Listening for specific information. (202)
g Giving instructions. (204,208)
h Stating a point of view and giving supporting evidence. (205)
i Understanding warnings and advice. (206,209)
j Asking for and giving information of an evaluative nature. (210)

---

198 | Talking and writing about people

Aims: 1 To practise giving biographical information.
2 To practise describing people.
3 To practise relative pronouns, prepositional phrases and other devices for producing complex sentences describing people and places.

Task   SB198a PB198

1 Students work in pairs. At the report back stage take their contributions and use them to illustrate.
1 Robert Peel was born in 1788 in Bury, Lancashire, which is a ...
2 He was a famous politician who is still well known because of the police force and so on. The most useful devices for combining sentences of this kind are: to use prepositional phrases, as in 1, or noun phrases with adjectives, as in 2, to link closely related information; and to use relatives like **which** and **who**, as in 1 and 2.

Task   SB198b

2 Go over the notes with students, answering any questions. Give them time to prepare their paragraphs in pairs before they write.

Task   SB198c

3 Ask students to work in pairs to produce the longest sentences they can. This should be done light-heartedly. It can be treated as a game rather than as a strict language practice exercise.
Alternatively, play a game in which someone begins with a short description:
The man on the left has fair hair.
The next player carries this description in mind and adds to it:
The man on the left has fair hair and he's wearing a brown jacket.
and so on. Students can play as individuals, as pairs or as groups. Again this should be a light-hearted activity simply to focus students' attention on important cohesive devices in English. The most likely ones in this context are probably those listed above in 198a. Prepositional phrases such as:
... the man with fair hair ...
... the man in the leather jacket ...
will be very useful.

---

199 | Talking about places

Aims: 1 To practise describing places.
2 To practise using relative pronouns, prepositional phrases and other devices for producing complex sentences describing people and places.

Report   SB199 PB199

Key: Students work in pairs. Make sure they know that they should write their descriptions of Keswick as accurately as they can.

You may wish to refer students back to Units 3 and 10 before they write the descriptions of Keswick. Basically all they need to do is review the work done in those units.

2 Individually students write their descriptions of a place they know for a purpose – to enable a classmate to recognise the place.

3 Ask students either to read out their description or give it orally without reference to their notes, and see if other students can recognise the place.

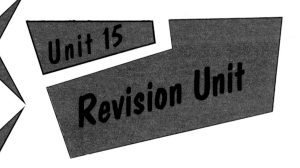

[198] Talking and writing about people

a   Can you make these into one sentence?

Sir Robert Peel was born in 1788.
He was born in Bury.
Bury is in Lancashire.
Bury is a small industrial town in the north of England.

And these?

He was a politician.
He was famous
He is still well known.
The police force he created still exists today.

b   Here are some notes about the author of *The Hitch-hiker*.

Roald Dahl, writer (short stories, e.g. *Kiss Kiss*; children's books, e.g. *Charlie and the Chocolate Factory*). B. 1916, Llandaff, South Wales, M. Patricia Neal, actress (3d., Is.). Lives Buckinghamshire, SE England.

> Write a short paragraph about Roald Dahl.

c   Study this picture carefully. How many things can you say about the people? Begin with a simple sentence and then add to it. For example:

The man on the left is wearing a brown jacket.
The man on the left in the brown jacket has fair hair.
The man on the left in a brown jacket with fair hair is reading a newspaper.

[199] Talking about places

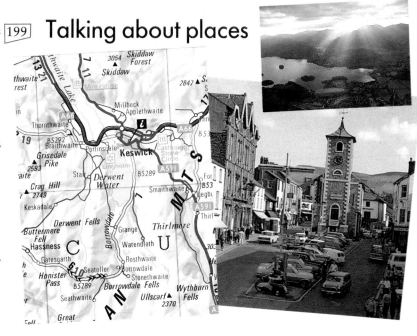

KESWICK 5,635 Cumbria (STD0596) Map 39NY22 EcWedMdSat
Carlisle 31, Kendal 30, London 304, Penrith 18, Windermere 22
***Derwentwater Portinscale (IH) Tel 72538 43rm (33 bath) 60P B&B(c)
***Keswick Station Road (THF) Tel 72020 C64 bath 50P B&B(e)

Here are some pictures and a map of Keswick, together with the entry from the *AA Member's Handbook*. Use this information to write a short description of the place.

> Write a short description of a place you know. Leave out the name and see if anyone else in the class can recognise the place.

200 The Hitch-hiker

A dramatisation

Here is a brief dramatisation of the first three parts of the story. (See sections 97, 114 and 121.)

200

Driver (*to audience*): I was driving up to London one day in my new BMW when I saw a man by the side of the road thumbing a lift. I always stop for hitch-hikers, because I used to do a lot of it myself, so I came to a stop and offered him a lift . . .

[Sound of a powerful car engine dying down as the car comes to a halt]

Hitch-hiker: Going to London, guv'nor?

Driver: Yes, jump in.

HH: Thanks.

○ [The car sets off again]

D: What part of London are you heading for?

HH: I'm goin' right through London. I'm goin' to Epsom for the races – the Derby.

D: Great. I love racing.

HH: I don't. It's a waste of time.

D: Why do you go then?

HH Ah well . . . I just do.

D: I see, it's part of your job is it? Do you mind me asking what you do? I'm very curious, I'm afraid. Perhaps it's because I'm a writer.

○

HH: You must be a good writer if you're drivin' round in a car like this. Writing's a skilled trade like mine. How fast will this car go anyway?

D: One hundred and twenty-nine miles an hour.

HH: I bet it won't. All car makers are liars. They always say they'll go faster than they really will. Go on. Open 'er up. I bet she won't do a hundred and twenty-nine.

Choose one other episode and write a dramatised version. Decide what sound effects you might need, and include them in the script in square brackets [ ].

201 Song

In English, people often talk about life in the same way as a journey.

. . . as you go through life . . .
. . . when you reach the age of twenty . . .
. . . you meet a lot of troubles on the way.
. . . he is approaching middle age . . .
etc.

Do you talk about life as a journey in your language?

This is an old music hall song that was first sung by a famous Scottish comedian, Harry Lauder, during the First World War. Harry Lauder was so popular that before he died he was knighted and became *Sir* Harry Lauder.

Keep right on to the end of the road

Every road through life is a long, long road,
Filled with joys and sorrows too,
As you journey on how your heart will yearn
For the things most dear to you,
With wealth and love 'tis so
But onward we must go

Keep right on to the end of the road,
Keep right on to the end.
Though the way be long let your heart be strong,
Keep right on round the bend.
Though you're tired and weary, still journey on
Till you come to your happy abode,
Where all you love and you're dreaming of
Will be there at the end of the road.

201

200 The Hitch-hiker

Aim: To give students practice in summarising a story and producing a dramatised version.

Lexis: **curious**

Task SB200 PB200

1 Students will need a good deal of help with this exercise. Point out the importance of a narrator and of sound effects.

2 Students should work in groups. When they have finished, they should act out or record their dramatisations.

201 Song

Aim: Verbs of motion used to describe passage of time.

Lexis: **dear**, **round**, **wealth**

Reading and listening SB201 PB201

1 Go through the examples illustrating how verbs of motion are used to describe a 'journey through life'. Point out that they are used to talk in general about the passage of time or of an event:
When we **get to** the end of the lesson . . .
We only have **a short way to go** to the end of the course . . .
and so on.

2 Introduce a discussion of how far students' own language or languages use this same device. It is certainly a powerful feature of English but probably happens in many other languages to a greater or lesser extent.

3 You may, if you wish, point out to students that they are coming to the end of their course. Have they found it difficult at times? Did they sometimes despair of **getting to the end**? Did they sometimes have to do their homework or come to class even though they felt tired? If so they will readily understand the words:
Keep right on to the end of the road,
Keep right on to the end.
Though the way be long let your heart be strong,
Keep right on round the bend.
Though you're tired and weary, still journey on . . .

4 Students read the instruction to the song. Go over any problems they have understanding it. Have the class sing the song.

202 Telling stories and summarising

Aims: 1 To give students practice in listening for specific information.
2 To give students practice in summarising a story.

Lexis: being, occasion

Listening SB202a * PB202

1 Students have already heard one version of Monica's story, but they will still probably need to hear this recording more than once. You might play it once, ask them to read the summary and see if they can find the mistakes, and then ask them to listen again to see if they are right.

Task SB202b

1 Students work in groups. Make sure that the class as a whole covers some three or four tapescripts. You need not do them one after another in this spot. You could, for example, get all the summaries written now and have the class as a whole listen to one of them and spot the mistakes. They could then work on the other three transcripts and summaries at stages spaced out through the unit.

Key: 1 In the first robbery the thieves got in through an open window, not by breaking a window.
2 In the second robbery the thieves tried to get in by battering a door down but failed. They then broke the window to get in.

203 Wordpower

Aim: To illustrate and practise some of the meanings and uses of **mind**.

SB203

1 Students do a–i individually, and then check their answers in pairs.

Key: a 1 b 3 c 4 d 2 e 6 f 8 g 9 h 5 i 7

2 Students could choose three of the illustrated situations and act them out. Then ask them to prepare and act out short parallel role-plays.

202a **a**   In section 178 we heard Monica talking to Caroline about her two burglaries. This is a slightly different account of the same story. Listen carefully.

b   Look at this summary. There are two mistakes in it. Can you spot them?

Monica told Caroline that her house had been burgled twice, once when she was living in Cambridge and once in Bristol. The first time the thieves got in by breaking a window while Monica and her husband were out. The second time the thieves got in by battering the door down. On each occasion a video was stolen. Monica found the second occasion more frightening because they were at home when it took place.

> Choose one of the transcripts you have studied. Write a summary of it which includes two mistakes. Give your summary to another group and see if they can spot the two mistakes.

203 *Wordpower* ··

mind

Your **mind** (noun) is:
1 where your thoughts are. People often use the word **mind** as if it is a box that thoughts come into or go out of. When something is 'in your mind', you are thinking about it. If you say 'Her name has gone right out of my mind' you mean that you have forgotten her name.

2 your ability to think, your intellectual ability

You have a good mind.

Anne's got a scientific mind.

He's now 82 and very absent-minded. (= he forgets a lot)

Find the phrases with **mind** in these examples. Then find phrases in the boxes below each set which express similar meanings to the phrases in colour.

a He went over it in his mind.
b The little talk took our minds off the awful things that were happening.
c That place just sticks in my mind.
d It was a weight off my mind.

> 1 thought about it carefully
> 2 I stopped worrying about it.
> 3 helped us forget
> 4 I can't forget

e Make your mind up! Which do you want?
f He's always changing his mind at the last minute.
g He must have read my mind.
h She's in two minds about it.
i It's a stupid plan. She must be out of her mind!

> 5 to be uncertain, unsure what to do
> 6 to make a decision, to decide one way or another
> 7 to be crazy
> 8 to change a decision, or make different plans
> 9 He knew what I was thinking.

What about **mind** as a verb?

204 # How to do things

a Divide into A students and B students. A's look at the *X-ray vision* trick opposite. B's look at the *Magic birthday* trick on page 110. When you have practised these tricks you can try them out on each other.

Preparation

Take a telephone directory and memorise the tenth name on page 89. Have the directory with you when you do the trick.

X-ray vision *A students*

1 Tell your audience that you have X-ray vision.
2 Ask someone to think of a three figure number, for example 329.
3 Ask them to reverse the number and to subtract the smaller from the larger:
$$923 - 329 = 594$$
4 Ask if the resulting combination has three digits. If not ask them to put 0 in front of it. If, for example, they have thought of 322, then $322 - 223 = 99$, so they must put 099.
5 Ask them to reverse this number and add the two together:
$$594 + 495 = 1089$$
or $$099 + 990 = 1089$$
6 Pick up the telephone directory and stare at it saying 'I am trying to read the 10th name on page 89. Yes, yes ... I think I have it. Yes, it's ...

b   Another magic banana

Do you remember the magic banana trick in section 171? Well here's another banana trick. The banana in section 171 cut itself into a number of pieces. The banana in this trick will peel itself. Try to work out from the pictures how to do the trick.

▶ When you have worked it out write numbered instructions for the trick. ◀

▶ How do you think it works? Write a short explanation. ◀

205 # Stating your case

Say whether you agree or disagree with the following statements. If possible relate something from your own experience, or that of someone you know, which supports your opinion. For example:

You should always lock up carefully when you go out.
Monica left a window open and that's how someone got into her house and stole a video recorder.

a *You should always lock the house up carefully when you go out.*
b *Fines for parking in the wrong place ought to be much higher.*
c *Television programmes give a very bad impression of the police.*
d *Parents should be much stricter with their children.*
e *Men work harder than women.*
f *Tourist brochures often give the wrong impression of a place.*

Aims: 1 To practise giving instructions.
2 To practise the use of the imperative with instructions.
3 To illustrate the differences in meaning of **ask to** and **ask if.**

Lexis: **instructions**, **minus** [T], **multiply**, **practice**, **practise**, **preparation**

Aims: 1 To practise stating a point of view and giving supporting evidence.
2 To practise expressions of opinion followed by a **that** clause.
3 To practise pointing to a personal anecdote to show its relevance in support of a point of view.

Lexis: **brochure**
Revision: **impression**, **support**

Task SB204a PB204

1 You will have to divide your time between the A and the B group to see that they both understand how to do the trick, and to encourage them to rehearse it.
If you have any capable mathematicians in your class they may be able to explain how the X-ray vision trick works. The Magic Birthday trick works because if you multiply any number by 9 (or multiply by 3 and then again by 3) the sum of the digits will be 9 or a multiple of 9 (18, 27, 36 etc). If the number you start with is 31 or less then the sum of the final digits will be either 9 or 18. If it is 18 then it will be reduced to 9 at stage 5.

Report

2 Give one student from each group a chance to do their trick.

Task and report SB204b

3 Go over the lexis needed for this task by asking students to tell you what the items in the pictures are. The word 'tweezers', for example, might prove difficult for them. In pairs students write their instructions for the trick. Go round the class providing assistance and encouraging them to use appropriate imperative forms, e.g. **hold** the rolled up bit of paper in the tweezers and light it with the match. **Then** . . .

Key: A possible set of instructions for the Magic banana trick:

1 Take a small piece of paper crumpled into a ball, a pair of tweezers, a box of matches, a milk bottle and a banana.
2 Peel back the skin of the banana about ¾".
3 Holding the paper in the tweezers, light it and when it is burning well drop it quickly into the milk bottle.
4 Place the part of the banana you have peeled firmly in the top of the bottle.
5 As the paper burns, a vacuum is created and the banana is drawn down into the bottle, thus 'peeling' the banana.

SB205 PB205

1 Give students time to discuss these issues in groups and to reach their own conclusions on them.

2 Lead into a class discussion of the issues, giving individual students a chance to make their contributions.

*Aim 3 of those listed above is a very difficult skill to master. Even native speakers are not always clear in showing the relationship between two clauses or sentences. In the example given in the Students' Book the words **that's how** are used to emphasise the relationship between the open window and the thieves' entry. In the spoken form this would probably be reinforced by intonation. You cannot list ways of realising this relationship. All you can usefully do here is listen to what the students have to say and rephrase it where necessary.*
E.g. Too many people are parking illegally. Parking fines should be higher.
could be rephrased as:
Parking fines should be higher because that might reduce the number of people parking illegally.
If students are exposed to this kind of exercise often enough, they will gradually extend their repertoire.

Aims: 1 To practise understanding and giving advice.
2 To practise the use of **if** with **would** for giving advice.
3 To practise expressions of advice.

Lexis: alone, attack, dreadful, exchange, ignore, lonely, method, plus, relatively, risk, risky, sympathy, warning
Revision: **contract, crush, cure, emergency, ignore**

Aim: To practise words and phrases for describing various degrees of certainty.

SB207 PB207

1 Students work in pairs. Go over with them the words and phrases which express certainty before they do the gap-filling exercise. Ask students if they can suggest any other ways of expressing certainty or uncertainty and put these on the board. Also point out to students that the modals **might, must, may** and **could** with **have** refer to the past.

Key: Certainty: certainly, must (have), definitely
Uncertainty: the rest

2 Questions a–p could all take more than one answer. Ask students in groups to go through these, using their linguistic knowledge and their knowledge of earlier sections in the book to decide what words could go in the blanks. If students are not sure, encourage them to think of 2 or 3 possibilities. (It is more important that students are able to suggest good linguistic and contextual possibilities, than that they are able to come up with the original answers.)

3 As a final check, each pair of students could be given a few of the examples to look up in the earlier units.

Key: (The original sentences contained these words but others are also possible, e.g. 'maybe' in a.)
a Perhaps
b might
c Maybe
d Maybe
e probably
f certainly
g Perhaps
h Perhaps
i may have
j could [not in notes for this section]
k could
l probably
m must be
n might
o must have
p Maybe

Task SB206a

1 Direct students' attention to the picture and go over any useful lexis. Use the pictures to lead a class discussion of theft and security. Students work in pairs to discuss the questions and make notes.

Key: 1 crowded places: undergrounds, escalators, shops; lonely places, particularly at night
2 The second, third and fifth people on the escalator. They should hold their money/bags in their hand or next to their body. They should use closed bags and hide their purses/wallets from view.

2 When students in pairs have discussed their notes and stories with another pair, ask each group to report back on one of the questions 1–3. The others should listen to see if they agree, and if they have anything to add.

3 Lead a class discussion for the last two questions. You might wish to start by telling students about any experiences you have had.

Listening SB206b [206b] *

4 Students should listen to the tape and discuss the questions in groups, and then report back informally.

Key: Caroline came off worst because she was carrying such a lot of money when she was robbed.
Monica should have kept her bag closed and kept it closely by her. Caroline shouldn't have been carrying so much money and she should have kept her bag on her instead of leaving it lying in a supermarket trolley.

Reading SB206c [206c]

5 This is essentially a scanning exercise. Encourage students to read the extract through quickly the first time, to answer the questions. Students can be given more time on a second reading.

Key: Both Caroline and Monica forgot that crowded places are high risk areas. As a result they forgot to keep a close watch on their bags.

Warnings and anecdotes

Personal security

a Prepare to discuss these questions.

1 What kind of areas are the most risky? Make a list.
2 Which people in this picture are most at risk? What ought they to do in order to lessen the risk of having a bag or money stolen?

3 Do you know anything about the methods that pickpockets use? Tell each other.
4 Have you ever been pickpocketed or had any money etc. stolen?

▷ Find another pair and compare notes and stories. ◁

What would you do if you saw a pickpocket or a shoplifter at work?

206b b Monica and Caroline exchange stories. Which of them came off worst? Who do you feel most sympathy with?
What should they have done to avoid this kind of misfortune?

206c c This is what one English magazine wrote for a teenage audience, the majority of whom may never have been to London. Read it quickly and say which advice Monica and Caroline ignored.

PREVENTION IS BETTER THAN CURE

Here are some general warnings

■ Never carry your purse in your back pocket or in an open handbag. High risk areas are at bus stops, in the crush in the underground and in crowded markets or shops, so be sure you know exactly where your purse is in any of these situations, and don't carry vast amounts of cash with you. Take enough to cover the day's needs plus an extra £5 to cover emergencies.

■ London, as capitals go, is relatively safe, but don't walk alone at night in lonely places like parks and commons.

LOSS OR THEFT

Report all losses or thefts to the police; this will validate your insurance claim should you later make one. Phone numbers of local police stations will be listed in the local press, or ring directory enquiries on 142 and ask for the nearest one to you. Don't ring 999 unless you were attacked at the time of the theft.

Watch out!
There's a thief ab ut
If you see anything suspicious, dial 999

Lock it or lose it

Help fight crime... dial 999
If you see anything suspicious – call the police immediately.

Grammar •

Possibility, probability and certainty

Which three of these words and phrases express *certainty*, and which express *uncertainty*?

I suppose	maybe
certainly	definitely
perhaps	probably
might (have)	may (have)
must (have)	could (have)

Which words fit where?

a _____ the writer got up early, leaving his wife sleeping in bed. (95)
b Think of three things the driver _____ ask the hitch-hiker next. (97)
c _____ he is a pickpocket. (114)
d _____ the pilots had noticed, but certainly nobody else on board had noticed. (104)

e It's _____ very scenic with Middleton Moor behind it. (133)
f I would _____ pull over. (136)
g _____ there's a woman in the back having a baby. (147)
h _____ your house is on fire and you're dashing home to rescue the family from upstairs. (147)
i He _____ had experience as a hod carrier. (152)
j Discuss what trade he _____ be in. (161)
k He _____ be a thief that's proud of his trade. (167)
l He'll _____ get a fine and an endorsement on his licence. (161)
m The lie _____ be about being an 'od carrier. (161)
n I'll try not to worry about things that _____ never happen. (186)
o The policeman _____ have been doing 130. (147)
p _____ it's because I'm a Londoner, that I love London so. (139)

208 How to do things

a Magic birthday

B students

1 Ask someone to think of the day of the month on which they were born. If they were born on the 17th September, for example, they will think of the number 17.
2 Ask them to multiply this number by 3.
   $17 \times 3 = 51$
3 Ask them to multiply this number by 3.
   $51 \times 3 = 153$
4 Ask them to add up the digits of this number.
   $1 + 5 + 3 = 9$
5 Ask them if the answer is an odd number or an even number. If it is an even number ask them to divide it by 2. The answer at this stage is *always* 9.
6 Ask them to add this number to the date of their birthday and tell you the answer.
   $9 + 17 = 26$
7 All you have to do now is take away 9 from the number you are given to find the person's birth date.
   $26 - 9 = 17$

How do you think the trick works?

210 *Evaluation*

Have you enjoyed your English course? What have you learned that is particularly useful?

> Write down ten questions which could be used in a questionnaire to give a student's evaluation of the course and also to find out what parts they enjoyed most, what they found boring, and so on.

209 Giving advice

How best to learn English

We asked some students from a language school in the south of England to give some advice to other students of English from abroad. Read what they wrote.
Which four pieces of advice do you think are the best?
Write a few sentences giving advice to other students from your country who are about to start an English course.

You should try to speak to British people as much as you can.
It's a good idea to have an English friend who you can spend a lot of time with.
Emiko Suzuki

Spend a holiday at a language school in England.
Have you tried getting an English pen-friend?
Listen to English or American radio.
Joachim Burbiel, Germany

If I were you, I'd read some English books.
Listen to English tapes.
Have you tried looking at a newspaper?
Live with an English family.
Go to an English language school.
Judith Lenz, Germany

If I were you, I'd go to England.
Find an English girlfriend.
Practice speaking English all the time.
Tong (Thailand)

Listen to English radio programmes.
Make friends with English people.
Chidun Asakawa, Japan

Read something written in English every day.
It is best to go to England.
Nasako Eder (Japan)

You shouldn't speak your own language in class.
Have an English boyfriend!
Harumi

Listen as much as possible to English on the radio or T.V. and practise listening and speaking it with native speakers or people like you who are also learning. Use it at every opportunity.
Munling Shields

Important words to remember (850)				
attack	dreadful	minus	practice	risk
being	exchange	multiply	practise	sympathy
brochure	lonely	occasion	preparation	warning
curious	method	plus	relatively	wealth

Giving advice

> **Aim:** To give students further practice in using and
> understanding expressions of advice.

Task SB209

1 Students work in groups. They could be referred to Unit 1,
section 12, if they need help thinking of advice to give.

210
Evaluation

> **Aims:** 1 Asking for and giving information of an
> evaluative nature.
> 2 Asking for and giving evaluation: **What do you think
> ...? I think ...**

Task SB210 PB210

1 Students will probably need help with this activity. Draw
their attention to the various components of the course
and ask them what sort of evaluation questions they could
write about these. If you wish, do one or two example
questions with the class on the board.

2 When groups have completed their questionnaires, ask
them to exchange them with another group and to
complete the one they receive.

3 The results could be summarised and sent to:
COLLINS ELT
8 Grafton Street
London W1X 3LA
together with any suggestions for improvement.

Sample key:
1 Which topics did you find:
the most interesting?
the least interesting?
2 Which of the stories in the book did you enjoy the most?
3 Which exercises did you find:
the most interesting?
the least interesting?
the most useful?
the least useful?
4 Which of the language exercises were the most useful?
5 List two units you enjoyed and say why.
6 List two units you found boring and say why.
7 Were there any texts or exercises which were too
easy?
8 Were there any texts or exercises that were too
difficult?
9 Say whether you like or dislike these features of the
course:
authentic speech.
discussion page at the beginning of the unit.
wordpower exercises.
Lexicon.

LEXICAL OBJECTIVES

Level 1 words (see page 129T):
alone, **mind**

attack 1 *Don't ring 999 unless you were
attacked at the time of the theft.*
2 an attack: as 1.
2.1 *an attack of illness*
being a creature. *I knew it wasn't a
supernatural being. a human being*
brochure 1 pamphlet. *Tourist
brochures often give the wrong
impression of a place.*
curious 1 anxious to find out something.
*I'm very curious, I'm afraid. Perhaps it's
because I'm a writer.*
2 strange, unusual. *What a curious idea!*
T
dreadful 1 very bad. *I didn't get paid for
about four months. It was dreadful.*
exchange 1 to give one thing for
another. *Monica and Caroline
exchanged stories.*
2 the giving of one thing for another. ...
an exchange of stories, ... in exchange.
3 **foreign exchange** = foreign money
lonely 1 alone and unhappy. *She was
very lonely as a child.* T
1.1 a place where there is nobody
around is lonely. *Don't walk at night in
lonely places.*
method a way of doing something. *Do
you know anything about the methods
that pickpockets use?*
mind See SB203
minus 1 less. *Five minus two is two.*
2 **a minus** = a minus sign
3 'minus four', 'minus seven' etc. = less
than zero. *Temperatures there are
colder than minus 120 degrees
Centigrade.*
4 *An A minus is a better grade than a B
plus.* T
5 without. ... *minus a leg* T
multiply *Multiply this number by 3.*
occasion happening. *On each occasion
a video was stolen.*
plus in addition. *Take enough to cover
the day's needs plus an extra £5 for
emergencies.*
1.1 *Two plus two equals four.* T
practice *You will be able to do these
tricks after a bit of practice.*
practise to do something in order to get
better at it. *When you have practised
these tricks you can try them out on
each other.*
preparation getting ready. *Preparation:
Take a telephone directory ...*
relatively 1 more than average.
London, as capitals go, is relatively safe.
risk 1 **to take a risk** = to do something
dangerous
2 **to be at risk** = to be in danger. *Which
people in this picture are most at risk?*
sympathy 1 to feel sympathy with/for
someone means to understand their
feelings, to feel sorry for them. *Who do
you feel most sympathy with?* [15]
warning a warning is advice not to do
something, or information that
something bad is about to happen. *Here
are some general warnings.*
wealth riches. *With wealth and love 'tis
so.*

Lexicon Index

This 15-page *Lexicon* appendix contains information on selected words from the Level 2 syllabus. All the words featured here are marked 'L' in the *Wordlist* on pages 126–128.

These Lexicon entries are not necessarily comprehensive. They focus on the important meanings of a word. Most of the categories given in an entry include one or more examples, which illustrate the particular meaning that has been described. Many of the examples are drawn directly from the Student's Book material, and a cross-reference to the section where each occurs is given in brackets after the example.

Numbers after headings give the Student's Book Unit(s) where a Lexicon word is referred to or practised. Additional exercise material relating to the Lexicon is included in the *Practice Book* for Level 2.

about 1

1 If you talk or write **about** a particular thing, you talk or write on that subject. EG *Catherine wrote about John.* (2)
2 Characteristic of. EG *What I like about him is his sense of humour.* (4)
3 Approximately. EG *Parking for about 200 cars.* (7)
4 That's all, it's finished. EG *... that's about it.*
5 Referring to the future. EG *We're about to start the lesson.*
6 With some verbs: **bring about** means make happen; **go about** means start, do. EG *Excuse me – I'm not sure how to go about this!*
7 Around. EG *They sat about doing nothing.*

above 10

1 In a position that is higher and directly over something. EG *The sky above us.*
2 Earlier in a text or on a page. EG *Which of the pictures above do you think might be part of the story?*
3 Higher in rank. EG *He's a senior manager, above me.*
4 More than. EG *It cost above a hundred pounds.*

account 8

1 An **account** is a written or spoken report which gives you all the details of something that has happened. EG *The police did not accept his account of the accident.*
1.1 When you say that something is the case **by all accounts**, you mean that everyone says that it is so.
2 **Accounts** are a detailed record of the money that a person or organisation receives and spends. EG *He had to submit accounts of his expenditure.* 2.1 If you have an **account** with a bank or a similar institution you leave money with them and ask for it when you need it. EG *How much is there in my account please?* 2.2 If you have an **account** with a shop you can buy goods there and pay for them at a later date. EG *Could you put it on my account please?*
3 If you say '**On no account** go home alone', you mean 'whatever you do do not go home alone'.

4 If you say 'He was not sent to jail **on account of** his youth', you mean 'because of his youth he was not sent to jail'.
5 **account for**. If you say you can **account for** something you mean you can explain it.

against 10

1 In opposition to. EG *In their first match against Manchester United ... Make a claim for damage against the other driver's insurance company.* (112) *I'd advise him against doing that.*
2 Referring to objects that may be touching each other or pressing each other. EG *... the water molecules in the food vibrating against each other.* (91) *I had the accelerator jammed right down against the floor and I held it there.* (136)
3 Used when expressing contrast or comparison, often with reference to a visual background. EG *You could see the trees against the sky ... If you go shopping, do you not particularly choose, say, a blue shirt against a pink shirt?* (128)

ahead 10

1 In front. EG *Up ahead I see the lights of the town.*
2 Leading. EG *Two people were ahead of us, and travelling fast.*
3 Winning, in the lead. EG *Liverpool were ahead by two goals.*
4 If someone goes on **ahead**, they go first and you follow. EG *The rest of the family went on ahead.*
5 In the future. EG *I see a lot of trouble ahead.*

allow, allowed 11

1 Permitted to do something. EG *You're not legally allowed to park.* (150)
2 To make something possible. EG *Railways allow quick travel from place to place.*
3 With time, space, distance etc. EG *I'm allowed a half hour break ...* (47) *Allow one centimetre between each line.*

111

among 7

1 When someone or something is **among** a group of people or things, they are in the middle of them. EG *We were occupying a small table in among many other tables.*

2 When something is **among** a group or collection of things, it is one of them, it is part of the group or collection. EG *I found a photograph of Peter among her things.*

3 If you say something is one example **among** others, you are saying that there are many other examples you could have mentioned. EG *Your father was, among other things, a very private person.*

4 If something is divided **among** two or more people, it is divided between them, usually so that they all have an equal share. EG *Half a chicken among four won't go very far.*

5 If you talk, argue etc **among** yourselves, you are talking together as a group. EG *They talked quietly among themselves at the far end of the room.*

apart 1

1 Separated, not together. EG *Their chairs were two metres apart ... He stood with his legs apart.*

2 Separated in time. EG *Our birthdays are just one month apart.*

3 **apart from** means except for. EG *Well, apart from English and American, which is similar, I can get by in French .... (12)*

appear 7

1 When you can see something for the first time, you say it has **appeared**. EG *Two men suddenly appeared at the top of the hill ... Then, as if from nowhere, a lighter appeared in his hand. (167)*

2 In a newspaper or magazine. EG *Here is a recipe for scrambled eggs which appeared in the teenager's section of a Sunday newspaper. (87)*

3 To be seen in public on stage or in a film or in court. EG *He has appeared in more than twenty films ... You will have to appear in court.*

4 To seem. EG *The baby appears to be hungry ... I am forced to appear as if writing you this note to apologise. (112)*

appearance 7

1 The **appearance** of someone or something in a place is their arrival, often sudden. EG *The sudden appearance of two men at the top of the hill ...*

2 An **appearance** on television, or in a play.

3 The way you look. EG *... a good appearance ... The two girls are very alike in appearance.*

4 To **put in an appearance** means to be somewhere for a short time. EG *I must put in an appearance at work.*

attention 5

1 If you give a subject or activity your **attention**, you look at it, listen to it, or think about it carefully. EG *He was finding it a strain to hold his students' attention ... Please pay attention!*

2 **Attention** to something is the act of dealing with it or caring for it. EG *The children are crying – they need my attention.*

back 2

1 In the opposite direction. EG *... he stepped back.*

2 To **go back** means to return to a place where you've been before. EG *Do you remember Ireland at all? Oh, I go back there every year ... (9)*

3 Used with words that describe positions. EG *Stand back from the edge ... The house is set back from the road ... She pushed her hair back from her face ... He sat back and smiled. (167)*

4 Used to say that something or someone is once again in the state or situation in which they were before. EG *He went back to sleep ... ... back to work ... You'll get the money back ... She put it back on the shelf ...*

5 Earlier in time. EG *... way back when I was a paperboy. (46)*

6 In reply (writing, telephoning, etc). EG *I shall call you back ...*

7 The part of your body which goes from your neck to your bottom. EG *We lay on our backs under the tree.*

8 Not the front. EG *... the back of her hand ... ... at the back of the book ... ... the back of the building ... The back door ... ... in the back of the police car.*

background 2

1 Personal details and experience. EG *The background of the person you talked to.*

2 The **background** to an important event or situation is the conditions behind it. EG *The economic background to the present political crisis ...*

3 The scenery behind an activity or object. EG *With the sea for a background, you can play golf ... (35) There were some lovely trees in the background.*

basic 4

1 Main or general. EG *... the basic problem is ... For my basic 40 hour week, I get £1.20 an hour. (47)*

2 Simple or essential. EG *... basic English ... ... basic food ... It's very basic ...*

basically 9

To show the most important feature or point. EG *... to tell the Willises about the holiday and basically to suggest that they pick them up. (33)*

behaviour 12

The way people or animals generally act. EG *... the behaviour of certain types of animal ... ... bad behaviour ...*

behind 10

1 At the back of, on the other side of. EG *The sun went behind a cloud.*

2 The events **behind** something are the cause of it. EG *Nobody knew what was behind his strange behaviour.*

3 The person **behind** something is the person responsible for it. EG *We know that there was a lot of trouble, but we don't know who was behind it.*

belief 12

The feeling that something is true. EG *... belief in God.*

believe 12

1 If you **believe** something is the case, you have that idea or opinion. EG *people used to believe the earth was flat.*

2 If you **believe** someone, you accept that they are telling the truth. EG *You mustn't believe what 'ee said to you about goin' to prison. (161)*

3 To think (if you are not completely sure). EG *Paris by train – I believe that's quite quick. (6)*

4 To show surprise. EG *I don't believe it! (78)*

5 **believe in.** EG *Fortune telling? Don't you believe in it? (14)*

below 10

1 In a lower position. EG *From the hills you can see the town below.*
2 Underneath. EG *The author's name was written below the title.*
3 In a text or on a page. EG *Look at the list of jobs below.* (43)
4 Less than. EG *The temperature was below zero.*

beyond 10

1 On the other side of, further than. EG *He pointed to the house and the street beyond it. . . . going beyond my destination.* (110)
2 Except for. EG *I'm very tired. Beyond that I have nothing to say.*
3 Later than. EG *Few children stay at school beyond 16.*
4 If you say something is **beyond** you, you mean you do not understand it or you cannot do it. EG *I'm afraid the mathematics is beyond me.*

bit 2

1 A small amount, piece or part (often of something larger); used mainly in informal spoken English. EG *I know a tiny bit of Italian . . . Would you like a bit of cake?*
2 To a small degree or extent; used mainly in informal spoken English. EG *. . . he looks a bit like Clive Sinclair. . . . looking a bit angry . . .*
3 For a short length of time. EG *. . . we stopped to walk for a bit.* (29)
4 To quite a large extent or degree. EG *. . . quite a bit of money . . . I have to reply to his letters. Well, that's a bit rough!*
5 Used with a negative, to mean 'not at all'. EG *You haven't changed a bit! . . . Are you hungry? Not a bit.*
6 A particular part, section or area. EG *The crowded bits of Spain.*
7 In computing, a **bit** is the smallest amount of information that is held in the computer's memory.
8 The past tense of the verb 'bite'. EG *. . . the dog bit her.*

board 3

1 A flat, thin, rectangular object made of wood, cardboard, plastic or similar material. **Boards** are made in a wide variety of sizes and can be used for many purposes. EG *Bread board . . . . . . the blackboard . . .*
1.1 **The board** is also used when referring to something which has 'board' as part of its name, for example 'diving board', 'notice board', 'blackboard'. EG *Look at the board, please.* 1.2 A **board game** is a game such as chess or ludo, which people play by moving small objects around on a board.
2 The **board** of a company or organisation is the group of people who control it and direct it. EG *The London Tourist Board . . . The Milk Marketing Board.*
3 If you **board** a train, ship or aircraft, you get on to it in order to travel somewhere. EG *. . . as you board the bus . . . I've already boarded this flight five times.* (34)
3.1 When you are **on board**, you are on or in a train, ship, or aircraft. 3.2 If you **take on board** an idea, knowledge, etc, you understand or accept it; an informal expression.
4 If you **board with** someone, you stay in their home for a period of time, usually in return for payment. EG *He boarded with an Italian family.* 4.1 **Board and lodging** is food and a place to sleep. (Full board – with all meals. Half board – with some meals.) 4.2 A **boarding school** is a school where some or all of the pupils live at the school during term time.
5 If you **board up** a door or window, you fasten boards over it so that it is covered.

bound 11

1 Sure to. EG *He's bound to come late.*
2 Obligation. EG *He's bound by law to pay the money.*
3 Concerned, worried. EG *The driver is so bound up with the fact that he's being booked for speeding.* (152)
4 To travel in the direction of. EG *He was bound for New York.*

break 12

1 When something **breaks** or when you **break** it, it splits into pieces. EG *They broke the window . . .* (184) *I've never broken any bones so far . . .* (18) *Break the eggs into the bowl.* (87)
2 If you **break** a law, you do something that is wrong. EG *Along with all the other criminals who break the law.* (161)
3 A **break** is a short period of time when you stop what you are doing in order to have a rest. EG *Wake me up for coffee break . . .* (55) *Mums get a good break from the kitchen . . . I'm taking a break.*
4 **break down.** EG *Has your car ever broken down on a motorway?*
5 **break in.** If someone **breaks in** or **breaks into** a building, they get into it by force. EG *My home has been broken into.*
6 **break into.** 'He broke into a run' means 'he started running'.
7 **break off** means to stop or put an end to. EG *I've broken off my engagement*
8 **break up.** 8.1 If you **break up** with your girlfriend, boyfriend etc, your relationship with that person ends. EG *Tim and I broke up . . . Their marriage is breaking up.* 8.2 To put an end to something, to stop it. EG *The police broke up the fight.* 8.3 To finish school for the holidays.

bring 1

1 To come with something. EG *Bring your books with you . . . Be sure and bring a passport size colour photograph of yourself.* (82)
2 **bring up.** When you **bring up** a child, you look after it until it is grown up. EG *She brought up two children alone.*
3 **bring down** can mean reduce. EG *. . . brings the cost down.* (162)

burn 13

1 To be on fire. EG *The dogs jumped through burning hoops.* (171)
2 To set on fire, destroy. EG *We burnt all the papers.*
3 To injure (yourself). EG *I burnt myself while lighting the gas.*
4 To spoil food by cooking it too much. EG *It's a pity she burnt the cake.*

business 8

1 Work relating to the production, buying, or selling of goods or services. EG *He had made a lot of money in business.*
2 A **business** is a company or organisation that sells goods or services. EG *. . . someone whose office or business is in Central London.*
3 Work that you do as part of your job, often contrasted with pleasure. EG *Are you in London on business or pleasure?*
4 The **business** you are in is the field in which you work in order to make money. EG *My brother is in the travel business.*
5 Something that concerns you personally and that other people have no right to ask or advise you about. EG *It's none of my business what you do.* (121)
6 You describe a task, activity or event as **a business** when you find it difficult, annoying or boring. EG *It's a dreadful business.*

113

case 9

1 Used in phrases, meaning 'in X's situation', 'as far as X is concerned'. EG *Bed and Breakfast: In most cases it will be run by the owner* ... (39) *We asked a group of people to talk about their journeys to work. In Myf's case, this was difficult, because she didn't go out to work.* 1.1 As part of a phrase with the verb 'be' to show that something is true. EG *Is that still the case today?*
2 **In any case** can mean 'Anyway ...' and is often used to mark a closing point in a conversation, or a new stage in a story or meeting. EG *In any case, I should go now really. It's late* ... *Well, I don't know a thing about cars, in any case. Ask Rob – he might.*
3 **In case** is used to refer to the possibility of something happening. EG *Take your umbrella just in case it rains* ... *I've got some extra money in case we see something we want to buy.*
4 The **case** for or against a particular plan or idea. EG *Most people argue the case against using nuclear power.*
5 A **case** is also a person with a particular illness or problem, who is being treated by a doctor or social worker. EG *Who's dealing with her case? Dr Adams.*

choice 3

1 The one you want. EG *Which one did you choose, what was your choice?*
2 The things from among which you choose. EG *Inns, guesthouses and farmhouses provide a wide choice of accommodation.* (35)

choose 3

To decide which one you want. EG *Did Catherine choose the same route as you?* (131)

claim 8

1 If you **claim** something is true you are saying that it is true even if other people say that it is not true. EG *I have a friend who's a waitress who claims that she gets about $20 an hour.* (42) *I thought he was wrong but he claimed it was true.*
2 If you **claim** something, you are saying that it is yours and should be given to you. EG *Tell the shop you want to claim refund of VAT before making your purchase.* (126)
3 A **claim** is a statement that something is true. EG *I could not accept his claim.*
4 A **claim** is the right to have something. EG *I want to make a claim for a refund.*

class 6

1 Social grouping. EG ... *a middle-class society* ... *He has an upper class background.*
2 A group of students who are taught together. EG ... *students in your class.*
3 An indication of quality. EG *He travelled first class* ... *It's a top class restaurant* ... *As a tennis player, he's in a class of his own.*
4 To **class** someone means to categorise them. EG *At the age of 19, you're still classed as a teenager.*

clear, clearly 4

1 Easy to understand, free from confusion, and with all the details well explained and in a sensible order. EG *Excuse me, but I'm not clear about* ... *erm* ... *He explained it all very clearly.*
2 Obvious and evident. EG *It wasn't clear whether the meeting had begun or not* ... *Women are clearly underpaid in some jobs they do.*
3 Easy to see or hear. EG *Write your address in clear handwriting* ... *He speaks very clearly.*
4 Easy to see through. EG *The sea was so clear that you could see everything on the bottom.*
5 To **clear** a surface or a place means to remove things from it. EG *He cleared some newspapers off a chair.*

community 1

1 All the people who live in a particular area or place. EG *What is best for the community?* ... *It's quite a close community.* (27)
2 A particular group of people who are all alike in some way. EG ... *the business community.*

complete, completely 4

1 Totally. EG ... *we've got it completely wrong* ... (49)
2 Finished. EG ... *began in 1974, completed last year* ... *Can you complete the story?*
3 To fill in a form. EG *Take your completed form to the point marked 'Service'* (117) ... *Just complete the attached form* ... (82)
4 Having everything. EG ... *a house complete with swimming pool.*

concern 14

1 Worry. EG *Growing public concern over the economy. Lack of teachers is a matter of serious concern.*
2 To be affected by something, or involved in it. EG *Crime prevention concerns everyone.* (178)
3 To be about. EG *Do you know any stories concerned with fortune-telling?* (188)

condition 2

1 The particular state that someone or something is in. EG *You can't go home in that condition* ... *Second hand car for sale – in a very good condition.*
2 The **conditions** in which you live or work are all the factors such as heating, hygiene, safety, etc. which affect the quality of your life or job. EG ... *living conditions* ... ... *bad housing conditions* ...
3 The **condition** of a group of people is their situation in life. EG ... *the condition of black people in the United States.*
4 A **condition** is something which must happen, be true, or be done first before it is possible for something else to happen. EG *What is the condition that you have to satisfy?*
5 Someone's state of health. EG *He was in good physical condition.*

consider 2

1 If you **consider** a person or thing to be something, you have the opinion that this is what they are. EG *They consider themselves to be very lucky* ...
2 If you **consider** something, you think about it carefully. EG *He had no time to consider the matter.*

contact 7

1 If you **contact** someone, you telephone or write to them in order to ask or tell them something. EG *If you have any problems contact us and we'll try to help.* (91)
2 To be **in contact with** someone means to communicate or spend time with them. EG *I'm in contact with a number of students in other classes.*

control 8

1 **Control** of a country or organisation is the power to make the important decisions about the way it is run. EG *The Communist Party has control of the country.*
2 **Control** of something is **2.1** the ability to make it do what you want it to do. EG *You should have control of your car at all times.* **2.2** the ability to prevent yourself behaving in an excited or emotional way. EG *Don't get angry, keep control of yourself.*
3 If you are **in control** of something you are able to make it do what you want. EG *Man was not yet in control of his environment.*
4 If something is **under control** it is being dealt with successfully. EG *Everything is under control.*
5 To **control** a country or organisation (refer also to 1 above). EG *His family had controlled The Times for more than a century.*
6 To **control** something (refer also to 2.1 above).
7 **Controls** are **7.1** the methods that a government or other organisation uses to prevent prices, wages, etc from increasing. EG *If we remove controls, prices will rise rapidly.* **7.2** the parts of a machine that enable you to make it do what you want. EG *The ship was sinking but the captain stayed at the controls.*

cover 9

1 If you **cover** something you place or spread something over it. EG *Cadbury's take them and they cover them with chocolate ...* (120) *... chocolate covered nuts.*
2 To travel, go. EG *We covered two hundred miles.*
3 To **cover** a topic means to explain it or talk a lot about it. EG *We covered a lot of words last lesson.*
4 To have enough money, food etc for your needs. EG *Enough to cover the day's needs plus an extra £5 to cover emergencies.* (206).
5 To **cover up** can mean to hide, or not to tell. EG *He covered up his plan to escape.*
6 You can be **covered by** insurance.

dead 6

1 No longer living. EG *The person who'd had the bag had been dead for a year.* (78)
2 Not lively; used in informal English. EG *The place is dead.*
3 Not working. EG *The batteries are dead.*
4 Exactly, completely. EG *It landed dead in the centre.*
5 Very; used in informal English. EG *He's dead nice.*
6 A **dead-end** is a road that stops, so you have to turn round and go back.

deal 1

1 A lot. EG *A great deal of rain fell in the night.*
2 An agreement in business. EG *That was the best business deal I ever did.*
3 To **deal in** means to sell. EG *He deals in cars.*
4 To **deal with** something means **4.1** to take action about it. EG *They can deal with any kind of emergency.* **4.2** to be the subject of something. EG *The film deals with a meeting between two men.*

dear 14

1 Used as a form of address. EG *How are you, dear?*
2 Used at the beginning of a letter. EG *Dear Sir,*
3 Used as an exclamation. EG *Oh dear! ... Dear me!*
4 Very fond of. EG *Her mother is very dear to her.*
5 Costing a lot. EG *I can't afford it. It's very dear.*

degree 1

1 Amount, how much. EG *We can do it by degrees ... She speaks with a high degree of accuracy.*
2 A unit in measuring. EG *The temperature was still 23 degrees centigrade ... ... an angle of 45 degrees.*
3 A course of study taken at a university or the qualification you get when you pass the course. EG *He had taken a degree in music at Cambridge.*

depend 6

1 If you **depend** on someone or something, **1.1** you need them. EG *Children usually depend on their parents until well into their teens.* **1.2** you trust them. EG *You can depend on me.*
2 If you say that something **depends** on something else, you mean that it might only happen under certain circumstances. EG *It really depends on the time you've got available ...* (69) *It really depends how long you've got though, doesn't it?*

direct 9

1 Moving in a straight line. Of an aeroplane, without stopping. EG *Flying direct from Sydney.* (33)
2 Not involving any intermediate stage or action. EG *... London stores are able to send goods direct to an overseas address ...* (126)
3 Plain, frank, honest. EG *She's very direct.*
4 To show someone where to go. EG *Can you direct me to the Post Office?*
5 To lead or organise a group of people or a project. EG *The film Dreamchild was directed by Gavin Millar.*

discover 3

1 To find out about something for the first time. EG *Discover the North Pennines.* (35) *He discovered the door had locked itself.* (104)
2 If you **discover** someone or something, you find them, often by accident. EG *A false wall was discovered in the ...*
3 To find a place, substance or fact which nobody knew about before. EG *Columbus discovered the largest island in the Caribbean ... Penicillin was discovered by Alexander Fleming.*

draw 4

1 To make a picture. EG *... draw maps for a new book ... I can't draw.*
2 If a vehicle **draws away, draws out, draws off**, etc it moves away, out or off etc smoothly and steadily. EG *Before she could reach the bus stop, the bus had drawn off ...*
3 If you **draw away, draw near** etc you move away, near etc. EG *As the people drew near ...*
4 If an event or a period of time is **drawing near**, it is approaching. EG *Their wedding day was drawing nearer all the time.*
5 To pull something smoothly. EG *Can you draw your chair in a bit further, please?*
6 To pull across. EG *He drew the curtains.*
7 To take out money from a particular source. EG *... draw money from or out of a bank ... He drew fifty pounds ...*
8 To **draw** a conclusion means to arrive at that conclusion.
9 To attract. EG *The film was drawing huge crowds.*

drop, dropped 6

1 If you **drop** something, you let it fall. EG *I dropped a glass and broke it ... He dropped the belt on his lap.* (179)
2 To leave out. EG *He played so badly that he was dropped from the team.*
3 You **drop** someone when they get out of your car. EG *Every day he says to me when I've dropped him: 'Don't know when I'll finish. I'll get back on my own.'* (75)
4 To **drop** something can mean to stop doing it. EG *I'm not very good at English. I think I'll drop it.*

due 12

1 If something is **due** at a particular time, it is expected to happen or be ready at that time. EG *We were due in London at 2 a.m. ... When is our homework due in?*
2 Used of something that is owed to someone. EG *That money was due to me and I have not had it ... Thanks are due to all the students who took part.*
3 Because of. EG *His death was due to natural causes, not poison.*
4 **Due** north, south etc means exactly in the direction of north, south etc.
5 **Due** attention, consideration etc is the proper amount of it under the circumstances. EG *He gave my comments due consideration.*

easily 2

1 You use **easily** 1.1 to emphasise that something is very likely to happen. EG *She might easily decide to cancel the whole thing.* 1.2 to emphasise that there can be no doubt that something is the case. EG *This car is easily the most popular model.* 1.3 to say that something happens more quickly than is usual or normal. EG *I make friends very easily.* (27)

enable 12

1 To make it possible for someone to do something or for something to happen. EG *Safety systems would have enabled the pilot to land safely.*

energy 2

1 Ability and strength. EG *You must eat to give you energy.*
2 Determination and enthusiasm. EG *Michael praised Tony's diligence, energy and ambition.*
3 **Energy** is also the power from electricity, coal, wind, etc that makes machines work. EG *Wood is an efficient source of energy.*

eventually 10

1 After some time or some distance. EG *The B6279 eventually runs into the B6278.* (132)
2 At the end of a situation or process, after many delays. EG *We eventually finished work just before midnight.*

expect 3

1 If you **expect** something to happen, you think that it will happen, because of what you know about the situation. EG *You have to expect rain.*
2 If you **expect** a person, you are waiting for them to arrive, because you have invited them or arranged to see them. EG *She would expect him at eight.*

3 If you **expect** someone to do something, you require them to do it as a duty or obligation, for example as part of their work. EG *He is expected to put his work before his family.*
4 If you **expect** to do something, you plan to do it or hope to achieve it. EG *I don't expect to be in England very long ...*
5 If you say that a woman is **expecting** a baby, she is pregnant.

experience 8

1 Knowledge and skill in a particular job, gained by doing that job for a certain time. EG *My experience as a teacher is valuable.*
2 All the events, knowledge and happenings that make up someone's life. EG *In my experience it doesn't happen very often.*
3 Something that happens to you or something that you do, especially something important that affects you. EG *A friend of mine had a similar experience on a Greenline bus.* (110)

express 7

1 If you **express** an idea or feeling, 1.1 you put it into words. EG *We hope that students will express their ideas to us.* 1.2 you show it by the look on your face or by your behaviour. EG *Her eyes expressed her excitement.*

fact 14

1 Something that really happened. EG *How much of the book is fact and how much is fiction?*
2 A **fact** is a piece of information or knowledge. EG *The report is full of facts and figures.*
3 **The fact that** ... is a way of referring to a particular situation or state of affairs. EG *... the fact that there was going to be this neat twist.* (193)
4 **In fact** ...; **in actual fact** ...; **as a matter of fact** ... mean really or truly. EG *This is in fact what happened.*

fall 2

1 If someone or something **falls**, they suddenly move downwards, especially by accident. EG *Be careful, don't fall in the water ...*
2 If a building **falls**, it collapses onto the ground. EG *... fallen buildings after the bombing.*
3 To go down. EG *The US $ fell sharply ... Falling numbers of students in school. ... The temperature fell at night.*

fear 7

1 **Fear** or **a fear** is the feeling you have when you think that something unpleasant is going to happen or something is going to go wrong. EG *Early fears about safety have now been largely dispelled.* (91)
2 If you **fear** someone or something you are frightened because you think they may be harmful in some way. EG *He is very brave. He fears nothing.*
3 If you **fear** something unpleasant you are worried that it has happened or is going to happen. EG *When I heard about the accident I feared that you might be badly injured.*
4 If you take a course of action **for fear of** something, you take that course of action because you do not wish that thing to happen. EG *They did not mention it for fear of offending him.*
5 If you say there is **no fear** of something happening you mean that it is not going to happen so there is no need to worry. EG *There's no fear of rain today.*

feel 11

1 If you **feel** a particular emotion or physical state, you experience it. EG *You'd feel exhausted when you got there . . . I still feel at home when I go back there.* (9)
2 To believe, to be of the opinion that. EG *I've taken you onto Broads because I feel it's far more scenic.* (131)
3 If you **feel like** something, you want it or you want to do it. EG *I feel like something to eat . . . We felt like going home . . . I'll feel like putting on clothes of a different colour.* (128)

feeling 11

1 An emotion that you experience. EG *Just a sort of sinking feeling . . .* (152) *Some people cannot put their feelings into words.*
2 Physical sensations. EG *A feeling of hunger . . . I've got a funny feeling in my arm.*
3 An attitude, opinion, thought or idea. EG *I have a nasty feeling that something's going wrong . . . I have mixed feelings about it.*

fight 13

1 To try to stop something happening. EG *Fight crime – protect your home!* (176)
2 To make something happen. EG *Fight for your rights!*
3 To take part in a war. EG *They fought in the First World War.*

figure 6

1 A person. EG *I saw a tall figure running towards me.*
2 An amount or price. EG *Could you give me some sort of a figure for your expenses?* (80)
3 An important person. EG *He's a controversial figure.*
4 A picture or diagram. EG *. . . see Fig.1.* (68)

find 3

1 To discover someone or something that you have been looking for. EG *. . . to find a partner . . . . . . be sure of finding comfortable accommodation . . .*
2 To work out an answer to a problem. EG *Did you find it easy to get here today?* (140)
3 To have an opinion about someone or something. EG *Oh! I find it very difficult to tell anybody anything about . . .* (20)

follow 5

1 To go along behind someone or something. EG *He followed her.*
2 To happen after something else. EG *Then followed a much longer pause before the waitress returned.*
3 To be true as a result of something else. EG *If x = 2, it follows that 3x = 6.*
4 To come next in a piece of writing. EG *If you are in London with no place to stay, ring one of the following: . . .* (162)
5 To watch something that is moving. EG *Eric and the others could follow the man's finger as it moved across the map.*
6 If you **follow** advice, instructions etc, you do as you are advised. EG *Follow the directions on the London Underground.*
7 To understand. EG *The story was very difficult to follow . . . Do you follow me?*
8 To take an interest in. EG *Do you follow any particular sport?*

foreign 1

1 Belonging to, coming from or made in a country which is not your own. EG *. . . foreign imports . . .*
2 Not naturally part of and coming from outside an organism or substance. EG *He found some foreign object in the bottle of milk.*
3 Not characteristic of something or not usually experienced as belonging to something. EG *Such beliefs seem foreign to our way of thinking.*

form 6

1 A **form** of something is a type or kind of it. EG *Bus and coach travel are probably the cheapest forms of transport . . .* (69) *Bed and breakfast is a form of holiday accommodation.* (39)
2 A paper where you write facts or answers to questions. EG *An application form . . .* (2) *She had to fill in this form.* (80)
3 To develop an opinion or habit. EG *He formed the habit of taking long walks.*

general 4

1 **General** is used to summarise a situation or an idea. EG *The general standard of education there is very high . . . I think in general they don't get equal pay.* (47)
2 **General** is used to describe a statement that does not give details. EG *In very general terms . . . They went in the general direction of the school.*

ground 8

1 The **ground** is 1.1 the surface of the earth. EG *. . . on the ground. . . . . . . 1.2 the soil and rock on and beneath the earth's surface. EG *The ground all round was very wet.*
2 A reason for something. EG *You have no real grounds for complaint.*

grow 5

1 To increase in size. EG *How tall our girl is growing!*
2 If you **grow** a plant, you put a seed or a young plant in the ground and look after it.
3 To change gradually. EG *The sun grew so hot that they were forced to stop working.*
4 **grow up.** To gradually change from being a child to being an adult. EG *It was not a very pleasant place to grow up in.*

hang 4

1 To attach something in a high place or position so that it does not touch the ground. EG *He should hang up his clothes.* (186)
2 Something that **hangs** somewhere is heavy or loose so that it swings slightly or can move freely. EG *There's something definitely hanging down.* (49)
3 To kill someone by tying a rope around their neck and making them fall. EG *He tried to hang himself.*
4 To **get the hang of** something means to understand or realise how a particular thing is done.
5 To **hang about** or **hang around** means to stay in the same place doing nothing.
6 To **hang on** means to wait.
7 To **hang up** the phone means to end a telephone call, by putting back the receiver. EG *'Thank you. Goodbye.' He hung up.*

heavy 4

1 Weighing a lot or weighing more than is usual; difficult to move. EG *... carrying heavy weights about ...* (47)
2 Great in amount, degree, or intensity. EG *... heavy rain ... The traffic is heavy now ... A man with heavy shoulders ... Heavy meals ...*
3 Very large and powerful, used for example of machines. EG *Heavy industry ...*
4 Involving a lot of work. EG *I've had rather a heavy week.*
5 Using a lot of something. EG *Our old car was very heavy on petrol.*

hold 14

1 To have something in your hand or arm. EG *He held it carefully in his hand.*
2 To contain. EG *This box will only hold about twenty bottles.*
3 To keep in the same place. EG *He held it there with his foot.*
4 To **take hold** means **4.1** to take something firmly in one's hand. EG *Here, take hold of this.* **4.2** to become established. EG *When the disease takes hold ...* (191)

hope 2

1 To want or wish. EG *I hope to see more of the world in the next ten years ... Can you come? I hope so.*
2 A wish or desire. EG *She expressed a hope to see more of the world.*

huge 8

Very large or surprisingly large in size or degree. EG *He looked like a huge human rat.*

idea 3

1 Something in the mind, a thought. EG *Tell each other the ideas you have.* (189)
2 A plan or suggestion. EG *Here are some ideas on how to enjoy yourself for absolutely nothing.*
3 A belief. EG *Some people have funny ideas about how to bring up children.*
4 Knowledge of something. EG *I can't remember where you stayed. Got absolutely no idea.* (29)

imagine 7

1 If you **imagine** something, your mind forms a picture or idea of it. EG *Imagine you were writing to a computer dating agency.* (20)
2 You say 'I imagine ...' or 'I would imagine ...' when you are not sure about something or when you are being polite. EG *I would imagine ...* (7)

immediately 10

1 If something happens **immediately**, it happens without delay or hesitation. EG *You turn left in Eggleston and then immediately right.* (132)
2 You use **immediately** **2.1** to refer to something that can be seen, understood, used, etc without any delay. EG *It was immediately obvious.* **2.2** to refer to someone or something that is closely involved in a situation. EG *We were not immediately concerned with the problem.* **2.3** to refer to something that is next to or very close to a particular thing or place. EG *Immediately to the right of the school is the shop.*

interest 3

1 A desire to pay attention to something and learn or hear more about it. EG *People who have taken an active interest in the project ... No one took any interest in me as a child.*
2 A sum of money that is paid as a percentage of a larger sum of money. EG *You receive interest on money that you invest and pay interest on money that you borrow.*
3 The advantages, well-being, success and happiness of a person or group of people. EG *They were acting in their own interests ... ... in the public interest.*
4 If you are **interested** in something, you are keen to know more about it or to do it. EG *I'm fairly interested in sport.*
5 If you find something **interesting**, it attracts your attention. EG *That's a very interesting question ... ... some very interesting people.*

involve, involved 8

1 If something **involves** a particular type of activity or behaviour, that activity or behaviour is part of it. EG *Social activities which involve meeting and talking with people ... Write about what you have done in the past and say, very briefly, what it involves.*
2 If you are **involved** in something you take part in it. EG *Have you ever been involved in an accident like one of these?* (106)

lead 8

1 To be in the front of a line of moving people or things. EG *Jenny was leading, Chris was behind her and I was at the back.*
2 To take someone to a place by going with them. EG *He led the way there.*
3 To go to a particular place. EG *Roads leading to the forts can be crowded ... ... stairs leading up to a house ...*
4 A **lead** is a length of wire covered in plastic that is used to carry electricity. EG *Make sure that you've got the leads plugged in to the correct sockets.*
5 The position of being ahead in a competition or contest at a particular time. EG *New Zealand went into an early lead ... Manchester are in the lead by 3 goals to 1.*
6 To be the most successful or the most advanced. EG *Japan and America now lead the world in computing science research.*
7 To be in control or in charge of a group of people. EG *The Labour Party is led by Neil Kinnock.*
8 The most important thing or person. EG *She's the lead singer in their rock group ... ... the lead story in a newspaper.*
9 **lead to** means to result in. EG *It will lead to trouble.*
10 To pass or spend your life in a particular sort of way. EG *I lead a hectic social life.*
11 **Lead** is a soft, grey, heavy metal that can be poisonous.

least 4

1 **At least** means **1.1** a minimum of. EG *... seven at least ...* (18) *That's at least 8+ hours work each day.* (47) **1.2** a good point despite something bad. EG *... had left his name and address so, at least, he could make a claim ...* (112)
2 **At least** can be used to modify what you have already said. EG *This is an island – at least I think it is!*
3 **The least** means that an amount of something is as small as it can be. EG *My least favourite ...* (58) *... which person spends the most and the least money ...* (80)

leave 1

1 To go away or to depart from places, people and institutions. EG *My last train leaves Euston at 11.30 ... It's a very pleasant school and I'd be sorry to leave it.* (2)
2 To allow or cause to remain in a particular condition or place. EG *We decided to leave the office as it was ... Can you leave the door open?*
3 Remaining. EG *I hope there's enough left ... I'm the only one left ... Which sentences are left over?* (13)

line 7

1 **Line** is used in the following ways. **1.1** A **line** on a surface is a long thin mark which is drawn, painted, printed, etc. EG *We did a line across the middle of the cake.* (100) **1.2 Lines** are found on paper, for writing on; on a road, to show where you can park your car; on sports fields and pitches; on someone's face when they grow old. EG *A plumber had parked on a double yellow line.* (150)
2 A **line** of people or things is a number of them standing side by side or one after the other forming a continuous row.
3 **Line** is used to refer to groups of words, numbers etc in a piece of work such as a book, speech, song or play. EG *Can you guess the last line of the story?*
4 **Line** is used to refer to a long, narrow piece of string, wire, pipe or metal on which you hang wet clothes to dry; with which you catch fish; along which electricity or telephone messages are sent; along which trains run. EG *Get the Victoria Line.*

little 1

1 Small. EG *A little village.*
2 Young. EG *Two little girls, Marion and Mabel.*
3 A small amount of. EG *I speak a little bit of Italian, a little Spanish, and a tiny bit of Greek.*
4 Not much or not enough. EG *John and I had very little money left ... I studied Latin and French, but they made little impression.* (12)

live 1

1 To stay in a place which is your home. EG *Where do you live?*
2 To behave in a particular way. EG *My sister and I lived very different lives ... We lived very simply.*
3 To be alive. EG *We need water to live ... People cannot live without air.*

machine 8

1 A piece of equipment that does a particular type of work. EG *A washing machine.*
2 A well-controlled system or organisation. EG *A propaganda machine.*
3 If you **machine** something, you make it or change its shape using a machine; a technical term.

make 9

1 **Make** is one of the most common verbs in English. It is often used in expressions where it does not have a very distinct meaning of its own, but where most of the meaning is in the noun that follows it. EG *Make a purchase ...* (126) *Even if you do not intend to make a claim.* (108)

2 If you **make** something, you produce it. EG *Some days I am a receptionist, other days I make the tea.* (52) *I usually make a cheese flan.* (86)
3 To cause someone to be angry, happy, sad, etc. EG *This made him very happy.* (179)
4 A **make** is a type of product. EG *What make of car do you have? A Ford.*

mark 9

1 A **mark** is a small part of a surface which is a different colour because something has been dropped on it. EG *A dirty mark ... ... grease marks.*
2 A **mark** is a written or printed symbol. EG *An exclamation mark ... ... a question mark.*
3 If you **mark** something, you put a written symbol on it. EG *Teachers were marking children's writing.*
4 A point on a scale. EG *Unemployment is now over the 3 million mark.*
5 To label. EG *Can you mark where your house is on the map?*
6 German currency. EG *The German Mark was worth about 25p.*

matter 9

1 An event, situation or subject which you have to deal with or think about, especially something that involves problems. EG *That's a different matter ... It's a personal matter.*
2 If something **matters**, it is important, it is something that you care about or that worries you. EG *Your happiness – that's the only thing that matters.*
3 **Matter** is written material, especially books and newspapers. EG *Reading matter ...... printed matter ...*
4 You say 'What's **the matter**?' to someone when you want to know what the problem is. EG *What's the matter with your arm? I broke it playing football.*
5 You say 'It doesn't **matter**' to tell someone who is apologising to you that you are not angry or upset.

meet 2

1 To make a new friend; to get to know someone for the first time. EG *I would need to meet somebody who also had a sense of humour.* (20)
2 To come together, usually for a particular purpose. EG *Let's meet at 11 o'clock tomorrow.*
3 Roads, rivers etc **meet** when they come together. EG *... the B6274 will meet the A688 ...* (131)

nor 6

1 **Nor** is used after 'neither' in order to introduce the second alternative in a negative statement. EG *Neither Margaret nor John was there ... He could neither read nor write.*
2 **Nor** is used after a negative statement in order to add something else. EG *That wasn't the whole story, nor anything like the whole story.*
3 **Nor** is used after a negative statement to express agreement with that statement. EG *'I haven't got a car.' '... nor have I.'* (69)

notice 8

If you **notice** someone or something, you become aware of them. EG *I think maybe the pilot had noticed, but certainly no one else on board had noticed ...* (173) *He couldn't help noticing a note to his secretary ...* (55) *Noticing a woman reading the menu ...* (93)

119

obviously 10

1 Used to show that you expect your hearer to know or understand something. EG *Obviously we'll have to think carefully about it.*
2 Used when something is clear or evident. EG *One of the beds had obviously been slept in.*

odd 5

1 Strange or unusual. EG *Isn't that a bit odd? ... We thought she was rather odd.*
2 **The odds** are a measurement of how probable it is that something will or will not happen. EG *The odds were against me, so I gave up the plan ... ... The odds are that it will rain tomorrow.*
3 Various. EG *Odd jobs ... Odd bits of shopping.*

offer 9

1 To ask someone if they would like to have something. EG *He offered her his chair ... It was always the smaller cars that offered you a lift.* (97)
2 To say you are willing to do something. EG *'We could do it for you,' offered Dolly.*
3 An **offer** is something that someone says they will give you or do for you. EG *Thanks for your offer of help.*
4 You can **offer** someone information, advice, help, an explanation, congratulations, thanks, friendship etc. EG *May I offer my congratulations.*
5 To provide. EG *Some stores offer relief from VAT.* (126)
6 Referring to a quality that makes things attractive, useful etc. EG *The latest that computer technology has to offer ... The best of everything that London has to offer.*
7 If something is **on offer**, its price is specially reduced.
8 To say you will pay a certain sum of money. EG *Make me an offer ... The original price was £10, but I'm open to offers.*

operation 12

1 An activity that involves many actions. EG *The speed with which he performed this difficult operation was incredible.* (126)
2 A planned series of military actions. EG *The Cambodian adventure had been the most successful operation of the war.*
3 A business or company. EG *The whole of the Vauxhall operation in Britain.*
4 A form of medical treatment in which a doctor cuts open part of the patient's body in order to repair it or to cure a disease. EG *Some 200 heart operations a year are performed there.*

part 5

1 One of a number of things that makes up a whole. EG *... a part of London.*
2 To **take part in** something means to do something or share an activity. EG *Even taking part in sport?*

partly 5

To some extent, but not completely. EG *The door was partly open ... That's partly because they live in unattractive conditions.* (25)

period 12

1 A length of time, usually a fixed length. EG *The payment period is within ten days of completion of the job.*
2 A particular time in history. EG *British paintings of all periods.* (157)

pick 14

1 To choose. EG *You can pick whichever one you want.*
2 **pick up** means **2.1** To lift up. EG *A million housewives every day pick up a can of beans and say ...* (120) **2.2** To give someone a lift in a car. EG *A motorist who had a brand new BMW car picked up a hitch-hiker.* **2.3** To find or collect. EG *You're quite likely to pick up a few bargains ... Pick up a copy at your nearest newsagent.*

plain 12

1 A large, flat area of land with very few trees on it.
2 Entirely in one colour and without a pattern, or without printing, writing, etc; used of surfaces and of cloth, paper, etc. EG *I'll tell them to put it in a plain envelope.*
3 Designed or prepared in a very simple way; used of buildings, clothes, food etc. EG *She was wearing a plain black dress ... Good plain food.*
4 Easy to recognise or be aware of; used of facts, and of difficulties, advantages, etc. EG *I'd say it's pretty plain that they got the baby to cry somehow.* (164)
5 Not beautiful. EG *A plain, plump person.*

point 12

1 Something that has just been said. EG *He makes a good point about people keeping dogs who know nothing about their real needs.*
2 A detail that occurs as part of a fixed procedure or process. EG *The main point on the agenda was left till the end of the meeting.*
3 Used to refer to a particular part of someone's character or abilities. EG *That's his best point, I think.*
4 The reason for saying or doing something, often used in negative expressions or questions, to show that something is useless or not worthwhile. EG *But that's not the point! What jobs need skilled hands?* (167)
5 A particular place or position, especially a precise one. EG *The two roads would merge at that point.* (131)
6 The sharp end of a pin, needle, or knife.
7 A particular time or moment. EG *At some future point, he may have to think again.*
8 **Up to a point** means partly but not completely. EG *Up to a point I agree with Catherine.*
9 A score in a game. EG *We won by five points to three.*
10 If you **point** to or at something, you show it to people. EG *She pointed to the bathroom door.*
11 To face a particular direction. EG *One of its four toes pointed backwards.*
12 To hold something, especially a weapon, so that it points towards someone. EG *My kids are forbidden even to point toy pistols at people.*
13 **point out** means to give an important piece of information. EG *Japan, he pointed out, has a huge population.*

policy 8

1 A **policy** is a general set of ideas or plans agreed by a government or party. EG *Washington has changed its policy with regard to the Soviet Union.*
2 An agreement with an insurance company. EG *You have to renew the policy every year.*

position 12

1 An attitude or point of view. EG *That is my position and I'm not going to change my mind.*
2 A condition or situation. EG *The party making an official statement is in a better position than the one who does not.* (108)
3 The place where something or someone is. EG *It stands in a good position overlooking Belfast.*
4 A job. EG *John anticipates some difficulty in finding a suitable position.* (52)

post 9

1 The **post** is the public service offered by the Post Office for collecting and delivering letters. EG *Send it by first class post ... Write by return of post.*
2 A strong pole made of wood or metal. EG *... a lamp-post ... The ball hit the goalpost ... The finishing post at the races.*
3 A job or position at work. EG *John was applying for a new post, the post of head of department in a school.*
4 **post-** is used to form words that describe something taking place after a certain date, event, or stage of development. EG *... post-war housing ...... post-graduate students ...*

powerful 7

1 A person, organisation or government is **powerful** if they are able to control other people and events. EG *... powerful and effective trade unions ...*
2 A person or animal that is **powerful** is very strong.
3 A machine or engine is **powerful** if it can exert a lot of force. EG *The powerful engine growled and grunted impatiently.* (97)
4 Other things that can be described as **powerful** are smells, lights, voices, blows or kicks.

produce 11

1 To cause or create. EG *With the hovercraft, the cushion is produced by a ring of airjets ... (73) ... once the door is opened, the microwaves stop being produced.* (91)
2 To manufacture. EG *Factories producing electrical goods ... It produces a third of the nation's oil.*
3 To show or supply. EG *From his pocket he produced a small black notebook.* (152).
4 To manage or organise. EG *They produce their own plays at school.*

professional 4

1 Relating to the work that a person does. EG *He started his professional life as a singer.*
2 Having an occupation that requires special training and education. EG *The flat is ideal for the professional single person.*
3 Having a job in which you receive money for doing an activity that many people do as a hobby, for example sport, music, or acting. EG *A professional footballer.* (43)
4 Showing great skill and high standards. EG *Piers Paul Read's a very professional writer.*

provide 3

1 To give or lend. EG *All meals will be provided by the hotel.*
2 Used to introduce a condition. EG *You can get a Cheap Day Return ticket at a reduced rate, provided that you do not start your journey before 09.30 hours.*

pull 11

1 Of a car, **1.1** to **pull in** or **pull over**. EG *I would say he would probably pull in to the side if he were by himself ... (136) If there was a policeman beside me telling me to pull over I would certainly pull over.* (136) **1.2 Pull up** means stop. EG *He pulls up at a traffic light.* (78)
2 To move something by getting in front of it and drawing it towards you. EG *Can you help me pull these things over here?*

push 5

1 To press something or someone, for example with your hand. EG *She pushed the button that locked the door.*
2 The act of pressing something or someone. EG *I gave her a push.*
3 To move something along. EG *Castle pushed his bicycle up King's Road.*
4 To try to cause someone to make progress by constantly persuading and encouraging them. EG *They didn't push you in that direction.*
5 **push on** means to travel onwards. EG *We must push on before nightfall.*

raise 11

1 If you **raise** something, you move it so that it is in a higher position. EG *Raise your hand if you want to ask a question.*
2 To increase in some way. EG *When he spoke next he raised his voice so loud that I jumped.* (147)
3 To grow. EG *Farmers raise crops.*

rate 6

1 The speed at which something happens. EG *... the rapid rate of change in the modern world ...*
2 The number of instances of something that occur during a period of time. EG *What is your success rate? ... A rising divorce rate among the middle classes.*
3 The level or amount. EG *... bargain rates ... Children at half the adult rate ... Interest rates rising to 12%.*
4 **Rates** in Britain are a local tax paid by house-owners (rate-payers), to pay for water, roads and other local services in their area.
5 To **rate** someone or something means to think a lot of them. EG *He was a highly rated goalkeeper.*
6 **At any rate** can mean 'anyway'. EG *I don't know exactly what he did, but at any rate he was very successful.*

reach 3

1 To come to a place or person. EG *It was dark by the time I reached their house.*
2 To speak to or send a message to someone. EG *I tried to reach you at home several times, but no-one answered the phone.*
3 To touch or take hold of something by stretching out your arm. EG *I can't reach that shelf unless I stand on a chair.*

relationship 5

1 The connection between two people or two groups of people. EG *The relationship between friends.*
2 The connection between two things, events, or ideas. EG *My exams bore no relationship to my being a doctor.* (64)
3 The type of family connection between two people. EG *'What is your relationship to the patient?' 'I'm his daughter.'*

remain 1

1 To stay in a particular condition and not to change. EG *Mrs Oliver remained silent ... Her husband remained standing. ... important that we should remain Irish ...* (9)
2 To stay in a particular place and not move away. EG *I was allowed to remain at home.*
3 To still exist, especially when other parts or other similar things no longer exist. EG *He was cut off from what remained of his family.*
4 To still exist and to be unanswered or unsolved, in spite of what people have said or done; used especially of problems and facts. EG *These problems remain ... The fact remains that they mean to destroy us.*

remember 14

1 If you **remember** people or events, your mind still has an impression of them. EG *Some of 'em can't even remember their own names ...* (193) *Do you remember Ireland at all?*
2 If you **remember** to do something, you do it when you intended to. EG *Remember to lock the door when you go out ... I remembered to put all my things away.*

repeat 1

1 To say or write something again. EG *'Is she quite dead?' – 'Quite dead', he repeated.*
2 To do or make something again. EG *I try not to repeat silly mistakes.*
3 A **repeat** is something which happens again. EG *... a repeat of the programme ...... a repeat performance of the play ...*

rest 6

1 What remains. EG *Let's turn over and read the rest.*
2 A period of time during which you do not do anything active. EG *I need a rest.*
3 To relax, and stop working or doing anything active. EG *'Try to rest', the doctor said.*
4 If a duty or responsibility **rests** with a person, that person must do the duty. EG *The decision rested with the headmaster.*
5 To lean on. EG *No more than a couple of fingers resting lightly on the wheel to keep her steady.* (97)

rich 14

1 Having a lot of money or possessions. EG *It must be nice to be rich.* **1.1** ' **The rich**' means people who are rich. EG *I only go after them as can afford it. The winners and the rich.* (189)
2 **Riches** are valuable possessions. EG *The young man set out in search of adventure and riches.*
3 The word **rich** is used to describe: **3.1** food, containing a lot of fats, eggs, cream etc. **3.2** soil that is very good for growing crops. **3.3** clothes that are beautiful and valuable. **3.4** voices and musical sounds that are strong in a pleasing way.

round 13

1 Of shape, position or direction. EG *... the belt from round the driver's waist ...* (174)
2 Near to, or moving from place to place within a certain area. EG *The policeman came round to my open window ...* (147) *Can you picture me goin' round kids' parties ...?* (174)
3 Approximately. EG *We should get there round four o'clock ... They live round about here.*
4 To **get round** something means to solve a problem. EG *If you don't know whether to put Miss or Mrs, you can get round it by writing Ms.*
5 A **round** can be: in sport – a round of golf; in politics – a round of talks.

scene 4

1 A part of a play, film, novel etc. EG *All we saw was about three scenes ... ... great love scenes ...*
2 A picture of a particular place or kind of activity. EG *It seems to be a street scene.* (49)
3 The place where something in particular has happened. EG *The scene of the accident.* (108)
4 A particular activity or part of life.
5 A fight or argument. EG *There was a scene, and Father called Christopher a lot of rude names.*

secret, secretly 4

1 Something that is known about by only a small number of people, and not told or shown to anyone else. EG *We had to promise to keep the secret.*
2 Happening or acting privately, with the intention of preventing other people from finding out. EG *They met secretly to discuss the plans.*
3 Something that is the best or only way of achieving a particular result. EG *He asked the popular one for her secret.* (55)
4 Something that has never been explained or understood. EG *The secret of life is to become very, very good at something that's very hard to do.* (121)

security 13

1 The precautions (safety measures) that are taken to protect a country from spying, to protect people from being attacked, to prevent prisoners from escaping etc. EG *Airport Security Check ... Top security prisons.*
2 A feeling of **security** means a feeling of safety. EG *People need job security.*

sense 5

1 If you have a **sense** of something such as justice, you believe in it. EG *a sense of right and wrong ... She's gained a sense of independence ... ... a sense of humour.* (20)
2 Meaning. EG *In the strict sense of the word ...*
3 The five **senses** of touch, hearing, smell, taste, sight.

serious 12

1 Causing worry or fear. EG *I suppose you know you're in serious trouble ...* (161) *... serious illness ... ... seriously ill ...* (145)
2 Important. EG *I think this is a serious point.*
3 Dealing with important matters. EG *A serious newspaper.*
4 Not joking or pretending. EG *At first I thought he was continuing the joke, but he was serious.*
5 Thoughtful, quiet, not joking. EG *A rather serious girl ... Don't look so serious!*

service, services 6

1 An organisation or system that provides a public need, especially related to transport or communications, health, education etc. EG *Bus services within the county.* (82)
2 The Army, Navy or Air Force.
3 Help or aid given as part of a job. EG *Thank you for your services.*
4 Being served in a shop or restaurant or hotel. EG *They give excellent service.*
5 The state of being used. EG *New vehicles brought into service ... This computer has been in service for years.*

sharp 11

1 A **sharp** object has a very thin edge that is good for cutting things. EG *A sharp knife.*
2 Clear. EG *... the photo was so sharp ...*
3 Sudden, quick. EG *Car prices have risen sharply.*
4 Spoken abruptly, often with anger, without warning. EG *'Who are you', he asked sharply.*
5 Exact time. EG *The train leaves at 8 o'clock sharp!*

sight 12

1 The ability to see. EG *For man, sight is the most important sense.*
2 An occasion of seeing. EG *We tried to get a sight of the president as his car shot past.*
3 Places, especially in a city, that are interesting to see and are often visited by tourists. EG *... the sights of London ...*
4 The distance or area within which it is possible to see someone or something. EG *He roared off up the road out of sight.* (161)

simple 7

1 If something is **simple** it is easy to understand; if a problem is **simple** it is easy to understand or solve. EG *The problem is a simple one.*
2 Something which is **simple** is straightforward without any unnecessary parts or complications. EG *Very simple language ...* (95) *A recipe for a simple dish.* (87)

simply 8

1 Used to give emphasis. EG *I simply can't believe it.*
2 Used to show that there is only one thing, reason etc. EG *I simply didn't look.* (106)
3 If you say or write something **simply** you do it in a way that is easy to understand. EG *Let me put it quite simply ...*
4 If you live **simply** you have an uncomplicated and cheap way of life.

somehow 14

1 You use **somehow** to show that you do not know how something was done. EG *It has somehow come out that way.*
2 To show that you do not know why. EG *Somehow I couldn't get to sleep.*

sorry 1

1 Used to apologise. EG *I'm sorry I'm so late ... I'm sorry about this but there's nothing I can do right now.*
2 Unhappy. EG *It's a pleasant school and I'd be sorry to leave it.* (2)
3 Used to disagree with someone. EG *I don't agree with you, I'm sorry.*

source 12

1 A person, place, or thing from which you get something that is useful or needed. EG *One of the world's main sources of uranium.*
2 A person or thing that provides information, especially about events that are reported in the news. EG *Sources close to the President report that ...*
3 The point or circumstance from which something comes or where something has its origin. EG *They're trying to trace the source of the trouble ... They come in useful as a source of disruption, I suppose, babies.* (164)

special 6

1 Different from normal, more important than usual. EG *Do you have any special skill, like typing?*
2 Particular: something that belongs to/is relevant to/is intended for one particular person, group, place, situation. EG *Travelcard is a special ticket.* (82)
3 Greater than usual. EG *Pay special attention to spelling ... He made a special effort to be helpful ... My special interest is music.*
4 Specialised. EG *Special schools for handicapped children.*

spread 2

1 To open, arrange or extend something, often over a place or surface, with the result that all of it can be seen or used easily. EG *He took the envelope and spread the contents on the table ...*
2 To put a thin layer of something over a surface. EG *... spreading jam on bread.*
3 To move outwards in all directions; to travel further. EG *... stop the fire getting out of control and spreading ... ... rats can spread disease.*
4 The activity or process of spreading. EG *... a result of the spread of fire ...... the spread of higher education.*
5 **spread out**. To move away from each other. EG *They followed him and spread out nervously in the forest.*

stage 7

1 A **stage** is a particular point in a continuous process. EG *To get creamy scrambled eggs be careful at this stage.* (87)
2 If you do something **stage by stage** you complete one part after another. EG *You must work through it very carefully stage by stage.*
3 A **stage** is a platform in a theatre on which the performances take place. EG *I walked on to the stage and started to sing.*
4 **The stage** is the profession or career of acting, or the activities connected with the theatre. EG *My Aunt Mabel was on the stage.*

step 10

1 A pace. EG *She took a step back ... I had to retrace my steps.* (140)
2 To **step on** means to put your foot on. EG *She stepped on his toe.*
3 A **step** is a stair outside a building. EG *She was sitting on the top step.*
4 A **step** is also a stage in achieving something. EG *This is a step on the road to victory.*

strong 13

1 **Strong** people can carry heavy things, work very hard, or are powerful. EG *Though the way be long, let your heart be strong ...* (201) *... some strong thread.* (172)
2 You use **strong** to describe something which affects you very much. EG *... strong feelings about ... She felt and argued strongly in support of equal pay for women.*

123

struggle 1

1 To try very hard to get or to do something that is difficult for you and that other people often are trying to stop you from achieving. EG *A nationalist movement that has had to struggle for independence ... I struggle through reading Italian.*

2 Very great efforts that you make to get or to do something that is difficult for you and that other people often are trying to stop you from achieving. EG *The conference called for a renewed struggle against racism.*

3 To twist, kick, and move violently in order to get yourself free when you are being held by another person or by a trap or ropes. EG *The guard was standing hitting him whenever he struggled.*

4 To manage with very great difficulty to move through a place, or to stand up, sit down, etc, for example because you are tired or ill. EG *He struggled forward for about half a mile.*

5 An activity which is very difficult for you to do and which you have to try very hard to achieve. EG *Reading, on the whole, was a struggle.*

support 13

1 If you **support** a political party, or a sports team, you want them to do well. EG *He supported Manchester United.*

2 To help people by paying for their food, clothes etc or by giving them practical advice, kindness, etc.

3 To take the weight of. EG *Will this shelf support all those books?*

supposed 8

1 If something is **supposed** to be done or not **supposed** to be done, you mean it should or should not be done because of a law, custom or rule. EG *You are supposed to report it to the police as soon as possible.*

2 If you say something is **supposed** to happen you mean it is expected or intended to happen. EG *Where are you supposed to be going?*

3 When you say something is **supposed** to be true you are reporting a statement or belief that is not your own. EG *It's supposed to be very difficult, but I don't know.*

surely 11

1 Used when making a statement to express surprise, or to contradict the other person. EG *Surely he must have known? ... You haven't finished all that yet, surely!*

2 In American English, **surely** means 'yes, certainly'. EG *Will you excuse me for a second? Surely!*

surprise, surprised 4

1 A sudden or unexpected event, or something that happens in a way that you do not expect. EG *The British government might be in for a surprise when the report is published.*

2 Something unexpected, especially something pleasant, such as a gift. EG *What a lovely surprise! ... I have a surprise for you.*

3 Feeling slightly shocked because of something unexpected, for example an unexpected event or piece of information. EG *'I'm not surprised,' said the plumber. 'Neither did I when I was a ...' Were they surprised when you went to University? (64)*

take 13

1 To move something from a place to another place. EG *Just complete the attached form and take it to any of the places listed here ... (82) What's the use of taking an umbrella when it's not raining ... They broke the window and they came in and took the video. (178)*

2 If something **takes** a certain amount of time, you need that amount of time in order to do it. EG *It takes me about twenty minutes I suppose to come in ... (80) He took plenty of time slowing down. (147)*

3 If you **take** a road, you choose to travel along it. EG *Take the second road on the left.*

4 The most frequent use of **take** is in expressions where it does not have a very distinct meaning of its own, but where most of the meaning is in the noun which follows it. EG *It is negative to take the attitude that 'It cannot happen to me ...' (178) Please take note of these points. (178)*

test 7

1 A **test** is **1.1** an event that makes clear how well something works or what it is like; EG *Stringent tests for electrical safety and microwave leakage. (91)* **1.2** a series of questions you must answer in order to show how much you know. EG *An English test.*

thick 7

1 Something that is **thick** **1.1** has a particular distance between its two opposite surfaces. EG *The piece of wood was about six centimetres thick.* **1.2** has a greater distance than you would expect between its two opposite surfaces. EG *A thick stone wall.*

2 Someone who is **thick** is stupid. EG *He's a bit thick.*

3 **Thick** liquids are fairly stiff and solid. EG *I made the sauce too thick.*

top 3

1 The highest point. EG *Very lucky to get to the top of it ... (24) We actually managed to reach the top. (29)*

2 More important or better than other people or things. EG *... Top twenty records ... The very top of the profession. (189)*

3 A woman's shirt or blouse. EG *That's a nice top!*

towards 10

1 The form **toward** is also used. In the direction of. EG *The policeman came strolling slowly toward us. (147)*

2 Of attitude. EG *He felt friendly towards them.*

3 Just before. EG *Towards the end of 1987.*

trade 9

1 The activity of buying, selling or exchanging goods or services between people, firms or countries. EG *France is dependent on foreign trade ... Trade with Eastern Europe.*

2 A business. EG *The tourist trade.*

3 A kind of work. EG *I'm in a skilled trade. (121)*

4 A **trade union** is an organisation formed by the workers to improve their working conditions and wages. EG *He will meet the trade union leaders tomorrow.*

treat 9

1 If you **treat** someone in a particular way, you behave that way towards them. EG *You will be treated as a royal guest.* (39)
2 If you **treat** something in a particular way, you deal with it that way. EG *Electricity is dangerous so treat it with respect ... Treat it as a joke.*
3 To **treat** an illness, an injury, or sick people. EG *Only two doctors and eight nurses treat 300 patients.*
4 To give someone something they will enjoy. EG *A finger of fudge is just enough to give your kids a treat!* (120)

trouble 4

1 Difficulties or problems. EG *My bank manager had a lot of trouble with his hot water system ...* (45) *What's the trouble, mate?* (103)
2 To make someone feel worried, doubtful or uneasy. EG *What's troubling you?*
3 A problem. EG *Our flight was delayed because of engine trouble.*
4 A situation in which someone is angry with you because of something you have done. EG *I don't want to get you into trouble.*
5 Unpleasant or strongly felt disagreement which may result in bad quarrels or even fighting. EG *He's the sort of person who always makes trouble ... ... trouble in Poland ...*
6 Someone or something that causes you a problem in some way. EG *If it wouldn't be a trouble to you, could I ask you to give me a lift? ... Please don't go to a lot of trouble on my behalf.*
7 To do something that requires a special effort or that is difficult. EG *I'm sorry to trouble you, but I wondered if we could have a word some time ... I do apologise for troubling you, especially on a Sunday.*

union 4

1 An organisation which has the aim of improving working conditions. EG *If it was union work, a union would insist on a wage of at least £108 a week.*
2 A group of countries or states which have been joined into one for political reasons. EG *The Soviet Union.*
3 The act of joining two or more things so that they become one; also the state of being joined in this way. EG *... the union of the two countries.*

various 8

1 **Various** means that there are several different things of the type mentioned. EG *Various kinds of sweets.*
2 **Various** can mean 'varied'. EG *His excuses are many and various.*

view 12

1 A belief or opinion. EG *To give vent to their views on politics, the price of butter, religion, anything.* (157)
2 You say '**In my view ...**' when you want to emphasise that you are stating a personal opinion. EG *In my view, it's a long way to a United States of Europe.*

3 To think of something in the particular way that is mentioned. EG *Once you see China, it's impossible ever again to view America as you always had.*
4 Something which is seen from a particular place, especially something which is thought to be beautiful. EG *From the top there is a fine view of the sea.*

voice 11

1 When someone speaks, you hear their **voice**. EG *He spoke in a deep voice ... He raised his voice so loud ...* (147)
2 People's opinions. EG *The powerful voice of the people ... The voice of reason.*

way 6

1 **Way** refers to the manner in which a person or thing behaves or acts, or the certain style someone or something has, or feeling or attitude of a person. EG *Just look at the way he eats! It's horrible!*
2 **Way** refers to the means or method by which something is done, or how it happens. EG *The best way of getting to Paris is by train and boat.* (64)
3 Used with reference to a direction, distance, route, road, path or journey somewhere. EG *'Which way do I go?' 'Turn right at the shops, and go all the way down that road.'*

while 6

1 During the time that. EG *Maybe she sneaked out while he wasn't looking ...* (78) *It was fun while it lasted.*
2 A short time. EG *... for a little while ...*
3 Although. EG *While I like his paintings, I would not want to spend all that money.*

wish 8

1 A **wish** is a longing or desire for something. EG *She told me of her wish to leave.*
2 To want, desire. EG *I wish I were going with you.* (114)

wonder 12

1 To want to know something. EG *I wonder how they made it cry.* (164)
2 Used to make what you are going to say sound more polite. EG *I wonder if you'd mind closing the window?*
3 To think or silently ask yourself about something, especially because you feel doubtful, uncertain, or worried about it. EG *I am beginning to wonder why we ever invited them.*
4 A surprising thing that you would not have expected. EG *It was a wonder that she managed to come at all; she's so busy nowadays.*
5 Greatly admired or widely praised because of having surprisingly good results or more skill than anyone else. EG *The wonder boy of American racing.*

Wordlist

Words followed by a star (*) occurred in Level 1 of the Course, but further new uses are covered here. Words followed by 'L' are explained in the Lexicon on pages 111–125. Figures refer to sections where examples of the word can be found, either in the Student's Book or in the transcripts. 'T' after a reference means students may need to be given the word to complete the section as it does not actually appear in the text. To locate each unit, refer to the table at the top of the page.

ability 126T
able* 121, 126
about* 4, 13
above* 142
abroad 126T, 130
absolutely 14, 27
absorbed 91
academic 14
accept 153, 156
accident 103
accommodation 35, 39
account L 115
across* 100
action 108
active 28, 29
activity 28T
actually* 132
add 164, 170
addition 161
additional 161T
adult 82
advance 157, 162
advantage 91, 93
advertising 120
advice 162, 170
affair 178
afford 34
after* 186, 189, 197
afterwards 18
against L 112, 142
agency 20
agreement 84
ahead L 142
air* 68
aircraft 68, 69
airport 82
allow L 143, 150, 156
almost* 157
alone* 206
along* 67
alright 13
although 68, 69, 84
altogether 161, 167
among L 93
amount 47
analysis, analyses 120
ancient 28
angry 78
animal 25, 26
announce 193
annoyed 103
annoying 103, 130
anybody 42, 57
anyway* 57
anywhere 49
apart L 12
apology 112
apparent 18
appeal 95
appearance L 112T, 87T
appear L 87, 112
apply 52, 57
approach 144, 147
area 176
argument 21, 27
arms* 63
around 165, 179, 184
arts 157, 158
artists 157, 159
ask* 136, 137

assistant 43, 55
associated 78
association 80
atmosphere 35
attach 82
attack 206
attempt 178, 184
attention L 64
attitude 157
audience 157
authority 178
away* 57, 67
awful 57, 103, 130
back*L 27
background L 17
bad* 186
ball 188
bar 161
bargain 116, 126
base 73
based 82
basic L 89, 47
basically L 122
be* 8, 37, 66
beach 28, 35
beautiful 28, 35
beauty 35T
because*69, 80
become* 131
bed* 39
beer 93T
before* 120, 126
behave 164, 165
behaviour L 12
behind* L 133, 141, 142
beings 202
belief 161T
believe L 69, 161, 185
belong 171
below L 142
bend, bent 179
beneath 142
beside 136, 142
beyond L 136, 142
bill 117, 130
bird 25
bit L 24, 27
blame 106
blind 189
block 150
blood 63
board L 39
boat 29
bored 14, 26
boring 14T, 26T
body* 63
boss 75
bothered* 152, 156
bottle 93
bound L 152
box 117, 124, 138
brain 63
branch 131
bread 101T
break, broke, broken, breaking
  L 161
breast 152
breath 188T
breathe 188
brick 152

brief 52
bright 128
brilliant 193
bring, brought L 9
brochure 205
building* 152, 156
burn, burned/burnt L 184
business* L 104, 114
but* 19, 27, 155
by* 91, 96
camp 133
capital L 1
captain 104
care 167
career 64
careful 147, 152, 156
careless 147T
case 123, 138
cash 117, 130
castle 131, 134
catalogue 117
catch 110
category 25
caught 110
cause* 76
central 41T
centre* 82
certain* 178
challenge 136
character 14T, 20T
characteristic 20
charge 68, 82
chest 63T
childhood 64
chin 49
choice L 35, 41
choose, chose, chosen L 35T
Christian 28
Christmas 38
circle 100
circumstances 150, 153
claim L 112, 115
class* L 68
clean 120, 130
clear L 48, 57
clearly L 48
close* 186
closely 186T
coast 29
cold* 95
collection 157
come, came, coming* 131, 142
comedy 157
comfort 35T
comfortable 35
community L 2, 9, 13
companion 93
company 2
compare 89, 134
completely L 49
computer 20
concern L 188, 197
condition L 25T, 108
confidence 152T
confident 152
connect 104T
connection 104
consequences 64
consider L 14
contact L 91

contents 171, 184
continue 131
control L 104, 115
conversations 97T
cook 86
cool 152, 156
copy 152
correct 186
corridor 172
could* 151
count 152
countless 152T
country* 33T
county 1, 2
course* 114
court 143, 161
cousin 78
cover L 120, 130
cream 87T
creature 25
crime 176, 178
criminal 176
cross 131
crowd 28
cry 189, 193
cup 85
curious 200
cut 18, 100, 138
damage 150
danger 58
dangerous 58
dead L 172
deal L 1, 25
dear L 188, 197
decided 55
decision 57
deep 73
definition 67
degree* L 12
dentist 42, 45, 54
department 52
depends L 69
design 116, 157, 159
details* 97
device 91
die* 172
diet 186
difficulty 52
direct L 126, 130
dirty 186
disappear 78, 167
discover L 35, 41
discovered 104
discuss 69
discussion 69T, 84
disease 25
distance 131T
divide 100
division 100T
do, did, done, doing* 32, 36, 162
dog 25, 26
dollars 46
doubt 176, 178
doubtful 176T
down* 170
draw L 52
dreadful 206
dream, dreamed/dreamt 64
driver 97
drop, dropped L 75

Level 1 Words

Additional categories of Level 1 words that have been covered in Level 2 are given below, in unit order. Examples mainly come from the unit where the word is dealt with; numbers in brackets are unit references.

UNIT 1

job 1 the work that a person does every day in order to earn money. *She got a good job as a secretary.*
2 a particular piece of work that you have to do. *I've got a few jobs to do.*
long 1 covering a great time or distance. *I have known you for a long time. It was a long walk to the bus. We still had a long way to go.*
2 size. *... about 30 miles long. His long legs stretched out.*
try 1 to make an effort. *John is trying to get a new job. I also tried to learn Russian. Keep trying!*
2 to do something to find out how helpful it is. *Have you tried looking at a newspaper?* [15] *Try going to bed early – you'd feel less tired.*
3 *I tried you in the office.* = *I tried to telephone you.* T
word/words 1.1 *What's this word?*
1.2 a short conversation or short text. *May I have a word with you? Write a few words about... A word of warning...* T
2 everything/nothing that someone has said. *I didn't understand a word! He went without a word.* T
3 the text. *... the words of the song.*

UNIT 2

how 3 in exclamations. *How awful!* T *How lovely!* [3]
love to like very much. *I love to be with friends and lead a hectic social life.*
meeting 1 *I like meeting people.*
2 *You turn up for a meeting on the wrong day.* [11]
still 1 continuing even to this/that time. *While I was still living with my family.*
2 even so, nevertheless. *I still love you more than basketball!*

UNIT 3

bed 1 *asleep in bed...* [7] *... bedrooms.*
2 *river bed, sea bed.* T
country 3 countryside = scenery.
for 2 expressing purpose. *A good place for walking.*
See also section 94.
4 distance. *You can drive for miles.*
forward 1 towards the front. *Move your chair forward.*
2 *I think it's going to be a very relaxing time. I'm looking forward to it.*
3 *put forward a view, some points, etc. Bring forward a meeting.*
last 4 to continue. *The holiday lasted two weeks.*

miss 3 to feel lonely without someone. *I miss you lots.* [3]
pass 1 *to pass another vehicle.*
2 *Time passed slowly. How do you pass the time? Sports and pastimes.*
3 *The road passes through the city.*
4 *Look at the picture... which I'll just pass round.* [2] *He passed me the book.*
5 *I hope you pass your exam.*
6 *The pain soon passed. His anger soon passes.*
7 *British Rail pass. Bus pass.*
top 1 the highest point. *Very lucky to get to the top of it. We actually managed to reach the top.*
2 more important or better than other people/things. *That must be top of the lists.* [4] *The top of the profession.* [4]
3 bottle top. *Take the top off!*
4 woman's shirt/blouse. *That's a nice top!*

UNIT 4

anyway 1 in any case. *It was bound to happen anyway.* T
2 closing point in conversation, boundary, change of topic. *Anyway, what can I do for you?*
2.1 colloquial: *What's the matter with you, anyway?* T
3 at least, as a qualification. *Money has got to be the reason, a primary reason, anyway.* T
during 1 at a point in time. *I'll ring during the week.*
2 throughout. *... during his ten-year career.* [2] *... during the summer I work to make some money...*
especially particularly (to emphasise). *There's plenty of entertainment too, especially in the larger towns.* [3]
everybody = everyone.
less 1 comparative of 'a little', a small extent/amount. *... the most attractive and less well-known parts of the country...* [3] *... a shop assistant probably gets even less.*
2 with adjective: *less interesting. Less polite* = not so polite as before. T
3 more or less. *... we felt more or less the same...* [7] *That's right, isn't it? 'More or less,' I said.* T
neither *Neither did I when I was a bank manager.*
nothing 1 none; used when talking about objects, events or ideas, but not when talking about people. *The man nodded but said nothing...*
2 *A fight started over nothing.* = it started over something trivial. T
3 very little. *They sold their land for nothing.* T

nuclear 1 to do with atomic energy. *I reckon a nuclear scientist is paid reasonably well.*
often 1 frequency. *I often think... I often work past 3pm.*
2 in many cases. *Men often get more money than women.*
once 1 one time only. *I have only been back once since then.* [1]
2 at a time in the past. *Once I had to show a visitor from Korea round... Jenny once had a silly accident.* [8]
or or somebody/something: used when you are not sure. *Perhaps it's the queen or somebody like that. A bag or something.*
process 1 *... the process of applying for jobs... a slow process.*
2 a manufacturing process... *a bottling process...* T
3 in the process of = in the middle of
system group of related parts operating together, used of equipment and institutions. *A bank manager had a lot of trouble with his hot water system. The Education system.*
wrong 1 something the matter. *What's wrong?*
2 made a mistake. *We've got it completely wrong!*
3 sinful. *It's wrong to tell lies.* T

UNIT 5

arms 1 the arms of a chair.
2 Arms are weapons that are used to hurt or kill people, especially in a war. *They were not allowed to use arms... ... by force of arms.* If you **take up arms** against someone, you prepare to attack them and fight against them.
body 1 *... parts of the human body...*
2 *Government bodies, like the Equal Opportunities Commission.*
3 a car body. *The body was blue.* [7]
face 1 *His ratty little face.* [8]
2 *In Madame Tussauds you come face to face with the famous.*
3 *... red-faced.* [11] *... ratty faced.* [12]
4 *The face of a clock.*
feet/foot 1 *I pressed my foot hard down on the accelerator.* [10]
2 at the bottom. *... at the foot of the hills.*
3 unit of measurement. *3 feet is about 1 metre.*
hand 1 part of the body.
2 to pass something to someone. *Hand me that paper.*
head 1 *The hitch-hiker poked his head through the open window...* [7]
2 someone's mind. *He hasn't a thought in his head.*

3 leader, chief, manager. *He wants a promotion to Head of Department.* [4]
4 to go to, go towards. *"What part of London are you headed for?"* [8]
thank 1.2 *Fine thanks.*
3 *Thank goodness.*
wait to spend time doing very little before something happens. *"Wait a minute, Mum..." Wait a moment and I'll be with you.*
would 5 past habit. *I would deal with their insurance needs.* [1]

UNIT 6

air 1 a gas. *That's an air cylinder and that's a balloon.* [4] *The hovercraft can travel across both land and water on a cushion of air.*
2 The space around you. *... paradise for everyone who enjoys the open air.* [3] *... fresh air.*
3 *by air, air hostess, aircraft, aeroplane, airport.*
because (of) *Why can't you starve in the desert? Because of the sand which is there. (Sandwiches – get it??)*
centre 1 the middle of something. *... the centre of London.* [1]
2 a place where you can get advice or information. *Tourist Information Centre.* [3] *The Piccadilly Advice Centre* [12]
3 a place for shows and exhibitions. *The Barbican Centre.* [12]
each 1.1 *each of the...*
1.2 apiece. *They sell for 5p each.*
2 *each other.*
listen 1 *Listen to Myf checking her figures. Listen carefully.*
2 to take someone's advice. *I told you what to do but you wouldn't listen to me.*
modern 3 *modern art/modern legends.*
one personal pronoun = impersonal 'you', but formal. *I suppose one could drive. One tends to think of him as...*
travel 2 to move or go a distance. *I travelled 30 miles to buy those books!*
with 1 because of. *I can't see him standing in front of the TV. Mad with energy and boredom...* [2]

UNIT 7

across 1 from one side to another. *We did a line across the middle of the cake.*
2 on the other side. *There's a supermarket just across the street.* T
3 If something happens **across** a country or continent, it happens eveywhere in that country or continent. *He gave a number of speeches across the United States.* T
4 **across** is often used with parts of the body. *He had a severe pain across his chest.*
5 If you come **across** someone or something you meet them or find them by accident. *As a police officer I come across a lot of tourists.* [11]
cold 3 devoid of emotion. *A cold voice/look, cold eyes.*
details 1 an individual fact or piece of information. *What details can you remember about the car?*
2 If you examine or discuss something **in detail** you do it thoroughly, considering all the points. *We'll talk*

about it in more detail later on.
3 **into detail** *There's no need to go into detail right now.*
fine 1 OK, good, agreed. *Shall we go for a walk? Fine!*
1.1 *How are you? Fine, thanks.*
2 good. *soft leather of the finest quality.*
4 delicate, fragile, thin. *in fine detail/fine print.* T
5 noble, good. *a fine young man, a fine principle.* T
6 *a parking fine.* [11]
7 *fine weather...*
large 1 big. *The large, expensive cars seldom stopped.*
2 something that is important or serious. *There will be large changes.* T
mains 1 The **mains** are a system of wires or pipes supplying water, electricity or gas to a house. *... to convert mains electricity into heat.*
now 1 You start off by saying **now** when you want to get someone's attention and make sure they are listening before you continue. *Now, what would each of you cook if someone dropped in.*
pound 1 unit of money. *Pounds sterling.*
2 measurement of weight. *1 lb is just under ½ a kilo.*

UNIT 8

course 3 *in due course, in the course of his work, the course of history.*
force 1 violence. *use force to prevent...*
2 *I am forced to appear as if...*
3 social/economic/political forces. T
4 technical use: *the force acting on the joint work force.* T
instead 1 instead of = in place of. *Instead of going out, he decided to stay home and save money.*
1.1 *He brought us instead. Or: Instead, he...*
party 2 *Let's have a party.*
3 on a tour. *In a party of 12 people.* T
4 a person in a legal agreement or dispute. *... third party ...... the guilty party.*
state 1 to express clearly. *To state an opinion...* T
2 to say something, often as an official. *I will now state the government's position.* T
3 condition. *Everything was in an awful state.* T
4 belonging to the government. *I went to a state school.* [1]
5 part of a country. *California is the richest state in America.*
6 a country and its government. *Indonesia is one of six states belonging to ASEAN.*
through From one side to the other. *I'm going right through London and out the other side.*

UNIT 9

able 1 having the power/skill. *Many London stores are able to send goods direct to an overseas address.*
2 clever. *... an able child.* T
before 2 in front of. *A woman stood before them. Right before my eyes.*
ever 1 at any time. *If you ever go to London... If anybody ever asked me*

what I wanted to be... [5]
(NOTE: common in Conditional sentences; far less commonly used with the Present Perfect tense.)
2 after a comparison. *... bigger than ever before. The worst thing I've ever seen.* [12]
Misc: *ever so small* [2] = very small. *For ever and ever...*
exactly 1 accurately, correctly. *I forget who, exactly.* [6] *How come exactly the same stories...* [6]
2 often after a negative. *He didn't exactly block me, it wasn't exactly pleasant, but...* T
3 *"Like you", I said. "Exactly..."* (= I agree strongly.)
few 2 not many. *Very few banks open on Saturdays.* T
fine penalty. *A ticket for a parking fine.*
get 4 to cause someone to do something. *Get it stamped. Get your hair cut.*
have same use as 'get' above.
present gift. *What presents would you buy to send home to members of your family?*
provided/providing 1 to give or lend. *All meals will be provided by the hotel.* T
2 used to introduce a condition = on condition that... *This means provided you export what you have bought you can have the VAT amount refunded to you. You can see everything from the outside for nothing providing you're willing to walk or just take a bus.* [12]
say used to introduce an example. *If you go shopping, don't you particularly choose, say, a blue shirt against a pink shirt?* (= for instance)
show 1 to demonstrate, reveal, make apparent.
1.1 *... evidence to show that women do better.* T
1.2 to show affection/interest
1.3 to show physically. *I've got something to show you. Once I had to show a visitor around the office.* [4] *You will need to show your passport.* [9]
1.4 diagramatically. *The map shows... Differences are bound to show. Never mind, it won't show.* T
2 a TV show, show business, film show, *Show Times* [12]
under 2 *England under Mrs. Thatcher. Under the Retail Export Scheme...* [9]
until 1 up to the point in time. *I lived in Dublin until I was seven.* [1]
2 with a negative, meaning 'not before'. *I have nothing to say until I see my lawyer. You don't get the book until you've paid for it.* [9]

UNIT 10

actually 1 used to mark new information, or introduce a new topic. *Actually, the attempted burglary was worse than the real one.* [15]
2 in reality. *The 6278 actually comes in from the left.*
3 surprisingly. *We actually managed to reach the top.* [3]
4 a comment that is added by the way. *A woman, a friend of mine actually...*
5 'I'm afraid' – to soften a contradiction. *Actually, I don't think it's very good.*

ask 1 ask someone something = say something in the form of a question.
2 ask someone for/to do something = make a request. . . . *he was asked to leave. One day a man came up to my window and asked for a return ticket.*
far 1 *far bigger/more expensive; by far; far too much.*
2 a distance. *as far as; far from; far away.*
3 extent, degree. *It's gone too far. As far as possible . . . As far as I know . . .*
4 until or at a point in time. *The story so far . . . So far . . . That far ahead. This far . . .*
5 *As far as . . . is concerned, . . .* T
6 far from: *far from sure.* T
law 1 *It's against the law.*
2 *The law of averages/Parkinson's law.*
middle centre . . . *in the middle of a city.*
than 3 used in phrase **rather than** to express contrast. *These are called commons rather than moors.*

UNIT 11

building 2 . . . *the building of new houses . . . A hod carrier is one of the more menial jobs on a building site.*
feel 1 *You'd feel exhausted when you got there.* [6] *How are you feeling?* T
2 to believe, to be of the opinion that . . . *I've taken you on to B roads because I feel it's far more scenic.*
3 If you **feel like** something you want it or you want to do it. *I feel like something to eat. We felt like going home. I'll feel like putting on clothes of a different colour.* [9]
front 1 . . . *in front of me . . .* [1] *The front of the car . . .*
2 *front room/seat*
3 facing. *On the front of his T shirt . . .*
inside 1 preposition: *It's inside a boat.* [5]
2 adverb: . . . *went inside . . . plumber working inside.*
3 noun: the area within something. . . . *no sound from inside . . .* T
4 adjective: *inside pocket, inside information/story.* T
let 1 allow. *I just couldn't let you eat that pie.* [9]
2 *Let's turn the page.* [8] *Let's find out who it is.* [4]
3 to allow or cause the movement of something. *I would have let his tyres down. He was going to let all the air out of his tyres.*
4 to let someone know means to tell them. *Then I would have let the police know.*
5 If you **let** someone **off** you decide not to punish them. *Do you think they'll get let off?*
number 1 *A large number of tourists . . . A number of reasons why . . .*
2.1 verb: to number (off). *His days were numbered. Put the numbered instructions in order.* [7]
problem 1 a difficulty. *Parking problems.*
2 a puzzle which requires logical thought. *A mathematical problem.* T

used to 3 familiar with, accustomed to. *I'm not used to this car. You must get used to the ideas that . . . She had got used to walking everywhere.*
very 2 *From the very beginning . . . . . . right to the very end . . . The very same thing happened to me.* T

UNIT 12

almost very nearly, not completely. *Free, or almost, in London.*
hall a large room. . . . *concert hall . . .*
2 in a house or flat. *entrance hall.*
kind 1 type, sort. . . . *that kind of thing.* [1] . . . *some kind of very . . . trade.*
2 as a modifier (= sort of). *It was kind of funny . . .* (often American) T
3 nice, pleasant, generous. *'Like a lift into London?' 'You're very kind,' I said.* [6] *It was so kind of you to listen.* T
later 1 at a subsequent stage. *Later, you will find that . . . See you later!*
2 referring to the second or last part of a period in history. *She acted in two of his later plays.* T
3 . . . *not later than 24 hours after the accident.* [8]
mean 1 *What's meant by . . .? What does this mean?*
2 to be important to. *She means a lot to me.* T
3.1 *When you say we, do you mean . . . who . . .?* [3] *You see what I mean?* [9] *Does that mean that nobody else had noticed?* [8]
3.2 'I mean' as a filler. *I mean . . . you can see everything from the outside.*
4 to signify, indicate. *Although it was more expensive, it meant we had more time there.* [9]
5 *You mean prison? Did you really mean it about . . .*
6 *I meant to ring you but I forgot.* (= intended)
7 a method. *Which means of transport?* [6] *Use Jo as a means of jumping queues.*
8 by no means; in no way. *I'm fairly interested in sport but by no means football.* [2]
9 unwilling to spend money, or nasty. *The policeman is a pretty mean character.* [11] . . . *as mean as the devil.* [11]
quite 1 fairly; rather. *The driver's quite interested in what the trade is.* [12] *There's really quite a lot to do. It's quite a close community.* [1]
2 completely. *It was quite fantastic. It was quite a shock really.* [13] *I think that's quite true. You are quite right.* T
set 1 positioned. *A piece of wood, set at an angle . . .* [11]
2 *If you are set on booking in . . .* (= have definitely decided to)

UNIT 13

certain 1 particular. . . . *in certain areas . . ., Microwaves can reduce cooking times for certain foods.* [7]
2 sure. *Make certain that your home is really secure.*

possible 1 *As quickly as possible. Whenever possible . . .*
2 not so likely. *It's possible he'll come. There are two possible systems.* [7]
question 2 to express doubts about.
3 problem or point that needs to be discussed. *The question was – how did the fire start?*
3 an exam question.
take 1 'delexical' uses: *take the attitude that/take precautions/take place/take note of/take part in/take care to/take an interest in/take charge of/take an exam/take account of/take no notice.*
3 *It takes a long time./Take your time.*
4 holds. *It takes 280 cars.*

UNIT 14

after 1 later. *She likes . . . sweet things after lunch.* [2] *The day after tomorrow.*
2 If you are **after** someone or something you want them or it for some reason. *I think the police are after him.*
3 If you go after someone you follow them. *She ran after him as quickly as she could.*
4 used in phrasal verbs. *take/look after.*
bad 1 harmful, undesirable. . . . *to sweep out the bad luck and make a fresh start.*
2 'The bad' is used to refer to people of things that are bad. *The good or bad that came out of it was at least human bad or good.* T
3 evil. *He gave up his bad ways.* T
close *A close friend. A close relative. They are very close.*
lot 1.1 *I study a lot. Yes we do tend to use those rather a lot.*
new 3 beginning again. *New year's resolution.*
right 2 suitable. *At the right time . . . Do/say the right thing. The right decision.*
4 morally good. *It wouldn't be right to . . . You have no right to . . . Civil rights.* T
ring 2 *bells ringing.* T
4 a *familiar/classy/ring about it . . .* T
4 *A ring of faces. A key ring.* T
6 *A ring belonging to his wife.*
such referring back. *I prefer to have such men about me. There's no such thing as . . . at such a time.*
2.1 emphatic. *They made such a noise that we couldn't hear the music. The extent of the disaster was such that . . .*

UNIT 15

alone 1 on your own. *Don't walk alone at night in parks.*
2 only. . . . *costs based on petrol and parking alone.* [6]
3 lonely. *I felt alone.*
mind 1.1 where your thoughts are. *She let her mind wander.*
1.2 intellectual ability. *You have a good mind . . .*
2 way of thinking. *You have the mind of a child.*
3 objecting. *I want it back, if you don't mind.*

Words covered in Level 1

a
able
about
above
across
actually
address
afraid
Africa
after
afternoon
again
age
ago
agree
air
alive
all
almost
alone
along
already
also
always
am
America
American
an
and
another
answer, answered
any
anyone
anything
anyway
April
are
arm
army
arrangement
arrive, arrived
as
ask, asked
at
August
autumn
available
away
baby, babies
back
bad
bag
bank
be
because
become, became, become
bed
been
before
begin, begun, began
behind
bell
below
best
better
between
big
birth
bit
black
blue
body, bodies
book

born
borrow, borrowed
both
bottom
boy
bring, brought
Britain
British
brother
brown
building
bus
business
busy
but
buy, bought
by
call, called
can
car
carefully
carry, carried
cent
centre
century, centuries
certain
certainly
chair
chance
change, changed
cheap
check, checked
child, children
church
city, cities
class
close, closed
clothes
coast
coffee
cold
college
colour
come, came, come
common
compare
corner
cost
could
country
couple
course
cross, crossed
daily
dark
date
daughter
day
dead
December
decide, decided
definitely
degree
desk
detail
dialogue
did
difference
different
difficult
dinner
direction
do

doctor
door
double
down
drink, drank, drunk
drive, drove, driven
during
each
early
east
easy
eat, ate, eaten
education
eight
either
eleven
else
emergency
end
England
English
enjoy, enjoyed
enough
entrance
especially
Europe
even
evening
ever
every
everyone
everything
exact
exactly
examination
example
except
expensive
experience
eye
face
fact
family, families
famous
far
farm
fashionable
father
February
feel, felt
few
fifteen
fifty, fifties
figure
find, found
fine
finish, finished
fire
first
five
flat
floor
food
foot
for
forest
forget, forgot, forgotten
form, formed
forty, forties
forward
four
fourteen
France

free
French
Friday
friend
from
front
full
furniture
further
future
game
garden
general
get, got
girl
give, gave, given
glass, glasses
go, went, gone, going
good
goodbye
government
great
green
grey
ground
group
had
hair
half, halves
hall
hand
happen, happened
hard
hat
have
he
head
hear, heard
hello
help, helped
her
here
herself
high
hill
him
himself
his
history
hold, held
holiday
home
hope, hoped
hospital
hot
hour
house
how
however
hundred
husband
I
idea
if
ill
important
in
individual
information
inside
instead
instruction
interest, interested

132T

into
is
it
its
itself
January
job
July
June
just
keep, kept
key
kitchen
kind
know, knew, known
labour
lady
language
large
last
late
later
law
learn, learnt/learned
leave, left
left
less
let
letter
level
licence
lie, lay, lain
life, lives
light
like, liked
list
listen, listened
little
live, lived
London
long
look, looked
lose, lost
lot
love, loved
lunch
machine
magazine
main
make, made
man, men
many
map
March
married
matter
may
May
maybe
me
meal
mean, meant
meet, met
meeting
middle
might
mile
million
mind
mine
minute
miss
Miss
modern
moment
Monday
money
month
more
morning
most
mother
mountain

move, moved
Mr
Mrs
much
music
must
my
myself
name
national
nature
near
nearly
necessary
need, needed
neither
never
new
news
newspaper
next
nice
night
nine
no
none
normally
north
not
nothing
November
now
numbers
October
of
off
office
often
okay
old
on
once
one
ones
only
open
opposite
or
order
other
others
our
out
outside
over
own
page
paper
paragraph
parent
park
parliament
part
particularly
party, parties
pass, passed
past
pay, paid
people
per
perhaps
person
personal
phone, phoned
photograph
picture
pink
place
plan, planned
play, played
please
point
police

political
politician
possible
pound
power
practise
present
press, pressed
pretty
price
primary
private
probably
problem
public
put
quarter
question
quick
quite
radio
rain
rather
read
ready
really
reason
receive, received
recently
red
remember
repeat, repeated
reply, replied
report
rest
right
ring
river
road
roof
room
round
run, ran, run
same
Saturday
say, said
school
Scotland
sea
season
second
secretary, secretaries
see, saw, seen
seem, seemed
send, sent
sentence
September
service
set
seven
shall
shape
share, shared
she
shoe
shop
shopping
short
should
show, showed, shown
side
sign
since
single
sir
sister
sit, sat
situation
six
size
sky
sleep, slept
small

so
social
society
some
someone
something
sometimes
son
song
soon
sorry
sort
sound
south
speak, spoke, spoken
spend, spent
sport
spring
square
stairs
stand, stood
start, started
state
station
stay, stayed
still
stop, stopped
story, stories
straight
street
student
style
such
summer
sun
Sunday
supper
suppose, supposed
sure
surname
system
table
take, took, taken
talk, talked
tea
teacher
telephone
television
tell, told
ten
tend, tended
term
than
thank
that
the
their
them
themselves
then
there
therefore
these
they
thing
think, thought
third
thirty, thirties
this
those
thousand
three
through
Thursday
till
time
to
today
together
tomorrow
tonight
too
top

towards
town
traffic
travel, travelled
tree
trip
true
try, tried
Tuesday
turn, turned
twelve
twenty, twenties
two
type
under
understand, understood
university, universities
until
up
us
use, used
used
useful
usually
vary, varied
very
view
village
visit, visited
wait, waited
walk, walked
wall
want, wanted
war
warm
was
water
way
we
wear
weather
Wednesday
week
weekend
well
were
west
what
whatever
when
where
whether
which
while
white
who
why
wife, wives
will
window
winter
with
within
without
woman, women
word
work, worked
world
would
write, wrote, written
wrong
yeah
year
yellow
yes
yesterday
yet
you
young
your
yours
yourself
yourselves

Tapescripts and Transcripts

Collins COBUILD English Course 2 is accompanied by a set of three cassettes. These include both unscripted and scripted recordings. There is a booklet containing the transcripts of the unscripted recordings in the back cover of the Student's Book. Complete tapescripts and transcripts are given here. (* denotes an unscripted recording.)

UNIT 1

 *

JM: How old are your children?
CM: Erm, I've got two ... I've got erm, a three year old, a girl, called Lucy Claire and erm, a nearly one and a half year old, who's called Neil.

JM: My son's called Joe.
CM: How old is he?
JM: He's about 15 months, and er, just about learning to walk ...

JM: At the moment I'm looking for jobs, and erm, maybe moving out of London.

JM: I work in Hillingdon, which is, erm, West London.

CM: Before I had the children I was an insurance broker.

CM: I used to work at a desk and have files of, erm, clients, businesses, in front of me and I would deal through – with their insurance needs ...

2a *

CM: What do you teach?
JM: I teach English in a state school, and er, at the moment I'm looking for jobs, and erm, may be move, moving out of London, er –
CM: So you teach in London.
JM: Mm.
CM: Is it, do you work for the ILEA?
JM: No, I work in Hillingdon which is, erm, West London. It's a very, er, pleasant school, and er, I'd be sorry to leave it, but there's no chance of promotion there so I'm going to move on.
CM: So where will you look, do you think?
JM: Well, I'm just applying for a job in Telford, and we had to look on the map, er –
CM: Where's that? Near Birmingham, is it?
JM: It is, yes, but we had to look on the atlas to find where it was. Erm, it's ... erm, it's a new town I think, and er ....

5

Both of you decide exactly where you would hide something small. But don't tell your partner. For example, in the vase on the bottom shelf of the bookcase on the left of the fire.
See how quickly you can guess which place the other hid their small object in. Rule: The other person can only answer yes or no so you must phrase your questions accordingly.
Play once each. Try to guess in as few as possible questions. (Count them.)
See which of you used the least questions.
Then summarise in one sentence exactly where your partner hid their object.

F: OK, it's your turn. I've got a small bunch of keys and I've hidden them somewhere in that picture.
M: Ah, let me see. Are they, erm, inside the teacup on the table?
F: No.
M: Er ... beside the chair?
F: No.
M: No? Erm ... on top of the mantlepiece?
F: No.
M: Oh dear, er ... behind the clock?
F: No – that's four.
M: Erm ... in the flower vase?
F: No.
M: What about under the radio?
F: No.
M: Behind the radio?
F: No.
M: Erm ... inside the slippers?
F: No – that's eight.
M: Erm ... behind the knitting wool on the shelves?
F: No.
M: .. between the books on the shelves?
F: No.
M: Where can they be, where can they be? Er ...
F: Shall I give you a hint – that you were close?
M: I was close?
F: In the right area.
M: When I was between the books?
F: Mmm.
M: Er ... inside the pot on the shelves there?
F: No, but you're still close.
M: Behind the pot?
F: No.
M: Under the pot?
F: No.
M: Erm ... behind the lampshade?
F: No – that's thirteen!
M: Erm ... on the shelf?
F: No – fourteen.
M: In that – side that little jar there with a – a lid on?
F: That's it, you've got it in fifteen!
M: Oh dear, what a long time I took! Erm, now, I've hidden a pen.
F: Mhm mhm. You've hidden a pen.
M: Yes.
F: OK. Is it on top of the table?
M: No.
F: Is it underneath the carpet?
M: No.

134T

F: Is it in the ball of knitting wool?
M: No.
F: ... like the needles. Erm, is it amongst the books ...
M: No.
F: ... on the shelf? No.
M: Four questions.
F: That's four. Is it under the flower pot?
M: No – five.
F: Is it inside the pot there on the, erm, in front of the fire?
M: No.
F: No ... beside the box?
M: No.
F: In the pot of – in the vase of flowers?
M: No.
F: Oh dear, how many questions have I had?
M: One, two, three, four, five, six, seven, eight.
F: Oh dear, eight, eight. Erm, is it on top of the shelf, there above the box?
M: No.
F: Oh dear. Is it in the letter rack?
M: Yes.
F: Oh, wonderful! How many?
M: That's ten questions.
F: Ah, right, so you had the pen ...
M: Yes
F: ... in the letter rack, and I did it in ten.
M: And you hid a bunch of keys in the little pot on the right hand shelves up at the top there, and I did it in fifteen.
F: So I beat you by five.
M: Right, well done.

 *

CM: Where did you live when you were a child?
JM: I was born, er in fact, in the front room of the house where my parents still live. And that was in Warrington, which in those days was in Lancashire, but now it's in Cheshire.
CM: What was – Did you like where you lived? Was it ...?
JM: Erm ... sometimes. Erm, I hated being at school there. Erm, it was an all boys' school, and I didn't like it. Erm, but living there was –
CM: What do you mean, an old boys' school?
JM: An all boys' school.
CM: Ah! I beg your pardon!
JM: Erm. The – it was a boys' grammar school which was even worse. And erm, so my secondary school I didn't enjoy. Primary school, er, was okay, and Warrington itself, it's a – quite a close community or it was, then, and er, so you did feel at home, and I still feel at home when I go back.
CM: How long have you been away from there?
JM: Erm, I left when I was eighteen, when I –
CM: To go to university?
JM: Yes. And I haven't been back since really, for very long. But it's still home, it still seems to be home.
JM: Where were you, erm, born and brought up?
CM: Well, I was born, erm, and lived until I was seven, in Dublin.
JM: Mm.
CM: Ireland. And then –
JM: Yes. One could have guessed from –
CM: Yeah! From my accent?
JM: Mm.
CM: Erm, and then I, I was brought over here when I was seven. My parents came to live in England. And I've lived here ever since.
JM: Mm.
CM: But if I have an accent after so many years it's because we were a small Irish family in a very English community, and it was very important to my parents anyway, that we should remain Irish, and erm, that we, the children, should, erm, retain our Irish identity.
JM: So do you remember Ireland at all?

CM: Oh I go back there every year. In fact I'm going on my holidays there tomorrow!
JM: Oh great! And er, is it – do you have – is it, what, family and friends still there?
CM: Yes. Mummy and Daddy went back to Ireland, some time ago.
JM: Yeah. Oh, so that's good.

 *

SB: How many languages do you speak?
CM: Erm, well, I learnt, erm English, French and German at school, I know a tiny bit of Italian and a tiny bit of Greek, from travels, but I can't say that I really speak any of the foreign languages to any degree, any more.
SB: Well apart from English and American which is fairly similar, I can get by in French and I can struggle through reading Italian and that's about it.

12c

Meriel West, Travel Agent, currently working in New York.
We were taught French at school, but very badly. We had to memorise lists of verbs, instead of being given sentences to learn which we could use in everyday speaking. I took another French course a few years ago, and we learnt some quite useful things. I also tried to learn Russian, but I did not get very far, although it was interesting. In fact I found a number of words have nearly the same pronunciation in both Russian and English.

Richard H. Turner, student of Engineering at Loughborough University.
The foreign languages I was taught at school were Latin, German and French. However, the only language I actually learnt was French.
(Although I 'picked up' English at the early age of one.)
My French has been particularly useful. For example, reading the instructions on imported packets of French coffee. And on one occasion, whilst on holiday in France, when a vineyard owner explained how he produced champagne.
When in France, the most useful phrase is 'Parlez-vous anglais?'' which means 'Do you speak English?' However I once mistakenly asked a puzzled French man if he spoke French! (He did.)

Caroline Egerton, publisher.
I learnt French, German and Spanish at school and went on to study German at University. Later, I spent two months in Malay speaking countries, followed by two years in Thailand. Malay and Thai ought to feel quite different to speak from the European languages, but for some reason, when I tried to speak Malay, it was always Spanish that tried to come out. In Thailand, if I couldn't think of a particular word in Thai, it was always the German word that came into my head. I think it has something to do with the rhythms of the languages.

E. Turner, Cordon Bleu cook and caterer.
What did I learn at school? Not a lot! I studied Latin and French, but they made little impression. However, I enjoyed English, both language and literature. Reading was, and still is, a great source of pleasure.
French later became important when I took an advanced cookery course, and all the menus and specialist terms were in French. This caused dreadful problems for the Americans on the course who had only learnt Spanish at school, not French.

| 14b | *

CM: Erm, I'm Catherine McKinna. And, erm, who are you?
CF: I'm Caroline Frost.
JM: I'm John Mannion.
SB: I'm Stephen Bowden.
CF: I work for a publishers.
SB: I'm a graduate student in anthropology.
CM: I'm so sorry, I've forgotten your name again.
SB: Stephen Bowden.
CM: You're Stephen . . . Right.

| 15a | *

CF: Right.
MJ: Mm, he has er short hair –
CF: Mmm.
MJ: Er, dark erm, and he's small and thin and, erm, he's got on cord trousers and a belt.

CF: It's Alan!
MJ: Do you want to describe someone?
CF: Mm, yes. Okay . . . She has dark hair. She's quite small, medium height to quite small. Erm, she's wearing trousers and a yellowish cardigan and she's got a very strange accent, and she likes to eat sweet things after lunch.
MJ: Is it Jane?
CF: No, it's you!
MJ: Me, Oh! That's a good one. It didn't occur to me it might be me! Oh well.
CF: I thought, I thought you'd get it when I said about the accent.
MJ: Well, I was just . . . It didn't even even occur to me that you were describing me you see!

| 18b | *

CM: Right, we've got to look at the picture of this footballer which I'll just pass round. And erm . . . Ah I'm sorry. There are two. Erm, it summarises the injuries he has sustained during his ten-year career. Approximately how many injuries has he had? And then how many injuries have you had altogether as a group. Have you had as many as, or more than he?
CF: Mm. How many has he had?
SB: Broken ankle.
JM: Mm.
SB: Broken leg.
JM: Yes, erm, damaged fingers. Er –
CM: And a hand isn't it?
JM: Yes.
SB: Yeah. And either a broken collar bone or a broken arm. I think that's –
CF: And a broken nose, by the look of it.
JM: Yes.
SB: Er, yeah, there's an arrow pointing to his shoulder. One to his hip.
JM: Yes. Erm.
SB: So, one two, three four, five, six, about seven.
JM: Seven.
CF: Seven.
CM: At least.
JM: At least.
CM: They're the apparent ones.

| 18d | *

CM: I broke my collar bone when I was quite small. I fell off my bicycle. And erm, I, I'm, I have to say that was so painful, because it wasn't something that was apparent immediately and I had to spend a whole night, supposedly asleep in, in bed and knowing that I was really very unwell. And it wan't diagnosed until the next day when I was in plaster, well not in plaster, but in

bandages for a long time afterwards.
CF: I've never broken anything, but I've had lots of stitches. Erm . . . here.
CM: On your chin.
CF: My sister gave me the bumps on the seesaw, and I went and split my chin on the handle, the metal handle.
SB: I've broken one bone in the one hand, which I then had to sit and write an exam with – this broken hand which was not fun.
CF: Was it the right hand?
SB: The right hand.
CF: Oh dear!
SB: And, I also tore all the ligaments in one knee, on a skiing accident
JM: Mm . . . No, I've never broken any bones so far. Erm. Just some very nasty cuts. Once, erm, I – we'd been collecting firewood for a bonfire, and we got this old chair, and erm, we were chopping it up, and I got my little finger between the axe and, er the wood.
CF: Goodness me!
JM: And I nearly chopped my hand off, but, er my finger off.
SB: So that's about five?
JM: Yes, about five. Less than he had in ten years.
SB: Oh yes.

| 20b | *

JM: Er, the first thing on my list would be that erm . . . that I have a sense of humour, er, and that I would need to meet somebody who also had a sense of humour. I'm also, erm . . . I suppose, interested in the Arts. So, erm, it'd be – I'd need to – I'd want to meet somebody who was, erm, interested in the cinema and the theatre and so on. And, somebody who read a lot, because I do. And, who wasn't terribly interested in sport because I absolutely hate sport. But er –
CM: Even taking part in sport?
JM: Oh, participation in sport is even worse then actually having to watch the stuff . . . .
Erm. Yes. So, what er, would you put in your list?
CM: Ah, I find it very difficult to tell anybody anything about me. I suppose erm, I'd probably give them my physical characteristics, that fact that I'm, erm, not very tall. I'm five foot two and a half, and that half an inch is very important to me. And that, that I have red hair, and that I'm Irish. But probably they would get that anyway. And I would say that I'm, erm, I'm fairly interested in sport but by no means football, I couldn't meet anybody who was interested in football. Because I abhor it.
JM: Mm.
CM: Erm. And I, and I would say that I like, er meeting people. I like gregarious activities. And I like talking.
JM: Yes.
CM: And I like reading . . . .

| 21 |

San Francisco disc jockey Don Sherwood tells of an argument in a friend's house after a weekend of sports television. The wife complained, 'You love football more than you love me.'
The husband replied, 'Yeah, but I still love you more than basketball.'

| 23 | *

CM: Well, er, I, I haven't won money. Erm, I don't think I've won – oh, I, I have won money. Er, a couple of years ago, when I was pregnant with my first child, erm, my husband put a bet on – is it the Derby? – some, some big race, erm, or the National, is that the one that's at – ?
SB: With the fences at Aintree.
CM: Yes, that's the one.
SB: The Grand National.
CM: And I won. I won on Corbière I think the horse

was. I was so proud I jumped up and down. Erm, I was really really pleased. And I won the next year, but not as much as I'd won the first year. So that's the only time I've ever won money.

---

 *

SB: Well, you could start by categorising them just according to size. Whether they're big or small.
CF: Mm. And then into, what? Birds, and others. Reptiles, perhaps?
SB: Birds, reptiles, amphibians, fish, mammals, insects, spiders. And –
CF: You could categorise them subjectively. Which ones you like and which ones you don't.
SB: Yeah. I suspect that would probably come out the same way as which are mammals and which are not because people seem to prefer cats and dogs to snakes and, snakes and spiders . . .
CF: Mm, why do you think that is?
SB: It's, I suppose it's because they're warm.
CF: Mm. More like ourselves.
SB: Yeah.
CF: Perhaps.
SB: And they probably respond more to attention. I, I've never really seen a spider respond to attention very much.
CF: Mind you, a mouse is a mammal isn't it?
SB: Yeah.
CF: A lot of people don't like them.
SB: That's the old cliché about them running up skirts and things. I think they're quite cute.
CF: Well, my mother actually does stand on a chair, and scream. I was very surprised because she's quite rational.
SB: The mouse is probably far more terrified than she is.
CF: Yes.
SB: No, rats get a really bad deal.
CF: Mm. Mind you, they're not very attractive.
SB: I don't know. It's just they tend to live in unattractive conditions.
CF: Mm. And spread disease.
SB: Well, that's only because – that's partly because they live in unattractive conditions.

The Dog Lovers by Spike Milligan
So they bought you
And kept you in a
Very good home
Central heating
TV
A deep freeze
A very good home
No one to take you
For that lovely long run –
But otherwise
'A very good home'
They fed you Pal and Chum
But not that lovely long run,
Until, mad with energy and boredom
You escaped – and ran and ran and ran
Under a car.
Today they will cry for you –
Tomorrow they will buy another dog.

Holes In The Sky by Spike Milligan
There are holes in the sky
Where the rain comes in.
But they're ever so small.
That's why rain is thin.

Listen and see if you can hear the difference. For example:
M1: I'm fairly interested in sport – NEUTRAL
F1: Not very tall – NEUTRAL
M1: They're ever so small – STRONG
F1: It's a very pleasant school – STRONG
F1: She's got a very strange accent – STRONG
M2: . . . squash and tennis, though I'm not very good at them
F2: English and American, which are fairly similar
M1: I make friends fairly easily
F1: It's quite a close community
M2: It's quite a close community
F2: She's quite small
M1: She's quite small
F1: They are ever so small
M2: It was so painful
F2: It's extremely cold outside
M1: It can be terribly cold in winter
F1: . . . who was not terribly interested in sport
M2: I absolutely hate sport!
F1: I was really very very unwell
M1: she looks a bit tired
F1: You're a bit late!
M2: a bit shorter than you
F2: a lot shorter, in fact
M1: much shorter
F1: generally quite healthy
M2: generally quite healthy
F21: It's rather expensive
M1: It's rather expensive
F1: Extremely expensive
M2: That's quite enough!

UNIT 3

JM: Last year we had a holiday in Northumberland. We went up by car. Took a very long time getting there because we stopped to walk along Hadrian's Wall for a bit. Er, we stayed in a farmhouse for a week, did a lot of walking along the coast, swam in the sea.
JC: Whe- er, when you say 'we', d'you mean, who, who's – ?
JM: Oh, m- me and my two children.
JC: Just you and your two children?
JM: Just me and the children.
JC: Yep.
JM: Yes, er, we swam –
JC: Uhum.
JM: It was very cold in the North Sea, but was very nice. Went to Holy Island one day.
JC: Uhum.
JM: Er, went up the Cheviot one day.
JC: The what?
JM: The Cheviot –
JC: Oh.
JM: which is the highest hill in Northumberland, highest mountain in Northumberland, I think. Very lucky to get to the top of it, because people we met on it said they'd been many times before and never managed to get to the top, 'cause it was normally very boggy, but it was a very dry summer when we went –
JC: Oh I see.
JM: So we actually managed to reach the top.
JC: Uhum.
JM: Erm, had a very nice, active week's holiday, quiet and peaceful but active. Oh and we went out in a boat one day and saw seals and things round – I've forgotten where.
JC: Wh- ha- have you, erm –?
JM: Lindisfarne or –
JC: Have you erm, have you been before to, er – ?
JM: No, never been before to Northumberland, no.

JC: I see.
JM: That was why we wanted to go.
JC: It's qui- quite different,
JM: Yes, yeah.
JC: Okay.
JM: And that was how we spent our, our holiday

29b *

JC: Right, well there was, er, I think I got most of the answers, erm, you told me that it was you and your two children who went on holiday, so that's the three of you went and you went by car. How did they travel? By car. How long was the holiday? You went for a week. Where did you stay? I'm sure you told me where you stayed, but I can't for the life of me remember. Did you tell me where you stayed?
JM: Yes.
JC: You – must have been a hotel.
JM: Ah, I'm, I'm n- . . .
JC: In, oh, oh, in Ch- Ch- Cheviots. No. I, I just can't remember where you stayed. Got absolutely no idea. Erm, what was the weather like? Well you say it was a dry summer, so the weather must have been sunny and nice and well, you, you told me masses about how you spent the time walking up mountains, swimming in the cold North Sea, all that sort of thing. Have you been on a similar holiday before? Well, I had to actually ask you that one, and you said no you hadn't, and then I didn't quite manage to get in 'Will you go again?'. You weren't going to tell me that, so I don't er, I've got no idea whether you have, I mean, it sounds like you had a good time, so the answer is probably you would, yes, but, er, I don't know definitely what the answer to that is.

33b *

JM: Then we move, move on to Postcard Speculations. I'll read this one out. Er. There's a postcard for us to look at.
MJ: Are you supposed to read the back as well?
JM: Mm. Read the two postcards. Note where they come from. Spec- speculate about who the senders are, and their reasons for sending the postcards. Do you think they are both away on holiday? What do you think will happen as a result of each of these postcards?
MJ: Can I see that?
JM: 'Dear Dave, Jane, Jenny and Becky,' mine says. 'My sister lives very close to this picture. The Blue Mountains are spectacular. We're having a family time here till we leave on Friday the eleventh. This is to inform you that we've changed our flight. We're flying out on – from Sydney on QF1 E.T.A. 21.10 just in case you, you're thinking of coming to the airport. See you soon,' and then I can't read the signature. So, this one is obviously –
MJ: It's a friend of theirs that's gone to Australia? The Blue Mountains are in Australia, aren't they?
JM: That's right. Yes.
MJ: And erm, erm . . . The purpose of the postcard is, er . . . to tell, erm, the Willises about the holiday and basically to suggest that they might like to come and pick them up.
JM: Yes. It suggests – 'If you are thinking of' rather than, er, 'please be at the airport'. But yes, I imagine, erm, they probably will turn up. So what –
MJ: I can't read the name
JM: No, I can't read the name either.

33c *

MJ: Erm, the other postcard is a picture of, er, a bridge in Dublin, and, erm, it's written to Becky Willis and it says, 'Sorry you couldn't come to the airport. Miss you lots. Say hi to your parents from me. Thanks for the

138T

weekend. Please write. Anne Claire has my address. Amanda.'
JM: Mm.
MJ: Perhaps this, erm, this is a friend of Becky's who, er, left, erm, and was hoping Becky would be able to come to the airport and say goodbye to her.
JM: Mm. So it sounds as though, either maybe she lives in Ireland and, and er, has gone back, or has just moved to Ireland and er, won't be back for some time.
MJ: Mm.
JM: With the invitation to write.
MJ: It's, well, yes, I suppose so. 'Thanks for the weekend.' Do you suppose this, erm, this girl went to Singapore for the weekend from Ireland?
JM: Singapore?
MJ: Yes, it's written to Becky in Singapore.
JM: Oh, I see. Oh, erm. Mm.
MJ: I don't know.
JM: No, perhaps they, er –
MJ: I think we move on from here.
MJ: Erm, as a result of this postcard, erm, I think Becky will write back.
JM: Yes, probably. If she's still in Singapore or wherever.
MJ: Right. I think that's the end of that one.
JM: Okay.

38a *

CM: Future holidays. Where are you going for your next holiday, and what are you going to do?
SB: I don't know. I don't know when I'm next going to have a holiday. I – if I'm lucky, my room-mate next year will be able to get us tickets to go down to Jamaica for Christmas. So that will probably be my next holiday.
CM: That sounds really lovely.
SB: I'll just laze in the sun and keep warm.
CM: Why can he get you tickets?
SB: It's a she, but erm her father –
CM: Sorry! Beg your pardon.
SB: Her father, er, has a place there I think, and, erm, tends to provide her with tickets and she said she can usually get them for friends.
CM: How lovely!
SB: So –

38b *

CM: Erm, my next holiday is tomorrow, hopefully. Erm, I'm going, I'm going to the West Coast of Ireland and, er, I'm taking my two children with me. My husband is joining us in a week's time. I'm going to be driving, most of the time, on the journey. And, er, when we get there I'm going to be – we're going to stay with my parents. They've got a holiday house on the West Coast. And, er, I expect it will be – it's mainly going to be a very relaxing bucket-and-spade holiday for the children.
SB: It'll rain all the time.
CM: Well when you go to the West Coast of Ireland you have to expect rain, so we always pack our wellingtons, and our anoraks and cagoules, and erm, and then if we get sunshine that's just a bonus. So – but mainly I think it's just going to be a very relaxing time. I'm looking forward to it.
SB: Mm. Okay.

UNIT 4

43b *

SB: Look at this list of jobs. Decide which three of these jobs are the best paid in Britain, and which two are the worst paid. Do you think any of them are underpaid? So we have a nurse in a hospital, a miner at the coalface, a shop assistant, a car-assembly worker, a bank manager, a dentist, a schoolteacher, a

plumber, a top professional footballer, and a nuclear scientist.
CF: Mm.
SB: Well. I reckon a nuclear scientist is paid reasonably well.
CF: What about a professional footballer? They get a lot of money don't they?
SB: Too much.
CF: Mm.
SB: Yes, that must be top of the list. Bank manager must also be pretty high up.
CF: Got no idea.
SB: Anybody who handles money tends to get paid a lot.
CF: Mm. What about the lowest? Schoolteacher.
SB: A schoolteacher, or a nurse.
CF: Mm.
SB: Who are both I would say underpaid. But I think a shop assistant probably gets even less. I don't know whether it's – I'd say the shop assistant and the car-assembly worker were probably the two worst paid. But what about the dentist? He must get well paid.
CF: Mm. Dentists are well paid, I think. It's hard to know isn't it?
SB: Yeah. They're probably worth the money though. I think – I think the footballers are probably overpaid and I think – I think bank managers are overpaid, but then, anybody who's paid more than me is probably overpaid.
CF: So we both agree that teachers and nurses are underpaid.
SB: Teachers and nursers are definitely underpaid.
CF: Mm.

44a *

CF: Mm. What about the lowest? Schoolteacher.
SB: A schoolteacher, or a nurse.
CF: Mm.
SB: Who are both I would say underpaid. But I think a shop assistant probably gets even less. I don't know whether it's – I'd say the shop assistant and the car-assembly worker were probably the two worst paid. But what about the dentist? He must get well paid.
CF: Mm. Dentists are well paid, I think. It's hard to know isn't it?
SB: Yeah. They're probably worth the money though. I think – I think the footballers are probably overpaid and I think – I think bank managers are overpaid, but then, anybody who's paid more than me is probably overpaid.
CF: So we both agree that teachers and nurses are underpaid.
SB: Teachers and nurses are definitely underpaid.
CF: Mm.

45c

A woman went to a dentist in Baghdad to have a tooth out and was told it would be the equivalent of £30. 'But that's ridiculous!' she said. 'My husband has to work two hours for that.'
'Madam,' the dentist replied, 'If you like, I will take two hours.'

Liked that one did you, yeah, well here's another, here's another.

My bank manager had a lot of trouble with his hot water system. Finally he called a plumber who fixed everything in about half an hour and gave him a bill for £75. 'But that works out at £150 an hour. I'm a bank manager and I don't make that kind of money.'
'I'm not surprised,' said the plumber. 'Neither did I when I was a bank manager.'

---

46 *

CF: What's the lowest-paid job you've ever had?

SB: Probably way back when I was a paperboy. Or babysitting maybe. That's sixpence an hour –
CF: How old were you then?
SB: Must have been about eight.
CF: Babysitting at eight?
SB: Well, little sisters were even smaller than me, so –
CF: Yes, I think my worst pay was in a factory – cake factory when I was a student and I can't remember how much it was, it wasn't much more than a pound an hour. But it was pretty awful.
SB: Mm. I, I've got a friend who's a waitress who claims that she gets about twenty dollars an hour including tips.
CF: Mm.
SB: As a waitress. Which is, what, twelve pounds an hour.
CF: Mm.
SB: And sometimes even as much as two hundred dollars in a day.
CF: So that's mainly from tips.
SB: That's mainly from tips. I think if it wasn't for the tips she wouldn't be getting much money at all.
CF: Yeah.
SB: And I think that might be where women have a slight advantage. I think they tend to get tipped more generously than men.

47b *

CF: Mm. In general do you think women receive the same pay for the same work as men?
SB: I think in general they don't.
CF: Mhm.
SB: On the other hand, it's not always possible to – they're not always getting – doing exactly the same job.
CF: Mhm.
SB: So you don't always know whether it is. But I think generally yes, they do get less pay –
CF: Mm.
SB: – er, for the same amount of work or equivalent work.
CF: And do you think that's fair?
SB: No. Of course not.
CF: Mm . . .
SB: I think this is, is definitely underpaid. I think anybody who is expected to work eight and a half hours of work a day should be receiving more than just one twenty an hour, even it they are just from school.
CF: Mm.
SB: I don't think that should make that much difference. And if that was a union work, the union would probably insist on a wage of, well, at least a hundred and eight pounds a week.

49a *

JM: He's obviously some sort of business person.
CM: He looks a bit like Clive Sinclair –
JM: He does, actually.
CM: with a little bit more hair, to me.
JM: Mm. Yes. But he's got – is that, erm –
CM: Is he looking into a microscope, I wonder?
JM: Yes, he looks sort of business-like and scientific, doesn't he?
CM: Mm.
JM: With the glasses. Erm, add to that. But it looks a bit – Is it a tie? Or, is it a, erm, a piece of rope or something.
CM: No, well it looks like a piece of rope or .... Here let me have a look.
JM: Seems to be a street scene, because there are people behind him – looks like a pair of jeans. So it might be, erm –
CM: Well it looks like a window behind him to me.
JM: Oh.
CM: Sorry about that.
JM: That's okay.
CM: Yes, you're right. There's something definitely hanging down.

JM: Mm.
CM: From h-, from his chin.
JM: Erm, and he's concentrating ....

49b *

JM: Er, right, let's find out who it is. What now?
CM: What now? What – What –
JM: Oh I see. You get a bigger keyhole.
CM: Yes, that's right.
JM: Ah that's – erm –
CM: Well you take it over and have a good – Oh.
JM: It's a car, I think. Do you think this is a car?
CM: Oh yes, he's, he's looking into, in – he's probably talking to somebody, who's getting in or out of a car.
JM: Mm.
CM: Or he's taking something out of a car. I think you're right.
JM: Perhaps it's the Queen or somebody like that. I don't know. Erm. Or maybe he's he's putting something into the car because there's a – er –
CM: A bag or something.
JM: – a bag there, a plastic bag. Yes.
CM: Well, yes.
JM: Mm.
CM: Perhaps he's still a scientist and he's got a bagload of scientific –
JM: Mm. Yeah. And that piece of string doesn't appear to go anywhere, does it?
CM: Well –
JM: It's just hanging in the air.
CM: Could it belong to the door of the car?
JM: I think it's definitely over his shoulder.
CM: I don't know.
JM: Okay. Ah now. Those – Are those balloons?
CM: It certainly looks like it and I still can't see what he's got around his neck ... He's a sportsman, I – it looks like an airtex shirt, so perhaps he's some kind of sportsman.
JM: Yes. No, I don't – I think we've got it completely wrong. I –
CM: He's loading the boot of a car, isn't he?
JM: No. No, I think this is a boat. It's inside a boat and he's some sort of fisherman.
CM: No, I disagree. I think that's the boot of a car. You can see the symbols on the top there are the back window. That's what I would say, anyway.
JM: Mm. Oh yes, it, it would be a very expensive car. Erm ...
CM: That's right.
JM: Yes, definitely a car.
CM: It's a car.

51

JM: Ah. Are they – ? Yes. I, I, that's a – an air cylinder, and that's a balloon. So –
CM: He's an ... could he be – ? What are these up here?
JM: I think those are the balloons he's already inflated.
CM: Oh, so he sells balloons.
JM: Yes.
CM: Perhaps at a zoo or a fair or something like that.
JM: Yes ...
CM: Oh, those balloons that erm, are full of helium or something. Yes.
JM: Yes, full of hydrogen or helium. Yes. And er, so he's obviously –
CM: So what's this – what's all this around about? Is he in a car park somewhere?
JM: Yes. It looks like a car park. And here we are.
CM: Oh yes.
JM: Inflated balloons.
CM: And this one looks like a rabbit.
JM: Yes.
CM: Oh yes. They're rather nice shapes. Rather pretty.

JM: And that's a truck there.
CM: That's right.
JM: So, so it's obviously the sort of the, the back of a ... mm, fair or something where, erm –
CM: That's right. There's a seat there for somebody to sit down, so, er – Nice pretty colours there too.
JM: Yeah. Right.

52b *

CM: So, when, when you, you go off to Telford or wherever it is that you might end up, are you going for a head of departmentship?
JM: Er, yes. But erm, really I haven't had quite enough experience, but –
CM: So you're just trying to jump a few steps.
JM: Yes, yes.
CM: Good for you.
JM: We, I, I discovered the joys of word processing the other day and er, I put all my applications and things on CV – er, onto a word processor, and er, I intend just sending off for every job that comes up now because it's just a question of putting in the address, and deleting the irrelevant sections.
CM: Yes.
JM: And er, should make the whole process a lot easier.
CM: Mm.

 55

M1: On his first day selling ice-cream in the cinema, an assistant sold more during the interval than anyone had ever done before. When his success was repeated day after day, the manager decided to keep an eye on him. He found that ten minutes before the interval the enterprising assistant turned up the heating.

F1: In the sweet shop, one sales assistant always had customers lined up waiting while other assistants stood around with nothing to do. The owner of the shop asked the popular one for her secret. 'It's easy,' she said. 'The other assistants scoop up more than a pound of sweets and then start taking away. I always scoop up less than a pound and then add to it.'

F2: Upon returning to his office, my husband stopped at his secretary's desk to see if there were any messages for him. There were none, but he couldn't help noticing a note to his secretary from a recently hired young clerk-typist. It read: 'Dear Ida, I'm in the lounge. Wake me up for coffee break. Sally.'

UNIT 5

58a *

CM: We've each got to say a little bit about our favourite subject at school. And which were the ones, erm, that we liked the least and for what reasons. Why don't you start?
CF: Right. Well. My favourite was always English, I think because I liked writing stories. The least favourite was always maths. I was awful at it. I think I, erm, didn't concentrate on some vital bits and missed out and then it just got worse and worse. I used to sit at the back and giggle quite a lot. And er, so it was pretty disastrous, really.
SB: I liked science subjects, but I think that was because the teachers were very much better in that than in subjects like French which I really didn't like at all. I didn't mind things like maths and English, because I could do them, but it – the languages, French, Latin, Greek, got a bit, you know – I got a bit behind, and the teachers weren't that helpful, so I didn't like those as much –
JM: What did you dislike?
SB: Well, French ....

JM: Erm, my least favourite subject was sport. Er PE. I hated it.
CM: But why was that? Just because it required physical exertion?
JM: No I had a sadistic PE teacher.
CM: Oh really?
CF: Mm. We did as well . . .
CM: Did you?
CF: Yes. She wrote the most dreadful report on me I've ever had. It was 'Caroline's movements are so uncontrolled at times that she's a danger to herself and others.'
JM: Yes. They do that even now.

58b

Teachers by Michael Rosen
Rodge said,
'Teachers – they want it all ways –
You're jumping up and down on a chair
or something
and they grab hold of you and say,
"Would you do that sort of thing in your own home?"

'So you say, "No"
And they say,
"Well don't do it here then."

'But if you say, "Yes, I do it at home."
They say,
"Well, we don't want that sort of thing
going on here
thank you very much."

'Teachers – they get you all ways,'
Rodge said.

---

61 *

JM: Er, right, let's find out who it is. What now?
CM: What now? What – What –
JM: Oh I see. You get a bigger keyhole.
CM: Yes, that's right.
JM: Ah that's – erm –
CM: Well you take it over and have a good – Oh.
JM: It's a car, I think. Do you think this is a car?
CM: Oh yes, he's, he's looking into, in – he's probably talking to somebody, who's getting in or out of a car.
JM: Mm.
CM: Or he's taking something out of a car. I think you're right.
JM: Perhaps it's the Queen or somebody like that. I don't know. Erm. Or maybe he's he's putting something into the car because there's a – er –
CM: A bag or something.
JM: – a bag there, a plastic bag. Yes.
CM: Well, yes.

63a *

JM: How many words for different parts of the body can you find in the pictures? E.g. the head of a pin. So, there is the head of a pin.
MJ: The eye of a needle.
JM: Mhm. The mouth of a tunnel.
MJ: Er, the seat of a chair.
JM: Mhm. The –
MJ: The face of a clock.
JM: Yes. The foot of a mountain. Headmaster's door.
MJ: Mm, yes. The headma-, headmaster's door, yes. Erm, the –
JM: Legs of a table.
MJ: Legs of a table, yeah.
JM: And of a chair, obviously. Then there's a finger. Er . . . of erm, on that sign. And of course, back. Erm, what about the car? Erm, parts of the body. The boot. No, that's not part of a car. You wear that.
MJ: No, that's not a part of the body. It's not part of the body is it?
JM: No, no. Erm.

MJ: Erm.
JM: Well, I can't think of anything for a car. Erm . . . the arms of a chair. That's one.
MJ: The arms of a chair, yes.
JM: Erm.
MJ: What about the back entrance sign?
JM: Well, back. Erm.
MJ: Just your, your back?
JM: Yes, your back. But there is a finger there. Er.
MJ: . . . Perhaps we have got them all except the car.
JM: Mm. And there's those two guns.
MJ: Oh, the guns, yes.
JM: what do guns have? Handles, no. You have handles and you have . . . erm . . . triggers? No. Barrels?
MJ: Trigger's not part of the body, it it?
JM: Ah well. I don't think we did very well on that one!

64a *

JM: Right. Childhood dreams and ambitions. Erm, what did you want to do when you grew up? What ambitions did you have? How far have they come true?
CM: Ah, goodness me!
JM: Erm . . . Well you start.
CM: Yes. Well, when I was very young, if anybody ever asked me what I wanted to be, career-wise, erm, I always said I wanted to be a lady-doctor. How I could have been a man-doctor, I do not know. But I wanted to be a lady-doctor. Unfortunately that dream must have got, erm, I must have forgotten it somewhere along the line, because, when I was at school I took only arts subjects, so that by the time it came to choose what my career should be, erm, what I'd taken for my qualifications, my exams, bore no relationship to being a doctor.
JM: Mm, yes.
CM: So, in that way, my very young childhood dreams haven't been fulfilled at all. How about you?
JM: Erm . . . I, I think I wanted to be taller, and erm, sane –
CM: To be taller?
JM: Mm. And er, sort of sane and healthy. I didn't really have any career ambitions. Erm. Partly because my parents didn't expect us to have career ambitions. And –
CM: Where they surprised then when you went to university?
JM: Yes, yes. Erm –
CM: But they didn't push you in that direction?
JM: No, erm. I was the first member of the family to, to go to university, and my two brothers were older than me but they left school for A-levels. Er but my sister who's younger than me also went to university, and my parents were perfectly happy for – they would have been happy if we'd left school at sixteen. Erm, they were very unpushy in that direction. Erm, so, I didn't have dreams. Erm, so . . . here I am.

64d

Juster and Waiter by Michael Rosen
My mum had nicknames for me and my brother.
One of us she called Waiter
and the other she called Juster.
It started like this:
she'd say, 'Lend me a hand with the washing up
will you, you two?'
and I'd say, 'Just a minute, Mum.'
and my brother'd say
'Wait a minute, Mum,.'
'There you go again' – she'd say,
'Juster and Waiter'.

64e

SB: Juster and Waiter.
CM: Do you ever say 'Just a moment?'
SB: No I – I d'know, maybe I did when I was smaller,

but, I was too – I think I was too much of a good little boy and I'd do what I was told or suffer the consequences. So – you've got children?
CM: Well I –
SB: Are they like that?
CM: Well I find – no, they're not like that. I'm like that, because they're the ones who are saying that they need my attention for something or other, some terrific trick that they're doing or whatever, and I'm the one who's always saying 'Just hang on a bit' or, erm, 'Wait a moment and I'll be with you'. And so I think that they could justifiably say that my name is Juster and Waiter, both of them. But erm, I don't think – when I was smaller I don't think I used to say 'Just a minute' or 'Wait' 'cause I was always so happy just to get out of the house or to do something.
SB: Just to get out of the house.
CM: Yes! Well my mother says that I was always pretty handy going and running for the odd bit of shopping.
SB: Mm. I don't really like the poem, it's a bit childish and twee. But –
CM: What else can you say?

UNIT 6

 68d

F1: Air France announce the departure of flight AF807 to Paris. Passengers are requested to proceed to Gate number 10 for immediate boarding.

M2: Your tickets please. Right sir.
Four passengers, one car.
Now, if you follow route A for departure you'll be directed to the waiting area for your sailing to Boulogne. Just follow the marshall's instructions for parking before you board the ferry. Have a good crossing! Good day sir.

M1: Your attention please. All passengers departing on coach service 121 to Paris, at 21 hundred hours, please check in at the Continental Lounge.

M4: You want a lift to Dover?
M1: Please! Are you going all the way?
M4: Well, I'm turning off a mile or two before the town centre. That any use to you?
M1: Yes, fine. I can walk from there. Thanks.
M4: Hop in then. You can put your bag on the back seat.
M4: OK then? The seat belt's just there.
M1: Thanks a lot.

F2: Passengers' attention is directed to the safety instructions for this aircraft, which are contained on a card in the pocket immediately in front of you.

F3: This is the last call for the 12.30 sailing to Calais. Would all foot passengers please proceed through Immigration to the Departure Lounge.

F1: Good morning, madam. Do you have a booking?
F2: Yes, I have. It's the 519 hovercraft, it leaves at 11 doesn't it?
F1: Yes, eleven hundred hours to Calais. Do you have any luggage?
F2: Yes, just this one.
F1: Thank you . . . [Luggage is ticketed] You can collect it when you arrive in Calais – here's the ticket. And here's your boarding card. Now turn to the right and go to Passport Control and then into the Departure Lounge.
F2: Thank you. Er, how will I know what time to go on board?
F1: There are VDU screens in there. They'll give you all the information.
F2: Thank you.
F1: Thank you, madam.

 69a *

BG: What do you think's the best way of travelling from London to Paris in early July?
JV: Well, I actually did that last year. It really depends on the time you've got available. We chose to go by plane because although it was more expensive, it meant we had more time there –
BG: Yes.
JV: and we had so little time available anyway. I suppose the cheapest way would be to go by, by bus, but I think that would be very tiring. Horrible.
BG: Yes, you waste a lot of time and you feel exhausted when you get there.
JV: Exactly. Erm, I, a compromise might be the train. I believe that's quite quick.
BG: Yes.
JV: In fact, I know it is, I've done it.
BG: Oh, have you? Or boat, I suppose, but that hovercraft doesn't take very long, does it?
JV: No, but if you're going by train I think you're confined to the ferry.
BG: Yes.
JV: I suppose one could drive but I haven't got a car.
BG: No, no, nor have I.

69b *

JV: So, we've thought of how many ways to get there? Car –
BG: Car, train –
JV: train, hovercraft –
BG: Hovercraft.
JV: but that would entail having a car, really.
BG: Yes, true.
JV: And –
BG: Plane.
JV: plane.
BG: Right.
JV: Could cycle, I suppose.

69c *

BG: What's your advice on the best way to travel from London to Paris in early July?
DL: Erm, early July. Well, I always prefer flying, 'cause I don't like having to sort of walk too much and I've never been to the Charles de Gaulle airport either. So, I'd suggest flying. It's nice and quick. You have more time to spend in Paris . . .
BG: Yes, that's true.
DL: Although, early July, the weather should be fairly nice, beginning of summer. Erm, it might be, fairly pretty going by train.
BG: It really depends how long you've got though, doesn't it?
DL: That's right, yes. What else is there? So we've got – ?
BG: How many -
DL: We can go –
BG: alternative ways?
DL: So we can fly.
BG: Train.
DL: We can go boat train.
BG: Hovercraft. Car.
DL: Cycle? Would you take your bike? Hyde Park, Dover.
BG: If I had a lot of time, yes, that might be quite a good idea.
DL: Mmm, rucksack. Erm . . . we said drive, didn't we?
BG: That's about it, isn't it?
DL: I would have thought so, yes.

 70b

Look at the first four sentences in B.
M1: It really depends on the time you've got . . .
M2: It depends really on the time you've got . . .

M1: It depends on the time you've got really . . .
F1: That would mean having a car, really.
F2: That would really mean having a car.
F1: It really depends on how long you've got, though, doesn't it?
F2: It depends really on how long you've got though, doesn't it?
M1: Well, I really don't know.
M2: Well, I don't know really.

How is the word **really** said in these sentences? What does it mean in each case?

M1: Erm . . . God, this is really difficult!
F1: I really like that one!

And how is **really** used here?

M1: I quite like the red one, but I really wanted blue.
F1: Hi Mike! I was really looking for Roger, but you'll do.
F2: It's quite warm. Do you really think it'll rain?

Here are some examples.
M1: I was cooking dinner when he called.
F1: I was busy cooking dinner when she rang.
M2: I was in the middle of doing my homework when you came.

Here are some other examples.

F2: I'll just be back from work when you arrive.
We'll all be having dinner if you arrive at seven.
We'll just about be finished if you come around eight.
And if you get there after nine we'll all be watching tele . . .

M2: 'Something really weird happened to this friend of my sister's the other week. He lives down in Southampton and he's driving back from a Duran Duran concert when he sees this girl standing by the roadside hitching. He stops and it turns out he's going right past her door – she tells him the address, 110 Acacia Gardens or something, and off they go. She sits in the back as if she's a bit cautious maybe, but they have a nice chat. Then, when they're getting close, he can't quite remember the quickest way. He pulls up at a traffic light and turns round to ask the girl – but she's vanished.

 *

CF: So what do you think has happened to the girl? Do you think she actually has got out of the car?
JM: Well, that would be the most logical explanation but, erm, it's very difficult to, erm – She is a bit cautious, so, I suppose she may have sneaked out when he wasn't looking or when his attention was distracted, erm, but it is quite difficult to get out of the car without somebody noticing.
CF: Yes. Or it could be that she's just, you know, under the seat getting her bag or something.
JM: Yes. It sounds a bit modern to be a ghost story. Do ghosts go to Duran Duran concerts? Or go near Duran Duran concerts? There are a lot of ghost stories, er, associated with hitch-hikers, aren't there?
CF: Mm. Do you know any?
JM: Erm. There is one where, wh- about the man who, er, picks up a hitch-hiker, and in the course of, erm, talking finds out his address, and, er, leaves the person near the road. The person's left his bag or something, and, er, so the person, the driver goes to the house to return the bag, and finds that the person who had the bag has been dead for a year. That's one story. Erm, but, er, there are quite a lot, I think.
CF: So what do you think George's sister's friend does?

JM: Erm, I, I assume he shrugs his shoulders, and goes and, er, goes and tells his mates about disappearing hitch-hikers.
CF: Mm. Says turn over and read the rest.

M2: 'Of course, he's amazed, he can't think how she got out without him noticing. Anyway, he goes round to the address she's given him and a middle-aged woman in her dressing-gown answers the door, looking a bit angry as it's one in the morning by then. He stammers out what happened – feeling daft, it sounds so stupid – but the woman softens up and tells him he's the sixth person who's come along with the same story. The girl answers the description of her daughter who disappeared two years ago after telling her friends at a party that she was going to hitch-hike home!'
F1: 'No – I don't believe it!'
M2: 'No, honestly, it's really true. The bloke told my sister . . .'
M1: Well, maybe, George. My bet is it didn't happen to your sister's friend though. I know you have to keep it simple to let a story flow along but, own up, wasn't it your sister's friend's mate's cousin . . . who heard it from someone, forget who exactly, who read it in a newspaper, so it must be true?
F2: In other words 'The Vanishing Hitch-hiker' is a modern legend. It has been told, and believed, a million times throughout Britain, America and Europe with only the place names changing. And it's complete codswallop.

 *

MS: Erm, now what about, er, your journey to work, Jane? Do you have a long way to go to work?
JW: I don't have a journey to work because I work at home.
MS: Fair enough. Er, what about you Philip?
PK: Well we live about three miles away from the University and what I do is I take the children to school in the morning so it's a, a roundabout route but it takes me about twenty minutes I suppose to come in.
MF: About twen- twenty minutes by car?
PK: Uh huh, yes.
MF: Right, erm, and . . . what about you Ken?
KO: Erm, I come by bus and I leave at about eight o'clock and arrive at about eight forty-five. It's about five miles from the University.
MS: Uh hum, so it's about three quarters of an hour by bus . . .
KO: Uh huh.
MS: and how . . . is it expensive?
KO: Erm, I don't know. I have a Travelcard so I don't have to pay. I pay monthly which is about sixteen pounds.
MS: Sixteen pounds a month for your travel?
KO: Uh huh.
MS: (to Philip) Would you say erm, that coming by car you could give some sort of figure about your, erm, expenses for getting here.
PK: Yes, if I, if I think a moment, erm . . . probably costs about twenty, twenty five p, in petrol.
MS: A day?
PK: In the morning to come in.
MS: Yes. And then to go out again.
PK: Probably about, probably about forty p a day . . . in . . .
MS: Forty p a day.
PK: . . . in petrol, yes.
MS: Erm, right. I can write these now properly down and then check. I'd better check them.

 *

MS: Erm, so, erm, and then . . . for coming to work it took you about twenty minutes?

143T

PK: About twenty minutes, yes.
MS: . . . to get here, twenty minutes to get back. Is that in the rush hour?
PK: Erm, well I try to come in a little bit ahead of most of the traffic.
MS: Erm, right. And, er, and it was about forty p a day and for you about three quarters of an hour and, erm . . .
KO: That is in the rush hour as well.
MS: And that, that's, yes and it was sixteen pounds a month, so I'd have to work that out, er, er, so four pounds a week. Yes. That's right. So that comes to, erm, seven, four, it's rather more than, erm, Philip's actually. Right.

UNIT 7

 *

JV: Erm, now what would each of you cook if someone dropped in unexpectedly and stayed for a meal in the evening? Bridget, what would you cook?
BG: Sausages and baked beans.
JV: What would you cook, David?
DF: Erm, I'd rustle something up from the fridge!
BG: What? What would you rustle up?
DL: A paper bag?
DF: Whatever vegetables happened to be there. Erm . . . rice. I'd do something imaginative.
JV: What would you do, Danny?
DL: Would I have to cook them something, because I'd prefer to take them out for a meal.
JV: It says here 'What would each of you cook?'
DL: Erm.
JV: Supposing they arrived after the restaurants had shut.
DL: I'd probably cook an omelette, something like that.
JV: We have to summ . . .
DF: What would you do?
JV: I, I usually make a cheese flan –
DL: I think we'll all go round to her place!
JV: if that sort of thing happens, and baked potatoes, quite good too.
DF: Yeah, yeah.
DL: Oh yes. Especially in the microwave.
JV: I haven't got a microwave.
DF: Yes, yes, fine.
JV: So, to summarise, Bridget would cook sausage and beans, Danny would cook an omelette, David would cook something exotic that he'd rustled up from bits in the fridge, and I would cook a cheese flan.

87a

The trick to getting nice soft scrambled eggs is to cook the eggs over a very low heat and to turn off the heat about two minutes before you think the eggs are ready. Scrambled eggs should be soft and creamy not hard and lumpy.

The seasoning given here is for one egg. To cook for more than one person, just multiply the ingredients.

You will need: One egg per person, 2 tablespoons milk, a knob of butter, ¼ teaspoon salt, shake of pepper, saucepan, small bowl, fork, large spoon.

1 Break the egg into the bowl and add the milk, salt and pepper. Beat the egg gently just to mix in the ingredients.
2 Place the pan over the lowest heat possible and put the knob of butter in. Stir the butter around the pan.
3 As soon as the butter starts to melt, pour in the egg. Keep stirring the egg in the pan with a spoon to mix the cooked egg with the uncooked part.
4 To get creamy scrambled eggs, be careful at this stage. As soon as the egg in the pan is thick and there is almost no liquid left, turn off the stove. Keep stirring

to continue the cooking. The heat in the pan will cook the egg to the right consistency.

JV: Now I have to, we have to work out roughly how much it would cost to cook the meal for two or four people at home and compare with a restaurant or take-away price.
DF: Mmm.
JV: So, how much do you think it would cost to cook your potato at home, for two? Well, it would be four potatoes.
DF: Two baked potatoes, four baked potatoes?
JV: Four baked potatoes.
DF: Ten p each? I don't know. What are baked potatoes? I suppose it's about fifty p, and then some filling – depends what – cheese – a pound, maybe? It's very basic. A pound and butter and –
JV: It would probably cost you four times as that much in a restaurant.
DF: Yes.
JV: Scrambled egg on toast.
BG: About seventy p, I should think, for four people. Well, it depends. Six eggs, and four slices of toast?
JV: Yes.
DF: Yes.
JV: But in a restaurant, or in a cafe?
DL: That's one and half eggs each. You could always go down to one egg each.
JV: That would be really mean.
DL: Maybe they haven't got a large appetite?
BG: Yes, you'd use more than six eggs though wouldn't you, for four people?
JV: Mmm.
DF: Yea, eight. 'Cause it, 'cause it all shrinks when it's scrambled eggs.
BG: Yeah, and milk. Erm, let's say, one pound fifty.
DF: How much would that cost in a restaurant? In a cafe?
BG: For four people?
JV: Two pound?
DF: A pound a head.
BG: No, you wouldn't get it for fifty p each.
DL: It would be more than two.
DF: No, it's more than fifty p.
JV: No.
BG: About a pound a head, yeah. Four pounds.
DF: Yeah, terrible.
JV: Well, you went out to buy your pie anyway.
DL: Yes. My pie and mash would cost me seventy-six p. That's with, with the gravy.
JV: But er, and if you made it at home. It would probably cost you more to make it at home, actually, because you'd have to make the pastry and buy the meat and –
DL: If it was home, yes, if the pie was home-made, it would, would cost more . . . And then you got all the time, time-consuming work of mashing the potatoes.

89b *

JV: Right. So really, er, to summarise. It seems that for most people, their favourite cheap meal is something which – their favourite cheap meal that they cook at home is probably going to cost about a pound or so to feed four people, maybe one pound fifty. But in fact in a restaurant it would cost about four times that much. Whereas Danny's favourite cheap meal was one which would actually take a lot of time and trouble to prepare and would probably cost more to make yourself than to, than to buy out.

Lunching at a restaurant, I ordered the special low-calorie dish. Then I ordered apple pie. The waitress told me there was none left.

As I got up to go, I saw the same waitress serving apple pie to another table. Seeing my expression, she came over and explained, 'I just couldn't let you eat that pie after you had ordered the slimmer's lunch.'

93b

One evening we decided to go out to eat at a small pub, which turned out to be very busy. Noticing a woman reading the menu, I kept an eye on her until she put it down.
Rushing over, I muttered, 'May I?' and brought it back to my friends.
Triumphantly, I opened the menu to reveal – a photograph album!

93c *

CM: Right, well this is fast food. Er ... We once went for a meal in a fast food restaurant, intending to get home quickly. The service was so slow and the waitresses made so many mistakes that we spent over an hour there before we even got anything to eat. When we complained to the manager he was very very apologetic and told us the meal was on the house. Has anything like this ever happened to you?

93d *

CM: Can you think of any other ways of getting meals or anything else for nothing? Well has anything like that ever happened to you? ....
Well I've erm – This has happened to me twice. But in slightly different, erm occasions. The first one was er, when we were, I think – I was with one other person. I can't remember who it was. And, erm, we were occupying a, a small table in among many other tables and all of a sudden a large party came in and it was, erm, to the owner's advantage to have us moved from our table to a table on the periphery. So he, erm, suggested that we might move, and my companion suggested that for a bottle of wine we would. So we got a bottle of wine on the house which was very nice. And the second time was when we went to eat at a hamburger restaurant. Erm, erm, the people on the table next to us had ordered exactly the same meal, but they were ordering bigger hamburgers. So they had, I don't know, twelve ounce hamburgers or eight ounce hamburgers and, my companion and I were having four ounce hamburgers. And the waitress got the orders mixed up so we ended up eating these enormous hamburgers, and er, the people on the other table had the smaller hamburgers and, we both had our bills written off.

95

This is just to say by William Carlos Williams
I have eaten
the plums
that were in
the icebox

and which
you were probably
saving
for breakfast.

Forgive me
they were delicious
so sweet
and so cold.

97a

The Hitch-hiker by Roald Dahl
Part 1: **I had a new car**
I had a new car. It was an exciting toy, a big B.M.W. 3.3 Li, which means 3.3 litre, long wheelbase, fuel injection. It had a top speed of 129 m.p.h. and terrific acceleration. The body was pale blue. The seats inside were darker blue and they were made of leather, genuine soft leather of the finest quality. The windows were electrically operated and so was the sun-roof. The radio aerial popped up when I switched on the radio, and disappeared when I switched it off. The powerful engine growled and grunted impatiently at slow speeds, but at sixty miles an hour the growling stopped and the motor began to purr with pleasure.

I was driving up to London by myself. It was a lovely June day. They were haymaking in the fields and there were buttercups along both sides of the road. I was whispering along at seventy miles an hour, leaning back comfortably in my seat, with no more than a couple of fingers resting lightly on the wheel to keep her steady.

Ahead of me I saw a man thumbing a lift. I touched the footbrake and brought the car to a stop beside him. I always stopped for hitch-hikers. I knew just how it used to feel to be standing on the side of a country road watching the cars go by. I hated the drivers for pretending they didn't see me, especially the ones in big cars with three empty seats. The large expensive cars seldom stopped. It was always the small ones that offered you a lift, or the old rusty ones, or the ones that were already crammed full of children and the driver would say, 'I think we can squeeze in one more.'

The hitch-hiker poked his head through the open window and said,

'Going to London, guv'nor?'

'Yes,' I said. 'Jump in.'

He got in and I drove on.

97b *

SB: Okay?
CM: Mm, fine.
SB: What details can you remember about the car?
CM: It was erm, pale blue, with dark, er, leather seats – dark blue leather seats. It was a three – it was a BMW I think, a three point three litre.
SB: LI.
CM: LI.
SB: L for long-wheel base.
CM: Ah, is that right? I for fuel injection. Yes.
SB: I for fuel injection. Yes.
CM: Erm. Anything else?
SB: The radio aerial. When you switched on the radio, the aerial went up. When you switched off the radio the aerial went down again.
CM: Er, I didn't – Er, it had electric windows, and it had erm, something else, but I can't remember. I was just trying to think about it. Erm.
SB: Okay. Have you ever felt like he did about something new?
CM: Yes.
SB: Er I'm not sure. It doesn't really say much about how he felt apart from the fact he was excited about it. But yes, I know, I know, even when it's been just a leather jacket, and I felt it's like this. A new one, you wear it everywhere, you take the car everywhere, or whatever.
CM: Well, we got a fairly – well we had a fairly nice car, some years ago. About two or three years ago my husband got a new company car. Erm, a Porsche. And we felt more or less the same way about that. So that's still our car but I love it.
SB: If it's a Porsche I'm not surprised.
CM: Yes.

97c *

SB: Think together of three things that the driver might ask the hitch-hiker next.
CM: Erm, that the driver might ask the hitch-hiker?

145T

SB: Yeah. The hitch-hiker said he's go – he wants to go to London but that's all he said.
CM: Yes. And the driver said 'you get in'. So the driver might ask him where he's just come from or where he started that morning.
SB: And, why he was going to London.
CM: Yes. And erm . . .
SB: Maybe where in London he wanted to go?
CM: Or if he was – perhaps if he was a student. 'Cos I mean it's principally students who hitch-hike, don't you think?
SB: Yeah. I – it doesn't say anything about the man at all. As to what age he was, so –
CM: No, not yet.
SB: I suppose he could ask him what he, you know, what he was doing.
CM: Mm.

The memory game. Study the picture for one minute. Turn it over and take turns to begin, to make as long a sentence as possible, from memory, about the people or the things happening in the picture. Right, let's look at the picture then.
F1: OK. There was a policeman.
M1: There – there was a policeman with a helmet.
F2: There was a policeman with a helmet and he had a walkie talkie on his lapel.
F3: There was a policeman who had a helmet and a walkie talkie on his lapel . . . he was pointing to something.
M2: There was a policeman with a helmet who had a walkie talkie on his lapel and was pointing to something . . . erm . . . he was pointing to something and helping a woman in the street.
F1: There was a policeman who had a helmet and a walkie talkie on his lapel . . . he was pointing and giving a woman some directions . . . she was wearing a scarf.
M1: There was a policeman with a helmet and a walkie talkie on his lapel pointing the directions – er – pointing to something and giving the directions to a woman who was wearing a scarf on her head because it was raining.
F2: Oh, I can't remember all of those!
M1: There's a man posting a letter who's wearing a cap and an overcoat.
F1: There's a man posting a letter who's wearing a cap . . .
Can you continue? What more can you add?

DF: Right, what next?
JV: We have a cake and a knife. Well here's a picture of the cake. What is the smallest number of straight cuts with a knife you have to make to cut it into equal, eight equal pieces?
DF: Is it a circular cake?
JV: Yes.
DF: Four. Is it?
JV: Well, the best way to start would be draw a circle, wouldn't it?
DF: One, two –
JV: One, then across, that's two, that's four.
DF: Yeah . . .
JV: Three. One, two, three, four, five, six, seven, eight – four times.

DF: Good. So we did a line across the middle of the cake and then one at ninety degrees to that.
JV: That's right.
DF: And then two more similar lines at, at erm er at an angle of forty-five if we're going to be technical about it.
JV: That's right, yes.

146T

DF: So four big cuts, yes? One, two, three, four. Right.
JV: Right.

JV: Now – look at the cake.
DL: I am.
JV: How many times would you have to cut that – straight cuts with a knife – to get eight, equally-sized pieces?
DL: Cut it which – what, across the cake or, er . . . ?
JV: How – you've got, what you've got to work out is the fewest number of times you must cut that cake to divide it into eight equal pieces.
DL: Er, one, two, three.
JV: Yes. How – can you show me how you would do it, drawing.
DL: Yeah. I'd go – once, twice, three times.
JV: Brilliant. None of us had that spatial awareness where you thought of cutting it across ways.

UNIT 8

The auto-pilot
The flight ran several times a week taking holiday-makers to various resorts in the Mediterranean. On each flight, to reassure the passengers all was well, the captain would put the jet on to auto-pilot and he and all the crew would come aft into the cabin to greet the passengers.
Unfortunately, on this particular flight the security door between the cabin and the flight deck jammed and left the captain and crew stuck in the cabin. From that moment, in spite of the efforts to open the door, the fate of the passengers and crew was sealed.

Jumbo jet pilot
A show-off Jumbo pilot put the controls on automatic in mid-flight and took his entire crew for a stroll back down the aisle to meet the passengers, then discovered the cockpit door had locked itself and he had mislaid the key.

CM: Have you ever had a worrying or frightening flight? Oh, hold on. There are two of these, I'm so sorry.
SB: That's okay. Erm . . . Not really. I've flown across the Atlantic a few times and it's usually been the other passengers who have been terrified of terrorists and so on and afraid of landing and afraid of taking off. I really enjoy it. I erm, I don't believe that I'm likely to be terrorised. I never fly TWA.
CM: Oh.
SB: But –
CM: Yes.
SB: And . . . I – The trouble is when you fly in big planes they don't tend to do that sort of thing.
CM: Mm.
SB: How about you?
CM: I can't say that I've ever had a frightening flight. Er, my husband works in the aviation insurance business and, er, he assures me, well not assures me, but tells me that er, the most frightening, or the most dangerous time, when you're on a plane is, erm, take off and landing. And I find those the most exciting times. The rest of it I find very boring.
SB: Mm.
CM: There's only a little, little that you can do. And nobody's ever threatened anything and nothing's ever happened apart from a little bit of turbulence so . . . .

SB: Well my girlfriend's very frightened of flying, and she had a bad experience. She was flying home to

Texas and she looked out of the window, and she was frightened enough, and suddenly saw that one of the engines was on fire.
CM: Uh, heavens!
SB: She called over an air hostesses and pointed this out and they had to take the plane back to Heathrow.
CM: Does that mean that nobody else had noticed?
SB: I think maybe the pilots had noticed, but certainly nobody else on board had noticed and she was the first to see this, so they drugged her up with a mixture of alcohol and valium for the next flight, by when she she'd missed her connection in New York to Texas and so she had to go on.
CM: So that was frustrating as well as a frightening experience.
SB: Yes, she's never wanted to fly again.
SB: And she flew over, flew back to England but she says next time she goes back to America it'll be by the QE2.
CM: Yes, that's probably the best thing to do if you are really terrified of flying.

Jenny once had a really silly accident. Listen to the sound effects and see if you can work out what happened, when and where it took place, and what caused it.

[Opening car door; settling into seat; shutting car door; starting engine; putting into reverse; slowly moving; crunch as parked car is hit; exclamations of alarm from woman driver; opening car door and getting out].

F1: Oh no! What have I done! Oh, my goodness, I'd better go and tell him. What a silly thing to do – why didn't I look!

Write down some sentences describing what you think happened. Which of the pictures on the right hand side of page 53 do you think might be part of the story?

 *

BG: Have you or has anyone you know ever seen or had an accident? Have you ever had an accident?
JV: I once backed into my neighbour's car.
BG: Oh dear.
JV: I simply didn't look. He was parked in front of his house doing no harm to anyone. In fact he was indoors asleep and I backed out of the garage. I can't imagine why I didn't look and the next thing I knew there was a sort of crunch.
BG: Oh dear!
JV: And that was his car!
BG: What happened? Did he – was he quite nice about it?
JV: Well, he seemed to be more annoyed about being woken up.
BG: Oh dear!
JV: Erm, it was in Africa, all the other people around came and laughed at me. So I had to join in and laugh as well. It was incredibly embarrassing. I mean, there was no excuse at all.
BG: No, no.
JV: I mean, he was completely stationary, and not even in his car.
BG: You couldn't even blame him!
JV: No.

Advice on action to be taken after a motor accident
It is suggested that these notes be kept with your insurance certificate.

At the scene of the accident
Keep calm. Do not discuss who is to blame. If there is no injury, move your car to the side of the road so as not to disrupt traffic flow.

A Obtain the following information:–
1 Name and address of the other driver.
2 Name and address of the other driver's Insurers.
3 Insurance certificate number.
4 Name and address of independent witness.
5 Make, owner and registration number of other vehicle.
6 Sketch a diagram of the accident (including measurements, directions, etc.)
7 Weather and road conditions at the time.

B Note the date and time of the accident.

C Provide your own particulars to anyone who has reasonable grounds for wanting them.

After the accident
You should report to:

1 The police as soon as possible but not later than 24 hours after the accident if there is personal injury or damage to government property. If there is no injury a police report is optional by either party, but remember that the party making an official statement is in a better position than one who does not.
2 Your insurers as soon as possible even if you do not intend to make a claim – this is a condition of your policy.
(a) Report any statement made at the scene of the accident by any of the parties.
(b) You will be required to complete an Accident Report Form, obtainable from your Insurers upon request.

 *

BG: Okay. Describe a journey you had that went wrong. Why did it go wrong and what happened.
JV: Oh, I can think of lots of journeys that went wrong.
BG: Yes, I can too. Well, I remember going home – my parents live in Sussex – and I remember catching a train once on a Friday night to go home, go down to Sussex, and it usually takes about an hour and I was very tired and I fell asleep half-way and ended up in Hastings which is about two and a half hours, two hours, erm, which was really annoying, 'cause it meant I had to wait for another train to come back again.

 *

BG: Right. Describe a journey you had that went wrong. Why did it go wrong and what happened?
DL: After you.
BG: Well, I think – the worst journey I've had is going beyond my destination, because I fell asleep. Erm –
DL: At the end of the day.
BG: Yes.
DL: Hard day's work.
BG: That's right.
DL: Very tired.
BG: That's right.
DL: I know the feeling.
BG: And then you have to get on a train and come all the way back again. Very annoying.
DL: Mmm. That's why it's always better to catch a taxi, 'cause he'll wake you up when you get home.
BG: Yes.

 *

JV: A friend of mine had a similar experience on a Greenline bus after an office party, so you can imagine that he went to sleep and the Greenline bus went all the way to its terminus at one end and then all the way back to the other one and was on its third trip –
BG: Oh no!
JV: before they finally woke him up and said 'Are you sure – Where are you supposed to be going to?'

BG: Oh no! Goodness!
JV: I suppose that's a journey that went wrong.

 112b

Dear Driver,
I have just run into your car and made a hell of a mess of it. As a crowd has gathered, I am forced to appear as if writing you this note to apologise and to leave you my name and address. As you can see, however, this I have not done.
A Well-Wisher

 114a

The Hitch-hiker
Part 2: A small ratty-faced man
He was a small ratty-faced man with grey teeth. His eyes were dark and quick and clever, like a rat's eyes, and his ears were slightly pointed at the top. He had a cloth cap on his head and he was wearing a greyish-coloured jacket with enormous pockets. The grey jacket, together with the quick eyes and the pointed ears, made him look more than anything like some sort of a huge human rat.

'What part of London are you headed for?' I asked him.

'I'm goin' right through London and out the other side,' he said. 'I'm goin' to Epsom, for the races. It's Derby Day today.'

'So it is,' I said. 'I wish I were going with you. I love betting on horses.'

'I never bet on horses,' he said. 'I don't even watch 'em run. That's a stupid silly business.'

'Then why do you go?' I asked.

He didn't seem to like that question. His little ratty face went absolutely blank and he sat there staring straight ahead at the road, saying nothing.

'I expect you help to work the betting machines or something like that,' I said.

'That's even sillier,' he answered. 'There's no fun working them lousy machines and selling tickets to mugs. Any fool could do that.'

114c *

CM: From memory, see if you can describe what the hitch-hiker looked like.
SB: After you've finished look back at the text and check the details.
CM: Do this together. Right. He was a ratty-faced man with grey teeth.
SB: Pointed ears.
CM: Pointed ears.
SB: A grey cap? Was it – it was a cap of some description.
CM: And he had a grey jacket with pockets.
SB: Big pockets.
CM: Big pockets.
SB: And he looks more like a human rat than anything else. And he had shifty looking eyes.
CM: Yes, well done.
SB: Erm . . .
CM: And he sat staring straight ahead, did he?
SB: I thought he was, sort of shifting around. Has – Shall we –
CM: Yes, go back to the text now.
SB: Erm. His eyes were dark and quick and clever like rats' eyes.
CM: Er, he had a cloth cap on his head, that's right. And he was wearing a greyish colour jacket with enormous pockets.
SB: With big pockets.
148T   CM: And he looked like a huge human rat. So that's him!

SB: Yeah we got it about right.
CM: I think so.

114d *

SB: Where is he going? Can you guess why?
CM: He's going to Epsom because it's Derby Day. Or is it – ? He does mention that it's Derby Day.
SB: Yes, that's probably why he's going. And he says he's going for the races. But he's not going to bet, on horses. And he's not going to watch them run. And he's not even working the betting machines.
CM: So what is he going for?
SB: Maybe he's a pickpocket.
CM: I'm sure that the fact he's he's so small – I mean that we've heard so much about this – his ratty features. I'm sure that that's got something – it sounds rather ghoulish.
SB: What's a rat do at a race course?
CM: I don't know. Bite horses or something.
SB: Mm. But he's not really – He doesn't seem interested in horses at all. But he –
CM: Well it doesn't say that he's – does it say that he is not interested in the horses? It says he's not interested in betting.
SB: He says 'I don't even watch them run'.
CM: That's right. He doesn't. But it doesn't say that he's not interested in horses.
SB: – not interested in them at all. That's true. Oh well.
CM: Let's turn the page and see what happens next.
SB: Find out.

UNIT 9

 117a *

DF: Yes, the only thing I can think of here is in Foyle's here or in some shops abroad and I can't remember where, where you have to pay at a special cash desk and collect the receipt before you can take what you've bought out of the shop. So you have to go to two different people. You choose whatever you want and you say 'I want that', and the first person, the first shop assistant writes out the bill and then you take the bill to a special cash desk and pay –
BG: pay somewhere else.
DF: Yeah, get it stamped and then you come back and, erm, when you show that you've paid you can take whatever it is you want to buy and leave with it. Can you think of anything else? Is there any other –
BG: I can't.

117b *

BG: I can't think of anywhere I've been where it's different from here.
DF: Oh, I know, Argos. Erm, when you do that sort of, what is it, you know – bulk buy or whatever it is. No, you buy from a catalogue, so you – the catalogue's in the front of the shop and you fill out a form for it – you take down . . .
BG: And then they go –
DF: you take down the number and the price and then you pay for it and you go through a cash system and it – a cash till, a cash till, you take it to a cash till and they – you pay there and they stamp it and they do something with a computer, they enter the number into a computer and it goes down to the warehouse.
BG: And they find what you want.
DF: At the back, yes, and they send it up.
BG: Oh, right.
DF: Have you ever done that?
BG: No, I haven't.
DF: That's, that's Argos. Erm, so there are two possible systems.

*

BG: Right, well, you said that in Argos you walk into the shop and you fill out a form for what you want and then it goes down to the warehouse or whatever in the basement and they find what you want and then your goods are ready for you to pick up when you're ready to leave. Erm, and Foyle's where you'd, you get a receipt for what you've paid for and then –
DF: No, you haven't paid for it, where you get a receipt.
BG: Oh, you just get a receipt and then you take it to a cash desk to actually pay for it.
DF: And they keep the book. So you don't get the book until you've paid for it.
BG: Oh right, yes.
DF: You have to go back. It's a real drag.

---

 *

CM: Right, we've got to think of some advertising jingles and slogans. How many advertising slogans or jingles can you remember? Erm, and somebody's got to write a list of them.
JM: Oh well, I'll do the list.
CM: Oh well done John.
SB: Are these just for English ones, 'cause I've been bombarded with American television for about nine months and I have –
CM: Well, we probably wouldn't recognise them, but if you, if you know them, why not? If, if they come to mind.
JM: The one that I find most irritating is, 'The dirt said hot, and the label said not –'.
CM: '– said not.
JM: I absolutely hate it.
CF: Oh, that's awful.
CM: 'Ariel gets it clean!'
JM: That's the one, yes, I'd forgotten what it's for, but I remember how annoying I find it.
CM: I'm addicted to advertisements on the television. So, that's one. So that's Ariel.
JM: Right yes.
CM: Erm, I like, erm 'A finger of fudge is just enough–'
CF: That's what I was thinking of.
CM: 'to give your kids a treat.' I think that's quite a nice one.
SB: 'Only the crumbliest, flakiest chocolate tastes like chocolate never tasted before.' Which if you try and analyse it grammatically makes no sense at all.
JM: Mm. Yes.
CM: But it's quite a tongue twister.
JM: Yes.
CF: 'A million housewives every day pick up a tin of beans and say –'
JM: Yes.
CF: 'Beanz meanz Heinz.'
SB: They don't have that on TV any- still, do they?
CM: No.
CF: Erm yes. I saw it recently.
CM: Do they?
CF: Yes. I was very surprised. They're still dragging it out.
SB: The other one that's almost as old as that must be 'There are two men in my life –'
CM: Oh yes.
SB: 'to one I am a –'
CF: 'mother'
SB: 'mother, the other I'm a wife.'
JM: God! I haven't heard that one in –
CF: Shredded Wheat.
SB: That's Shredded Wheat . . .
CM: That must be very old. I don't remember that one.
JM: Yes, I remember it, which is . . .

SB: It was a contemporary with Cadbury's Whole Nut 'Cadbury's take 'em, and they cover them with chocolate'.
JM: Oh yes, that's, erm –

CM: What's the Smarties one? I –
SB: 'Smartie people are happy people.'
JM: 'They smile all the while.'
CM: No. No. That's not the one I'm thinking of.
JM: 'Only Smarties have the answer.'
CM: No. Erm, there were, there were some children singing in the Smartie advertisement. I, I . . . oh, it doesn't matter.
JM: Erm . . . no. An awful lot of advertisements have got erm, songs now like, erm, 'A wonderful world' and that . . . .

The Hitch-hiker
Part 3: **The secret of life**
There was a long silence. I decided not to question him any more. I remembered how irritated I used to get in my hitch-hiking days when drivers kept asking me questions. Where are you going? Why are you going there? What's your job? Are you married? Do you have a girl-friend? What's her name? How old are you? And so on and so forth. I used to hate it.

'I'm sorry,' I said. 'It's none of my business what you do. The trouble is, I'm a writer, and most writers are terrible nosey parkers.'

'You write books?' he asked.

'Yes.'

'Writin' books is okay,' he said. 'It's what I call a skilled trade. I'm in a skilled trade too. The folks I despise is them that spend all their lives doin' crummy old routine jobs with no skill in 'em at all. You see what I mean?'

'Yes.'

'The secret of life,' he said, 'is to become very very good at somethin' that's very 'ard to do.'

'Like you,' I said.

'Exactly. You and me both.'

'What makes you think that I'm any good at my job?' I asked. 'There's an awful lot of bad writers around.'

'You wouldn't be drivin' about in a car like this if you weren't no good at it,' he answered. 'It must've cost a tidy packet, this little job.'

'It wasn't cheap.'

'What can she do flat out?' he asked.

'One hundred and twenty-nine miles an hour,' I told him.

'I'll be she won't do it.'

'I'll bet she will.'

'All car makers is liars,' he said. 'You can buy any car you like and it'll never do what the makers say it will in the ads.'

'This one will.'

---

 *

SB: I d'know. But if they were liars they'd get into trouble with the advertising standards people.
CM: Well I think what they claim that a car does, it must be able to do, mustn't it? By the – by some some Act, the trades description or sale of goods or whatever.
SB: But under very special circumstances, perhaps. Like fuel economy but they'll only do it if you drive at a steady 55 miles an hour on an absolutely flat road with no wind. So –
CM: With no wheels.
SB: They tend to stretch the truth without actually lying.
CM: So it's not actually liars. Perhaps they're slightly deceiving, deceptive.

149T

SB: Yeah. What do you think will happen next.
CM: Oh well obviously I think the only thing that he can do is to prove that the car can go at 120 miles an hour.
SB: Can go to 120 miles an hour.
CM: That's right, so, that's obviously what's got to happen next.

122c *

SB: Okay?
CM: You read very fast.
SB: What can you guess about the hitch-hiker from the way he speaks? Well, he drops the 'g's from the ends of his 'ing's so it's 'in'. Doin' this and I'm doin' that.
CM: So what does that mean?
SB: Erm . . . I don't know. He's sort of – he speaks with a basically uneducated accent.
CM: That's right. Yes.
SB: He also drops 'h's and things.
CM: But it is an accent of a kind, isn't it? He drops his 'h's. So he probably – perhaps he's from, erm, the East End of London or somewhere like that.
SB: Yeah . . . Something like that.
CM: So, you think he's not particularly well educated.
SB: I think – I don't think he's got a university education or anything like that. But er, beyond that it's hard to tell. And he's – he claims he's got a skilled job.
CM: Yes, he also uses very – erm, he doesn't use erm, particularly . . . erm . . . big words or anything like that does he? Erm, he seems to use the word 'very' a lot like 'very very good' at something that is 'very very 'ard' to do, he says.
SB: Yeah.
CM: So he – perhaps he's not very good at describing.
SB: Not very well educated. Self taught.

124

I discovered a pom pom pom
As I was walking down the beach
One bright and sunny day,
I saw a great big wooden box
Afloating in the bay.
I pulled it in
I opened it up
And much to my surprise
I discovered a pom pom pom
Right before my eyes.

128b *

SB: What's your favourite colour and why?
CM: Right, if you'll just give me a sheet of paper, please.
SB: Here's some paper.
CM: Thank you. What's my favourite colour? Erm . . . I suppose it's blue. And I don't know why I like blue, except it's – I think it's probably the most popular colour for . . . a majority of the population.
SB: You think more than red?
CM: Well, if you look at erm, any any group of people together, like say in a football stadium or something like that, you'll find the predominant colour – I find the predominant colour invariably is, is blue. Blue jerseys and things like that.
SB: Not if it's Liverpool and they're all in red! I don't think I have a favourite colour. I just sort of wake up in the morning depending on what sort of day it is and I'll feel like putting on clothes of a different colour.
CM: But if you go and er – if you go shopping do you not particularly choose say, a blue shirt against a pink shirt? I know you're wearing a pink shirt at the moment!
SB: Well, I tend to buy – when I buy clothes most clothes I buy tend to be khaki or olive or grey, and then I have things with bright colours to go with them so – and it's very much a matter of mood. I have er, pink

shirts and blue shirts. Not green. I don't like green. I'm not too keen on yellow. But apart from that red, blue, purple, black, white.
CM: So, it probably would be better to say what is your least favourite colour because the rest of the colours are ones that you like.
SB: Yeah, I think so.

128d *

CM: And I don'tknow why I like blue, except it's – I think it's probably the most popular colour for . . . a majority of the population.

CM: Well, if you look at erm, any group of people together, like say in a football stadium or something like that . . .

CM: . . . if you go shopping do you not particularly choose say, a blue shirt against a pink shirt?

SB: . . . most clothes I buy tend to be khaki or olive or grey,and then I have things with bright colours to go with them so – and it's very much a matter of mood.

UNIT 10

131a *

CM: Erm, well, we're in Caldwell and I want you to head north on theB6274.
SB: B6274.
CM: And erm, some way along there, not very far, you'll, er, come across the A6-, 67 at a little place called Winston, and you just go straight across there.
SB: Go through it – across the A67?
CM: Yes, you cross the A67. So you're still on your little B road.
SB: Okay.
CM: So you're crossing a major road. And y-, erm, eventually the, erm, the B6274 will meet the A688.
SB: A688. When you say it will meet it, does that mean it ends there?
CM: It ends there.
SB: Right.
CM: And the A688 goes to the left and to the right. I want you to turn left, and you should –
SB: So that's west.
CM: Er, yes. Well done. And you should immediately come to a little village called Staindrop.
SB: Staindrop. S, T, A, I, N, D, R, O, P.
CM: D, R, O, P. And just at the end of Staindrop, erm, you . . . .

131b *

SB: Staindrop. S, T, A, I, N ,D, R, O, P.
CM: D, R, O, P. And just at the end of Staindrop, erm you – I want you to branch off to the right . . . onto a B road again.
SB: Branch right. So I'm going – the A688 goes through Staindrop, and then at the end there's this road off to the right.
CM: That's right.
SB: And it's called?
CM: Which is the B6279.
SB: 6279.
CM: All right?
SB: So far so good.
CM: And the B6279 eventually runs into the B6278.
SB: 6278.
CM: Yes. And, the B262 – B6279, I think, erm, fades out at that stage and the 6278 takes over.
SB: So it just changes its number?
CM: Well –
SB: Or do I have to make a turn?
CM: The 6278 actually comes in from the left, and

you're coming down from the right and the two roads would merge at the, that point and become the 6278.
SB: Okay, so I – but I can just keep going.
CM: Yes, in other words you're just carrying on straight but the road number has changed. And you come to a little town called – or probably it's a village called Eggleston.
SB: Eggleston.
CM: Yes.
SB: Yep.
CM: Now I want you to turn left, in Eggleston, and then immediately right.
SB: When you say left in Eggleston is there only one road?
CM: Erm. Yes. You have to turn left – you would still be continuing – sorry. Erm, the B6278 would go straight on.
SB: Right.
CM: In Eggleston, I want you to turn left, and then immediately right, onto the B6282.
SB: Then the B6282.
CM: And then continue on that road until you should end up in the middle of Middleton-in-Teesdale.

---

 *

CM: Well, we could have, we could have taken an A road. That would have taken you into, erm, Barnard Castle. But as I always avoid anything with a town centre, where you could get lost, I've taken you onto B roads because I feel it's far more scenic.
SB: This is the scenic route and y-, so, if we get lost, there'll be nobody to ask.
CM: Well, you've got all those lovely, erm, country people in Eggleston and Staindrop who'll probably be able to help you on your way.
SB: I see.

132b *

CM: Erm, well, we're in Caldwell and I want you to head north on the B6274.
SB: B6274.
CM: And erm, some way along there, not very far, you'll, er, come across the A6-, A67 at a little place called Winston, and you just go straight across there.

CM: Er, yes. Well done. And you should immediately come to a little village called Staindrop.

CM: Yes, in other words you're just carrying on straight but the road number has changed. And you come to a little town called – or probably it's a village called Eggleston.

CM: Now I want you to turn left, in Eggleston, and then immediately right ....

---

133 *

SB: So, am I supposed to tell you what Middleton looks like?
CM: That's right. I, I think so, yes.
SB: Well, it looks a fairly small village at the foot of a valley. So it's probably very scenic, with Middleton Common behind it.
CM: It's got – it's on a river isn't it? Or a tributary.
SB: It's on a tributary of the river Tees, which is logical since it's in Teesdale.
CM: Yes.
SB: And ... yeah, it's near waterfalls and camping sites, so it must be scenic.
CM: Lots of camping sites around, so it must be quite scenic.
SB: And there's – that looks like a waterfall and that looks like a stream with some little windy roads. So it's probably sheep country, erm –

CM: Yes, well it looks quite hilly, so it's obviously quite, erm –
SB: These are called commons rather than moors.
CM: What's the difference?
SB: Well, I think a common would be more gentle than a moor. I think you'd have grasses rather than bare rock. But it, higher up it gets into the moor. So I think – I think it's – it must be sheep farming country.
CM: Right.

136b

The Hitch-hiker
Part 4: 'Go on! Get 'er up to one-two-nine!'
'What can she do flat out?'
'One hundred and twenty-nine miles an hour', I told him.
'I'll bet she won't do it.'
'I'll bet she will.'
'All car makers is liars' he said. 'You can buy any car you like and it'll never do what makers say it will in the ads.'
'This one will.'
'Open 'er up then and prove it,' he said. 'Go on, guv'nor, open 'er right up and let's see what she'll do.'

There is a roundabout at Chalfont St. Peter and immediately beyond it there's a long straight section of dual carriage-way. We came out of the roundabout on to the carriage-way and I pressed my foot hard down on the accelerator. The big car leaped forward as though she'd been stung. In ten seconds or so, we were doing ninety.

'Lovely!' he cried. 'Beautiful! Keep goin'!'

I had the accelerator jammed right down against the floor and I held it there.

'One hundred!' he shouted ... 'A hundred and five!' ... 'A hundred and ten!' ... 'A hundred and fifteen! Go on ! Don't slack off!'

I was in the outside lane and we flashed past several cars as though they were standing still – a green Mini, a big cream coloured Citroen, a white Land-Rover, a huge truck with a container on the back, an orange-coloured Volkswagen Minibus ...

'A hundred and twenty!' my passenger shouted, jumping up and down. 'Go on! Get 'er up to one-two-nine!'

At that moment, I heard the scream of a police siren. It was so loud it seemed to be right inside the car, and then a policeman on a motor-cycle loomed up alongside us on the inside lane and went past us and raised a hand for us to stop.

'Oh, my sainted aunt!' I said. 'That's torn it!'

136c *

CM: I think we had guessed, except that, erm, I thought that, er, the driver might have just taken the challenge from the first page. In fact, he had to be challenged again, didn't he? The little man said 'Go on, open 'er up, go on guv'nor'.
SB: Yeah.
CM: I think we more or less got it right.
SB: Yeah. So what what happened, I mean, the guy got in and he started boasting about his new car and, the hitch-hiker made him prove it.
CM: Yes.
SB: And they didn't really get a chance to get the ultimate proof 'cause the police came along.
CM: Yes.

136d *

SB: What do you think will happen next? Will the writer stop or drive on even faster? What would you have done?

CM: Well, the way he says 'Oh my sainted aunt. That's torn it.' He's obviously – I – that to me sounds like a man who's who's usually remains well within the law. So the idea of having a policeman zooming up beside him on his motorcycle, erm, I would say he would probably pull in quite docilely to the side if he were by himself. I don't know what's going to happen.
SB: I think he'll probably want to do that, because a police motorbike can probably outrun –
CM: Yes.
SB: 129 miles an hour but –
CM: What will the influence of the ratty little man have?
SB: Yeah.
CM: Yes, I agree.
SB: He could well –
SB: What would you have done?
CM: Ah, I probably wouldn't have gone at 129 miles an hour. No, I might have. Certainly if there was a policeman beside me, telling me to pull over or flagging me down, I would certainly pull over.
SB: Yeah, I think I would do that.

---

 *

SB: I think the first thing he would do is ask to see the driver's licence.
CM: I – well I think the first thing he might say is, Do you know what speed you were doing, coming along that stretch between Chalfont St Peter and wherever it was? Yes and then he might say –
SB: Can I see your licence?
CM: Can I see your licence?
SB: Is this your car? What's the number plate?
CM: Where do you live? What's your address?
SB: That'll probably be on the licence.
CM: Yeah, but he'd still ask it. Erm, and, er, where are you going?
SB: In such a hurry.
CM: In such a hurry, yes. Or where have you come from or what's your business? And anything else that came into his mind.
SB: Yeah. It could be interesting if it's a new car and he asks for the number plate, because the driver might not know the number plate. But –
CM: No. I don't think that that would be particularly significant.
SB: I know, he must have the doc- He probably – he'll probably ask to see all the documents.
CM: And he probably – and the driver probably won't have them.
SB: Yeah. Okay?

Maybe it's because I'm a Londoner
Maybe it's because I'm a Londoner, that I love London so,
Maybe it's because I'm a Londoner, that I think of her wherever I go.
I get a funny feeling inside me when I'm walking up and down,
That maybe it's because I'm a Londoner, that I love London town.

SB: Do you have a good sense of direction? Have you ever been lost? Did you find it easy to get here today?
CM: Well, I do pride myself on having a good sense of direction. There not many things that I pride myself on, but I think it's not – I'm, I'm pretty good there. Er, have I ever been lost? Well not totally and utterly lost. I've always known how to get out of wherever I've been, even it's in a – in the middle of a city. Erm, often I just – it sounds really weird, but in the middle of a city I would look for the sun and follow that.
SB: Yeah.

CM: And erm, how about you?
SB: Well, I – if I – if I've ever been on a route, then I can follow it again, and I can go back the way I came. So, if I've ever been somewhere I can do it again. So I think I've got a good sense of direction in that respect. And if I look look up somewhere on a map I can work out what I'm supposed to be doing, and so I don't worry about that. And when I came here I looked it up in the A to Z before I left home and then I checked at the map at the Underground station when I got off, and had no trouble at all. I just – you know, the streets were all where they were supposed to be.
CM: Yes.
SB: I've never really been lo- – I've sometimes taken the wrong turning in Newhaven, when I was in a hurry and hadn't really been – it was dark and I'd never been there in the dark before, and had to retrace my steps to realise where I went wrong. But usually there are landmarks and you – suddenly realise that that shouldn't be in that direction and maybe you're heading the wrong way.
CM: Mm, you should be going backwards. Yes.

UNIT 11

---

 *

CF: What slang words do you know for the police beginning with these letters? B?
MJ: Bobby.
CF: Mhm. C?
MJ: Cop.
CF: F?
MJ: Flic.
CF: I was thinking of flic. That's French isn't it, really?
MJ: Yeah.
CF: L? The law?
MJ: The law, yeah.
CF: Mm. R. Oh, there's that old word. Erm, 'razzers' or something like that. what is it? Rozzers?
MJ: Oh yes, rozzers. Yes, that's right. I have heard that.

As a police officer in the Costwold village of Broadway, I come across large numbers of tourists. On duty one day, I was approached by an American mother and her four-year-old son. She asked whether I would pose for a photograph with the boy and, in the interests of good public relations, I naturally agreed. As I took the child's hand, however, he looked distinctly apprehensive. Noticing this, his mother said, 'Now don't worry, son. This is not a real cop. This is an English bobby.'

The Hitch-hiker
Part 5: **'This is real trouble'**
The policeman must have been doing about a hundred and thirty when he passed us, and he took plenty of time slowing down. Finally, he pulled into the side of the road and I pulled in behind him. 'I didn't know police motor-cycles could go as fast as that,' I said rather lamely.

'That one can,' my passenger said. 'It's the same make as yours. It's a B.M.W. R90S. Fastest bike on the road. That's what they're usin' nowadays.'

The policeman got off his motor-cycle and leaned the machine sideways on to its prop stand. Then he took off his gloves and placed them carefully on the seat. He was in no hurry now. He had us where he wanted us and he knew it.

'This is real trouble,' I said. 'I don't like it one bit.'

'Don't talk to 'im any more than is necessary, you

152T

understand,' my companion said. 'Just sit tight and keep mum.'

Like an executioner approaching his victim, the policeman came strolling slowly towards us. He was a big meaty man with a belly, and his blue breeches were skin-tight around his enormous thighs. His goggles were pulled up on to the helmet, showing a smouldering red face with wide cheeks.

We sat there like guilty schoolboys, waiting for him to arrive.

'Watch out for this man,' my passenger whispered. ''Ee looks mean as the devil.'

The policeman came round to my open window and placed one meaty hand on the sill. 'What's the hurry?' he said.

'No hurry, officer,' I answered.

'Perhaps there's a woman in the back having a baby and you're rushing her to hospital? Is that it?'

'No, officer.'

'Or perhaps your house is on fire and you're dashing home to rescue the family from upstairs?' His voice was dangerously soft and mocking.

'My house isn't on fire, officer.'

'In that case,' he said, 'you've got yourself into a nasty mess, haven't you? Do you know what the speed limit is in this country?'

'Seventy,' I said.

'And do you mind telling me exactly what speed you were doing just now?'

I shrugged and didn't say anything.

When he spoke next, he raised his voice so loud that I jumped. 'One hundred and twenty miles per hour!' he barked. 'That's fifty miles an hour over the limit!'

147c *

CM: He was a meaty looking man wasn't he?
SB: Red faced.
CM: And a big pot belly, big thighs with blue breeches pulled tightly over them.
SB: I don't remember that. Sounds like the standard American cop.
CM: It does sound ike an American, yeah.
SB: American cop. The type that you don't like to mix with.
CM: And he had – Oh no –
SB: He took his gloves off and he's got his goggles up on his helmet.
CM: On his helmet.
SB: Not the type of person I would like to meet.
CM: Not at all.

147e *

SB: Do you think they'll get let off?
CM: Well it sounds like the policeman is a pretty mean character, and erm, he's so sarcastic in his preliminary remarks that erm, I can't imagine him, er, being lenient, no, so I don't think they'll get let off.
SB: I don't think it'd be reasonable anyway. But this is a Roald Dahl story so you never know.

150b *

SB: Well, if it was me I would have let his tyres down, but I probably wouldn't have waited for four days. And I would also have told the local police.
CM: Can the police do anything about it?
SB: They can clamp him. They can ticket him.
CM: But surely, surely not unless he's –
SB: It's not – you're not legally allowed to park in front of a driveway.

CM: Oh you're not, right.
SB: So I think he could have got the police to tow it away, but I think that if the police hadn't co-operated I'd have let the tyres down. I wouldn't have done any damage like smash the windscreen or scratch the paint, but just nuisance value stuff.
CM: Mm. I think I would have advised the police, erm, or probably I would have erm sought advice from some friend, who could have given me, erm, the legal, erm, bits of it and let me know whether I had a case or not. Then I would have let the police know, and then I think, erm had they not done anything, I would have, erm, I would probably waited by the car for the culprit to return and really speak to him or her face to face and explain the situation.
SB: Mm.
CM: So shall we turn over and read what happened? Do you want to read what happened?
SB: He was going to let all the air out of the tyres but he realised that then the car couldn't have moved. He finally borrowed his wife's lipstick and wrote on the windscreen.
CM: Oh.
SB: That was a bit of a cop out.
CM: Yes.
SB: I wouldn't have –
CM: Then it says has anything like this ever happened to you?
SB: Not really, because I don't drive a car, and it's very difficult to block up a bicycle.
CM: Yes.
SB: Erm, so I've never really had that sort of problem.
CM: It's never happened to me because I don't have a private drive, erm, and I don't tend to be boxed in. I haven't, been boxed in in parking places or anything like that, so it hasn't happened to me either.

The Hitch-hiker
Part 6: 'Me? What have I done wrong?'
He turned his head and spat out a big gob of spit. It landed on the wing of my car and started sliding down over my beautiful blue paint. Then he turned back again and stared hard at my passenger. 'And who are you?' he asked sharply.

'He's a hitch-hiker,' I said. 'I'm giving him a lift.'

'I didn't ask you,' he said. 'I asked him.'

''Ave I done somethin' wrong?' my passenger asked. His voice was as soft and oily as haircream.

'That's more than likely,' the policeman answered.

'Anyway, you're a witness. I'll deal with you in a minute. Driving-licence,' he snapped, holding out his hand.

I gave him my driving-licence.

He unbuttoned the left-hand breast-pocket of his tunic and brought out the dreaded book of tickets. Carefully, he copied the name and address from my licence. Then he gave it back to me. He strolled round to the front of the car and read the number from the number-plate and wrote that down as well. He filled in the date, the time and the details of my offence. Then he tore out the top copy of the ticket. But before handing it to me, he checked that all the information had come through clearly on his own carbon copy. Finally, he replaced the book in his tunic pocket and fastened it.

'Now you,' he said to my passenger, and he walked around to the other side of the car. From the other breast-pocket he produced a small black notebook. 'Name?' he snapped.

'Michael Fish,' my passenger said.

'Address?'

'Fourteen, Windsor Lane, Luton.'

'Show me something to prove this is your name and address,' the policeman said.

My passenger fished in his pockets and came out with a driving-licence of his own. The policeman checked the name and address and handed it back to him. 'What's your job?' he asked sharply.

'I'm an 'od carrier.'

'A what?'

'An 'od carrier.'

'Spell it.'

'H-O-D C-A- . . .'

'That'll do. And what's a hod carrier, may I ask?'

'An 'od carrier, officer, is a person 'oo carries the cement up the ladder to the bricklayer. And the 'od is what 'ee carries it in. It's got a long 'andle, and on the top you've got two bits of wood set at an angle . . .'

'All right, all right. Who's your employer?'

'Don't 'ave one. I'm unemployed.'

The policeman wrote all this down in the black note-book. Then he returned the book to its pocket and did up the button.

'When I get back to the station I'm going to do a little checking up on you,' he said to my passenger.

'Me? What've I done wrong?' the rat-faced man asked.

'I don't like your face, that's all,' the policeman said.

'And we just might have a picture of it somewhere in our files.' He strolled around the car and returned to my window.

152c *

SB: Memory Test. Are you ready?
CM: Mm. Yes.
SB: What details did the policemen write down, and where did he write them?
CM: He wrote down . . . well, where he wrote them was in his, his notebook.
SB: But I – not all. I think he did some on his ticket. He wrote down the name and address of the driver and his car number plate on the ticket book.
CM: And gave him a ticket.
SB: And gave him a ticket.
CM: He gave him the –
SB: Having checked that the carbon's come through.
CM: Top copy, yes.
SB: And he then put the, put the ticket book back in his tunic pocket.
CM: I don't think I read that bit.
SB: That was just aft- – I mean that was . . . on the previous page I think.
CM: Right, I believe you.
SB: But he wrote down . . . the passenger's name, address, occupation, and the fact that he's –
CM: occupation, and that fact that he's unemployed.
SB: In his notebook.
CM: Yes, and he's going to check them on his – when he gets back to the station.
SB: Yeah.
CM: Where did he put it – did – and he returned his notebook to his pocket and he did up the button, didn't he?
SB: To his pocket. Yeah.

152e *

CM: Right. Do you think the passenger really is a hod carrier? Would that count as a skilled trade, do you think?
SB: Well he said he wanted to – he thought the best way to get by was to be very good with something that is very very hard. I don't think being a hod carrier fits

into that, but that doesn't mean he isn't a hod carrier and does whatever he does that's very very hard in his spare time.
CM: Well he obviously thinks that skilled work is very important and he obviously counts himself as a skilled worker. I wouldn't count a hod carrier as a skilled worker.
SB: Mm.
CM: I would imagine that's one of the more menial jobs on a –
SB: Building site.
CM: on a building site. So if he is a hod carrier, erm he's not skilled and if he's skilled, he's not a hod carrier.
SB: Yeah, but he could be somebody who – is officially a hod carrier but really you know – he's a – he may have had experience as a hod carrier, but because he's unemployed he does things which may be a bit shady, that he wouldn't go around telling a policeman.
CM: So you think that he might be skilled in erm, safe-breaking or something and be a a hod carrier as erm, his legitimate employment.
SB: Yes. Something like that.

152f *

SB: Just a sort of sinking feeling that there's a fine, an endorsement, who knows what else coming up.
CM: Well I think also the fact that the policemen has spat out this horrible gob of spit over his beautiful new car.
SB: Yeah, must be feeling pretty sick.
CM: Yes, he wants to get out there and throw a bucket of water over it and shine it up again I think.
SB: Summarise how you feel you think both characters in the story are probably feeling. Do you agree with each other? Well I think the driver is probably feeling very puzzled about this person next to him who's – because he said he was skilled and is now a, saying he is a hod carrier. He's probably a bit suspicious of him.
CM: Erm, well, I think he was suspicious of him from the very beginning, the way that he's, erm, described him. I still think that the driver is still so bound up with the fact that he's, he's being booked for speeding. I think he I think he must still be trying to recover from that. And the little man, I wonder if he's worried at all. Because the policeman said that he's going to go and check on him. Erm, back at the station.
SB: He strikes me as the type of person that's supremely confident in all he does.
CM: Mm.
SB: So he's probably feeling quite cool and relaxed and the other, and the driver's feeling just generally bothered and worried and flustered.
CM: Mm.
SB: And unhappy. I think the the ratty-faced man or the hod carrier or whatever is probably a lot more relaxed.
CM: I think so too. I, I feel that erm, he's the one who's going to come better out of this er, this particular situation.
SB: I think he knows what he's doing.

UNIT 12

157e *

SB: What things can a tourist do for nothing or next to nothing in London?
CM: Feed the pigeons, in Trafalgar square.
SB: But that's bad for them!
CM: Oh yes, but they can still do it for nothing, or next to nothing. They can sit on a park bench in one of the many parks.

SB: Or they could go to Covent Garden and listen to the street entertainers.
CM: Buskers, yes.
SB: Buskers who – there's a lot of them and they're very good.
CM: And they can just walk around the markets there, and erm, and see – what's to be bought and all the colours, I think.
SB: You can't really eat, much.
CM: What, on nothing or next to nothing?
SB: On next to nothing.
CM: Yes.
SB: But – I think there's a lot to do. And they can go to museums and art galleries which are still free. And it doesn't cost that much to get a bus pass or an Underground pass.
CM: And they can walk along the Thames. Just walk down all the famous streets in London. Mainly sightseeing, I think. You – I mean you can see everything from the outside for nothing, can't you? Providing you're willing to walk or just take a bus ride. So, there's really quite a lot to do.

161a *

SB: What punishment/penalty do you think the driver will get? What might the police find out about the passenger from their files. Read on, and see how well you guessed.
CM: What punishment/penalty do you think the driver will get? Erm, where had we got to? That er –
SB: He's had a ticket.
CM: Oh that's right!
SB: So he'll probably get a fine, and an endorsement on his licence.
CM: Yes, but what would the endorsement be? For careless driving? Or driving without due care and attention?
SB: That sort of thing.
CM: Erm, and he'll probably get a fine, a substantial fine. But don't you get fined something like a pound an hour over – not a pound – a pound per mile per hour over the speed limit.
SB: Per mile per hour over the speed limit. So it would be a fifty pound fine. Something like that.
CM: What might the police find out about the passenger from their files?
SB: Well, that he had a previous criminal record.
CM: Well that – if they'd got him on file, that would be obvious wouldn't it?
SB: They – I wouldn't be surprised if they didn't have anything on him at all . . . But –
CM: Now, you're anticipating a twist.
SB: Of course. Shall we read on?
CM: Read on.

161b

The Hitch-hiker
Part 7: **'In serious trouble'**
'I suppose you know you're in serious trouble,' he said to me.

'Yes, officer.'

'You won't be driving this fancy car of yours again for a very long time, not after we've finished with you. You won't be driving any car again, come to that, for several years. And a good thing, too. I hope they lock you up for a spell into the bargain.'

'You mean prison?' I asked, alarmed.

'Absolutely,' he said, smacking his lips.' In the clink. Behind the bars. Along with all the other criminals who break the law. And a hefty fine into the bargain. Nobody will be more pleased about that than me. I'll see you in court, both of you. You'll be getting a summons to appear.'

He turned away and walked over to his motor-cycle.

He flipped the prop stand back into position with his foot and swung his leg over the saddle. Then he kicked the starter and roared off up the road out of sight.

'Phew!' I gasped. 'That's done it.'

'We was caught,' my passenger said. 'We was caught good and proper.'

'I was caught, you mean.'

'That's right,' he said. 'What you goin' to do now, guv'nor?'

'I'm going straight up to London to talk to my solicitor,' I said. I started the car and drove on.

'You mustn't believe what 'ee said about goin' to prison,' my passenger said. 'They don't put nobody in the clink for just speedin'.'

'Are you sure of that?' I asked.

'I'm positive,' he answered. 'They can take your licence away and they can give you a whoppin' big fine, but that'll be the end of it.'

I felt tremendously relieved.

'By the way,' I said, 'why did you lie to him?'

161c *

SB: Well, the lie must be about being an 'od carrier.
CM: That's right. It has to be that and obviously he'd picked up on the fact.
SB: Because he couldn't – that he'd said about skilled jobs.
CM: About being a skilled –
SB: Because he couldn't have s-, have known that, whether or not he was lying about his name and address. That was about all he said. So can you answer? Why?
CM: Why did he lie to him? Well obviously to – well the, the only reason I could think of is that this, his –
SB: Skilled profession.
CM: His – yes – is something that would not – he would not want the police to know about. Certainly that he would not tell the police about.
SB: He's a crook in other words. So what punishment do you think he will get?
CM: Who? The driver, presumably.
SB: The driver, I sup- – yeah.
CM: Well, could it be the hod carrier for not being er, honest to the police.
SB: No, I don't think the hod carrier is – I think they mean the driver.
CM: Well. As you said the, the – as erm, the ratty faced man said to the driver that they'll give him a, probably a big fine and they'll endorse him. Didn't he say that ? They can take your driver's licence away and give you a whopping fine.
SB: Yeah. But they won't throw him in prison.
CM: Well I don't think people get sent to prison these days not certainly on first offences.
SB: Not for speeding.
CM: No.
SB: Prisons are overcrowded as it is. What do you think he'll say to his solicitor? Write a quick list of the points he'll probably include. Well, he'll tell his solicitor he was speeding. He'll say that the man encouraged him to do it. Or say that he co-operated with the police.
CM: Do you want to make a quick list of the points he'll probably include?
SB: Okay.
CM: He'll have to say that, what, what speed he was going and in what –
SB: What speed.
CM: And er, what was the maximum legal speed.
SB: What the limit was. That he pulled over as soon as he was –
CM: Yes. Signalled.

SB: That he had a witness.
CM: A witness for the fact that he was speeding.
SB: Well, he'll probably tell his solicitor there was somebody in the car with him.
CM: Yeah.
SB: Anything else?
CM: And perhaps some details of the witness. If he managed to retain erm, the erm – if he remembered – managed to remember –
SB: The name and address.
CM: – the hod carrier's name and address.
SB: Michael Fish. 14 something or other, Luton.
CM: What a memory.
SB: And so on.
CM: Yes.
SB: Okay?
CM: Is that enough?
SB: I think so. Let's go on to the next one.

163

Listen to the sentences a to r. In which two sentences is the 'do' stressed?

a. M1: If you do find yourself in London with no place to stay . . .
b. F1: So, there's really quite a lot to do.
c. M2: But they can still do it for nothing or next-to-nothing.
d. F2: It doesn't cost that much to get a bus pass . . .
e. M1: Well no . . . I don't think people get sent to prison.
f. F1: Don't you get fined something like a pound an hour?
g. M2: 'Phew!' I gasped. 'That's done it.'
h. F2: 'By the way,' I said, 'why did you lie to him?'
i. M1: What job do you think he does?
j. F1: 'So what do you do? I asked him.
k. M2: Doesn't strike me really as a surgeon.
l. F2: 'Do I look like a copper?' 'No,' he said. 'You don't.'
m. M1: 'I don't really care one way or the other.' 'I think you do care,' he said.
n. F1: I didn't like the way he read my thoughts.
o. M2: Didn't he say that?
p. F2: 'Well, what do you think?' he asked.
q. M1: Yes, that was how they did it.
r. F1: How do you think it ends?

164b *

JM: Getting things for nothing. Read the story about the baby in the cinema. How do you think it ends? So it's another one of these sort of things. Erm . . .
MJ: Well, I'd say it's pretty . . . clear that they got the baby to cry somehow and, erm, got their money back.
JM: Yes, yes.
MJ: I wonder how they made it cry.
JM: Oh, pinching it probably, yes.
MJ: Bit cruel, isn't it?
JM: Er . . . Yes . . . they can be useful as a source of disruption, I suppose, babies.
MJ: Do you find?
JM: Well, erm, I haven't had to use Joe, erm, as a means of jumping queues but I'm sure if I got Joe to be really, erm, badly behaved I could get him to sort of make people leave the room and, er, enable me to get, get to the front of queues in waiting rooms I suppose. This is apparently what, erm, some relatives of ours used to do all the time. They had two sons and they used to make them run around and they'd get boarded onto planes or onto boats more quickly because they were causing so much fuss.
MJ: Gosh, yes. Let's have a look and see. 'Shake little Johnny.' Yes. That was how they did it. They shook him and he cried.
JM: Mhm.
MJ: Poor little Johnny.
JM: Yes. Right.

167b *

CM: Stop after – and discuss what trade he could be in.
SB: That he's very proud of.
CM: He's proud of a trade in – but he's not likely to just tell it – well –
SB: Tell the police.
CM: Yes.
SB: He could be a thief that's proud of his trade or –
CM: He's, he's – 'I'm about as proud of my job as anybody could be in the entire world'. I wonder if he's as proud of his – he says – Yes, I wonder if he could – if he he really is as proud of his job or as proud of his skill.
SB: I think he's proud of the job but I don't know – I'm not sure what it would be unless it's something illegal.
CM: Yes, I – that's the only reason I can think why he wouldn't be willing to tell the police. And certainly, erm . . . have the police look him up in their files about –. Shall we go on?
SB: Yeah, shall we go on?
CM: Yes.

167d *

SB: I'm in some kind of a very-blank-trade.
CM: Skilled, again?
SB: I think something more like crooked . . . Because he's –
CM: Yes, it's not –
SB: 'Cause he's obviously quite interested in it. The driver is quite interested in what the trade is.
CM: Yes. And he says, I didn't like the way he read my thoughts. So what would the driver think he's doing? Well, we've already decided that we think he's crooked.
SB: I think the driver would as well.
CM: Yes.
SB: In the circumstances. I am in a very crooked trade.
CM: I'm in the most crooked trade of them all.
SB: I suppose so. Makes sense.
CM: I don't know.
SB: He waited for him to go on. How do I know you're not another – well that must be –
CM: Another p- –
SB: Policeman, or cop.
CM: Or a copper.
SB: Yeah.
CM: In plain clothes. Do I look like a co- – Well he's already used the word copper so –
SB: Yeah. Do I look like a copper? I think it's most likely that that's what that's all about.
CM: Mm. Er, he took from his pocket a tin of tobacco and a packet of cigarette papers and started to –
SB: Roll.
CM: Must have roll a cigarette. His tongue – he ran his tongue along the edge of the paper, stuck it down and –
SB: Placed the cigarette between his lips.
CM: Stuck.
SB: Something like that.
CM: I'd say it would be stuck. And as if from nowhere a lighter appeared in his hand. The lighter . . . flicked?
SB: Flared? – Flared?
CM: Or flicked yes. Flared, yes, lit no.
SB: Yes, 'c-cos th-the cigarette was lit, the lighter disappeared. It was altogether a . . .
CM: Magnificent.
SB: I'd go for professional.
CM: Or polished.
SB: Yeah, something like that.

167c *

SB: Tell us now with fresh evidence what job do you think he does. What job needs skilled hands?
CM: Write a list. I think a safebreaker.

SB: That's possible. But why's he going to Epsom on Derby Day? Where he . . .
CM: Or a pickpocket.
SB: Yeah, that's my first thought. He's a pickpocket. Erm . . . we're all being very suspicious of him.
CM: Well exactly, it's his . . . erm, what jobs need skilled hands, oh, what job do you think does? Can you say a pickpocket is a job?
SB: Yeah, I would have thought so if you made your money from it.
CM: Put down in your CV!
SB: Well, maybe not that much. Erm, a conjurer?
CM: M-mm.
SB: Or a con-man of some description.
CM: Er, surgeons need skilled hands.
SB: Doesn't strike me really as a surgeon.
CM: But that's not the point! What jobs need skilled hands?
SB: True, you can put him down as a surgeon.
CM: With a ratty face.
SB: A ratty faced surgeon . . . yes . . . erm . . . anything else?
CM: How many have we got?
SB: Four.
CM: Okay. Let's check the key to the missing words, see over . . .

The Hitch-hiker
Part 8: 'It was quite fantastic'
'Who, me?' he said. 'What makes you think I lied?'

'You told him you were an unemployed hod carrier. But you told me you were in a highly skilled trade.'

'So I am,'' he said. 'But it don't pay to tell everythin' to a copper.'

'So what do you do?' I asked him.

'Ah,' he said slyly. 'That'd be tellin', wouldn't it?'

'Is it something you're ashamed of?'

'Ashamed?' he cried. 'Me, ashamed of my job? I'm about as proud of it as anybody could be in the entire world!'

'Then why won't you tell me?'

[Can you guess what he does?]

'You writers really is nosey parkers, aren't you?' he said. 'And you ain't goin' to be 'appy, I don't think, until you've found out exactly what the answer is?'

'I don't really care one way or the other,' I told him, lying.

He gave me a crafty little ratty look out of the sides of his eyes. 'I think you do care,' he said. 'I can see it on your face that you think I'm in some kind of a very peculiar trade and you're just achin' to know what it is.'

I didn't like the way he read my thoughts. I kept quiet and stared at the road ahead.

'You'd be right, too,' he went on. 'I am in a very peculiar trade. I'm in the queerest peculiar trade of 'em all.'

I waited for him to go on.

'That's why I 'as to be extra careful 'oo I'm talkin' to, you see. 'Ow am I to know, for instance, you're not another copper in plain clothes?'

'Do I look like a copper?'

'No,' he said. 'You don't. And you ain't. Any fool could tell that.'

He took from his pocket a tin of tobacco and a packet of cigarette papers and started to roll a cigarette. I was watching him out of the corner of one eye, and the speed with which he performed this rather difficult operation was incredible. The cigarette was rolled and

ready in about five seconds. He ran his tongue along the edge of the paper, stuck it down and popped the cigarette betewen his lips. Then, as if from nowhere, a lighter appeared in his hand. The lighter flamed. The cigarette was lit. The lighter disappeared. It was altogether a remarkable performance.

'I've never seen anyone roll a cigarette as fast as that,' I said.

'Ah,' he said, taking a deep suck of smoke. 'So you noticed.'

'Of course I noticed. It was quite fantastic.'

He sat back and smiled. It pleased him very much that I had noticed how quickly he could roll a cigarette ....

UNIT 13

 *

JM: Once erm, er, when I was at University, and some friends put brown paper over, erm, the entrance to a friend's, er, room, and so, she opened the door in the morning and the corridor wasn't there, there was just this brown paper screen. And she said, 'I didn't know whether to sort of jump through it like jumping out of a hoop, you know, through a hoop, or, erm, whether to ignore it and just sort of calmly, erm, tear it down', but because, er, because she didn't know what was on the other side, she decided to calmly tear it down. But, er, the people watching found it all very amusing.

---

 *

SB: Well my girlfriend's very frightened of flying, and she had a bad experience. She was flying home to Texas and she looked out of the window, and she was frightened enough, and suddenly saw that one of the engines was on fire.
CM: Uh, heavens!
SB: She called over an air hostess and pointed this out and they had to take the plane back to Heathrow.
CM: Does that mean that nobody else had noticed?
SB: I think maybe the pilots had noticed, but certainly nobody else on board had noticed and she was the first to see this, so they drugged her up with a mixture of alcohol and valium for the next flight, by when she'd missed her connection in New York to Texas and so she had to go on.
CM: So that was frustrating as well as a frightening experience.

---

 *

SB: Some of the words in this episode have been blanked out. Discuss what you think they were.
CM: So we read it first and then discuss, right.

SB: Well, beautifully shaped, so long, slim and long and –
CM: elegant.
SB: straight.
CM: Right.
SB: Something like that.
CM: elegant.
SB: We didn't think that he might have been a piano player.
CM: Could be nimble
SB: Yes.
CM: Yes, he didn't look like a piano player. But it's interesting that they were the fingers of a brain surgeon.
SB: Or a watchmaker.
CM: Mm.
SB: It's a hundred more times difficult than playin' the piano.

CM: Any . . . fool –
SB: Any . . . any fool –
SB: Yes . . .
SB: can learn to do that
CM: can learn to do that.
CM: There's . . . something little kid's learnin' lots of . . . little kids?
SB: Yeah –
CM: Tons of . . .
SB: Yeah, something like that . . .
CM: Something like that . . . loads of, or something like that. Erm – You do, I think you, I know what you do I said. You do –
SB: conjuring tricks. You're a magician.
CM: tricks. You're a –
CM: or a conjurer. Me? he snorted, a –
SB: magician.
CM: conjurer.
SB: Can you picture me –
CM: Can you picture me –
CM: goin' round snively kids' parties, something like that..
SB: noisy.
CM: makin' rabbits come out of top hats.
SB: Then you're a card player. You get people in card games and
SB: you deal yourself –
CM: you deal yourself –
SB: excellent hands . . . winning hands –
CM: Erm, yes . . .
SB: Me! a rotten card sharp –
CM: card shark –
SB: Yes.
CM: Is it shark or sharp?
SB: I think sharp, for –
CM: Is it?
SB: Yeah.
CM: Card sharp. That's a miserable lie if ever I – oh.
SB: A miserable trade or a lie, yeah.
CM: a miserable –
CM: if ever there was one. It looks bigger than lie!
SB: Mm, I think trade, you know, it's a miserable –
CM: Mmm, right.
SB: occupation.
SB: Well, where did he get the belt from?
CM: Well, presumably he got it off the driver.
SB: Yeah, round the driver's waist, I suspect.
CM: That's right.

174c *

SB: Let's see those missing words. Elegant, you were right.
CM: Twerp, what did we say? Erm, they – any twerp – we said fool, didn't we? Any twerp. Titchy, I said snively.
SB: Yeah.
CM: Conjuring tricks, conjurer.
SB: Conjuring tricks, conjurer.
SB: Yes, titchy kids, learning to play piano, yes,
CM: Yeah. Can you picture me going round . . . was it –
SB: Erm –
CM: No, hold on . . . oh, and deal yourself crummy hands . . . well that would be right because to get erm –
SB: No, marvellous hands, surely . . . crummy kids and marvellous hands!
CM: Sorry!
SB: card sharper, yeah.
CM: Is, is it a card sharper? Yes.
SB: Mm, miserable racket.
CM: That's a miserable racket if ever there was one.
SB: Yeah. Okay.
CM: Good.

174f

The Hitch-hiker
Part 9: '**Any twerp can learn to do that!**'
'You want to know what makes me able to do it?' he asked.

'Go on then.'

'It's because I've got fantastic fingers. These fingers of mine,' he said, holding up both hands high in front of him, 'are quicker and cleverer than the fingers of the best piano player in the world!'

'Are you a piano player?'

'Don't be daft,' he said. 'Do I look like a piano player?'

I glanced at his fingers. They were so beautifully shaped, so slim and long and elegant, they didn't seem to belong to the rest of him at all. They looked more like the fingers of a brain surgeon or a watchmaker.

'My job', he went on. 'is a hundred times more difficult than playin' the piano. Any twerp can learn to do that. There's titchy little kids learnin' to play the piano in almost any 'ouse you go into these days. That's right, ain't it?'

'More or less,' I said.

'Of course it's right. But there's not one person in ten million can learn to do what I do. Not one in ten million! 'Ow about that?'

'Amazing,' I said.

'You're darn right it's amazin',' he said.

'I think I know what you do,' I said. 'You do conjuring tricks. You're a conjurer.'

'Me?' he snorted. 'A conjurer? Can you picture me going' round crummy kids' parties makin' rabbits come out of top 'ats?'

'Then you're a card player. You get people into card games and you deal yourself marvellous hands.'

'Me! A rotten card-sharper!' he cried. 'That's a miserable racket if ever there was one.'

'All right. I give up.'

I was taking the car along slowly now, at no more than forty miles an hour, to make quite sure I wasn't stopped again. We had come on to the main London–Oxford road and were running down the hill toward Denham.

Suddenly, my passenger was holding up a black leather belt in his hand. 'Ever seen this before?' he asked. The belt had a brass buckle of unusual design.

'Hey!' I said. 'That's mine, isn't it? It is mine! Where did you get it?'

 177c *

MJ: If you did lose your purse/wallet could you describe it to the police? Without looking at it, describe it as accurately as possible to your partner and then take it out and see if your partner agrees.
CF: I could try I suppose.
MJ: Go on.
CF: I've got to describe my purse?
MJ: Your purse or your wallet.
CF: And its contents or just the purse?
MJ: It just says your, no, it doesn't say contents.
CF: Okay, I know mine pretty well, because I was ripped off when I bought it . . . Erm, because it's an imitation Pierre Cardin.
MJ: Oh no!
CF: I bought it at the airport in Sydney, er, very foolishly. It's blue. I don't know if it's leather or not – it's about seven inches long and about four inches wide.
MJ: Uh huh.
CF: Erm, it's got a kind of metal 'R' on the front.

Inside, it's got a front pocket, and then, two side, two pockets either side of a zip container and a back folder place, folder place where you put credit cards. Do you want to have a look and see if I'm right . . . ?
MJ: Mm.
CF: Do you think it's leather?
MJ: Mm, yeah, I think it's leather.
CF: Well, that's something ....

---

 *

MJ: Have you ever had to call the police? Why? What happened?
CF: Well I don't think I have.
MJ: I have – recently. We were burgled twice in the last few months.
CF: Really!
MJ: Once in Cambridge and once in Bristol, erm, both times the video was stolen and the second one was a replacement for the first one – they were both rented.
CF: Oh.
MJ: And erm, Kas insisted on calling the police immediately and wanted to dial nine nine nine you know. Emergency! We must call the police even though it was four in the morning the second time and erm, they came round but they never caught the people that erm, broke in. The second time they actually broke the window, these people. Most unusual.
CF: Was it a ground floor window?
MJ: They smashed the window with a dustbin, got in and got out while er we were upstairs. By the time we got downstairs they, they already were half way down the street.
CF: Did you hear them?
MJ: Oh yes!
CF: Mm.
MJ: It was quite a shock really.
CF: Could they see the video from outside?
MJ: Yes, they did, they saw the, the light.
CF: Mm.
MJ: Erm they, there was a, we had an attempted burglary first of all, we were in the house that time as well and they tried to bash the door down, erm, it's what's called the three minute gang in Bristol. They erm, they come and they try and batter your door down and get something out before er you know, you have time to react really, in three minutes.
CF: Mm.
MJ: And erm, they didn't get the door down, though we had to get a new door because they damaged it with a crow bar, and then they came back and they'd evidently decided they must have this video, cause they'd seen the light, and after the attempted break in we did have a piece of paper over the light but they, they knew it was there.
CF: Mm.
MJ: They came back, and they got so frustrated they broke the window. But the police never caught them.
CF: Mm.

---

 *

SB: No more blanked words.
CM: If the hitchhiker had got the driver's belt, what other things might he have got and how? Why is he doing this? Read on and comment as you read if you like.
SB: Might have got the wallet.
CM: Well yes. Any – what other things, his watch perhaps? Anything of value that he'd have on his person.
SB: His tie . . . that might be a bit tricky!
CM: I don't think it will be of much value, anyway! Unless it was made of gold.
SB: Right.

The Hitch-hiker
PART 10: 'Nice bit of stuff, this!'
He grinned and waved the belt gently from side to side. 'Where d'you think I got it?' he said. 'Off the top of your trousers, of course.'

I reached down and felt for my belt. It was gone.

'You mean you took if off me while we've been driving along?' I asked, flabbergasted.

He nodded, watching me all the time with those little black ratty eyes.

'That's impossible,' I said. 'You'd have had to undo the buckle and slide the whole thing out through the loops all the way round. I'd have seen you doing it. And even if I hadn't seen you, I'd have felt it.'

'Ah, but you didn't, did you?' he said, triumphant.

He dropped the belt on his lap, and now all at once there was a brown shoelace dangling from his fingers. 'And what about this, then?' he exclaimed, waving the shoelace.

'What about it?' I said.

'Anyone around 'ere missin' a shoelace?' he asked, grinning.

I glanced down at my shoes. The lace of one of them was missing. 'Good grief!' I said. 'How did you do that? I never saw you bending down.'

'You never saw nothin',' he said proudly. 'You never even saw me move an inch. And you know why?'

'Yes,' I said. 'Because you've got fantastic fingers.'

'Exactly right!' he cried. 'You catch on pretty quick, don't you?' He sat back and sucked away at his home-made cigarette, blowing the smoke out in a thin stream against the windshield. He knew he had impressed me greatly with those two tricks, and this made him very happy. 'I don't want to be late,' he said. 'What time is it?'

'There's a clock in front of you,' I told him.

'I don't trust car clocks,' he said. 'What does your watch say?'

I hitched up my sleeve to look at the watch on my wrist. It wasn't there. I looked at the man. He looked back at me, grinning.

'You've taken that, too,' I said.

He held out his hand and there was my watch lying in his palm. 'Nice bit of stuff, this,' he sid. 'Superior quality Eighteen-carat gold. Easy to flog, too. It's never any trouble gettin' rid of quality goods.'

'I'd like it back, if you don't mind,' I said rather huffily.

He placed the watch carefully on the leather tray in front of him. 'I wouldn't nick anything from you, guv'nor,' he said. 'You're my pal. You're givin' me a lift.'

'I'm glad to hear it,' I said.

'All I'm doin' is answerin' your question,' he went on. 'You asked me what I did for a livin' and I'm showin' you.'

---

 *

SB: Well, we guessed right about the watch.
CM: Yes. We didn't guess about the shoelace.
SB: I never wear sh . . . Well, I do wear shoes with laces but not that often.
CM: Er, the question is why's he doing this? Erm, what other things? To show –
SB: To impress the other guy?
CM: Yes, and to show him that, er –
SB: To answer his question about what sort of job he does.

CM: He still isn't answering it, though.
SB: Well, he's a pickpocket.
CM: Yes, well, I don't know ... Anyway, yes, to impress the man, and to to to show him what he can do. Shall we go on?

UNIT 14

MJ: Mm. Well, for Kas, I've got, er, I will try not to –
CF: Who's Kas?
MJ: Kas is my husband.
CF: Right.
MJ: I will try not to finish everything at the eleventh hour. He always finishes everything at the absolute last minute. Like at the moment he's finishing off an MA thesis he's been doing for four years and we're leaving the country, erm, Friday week and he's in Cambridge at the moment, erm reading through the, erm, the computer script for it. He still needs to get it corrected and bound and submitted. Erm, I will always reply to letters within two weeks of receiving them. In fact he never replies to letters at all normally. I have to reply to his letters.
CF: That's a bit rough!
MJ: Yes. Yes it is really. And I will not leave tissues, money, etc. in my clothes and I will always unfold the sleeves of my shirts when I put them in the dirty clothes basket. That's a totally banal sort of thing but – I have to do all his washing you see.
CF: Why's that?
MJ: He doesn't get around to doing it. Well I have to put it in the washing machine for him. I don't know really. It somehow has come out that way. But erm, I'm always finding bits of tissue all over the clothes, and coins in the pockets and he never rolls his sleeves down so I think he should make a resolution to stop that.

186d *

MJ: Do you want mine or, my resolutions now or would you like to give me yours? I'll give you mine. Well Kas is always complaining that I don't clean the kitchen up, and I don't do the washing up, and he always has to do all the washing up, so I can make a resolution to regularly clean the kitchen and do some washing up.
CF: How regularly?
MJ: Well like, most days.
CF: Most days.
MJ: Erm, I'll try not to worry about things that might never happen. I'm a bit of a worrier. I tend to worry about – I lie awake at night thinking Oh my God such and such might happen, you know. Or really I ought to do this. Thinking of things to worry when there isn't any- – to worry about when there isn't anything to worry about. And I will keep regular track, track of the money I spend. Because it gets out of hand. You keep writing cheques and you don't know how much money you've spent. You suddenly realise that you've got an overdraft of four hundred pounds when you thought you had some money in the bank.
CF: Mm. Have you got, erm, plastic money?
MJ: Cards?
CF: Yes.
MJ: Yes. We do tend to use those rather a lot. Yes, as well. It adds up.
CF: They're the worst.
MJ: Yes, shocking. John Lewis, and er, Barclaycard and ... things. Yes.

188a *

JM: Have you ever erm ... had your fortune told?
CF: Mm. Yes. In India.
JM: Oh yes.

CF: Mm. In Delhi. A very plausible rogue. Accosted me in the street and took me off to this little carpet shop. And he was so charming, as only Indian men can be.
JM: Mm.
CF: Erm. He persuaded me to part with – I can't remember how many rupees now, I think it was about 200, which is quite a lot of money. And then proceeded to tell me all sorts of wonderful things. He told me, by this time next year – this time last year, I think it was in June actually – I would be married.
JM: Are you?
CF: And back in India. No, no, no. And I liked the idea of being back in India very much. And he told me I was going to win forty thousand pounds in a lottery, and various other things.
JM: Did anything come true?
CF: Absolutely nothing. I then went back to the hotel and found a New Zealander who'd had the – exactly the same story.

CF: I did have a friend who used to read tea-leaves. She learnt to do it in Jamaica. And, erm, one day she told me that I was going to – she saw me, sprawling in a ditch – erm, with a friend and there was a motor, motorcycle on the road.
JM: Oh dear.
CF: And that actually did happen.
JM: Oh.
CF: It was, er, I was on the back of my friend's motorbike and we were coming back, erm, to school, very early one morning, we'd stayed out the night before. And sh-, there was a lot of loose gravel on the road and the bike slipped, and we both ended up in the ditch, and I burnt my leg on the exhaust.
JM: My sister, erm, went through a phase of reading palms and, er, she read my palm and my wife's palm and, erm, according to my palm we're going to have three children, and according to hers we're going to have two which is a bit worrying.
CF: Two and a half!
JM: Yes. Erm ... But –
CF: You haven't ever had your palm –
JM: I've never, erm, been to a formal, er, fortune telling.
CF: Mm. Don't you believe in it?
JM: Erm, not really, no. Erm, I, erm ... I, I just don't think it's, it's likely that, erm, I believe in free will, you know, so it's not likely that er, er, things can be preordained.
CF: Mm.

188d

Mme. Wawanda tapped her crystal ball nervously and began to speak. "You soon will meet a tall, handsome man who looks something like Mayor John Lindsay," she told the young woman. "He owns 94 producing oil wells, two square blocks in downtown Minneapolis, and a yacht with a crew of 34. He will marry you and you'll be happy forever after."

"Sensational!" breathed her ecstatic customer. "But tell me just one more thing: ..."

CM: Summarise the things he has already taken. What else might he have got?
SB: Shoelace, watch, belt.
CM: Belt.
SB: What else might he have got?
CM: Wallet, erm, tie-pin if there had been one. You, you suggested a tie.
SB: Yeah.
CM: Well if he was so good he would well have done a – taken his tie away.

SB: Yeah.
CM: Erm, I believe they can take vests off without taking your shirt off.
SB: I think that's going a bit too far even with these, with that sort of hands –
CM: Well, I don't know –
SB: That's conjuring tricks.
CM: He seems to be pretty smart.
SB: Yeah, driving licence, or –
CM: Well, that'll probably be in the wallet.
SB: Key ring, or something, except that'd probably be in the ignition.
CM: Any of the contents of his, er, of his pockets.
SB: All the loose change from his pockets, or –
CM: That's right.
SB: What else, so what is his trade? He's a pickpocket.
CM: Yes.
SB: Must be.

The Hitch-hiker
Part 11: **'A Fingersmith'**
'What else have you got of mine?'

He smiled again, and now he started to take from the pocket of his jacket one thing after another that belonged to me – my driving-licence, a key-ring with four keys on it, some pound notes, a few coins, a letter from my publishers, my diary, a stubby old pencil, a cigarette-lighter, and last of all, a beautiful old sapphire ring with pearls around it belonging to my wife. I was taking the ring up to the jeweller in London because one of the pearls was missing.

'Now there's another lovely piece of goods,' he said, turning the ring over in his fingers. 'That's eighteenth century, if I'm not mistaken, from the reign of King George the Third.'

'You're right,' I said impressed. 'You're absolutely right.'

He put the ring on the leather tray with the other items.

'So you're a pickpocket,' I said.

'I don't like that word,' he answered. 'It's a coarse and vulgar word. Pickpockets is coarse and vulgar people who only do easy little amateur jobs. They lift money from blind old ladies.'

'What do you call yourself, then?'

'Me? I'm a fingersmith. I'm a professional fingersmith.' He spoke the words solemnly and proudly, as though he were telling me he was the President of the Royal College of Surgeons or the Archbishop of Canterbury.

'I've never heard that word before,' I said. 'Did you invent it?'

'Of course I didn't invent it,' he replied. 'It's the name given to them who's risen to the very top of the profession. You've 'eard of a goldsmith and a silversmith, for instance. They're experts with gold and silver. I'm an expert with my fingers, so I'm a fingersmith.'

'It must be an interesting job.'

'And that's why you go to the races?'

'Race meetings is easy meat,' he said. 'You just stand around after the race, watchin' for the lucky ones to queue up and draw their money. And when you see someone collectin' a big bundle of notes, you simply follows after 'im and 'elps yourself. But don't get me wrong, guv'nor. I never takes nothin' from a loser. Nor from poor people neither. I only go after them as can afford it, the winners and the rich.'

'That's very thoughtful of you,' I said. 'How often do you get caught?'

'Caught?' he cried, disgusted. 'Me get caught!' It's only pickpockets get caught. Fingersmiths never. Listen, I could take the false teeth out of you mouth if I wanted to and you wouldn't even catch me!'

'I don't have false teeth,' I said.

'I know you don't,' he answered. 'Otherwise I'd 'ave 'ad 'em out long ago!'

I believed him. Those long slim fingers of his seemed able to do anything.

We drove on for a while without talking.

Ring a ring o' roses

Ring, a ring o' roses,
A pocketful o' posies,
Hish-a, hish-a,
All fall down.

The big ship sailed
The big ship sailed on the Ally-Ally-O,
The Ally-Ally-O, the Ally-Ally-O.
The big ship sailed on the Ally-Ally-O
On the last day of September.

The big ship sank to the bottom of the sea,
The bottom of the sea, the bottom of the sea.
The big ship sank to the bottom of the sea
On the last day of September.

 *

SB: Well?
CM: How do you think the driver is feeling now?
SB: Nervous . . . and a bit of a fool.
CM: Mm, yes, I, I wouldn't say he's particularly – I, I, I don't think he's feeling nervous. Because . . .
SB: I suppose if everything is now . . . in plain view.
CM: Yes, and also that erm, the man is so . . . erm . . . proud of his profession, he calls himself a fingersmith, not a pickpocket and he spoke the word solemnly and proudly and so he's obviously very proud of his profession . . . er, he calls it a profession . . . erm . . . so I think that erm he said that he wouldn't, he wouldn't –
SB: Take anything from the driver because he was his friend –
CM: From the driver because he was his pal –
SB: Yeah.
CM: his friend so I think I wouldn't be feeling nervous in that situation so I don't see why the driver should.
SB: Impressed?
CM: Yeah, very impressed.
SB: Mm and I think, a bit, a bit sort of feeling that, how easy he's been taken for a ride or something.
CM: That he's easy prey.
SB: Yeah, er, a bit embarrassed about himself.

193c *

CM: Mm, well the thing is I'm sure there's going to be a twist to this . . .
SB: Mmm.
CM: So erm . . .
SB: I wouldn't be surprised if he's managed to pick the pockets of the policeman and taken out his notepad and ticket book.
CM: I – wou – that's probably exactly right, well done. But did the policeman come near enough to him?
SB: He came round to his side of the car to talk to him. And with fingers like that he didn't need to come that near.
CM: Do you believe me then that he said that . . . he, he could take his, his vest off?
SB: I think he could if the guy's wearing a vest. I mean, if he could take the false teeth out of his mouth without him noticing –

CM: Yes, you're probably quite right! I'm, so, erm . . . well, shall we say that that's one ending and the other ending probably is far more tame than that.
SB: That's one possible ending, yes.
CM: Erm . . . just that they get to London or wherever they're going.
SB: He picks the car from around the driver!
CM: . . . stuffs it, stuffs it in his pocket! Erm . . .
SB: Or else that they get, I don't know . . . somewhere th- . . .
CM: Just that he drops him off in London and breathes a sigh of relief . . . that the man has left his life and . . .
SB: I suppose so, mmm . . .
CM: That he's got to pick up the debris, of, the, the ticket and everything.
SB: Maybe the pickpocketing is so obvious that they'll have thought of a different ending, the picking the policeman's pocket is so obvious they'll have thought of something else.
CM: Well, shall we have a go?
SB: Okay.
CM: and have a look.
CM: Mmm, very well done . . . And say what you thought about the ending . . . well, it was only what I expected after you had anticipated it.
SB: Yeah, we never did get to find out whether the car could do a hundred and twenty nine miles an hour.
CM: Yes we did! Because he was booked for doing a hundred and twenty –
SB: He was doing, for doing a hundred and twenty.
CM: A hundred and twenty nine. The policeman must have been doing a hundred and thirty.
SB: Yeah, but he's, the policeman said you were doing a hundred and twenty because you were fifty miles over the speed limit.
CM: He did say you were doing a hundred and twenty nine. We'll go back and have a look at the, at the page earlier on.
SB: Well that's in the other – yes, oh yes, the ending was far too obvious. Anybody could have guessed it right from the start.
CM: Mmm.
SB: No, I think it's a very good ending. I think that you wouldn't necessarily have thought about it unless you'd read through everything slowly and carefully, like we did.
CM: I wouldn't have, sorry . . .
SB: I don't think – we would not have got, guessed it if we hadn't -
CM: No, that's true because it, it brought it right up neatly to the to the fact that there was going to be this neat twist where – erm especially he was, um, the ratty fellow was so complacent, smug and er that had to be based on something.
SB: Easiest job I've ever done.
CM: That's right.
SB: Yes.
CM: Thank you Guv'nor. It's always nice to be appreciated.
SB: Right.

The Hitch-hiker
Part 12: **'It's always nice to be appreciated'**
'That policeman's going to check up on you pretty thoroughly,' I said. 'Doesn't that worry you a bit?'

'Nobody's checkin' up on me,' he said.

'Of course they are. He's got your name and address written down most carefully in his black book.'

The man gave me another of his sly, ratty little smiles. 'Ah,' he said. 'So 'ee 'as. But I'll bet 'ee ain't got it all written down in 'is memory as well. I've never known a copper yet with a decent memory. Some of 'em can't even remember their own names.'

'What's memory got to do with it?' I asked. 'It's written down in his book, isn't it?'

'Yes, guv'nor, it is. But the trouble is, 'ee's lost the book. 'Ee's lost both books, the one with my name in it and the one with yours.'

In the long delicate fingers of his right hand, the man was holding up in triumph the two books he had taken from the policeman's pockets. 'Easiest job I ever done,' he announced proudly.

I nearly swerved the car into a milk-truck, I was so excited.

'That copper's got nothin' on either of us now,' he said.

'You're a genius!' I cried.

''Ee's got no names, no addresses, no car number, no nothin','' he said.

'You're brilliant!'

'I think you'd better pull in off this main road as soon as possible,' he said. 'Then we'd better build a little bonfire and burn these books.'

'You're a fantastic fellow,' I exclaimed.

'Thank you, guv'nor,' he said. 'It's always nice to be appreciated.'

UNIT 15

The Hitch-hiker: a dramatisation
M1: I was driving up to London one day in my new BMW when I saw a man by the side of the road thumbing a lift. I always stop for hitch-hikers, because I used to do a lot of it myself, so I came to a stop and offered him a lift . . .
M2: Going to London, guv'nor?
M1: Yes, jump in.
M2: Thanks.
M1: What part of London are you headed for?
M2: I'm goin' right through London. I'm goin' to Epsom for the races – the Derby.
M1: Great. I love racing.
M2: I don't. It's a waste of time.
M1: Why do you go then?
M2: Ah well . . . I just do.
M1: I see, it's part of your job is it? Do you mind me asking what you do? I'm very curious, I'm afraid. Perhaps it's because I'm a writer.
M2: You must be a good writer if you're drivin' round in a car like this. It's a skilled trade like mine. How fast will this car go anyway?
M1: One hundred and twenty-nine miles an hour.
M2: I bet it won't. All car makers is liars. They always say they'll go faster than they really will. Go on. Open 'er up. I bet she won't to a hundred and twenty-nine.

Keep right on to the end of the road.

Every road through life is a long, long road,
Filled with joys and sorrows too,
As you journey on how your heart will yearn
For the things most dear to you,
With wealth and love 'tis so
But onward we must go.

Keep right on to the end of the road,
Keep right on to the end.
Though the way be long let your heart be strong,
Keep right on round the bend.
Though you're tired and weary, still journey on
Till you come to your happy abode,
Where all you love and you're dreaming of
Will be there at the end of the road.

*

MJ: Yes, my home has been broken into. Erm, once in Cambridge and once in Bristol within the last six months, and a video was stolen each time. Erm, the first time, they came in through an open window, and we got back in the evening to find that someone had gone through the window, taken the video and gone out through the door. It wasn't really very traumatic because, erm, you feel that if you leave a window open, you know, people take that sort of opportunity. But the second time, we'd already had an attempted break-in and they attempted to batter the door down and then they broke the window and came in and erm, took the video and that was rather traumatic, both the attempted, erm, burglary and the, and the actual burglary.

CF: Hm.

MJ: Because you know, you hear that, you suddenly hear this terrific banging downstairs and someone's trying to get into your house, you know, it's really traumatic.

CF: Hm, I would imagine it would be very frightening.

MJ: Yes.

CF: Actually, the attempted burglary was worse than the real burglary because, er, it was the first time it had happened and because, because you didn't actually see the person. This – when the burglary took place, I stuck my head out of the window, I ran straight downstairs, no clothes on or anything, stuck my head straight out the window, saw this guy running down the road, and so it was a person. I knew it wasn't a supernatural being, whereas the first time, you know, I felt almost as if it was not a person at all, a thing, that was battering at the door, trying to get in.

CF: Hm.

MJ: Because I never saw them.

CF: Hm.

---

 *

CF: Oh, here we go. Have you ever been. pickpocketed, or seen a pickpocket at work, or had a bag snatched?

MJ: I have, actually.

CF: Yeah?

MJ: On the tube once.

CF: Really!

MJ: I had erm, my purse stolen out of my bag . . . and erm, later I got the purse back 'cos the, you know, their their method on the tube is to take everything out

and then sling it in a bin as quickly as possible. But the credit cards and money were gone. Erm, I mean, I don't know who did it, I didn't notice. After that I was very much more careful about keeping my bag closed, keeping my arm round it and so on.

CF: Mm. I've had it twice, once was in New Guinea when I, when I first went onto a contract, erm, I didn't get paid for about four months so it was dreadful, I had to borrow money left right and centre.

MJ: Oh!

CF: And I borrowed a large amount from a friend of mine, I think it was about five hundred kina which is about what, four hundred pounds. I just went to the bank and cashed the cheque and I went to the supermarket and I had my bag, my purse in my bilum which is their kind of string bag, in the supermarket trolley, and I just sort of turned round to get something and . . . well, I didn't see anything happen, but when I got to the checkout the purse wasn't in the bag anymore, so that was all that money just gone, it was terrible.

MJ: Could you claim? Did you have insurance?

CF: No. No.

F1: **Prevention is better than cure**

Here are some general warnings

Never carry your purse in your back pocket or in an open handbag. High risk areas are at bus stops, in the crush in the Underground and in crowded markets or shops, so be sure you know exactly where your purse is in any of these situations, and don't carry vast amounts of cash with you. Take enough to cover the day's needs plus an extra £5 to cover emergencies.

London, as capitals go, is relatively safe, but don't walk alone at night in lonely places like parks and commons.

M1: **Loss or theft**

Report all losses or thefts to the police; this will validate your insurance claim should you later make one. Phone numbers of local police stations will be listed in the local press, or ring directory enquiries on 142 and ask for the nearest one to you. Don't ring 999 unless you were attacked at the time of the theft.

Please return this questionnaire to:
Annette Capel, ELT Publishing Manager
Collins ELT, 8 Grafton Street, London W1X 3LA

QUESTIONNAIRE

Please help us to help you by commenting on this Collins ELT title.
Write your answers in the space provided or on additional sheets if necessary.
Thank you for giving us this invaluable feedback.

COLLINS COBUILD ENGLISH COURSE

YOUR CLASS		TIMETABLING	
Number of students		Length of lessons	
Age range		Number of lessons per week	
Level		Total length of course	
		Homework? Yes/No	

1 Did you complete this Level of the Course?

2 Were the materials at the right language level?

3 Did your students make noticeable progress in

Fluency	☐	Listening	☐
Accuracy	☐	Reading	☐
Vocabulary acquisition	☐	Speaking	☐
Writing	☐		

4 Was there sufficient recycling in the Course?

5   Were the topics/themes suitable for your students?

6   Did your students enjoy doing the tasks?

7   Did you use the Practice Book?

8   Was the Teacher's Book clear and informative?

9   What did you/your students particularly like about this Level of the Course?

10   What did you/your students dislike?

Further Comments

Name

Institution

Address